VISUAL QUICKPRO GUIDE

FINAL CUT PRO 6

Lisa Brenneis

 Peachpit Press

08 Oct 30
BT
39.99 (27.99)

Visual QuickPro Guide
Final Cut Pro 6
Lisa Brenneis

Peachpit Press
1249 Eighth Street
Berkeley, CA 94710
510/524-2178
510/524-2221 (fax)

Find us on the World Wide Web at www.peachpit.com.
To report errors, please send a note to errata@peachpit.com.
Peachpit Press is a division of Pearson Education.

Editor: Karyn Johnson
Production Editor: Connie Jeung-Mills
Compositor: WolfsonDesign
Indexer: Emily Glossbrenner
Cover Design: The Visual Group

ISBN-13: 978-0-321-50269-8
ISBN 10: 0-321-50269-8

9 8 7 6 5 4 3 2 1

Printed and bound in the United States of America

Painting by Marjorie Baer

Now that Marjorie Baer has retired from Peachpit Press, she can't prevent me from dedicating this book to her, nor improve this expression of my gratitude and love for her.

Acknowledgments

I feel very lucky to be working with editor Karyn Johnson who took the helm back in 2005 for the FCP 5 edition—she is smart and funny, and she races Ford Pintos at Altamont. Thank you, Karyn.

Thanks to the Peachpit Press people: publisher Nancy Ruenzel, executive editors Marjorie Baer and Nancy Davis; Production-Editor-for-Life Connie Jeung-Mills, compositor Owen Wolfson; Tonya Engst, Jill Marts-Lodwig, Lisa Theobald, and Kelly Ryer, the editors of the previous editions, who built a fine foundation for this edition.

Thanks to Ghretta Hynd and Jim Churchill for appearing in the book illustrations. Jim really isn't that stiff, but Ghretta really is a great yoga teacher.

Thanks to my dad, Jon Brenneis, for generously allowing the use of images that appear in this book.

Thanks to Marc Thompson, Jamie Muhoberac, and Jill Frazier for allowing the use of stills from the Chocolate Genius performance in this book.

Thanks to the whole Final Cut Pro team at Apple Computer, particularly Brian Meaney, Erin Skitt, John Malm, Kirk Paulsen and Paul Saccone—genuinely kind, helpful people who work very hard.

Thanks to my collaborator and friend Brett Spivey, who concocted the compositing and special effects chapters with me.

Thanks to Lauren Coyne who continues to astonish me with her mystical ability to spot errors where nobody else can. I'll have what she's having.

Thanks to all the men and women of the Final Cut Pro discussion forums: 2-pop.com, LAFCPUG.org, and Creative Cow. You lead the FCP community by example, and I am indebted to you. Keep posting.

Internet radio just keeps getting better and better. These are a few of the stations that make it a pleasure to work long hours: KEXP.org (Seattle), wefunkradio.com (Montreal), RadioDarvish.com (San Jose), davidbyrne.com/radio and those crazy ska lovers over at Ska Jerk Radio. Viva!

Thanks to a group of very important people who defy classification: Michael Wohl, Andrew Baum, Cawan Starks, Ross Jones, Philip Hodgetts, Josh and Michelle Mellicker, Larry Jordan, Elina Shatkin, Tom Wolsky, Bill Davis, Kevin Monahan, Michael Horton, Ken Stone, Ned Soltz, Lowell Kay, Michael Rubin, Steve Martin, Ramy Katrib, Ben Gardiner, Nick Meyers, Fred Huff, Bruce Heavin, Christopher Gray, Andreas Kiel, and Anders Holck Peterson.

Finally, eternal gratitude to the late Ralph Fairweather.

TABLE OF CONTENTS

Chapter 8: **Working with Clips in the Viewer** **227**

Chapter 9: **Basic Editing** **261**

Chapter 13: Creating Transitions   437

Chapter 14: Compositing and Effects Overview   455

Chapter 19: Creating Final Output 573

TABLE OF CONTENTS

INTRODUCTION

When the two Steves started Apple back in 1976, they dreamed of making a computer that people could use as a tool to change the world. Final Cut Pro is an Apple program worthy of the founders' vision. A community has formed around this tool, and people are making movies who weren't able to before. FCP is changing the way stories are told because it changes who's telling them.

In January 2003, Apple released Final Cut Express, a lower-cost, nonlinear editing and effects program. With Express handling the needs of entry-level users, Final Cut Pro is now free to develop into a bigger, faster, feature-rich, nonlinear beast.

Final Cut Pro is no longer available as a stand-alone application. FCP 6 was released in May 2007 as the central application of the Final Cut Studio 2 suite of professional post-production applications. The big changes in this latest edition of Final Cut Pro are all about power, performance gains and tighter integration with FCP's sister apps: Motion, Soundtrack Pro, DVD Studio Pro and Color. Day-to-day editing operations are largely unchanged.

This book, *Final Cut Pro 6 for Mac OS X: Visual QuickPro Guide*, is the sixth (!) revision of the original *Final Cut Pro for Macintosh: Visual QuickPro Guide*. I've added coverage of FCP 6's new features and (only because this book is now at its upper size limit) moved a few topics on to peachpit.com. When a topic has moved to the peachpit.com Web site, you'll see a note directing you to this url: **www.peachpit.com/finalcutpro6vqp**.

I'm reluctant to take material out of the print edition, but consider this: According to my calculations, moving 80 pages of content onto the Web will save more than half a million pages of paper over the projected print run of this book. That's 44 pulp trees, plus the 208 gallons of oil and 3575 gallons of water required to produce the paper—and that's just the paper.

This edition describes the operation of FCP 6. If you are using FCP 2, 3, 4, HD or 5, much of this book should be a useful guide, but if you are using FCP version 1.2.5 or earlier, you'll need a copy of *Final Cut Pro for Macintosh: Visual QuickPro Guide*. And you should seriously consider an upgrade.

Who should use this book

Final Cut Pro 6 for Mac OS X: Visual QuickPro Guide is designed to be used by intermediate to advanced Mac users with some basic knowledge of video editing terms and procedures; explaining basic video production and editing is beyond the scope of this book. Final Cut Pro is designed to be easy to use, but it's still a professional-level video editing and compositing program. If you are not new to the Macintosh, but you're completely new to video editing, consider some basic training in video editing fundamentals before you plunge into this program. Try Apple's free iMovie program—it's a great way to get a taste of basic video editing in a stripped-down program that's a little easier for beginners to use. Also consider Final Cut Express, a simplified version of Final Cut Pro; it's a good choice if you want to work your way up to the Pro version.

What's in this book

The first part of the book starts with a quick feature overview of the entire program, followed by hardware setup, program installation, and preferences specification. Part I ends with a chapter devoted to FCP's project structure and clip handling.

The next two sections introduce the Capture, Browser, and Viewer windows—the Final Cut Pro tools you use for capturing, importing, and organizing media in preparation for an edit.

The fourth part of the book details the variety of ways that you can use FCP's editing tools to assemble and refine an edited sequence. This section covers basic editing procedures and the operation of the Timeline, Canvas, and Trim Edit windows.

The fifth section is devoted to using the program's special effects and compositing tools. You'll find an overview chapter plus chapters devoted to creating motion effects, using filters, and creating titles and other generator effects.

The final section includes three chapters on finishing your FCP project; one covers real-time playback and rendering techniques; the next lays out your options for outputting a final product. The final chapter walks you through FCP's media management tools and offers some general project management tips.

How to use this book

This guide is designed to be a Final Cut Pro user's companion, a reference guide with an emphasis on step-by-step descriptions of specific tasks. You'll encounter the following features:

◆ "Anatomy" sections introduce the major program windows with large annotated illustrations identifying interface features and operation. If you're not a step-by-step kind of person, you can pick up quite a bit of information just by browsing these illustrations.

◆ "FCP Protocol" sidebars lay out the protocols (the programming rules) that govern the way Final Cut Pro works. These sections are highly recommended reading for anyone interested in a serious relationship with this program.

◆ Sidebars throughout the book highlight production techniques, project management ideas, and suggestions for streamlining your workflow.

◆ Tips are short bits that call your attention to a neat trick or a cool feature, or warn you of a potential pitfall in the task at hand.

Learning Final Cut Pro

Here are some tips to help you get up and running in Final Cut Pro ASAP.

Basic theory

Two sidebars, one in Chapter 1 and another in Chapter 4, are referred to throughout this book. You don't absolutely have to read these to operate Final Cut Pro, but understanding some of the basic concepts underlying the design of the program will make FCP much easier to learn.

"What Is Nonlinear, Nondestructive Editing?" in Chapter 1 explains how nondestructive editing works and how it affects the operation of Final Cut Pro.

"FCP Protocol: Clips and Sequences" in Chapter 4 explains the protocols governing clip and sequence versions, which are key to understanding how Final Cut Pro works.

FCP is context sensitive

The Final Cut Pro interface is context sensitive, which means that the options available in the program's menus and dialog boxes can vary depending on any of the following factors:

◆ The external video hardware attached to your system

◆ The setup configuration you specify when you install the program

◆ The program window that is currently active

◆ The program selection that you just made

The logic behind the context-sensitive design is sound: to simplify your life by removing irrelevant options from your view. However, because the interface is context sensitive, the menus and dialog boxes in your installation of Final Cut Pro may occasionally differ from those in the illustrations shown in this guide.

Test, test, test

Many times, what you are able to produce with Final Cut Pro depends on the capabilities of your external video hardware and the video format you are working in. So before you rush out and submit a budget or sign a contract, take your entire Final Cut Pro system, including your external video gear, for a test-drive.

LEARNING FINAL CUT PRO

Keyboard commands

Final Cut Pro was designed to support a wide variety of working styles ranging from heavy pointing, clicking, and dragging to entirely keyboard-based editing. More keyboard commands are available than those listed in the individual tasks in this book. You'll find a comprehensive list of commands in Appendix A, "Keyboard Shortcuts."

Shortcut menus

Final Cut Pro makes extensive use of shortcut menus. As you explore the program, Control-clicking items and interface elements is a quick way to see your options in many areas of the FCP interface, and it can speed up the learning process.

Buy a mouse

You'll be amazed how much a two-button mouse with a scroll wheel will improve your Final Cut Pro editing experience. The FCP interface is quite scroll-friendly; everything from major program windows to the parameter controls on the Viewer's effects tabs respond to the scroll wheel. Right-clicking a two-button mouse is equivalent to a Control-click, so FCP's shortcut menus are never more than a single click away.

Refer to the manual

I'm happy to be able to recommend the official *Final Cut Pro User Manual* that ships with the program (that's why the box is so heavy). Apple documenters continue to expand this 2000+ page reference work, adding more basic FCP information and explanatory sections for beginning editors, complete lists of FCP filters, shots of every shortcut menu in the program, 100+ pages devoted to working with audio, and so on. The FCP manual runs over four volumes for the Final Cut Pro 6 release. I'll occasionally refer you to a specific section of the official manual PDF that covers a topic in much more detail than this book can accommodate. (Still, the official manual did miss a few items covered here, and this Visual QuickPro Guide is much easier to carry around.)

Check out Apple Support

Apple posts a steady stream of valuable Final Cut Pro articles and updates in its online Apple Support site: www.apple.com/support/finalcutpro/.

Apple support is also the place to go for program update downloads, user manuals, and user forums. The company also posts information about FCP "known issues" (that's corporate-speak for bugs) as technical articles on the site.

The Web is your friend

Using the World Wide Web is an essential part of using Final Cut Pro. Apple, as well as the manufacturers of the video hardware you'll be using with Final Cut Pro, relies on the Web to inform users of the latest developments and program updates, and to provide technical support. You'll find a starter list of online resources on the Apple FCS Resources page: www.apple.com/finalcutstudio/resources/ and specific URLs sprinkled throughout this book. There are some great sources of information, technical help, and camaraderie out there. If you get stuck or encounter difficulties getting under way, go online and start asking questions. After you've learned the program, go online and answer questions. Helping other people is a great way to learn.

Welcome to Final Cut Pro

Welcome to Apple's Final Cut Pro—a combination digital video editing, compositing, and special effects program.

Final Cut Pro, now at the center of a mighty suite of professional media-making applications known as Final Cut Studio, is tightly integrated with Apple's Intel processors, FireWire highspeed data transfer technology, and QuickTime multimedia format. It supports a wide variety of digital video formats, from DV to HDV and DVCPRO HD, along with the latest HD (High Definition) digital formats. Final Cut Pro also supports non-broadcast formats such as M-JPEG; and all QuickTime formats, as well as QuickTime's built-in effects generators. It also supports Adobe After Effects and other third-party plugin filters.

Final Cut Pro provides professional editing functionality in a variety of styles, from strictly drag-and-drop edits to entirely keyboard-based editing.

Soon you'll be spending plenty of time working with clips, audio levels, and other editing minutiae, so let's start with the big picture. In this chapter, you'll find an overview of Final Cut Pro features, and a brief description of three additional special-purpose applications included in the Final Cut Pro 6 suite. You'll be introduced to the main interface windows used for editing and for creating effects, and you'll learn how to customize the arrangement of these windows in a variety of screen layouts.

You'll also learn about Final Cut Pro's media management tools, import and export options, and functions for undoing changes.

Your First Final Cut Pro Project: Start to Finish

Here's a road map you can use to chart a course through your first FCP project. This flowchart describes the production pathway of a typical DV project from hardware setup through output of the finished program. At each step, you'll find pointers to sections in this book that describe that part of the process in more detail.

1. **Set up hardware, install FCP, and choose an initial Easy Setup:** Use a FireWire cable to connect your DV camcorder to your computer. If you hook up your hardware before you install FCP, the program will select the correct initial settings automatically. (If you've already installed FCP, don't worry—those settings are easy to define at any time.)
   See Chapter 2, "Installing and Setting Up."

2. **Capture DV:** Use the controls in the Capture window to capture raw video and audio from your DV camcorder and save them to a hard disk.
   See Chapter 5, "Capturing Video."

3. **Import other media elements:** Add music or sound effects, or graphics elements such as digital stills or graphics created in Photoshop.
   See Chapter 6, "Importing Digital Media."

ROUGH CUT

4. Rough assembly: Review your raw video in the Viewer, and select the portions you want to use by marking In and Out points. Assemble the selected portions into a "rough cut" in an empty sequence in the Timeline. If your project includes narration, be sure to edit a "draft" narration into your rough cut. If you plan to base the rhythm of your cut on a piece of music, you should edit the music into the rough cut as well.

See Chapter 9, "Basic Editing."

5. Fine cut: Revisit your rough cut, and make fine adjustments to edit points directly in the Timeline, in the Trim Edit window, or by opening sequence clips and making adjustments in the Viewer.

See Chapter 11, "Fine Cut: Trimming Edits."

FINISHING

6. Finishing: When your fine cut is complete, use FCP's text generators (or the LiveType application) to add titles; apply the Color Corrector filter to tweak the video's color balance; and fill out the audio tracks with effects and music.

See Chapter 14, "Compositing and Effects Overview."

OUTPUT

7. Output: Output your finished program to DV tape or to a DVD-mastering program like Apple's DVD Studio Pro, or use the Compressor application to export in a compressed QuickTime format for distribution in another digital format like streaming Web video or CD-ROM.

See Chapter 19, "Creating Final Output."

YOUR FIRST FINAL CUT PRO PROJECT

What Is Nonlinear, Nondestructive Editing?

Final Cut Pro is a nonlinear, nondestructive editing program.

In a tape-based *linear* editing system, constructing an edit means selecting shots from one tape and then recording them in order on another tape. Once you've recorded the shots, you're limited to the shots as recorded and in the order recorded. If you want to go back and extend the length of a shot in the middle of your edited program, you'll also have to re-record every shot that came after it because you can't slip the back end of your program down the tape to make room. A computer-based *nonlinear* editing system uses the computer's random access capabilities to allow editors to swap, drop, trim, or extend shots at any point in an edited sequence, without having to reconstruct any other portion of the program.

Some nonlinear computer editing programs, like iMovie, offer random access but modify the original media files on your hard disk when you change a clip (in iMovie's case, when you empty the Trash). This is called *destructive* editing.

Nondestructive editing is a basic concept that distinguishes Final Cut Pro from other digital, nonlinear editing systems like iMovie. When you edit on a digital, nonlinear editing system like Final Cut Pro, constructing a digital edit means constructing a playlist, much like a playlist you would construct in iTunes.

In iTunes, your archive of song files is stored in the iTunes Library; an iTunes playlist is just a set of instructions that tells the iTunes jukebox how to sequence playback of songs you select. A single song file can appear in multiple playlists, and deleting a song from a playlist doesn't delete the actual song file from the Library. In Final Cut Pro, sequences operate like iTunes playlists.

An FCP sequence is a collection of instructions to the program to play a certain bit of Media File A, then cut to a bit of Media File B, then play a later bit of Media File A, and so on. The full length of each file is available to the editor from within the edited sequence. That's because in Final Cut Pro, the "clip"—the basic media element used to construct edited sequences—is only a set of instructions referring to an underlying media file. When you play back an edited sequence, it only looks as though it's been spliced together; in fact, Final Cut Pro has assembled it on the fly. Since you're viewing a simulation of an edited sequence, and the full length of each captured file is available at the edit point, extending a shot is simply a matter of rewriting the editing program's playlist to play a little more of Media File A before switching to Media File B. In Final Cut Pro, you do this by modifying the clip's length in your edited sequence.

Nondestructive editing is key to editing in a program like Final Cut Pro, which allows you to use media source files multiple times across multiple projects, or to access the same source file but process it in a number of different ways. Having many instances of a clip (which in Final Cut Pro is just a set of instructions) all referring to the same media file saves disk space and offers flexibility throughout your editing process.

When you reach the limit of Final Cut Pro's ability to assemble your edited sequence on the fly, it's time to render. The rendering process computes all the modifications, superimpositions, and transitions applied to the clip into a single new media file that resides on your hard disk and plays back as part of your edited sequence.

For more information on protocols governing clips, see Chapter 4, "Projects, Sequences, and Clips."

Final Cut Pro 6: Only Available in Final Cut Studio 2

Apple has reconfigured its ever-expanding professional applications software lineup yet again and —for the first time—Final Cut Pro is no longer available as a standalone application. FCP 6 is only available if you purchase the latest Final Cut Studio bundle, which includes updated versions of Final Cut Pro, Soundtrack Pro, Motion, and the same old DVD Studio Pro 4. Final Cut Studio 2 also introduces the latest "pro app": Color.

The Final Cut Pro 6 Suite

Final Cut Pro 6 ships with a suite of three special-purpose applications. Each application is independent, but has been designed to work closely with FCP.

Just covering Final Cut Pro has taken this book to its upper size limit, so coverage of the FCP suite is limited to the realm of importing and exporting material between these applications and FCP. Individual PDF manuals are available from the Help menu of each application.

Cinema Tools: This utility provides frame-rate conversion and generates negative cut lists for projects shot on film and edited in FCP. Cinema Tools can also be used to perform frame-rate conversions of 24P video.

Compressor: Compressor is a compression and transcoding utility, offering Apple's best and brightest video and audio compression algorithms and easy-to-use batch encoding. If you need to output your FCP project as DVD-ready MPEG files or Web-ready compressed QuickTime movies, Compressor is your best output option.

LiveType: Select a prefabricated animated type sequence from LiveType's library to create complex animated titles, or edit the stock animated fonts in the library to create your own customized library. You can even borrow the motion paths from a LiveType animated font to animate graphical or video elements in your FCP sequence.

Touring Your Desktop Post-Production Facility

Four program windows form the heart of the Final Cut Pro interface: the *Browser*, the *Viewer*, the *Canvas*, and the *Timeline* (**Figure 1.1**).

Because the program combines so many editing and effects creation capabilities in a single application, each of these windows performs multiple functions. Final Cut Pro's elegant use of tabbed windows to stack multiple functions in a single window makes maximum use of your screen real estate.

A small, floating Tool palette contains tools you can use to make selections, navigate, and perform edits in the Timeline and the Canvas.

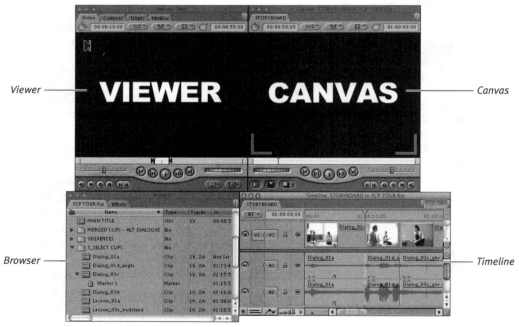

Viewer — VIEWER   CANVAS — Canvas

Browser —   — Timeline

Figure 1.1 The four main program windows in Final Cut Pro.

Figure 1.2 Tabs give you access to multiple functions in the Viewer window.

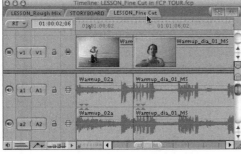

Figure 1.3 Tabs give you access to multiple sequences in the Timeline.

Figure 1.4 Rest the pointer over a button in the Tool palette, and a tooltip—a label with the tool's name—will appear. Tooltips also display keyboard shortcuts for tools and buttons.

Useful features

Following are a few useful features that apply throughout the program:

◆ **Tabbed windows:** Every major window in Final Cut Pro uses tabs. In the Viewer and User Preferences windows, tabs give you access to multiple functions within the window (**Figure 1.2**). In the Canvas, Timeline, and Browser, tabs provide access to multiple sequences or projects (**Figure 1.3**). You can drag a tab out of the Browser, Viewer, Canvas, or Timeline and display the tab as a separate window. You can also return a tab to its original window by dragging the tab back to the tab header of the parent window. You can find out more by reviewing "Creating Custom Screen Layouts" in Chapter 3.

◆ **Tooltips:** You can use tooltips to identify most of the controls in the Viewer and Canvas windows and on the Tool palette (**Figure 1.4**). Tooltips also display the keyboard shortcut for a tool or button. Rest the pointer over the button and wait a moment, and a label will appear. Activate tooltips on the General tab of the User Preferences window.

Menus, shortcuts, and controls

Final Cut Pro offers several methods for performing video editing tasks. Some people work fastest using keyboard shortcuts; others prefer to use the menu bar or shortcut menus as much as possible. Apart from the menu bar and window buttons, you can use several other means to access Final Cut Pro's functions; experiment to find out which control methods work best for you:

◆ **Shortcut menus:** Shortcut menus can speed your work and help you learn Final Cut Pro. Control-click an item in one of the four main interface windows and select from a list of common functions specific to that item (**Figure 1.5**). Control-click often as you learn your way around the program just to see your options in a particular area of the FCP interface.

◆ **Keyboard shortcuts:** You'll find a complete list of keyboard shortcuts in Appendix A. You may find that these shortcut keys help you work more efficiently.

◆ **Timecode entry shortcuts:** Final Cut Pro provides a number of timesaving shortcuts for timecode entry. See "FCP Protocol: Entering Timecode Numbers" in Chapter 8.

Figure 1.5 Control-clicking a sequence clip in the Timeline calls up a shortcut menu with a list of functions related to that clip.

Customizable interface

FCP's flexible interface can be custom-tailored to suit your needs. You can create and save multiple screen layout configurations to enhance different editing and effects-creation tasks. Personalize and save anything from a single keyboard shortcut to an entire screen layout for a multi-monitor setup.

◆ Create and save custom Browser column layouts, Timeline track display layouts, and full-screen layouts.

◆ Build custom keyboard configurations and shortcut button bars that can be saved and reloaded or transported to another FCP system.

See "Customizing Final Cut Pro" in Chapter 3.

Onscreen help

Onscreen help for FCP is a PDF version of the complete *Final Cut Pro User Manual* (all 2033 pages of it!). The PDF has a couple of advantages over the printed version. The PDF offers a single index that covers all four volumes, and index entries are hyperlinked; you can jump to a listing by clicking its page number. The PDF is also illustrated in full color.

To access onscreen help:

◆ Choose Help > Final Cut Pro User Manual.

You can display more than 60 sortable columns of information

Different projects appear on separate tabs

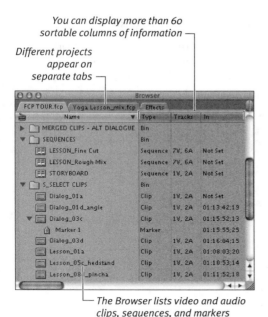

The Browser lists video and audio clips, sequences, and markers

Figure 1.6 Use the Browser window to organize the media elements in your projects.

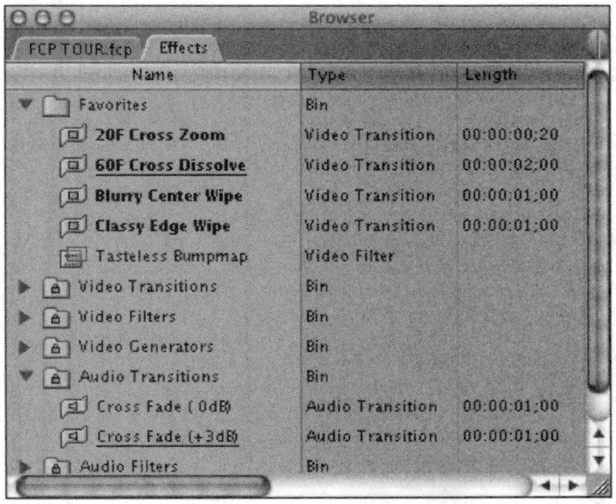

Editing and Effects Windows

The following brief descriptions of the features and functions of each of the four main windows are simplified summaries of the full list of features. Final Cut Pro's designers went all out to support a wide variety of editing styles, and they have produced a very flexible editing system.

The Browser

The Browser (**Figure 1.6**) is the window where you organize and access all the media elements used as source material for your projects. It also contains your projects' sequences: the data files that contain edited playlists.

The Browser's Effects tab is your source for effects, filters, and generators, including the text generator (**Figure 1.7**).

The Browser is not like a folder on your computer's Desktop—it's not a collection of actual files. Instead, a Browser item is a *pointer* to a file on your hard disk. It's important to keep in mind that file storage is independent of Browser organization. That means you can place the same clip in multiple Browser projects, and each instance of the clip will refer to the same media file on your hard drive. For detailed information about the Browser, see Chapter 7, "Organizing Clips in the Browser."

Figure 1.7 The Browser's Effects tab displays Final Cut Pro's effects, filters, and generators, as well as your own customized effects.

The Viewer

The Viewer is bursting with functions. When you're editing, the Viewer acts as your source monitor; you can review individual video and audio clips and mark edit points. You can also load clips from the current sequence into the Viewer to refine your edits, apply effects, create titles—and, as they say, much, much more.

The FCP interface offers a stack of tabs in the Viewer that organize and display audio and video plus provide controls for any effects you want to apply to a clip. Here are quick summaries of the functions available on each of the tabs.

The Viewer's Video tab

◆ **Video tab (Figure 1.8):** View video frames and mark and refine edit points. This is the default playback window for a video clip.

Different Viewer window functions appear on separate tabs

Enter a timecode in the Current Timecode field to navigate to a specific frame

Drag the playhead along the Scrubber bar to scrub through a clip

Use these controls to set In and Out points, markers, and keyframes

Use these onscreen transport controls —or keyboard commands or timecode entry— to move around in your clips

Figure 1.8 The Viewer's Video tab.

The Viewer's Audio tab

◆ **Audio tab** (**Figure 1.9**): Audition and mark edit points in audio-only clips. Set level and pan or spread settings. The Audio tab displays the audio portion of an audio+video clip. Clips with two channels display two audio tabs.

Use the sliders to set your audio levels and stereo pan position

The Audio tab displays waveforms of your audio track

Drag this hand icon. It's your handle for performing drag-and-drop audio edits

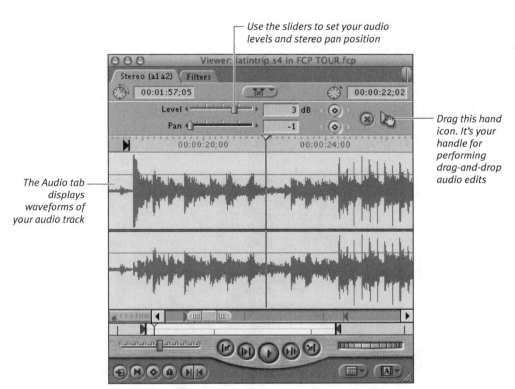

Figure 1.9 The Viewer's Audio tab contains a few controls that don't appear on the Video tab.

The Viewer's Effects tabs

◆ **Controls tab (Figure 1.10):** Adjust the settings for a generator effect, such as the text generator.

◆ **Filters tab:** Adjust the settings and set keyframes for any filter effects you have applied to a clip.

◆ **Motion tab:** Apply and modify motion effects.

◆ **Color Corrector tab:** Contains onscreen controls for adjusting the settings for the color correction filters. This tab appears only on clips with a color correction filter applied.

For more information on the Viewer, see Chapter 8, "Working with Clips in the Viewer."

To learn about creating effects, see Chapter 14, "Compositing and Effects Overview."

Enter your text here

Use these controls to specify settings for your text

Adjust keyframes in the keyframe graph; you can extend its display to the full width of your monitor

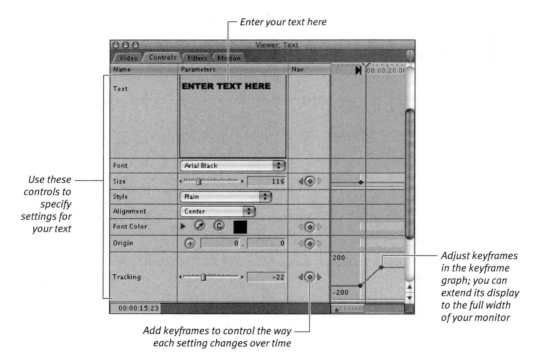

Add keyframes to control the way each setting changes over time

Figure 1.10 A text generator on the Viewer's Controls tab. The Controls tab contains the tools you need to adjust the settings for a generator effect. The Filters tab and the Motion tab each perform this function too, but for different classes of effects.

The Canvas

The Canvas is a monitor where you view playback of your edited sequence. The Canvas and the Timeline work together; the Canvas always displays the frame at the current position of the Timeline's playhead.

The Canvas (**Figure 1.11**) looks similar to the Viewer and has many of the same controls. You can use the controls in the Canvas to play sequences, mark sequence In and Out points, add sequence markers, and set keyframes.

Multiple open sequences appear on separate tabs

Drag the Canvas playhead along the Scrubber bar to scrub through a sequence

Click an edit button to perform one of seven types of edits

The Canvas and Viewer transport controls operate in the same way; you can also edit with keyboard commands or timecode entry

Figure 1.11 The Canvas window.

The Timeline

The Timeline displays your edited sequence as clips arrayed on multiple video and audio tracks along a time axis (**Figure 1.12**). The Canvas and Timeline are locked together; you view Timeline playback in the Canvas. If you have multiple sequences open, both the Timeline and the Canvas will display a tab for each sequence. You can edit by dragging clips directly from the Browser or the Viewer and dropping them in the Timeline; see Chapter 10, "Editing in the Timeline and the Canvas."

Transitions appear in the same track as the clips they are applied to —

Adjust a clip's opacity by dragging the clip overlay line up or down

Multiple open sequences appear on separate tabs in the Timeline window

Drag the playhead along the ruler to scrub through a sequence

Adjust keyframes for effects and motion properties in the keyframe editor

Shortcut menus provide information and task shortcuts for individual clips

Sequence clips appear on multiple tracks

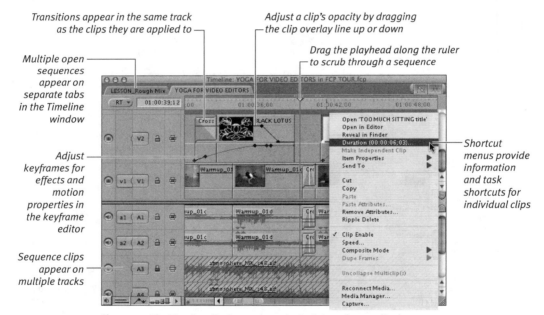

Figure 1.12 The Timeline displays a chronological view of your edited sequence.

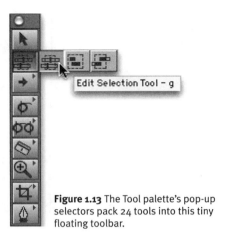

Figure 1.13 The Tool palette's pop-up selectors pack 24 tools into this tiny floating toolbar.

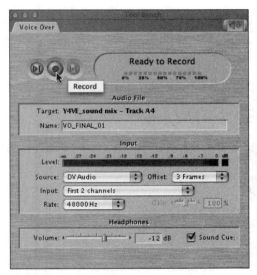

Figure 1.14 The Voice Over tool records synchronous audio directly into FCP.

The Tool palette

The Tool palette (**Figure 1.13**) contains tools for selecting and manipulating items in the Timeline, Canvas, and Viewer. For a listing of each tool, see Chapter 9, "Basic Editing."

The Tool Bench

FCP's tool collection has grown steadily; Apple designers have added the Tool Bench window to store all those miscellaneous tools and keep the interface organized. Tool Bench tools include:

◆ **Voice Over tool (Figure 1.14):** Use the Voice Over tool to record audio inside Final Cut Pro. Specify a section of your sequence in the Timeline; then record a voiceover as you play. See "Recording Audio with the Voice Over Tool" in Chapter 12.

◆ **Audio Mixer:** This Tool Bench window displays virtual audio faders and meters. Use the mixer to record audio mix moves in real time; FCP records your fader moves as audio level or pan keyframes. See "Using the Audio Mixer" in Chapter 12.

◆ **Video Scopes:** FCP has a suite of image calibration tools you can use to check the balance and levels of captured footage. For details on using these tools in a color correction process, see "Using Color Correction Filters" in Chapter 16.

◆ **QuickView:** When you adjust a composited shot that requires rendering, QuickView stores a RAM preview of it so you can review adjustments without having to stop and render.

Select any of these tools from FCP's Tools menu, and that tool will appear in the Tool Bench.

Input and Output Windows

Although you perform most editing tasks in Final Cut Pro's main editing and effects windows, you'll need to use a couple of other windows to shape your program's input and output.

Log and Capture

Use the Log and Capture window (**Figure 1.15**) to capture video and audio media in Final Cut Pro. Log and Capture supports a range of capturing options, from live video capture on the fly to automated batch capture with full device control. Log and Capture functions are explained in detail in Chapter 5, "Capturing Video."

Figure 1.15 The Log and Capture window supports a range of capturing and logging techniques, including automated batch capture after you've logged all your reels.

Media Management Tools

The following tools can help you manage your wonderland of media files. See Chapter 20, "Managing Complex Projects," for the full rundown.

Media Manager

The Media Manager is the Swiss Army knife of project management tools. You can copy or move sequences and clips, along with their source media files, to another drive location. You can create offline versions of your sequence for batch recapture. You can transcode project media into another format as you copy, move, and trim. You can also delete all or part of a media file from inside the program. That means that you can trim the unused portions of the clips you're using in your sequence and actually delete them from your drive (**Figure 1.16**).

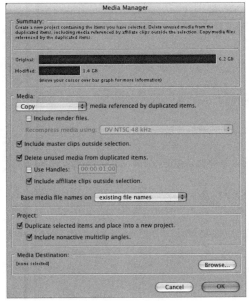

Figure 1.16 Use the Media Manager to trim unused portions of your source media files from a project.

Other media management tools

You use FCP's other media management tools to control the links between Final Cut Pro projects and their associated media and render files.

◆ Use the Reconnect Media command to restore links between projects and their media or render files.

◆ Control-click a clip (or multiple clips) and choose the Make Offline command, which offers three options: break the clip's link to its source media file but leave the source file on the disk; move the source file to the Trash; or delete the source file from the disk.

◆ Use the Render Manager to delete render files for deleted or obsolete projects and to remove obsolete render files from your current projects. The Render Manager finds and lists render files from unopened projects as well as open projects, and displays their modification dates to help you decide which files to remove. For information on the Render Manager, see Chapter 18, "Real Time and Rendering."

Import and export options

Final Cut Pro's media handling is based on Apple's QuickTime, and that means you have a lot of import and export format options. If QuickTime can handle it, so can Final Cut Pro. You can also import and export Edit Decision Lists (EDLs), FXBuilder scripts, and logging information.

◆ You can import QuickTime-compatible media files into a Final Cut Pro project.

◆ You can import audio directly from a CD.

◆ You can import still images in a full range of formats.

◆ You can import a layered Adobe Photoshop file (**Figure 1.17**). Final Cut Pro preserves the layers, importing the file as a sequence. Each layer in Photoshop corresponds to a video track in the sequence.

◆ You can import an EDL created on a linear editing system or another non-linear editing system and use it to create sequences.

◆ You can export clips, sequences, or portions of either as QuickTime movies or in a variety of image and sound formats.

◆ You can use Compressor, FCP's affiliate application, to perform high-quality batch transcoding operations.

◆ You can export a sequence as an EDL and use this to create sequences on another linear or nonlinear editing system.

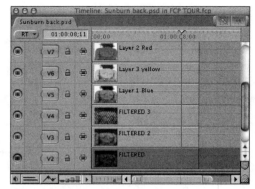

Figure 1.17 When you import a layered Photoshop file into Final Cut Pro, you can maintain control over the individual layers.

MEDIA MANAGEMENT TOOLS

Installing and Setting Up

2

This chapter walks you through the process of assembling the necessary hardware, hooking everything up, and installing Final Cut Pro. Topics include Final Cut Pro system requirements as well as hardware selection and configuration for both a basic setup and a more full-featured system.

The chapter ends with suggestions for optimizing performance, including recommendations for running Final Cut Pro on a minimal "base-case" system and tips for troubleshooting Final Cut Pro.

As each successive release of FCP increases the range of hardware options and software plugins, it's never been more important to get current information before you commit to a particular system. The perfect time to get the latest news on Final Cut Pro and your hardware options is *before* you commit to a particular system. There's a bustling community of resources for Final Cut Pro. FCP Web sites, FCP user group meetings, and reputable vendors are my favorite sources.

It's possible to do great work on a simple, low-cost Final Cut Pro system, but if that money is just burning a hole in your pocket, there are a number of ways to spend your dough and upgrade your FCP system.

System Requirements

Final Cut Pro 1.0 was conceived as a DV post-production system that would run on a Macintosh G3 computer. Each new version of Final Cut Pro stiffens the minimum system requirements a bit more (FCP 6 requires a minimum 1.2 GHz G4 processor), but because fast CPUs and built-in FireWire ports have spread throughout the Macintosh product line, FCP wanna-bes can keep pace on just about any recent Mac. If you're unsure whether your Power Mac makes the grade, go to the Specifications page on Apple's Web site, and look up its complete specifications at support.apple.com/specs/.

Apple is continuously testing and qualifying third-party software and third-party external devices for compatibility with Final Cut Pro. To review the latest list of Apple-approved video hardware and software, go to the Final Cut Pro Web site at www.apple.com/finalcutstudio/finalcutpro.

Real-Time System Requirements

FCP's real-time technology (dubbed "RT Extreme" by Apple marketing wizards) performs its effects-previewing magic without additional hardware. FCP minimum system requirements now support minimal real-time effects previewing.

FCP has been programmed to check the processor speed of your Mac and to scale the quantity and quality of real-time effects available. Macs with faster processors (or dual processors) can process and preview multi-layer scaling, motion effects, and selected transitions.

For more information on real-time system capabilities, see Chapter 18, "Real Time and Rendering." Why are real-time effects discussed in the rendering chapter? Because you can preview all sorts of FCP effects while you edit your show, but you still have to render many of them before you can output a full-resolution final program.

HDV: HD for the Masses

Now HDV cameras with retail prices well under $1,000 are commonplace. These inexpensive cameras make entry-level HD video available to those thousands of us with more limited means. Final Cut Pro (even the latest editions of iMovie) can now capture HDV via FireWire, edit in a format called "HDV-native," and then output via FireWire—all without an additional hardware card. HD capture without a hardware card? Here's how it works:

High definition video is a growing family of formats with a wide variety of frame sizes and frame rates ranging from ultra-compressed HDV 720p (1280 x 720-pixel frame size and a data rate of 19 Mb/s) to uncompressed 10-bit 1080i60 (1920 x 1080-pixel frame size and a data rate of 932 Mb/s).

HDV uses MPEG-2, a compression algorithm that reduces the size of the HDV datastream by reducing the number of frames that contain complete picture information. One of these complete frames (called I-frames) is followed by a sequence of reduced-image data frames (called B-frames and P-frames). HDV operates at data rates similar to DV—that's a data rate that FireWire can handle. FCP can capture the HDV datastream without converting it to an intermediate codec. As you edit, FCP generates complete image and audio information for each frame in real time. For more information, see Apple's *Final Cut Pro User Manual*.

Real-Time Effects: More Hardware Options

Final Cut Pro's open program architecture is designed to allow video hardware manufacturers to develop products that integrate smoothly with FCP's operation. In the years since FCP was released, the list of compatible hardware has grown to include decks, cameras, and capture systems that range from simple consumer-quality DV camcorders to systems capable of editing uncompressed, high-definition (HD) video.

Hardware-assisted real-time video effects were introduced in FCP 2; FCP's RT Extreme is now powerful enough to preview many DV- and compressed HD-format effects in real time, and to output these previews to your external video deck and monitor via FireWire. Now that the Mac processor has taken over effects previewing chores for DV, video hardware manufacturers are focusing on producing card/breakout box combos that provide real-time effects previewing for higher-quality video formats, such as SD and uncompressed HD.

The FCP program design lets video card developers pick and choose which individual effects their real-time systems support. Effects that aren't programmed into a system's hardware are handled by Final Cut Pro, but they don't play back without rendering. Because different real-time systems offer different capabilities, you need to pay close attention to the specifications of any system you consider. A good place to start your investigation is Apple's Final Cut Pro Web site, which offers a list of compatible products and the latest FCP news: `www.apple.com/finalcutstudio/finalcutpro/specs.html`.

What's the Difference Between DV and Digital Video?

When you refer to *digital video*, you could be talking about any video format that stores image and audio information in digital form—it's digital video whether you store it on a DV tape or on a DVD disc.

DV is a specific digital video format whose identifying characteristic is that the conversion from analog to digital information takes place in the DV camera. So *DV* is a camera-based digital video format.

There are a few different flavors of DV; the differences between them come down to tape format and tape speed:

◆ DV usually refers to MiniDV, used by most consumer digital camcorders.

◆ DVCAM prints the same DV bitstream to a larger, more robust tape stock.

◆ DVC Pro uses a professional-grade tape as well, and it supports a high-quality mode—DVC Pro 50—which digitizes at twice the data rate as DV.

◆ DVCPRO HD uses the same DVC Pro tape stock to record a compressed 720:1080 pixel hi-def frame at data rates up to 14 Mbytes/sec.

◆ HDV uses the same miniDV tape stock to record compressed digital video with frame sizes up to 1080:1440 pixels at data rates similar to standard DV rates.

Hardware Selection and Connection

You'll need a few additional items to transform your Macintosh into a video production studio. This section describes four possible setups—the basic system is the bare minimum required; the recommended setup is, well, highly recommended for anyone with more than a passing interest in making movies. The third setup uses an analog video card for capture. The fourth configuration (recommended for handling higher-resolution video formats) uses a FireWire-equipped breakout box as the interface between a variety of video and audio sources and Final Cut Pro.

A basic hardware configuration (Figure 2.1) includes a DV camcorder or deck, a computer, and a high-resolution computer monitor. The beauty of the basic system is its simplicity—a DV camcorder connected to your Macintosh with a FireWire cable. That's all there is to it.

Here's a rundown on the function of each piece of the system.

DV camcorder or deck: The DV camera or deck feeds digital video and audio into the computer via FireWire and records DV output from Final Cut Pro. During video capture, you must monitor audio through your camera's or deck's audio outputs; computer speakers are muted.

Computer: Final Cut Pro, installed on the Mac, captures and then stores digital video from the DV camera or deck on an A/V hard drive. Qualified Macs are equipped with FireWire; no additional video digitizing card is needed. You use your computer's speakers to monitor your audio. You edit your DV footage with Final Cut Pro and then send it back out to tape through FireWire to your DV camcorder or deck.

High-resolution computer monitor: You view the results of your work on the computer's monitor.

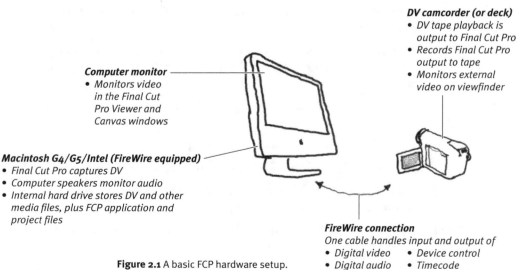

Computer monitor
• *Monitors video in the Final Cut Pro Viewer and Canvas windows*

Macintosh G4/G5/Intel (FireWire equipped)
• *Final Cut Pro captures DV*
• *Computer speakers monitor audio*
• *Internal hard drive stores DV and other media files, plus FCP application and project files*

DV camcorder (or deck)
• *DV tape playback is output to Final Cut Pro*
• *Records Final Cut Pro output to tape*
• *Monitors external video on viewfinder*

FireWire connection
One cable handles input and output of
• *Digital video* • *Device control*
• *Digital audio* • *Timecode*

Figure 2.1 A basic FCP hardware setup.

A recommended DV/HDV setup (Figure 2.2) adds a dedicated hard drive to store your media, and enhances your monitoring capabilities with the addition of an NTSC or PAL video monitor and external speakers.

Dedicated hard drive: Adding a dedicated drive for your media improves the performance as well as the storage capacity of your system. For more information, see "Storage Strategy for Final Cut Pro," later in this chapter.

NTSC monitor: Most DV camcorders feature a built-in LCD display that you can use as an external video monitor, but if you're producing video to be viewed on television, you should preview your video output on an NTSC monitor as you edit. A real studio monitor is best, but even a consumer TV will give a much more accurate idea of how your program looks and sounds. Connect the NTSC or PAL monitor to your video deck or camcorder using the component, S-video, or composite output jacks.

External speakers: Monitoring audio output from your video camcorder or deck with external speakers provides higher-quality audio output.

✔ Tip

■ If you plan to use an external NTSC or PAL monitor as you edit, connect your external speakers to monitor the audio output of your camcorder or deck, so that the audio from the external speakers will be synchronized with the video displayed on the video monitor. You need to do this because audio from your computer's built-in audio outputs will be slightly out of sync with the NTSC or PAL monitor.

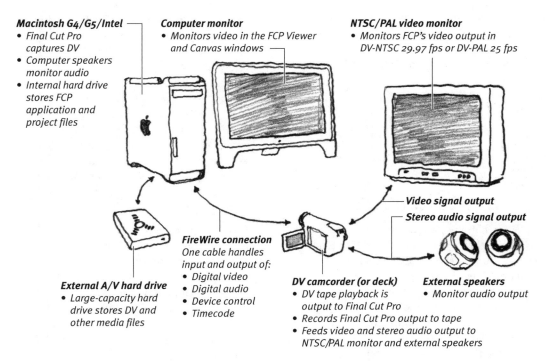

Macintosh G4/G5/Intel
- Final Cut Pro captures DV
- Computer speakers monitor audio
- Internal hard drive stores FCP application and project files

Computer monitor
- Monitors video in the FCP Viewer and Canvas windows

NTSC/PAL video monitor
- Monitors FCP's video output in DV-NTSC 29.97 fps or DV-PAL 25 fps

Video signal output

Stereo audio signal output

External A/V hard drive
- Large-capacity hard drive stores DV and other media files

FireWire connection
One cable handles input and output of:
- Digital video
- Digital audio
- Device control
- Timecode

DV camcorder (or deck)
- DV tape playback is output to Final Cut Pro
- Records Final Cut Pro output to tape
- Feeds video and stereo audio output to NTSC/PAL monitor and external speakers

External speakers
- Monitor audio output

Figure 2.2 A recommended DV hardware configuration.

A breakout box/FireWire configuration (**Figure 2.3**) is a scheme recommended by Apple for capture and edit of uncompressed analog or digital video. There's no "capture card" in this setup; the analog capture card's digitizing function is taken over by the Mac's G4 or G5 processor. The breakout box is not a capture device; it serves as a central patch point for media input and output from analog or digital VTRs, DAT recorders, or multichannel audio formats like ADAT. The breakout box also routes RS422 device control signals and any reference video signals used for timecode synchronization. The breakout box's sole connection to the Mac (and to FCP) is the FireWire connector. All signals traveling in or out of FCP—analog and digital video, audio, device control, and timecode reference—move along that single FireWire cable.

✔ Tip

■ Uncompressed video's data transfer rate and file size demands serious hard disk arrays; FireWire drives are out of the question. For more information, see "Storage Strategy for Final Cut Pro."

FCP Protocol: Disk Names

When naming hard drives, partitions, and folders that you intend to use with Final Cut Pro, you should observe a special naming requirement—each hard disk must have a name that does not contain the entire name of another disk or partition. For example, naming disks "Inferno" and "Inferno 1" could cause FCP to have trouble finding your files later.

Monitor Video on a Computer Display

FCP's Digital Cinema Desktop Preview is a terrifically useful option for external video display: You can attach a second computer display to your Mac and use it as a dedicated video monitor, or use the Desktop Cinema display option with a single display to enjoy gorgeous full-screen monitoring.

Digital Cinema's full-screen playback is wonderful for editing on a PowerBook because you don't need to tie up your FireWire port with the deck or camcorder that's feeding your external video monitor.

The playback quality is decent enough for rough edit monitoring, and you can skip the FireWire traffic jam that ensues when you're trying to get FireWire drives and your external video device all hooked up and playing nicely together on the PowerBook's single FW bus. Choose View > Video Playback > Digital Cinema Desktop Preview, then switch in and out of full-screen preview using the external video keyboard shortcut—Cmd-F12. (You can use the customizable keyboard feature to reassign your full-screen preview toggle to something more convenient; try Shift-1.)

If you're working in an HD format such as HDV, you can monitor your HDV output on a computer display rather than an expensive HD broadcast monitor. This is good news for entry-level HD producers and others looking for a low-cost way to monitor HD video. For more information, see page 216 of Apple's *Final Cut Pro User Manual* PDF.

HARDWARE SELECTION AND CONNECTION

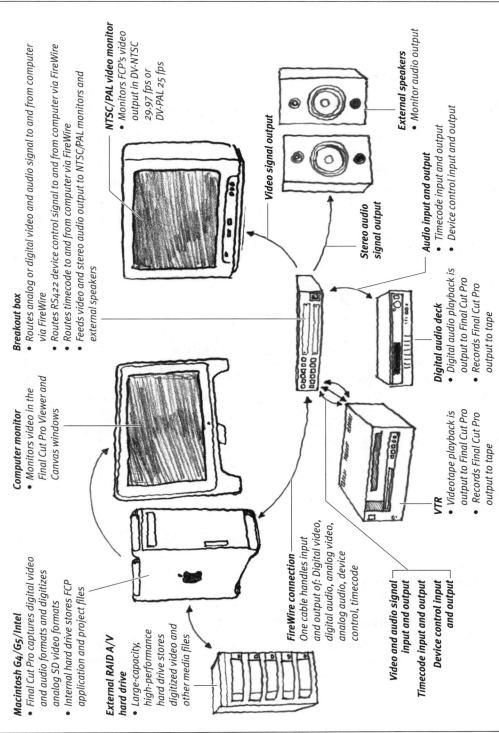

Macintosh G4/G5/Intel
- Final Cut Pro captures digital video and audio formats and digitizes analog SD video formats
- Internal hard drive stores FCP application and project files

External RAID A/V hard drive
- Large-capacity, high-performance hard drive stores digitized video and other media files

Computer monitor
- Monitors video in the Final Cut Pro Viewer and Canvas windows

FireWire connection
One cable handles input and output of: Digital video, digital audio, analog video, analog audio, device control, timecode

Video and audio signal input and output
Timecode input and output
Device control input and output

VTR
- Videotape playback is output to Final Cut Pro
- Records Final Cut Pro output to tape

Digital audio deck
- Digital audio playback is output to Final Cut Pro
- Records Final Cut Pro output to tape

Audio input and output
- Timecode input and output
- Device control input and output

Stereo audio signal output

Video signal output

External speakers
- Monitor audio output

NTSC/PAL video monitor
- Monitors FCP's video output in DV-NTSC 29.97 fps or DV-PAL 25 fps

Breakout box
- Routes analog or digital video and audio signal to and from computer via FireWire
- Routes RS422 device control signal to and from computer via FireWire
- Routes timecode to and from computer via FireWire
- Feeds video and stereo audio output to NTSC/PAL monitors and external speakers

Figure 2.3 A basic breakout box/FireWire hardware configuration.

HARDWARE SELECTION AND CONNECTION

Storage Strategy for Final Cut Pro

Digital video files are big—really, really big. In the Olde Days (five years ago), big hard drives were an expensive proposition; these days, $300 will get you a reliable 500 GB FireWire drive that will store almost 40 hours of DV. If you're going to edit anything substantial at all, consider additional hard drive storage for your system.

Here are some overall considerations when selecting a storage option:

Any storage system you select must be fast enough to keep up with required data transfer rates (some experts recommend a minimum transfer rate of 7 or 8 MB per second). Many storage formats do meet the speed requirement, but as you weigh your speed/capacity/price trade-offs, don't shortchange yourself in the speed department.

If you plan on capturing any uncompressed video format, your required data transfer rate jumps to a minimum of 50 MB per second. A RAID (Redundant Array of Independent Disks)—a multiple disk array that shares the work of transferring and storing data—can be configured to improve your system's performance by increasing the speed of data transfer. RAIDs are unnecessary for editing DV in Final Cut Pro but are in wide use on high-performance systems.

Hard disk storage is available in a variety of formats, and the number of formats is always growing. Rather than discuss a variety of specific hard disk options, here's a set of strategic questions to help steer you to the storage option that's best for you.

How much space do I need?

DV requires 3.6 MB of storage space per second of program material.

That's 216 MB of space per minute of DV.

Or 1 GB of space per five minutes of DV.

When calculating your storage needs, remember that a good rule of thumb is to add the final program lengths of the total number of projects you want to keep online, and then multiply by four to accommodate any render files, undos, scratch copies, and test exports you may generate while editing. Be more generous if you want to capture much more footage than you ultimately use.

Do I need a dedicated drive just for media storage?

A dedicated drive for storing your media will improve the performance of your system because it contains no operating system software, other applications, or files that can fragment the disk. Fragmentation can interfere with the continuous data flow of video and audio to and from the disk.

Here's another reason to keep your media files and program files on separate drives: Your media drive, because it works harder, is more likely to crash than your program drive. In the event of a media drive crash, you may lose your media files, but you won't lose your edit data, which should make it easier to recover from the crash. A dedicated drive or drives for media storage are almost always a great investment.

Should I go with internal or external storage?

What kind of workflow do you anticipate? Whether to invest in internal drives (which could be less expensive) or external drives (which allow you to switch between projects quickly by swapping out drives on your workstation, or move a project and its media from one workstation to another quickly) depends on your individual needs.

About Apple FireWire

Apple FireWire is a high-speed serial bus that allows the simultaneous transfer of digital video, digital audio, timecode information, and device control, all through a single cable. All qualifying Macs come with built-in FireWire ports on the back. FireWire's usefulness is not limited to digital video, however; the future should bring a wider variety of hard drives, printers, scanners, audio mixers, and other peripherals that take advantage of FireWire's high speeds and advanced features.

FireWire (IEEE 1394) is currently supported by many professional- and consumer-level camcorders and decks. However, not all manufacturers have implemented the full FireWire specification in their products, so some decks and camcorders won't fully support Final Cut Pro's device control. That is why Final Cut Pro provides two versions of the FireWire protocol in its Device Control presets: Apple FireWire and Apple FireWire Basic.

If your deck or camcorder uses FireWire, try selecting the Apple FireWire protocol first. This is the default protocol if you select DV during the installation setup. With Apple FireWire as your selected device protocol, your FireWire deck or camcorder should support the most basic functions like returning timecode and accepting basic transport commands. If you discover that your deck or camcorder does not accurately go to specified timecodes or fails to execute special commands, switch to the Apple FireWire Basic protocol. To learn how to switch between FireWire protocols in Final Cut Pro, see "Specifying Device Control Settings" in Chapter 3.

Connecting video devices

Connect video devices to your computer through a FireWire connection or a dedicated video capture card (such as a Kona or Blackmagic card).

◆ Connecting a DV camcorder or deck to your computer couldn't be simpler. All you need is a single FireWire cable, which transmits device control data, timecode, video, and audio between the DV device and your Mac.

◆ If you are using an analog video capture card, device control and timecode signals are transmitted over one cable, while video and audio data use a separate set of cables. The type of audio and video connection cables depends on the type of analog video device you're connecting. See your video capture card's manual or consult the manufacturer's Web site for details.

◆ If you are using a breakout box (such as AJA's Io), the box becomes your central patch point for video and audio signals, plus the device control and timecode signals, from your VTR. The breakout box uses a single FireWire cable for the input and output of all these signals to your Mac.

HARDWARE SELECTION AND CONNECTION

To connect a DV device to your computer with FireWire:

1. Start with a 6-pin-to-4-pin FireWire cable (**Figure 2.4**). Plug the 6-pin connector into the 6-pin Apple FireWire port (**Figure 2.5**) and the 4-pin connector into your video device's DV port. (FireWire ports on external devices are sometimes labeled IEEE 1394, DV IN/OUT, or iLink.) Both connectors snap into place when engaged properly.

2. Turn on the DV camcorder or deck.

3. Switch the DV device to VCR mode (sometimes labeled VTR).

✔ Tips

- If your DV device is Apple FireWire compatible, connect it to the computer and turn it on before installing Final Cut Pro so that the installation program can automatically receive setup information from your DV camcorder or deck.

- Whenever you want to use a DV deck or camcorder with Final Cut Pro, connect the device and turn it on before opening the application so that FCP can detect the device.

- If you want to use a camcorder as your playback/record deck, you must switch it to VCR mode. In VCR mode, the camcorder uses the video and audio connectors or FireWire for input and output. Because a camcorder in Camera mode has switched its inputs to receive information from the CCD sensor and microphone, Final Cut Pro cannot record to the camcorder while it is in Camera mode.

  For more information on controlling your deck or camcorder during video capture, see Chapter 5, "Capturing Video."

  For more information on controlling your deck or camcorder as you output to tape, see Chapter 19, "Creating Final Output."

Figure 2.4 A 6-pin-to-4-pin FireWire cable. The 6-pin (big) end goes into your Mac's FireWire port; plug the 4-pin (small) end into your DV camcorder.

Figure 2.5 The FireWire logo labels the FireWire ports on the back of your computer.

FireWire Cables: Handle with Care

Before you hook up your FireWire connectors, take a careful look at the connector ends (the 4-pin connector is the smaller end). They are easy to connect, but the 4-pin connectors and ports can be especially fragile. Before connecting a 4-pin connector to its corresponding port, be sure to align it properly by matching an indent on the connector to the indent in the port. Do not force the two together.

The 6-pin connector (the larger end) plugs into one of the FireWire ports on the back of your Mac. Don't try to force the 4-pin connector into the computer's 6-pin FireWire port.

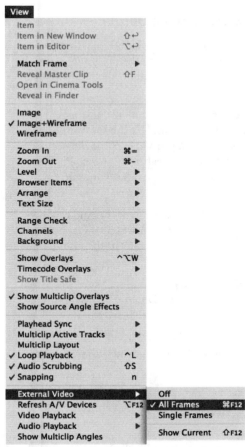

Figure 2.6 Choose View > External Video to check or modify your external video output settings.

Connecting an external NTSC or PAL video monitor

Final Cut Pro is designed to use the audio and video outputs of your DV deck or camcorder to feed an external NTSC or PAL monitor. Because the monitor receives output from Final Cut Pro through your device's outputs, you must have your device on and the FireWire connection to your computer established, or you won't be able to view output on your monitor while you work in Final Cut Pro.

To connect an external NTSC or PAL monitor:

1. Position your video monitor at a comfortable viewing distance from your position in front of the computer.

2. *Do one of the following:*
   - ◆ Connect the audio and video outputs of your video deck or camcorder to the audio and video inputs of your NTSC or PAL monitor.
   - ◆ If you are using additional external speakers, or if your video monitor has no speakers, connect only the video output from your video device to the video input of your monitor. Use your video device's audio outputs to feed your external speakers.

3. After you install Final Cut Pro, you can check or modify your viewing settings by choosing View > External Video (**Figure 2.6**). See the next section, "FCP Protocol: Controlling External Video Output" for details on configuring your external video output options.

✔ Tip

- ■ Choose View > Refresh A/V Devices menu command to re-scan all input/output busses and detect your external devices—convenient when you've forgotten to power up your deck before launching FCP.

FCP Protocol: Controlling External Video Output

The external video display options in Final Cut Pro require a little explanation. Using an external video monitor while editing is really the best way to work, so the program assumes you'll be working in this way and was designed to output video and audio via FireWire whenever a video device is connected to the system.

There are two control points. The first, the View > Video Playback submenu, is where you select an output format and/or a destination for your video output. Use the separate View > Audio Playback menu to route FCP's audio output—Audio Follows Video is the default choice, but if you are using separate audio hardware it should appear in the Audio Playback submenu. This menu is context sensitive; you will see only the options that your currently connected hardware supports.

The same View menu options can also be accessed on the Summary tab of the Audio/Video Settings window. If your video hardware is connected and powered on when you launch FCP for the first time, these playback options should be set automatically in the initial setup process.

Your second point of control is also accessed from the View menu. Think of View > External Video as a valve at the end of a pipe, which can be closed (Off), activated on demand (Single Frame), or wide open (All Frames).

When you're building some heavy effects, waiting for all your frames to render before you can watch playback on your external monitor may be too time consuming, and that's where the View > External Video settings come in handy.

◆ If you choose View > External Video > All Frames, FCP will play all video that does not require rendering, and it will also render the currently displayed frame automatically whenever you are parked on a frame.

◆ If you choose View > External Video > Single Frames, FCP will play all video that does not require rendering, but will render and display a single frame only when you press Shift-F12. This setting lets you preview a single frame of an effected clip on your NTSC or PAL monitor before committing to a full rendering operation.

◆ If you choose View > External Video > Off, you shut off the external video output.

Controlling Video Devices with Final Cut Pro

Final Cut Pro can control external video devices through a FireWire cable or a serial cable.

You can also connect DV and non-DV camcorders or decks that do not support device control to capture video clips and export edited sequences.

Whenever you want to use an external video device, connect and turn on the device before opening Final Cut Pro so the application can detect the device.

If you want to use a camcorder as your playback/record deck, you must switch it to VCR mode. In VCR mode, the camcorder uses the video and audio connectors or FireWire for input and output. Because a camcorder in Camera mode has switched its inputs to receive information from the CCD sensor and microphone, Final Cut Pro cannot record to the camcorder while it is in Camera mode.

For more information on controlling your deck or camcorder during video capture, see Chapter 5, "Capturing Video." For more information on controlling your deck or camcorder as you output to tape, see Chapter 19, "Creating Final Output."

Installing Final Cut Pro

It's a good idea to set up and connect your additional hardware before you install Final Cut Pro because the type of capture hardware you use with Final Cut Pro determines how the software is configured during installation. If you have not yet installed and configured the additional hardware you will be using with your computer, read "Hardware Selection and Connection," earlier in this chapter. If your system is already configured with capture hardware and a camcorder or deck, insert the Final Cut Pro DVD into your DVD drive and follow the onscreen installation instructions.

Where to install FCP?

Here's a recommended installation configuration for a Final Cut Pro system with two hard drives available:

You should leave your fastest drive completely free for media files only. Media files include captured audio and video, as well as rendered media files and any computer-generated graphics or motion graphics.

Keep your Final Cut Pro project files on the same drive as the application.

You should also back up your project files to removable media with such frequency that your behavior seems obsessive to a casual observer. Go ahead, let 'em laugh.

✔ Tips

- For each user, Final Cut Pro creates a separate Final Cut Pro User Data folder and generates a separate Custom Settings folder and Final Cut User Preferences file (**Figure 2.7**).

- One big benefit of personal FCP Preference files is that your individual Scratch Disk preferences stay put, even when you're sharing your FCP system with the masses. As long as you remember to log in to your own identity before you start work, your preferences will load from your User Data folder when you launch FCP.

Figure 2.7 For each user, FCP creates a Final Cut Pro User Data folder. You can find it in each user's Preferences folder (in the user's Library folder).

FCP Protocol: Installing the FCP Suite of Applications

Final Cut Studio is huge—60 GB worth of applications and associated media libraries. Even if you restrict yourself to installing FCP solo, it's wise to consider where to install your new media horde. Final Cut Pro ships with a trio of helper applications—LiveType, Compressor, and Cinema Tools. LiveType includes a big media library, which pushes the minimum disk space required to 13 GB for a default FCP installation. That 12 GB of LiveType media must be installed on your boot drive—unless you take steps. Here are a couple options:

◆ Create a folder called "LiveType Data" on the drive where you want to install the LiveType media, and then install the LiveType media into that folder. Next, create an alias of that folder (the alias must be called *exactly* LiveType Data), and put the folder alias on your boot drive here: `Library/Application Support/LiveType/LiveType Data`. The alias will direct LiveType to the location of its stock media folder.

◆ Install individual LiveType fonts from the application DVD on an as-needed basis. LiveType supports this option; you can preview the fonts and textures without installing the multi-gigabyte LiveType data.

Figure 2.8 If you see scroll bars on the edge of the Canvas's image area, you're zoomed in too far for optimal playback performance, and your external video playback will be disabled. Choose Fit to Window from the Canvas View pop-up menu to bring the entire frame back into view.

Optimizing Performance

Trying to eke out the best possible performance from Final Cut Pro? Here's a rundown of settings and maintenance tips that can help FCP perform more efficiently:

Settings

◆ Turn off file sharing.

◆ Avoid running processor-intensive operations in other open applications while you're working in Final Cut Pro (especially when capturing video).

Display

◆ Make sure the entire image area is visible in windows playing video. If you see scroll bars on the edge of the Viewer or the Canvas (**Figure 2.8**), you're zoomed in too far for optimal performance.

◆ Don't place program windows so that they split across dual monitors.

Disk maintenance

- Store project files on your startup disk, and store media and rendered files on a separate hard disk.

- Maintain 10 percent free space on each disk drive. If you fill your disk to the last megabyte, your performance will take a dive—and that's the *best*-case scenario.

- Defragment disk drives regularly, especially those you use for capturing. You can use a defragmentation utility; or, make a complete backup of your data, erase the disk, and restore your data.

- When a project is finished and archived, delete all files from the disk you used to create the project, and defragment the drive. This helps prepare the disk for the next project.

- Final Cut Pro performs poorly if you try to work with remote media files over a network connection. Copy files from the network to a local disk before importing them.

- It's a good idea to run Disk First Aid, a component of Apple's Disk Utility application, once or twice a month to check your drive's data directory.

The Bottom Line: Running FCP on a "Base-Case" Mac

To get the best performance possible from Final Cut Pro running on a slower G4, you'll have to give up a little flexibility in your display options, but you may find that the improved responsiveness and playback quality are worth it.

1. Eliminate display scaling. Scaling the video to match the size of the playback window in the Viewer or the Canvas is handled by the computer's video card, but it takes a lot of processing power to pull off. To reduce the card's demands on your CPU, set your display option to match DV's native display format: 50 percent, non-square pixels. Go to the Zoom pop-up menu in the Canvas, set the View size to 50 percent, and then uncheck the View as Square Pixels box.

2. In the Monitors preference pane, set your monitor resolution to 1024 by 768 or lower and your color depth to Millions.

3. On the General tab of the User Preferences window, reduce the number of undos as well as the number of recent items. These changes will free up more RAM.

4. Keep your projects lean by deleting old versions of sequences that you no longer need to reference. Smaller projects reduce the amount of RAM necessary to track an open project file.

5. Reinitialize your drives. Quite often, old drive software and/or drivers will impair performance.

OPTIMIZING PERFORMANCE

Troubleshooting

You probably won't encounter any of these problems. But if you run into snags after installing Final Cut Pro and configuring your hardware, the following tips may help.

Many of the tips presented here involve checking and adjusting preferences. But before you start changing individual preferences, try this: Choose Final Cut Pro > Easy Setup, and make sure you're still using the correct Easy Setup for your video format and hardware.

Also, make sure you're running the latest version of Final Cut Pro by checking Apple's Web site.

You'll find a complete guide to setting preferences and presets in Chapter 3, "Presets and Preferences."

You can't establish a device control connection with your camcorder or deck.

◆ Make sure the FireWire cable connecting your computer and DV camcorder is connected properly.

◆ Verify that the camcorder is set to VCR mode.

◆ If your device has a Local/Remote switch, be sure it's set to Remote.

◆ Turn the device off and back on, and then restart Final Cut Pro.

You can't control certain functions of your camcorder or deck.

◆ Make sure the FireWire cable connecting your computer and DV camcorder is connected properly.

◆ If you are using a device with FireWire, try switching the device control protocol from Apple FireWire to FireWire Basic.

◆ If your device has a Local/Remote switch, make sure it's switched to Remote.

You see a "Missing scratch disk" warning.

◆ Make sure your scratch disks are powered up and mounted properly. You should see your disks on the Finder Desktop.

◆ Make sure your designated Capture Scratch folder is in its proper location.

◆ If you are sharing Final Cut Pro with other users on a multiuser system, make sure you are logged in as the current user—FCP creates a separate set of preference settings for each user.

TROUBLESHOOTING

You don't hear audio on your computer's speakers when playing video from your camcorder or deck.

◆ Make sure your audio cables are connected properly.

◆ When you enable your external video output to monitor video externally (by choosing All Frames from the View > External Video menu), your audio and video are routed to your external monitor or video device, and your computer's speakers are not receiving any audio. Make sure your external monitor and speakers are on and that the volume is turned up. To disable external video output, choose View > External Video and select Off.

Video is not visible on an external NTSC or PAL monitor.

◆ Make sure your cables are connected properly and that your monitor is on.

◆ Verify that the camcorder is set to VCR mode.

◆ Choose View > Refresh A/V Devices to re-scan all input/output busses and detect all external devices that are properly powered up and connected.

◆ Confirm that external video output is enabled. Choose View > External Video, and make sure the All Frames option is checked.

◆ Make sure the Capture window is closed.

You notice dropped frames on your NTSC or PAL monitor during DV playback from the Timeline.

Like the common cold, dropped frames are frequently a symptom of an overworked system. Refer to page IV-438 of Apple's *Final Cut Pro User Manual* PDF, "Solutions to Common Problems," for a comprehensive list of possible causes of dropped frames. Here are a few easy things to try first:

◆ In the Canvas, choose Fit to Window from the View pop-up menu to ensure that the image area displays the entire frame.

◆ Reduce the Canvas or Viewer view size to 50 percent.

◆ Disable Show as Square Pixels in the Zoom pop-up menu.

◆ Turn off Mirror on Desktop During Playback on the A/V Settings tab of the Audio/Video Settings window.

◆ Set the Audio Quality Playback to Low Quality, and reduce the number of Real-Time Audio Mixing tracks specified on the General tab in the User Preferences window.

◆ Turn off AppleTalk and file sharing.

◆ Make sure your media drives are fast enough to feed media files to FCP and that the drives have not become so fragmented that their performance is impaired.

PRESETS AND PREFERENCES

3

Final Cut Pro's designers have carefully organized the tools you use to configure settings and preferences. The goal of this organization is to make it much easier for editors using the most common hardware and video formats to configure FCP—and much more difficult for users to unintentionally modify individual settings within a preset configuration.

FCP's preset principle is balanced by a highly customizable interface. At the end of this chapter you'll learn about options for reconfiguring Final Cut Pro's interface to complement your personal working preferences.

About Easy Setups, Presets, Settings, and Preferences

Capture, device control, and sequence settings are all organized into preset configurations, and these Audio/Video presets are grouped into master presets called *Easy Setups*.

Any of these preset configurations are completely customizable, but most FCP users should be able to choose an Easy Setup based on their hardware and video format, specify a scratch disk for media capture on the Scratch tab of the System Settings window, and forget about settings until they change their external hardware.

FCP preference settings are accessed from four menu choices: Easy Setup, Audio/Video Settings, User Preferences, and System Settings (**Figure 3.1**).

Easy Setup

An Easy Setup is a master preset configuration of multiple Final Cut Pro settings: presets for a Device Control preset, a Capture preset, a Sequence preset, and Audio/Video Playback settings. Instead of choosing several presets and Video and Audio Playback settings using various tabs, you can make one selection in a single window: Easy Setup. FCP offers several standard Easy Setups, but you also have the option of customizing an Easy Setup.

Any customized setups you create are stored in the Custom Settings folder in the Final Cut Pro Documents folder, which makes your custom setups portable.

Figure 3.1
Access preference settings from four Final Cut Pro menu choices: Easy Setup, Audio/Video Settings, User Preferences, and System Settings.

How to "Trash Your Prefs"

FCP has made setting up preferences simple, but you still may find that you need to delete your FCP preferences files (or "trash your prefs") to force FCP to restore all your program settings to their default values. You will need to delete four files:

1. Quit Final Cut Pro.

2. Go to User/Library/Preferences/ and remove the file called com.apple.FinalCutPro.plist.

3. Then go to User/Library/Preferences/ Final Cut Pro User Data/ and remove the other three preferences files, called Final Cut Pro 6.0 Prefs, Final Cut Pro Obj Cache, and Final Cut Pro Prof Cache.

After deleting the files, relaunch Final Cut Pro with all your external hardware on and connected. You'll see the Choose Setup dialog box. Here's your chance to reset your preferences from scratch.

If you'd like an easier way to backup, restore, and trash your FCP preference files, Anders Holck, a community-minded FCP user in Denmark, has created a freeware program called "FCP Rescue" to do exactly that. Download Anders's helper at: http://fcprescue.andersholck.com.

Audio/Video settings

FCP's Audio/Video settings have their own preference window, called Audio/Video Settings. That's where you can make detailed adjustments to your Sequence presets, Capture presets, Device Control presets, Video Playback, and Audio Playback settings, should the need arise. Your Audio/Video settings are summarized on the Summary tab. If for some reason you want to modify your underlying basic QuickTime settings, you can access them through the tabs in the Audio/Video Settings window.

User Preferences and System Settings

Unlike the Audio/Video settings, which are largely dictated by your hardware and video format, a preference is a setting that specifies how *you* want to work with your media in Final Cut Pro. FCP preferences have been divided between two different windows: User Preferences and System Settings. The settings in these windows affect all your Final Cut Pro projects.

Modifying the Settings of an Existing Item

If you change the settings on the Easy Setup, Audio/Video, or Timeline Options tab of the User Preferences window, your change will be reflected in new projects, sequences, or items created after you changed the settings. Here's how and where you modify the settings of a project, sequence, or clip you've already created:

◆ **Item Properties:** Control-click the item's icon in the Browser or Timeline, then select Item Properties from the shortcut menu.

◆ **Sequence Settings:** Control-click the sequence's icon in the Browser, then select Settings from the shortcut menu.

◆ **Project Properties:** Open the project and then choose Edit > Project Properties.

Accessing preferences and settings

Frequently, Final Cut Pro provides more than one route to access your settings for presets and preferences. For example, you can access the capture preferences from the Capture Presets tab in the Audio/Video Settings window, and also directly in the Log and Capture window by selecting a preset from the Capture/Input pop-up menu located on the Capture Settings tab (**Figure 3.2**). The list of Capture presets you access directly from the Log and Capture window is labeled Capture/Input, but the preset list is the same, and any changes you make on the Log and Capture window's Capture Settings tab will be reflected on the Audio/Video Settings window's Summary tab (**Figure 3.3**) and in the Easy Setup window (**Figure 3.4**).

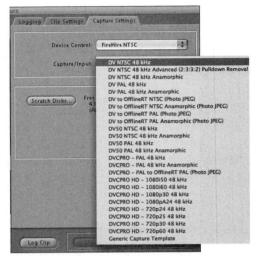

Figure 3.2 Select a different Capture preset from the Capture/Input pop-up menu.

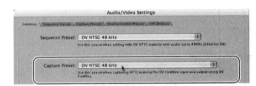

Figure 3.3 Your change is reflected on the Summary tab of the Audio/Video Settings window.

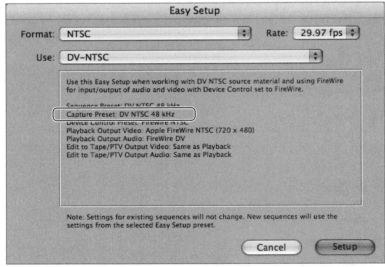

Figure 3.4 You'll also see your Capture preset change in the Easy Setup window. All three windows reference the same set of Capture preferences.

EASY SETUPS/PRESETS/SETTINGS/PREFERENCES

One of the reasons FCP's designers based their configuration scheme on presets is that they wanted to make it easy to completely configure the program settings without having to alter individual settings. And it is easy to get confused. Some settings windows look the same but actually modify different program settings. For example, Sequence presets and Capture presets have separate QuickTime settings options. A mismatch between capture settings and sequence settings makes clips play back poorly when you start to edit them in the Timeline, and a settings mismatch is one of the primary causes of user difficulties with FCP.

So how can you avoid problems and confusion? When you launch Final Cut Pro for the first time after installing it, your answers to the Initial Setup questions determine the settings you see in the Easy Setup, Audio/Video Settings, and User Preferences windows. It's best to start with the default settings, use the recommended Easy Setup, and make changes only if you have a specific problem. If you do make changes, your troubleshooting will be most effective if you make one change at a time.

Finding Additional and Third-Party Presets

Final Cut Pro loaded its default preset files when you installed the program, but you may want to install custom presets for any third-party hardware or software you are using with FCP. Check with the hardware manufacturers; they may have created a custom FCP preset. Having the correct custom preset for your external hardware can make configuring Final Cut Pro a whole lot easier.

To install additional and third-party presets, just copy them into the correct folder. Here is the directory path to that folder: **Library/Application Support/Final Cut Pro System Support/Plugins/**.

The next time you open Final Cut Pro, the presets will be available in the Audio/Video Settings window.

EASY SETUPS/PRESETS/SETTINGS/PREFERENCES

Using Easy Setups

An Easy Setup is a single preset configuration of multiple Final Cut Pro settings: a Device Control preset, a Capture preset, a Sequence preset, and Video and Audio Playback settings. FCP offers several standard Easy Setups, but you also have the option of customizing an Easy Setup.

You selected an Easy Setup as part of the initial setup process. Once you have an Easy Setup that works for your Final Cut Pro system, you shouldn't need to change it unless you change your video hardware or video format. If your FCP system includes a variety of external hardware, Easy Setups make it simple to switch FCP's configuration quickly and accurately.

Easy Setups are portable; you can create a custom Easy Setup and install it on another FCP system or email it to a colleague. In this section, you'll learn how to choose the right Easy Setup, how to switch to a different Easy Setup, how to find the folder where Easy Setups are stored so you can add and remove Easy Setups, and how to customize an Easy Setup.

How to choose an Easy Setup

The Easy Setups window displays the currently selected presets for each setting—Sequence, Capture, and Device Control, plus Audio and Video Playback—that make up your current Easy Setup, plus a brief description of when you should use the currently selected setup.

FCP's default DV-NTSC (or DV-PAL) setup will be fine for most FCP users working with DV hardware. FCP supports a staggering number of video formats; if you'd like to see the entire list, choose (all formats) from the Format and (all rates) from the Rate pop-up menu, and then you'll see a long list of other setups to choose from in the Use pop-up menu (**Figure 3.5**).

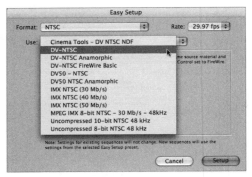

Figure 3.5 The Easy Setup window. Choose the option that matches the format of the video you want to capture.

When should you switch to another Easy Setup? The basis for selecting a preset is always *matching*:

◆ You want your Capture preset to match the recorded format of the DV tape you're capturing. If the tape was recorded with 16-bit, 48 kHz audio, then the default DV-NTSC setup is fine. If you're capturing DV with 12-bit, 32 kHz audio, you'll need to switch to an Easy Setup with the same settings. If you're capturing DV that was shot in anamorphic (wide-screen) format, switch to a setup that includes anamorphic settings.

◆ Your Sequence preset must match the format of your Capture preset. All Easy setups in FCP take care of this for you.

◆ Your Device Control setting must match the requirements of the video hardware you're controlling. Final Cut Pro is pretty good at automatically selecting the correct device control setting, but if you're having trouble controlling your video device from inside FCP, check the Final Cut Pro Qualified Devices page at `www.apple.com/finalcutpro/qualification.html`. Your equipment may require a different device protocol or an additional helper script.

◆ Your Video Playback settings must match the video format (DV or PAL) of the device you're outputting video to.

✔ Tip

■ DV-NTSC, FCP's default setup, is designed to complement the recommended settings on most DV decks and camcorders. (The default settings are the same in the two video standards that FCP supports: NTSC and PAL.)

Easy Setups to Go

One of the great things about Easy Setups is that they're portable. You can copy your customized Easy Setups from the folder where Final Cut Pro stores them and take them with you if you move to a different FCP system. You can even email them to a client or colleague (or to your dad when he's having trouble configuring his FCP system).

Here's the protocol for FCP's Custom Settings folders:

Customized Easy Setups can be stored in either of two Custom Settings folders. Setups you want to reserve for your own use should be stored with other personal preferences in your Final Cut Pro User Data folder. Here's the directory path: (*Your User Name*)/**Library/Preferences/Final Cut Pro User Data/Custom Settings.**

FCP's stock Easy Setups files are stored in the general access Custom Settings folder. Here's the directory path: **Library/Application Support/Final Cut Pro System Support/Custom Settings.**

Add or remove Easy Setups by copying them or deleting them in either of the Custom Settings folders.

To switch to a different Easy Setup:

1. Choose Final Cut Pro > Easy Setup.

2. *Do one of the following:*

   ◆ Specify the format and frame of your project's media in the pop-up menus; you'll see a restricted list of Easy Setups.

   ◆ Choose (all formats) from the Format pop-up menu and (all rates) from the Rate pop-up menu to see the complete list of available Easy Setups.

3. From the Use pop-up menu, select an Easy Setup (**Figure 3.6**).

   A summary of your selected Easy Setup appears below the pop-up menu (**Figure 3.7**).

4. Click Setup.

   The new Easy Setup affects only new projects and sequences and doesn't change settings for existing projects and sequences.

To create a custom Easy Setup:

1. Choose Final Cut Pro > Audio/Video Settings.

2. On the Summary tab, select from the preset pop-up menus to compose your custom Easy Setup (**Figure 3.8**), or make more specific preset modifications on the settings tabs. Information on specifying presets appears later in this chapter.

3. Specify Video and Audio Playback settings.

4. Click Create Easy Setup.

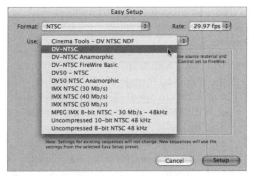

Figure 3.6 From the Use pop-up menu, select an Easy Setup.

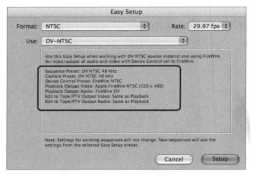

Figure 3.7 A summary of the Easy Setup you chose appears below the pop-up menu.

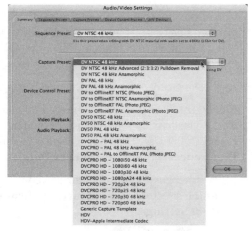

Figure 3.8 Select from the preset pop-up menus on the Summary tab of the Audio/Video Settings window to compose your custom Easy Setup.

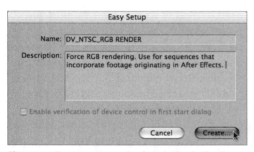

Figure 3.9 Type a name and a description in the Easy Setup dialog box. Specify whether you want FCP to check the device control status each time you launch the program, then click Create.

5. In the Easy Setup dialog box, enter a name and a description. Check Enable Verification of Device Control in First Start Dialog if you want FCP to check the device control status each time you launch the program; then click Create (**Figure 3.9**).

6. The Save dialog box appears, with the Custom Settings folder (the default storage location for Easy Setups) selected. Enter a filename and navigate to your desired folder location if you don't want to use the default.

7. Click Save.

Your new Easy Setup becomes the selected Easy Setup and appears in the Setup For pop-up menu of the Easy Setup window (**Figure 3.10**).

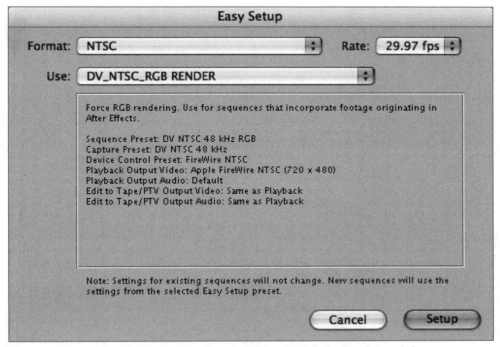

Figure 3.10 Your new Easy Setup appears as the selected Easy Setup in the Easy Setup window.

Using Audio/Video Presets

A preset is a group of saved settings that are automatically applied any time you create a new project or sequence. The beauty of a preset is that you can configure all your settings correctly with a single selection because these settings have already been tested with your video hardware and format.

In the Audio/Video Settings window, the Summary tab (**Figure 3.11**) displays the currently selected preset for each setting—Sequence, Capture, and Device Control, plus your Video and Audio Playback settings—that makes up your current Easy Setup. If you

need to modify your current Audio/Video preset settings, you can select a different preset from the pop-up menus on the Summary tab, or you can open the tab for the setting you need to modify and specify custom settings. Try to use the stock presets before you start tinkering with your settings. This section will explain how to choose, edit, and delete an existing preset and how to create a new preset. For detailed information on your settings options for the different types of Audio/Video presets, see "Specifying Sequence Settings," "Specifying Capture Settings," "Specifying Device Control Settings," and "Using Video and Audio Playback Settings," later in this chapter.

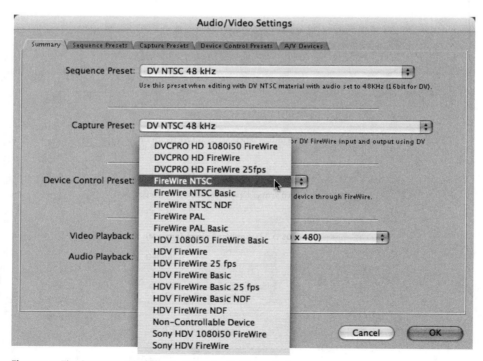

Figure 3.11 The Summary tab of the Audio/Video Settings window.

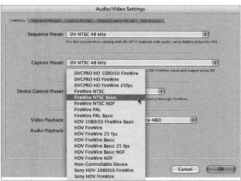

Figure 3.12 You can modify your Easy Setup by switching to a different preset on the Summary tab of the Audio/Video Settings window.

Figure 3.13 Your Easy Setup designation switches to Custom, and your new settings are summarized in the Easy Setup window.

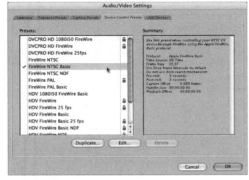

Figure 3.14 Click the preset's name to view its settings in the Summary box on the right side of the preset tab. Careful: If you click in the leftmost column of the Presets box, you'll switch the default preset.

To switch to a different preset in your current Easy Setup:

1. Choose Final Cut Pro > Audio/Video Settings.

2. On the Summary tab, choose a different preset from one of the pop-up menus (**Figure 3.12**); then click OK.

   If your newly selected preset configuration doesn't match an existing Easy Setup, Final Cut Pro switches your Easy Setup designation to Custom Setup and summarizes your new settings in the Easy Setup window (**Figure 3.13**). If your new settings match an existing Easy Setup, FCP switches to that Easy Setup.

To view settings for a preset:

1. Choose Final Cut Pro > Audio/Video Settings.

2. In the Audio/Video Settings window, click the tab for the preset settings you want to view.

3. On the tab for your preset, click the preset's name in the list (**Figure 3.14**).

   The Summary box lists the properties of the selected preset. The default preset is indicated by a checkmark in the left column of the Presets box.

4. When you're done, click OK to close the Audio/Video Settings window.

USING AUDIO/VIDEO PRESETS

To edit an existing preset:

1. Choose Final Cut Pro > Audio/Video Settings.

2. In the Audio/Video Settings window, click the tab for preset type you want to edit (**Figure 3.15**).

3. On the preset tab, click the preset you want to edit; then *do one of the following*:

   ◆ Click Duplicate to open an editable copy of this preset in the Preset Editor. This is the only way to edit Final Cut Pro's presets, which are locked by default.

   ◆ Click Edit to modify an existing unlocked preset.

   The Preset Editor window appears, with settings for the selected preset displayed.

4. In the window, enter a new name and description for your preset; modify its settings (**Figure 3.16**); then click OK.

   The modified preset becomes the currently selected preset, appearing in the appropriate Summary tab pop-up menu (**Figure 3.17**).

5. When you've finished making changes in the Audio/Video Settings window, click OK to save your changes.

To create a new preset:

◆ There is no way to create a new preset entirely from scratch. Duplicate and then edit the preset whose settings are closest to the custom preset you require.

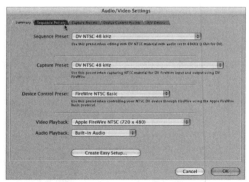

Figure 3.15 In the Audio/Video Settings window, click the tab for the type of preset you want to edit.

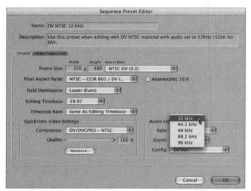

Figure 3.16 Enter a new name and description for your preset; then modify its settings.

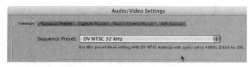

Figure 3.17 The modified preset becomes the currently selected preset and appears on the appropriate Summary tab pop-up menu.

USING AUDIO/VIDEO PRESETS

To delete a preset:

1. In the Audio/Video Settings window, click the tab for the type of preset you want to delete.

2. On that tab's list of presets, click the preset you want to delete; then click Delete (**Figure 3.18**).

✔ Tips

- You won't be able to delete the currently selected preset (that's the one with the checkmark next to it) or a locked preset (any preset with a lock icon displayed in the right column).

- Think before you delete a preset because you can't undo this action. Once you delete a preset, it's gone. You can restore FCP's stock presets, though, by reinstalling the program.

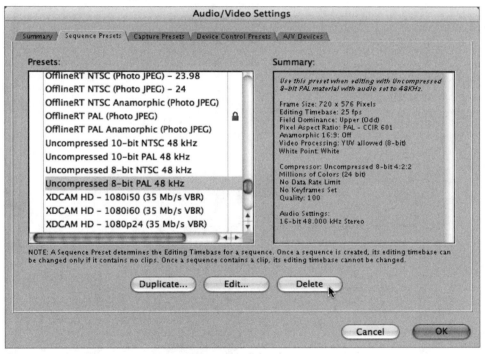

Figure 3.18 Select the preset you want to delete; then click Delete.

USING AUDIO/VIDEO PRESETS

Specifying Sequence Settings

Final Cut Pro provides a selection of stock sequence setting presets. Using a preset ensures that each new sequence you create will have the same settings. You can also choose to be prompted to specify the preset for each new sequence you create. The Preset Editor window allows you to duplicate and edit existing sequence presets to create new ones. The preset you choose will be applied to all new sequences until you change it. Sequence settings for existing sequences are not affected.

You can open and review or modify an existing sequence's settings in its Sequence Settings window. For more information, see "Changing the Settings of an Existing Sequence" in Chapter 4.

To edit general sequence settings for the current preset:

1. On the Sequence Presets tab of the Audio/Video Settings window, select a preset (**Figure 3.19**); then click the Edit button.

   If the preset is locked, a dialog box appears indicating that a copy will be made for editing; then the Sequence Preset Editor window appears. Sequence settings are available on the Sequence Preset Editor's General tab and Video Processing tab.

2. Enter a name and description for the preset. If it's based on an existing preset with one or two changes, you might note the base preset plus the changes.

3. On the General tab, you can modify the default settings for any of the following (**Figure 3.20**):

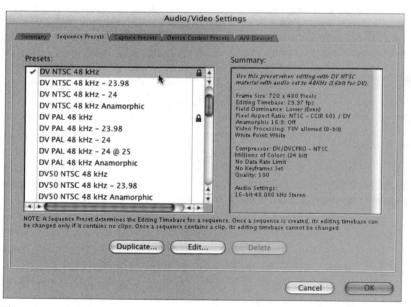

Figure 3.19 Select the preset you want to edit on the Sequence Presets tab of the Audio/Video Settings window; then click the Edit button.

◆ **Frame Size:** Specify the frame size for the output of the sequence. Enter a custom frame size in the Width and Height fields, or choose a pre-defined frame size in the Aspect Ratio pop-up menu.

◆ **Pixel Aspect Ratio:** Specify a pixel aspect ratio that is compatible with your source video.

◆ **Anamorphic 16:9:** If your source video is 16:9, checking this box ensures that FCP will interpret and display your source media's pixel aspect ratio properly.

◆ **Field Dominance:** Specify the field to be displayed first on an NTSC monitor. DV defaults to the Lower (Even) setting. If field dominance is set incorrectly, moving areas of the image will have jagged edges.

◆ **Editing Timebase:** This field displays the currently selected editing timebase. The editing timebase should be identical to the frame rate of the source clips in the sequence. All source clips with a frame rate that does not match the editing timebase are converted to the sequence's editing timebase and will require rendering. You can modify an existing sequence's timebase only if there are no clips in it.

◆ **Timecode Rate:** The default setting—Same as Editing Timebase—matches the timecode playback rate to the Editing Timebase setting for this sequence preset. Always use this default setting unless your project requires a different timecode playback rate; for example, if you are editing 24 fps film that's been transferred to 25 fps PAL video.

◆ **QuickTime Video and Audio Settings:** The current video compression codec settings for the selected sequence preset are displayed under QuickTime Video Settings. The current audio sample-rate setting for this preset is displayed under QuickTime Audio Settings. Unless you have a specific reason to make a change, stick with the default settings. Selecting the appropriate sequence preset in the main Audio/Video Settings window should load the correct values for all other settings. Refer to Apple's *Final Cut Pro User Manual* PDF for details on other QuickTime settings options.

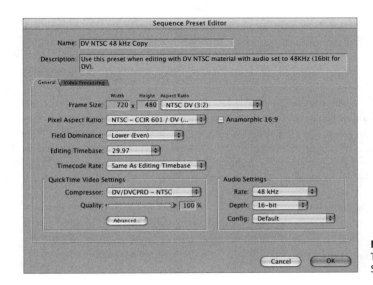

Figure 3.20
The General tab of the Sequence Preset Editor.

Specifying video processing settings for a Sequence preset

The settings on the Video Processing tab allow you to specify how FCP will interpret color space when rendering clips used in sequences created with this sequence preset.

Older versions of QuickTime used DV codecs that converted YUV (the color space that DV video uses) to RGB (the color space that computers use) whenever rendering was required. This conversion could generate noticeable color or luminance shifts. Now, because QuickTime has added support for rendering in YUV (also known as YCrCb) color space, you have a choice. If you select a QuickTime codec that supports YUV color space, you'll be able to set additional options on the Video Processing tab.

To edit video processing settings for the current preset:

On the Video Processing tab of the Sequence Preset Editor window (**Figure 3.21**), you can modify the following default settings:

- **Always Render in RGB:** Check this box to force codecs that normally process color using the YUV (or YCrCb) color space to render in RGB color space. This may cause slight color shifts in rendered material.

- **Render in 8-bit YUV:** Choose 8-bit YUV rendering if you are working with 8-bit source video (DV/DVCAM) or using a capture card that handles 8-bit YUV video.

- **Render 10-bit material in high-precision YUV:** Choose this option if you are working with 10-bit source video.

- **Render all YUV material in high-precision YUV:** Choose this option to use additional video bit depth to improve the quality of 8-bit video that requires complex render processing. 10-bit render files take longer to compute.

- **Process Maximum White As** (note that this pop-up menu appears only if Always Render in RGB is not selected):

  - **Super-White:** Choose this to match the maximum brightness of imported clips from RGB color space to the super-white levels of clips from DV camcorders.

  - **White:** Choose this to limit the maximum brightness of imported clips created in RGB color space to 100 IRE.

  This setting allows you to match the brightness levels of DV video source clips to integrate better with RGB elements. Many DV camcorders record video with white values that are brighter than 100 IRE (known as super-white). Brightness

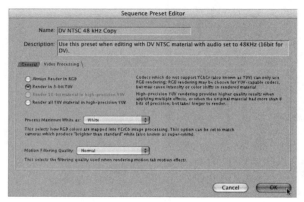

Figure 3.21 The Video Processing tab of the Sequence Preset Editor window.

levels in these DV clips with super-white white values may not match other elements in your sequence—for example, imported graphics files or Adobe After Effects clips created in RGB color space.

◆ **Motion Filtering Quality:** Choose a rendering quality for motion effects from this pop-up menu. Fastest is equivalent to pre-FCP 6 motion-effect rendering quality. Normal and Best offer superior resolution and motion smoothness, but require more processing power for real time and rendering.

✔ **Tip**

■ You might choose Always Render in RGB if you want to use After Effects filters and Final Cut Pro filters in the same project. After Effects filters can render only in RGB space, so you'd choose this option to force the Final Cut Pro filters—which render in YUV by default—to render in RGB as well, thus ensuring a consistent result.

RGB or YCrCb: Choosing a Color Space

When you choose RGB or YCrCb (also known as YUV) color space on the Video Processing tab of the Sequence Settings window, you are specifying the color space in which the rendered sections of your sequence will be processed.

Rendered material is frequently intercut with unprocessed footage, so if you want your rendered footage to blend seamlessly with the unprocessed sections, it's critical that you understand how the choice of RGB or YCrCb color space in your sequence settings can affect the image quality of your rendered material.

DV video and computers use different schemes for interpreting image data, and this can cause headaches for the FCP user.

YCrCb (the color space used by DV video) organizes stored image data into three values for each pixel: one for luminance (Y) and two for color information (Cr and Cb).

RGB (the color space used by computers) also stores three values for each pixel, but all three represent color data: one each for the red, green, and blue components of the image.

Older versions of QuickTime used DV codecs that required the conversion of YCrCb (the color space used by DV video) to RGB (the color space used by computers) whenever rendering was required.

Because RGB allows a wider range of color and luminance values (0 through 255) than YCrCb, which usually has a more restricted range (16 through 235), the most intense RGB colors (including blacks and whites at the far ends of the luminance scale) can get clipped when you convert them back to the YCrCb video color space. The results: "chroma clamping," when RGB colors lose their saturation, and "luma clamping," when an RGB white value greater than 235 is clipped back to the 235 maximum on conversion back to YCrCb.

Since QuickTime has added support for rendering in YCrCb color space, you have a choice. The settings on the Video Processing tab allow you to specify how FCP will interpret color space when rendering clips used in sequences created with this sequence preset.

SPECIFYING SEQUENCE SETTINGS

Specifying Capture Settings

Capture settings determine the quality at which Final Cut Pro captures video, and you must set your capture preferences before you can capture any media. Your capture settings will determine your clip's native format. Capture preferences specify the capture board you are using, compression method, frame rate, frame size, and audio sampling rate. Final Cut Pro sets capture preferences for you automatically when you install the program, so unless you change your hardware or know the change you want to make, don't feel you need to alter the default settings. One exception to this guideline: Before you capture, you'll want to check the audio settings to specify which audio channels you want captured, adjust your audio input levels, and specify a sample rate. For more information, see Chapter 5, "Capturing Video."

✔ Tip

- If you are using a third-party video capture card with your Final Cut Pro system, check the manufacturer's documentation or Web site for the latest information on configuring the product to work smoothly with Final Cut Pro. A custom preset may be available for you to download and install, or you may find details on configuring the Capture preset correctly.

Specifying QuickTime Settings for Video and Audio Capture

Final Cut Pro has incorporated the QuickTime settings you use the most into pop-up menus in the Capture Preset Editor. You can modify most QuickTime settings for your Capture preset right in the Capture Preset Editor window.

The video and audio options that appear in the QuickTime Video Settings and Audio Settings pop-up menus depend on which video hardware is connected to your FCP system. It's critical that your capture settings match the hardware you're using. Unless you have a specific reason to make a change, stick with the default settings that match your capture hardware. Selecting the appropriate Capture preset in the main Capture Presets window should load the correct values for all other settings.

To edit settings for the current Capture preset:

1. On the Capture Presets tab of the Audio/Video Settings window, select a preset; then click the Edit button.

If the preset is locked, a dialog box appears indicating that a copy will be made for editing; then the Capture Preset Editor window appears (**Figure 3.22**).

2. You can modify default settings for the following:

- **Name:** Enter a name for the preset.

- **Description:** Enter a description of the preset. If it's based on an existing preset with one or two changes, you might note the base preset plus the changes.

- **Frame Size:** Choose a preset frame size from the Aspect Ratio pop-up menu, or choose Custom and then enter a custom value in the Width and Height fields.

- **Anamorphic 16:9:** Check this box if you are capturing 16:9 media.

- **Capture Card Supports Simultaneous Play Through and Capture:** Check this box if your video capture card is equipped to display video on an external video monitor while the Log and Capture window is open and you're capturing video. Check your capture card's documentation.

- **Remove Advanced Pulldown (2:3:3:2) From DV-25 and DV-50 Sources:** Check this box to remove 2:3:3:2 pull-down from 24P video material that has been converted to conform to a 29.97 fps DV stream. This feature will remove redundant frame fields created by the pull-down, allowing you to edit in 23.98 fps progressive video. For more information on editing 24-frame material, see Apple's Cinema Tools documentation.

- **High-Quality Video Play Through:** Check this box to enable high-quality DV playback in the Log and Capture window.

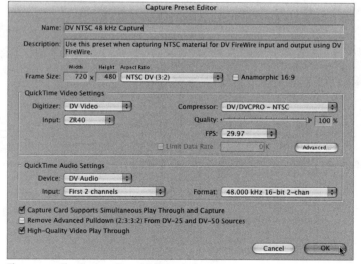

Figure 3.22 The Capture Preset Editor window.

SPECIFYING CAPTURE SETTINGS

Specifying Device Control Settings

Before you can begin logging and digitizing source footage, you need to specify device control settings. Even if your external video deck or camcorder doesn't support device control, you'll still have limited capture and output capabilities, but to get the benefits of Final Cut Pro's batch capture and recapturing functions, device control is a must. Before you modify the default settings, try the recommended Device Control preset for your external deck or camcorder. The Device Control Preset Editor window allows you to create and edit device control presets.

To edit settings for the current Device Control preset:

1. On the Device Control Presets tab of the Audio/Video Settings window, select a preset; then click the Edit button.

   If the preset is locked, a dialog box appears indicating that a copy will be made for editing; then the Device Control Preset Editor window appears.

2. You can modify the default settings for any of the following (**Figure 3.23**):

   ◆ **Name:** Enter a name for the preset.

   ◆ **Description:** Enter a description of the preset. If it's based on an existing preset with one or two changes, note the base preset plus the changes.

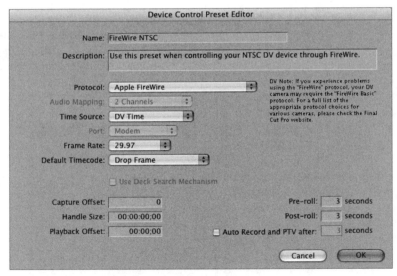

Figure 3.23 The Device Control Preset Editor window.

◆ **Protocol:** Choose the device control protocol your camcorder or deck uses:

    ◆ **FireWire (IEEE 1394):** If your deck or camcorder uses FireWire, try selecting the Apple FireWire protocol first. This is the default protocol if you select DV during the installation setup. With Apple FireWire as your selected device protocol, your FireWire deck or camcorder should support the most basic functions, such as returning timecode and accepting basic transport commands. If you discover that your deck or camcorder can't move to specified timecodes or fails to execute special commands, switch to the Apple FireWire Basic protocol. For more information, see "About Apple FireWire" in Chapter 2.

    ◆ **Other protocols:** Check your deck or camcorder manual for the correct protocol type; then select it from the Protocol pop-up menu.

◆ **Audio Mapping:** Choose an audio track configuration compatible with the record deck you use for Edit to Tape operations. Check your deck's manual for details. If you're using a DV device, there's only one option available.

◆ **Time Source:** Specify the timecode format supported by your deck or camcorder. Check the device's manual for timecode specifications.

    ◆ **LTC:** Longitudinal timecode is recorded on a linear track of the tape and can be read while the tape is moving.

    ◆ **VITC:** Vertical interval timecode is contained in the vertical blanking of a signal and can be read when the tape is paused on a frame.

    ◆ **LTC+VITC:** A combination of longitudinal timecode and vertical interval timecode ensures that timecode can be read while the tape is in motion or paused.

    ◆ **Timer:** This format specifies a clock-based value as the timecode.

    ◆ **DV Time:** Digital video timecode is available for FireWire, Sony VISCA, and LANC protocols and should be selected when using DV formats.

◆ **Port:** Choose a port to specify the computer port to which your device control cable is connected.

◆ **Frame Rate:** Select the correct frame rate for your system's broadcast standard. For NTSC, select 29.97. For PAL, select 25.

continues on next page

◆ **Default Timecode:** Choose a default timecode format. If you usually work with DV tapes, choose a drop-frame format.

The Default Timecode setting is designed to speed FCP's identification of your timecode format when you capture with a DV/FireWire setup. Typically it takes several seconds of playback before FCP can determine whether a newly loaded tape is using drop-frame or non-drop-frame timecode. The Default Timecode control gives FCP a hint and reduces the delay.

If you load a tape with a timecode format that's different from what you specify here, FCP will still detect and correctly identify your tape's format, but it could take several seconds.

◆ **Use Deck Search Mechanism:** Check this box to use a deck's internal search mechanism. Turn off this option if your deck has problems shuttling the tape to a specified timecode during capture. This option is available only for systems using serial device control.

◆ **Capture Offset:** Enter a value to calibrate your system to your tape deck when using Log and Capture. You may not need to offset your timecode, but if the timecode you capture doesn't match the timecode on your video deck, you may need to change the capture offset or playback offset. See Chapter 5, "Capturing Video."

◆ **Handle Size:** Enter a duration (in seconds) to determine handle sizes for batch-captured clips. Handles provide extra frames on either end of the captured clip for editing flexibility.

◆ **Playback Offset:** Enter a duration (in seconds) to delay FCP's playback. You use this to compensate for delays between the start of playback and the start of recording on the deck when you edit to tape. Playback offset normally is set to

zero. Enter a positive number to start playback before your deck starts to record. Enter a negative number to start playback after recording begins. If you discover that the first few frames laid to tape during an Edit to Tape operation are duplicates, enter a positive value in this field equal to the number of frames being repeated.

◆ **Pre-roll:** Enter a duration to determine the amount of video your deck or camcorder will play before the Capture In point you specify in the Log and Capture window. If your deck is having problems cuing up during capture, increase this duration.

◆ **Post-roll:** Enter a duration to determine the amount of video your deck or camcorder will play after the specified Capture Out point.

◆ **Auto Record and PTV After:** Check this box to enable FCP to automatically place your deck or camcorder into Record mode during a Print to Video operation. Enter a duration (in seconds) in the Seconds field to delay FCP's playback during the Print to Video operation. If you leave the box unchecked, you'll be prompted to put your deck into Record mode manually, which is how Print to Video worked in earlier versions of FCP.

✔ **Tip**

■ After you've specified Device Control preferences, you should capture some footage from a tape with burned-in timecode to determine whether you need to calibrate your system. You may not need to offset your timecode, but if the timecode you capture doesn't match the timecode on your video deck, you may need to change the timecode offset or playback offset. See Chapter 5 for more information on calibrating timecode offsets.

Using Video and Audio Playback Settings

External Video and Audio Playback settings specify how Final Cut Pro feeds video and audio to your external video and audio hardware, which in turn feeds your external video monitors and audio speakers. If you're using a single external deck or camcorder for both audio and video output, you don't need to configure separate Audio Playback settings; FCP's default settings will automatically configure compatible Audio Playback settings to match your selected video device. Because FCP supports output of multiple audio channels, you can use qualified audio hardware for separate audio capture and output. If you do, you must configure video and audio output settings separately.

You control Final Cut Pro's external video settings in three locations:

◆ The Video Playback pop-up menu on the Summary tab of the Audio/Video Settings window displays the external video setting for your current Easy Setup. You can use the pop-up menu on the Summary tab to select a different setting. FCP will use this setting to route video output for both playing and recording. This menu is context sensitive; you will see only the options that your currently connected hardware will support.

◆ The A/V Devices tab of the Audio/Video Settings window offers the complete array of external video settings. You can select one output destination for playing your video output and a different output routing for recording video output.

◆ The View > External Video menu selection is the third control point for external video output. You can use this control to turn off FCP's external video output or to control display of rendered frames on external video monitors. To learn more about choreographing FCP's external video settings, see "FCP Protocol: Controlling External Video Output" in Chapter 2.

To select a Video Playback setting from the Audio/Video Settings Summary tab:

1. Choose Final Cut Pro > Audio/Video Settings.

2. From the options in the Video Playback pop-up menu on the Summary tab (**Figure 3.24**), *choose one of the following*; then click OK:

   ◆ **None:** Choose this option to turn off external video output.

   ◆ **Apple FireWire NTSC:** Choose this option to send the contents of the Canvas or Viewer to the connected NTSC FireWire device.

   ◆ **Apple FireWire PAL:** Choose this option to send the contents of the Canvas or Viewer to the connected PAL FireWire device.

   ◆ **Other video capture interface:** If you are using FCP with a third-party capture system, it will appear as an option in this menu. Choose this option to send FCP's video output to your capture system.

To select an Audio Playback setting from the Audio/Video Settings Summary tab:

1. Choose Final Cut Pro > Audio/Video Settings.

2. From the options in the Audio Playback pop-up menu on the Summary tab, *choose one of the following*; then click OK:

   ◆ **Built-in Audio:** Choose this option to route audio output to your computer's built-in audio interface. This is the default setting if FCP cannot detect an external DV camcorder or deck, a compatible video capture card with audio outputs, or other compatible audio hardware.

   ◆ **FireWire DV:** If FCP detects an external DV camcorder or deck, the combined audio and video output is routed to the device via FireWire, and FireWire DV becomes the default option.

   ◆ **Other audio hardware:** If you are using FCP with a third-party capture system or audio hardware, it will appear as an option in this menu.

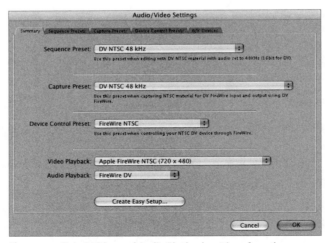

Figure 3.24 Select Video and Audio Playback settings from the pop-up menus on the Audio/Video Settings Summary tab.

Specifying Audio/Video Output Settings

The A/V Devices tab of the Audio/Video Settings window contains two sets of controls for configuring Video and Audio Playback settings: Playback Output and Different Output for Edit to Tape/Print to Video. Both control sets contain identical options—the same video and audio output settings that appear on the Summary tab—but the two independent routing controls allow you the option of selecting one output destination for external monitoring, and a different routing for video or audio output you're recording to tape. You can also enable or disable mirroring (video playback in the Canvas or Viewer) while playing back external video.

To configure additional Audio/Video output settings:

1. Choose Final Cut Pro > Audio/Video Settings.

2. On the A/V Devices tab (**Figure 3.25**), modify any of the following default settings; then click OK:

   ◆ **Playback Output:** Choose video and audio output routing for Final Cut Pro playback.

      ◆ **Video:** Choose an external video output routing to use when playing sequences and clips from the Viewer or Canvas. See step 2 of "To select a Video Playback setting from the Audio/Video Settings Summary tab" for a list of your options.

continues on next page

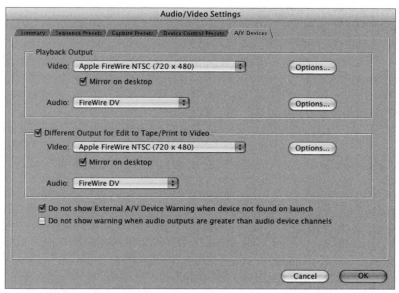

Figure 3.25 Specify how and where you monitor your video on the A/V Devices tab of the Audio/Video Settings window.

SPECIFYING AUDIO/VIDEO OUTPUT SETTINGS

- ◆ **Mirror on Desktop:** Check this box to display video in the Viewer or Canvas window on your computer monitor when playing back external video.

  Disable this option if you notice dropped frames in your external output during video playback.

- ◆ **Audio:** If you want, you can choose a different output routing for audio playback and monitoring. See step 2 of "To select an Audio Playback setting from the Audio/Video Settings Summary tab" for a list of your options.

- ◆ **Options buttons:** Your video or audio hardware may offer additional configuration options. Check your hardware documentation for more information.

- ◆ **Different Output for Edit to Tape/ Print to Video:** Check the box to enable a second set of output routing controls for specifying video and audio outputs to be used during Edit to Tape or Print to Video operations. The settings options are identical to those for the Playback Output section.

- ◆ **Do not show External A/V Device Warning when device not found on launch:** Check this box to disable the warning dialog box that appears when you launch FCP without first turning on your external video and audio hardware. This option is recommended for editors working on an FCP system with no external hardware attached.

- ◆ **Do not show warning when audio outputs are greater than audio device channels:** Check this box to disable the warning dialog box that appears when you assign to a sequence more audio output channels than your currently selected audio output device can provide.

Specifying User Preferences and System Settings

The settings in the User Preferences and System Settings windows affect all of your Final Cut Pro projects. The User Preferences window contains six tabs: General, Editing, Labels, Timeline Options, Render Control, and Audio Outputs. The System Settings window offers another six tabs' worth of additional preference settings: Scratch Disks, Search Folders, Memory & Cache, Playback Control, External Editors, and Effect Handling. System Settings window preference options are covered in the second half of this section.

To set General preferences:

1. Choose Final Cut Pro > User Preferences. The General tab will appear as the front tab in the User Preferences window (**Figure 3.26**).

2. You can specify settings for the following:

   ◆ **Levels of Undo:** Specify the number of actions that can be undone. Specifying a large number of undos can make significant demands on your available RAM, however.

   ◆ **List Recent Clips:** Set the number of recently accessed clips available on the Viewer's Recent Clips pop-up menu.

   continues on next page

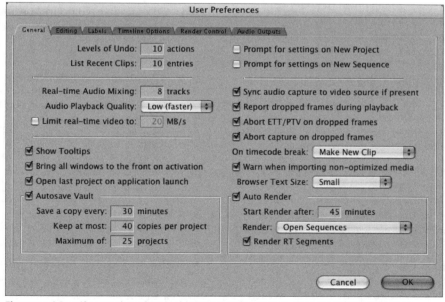

Figure 3.26 Specify a number of general program preferences on the General tab of the User Preferences window.

USER PREFERENCES AND SYSTEM SETTINGS

◆ **Real-time Audio Mixing:** Specify the number of audio tracks that Final Cut Pro mixes in real time. The default setting is eight tracks. The maximum number of tracks you will be able to mix depends on multiple factors. Reduce the number of tracks if you experience audio playback problems, such as video stuttering or audio pops or dropouts.

◆ **Audio Playback Quality:** Choose the quality of sample-rate conversion when you import audio files with sample rates that differ from your sequence's rate. At the lowest playback quality, Final Cut Pro can reserve more processing power for real-time mixing operations. If you choose the highest playback quality, your sample-rate-converted audio will sound better, but you won't be able to stack up as many simultaneous audio tracks before FCP needs to mixdown (render) your audio. Higher quality settings will take more processing time, so the default is set to Low. In general, choose Low when editing. FCP automatically defaults to the highest audio quality during all rendering, audio mixdown, editing to tape, printing to video, and OMF operations, so you won't need to switch the setting here when you're ready to output your program.

◆ **Limit real-time video to n MB/s:** Check this preference, then enter a maximum data rate if you want to enable a hard limit on the number of video streams your FCP system will attempt to play back in real time. Calculate the data rate by multiplying the number of video streams by the data rate for the video format you are using. A single stream of DV has a data rate of 3.6 MB/sec.

✔ **Tip**

■ Here's a method for testing your FCP system to determine the maximum data

rate your drives can sustain. Stack a few video clips on multiple Timeline tracks, then adjust each clip's opacity below 100% to force FCP to display multiple tracks. Keep adding video tracks to your stack until FCP interrupts playback and displays the dropped frames warning—you've reached the maximum data rate for your FCP system and drives.

◆ **Autosave Vault:** Check this box if you want FCP to save backup copies of all your open projects automatically at regular intervals. Enter a number to specify a time interval in minutes. For more information, see "Using the Autosave Vault" in Chapter 4.

　◆ **Save a Copy Every n Minutes:** Enter a number of minutes to specify a time interval between backup operations.

　◆ **Keep at Most n Copies per Project:** Enter a value to specify how many autosaved backup copies of each project file you want Final Cut Pro to store.

　◆ **Maximum of n Projects:** Enter a value to specify the maximum number of projects you want to back up in the Autosave vault. If the number of open projects exceeds the number specified here, Final Cut Pro will override the maximum you set and autosave all open projects.

◆ **Show Tooltips:** Check this box to toggle the display of tooltip labels on buttons and tools.

◆ **Bring All Windows to the Front on Activation:** Check this box to specify that whenever FCP is in the background, clicking any single FCP window to activate the application will bring all open FCP windows to the front of the Desktop.

◆ **Open last project on application launch:** Check this box if you want FCP to automatically reopen your last saved project when you launch the application. Uncheck the box if you want FCP to create a new empty project on application launch.

◆ **Prompt for settings on New Project:** Check this box if you want the option to modify project properties each time you create a new project.

◆ **Prompt for Settings on New Sequence:** Check this box if you want to see a list of sequence presets each time you create a new sequence.

◆ **Sync Audio Capture to Video Source if Present**: Check the box to ensure that the timecode from any genlocked audio deck is referenced to the timecode of the genlocked video source during audio capture, thus ensuring sync accuracy during long sync audio captures from device-controllable audio decks.

◆ **Report Dropped Frames During Playback:** Check this box if you want Final Cut Pro to display a warning dialog box whenever frames are dropped during playback.

◆ **Abort ETT/PTV on Dropped Frames:** Check this box to automatically stop any Edit to Tape or Print to Video operation if dropped frames are detected.

◆ **Abort Capture on Dropped Frames:** Check this box to automatically stop the capture process if dropped frames are detected during a capture.

◆ **On Timecode Break:** This pop-up menu offers three different ways to direct FCP's behavior when it encounters a timecode break during a capture operation.

   ◆ **Make New Clip:** When FCP detects a timecode break, it will save a media file containing all video captured up to the break, setting the frame before the break as that file's Out point. FCP continues capturing video after the break as a second media file.

   ◆ **Abort Capture:** FCP automatically stops capturing if it detects a timecode break during the capture process.

   ◆ **Warn After Capture:** FCP will report the timecode break after your capture operation is complete, and will retain that captured media file. Clips containing timecode breaks can't be recaptured accurately, so select this option only if you never, ever need to recapture this clip ever, ever again.

◆ **Warn when importing non-optimized media:** Check the box if you want FCP to alert you when you import media files created or captured using a codec that cannot be optimized for real-time playback.

◆ **Browser Text Size:** Choose Small, Medium or Large from the pop-up menu to specify text size displayed in the Browser and Timeline.

continues on next page

- **Auto Render:** Check the box to enable the triggering of automatic rendering when FCP is idle for a specified period.
  - **Start Render After:** Enter a number of minutes to specify how long FCP should be idle before automatic rendering is triggered.
  - **Which Sequences:** Select Open Sequences to render all sequences currently open in the Timeline, select Current Sequence Only to render just the active sequence on the front tab of the Timeline, or select Open Except Current Sequences to render all open sequences except the active sequence on the front tab of the Timeline.
  - **Render RT Segments:** Check the box to include those sections of your sequence that use real-time effects in the auto-render operation.

✔ Tip

- Displaying video on the computer monitor while printing to video or editing to tape taxes the computer's processing power and can cause performance problems. If you notice dropped frames in your output when performing these operations, check out the tips for optimizing performance in Chapter 2, "Installing and Setting Up," before giving up and disabling Desktop video playback. You may want to increase the size of your thumbnail caches if you are working with a large number of clips and want to display thumbnails, or if you are using the Browser's Icon view. If you often scrub through thumbnails in Icon view, you can optimize the performance of this feature by increasing the size of the thumbnail RAM cache on the Memory & Cache tab of the System Settings window.

Setting Editing Preferences

Preference settings on this tab are all directly related to editing and trimming operations. Many of these preferences can be modified without opening the User Preferences window; for example, the Trim preferences can be toggled without leaving the Trim Edit window by using keyboard shortcut equivalents.

To set Editing preferences:

1. Choose Final Cut Pro > User Preferences.

2. Click the Editing tab. On the tab (**Figure 3.27**), you can specify settings for the following:

   ◆ **Still/Freeze Duration:** Enter a duration (in seconds) to specify a default duration between In and Out points for imported still images, generators, and Adobe Photoshop files. Feel free to change this setting to increase your efficiency—for example, when you're producing a series of freeze-frames of a uniform length. The same Still/Freeze duration also applies to any freeze-frames you create from clips opened in the Canvas or Viewer.

   ◆ **Preview Pre-roll:** Enter a number of seconds to specify how much media to play before the edit point when you click the Play Around Current button or the Play Around Edit-Loop button.

   ◆ **Preview Post-roll:** Enter a number of seconds to specify how much media to play after the edit point when you click the Play Around Current button or the Play Around Edit-Loop button.

continues on next page

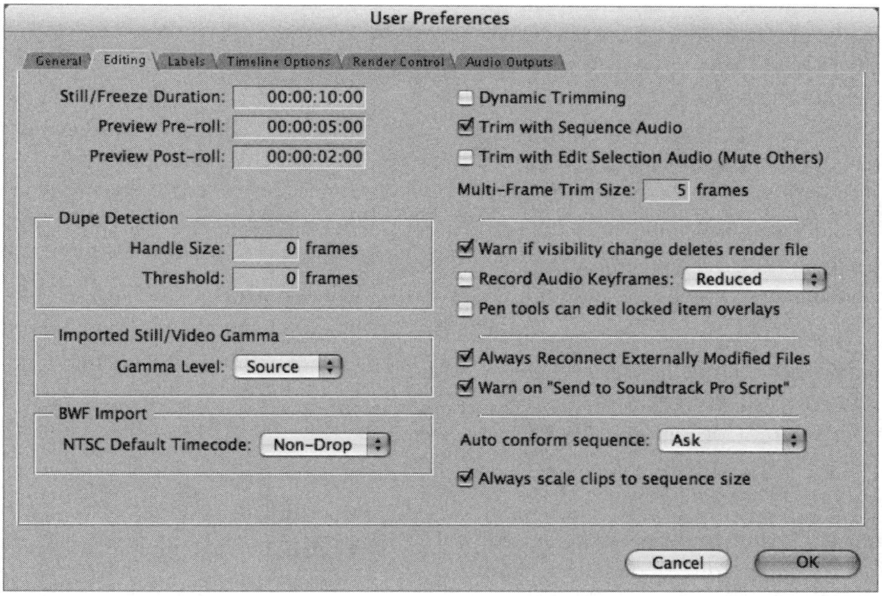

Figure 3.27 The Editing tab of the User Preferences window.

◆ **Dupe Detection:** In film post-production, the negative for any frames appearing more than once must be duplicated. With this feature enabled, FCP will track any frames that are duplicated elsewhere in the sequence.

  ◆ **Handle Size:** Enter the number of extra frames you need to accommodate the frames required for the physical splicing and cementing of the film negative.

  ◆ **Threshold:** Enter the number of consecutive dupe frames FCP must detect before the dupe detection overlay indicator appears.

◆ **Imported Still/Video Gamma:** Choose one of the following options from the Gamma Level pop-up menu:

  ◆ **Source:** Choose Source if you're importing media that has already been adjusted to work with previous versions of Final Cut Pro. This option uses QuickTime to interpret the gamma of imported media files.

  ◆ **1.8:** Choose 1.8 if you're importing media files created with the Mac OS or any files you know to have a specified gamma value of 1.8.

  ◆ **2.2:** Choose 2.2 if you're importing media files created with non–Mac OS systems or any files you know to have a specified gamma value of 2.2.

  ◆ **Custom:** Specify a custom gamma value in this field.

◆ **BWF Import:** From the NTSC Default Timecode pop-up menu, specify the default timecode mode (drop frame or non-drop frame) for imported Broadcast Wave Format (BWF) files recorded using NTSC frame rates.

◆ **Dynamic Trimming:** Check the box to enable Dynamic Trim mode in the Trim Edit window. You can also enable this mode in the Trim Edit window.

◆ **Trim with Sequence Audio:** Check the box to monitor all audio tracks at the playhead position while trimming an edit in the Trim Edit window. Uncheck this option to limit audio monitoring in the Trim Edit window to the selected clip's audio.

◆ **Trim with Edit Selection Audio (Mute Others):** Check the box to monitor only the audio tracks included in the edit selected for trimming in the Trim Edit window.

✔ Tip

■ The two Trim Edit preferences settings listed above apply only when you are using the JKL keys to playback or trim—they have no effect if you're using the spacebar or Transport control buttons. See Chapter 11, "Fine Cut: Trimming Edits," for more information.

◆ **Multi-Frame Trim Size:** Set the multi-frame trim size by specifying the number of frames (up to 99) in this field. The specified number appears in the multi-frame trim buttons in the Trim Edit window.

◆ **Warn if Visibility Change Deletes Render File:** Check this box if you want Final Cut Pro to display a warning dialog box whenever making tracks invisible would cause render files to be deleted.

◆ **Record Audio Keyframes:** Check the box to enable the real-time recording of audio keyframes in the Audio Mixer or Filters tab as you make level or pan adjustments on the fly. From the pop-up menu, choose one of three levels of resolution for your automated audio keyframe recording:

  ◆ **All:** Records the maximum number of keyframes possible and tracks your moves very precisely, but produces dense clusters of many keyframes.

- ◆ **Reduced:** Tracks your moves, but records fewer keyframes.

- ◆ **Peaks Only:** Sets keyframes only at the highest and lowest levels in each mixer move.

◆ **Pen Tools Can Edit Locked Item Overlays:** Check this box to enable the Pen tools to edit keyframe overlays on items on locked tracks in the Timeline.

◆ **Always Reconnect Externally Modified Files:** Check the box to allow FCP to automatically reconnect any files that have been modified in another application. Uncheck the box to restrict automatic reconnection to files you have opened and modified using the Open in Editor command. Checked is convenient, but unchecked is safer.

◆ **Warn on "Send to Soundtrack Pro Script."** Check this box if you want Final Cut Pro to display a dialog allowing you to choose how your media files are processed when you choose the Send To > Soundtrack Pro Script command.

◆ **Auto conform sequence:** From the Auto Conform Sequence pop-up menu, select Always to automatically conform sequence settings to the settings of the first clip added. Select Ask and you'll see a dialog when you add a non-conforming clip to your sequence.

◆ **Always scale clips to sequence size:** Check the box to automatically scale up any clips whose frame size is smaller than the frame size of the current sequence so they match when you edit them into that sequence. This setting applies to scaling up only, and will not automatically scale down clips.

Setting Label Preferences

Final Cut Pro offers color-coded icons with customizable names. You can apply these labels to Browser and Timeline clips and use the Label and Label 2 columns in the Browser to sort by label type. Label colors are not customizable.

To customize label names:

1. Choose Final Cut Pro > User Preferences.

2. Click the Labels tab.

3. Click the text field to make it active; then enter your custom label name (**Figure 3.28**).

4. Click OK.

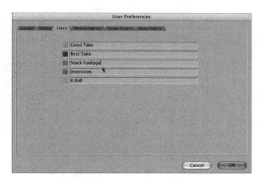

Figure 3.28 Enter a custom label name in the text field.

Customizing the Timeline Display

The Timeline display options you specify on the Timeline Options tab in the User Preferences window will become the default display settings for subsequent new projects and sequences. If you want to modify the Timeline display options for an existing sequence, you will need to make the change in the Sequence Settings window for that sequence. See "Changing the Settings of an Existing Sequence" in Chapter 4.

To customize your default Timeline display settings:

1. Choose Final Cut Pro > User Preferences.

2. Click the Timeline Options tab. On the Timeline Options tab (**Figure 3.29**), you can modify the default settings for any of the following:

- **Starting Timecode:** Enter a value to set the starting timecode for your sequence. The hour value can help you identify sequences. The default starting timecode is 01:00:00;00.

- **Drop Frame:** Check this box if you want drop-frame timecode displayed in the sequence Timeline.

- **Track Size:** Choose a setting to specify a default track size.

- **Thumbnail Display:** Select one of three thumbnail display options:

  - **Name:** Choose Name to display just the name of the clip.

  - **Name Plus Thumbnail:** Choose this option to display the first frame of every clip as a thumbnail image, along with the name of the clip.

  - **Filmstrip:** Choose Filmstrip to display as many thumbnail images as possible for the current zoom level of the Timeline.

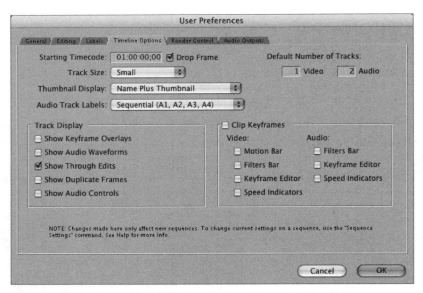

Figure 3.29 Customize your default Timeline display options on the User Preference window's Timeline Options tab.

◆ **Audio Track Labels:** Select one of two track labeling options:

  ◆ **Paired (A1a, A1b, A2a, A2b):** This is a good labeling scheme if you are working with stereo tracks.

  ◆ **Sequential (A1, A2, A3, A4):** This is a good labeling scheme if you are working with a collection of single tracks, such as dialog tracks.

◆ **Track Display:** Check the boxes next to the Timeline features you want to display by default in new sequences.

  ◆ **Show Keyframe Overlays:** Display opacity keyframe overlays on video clips and audio level keyframe overlays on audio clips in the Timeline.

  ◆ **Show Audio Waveforms:** Display audio waveforms on audio clips in the Timeline.

  ◆ **Show Through Edits:** Display a Through edit indicator at edit points in the Timeline joining two clips with the same reel number and contiguous timecode (such as a clip you've divided in two with the Razor Blade tool). See "About through edits" in Chapter 11 for more information on working with through edits.

  ◆ **Show Duplicate Frames:** Display color-coded overlays at the bottom of clips containing frames used more than once in a sequence. The color code indicates how many times the frames have been duplicated. See "Options for Displaying Duplicate Frames" on page I-130 of Apple's *Final Cut Pro User Manual* PDF for details on dupe frame detection.

  ◆ **Show Audio Controls:** Reveal the Audio Mute and Audio Solo buttons in the track controls.

◆ **Clip Keyframes:** Check this box to show Clip Keyframe tools and indicators below your Timeline tracks; then check the boxes next to the specific Clip Keyframe features you want to display by default in new sequences. You must specify audio and video features separately. You can also modify these selections by control-clicking the Clip Keyframes button in the Timeline and making your selections there. For more information on using these and other keyframing tools, see "Working with Keyframes in the Timeline" in Chapter 14.

  ◆ **Motion Bar:** Display Motion bars below Timeline clips. This option is available only for video clips. The Motion bar displays keyframes for motion effects applied to a clip. Double-click the bar to open the settings in the Viewer window.

  ◆ **Filters Bar:** Display Filters bars below Timeline clips. The Filters bar displays filter keyframes and works like the Motion bar.

  ◆ **Keyframe Editor:** Display keyframe editors below Timeline clips. These compact keyframe editors can be used to add and edit keyframes in the Timeline, but are limited to displaying keyframes for one parameter at a time.

  ◆ **Speed Indicators:** Display speed indicators below Timeline clips. These indicators show the frame rate for the playback of speed-modified clips.

◆ **Default Number of Tracks:** Specify the number of video and audio tracks to be included in a new sequence.

CUSTOMIZING THE TIMELINE DISPLAY

Specifying Render Control Settings

Render Control tab settings affect the image quality of rendered material in your sequence. You can selectively disable non-critical aspects of render processing that improve image quality but slow your work. Most of the choices you will make relate to balancing the quality of the render file with the speed of the rendering process. These Render Control tab settings apply during all FCP operations, including real-time playback, rendering, video output, and QuickTime output, so be sure to specify full-quality rendering before your final output.

The settings you define in this window become the default render quality settings for subsequent new projects and sequences. If you want to modify Render Control settings for an existing sequence, you will need to make the change in the Sequence Settings window for that sequence. See "Changing the Settings of an Existing Sequence" in Chapter 4.

✔ Tip

■ Render Control settings define the image quality of rendered material. On the Playback Control tab in the System Settings window, you'll find the Record option, which determines whether rendered material will always be recorded to tape at the highest image quality (which could require rendering), or at the same image quality you've selected for real-time playback. For more information, see "Specifying Playback Control Settings," later in this chapter.

To customize your default Render Control settings:

1. Choose Final Cut Pro > User Preferences.

2. Click the Render Control tab. On the tab (**Figure 3.30**), modify the default settings for any of the following; then click OK:

Render & Playback options:

- **Filters:** Check this box to include filters when rendering. Filters will be applied only to clips you have specified. Excluding filters from a render quality setting is another way to speed up rendering.

- **Frame Blending for Speed:** Check this box to enable any motion-smoothing effects you have previously applied to speed-modified clips.

Render options:

- **Frame Rate:** Set the frame rate for the render quality to 25%, 33%, 50%, or 100% of the sequence editing timebase.

- **Resolution:** Select an option from this pop-up menu to set the resolution (frame size) for the render quality to 25%, 33%, 50%, or 100% of the resolution set for the sequence.

- **Codec:** For native HDV and XDCAM HD format sequences only. Choose whether to render in the native codec or in the Apple ProRes 422 codec.

Master Templates and Motion Projects options:

- **Quality:** Choose a render quality from this pop-up menu for sequence material originating in Motion.

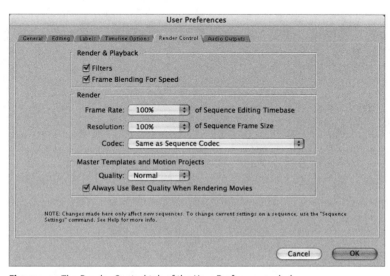

Figure 3.30 The Render Control tab of the User Preferences window.

Specifying Audio Output Settings

The Audio Outputs tab of the User Preferences window lists FCP's audio output presets. In the Audio Outputs Preset Editor (**Figure 3.31**), you can create preset configurations that map your sequence's audio tracks to multiple audio channel outputs. To make use of multiple-channel audio output, you must use Final Cut Pro with audio hardware that supports multiple-channel output. Final Cut Pro's default audio output configuration is a two-channel stereo output, so unless you are using FCP-compatible audio hardware, you don't need to alter the default audio output settings.

Audio hardware that is compatible with Mac OS X 10.2 or later should work with FCP, though Apple does not qualify individual audio interfaces for use with Final Cut Pro. If you are using third-party audio hardware with your Final Cut Pro system, check the manufacturer's documentation or Web site for the latest information on configuring the interface to work smoothly with Final Cut Pro.

For more information on configuring audio output presets, see "About Audio Output Presets" on page III-40 of Apple's *Final Cut Pro User Manual* PDF.

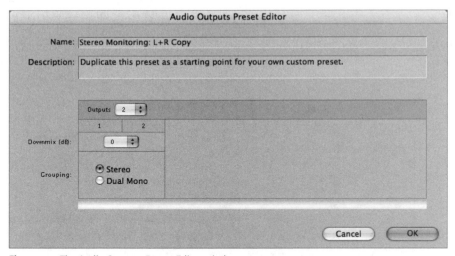

Figure 3.31 The Audio Outputs Preset Editor window.

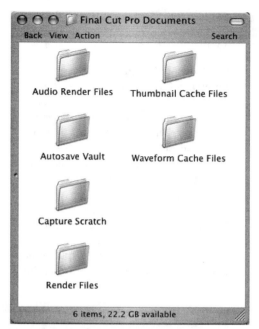

Figure 3.32 The Final Cut Pro Documents folder contains a subfolder for each type of media file that your project will generate.

Setting Scratch Disk Preferences

A *scratch disk* is a folder on a hard disk where Final Cut Pro stores your captured media source files and render files. The default scratch disk location is the same hard disk where your Final Cut Pro application is installed. You can specify multiple scratch disk locations, either to improve performance by capturing audio and video on separate drives (not recommended for DV) or to provide the necessary storage capacity for your project media.

You should assign your scratch disks to your fastest disk drives. For best performance, avoid using the system hard disk as a scratch disk.

When a disk or folder is added to the scratch disk list, Final Cut Pro automatically creates a folder on that disk called Final Cut Pro Documents. That folder contains subfolders (one for each type of media file your project will generate) named Capture Scratch, Audio Capture Scratch, Render Files, Audio Render Files, Thumbnail Cache Files, and Waveform Cache Files (**Figure 3.32**). If you are capturing DV, your captured media files will be stored in a folder bearing your project's name inside the Capture Scratch folder.

✔ Tip

■ Final Cut Pro requires that each hard disk have a distinct name that does not contain the entire name of another media drive. For example, the program will not reliably distinguish between two drives named Media and Media 1, but Media 1 and Media 2 are acceptable names. Bear this in mind when you are assigning names to hard drives you are using with Final Cut Pro.

FCP Protocol: Scratch Disks

Unless you specify otherwise, Final Cut Pro uses the disk with the most available space as its storage area for rendered files. If you specify multiple scratch disks, Final Cut Pro will use the next disk in the list with the most available space when the current disk runs out of space. You can specify separate disks for captured video and audio files to obtain better capture quality at higher data rates and improved playback performance. If you're capturing DV, however, you should always specify the same scratch disk for captured video and audio.

To specify Scratch Disk preferences:

1. Choose Final Cut Pro > System Settings. The Scratch Disks tab appears as the front tab of the System Settings window (**Figure 3.33**).

2. You can specify settings for the following:

   ◆ **Video Capture, Audio Capture, Video Render, and Audio Render:** Check these boxes to specify the types of files to be stored on each disk. Specify more than one disk for increased storage space. When the current disk runs out of space, Final Cut Pro automatically switches to the next specified disk for storing capture files or to the disk with the most space available for storing render files.

   ◆ **Clear:** Click to remove a disk from the list of available disks.

   ◆ **Set:** Click to choose a disk or a folder on a hard disk. You can specify up to 12 disks.

   ◆ **Capture Audio and Video to Separate Files** (not recommended for DV): Check this box to optimize playback for QuickTime files with higher data rates. This feature allows you to write the video and audio tracks in a QuickTime movie to separate files on separate disks during the capture process. Video and audio files have the same name, with _v appended to video files and _a appended to audio files. Note that separate files must be captured to different disks; you cannot capture the two files to different directories on the same disk.

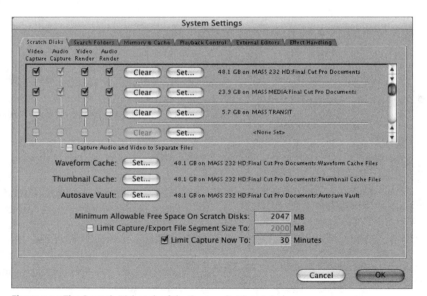

Figure 3.33 The Scratch Disks tab of the System Settings window.

◆ **Waveform Cache:** Click the Set button to specify a folder or disk to store waveform cache files (graphical representations of audio signals). The default location is the Final Cut Pro Documents folder on your scratch disk.

◆ **Thumbnail Cache:** Click the Set button to specify a folder or disk to store thumbnail cache files. The default location is the Final Cut Pro Documents folder on your scratch disk. You specify the size of this cache on the Memory & Cache tab.

◆ **Autosave Vault:** Click the Set button to specify a folder or disk to store FCP's automatic backup copies of your project files. The default location is the Final Cut Pro Documents folder on your scratch disk. For more information on the Autosave Vault, see Chapter 4.

◆ **Minimum Allowable Free Space on Scratch Disks:** Enter a limit value. When disk space falls below this minimum, a disk will no longer be used as a scratch disk, and files will be stored on the next disk in the list.

◆ **Limit Capture/Export File Segment Size To:** Enter a limit value. The default value is 2 GB. Final Cut Pro allows the capture and export of single files larger than 2 GB, but if you plan to move your files to another system that has a file size limitation, or if you share media files over a network, you should enable this option. Files that are larger than your specified limit will be spanned (written as separate, but linked, files).

◆ **Limit Capture Now To:** Enter a limit value. The default limit is 30 minutes.

✔ Tip

■ FCP automatically calculates a safer, saner default value for Minimum Allowable Free Space (MAFS) on Scratch Disks. Previous versions of FCP used 10 MB as the default minimum—too low for comfort.

Each time FCP generates a new preference file, it checks the capacity of the first scratch disk selected in the Scratch Disks tab, and automatically sets a default value for MAFS that is based on a percentage of the disk's capacity. FCP allows 5% if the scratch disk is a boot drive, and 1% for a non-boot hard drive. You can always set a higher MAFS. If you're interested in preserving the performance and reliability of your captured source media, you should set a much higher minimum. Many users set aside 10 percent of each drive's capacity as "headroom"—and sleep better for it.

SETTING SCRATCH DISK PREFERENCES

Specifying Search Folder Preferences

The Search Folders tab of the System Settings window speeds the reconnection of offline files by restricting the Reconnect window's search to the folders or drives you specify. If you're not sure where your source media files are located, the Reconnect Files feature still offers you the option of searching every volume available to your FCP system, including remote volumes accessible over a network. See "Reconnecting Offline Files" in Chapter 20 for more information.

To specify a search folder:

1. Choose Final Cut Pro > System Settings.

2. Click the Search Folders tab.

3. Using the Clear and Set buttons, specify the folders or drives you want to search in the Reconnect Files window. (**Figure 3.34**):

    ◆ **Set:** Click the Set button, navigate to the folder location you want to specify, and then click Choose.

    ◆ **Clear:** Click the Clear button next to a folder location to remove that folder from your list of specified folders.

The pathname and the folder name appear next to the Set button in the Search Folders tab. All folders specified on this tab appear in the Reconnect Files window's Search Folders pop-up menu.

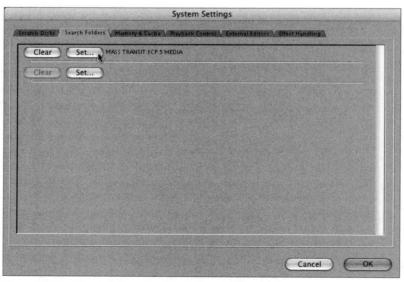

Figure 3.34 The Search Folders tab of the System Settings window.

Specifying Memory & Cache Settings

Settings on the Memory & Cache tab determine how much of your computer's available RAM can be used by Final Cut Pro, and how that assigned RAM will be apportioned.

Final Cut Pro makes extensive use of your computer's RAM to support real-time playback and preview. You don't have to set hard memory allocations for applications running in OS X, but it is advisable to set an upper limit on the amount of RAM that FCP can use. If you like to keep multiple applications open while you edit, setting aside some RAM will minimize OS X's use of virtual memory to accommodate the processor load, which helps maintain FCP's performance.

1. Choose Final Cut Pro > System Settings.

2. Click the Memory & Cache tab. On the tab (**Figure 3.35**), modify the default settings for any of the following; then click OK:

    ◆ **Memory Usage:** Assign an upper limit to FCP's RAM usage, and allocate a percentage of that total for use by the still cache.

◆ **Application:** Use the slider or enter a maximum percentage of total available RAM to make available to Final Cut Pro. The numeric value of the total megabytes assigned to FCP appears to the right of the percentage slider.

◆ **Still Cache:** Use the slider or enter a percentage value to allocate a portion of the RAM allotted to FCP for use by the still cache. The recommended minimum is 25 MB, but you should increase this value if your projects include large amounts of graphics. The numeric value of the total megabytes appears to the right of the percentage slider.

◆ **Thumbnail Cache:** If you use Large Icon as your Browser view, or if you're working on a large project containing many clips and want to display thumbnails in the Browser or Timeline, you should increase the amount of RAM available for displaying thumbnails to improve FCP's performance and the image quality of your thumbnails.

    ◆ **Disk:** Specify the amount of disk space to allocate for storing thumbnails.

    ◆ **RAM:** Specify the amount of memory to allocate for storing thumbnails.

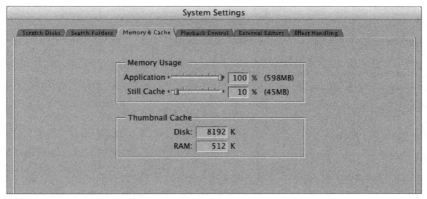

Figure 3.35 The Memory & Cache tab of the System Settings window.

Specifying Playback Control Settings

Playback Control tab settings help you strike a balance between the number of effects you can see in real time versus the visual quality of the playback by adjusting the image quality and frame rate of real-time playback.

FCP offers two locations where you can access Playback Control settings. The complete set of controls appears on this tab; the RT pop-up menu in the Timeline gives you access to most of the same settings. An overview of these settings follows; for more information, see Chapter 18, "Real Time and Rendering."

✔ Tips

- As you shift from basic assembly to multi-layer effects and finishing work, your playback quality needs may change frequently. FCP's Dynamic quality and frame rate settings look at the frames ahead, calculating and displaying the best real time performance your system can produce on a particular section of your sequence.

- FCP calculates the Safe RT playback rate for your system based on the speed of your computer's CPU, but if your scratch disk is slow, you could still see dropped frames. If you experience dropped frames with Safe RT selected, you might need to adjust the real time data rate limit manually by setting the Limit real-time video to *n* MB/s option on the General tab of the User Preferences window. See "To set General Preferences" earlier in this chapter.

To specify Playback Control settings:

1. Choose Final Cut Pro > System Settings.

2. Click the Playback Control tab. On the Playback Control tab (**Figure 3.36**), modify the default settings for any of the following, and then click OK:

   - **RT:** Choose a default image quality level for the playback of real-time effects.

     - **Safe:** Final Cut Pro limits real-time effects processing to a level that can be sustained without dropping frames during playback.

     - **Unlimited:** Final Cut Pro allows real-time effects processing to exceed the level that your computer can handle without dropping frames during playback. Unlimited playback is useful if quick previewing is more important than image quality or playback integrity.

   - **Video Quality:** This option is available for DV and other codecs that support playback at multiple quality levels. Choose one of four image-quality levels:

     - **Dynamic:** FCP adjusts the video quality as necessary to achieve the highest quality playback with the most effects.

     - **High:** Full-frame, full-resolution playback, which preserves video interlacing.

     - **Medium:** High-quality, quarter-frame-resolution playback of non-interlaced video.

     - **Low:** Low-quality, quarter-frame-resolution playback of noninterlaced video.

◆ **Frame Rate:** By adjusting the playback frame rate options, you can choose to calculate real time effects at a reduced frame rate to improve real time image quality or increase the number of simultaneous effects possible in real time. Playback speed is constant, but the number of frames displayed per second is reduced. Choose from the following frame rate options:

◆ **Dynamic:** FCP adjusts the frame display rate as necessary to achieve the highest quality playback with the most effects.

◆ **Full:** Set the number of frames displayed per second to the full frame rate (editing timebase) assigned in Sequence Settings.

◆ **Half:** Set the number of frames displayed per second to half of the full frame rate.

◆ **Quarter:** Set the number of frames displayed per second to one quarter of the full frame rate.

◆ **Pulldown Pattern:** Pulldown allows the output of 23.98 fps sequences to be converted to the NTSC standard 29.97 fps timebase in real time. This setting applies only to the 23.98 fps timebase. For more information, see Apple's Cinema Tools documentation.

◆ **Gamma Correction:** Choose Accurate for precision gamma adjustment to displayed images, or choose Approximate to improve real time effects performance at the expense of color and brightness accuracy of displayed images.

◆ **Frame Offset:** Adjust the frame offset value to delay playback in the Canvas and Viewer the precise number of frames necessary to synchronize playback between your computer display and external video and audio monitoring. The default frame offset delays Canvas and Viewer playback by 4 frames. If your internal and external playback is out of sync at the default frame offset, you can adjust the offset here.

continues on next page

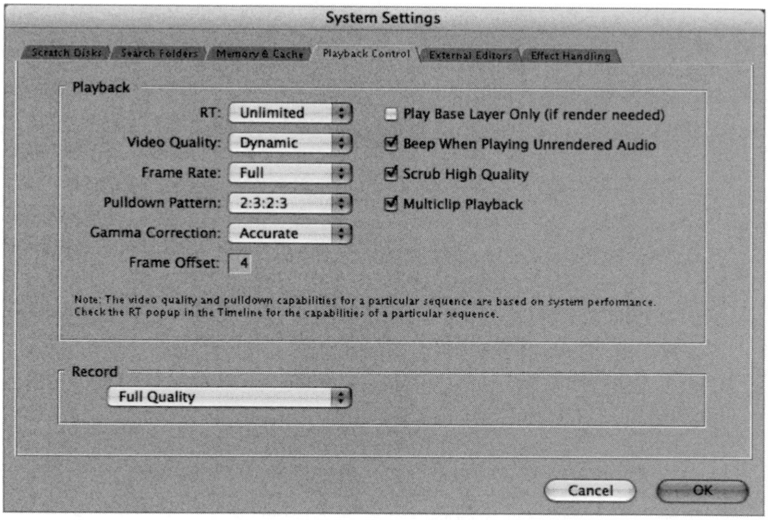

Figure 3.36 The Playback Control tab of the System Settings window.

- **Play Base Layer Only (if Render Needed):** Check this box to play only the base tracks (V1 and all audio tracks up to the real-time audio mixing track limit you set in General preferences) and cuts. Cuts will be substituted for unrendered or non-real-time transitions. Motion will not be applied to clips or sequences when played back in the Viewer. Play Base Layer Only is optimized to allow playback with minimal rendering. Unrendered sections will display the red render status indicator.

- **Beep When Playing Unrendered Audio:** Check this box to enable the unrendered audio warning beeps that alert you when you play audio clip items that require rendering. Uncheck the box to silence the warning beeps.

- **Scrub High Quality:** Check this box to specify full quality image display whenever video is paused or when you scrub. Uncheck the box to use the current Video Quality setting during scrubbing. Reduced image quality during scrubbing can improve scrubbing performance.

- **Multiclip Playback:** Check this box to enable multiclip playback mode in the Viewer.

✔ Tip

- After you enable the multiclip playback option here, choose Open from the Viewer's Playhead Sync pop-up menu to complete the multiclip playback mode setup. For more information on multiclip editing, see Chapter 9, "Basic Editing".

- **Record:** Choose a default image quality level for output during Edit to Tape or Print to Video.

  - **Full Quality:** FCP's output will always be recorded to tape at the highest image quality, but it could require rendering before output.

  - **Use Playback Settings:** FCP's output will be recorded to tape at the same image quality you've selected for real-time playback.

Setting External Editors Preferences

When you're coaxing a stack of graphic elements you've created in a layered Photoshop file into a seamless match with your video elements, you can find yourself making many, many trips back and forth between FCP and Photoshop. The External Editors preferences are designed to speed the process of modifying a media file you've created in another application and then imported into FCP.

In this preferences window, you can specify which application will become the default editing application for each of three different media types: still image, video, and audio.

To specify External Editors preferences:

1. Choose Final Cut Pro > System Settings.

2. Click the External Editors tab.

3. Using the Clear and Set buttons, specify an external editing application for the file types listed (**Figure 3.37**):

   ◆ **Clear:** Click the Clear button next to a file type to reset the External Editor for that file type to the default application used by your Mac's Finder.

   ◆ **Set:** Click the Set button, navigate to the folder location of the editing application you want to specify, and then click Open.

The pathname and the application name appear next to the file type in the External Editors tab.

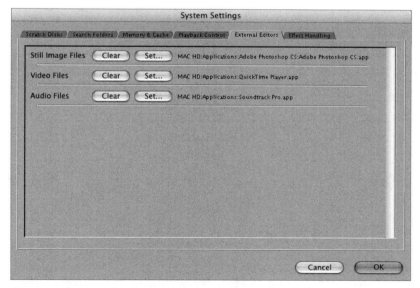

Figure 3.37 The pathname and the application name appear next to the file type in the External Editors tab.

Specifying Effect-Handling Preferences

If you're fortunate enough to be running a Final Cut Pro system enhanced with high-tech capture or effects-handling hardware cards, you can make use of the Effect Handling tab's options to assign effects handling to your hardware. For Final Cut Pro systems without additional hardware, real-time effects handling for all codecs listed on this tab will be assigned to Final Cut Pro. Final Cut Pro is the default setting.

To specify real-time Effect-Handling preferences:

1. Choose Final Cut Pro > System Settings.

2. Click the Effect Handling tab.

3. To modify any of the default settings listed on the tab (**Figure 3.38**), choose one of the following options from the pop-up menu for the codec you want to reassign; then click OK:

   ◆ **None:** Disables real-time effects handling for the selected codec.

   ◆ **Final Cut Pro:** This setting, the default for all codecs listed on this tab, uses FCP to process any real-time effects.

   ◆ **Other hardware:** If your FCP system includes third-party hardware capable of real-time effects processing, the hardware appears in the pop-up menu of all the codecs it supports and can be selected as a real-time effects handler.

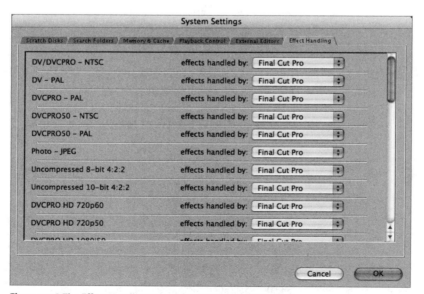

Figure 3.38 The Effect Handling tab of the System Settings window.

Customizing Final Cut Pro

Each successive version of Final Cut Pro has expanded its list of customizable options. You can customize and recall everything from a single keyboard shortcut to an entire screen layout for a multi-monitor setup.

◆ You can create and save custom Browser column layouts, Timeline track display layouts, and full-screen layouts.

◆ You can turn any command used in Final Cut Pro into a custom button or a custom shortcut, building custom keyboard configurations and button bars that can be saved and reloaded, or transported to another FCP system. And that's just the custom interface options, folks.

◆ You can also create and save custom filters, transitions, and even motion effects as Favorites.

◆ You can use FXBuilder script to build FCP visual effects from scratch or edit existing effects.

In this section, you'll learn how to create custom screen layouts, keyboard configurations, and button bars. Custom Browser layouts are covered in Chapter 7; custom Timeline track layouts are covered in Chapter 10.

Creating Custom Screen Layouts

The power of the Final Cut Pro interface lies in its flexibility. You perform a wide range of tasks in FCP—database management, editing, effects design, titling, and many others. Here are a few sample screen layouts that can help you make the most of your screen real estate. Final Cut Pro saves every detail of your workspace status each time you quit the program, so the next time you relaunch Final Cut Pro, each program window will contain the same project, sequence, clip, and frame—just as you left them.

Figure 3.39 is an example of a screen layout with a wide view of the Timeline.

Figure 3.40 is an example of an effects creation layout, with the Viewer's Motion tab expanded for a better view of the keyframe graphs.

Figure 3.41 is an example of a video-editing layout, with large picture-viewing monitors.

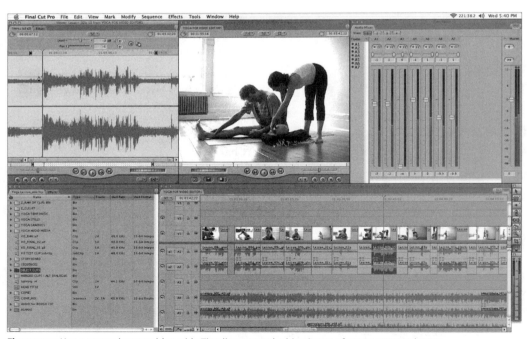

Figure 3.39 Use a screen layout with a wide Timeline to get the big picture of your sequence layout.

Figure 3.40 Use a screen layout with an expanded Effects tab to improve your access to effects controls and keyframe graphs.

Figure 3.41 This screen layout features large monitor views for video editing.

To select a preset screen layout:

◆ Choose Window > Arrange (**Figure 3.42**); then select a screen layout from the five presets and two custom layouts available.

To customize a screen layout:

1. Arrange the four main windows in the layout and sizes you want.

2. Hold down the Option key, and choose one of the two custom layouts from the Arrange submenu of the Window menu (**Figure 3.43**).

   The next time you open Final Cut Pro, you can choose the layout you created from the Arrange submenu of the Window menu.

✔ Tip

■ You can save an unlimited number of custom screen layouts (with custom names!) by arranging the screen as you like it and then choosing Window > Arrange > Save Window Layout. Your custom layout will be saved with your FCP preferences. The default location is: (*Your User Name*)/**Library/Preferences/ Final Cut Pro User Data/Window Layouts.**

Figure 3.42 Choose Window > Arrange; then select from five preset and two custom screen layouts.

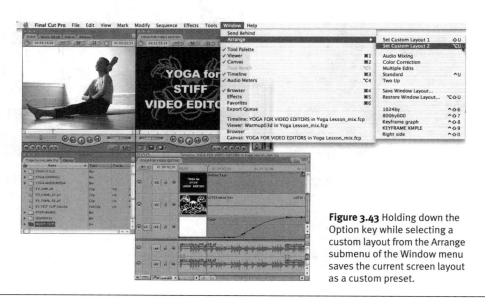

Figure 3.43 Holding down the Option key while selecting a custom layout from the Arrange submenu of the Window menu saves the current screen layout as a custom preset.

Creating Custom Keyboard Layouts

Ever since Final Cut Pro's debut in 1999, editors with experience on other professional nonlinear editing systems have been requesting custom keyboard layouts; Final Cut Pro 4 delivered the goods. You can:

◆ Completely reconfigure your keyboard layout.

◆ Reassign an existing shortcut to a different key.

◆ Create an entirely new keyboard shortcut.

◆ Select and reconfigure a foreign language keyboard layout.

◆ Save multiple keyboard layouts, and import and export layouts from other sources.

◆ Save a keyboard layout as a text file, so you can document your custom layout.

The Keyboard Layout window (**Figure 3.44**) makes it dangerously easy to completely rewire your keyboard shortcuts. Take special note of the Reset button, which will return all keyboard shortcuts to Final Cut Pro's default settings with a single click. For a complete rundown on custom keyboard layouts, see "Ways to Customize Keyboard Shortcuts" on page I-146 of Apple's *Final Cut Pro User Manual* PDF.

CREATING CUSTOM KEYBOARD LAYOUTS

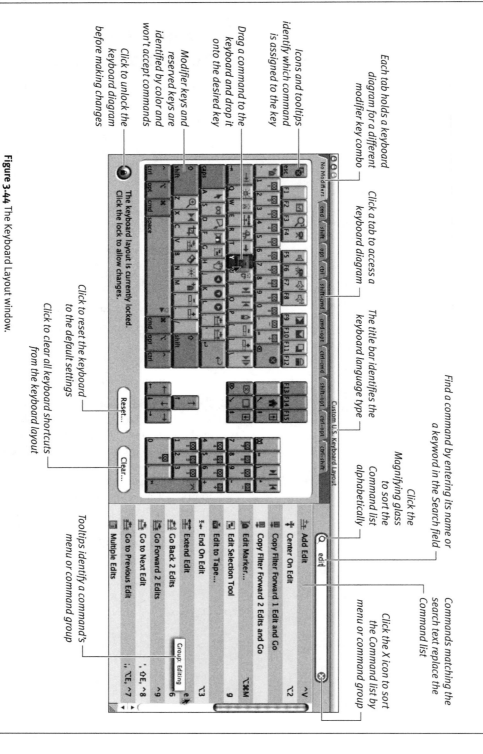

Figure 3.44 The Keyboard Layout window.

Each tab holds a keyboard diagram for a different modifier key combo

Icons and tooltips identify which command is assigned to the key

Drag a command to the keyboard and drop it onto the desired key

Modifier keys and reserved keys are identified by color and won't accept commands

Click to unlock the keyboard diagram before making changes

Click a tab to access a keyboard diagram

The title bar identifies the keyboard language type

The keyboard layout is currently locked. Click the lock to allow changes.

Click to reset the keyboard to the default settings

Click to clear all keyboard shortcuts from the keyboard layout

Find a command by entering its name or a keyword in the Search field

Click the Magnifying glass to sort the Command list alphabetically

Commands matching the search text replace the Command list

Click the X icon to sort the Command list by menu or command group

Click the Command list by menu or command group

Tooltips identify a command's menu or command group

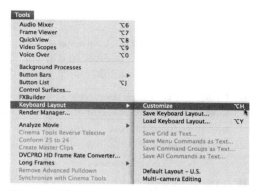

Figure 3.45 Choose Tools > Keyboard Layout > Customize to open the Keyboard Layout window.

To create a custom keyboard shortcut:

1. Choose Tools > Keyboard Layout > Customize (**Figure 3.45**).

   The Keyboard Layout window appears. Keyboard layout diagrams are arranged by shortcut modifier key and appear on multiple tabs. A complete list of commands, sorted by command group, appears at the right side of the window.

2. To find the command you want to assign to the keyboard, *do one of the following:*

   ◆ Click the expansion triangle next to the name of the command's menu group to reveal the command in the list (**Figure 3.46**).

   ◆ Enter the command's name or a keyword in the Search field. Matching commands display automatically.

   ◆ Click the Search field to view the command list alphabetically.

3. Click the Lock button to unlock the current keyboard layout diagram.

continues on next page

Figure 3.46 Clicking the triangle next to a group name reveals a complete list of commands available in that group.

CREATING CUSTOM KEYBOARD LAYOUTS

4. To assign the command to a key, select the command in the list and *do one of the following:*

- ◆ Press the key or key combo you want to assign as the new shortcut for that command. If the shortcut is already in use, a dialog box appears asking you to confirm your choice. If you want your new command choice to replace the key's current assignment, click Yes.

- ◆ If your new keyboard shortcut uses no modifier key, drag the command from the list and drop it on the appropriate key in the keyboard diagram.

- ◆ If your new keyboard shortcut is a key combined with a modifier key, select the keyboard diagram for that modifier key by clicking its tab, and then drag the command from the list and drop it on the appropriate key (**Figure 3.47**).

5. To save your changes, close the Keyboard Layout window.

✔ Tips

- ■ You can reassign a keyboard shortcut by dragging it from one key to another in the keyboard layout diagram.

- ■ Heads up: When you reassign a keyboard shortcut by dragging it to a key on the keyboard layout diagram, the change takes effect without any confirming dialog box.

- ■ You can't assign more than a single command to a key.

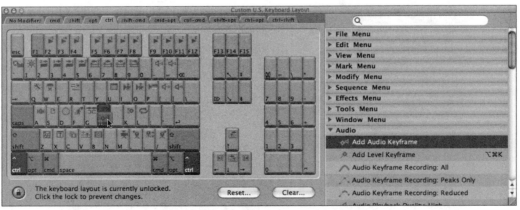

Figure 3.47 Drag the command from the list to the keyboard diagram, and drop it on the appropriate key.

Figure 3.48 You can arrange shortcut buttons in the button bar found at the top of major program windows. You can group and color-code buttons, and save and load custom button bar sets.

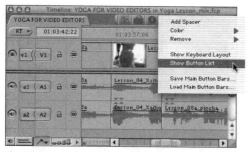

Figure 3.49 Control-click; then choose Show Button List from the button bar's shortcut menu.

Creating Custom Shortcut Buttons

If you like the idea of custom controls but don't want to mess around with custom keyboard layouts, consider a more decorative alternative: Final Cut Pro's button bar (**Figure 3.48**). You can:

◆ Add custom shortcut buttons to the button bar located at the top of the Viewer, Canvas, Browser, Timeline, and Tool Bench windows.

◆ Rearrange the button order.

◆ Add spacers to organize your buttons into groups.

◆ Change the color of a button.

◆ Copy or move a button from one window to another.

◆ Save custom button bars.

For all the details on managing custom buttons, see "Working with Shortcut Buttons and Button Bars" on page I-155 of Apple's *Final Cut Pro User Manual* PDF.

To create a custom shortcut button:

1. Control-click the button bar area at the top of the window; then choose Show Button List from the shortcut menu (**Figure 3.49**).

   The Button List window appears, displaying a complete list of commands.

continues on next page

2. To find the command you want to make into a shortcut button, *do one of the following:*

◆ Click the expansion triangle next to the name of the command's group to reveal the command in the list.

◆ Enter the command's name or a keyword in the Search field. Commands matching the search term display automatically (**Figure 3.50**).

◆ Click the Search field to view the command list alphabetically.

3. Drag the command from the list to the button bar location where you want the button to appear (**Figure 3.51**).

The button appears in the location you've selected (**Figure 3.52**).

4. Close the Button List window.

To delete a button:

Do one of the following:

◆ Control-click the shortcut button, and then choose Remove > Button from the shortcut menu.

◆ Drag the button off the bar and release the mouse button.

The button disappears in a puff of animated smoke (**Figure 3.53**).

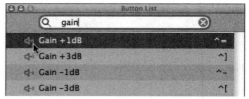

Figure 3.50 Searching the button list for commands containing the word *gain* returns four Gain commands.

Figure 3.51 Drag the command from the list to the button bar.

Figure 3.52 The button appears in the new location. You can use the color-coding options in the button bar shortcut menu to tint the buttons.

Figure 3.53 Drag the shortcut button off the button bar and watch it disappear in a puff of smoke—kinda like Road Runner.

PROJECTS, SEQUENCES, AND CLIPS

A Final Cut Pro project is more than a collection of media files. The real power of Final Cut Pro lies in the way the media is controlled by the intelligence of the program's data structuring. To take advantage of that power, you must take control of the data.

This chapter introduces Final Cut Pro's system of organizing your video projects. You'll get an overview of Final Cut Pro's organizing frameworks—projects, sequences, and clips. You'll also learn how to manipulate that organizational framework so that your projects, sequences, and clips stay sound and organized.

"FCP Protocol: Clips and Sequences," found later in this chapter, explains the rules you really need to know in order to understand how this program constructs edits.

Anatomy of an FCP Project

A Final Cut Pro project breaks down into the following key components.

- **Project file:** The top level of the FCP organizing framework, a *project* file stores references (file location information) to all the media files you use to complete a particular program, along with the sequencing information (your "cut") and all settings for special effects you apply to any clip in the project. The project file contains no media—it's strictly the "brains" of your project—but this one file is your project's most valuable asset. All your editing genius is stored in this modest data file.

- **Sequence:** The middle level of the Final Cut Pro organizing framework, a *sequence* is an edited assembly of audio and video clips. A sequence is always part of a project, and you can have multiple sequences in a project, but you can't save a sequence separately from a project. However, you can copy a sequence from one project and paste it into another project.

- **Clip:** The ground level of the FCP organizing framework, the *clip* represents an individual unit of media in Final Cut Pro. A clip can stand for a movie, a still image, a nested sequence, a generator, or an audio file. Clip types appear in the Browser's Type column, and each type of clip displays an identifying icon.

Figure 4.1 diagrams the FCP organizing framework.

Figure 4.2 shows how the FCP project structure plays out in the Browser and Timeline windows.

Project item types

On a project's Browser tab, you'll find quite a few different clip types, but you'll also find containers for holding clips—sequences and bins. The Browser's Effects tab contains other types of non-clip project items, audio and video filters and transitions, and generators. See "Browser Window Icons" in Chapter 6 for descriptions of each type of item you'll encounter in a project.

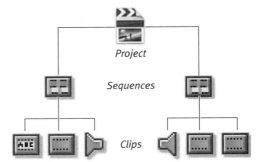

Figure 4.1 The project file is at the top level of FCP's organizing framework. You organize multiple clips and sequences inside a project file.

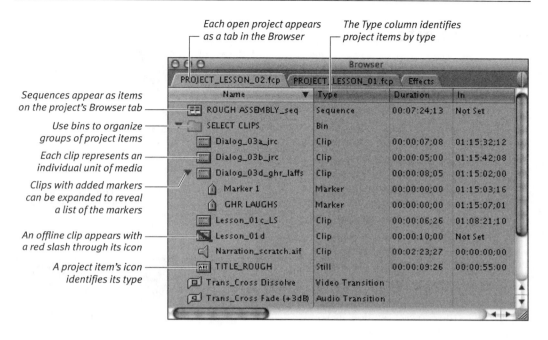

Each open project appears as a tab in the Browser

The Type column identifies project items by type

Sequences appear as items on the project's Browser tab

Use bins to organize groups of project items

Each clip represents an individual unit of media

Clips with added markers can be expanded to reveal a list of the markers

An offline clip appears with a red slash through its icon

A project item's icon identifies its type

The selected sequence and project name appear in the Timeline title bar

Each open sequence appears as a tab in the Timeline

Timeline clips appear on tracks

Linked clips appear with underlined names

Offline clips are color-coded white

Figure 4.2 The Browser (top) and Timeline (bottom) interfaces provide a variety of information about your project.

ANATOMY OF AN FCP PROJECT

About Projects

Project files store disk location information for all the media files used in a program, along with the sequencing information for your edited program plus the settings for special effects applied to any clip in the project. The data stored in a project file is used to re-create the timing, sequencing, and transitions and effects you specify for a particular cut, *without altering or changing the storage location of your original source files*. (Note: If you haven't read the section "What Is Nonlinear Nondestructive Editing?" in Chapter 1, please do so now. It's key to understanding how Final Cut Pro works.)

To get started in Final Cut Pro, you create a new project and then start adding clips and sequences to the Browser window as you shape your project. Sequences can be exported independently as movies or clips, but they can't be saved separately from a project.

To create a new project:

◆ Choose File > New Project (**Figure 4.3**); or press Command-Shift-N.

A new project tab appears in the Browser window (**Figure 4.4**).

To open a project:

1. Choose File > Open; or press Command-O.

2. Locate and select the project file you want to open (**Figure 4.5**).

3. Click Choose.

Figure 4.3 Choose New Project from the File menu.

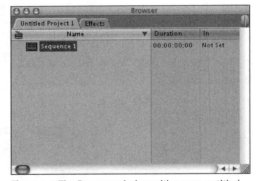

Figure 4.4 The Browser window with a new, untitled project. Sequence 1 appears automatically when you create a new project.

Figure 4.5 Locate the project file you want to open.

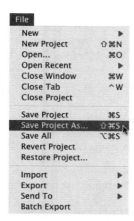

Figure 4.6 Choose Save Project As from the File menu.

Figure 4.7 After you've typed the new name for your project, click Save.

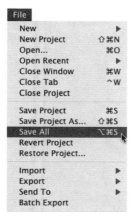

Figure 4.8 Choose Save All from the File menu.

To save a project:

◆ Choose File > Save Project; or press Command-S.

To save a project with a different name:

1. Choose File > Save Project As (**Figure 4.6**); or press Command-Shift-S.

2. In the dialog box, type a name for the project in the Save As field.

3. Choose a destination folder.

4. Click Save (**Figure 4.7**).

To save all open projects:

1. Choose File > Save All; or press Command-Option-S (**Figure 4.8**).

2. If you created one or more new projects that haven't yet been saved, type a name for the first one in the dialog box.

3. Choose a destination folder.

4. Click Save.

   Repeat steps 2 through 4 for each new project that you want to save. Previously saved open projects are saved automatically.

Using Save As to Protect Your Work

Opening, modifying, and then saving the same project file day after day increases the chance that your precious project file will become corrupt and unusable.

Use the Save As command to back up your project file every day or so. Save As makes a fresh copy of the current version of your project file.

Give the original project file a version number, revert the name of your fresh duplicate to the base name of your project, and then continue working in the new duplicate version.

FCP automatically creates a new, separate capture folder every time you change the name of your project. For this reason, to avoid the complications that arise from changing the name of your project file (multiple capture folders), you'll need to add an identifying version number to your older project file, and then be sure that your active project file always has the same original name (**Figure 4.9**).

FCP's vault system, which automatically saves and then archives multiple versions of your project, provides you with a fail-safe backup, but some editors still prefer to retain control over the process. Good habits are hard to break.

Figure 4.9 Rename your older project file with an identifying version number, and use the original project filename on your fresh copy.

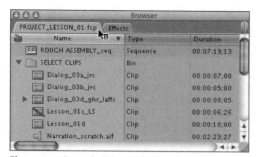

Figure 4.10 Control-click a project's tab to bring up the shortcut menu; note the special pointer.

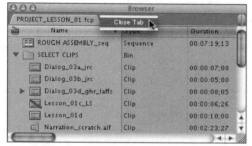

Figure 4.11 Control-clicking the project's tab will result in only one choice; choose Close Tab to close the project.

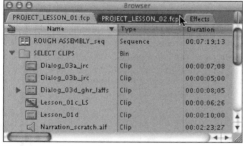

Figure 4.12 Click a project's tab to bring it to the front of the Browser.

To close a project:

1. In the Browser, Control-click the project's tab (**Figure 4.10**).

2. From the shortcut menu, choose Close Tab (**Figure 4.11**).

Or do one of the following:

◆ In the Browser, click the project's tab to bring it to the front (**Figure 4.12**). Then choose File > Close Project.

◆ In the Browser, press Command-W. For all projects you've modified, Final Cut Pro will ask which projects you want to close.

✔ Tip

■ To close all open projects, close the Browser window.

Viewing and setting project properties

Each project has a set of properties that are saved with it. The project's properties apply to all sequences in a project and are independent of the project's Sequence presets.

To view or change the properties of a project:

1. In the Browser, click the Project tab, then choose Edit > Project Properties (**Figure 4.13**).

2. In the Project Properties window (**Figure 4.14**), *do any of the following*:
   - ◆ Display project durations as timecode or as frames. Choosing Frames displays the total number of frames for clips and sequences in the Browser's Duration column, as well as in the Timeline, Canvas, and Viewer.
   - ◆ Set the time mode of all project clips to Source Time (which matches the timecode rate of the clip's source media file) or Clip Time (which starts with the timecode value of the first frame in the clip, then calculates and displays timecode based on the current frame rate assigned to the clip). Source Time and Clip Time are identical in most cases; speed-modified clips and 24P video clips captured from 29.97 fps videotapes are two examples of clips whose Source Time and Clip Time do not match. For more information, see "About Timecode Viewing Options," later in this chapter.
   - ◆ Toggle View Native Speed mode for all clips in the project. For more information, see "About Timecode Viewing Options," later in this chapter.
   - ◆ Edit the heading labels for the Comment columns that appear in the Browser window.

3. After you make your changes, click OK.

Figure 4.13 Choose Project Properties from the Edit menu.

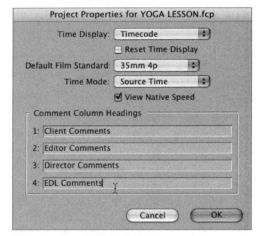

Figure 4.14 You can rename Comment column headings and choose the timecode or frame display format from the Project Properties window.

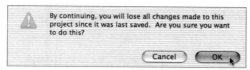

Figure 4.15 After you choose File > Revert Project, you'll see a dialog box warning you that your unsaved changes will be lost.

Figure 4.16 Choose Restore Project from the File menu.

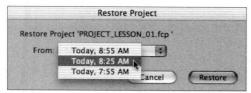

Figure 4.17 Select the archived project you want to restore; then click Restore.

To revert a project:

1. Choose File > Revert Project.

2. In the warning dialog box, click OK (**Figure 4.15**).

   Final Cut Pro reverts the current project file to its condition at the last time you saved the file.

To restore a project:

1. Choose File > Restore Project (**Figure 4.16**).

2. In the Restore Project dialog box's pop-up menu, select the archived project file you want to restore (**Figure 4.17**).

3. Click Restore.

   Final Cut Pro opens the selected archived project from the Autosave Vault.

✔ Tip

■ If you want to replace the current version of your project with this dated archived version, you should save the archive copy with the same project name as your current version. This will maintain continuity in capture folders and Autosave archives.

Using the Autosave Vault

Final Cut Pro's Autosave Vault automatically saves all open projects as you work, at a time interval that you select. The vault stores multiple, dated backup copies of your project. This archive can come in handy. For example, maybe you're at the point in a project where you are trying new approaches to refine your cut, and you want to discard your last experiment. Or maybe you and your collaborator just don't agree, and she's completely recut your program while you were away for the weekend.

Each autosaved version is a backup copy that includes all changes you've made (up to the last autosave time) in the project file that you're currently working on. (That project file is modified only when you invoke the Save or Save All command.) If you haven't made any changes in an open project file since the last backup copy was autosaved, FCP won't archive another backup in the Autosave Vault until you do.

Setting Autosave Vault location and preferences

You can set Autosave preferences on the General tab of the User Preferences window. See "Specifying User Preferences and System Settings" in Chapter 3 for details on your settings options.

The backup copies of your project files are archived in a folder located inside your Final Cut Pro Documents folder (**Figure 4.18**). If you want to store your archive of backups elsewhere, specify another location on the Scratch Disks tab of the System Settings window (**Figure 4.19**).

Figure 4.18 In the Autosave Vault, dated backup copies of your project files are archived in a folder.

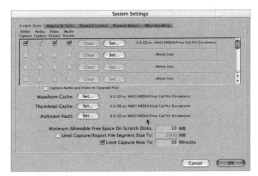

Figure 4.19 Set the Autosave Vault location on the Scratch Disks tab of the System Settings window.

When the number of backup copies in the Autosave Vault reaches the limit you set in User Preferences, FCP deletes the oldest Autosave file (or project folder) to make room for the newest Autosave file, unless the oldest project archived in the vault is currently open. FCP overrides the maximum projects limit you set if the number of open projects exceeds your specified limit when a scheduled Autosave occurs.

Using Autosave to recover from a crash

If your computer powers off or crashes while you're working, the last saved version of your project file will open when you relaunch Final Cut Pro. The choice is yours—continue to work in your original file, or use the Restore Project command to open your most recent autosaved backup copy. Here's the drill.

To use Autosave to recover from a crash:

1. After you restart, go to the folder where you archived your current original project file (that's the file you just crashed out of) and rename that file so it won't be overwritten and you can return to it, if need be.

2. Launch FCP, then use the Restore Project command to go to the Autosave Vault, and open the most recent Autosave backup version of your project file in FCP.

3. After you've checked out the integrity of the autosaved file in FCP, save the autosaved project file with your original project name.

You Need Backup

◆ The Autosave Vault should not be used as a substitute for your own systematic archiving of your project files. The Autosave Vault folder is not locked, and the oldest backups are purged regularly.

◆ Be consistent about where you store your project files. Make sure that all files relating to a project are stored in the same place.

◆ Back up project files on your FCP system and again on a removable disk or in another safe location to avoid losing files in case of a power outage or another technical problem. Project files contain all your time and hard work. Without the editing information in the project files, your media files have no sequencing information. Protect it. OK—end of lecture.

USING THE AUTOSAVE VAULT

Undoing Changes

You can undo every type of action you perform in your projects, sequences, and clips, as well as redo actions that you have undone. FCP can store up to 99 actions across multiple projects—you set the number of undos on the General tab of the User Preferences window.

To undo the last action:

◆ Choose Edit > Undo (**Figure 4.20**); or press Command-Z.

To redo the last undone action:

◆ Choose Edit > Redo; or press Command-Shift-Z.

To specify the number of actions that can be undone:

1. Choose Final Cut Pro > User Preferences.

2. On the General tab of the User Preferences window, set the levels of undo actions to a number between 1 and 99 (**Figure 4.21**).

Figure 4.20 Choose Edit > Undo to undo your last action.

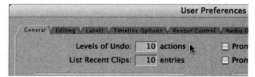

Figure 4.21 You can set the levels of undo actions to any number between 1 and 99 on the General tab of the User Preferences window.

FCP Protocol: Undoing Changes in Multiple Projects

FCP's Undo feature can track up to 99 changes across multiple projects, but it makes no distinction between projects.

If you are working with more than one sequence or project, check to be sure that you are in the correct one when you choose Undo. Even so, the change you undo may not occur in the current project, so take care when undoing multiple changes.

Figure 4.22 Creating a single user ID for all project collaborators can simplify file access on shared FCP projects.

Setting Up for Multiple Projects and Users

Mac OS X was designed as a multiuser environment. The operating system's hierarchy of users and file access privileges is built on the assumption that multiple people are sharing the data and applications stored on your computer. For Final Cut Pro users, this has a few specific effects.

File access

How you choose to set up your file access depends on your individual circumstances.

◆ If you are a solo user running Final Cut Pro on a computer that you own, you should already be set up as the computer's Owner-User. This gives you access to any file in the system that you created.

◆ If you are collaborating on a project with a small group of trusted colleagues sharing Final Cut Pro, you'll need to decide how you want to handle access to Final Cut Pro's project and media files. You can choose to administer the project in OS X's multiuser domain and allow multiple users access to the project files, or you might find it simpler to create a single user ID for the entire group (**Figure 4.22**). In the latter case, everyone in the group logs in as that Project User and has the same read/write privileges to the project and media files.

◆ If you are sharing a Final Cut Pro system with many users working on different projects, you'll want to configure your file access for maximum privacy.

Creating and saving files

Solo users can save their project files in a public or private Documents folder (save in your private Documents folder if you have any security concerns); groups collaborating on an FCP project should save common project files in the Shared folder (**Figure 4.23**), located inside the Users folder, so that all users can access the shared documents.

In OS X, any time you create a new file—by saving a project file, capturing media, or creating graphics—that file's access privileges are set to the system default: Read & Write for the file's owner, and Read Only for all other users (**Figure 4.24**). You may occasionally need to modify file access privileges to allow other users access to your project and its media.

Figure 4.23 Groups collaborating on a Final Cut Pro project should save common project files in the Shared folder so all group members have access to them.

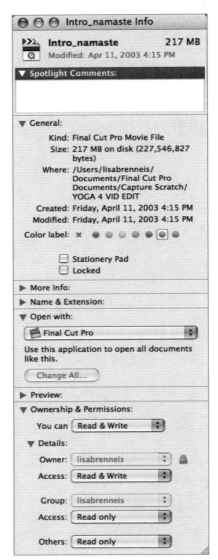

Figure 4.24 The Mac OS X default file access for new files is Read & Write for the file's owner and Read Only for all other users.

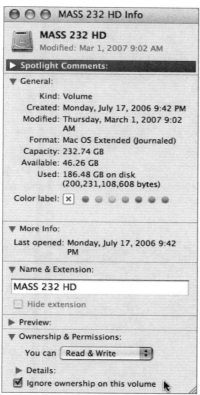

Figure 4.25 In the disk's Info window, check Ignore ownership on this volume to make all files on the volume accessible to all users.

✔ Tips

■ A non-bootable hard disk may offer Read & Write privileges to all users by default, but that doesn't mean individual files and folders on that drive are accessible to all. To set open access for all files on a disk volume, check Ignore ownership on this volume in the drive's Info window (**Figure 4.25**).

■ Mac OS X considers FireWire drives to be removable media (because they're hot-swappable) and offers Read & Write privileges to all users for the entire contents of the drive by default.

What's a Sequence?

A sequence is an edited assembly of audio and video clips. Sequences are the middle level of the Final Cut Pro organizing framework. A sequence is always part of a project, and you can have multiple sequences in a project. Sequences can be exported independently as movies or clips, but they can't be saved separately from a project.

Once you've assembled a sequence, that sequence can be manipulated as if it were a single clip. You can open a sequence and play it in the Viewer, mark In and Out points, and insert all or part of that sequence into another sequence, just as if it were a clip. Inserting a sequence into another sequence creates what's known as a nested sequence. (See "Working with Multiple Sequences," later in this chapter.)

Creating a new sequence

A new project created in FCP automatically generates a new, untitled sequence in your default sequence format.

Note that you probably won't need to change Sequence presets unless you change your audio or video input device. Final Cut Pro selects an Easy Setup with your default preset based on setup information you supplied when you installed the program. See "How to Choose an Easy Setup" in Chapter 3.

To add a new sequence to the current project:

1. Choose File > New > Sequence; or press Command-N.

   A new sequence with a default, highlighted name appears at the top level of the current bin (**Figure 4.26**).

2. Type a new name for the sequence to rename it (**Figure 4.27**).

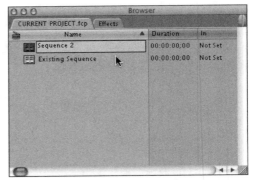

Figure 4.26 A new sequence with a default, highlighted name appears in the current bin.

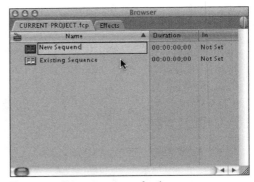

Figure 4.27 Type a new name for the sequence.

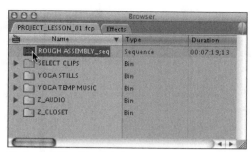

Figure 4.28 Double-click the sequence's icon in the Browser to open it for editing.

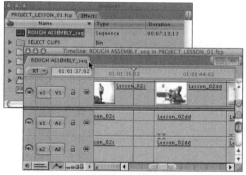

Figure 4.29 The sequence opens in the Canvas and the Timeline.

To open a sequence for editing:

Do one of the following:

◆ Double-click the sequence in the Browser (**Figure 4.28**).

◆ Control-click the sequence's icon; then choose Open Timeline from the shortcut menu.

◆ Select the sequence; then choose View > Sequence In Editor.

The sequence opens in both the Canvas and the Timeline (**Figure 4.29**).

✔ Tip

■ The new Auto-Conform Sequence feature in FCP 6 can identify the format settings of the first clip you add to a new sequence and automatically conform sequence settings to match. Does this mean you'll never render unnecessarily again? For the answer to that question and more, see Chapter 18, "Real Time and Rendering."

Time Stamp for Sequences

The Last Modified column in the Browser makes it easy to find the most recently revised version of your sequence—a real lifesaver when you're returning to a project after a long absence.

WHAT'S A SEQUENCE?

To duplicate a sequence:

1. Select the sequence in the Browser (**Figure 4.30**).

2. Choose Edit > Duplicate (**Figure 4.31**); or press Option-D.

3. In the Browser, rename the sequence copy with a unique name (**Figure 4.32**).

✔ Tip

■ The copy procedure described here is a convenient way to "safety copy" a version of a sequence and associated media files after a long rendering process. With a safety copy of the rendered sequence, you can feel free to experiment with changes that could cause a re-render because any changes you make to the duplicate sequence will not affect the original sequence or its render files.

To copy a sequence from one project to another:

1. Select the sequence in the Browser.

2. Choose Edit > Copy; or press Command-C.

3. Open the second project and select its tab in the Browser.

4. Choose Edit > Paste; or press Command-V.

   The sequence now appears in both projects. The two copies of the sequence reference the same source media files on disk, but you'll need to re-render any previously rendered sequence material in the new project location.

✔ Tip

■ You can also create a copy of a sequence by dragging it from a project window and dropping it on the destination project's Browser tab.

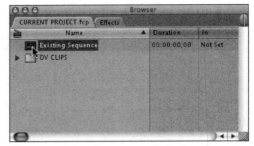

Figure 4.30 Select the sequence in the Browser.

Figure 4.31 Choose Edit > Duplicate.

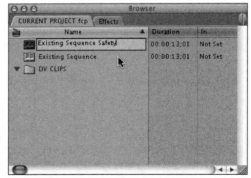

Figure 4.32 Rename the sequence copy.

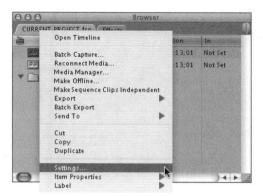

Figure 4.33 Control-click the sequence icon; then choose Settings from the shortcut menu.

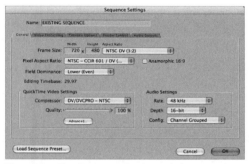

Figure 4.34 The Sequence Settings window contains the same options as the Timeline Options tab, plus Render Control and Audio Outputs settings tabs. Modifying a sequence's settings in the Sequence Settings window changes the settings for that sequence only.

Changing the Settings of an Existing Sequence

You can open and review or modify settings for an existing individual sequence in the Sequence Settings window. The Sequence Settings window contains the same main display options as the Timeline Options tab in the User Preferences window, but you'll also find Video Processing, Render Control, and Audio Output tabs. When you modify any settings for an individual sequence, you are changing the settings for that sequence only.

You can use this window's Load Sequence Preset button to switch to a different Sequence preset, but unless you're sure that's what you need to do, it's not advisable.

To change the settings for an individual sequence:

1. Control-click the sequence's icon in the Browser.

2. Choose Settings from the shortcut menu (**Figure 4.33**).

3. Modify your Sequence settings (**Figure 4.34**); then click OK. (For more information about the Sequence Settings window, see "Customizing the Timeline Display," "Specifying Sequence Settings," "Specifying Render Control Settings," and "Specifying Audio/Video Output Settings" in Chapter 3.)

To switch a sequence's settings to a different Sequence preset:

1. Make the sequence active by selecting it in the Browser or Timeline.

2. Choose Sequence > Settings.
   The Sequence Settings window appears.

3. Click the Load Preset button at the bottom of the General tab.

4. Choose a different preset from the Select pop-up menu in the Select Sequence Preset dialog box (**Figure 4.35**); then click OK.

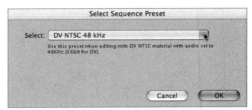

Figure 4.35 Choose a different Sequence preset to replace the settings of your selected sequence.

Working with Multiple Sequences

In Final Cut Pro, you can edit a sequence into another sequence in the same way you would a clip: Drag the entire sequence from the Browser to another open sequence in the Timeline or Canvas. Alternatively, you can drag the sequence from the Browser and drop it on the Viewer's image area and then edit it into your open sequence as you would a clip.

Unlike clips, nested sequences are actually pointers or references to the original sequence, not copies. You can nest a sequence into multiple projects; then, if you change the original sequence, all the projects in which that sequence is nested will be updated.

Assembling multiple sequences into a master sequence is useful for a number of purposes, from reusing a previously edited and rendered segment such as a logo or a credit sequence to assembling a final master sequence from shorter segments produced by multiple editors.

Nesting and Sequences: A Glossary

What's the difference between a nested sequence and a sub-sequence? Here's a short glossary of terms related to nesting sequences as used in this book.

- **Main sequence:** A sequence containing one or more nested sequences. Sometimes referred to as a *parent sequence*.

- **Nested sequence:** Any sequence that has been nested within another sequence. Sometimes referred to as a *child sequence*. A nested sequence can range from a clip on a single track to an entire sequence. What designates a sequence as nested is its placement in a parent sequence. The word *nest* can also be used as a verb, as in "nest a sequence," which refers to editing all or a portion of an existing sequence into another sequence.

- **Sub-sequence:** Can be used interchangeably with the term *nested sequence*. Nested sequences function as sub-sequences in their parent sequences.

Creating nested sequences

You can select a group of sequence clips or a portion of a Final Cut Pro sequence and convert that selection to a self-contained sub-sequence. Converting a group of clips to a nested sequence has several advantages:

◆ Nesting a group of clips can simplify the process of moving them around within a sequence or placing them in another sequence.

◆ Using Nest Items to convert a series of edited clips into a single nested sequence allows you to create a single motion path for the nested sequence rather than having to create separate motion paths for each clip.

◆ Nesting a group of clips allows you to apply and adjust a single copy of a filter to a series of clips, rather than having to apply and adjust filters for each individual clip.

◆ You can nest clips that are stacked on multiple tracks (such as layered title elements) and animate them as a single sub-sequence.

◆ You can nest a clip containing an element you want to blur. By increasing the frame size when you nest, you can create a roomier bounding box that will accommodate the larger size of your blurred element.

◆ Nested sequences can help preserve your render files—most render files associated with the nested sequence are preserved within the nested sequence, even if you move it around or change its duration. For more information on nested sequences and rendering protocol, see "Using nested sequences to preserve render files" in Chapter 18.

◆ In a sequence with multiple effects applied, nesting a clip can force a change in the rendering order.

FCP Protocol: Selecting Items for Nesting

◆ FCP includes any video and audio sequence material that you select in the nested sequence; you can include as many multiple tracks as you wish.

◆ Any linked audio and video will be included in the nested sequence unless you turn off Linked Selection.

◆ Only whole clips can be selected.

◆ All nested audio will appear as a stereo pair on two tracks, even if the sub-sequence contains only a single channel of audio.

Figure 4.36 Select the Timeline items you want to nest.

Figure 4.37 Choose Sequence > Nest Item(s).

Figure 4.38 Specify settings for your nested sequence in the Nest Items dialog box.

Figure 4.39 At the selected clips' previous location in the Timeline, a new, nested sequence appears as a sub-sequence.

To nest items in a sequence:

1. In the Timeline, select the items to be nested (**Figure 4.36**).

2. Choose Sequence > Nest Item(s) (**Figure 4.37**).

   The Nest Items dialog box appears.

3. Using the Nest Items dialog box (**Figure 4.38**), *do any of the following*:

   ◆ Enter a name for the new nested sequence.

   ◆ Specify another frame size, but only if you want the nested sequence to have a frame size different from that of the main sequence. (This is specifically useful for increasing the frame size of a sequence to accommodate a blur that exceeds the size of the current item.) All other sequence properties are copied from the parent sequence.

   ◆ If you've selected only one clip, leave Keep Effects, Markers, and Audio Levels with Clip deselected if you want the clip's current effects to be applied to the entire nested sequence.

   ◆ Check Mixdown Audio if you want to create a render file of any audio tracks included in the nested sequence.

4. Click OK.

   A new, nested sequence appears as a sub-sequence at the selected clips' former location in the Timeline (**Figure 4.39**). The new sequence also appears in the same Browser bin as the main sequence.

Making changes to a nested sequence

You can open a nested sequence and add, remove, or trim clips. When you return to your main sequence, you'll see that the duration of the nested sequence has been adjusted to reflect your changes. Clips to the right of the nested sequence will be rippled to accommodate the change to your nested sequence duration. You'll still need to open the nested sequence to make changes to the clips inside.

To make changes to a nested sequence:

Do one of the following:

◆ In the main sequence in the Timeline, double-click the nested sequence (**Figure 4.40**).

◆ In the Browser, double-click the icon for the nested sequence.

The nested sequence opens as the front tab of the Timeline (**Figure 4.41**). If you opened the nested sequence from inside the main sequence, the main sequence is still open on the rear tab (**Figure 4.42**).

To "un-nest" a sequence:

◆ There's no "Un-nest" command in Final Cut Pro. If you want to replace a nested sequence that you have placed in your main sequence with the clips contained in that nest, you should first open the nest in the Timeline, and then copy the clips from the open nest and paste them back over the nested sequence's original location in the main sequence. For more information, see "Copying and pasting from sequence to sequence," next.

Figure 4.40 In the main sequence in the Timeline, double-click the nested sequence.

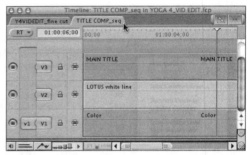
Figure 4.41 The nested sequence opens as the front tab of the Timeline.

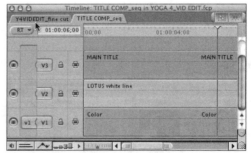
Figure 4.42 The main sequence is still open on the rear tab of the Timeline.

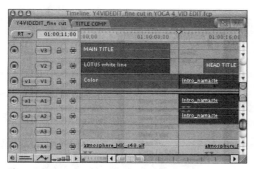

Figure 4.43 In the Timeline, select the clips you want to cut or copy. In this example, the selected clips are on Tracks V1, V2, and V3.

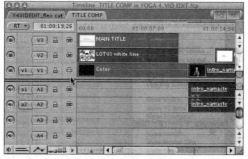

Figure 4.44 Press Command-V to paste the sequence tracks into your destination sequence. As long as you make no change to the Auto Select controls between cutting and pasting commands, the pasted clips are assigned to the same tracks they occupied in the source sequence. In this example, Auto Select control settings have been overridden, and the clips are pasted into the destination sequence on Tracks V1, V2, and V3.

Copying and pasting from sequence to sequence

Moving selected clips into a new, separate sequence is the first step in nesting a selection of clips inside your master sequence. Moving material from sequence to sequence is easy; simply copy (or cut) material from one sequence and paste it into another sequence. You can copy and paste the entire contents of a sequence, or you can select a single clip.

Copying and pasting between sequences is governed by the same rules that govern copying and pasting within the same sequence: When you paste, the clips paste themselves into the destination sequence on the same tracks you cut them from *unless you make a change to the Auto Select controls of the destination sequence after you cut (or copy) but before you paste.* If you do, then the Auto Select controls determine the track destination of pasted tracks. Clips will be pasted starting at the lowest-numbered Auto Select–enabled track.

To copy and paste clips between sequences:

1. In the Timeline, select the clips you want to copy into the destination sequence (**Figure 4.43**) and then *do one of the following:*
   - ◆ To copy the selected clips, press Command-C.
   - ◆ To cut the selected clips, press Command-X.

2. In the destination sequence, position the playhead where you want to paste the clips, then press Command-V.

   The clips are pasted into your destination sequence according to the protocols described above (**Figure 4.44**).

✔ Tip

- ■ You can also select and then Option-drag items from one sequence to another.

To paste the entire contents of a sequence into another sequence:

1. Open the destination sequence in the Timeline, and mark a sequence In point where you want to paste the contents of your source sequence.

2. In the Browser, select the sequence whose contents you want to copy into a second sequence.

3. Hold down the Command key as you drag the sequence's icon from the Browser into the destination sequence (**Figure 4.45**).

   All the clips from the selected sequence are pasted into the destination sequence (**Figure 4.46**).

✔ Tip

- Drag a sequence into another open sequence in the Timeline without holding the Command key, and you will nest the sequence.

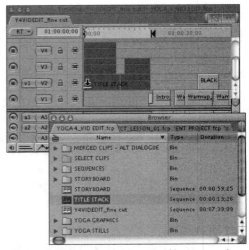

Figure 4.45 Hold down the Command key as you drag to paste the entire contents of a sequence into your destination sequence.

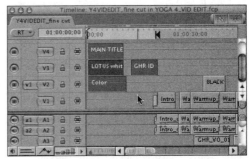

Figure 4.46 The clips from the sequence you dragged are pasted into the destination sequence.

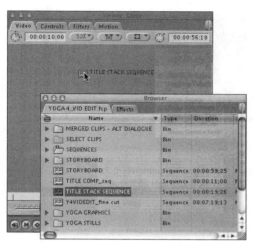

Figure 4.47 To open a sequence in the Viewer, drag the sequence's icon from the Browser and drop it on the image area in the Viewer window.

Figure 4.48 Your edited sequence opens in the Viewer window. You can edit the sequence into an open sequence in the Timeline, just as you would a clip.

Editing a sequence into another sequence

You can use sequences as source clips and edit them into another sequence. Your source clip sequence could be a preexisting sequence you drag into the Viewer or Timeline from the Browser, or it could be a nested sequence located inside a parent sequence in the Timeline. Opening a sequence in the Viewer is not quite as easy as opening a clip. Once you've loaded a sequence into the Viewer, however, you can edit it into a sequence just as you would a clip.

If you need more information on how to perform edits in Final Cut Pro, see Chapter 9, "Basic Editing."

To load a sequence into the Viewer:

In the Browser, select the sequence you want to edit into your main sequence; then *do one of the following:*

◆ Choose View > Sequence.

◆ Drag the sequence's icon from the Browser and drop it on the image area in the Viewer window (**Figure 4.47**).

Your edited sequence opens in the Viewer, ready to be used as source media (**Figure 4.48**). If the sequence you select is open in the Timeline and the Canvas, it closes automatically when you load it into the Viewer.

To load a nested sub-sequence into the Viewer:

In the Timeline, *do one of the following:*

◆ Control-click the nested sequence, and then choose Open in Viewer from the shortcut menu (**Figure 4.49**).

◆ Double-click the nested sequence while holding down the Option key.

Your nested sequence opens in the Viewer window, ready to be used as a source clip.

✔ Tips

■ When you load a nested sequence from the Timeline and edit it back into your main sequence, you are creating a duplicate of the nested sequence—an independent copy of the original sequence that will not reflect changes you make to the original. If you want all copies of your nested sequence to update when you make changes, use the Browser version of your nested sequence as your source clip instead.

■ All nested audio appears as stereo pairs on two tracks, even if the sub-sequence contains only a single channel of audio.

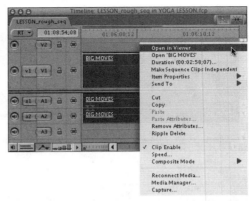

Figure 4.49 In the Timeline, Control-click the nested sequence, and then choose Open in Viewer from the shortcut menu.

FCP Protocol: Updating Nested Sequences

When you insert a clip from the Browser into a sequence, the clip is copied into the sequence. The copy of the clip you placed in the sequence refers directly to the actual media file on the disk and is not a reference to the clip in the project file. Changes you make to the sequence version of the clip will not be reflected in the Browser version.

Nested sequences update globally

The protocol governing sequence versions is different, and it is also central to understanding Final Cut Pro. Unlike clips, sequences nested inside another sequence are actually pointers, or references, to the original sequence, not copies. *If you make changes to a sequence after you've edited it into a number of other master sequences, any changes you make to the original **will be reflected** every place you have used it. You'll need to make a duplicate of the sequence and make changes to the copy if you want to avoid a global update.*

For example, you could create a standard credit sequence and edit that sequence into every program in your series. If your credits require any last-minute changes, you can make the changes in the original sequence, and all the projects in which that sequence is nested will be updated.

But duplicate sequences are independent copies

Keep a close watch on nested sequences that you're using in multiple locations.

Multiple nested copies of the same sequence point to the original sequence IF (that's a big *if*) you always use the original Browser version of your sequence as your source when you nest the sequence in multiple locations.

*If you duplicate the original sequence in the Browser, the duplicate sequence you create is an independent copy of the original sequence that **will not reflect** changes you make to the original.* Duping a sequence is a good way to preserve render files, but it's bad news if you want to nest an identical sequence in multiple locations and take advantage of the global updating feature.

Copying and pasting a nested sequence to multiple locations within the master sequence in the Timeline produces the same result: independent duplicates of the original that don't update.

If you need to place multiple copies of a nested sequence you created in the Timeline, always use the Browser version of your nested sequence (it appeared when you performed the Nest Items command) to place the sequence in multiple locations.

Assembling Nested Sequences with Transitions

Building your program as a series of separate sequences and then assembling your sequence "scenes" into a final master sequence is a common post-production strategy. If you want to use transitions to join your scenes together, you'll need to allow extra media handles at the start and end of your nested sequences. When you're ready to assemble your master sequence, load each sub-sequence into the Viewer. Mark the frames you want to appear as the center point of your scene-to-scene transition as the sub-sequence's In and Out points before you edit them into the final master sequence (**Figure 4.50**).

Figure 4.50 If you want to use a transition to join two sub-sequences, mark In and Out points that allow handles on your sub-sequences, in order to establish the extra frames your transition will require.

About Clips

Final Cut Pro has always used clip types—audio, video, graphic, and generated—to identify clips that reference different types of source media. FCP uses a different class of clip types—subclip, merged clip, and sequence—to identify clips that reference a portion of another clip (like a subclip) or multiple clips (like merged clips, multiclips, and sequences).

FCP 4 introduced three new clip types—master, affiliate, and independent—to identify clips that are linked by shared properties (like master and affiliate clips) or clips whose properties and behavior are independent of other clips (like independent clips). The new clip type classifications and behavior are designed to ease media management by automatically updating all affiliated clips when you make a change to a shared property on any of the individual affiliates anywhere in the project. The master/affiliate clips' shared properties are all related to media management; clip properties that remain independent—In and Out points, markers, and applied effects—are all modified during the normal course of editing and must remain independent in each clip copy you use.

Here's an example: You have a master clip in the Browser, and you edit it into your sequence. An affiliate copy of that master clip appears in the sequence. Rename the affiliate copy, and the name of its master clip is also renamed. Change the reel name of the master clip, and the reel name of the affiliate clip in the sequence reflects the same change.

The master/affiliate clip-handling scheme keeps your clip duplicates in sync, which can simplify your life when you're media-managing certain types of projects. Projects best suited to master/affiliate clip handling are well logged, with discrete clips that you don't plan on subdividing much.

If your preferred editing method is to capture large chunks of media and then subdivide and rename the clips post-capture, there's no easy way to rename a portion of an affiliate clip without renaming its master and all other affiliates. You could convert your subdivided clip into a subclip before renaming, or you could convert your master clips to independent-type clips before you start dicing them up. Converting your clips to independent-type could save you from the headache and confusion of converting (and tracking) each clip's type separately; however, Apple warns that independent-type clips can be more trouble when you go to media manage your project later because their offline/online status is tracked independently of the master clip they were derived from. For more information on clip affiliation protocols, see "Working With Master and Affiliate Clips" on page IV-43 of Apple's *Final Cut Pro User Manual* PDF.

Here's a rundown of FCP's clip types:

Format-based clip types

◆ **Audio, Video, and Graphics clip:** These clip types are determined by the type of source media the clip is referencing.

◆ **Generated clip:** Create a generated clip by opening a generator from the Viewer's Generators pop-up menu. Generated clips are created as master-type clips. For more information, see Chapter 17, "Titles and Generators."

Relationship-based clip types

◆ **Master clip (Figure 4.51):** Any clip that can generate affiliate clip copies is a master clip. See **Table 4.1** on page 138 for a complete list of ways to create one.

◆ **Affiliate clip (Figure 4.52):** An affiliate clip is a copy of a master clip that is created by inserting the master clip into a sequence or duplicating the master clip in the Browser. Copies of affiliate clips remain linked to their master clip originals; the linked relationship extends to the clip name, reel name, source timecode, labels, subclip limits, and online/offline state of all affiliate clips. Change one of these shared properties in any one of the affiliated clips, and the change will appear in all the affiliated clips. Markers, In and Out points, and applied effects or motion properties remain independent in master/affiliate clips. See Table 4.1 for a complete list of ways to create an affiliate clip.

◆ **Independent clip (Figure 4.53):** Each copy of an independent clip refers directly back to its source media and does not synchronize clip naming or any other properties with any other independent clip copy. All clips in pre-FCP 4 projects are independent clips. See Table 4.1 for a complete list of ways to create an independent clip.

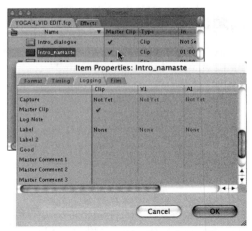

Figure 4.51 It's not easy to identify master, affiliate, and independent clips in the FCP interface. Master clips are easiest to spot; a checkmark in the Master Clip column identifies a master clip in the Browser and on the Logging tab of the clip's Item Properties window. Master clips never appear in a sequence.

Figure 4.52 Affiliate clips have no checkmark in the Browser's Master Clip column. In a sequence, the only way to identify an affiliate clip is to open the clip's shortcut menu. If the Make Independent Clip command is available and not dimmed, the clip is an affiliate clip.

Figure 4.53 In a sequence, you can identify an independent clip by opening the clip's shortcut menu. If the Make Independent Clip command is dimmed, the clip is already an independent clip. Independent clips appear in the Browser only when you open a pre-FCP 4 project file.

FCP Protocol: Sequence Clip Terminology

FCP uses slightly different terminology when referring to clips that have already been placed into a sequence:

A *sequence clip* is simply a clip that's already been edited into a sequence in the Timeline. When you double-click a sequence clip in the Timeline, it opens in the Viewer with two rows of dots in the Scrubber bar, indicating that you've opened a sequence clip.

Recent versions of Final Cut Pro have started to refer to the video and audio tracks that comprise a sequence clip as *clip items*. A standard DV clip edited into a sequence would be composed of one video and two audio clip items. FCP's clip-handling scheme tracks all clip items independently—even those captured together as a single clip—in order to accommodate the need to reliably track complex merged clips and multiclips where a video clip can be linked to multiple tracks of audio from different sources.

♦ **Merged clip:** Create a merged clip by combining video and audio from separate sources into a single clip. Merged clips are always created as master-type clips. For more information, see "Working with Merged Clips," later in this chapter.

♦ **Subclip:** Subclips are shorter clips you create from a section of a longer master clip. A subclip is always created as a new master-type clip, with no affiliate relationship to the clip it was created from. For information on subclips, see Chapter 8, "Working with Clips in the Viewer."

♦ **Multiclip**: Like merged clips, multiclips are created by grouping and synchronizing multiple clips (called multiclip *angles*) into a structured unit. In multiclip editing mode, you can create your edit by switching between multiclip angles in real time. For more information on multiclip editing, see Chapter 9, "Basic Editing."

♦ **Offline Clip:** Any clip that currently has no valid link to its source media file is considered an offline clip. A clip can be offline because it has been logged but not captured yet, or a clip's status can switch from online to offline because its source media has been moved or deleted. See "Reconnecting Offline Files" in Chapter 20 for more information on offline clips.

✔ Tip

■ You can find a list detailing which clip properties are controlled by the Master-Affiliate clip relationship, which properties are unique to Affiliate clips, and which properties are written into the source media file on Page IV-45 of Apple's *Final Cut Pro User Manual* PDF.

FCP Protocol: Clips and Sequences

A *clip* is the basic unit of media in Final Cut Pro.

A clip can represent a movie, still image, nested sequence, generator, or audio file.

A clip is a reference to the actual media file stored on your hard disk. But a clip can also reference material that is not currently online. If you delete the original media file, the clip will still appear in the Browser and Timeline, but you won't see its frames and you won't be able to play it.

When you apply special effects and perform edits on clips, you are *not* affecting the media file on disk.

Before FCP 4, all clips were governed by the same clip-handling protocols. FCP 4, 5, and 6 use three clip types: master, affiliate, and independent. Master and affiliate clips use one set of behavior protocols; independent clip behavior is governed by a different set of rules.

Using Master and Affiliate Clips in Sequences

When you insert a master clip from a project into a sequence, FCP inserts a copy of the master clip, known as an *affiliate clip*. That affiliate copy in the sequence shares certain properties with the master clip but maintains independent control over other properties.

This protocol is important to understand because it affects how and where you should make changes to master/affiliate clips, and it illuminates what's different about independent clip behavior. So, let's lay out the rules.

When you modify a master or affiliate clip's name, reel name, source timecode, or labels; remove its subclip limits; or change its online/offline state:

◆ The change you make is applied to all affiliated clips in the project. It doesn't matter if you make the change to the master clip or its affiliate—the result is the same.

◆ Master and affiliate clips' shared property behavior only applies within a single project; your changes will not be applied to other projects.

When you apply markers, In and Out points, effects, or motion properties to a master clip or its affiliate clip copy:

◆ You can open the clip from the Browser (outside a sequence) or from the Timeline (within a sequence).

◆ If you make changes to the clip in the Browser and then insert that clip into a sequence, the clip copy that is placed in the sequence *includes* the changes that have been made in the Browser.

◆ Any changes you make to a clip from within a sequence are *not* made to the clip in the Browser.

continues on next page

ABOUT CLIPS

FCP Protocol: Clips and Sequences *continued*

◆ After you've inserted a clip into a sequence, any further changes you make to that clip from the Browser will not be reflected in any sequence where the clip is used.

◆ Clips that appear in multiple sequences are independent of one another. Changes to one will not affect the others.

◆ If you want to make further revisions to a clip that's already in a sequence, open the clip from the Timeline and then make the changes.

◆ If you want to make changes to a clip and have the changes show up in all the sequences in which that clip is used, open the clip from the Browser and make the changes. Then reinsert the revised clip into each sequence in which you want the updated clip to appear.

◆ Final Cut Pro identifies clips that have been opened from the Timeline by displaying two lines of dots in the Scrubber bar. No dots appear in the Scrubber bar of clips that have been opened from the Browser.

Using Independent Clips in Sequences

When you convert an affiliate-type sequence clip to an independent-type clip, that independent clip refers directly back to the source media file on the disk, and any clip property can be modified independently from any master or affiliate clip referencing the same source media file.

Because each independent clip copy maintains independent control over all its properties, the same rules that apply to the In and Out points of master and affiliate clips (listed above) apply to all properties of independent clips.

FCP 6 Update: Master Clip Identity Now Travels Across Multiple Projects

Copy a clip from one FCP 6 project to another, and FCP will now check to see if the added clip shares a master clip identity with any clips in the destination project. If FCP detects a match, the added clip will become an affiliate of the existing master clip. If FCP detects a conflict between the master clip properties of the added clip and the existing clip, it will display a dialog box allowing you to sort out which master clip properties to preserve and which to replace; the same box offers the option of resolving this conflict by creating a new master clip and preserving both sets of master clip properties.

If you're copying an entire sequence into a project, FCP will check every clip in that sequence in the same way. You can choose to deal with your clips individually or globally.

ABOUT CLIPS

Table 4.1

FCP Clip Type Relationships			
TYPE	**MASTER?**	**HOW TO CREATE**	**BEHAVIOR**
Master clip	yes	Capture new video or audio. Import video or audio. Create a subclip. Create a freeze-frame. Create a merged clip. Drag a merged clip from the sequence back to the Browser. Import an EDL or batch list. Use the Duplicate as New Master clip command. Use Modify > Make Master Clip on an affiliate or independent sequence clip. Delete an affiliate's master clip. Affiliate clips in the Browser are converted to master clips.	Synchronizes clip name, reel name, source timecode, labels, subclip limits, and online/offline state with all affiliate clips. Does not synchronize markers, In and Out points, applied effects, or motion properties. Master clips appear only in the Browser.
Affiliate clip	no	Edit a master clip into a sequence. Duplicate a clip in the Browser or in a sequence. Copy and paste a clip in the Browser or in a sequence. Drag a sequence clip back into the Browser.	Synchronizes clip name, reel name, source timecode, subclip limits, and online/offline state with all affiliated clips and the master clip. Does not synchronize markers, In and Out points, applied effects, or motion properties. Affiliate clips can appear in the Browser or Timeline.
Independent clip	no	Delete an affiliate's master clip. Use the Make Independent Clip command on a sequence clip. Edit a clip opened outside the project directly into a sequence. Open a FCP 3 project in FCP 4, 5, or 6; all project clips will be independent.	Maintains independent clip name, reel name, source timecode, remove subclip limits, online/offline state, markers, In and Out points, and applied effects or motion properties. Independent clips appear only in the Timeline, except when a pre-FCP 4 project is opened.

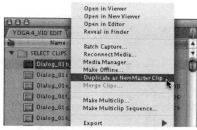

Figure 4.54 Control-click the Browser clip, and then choose Duplicate as New Master Clip from the clip's shortcut menu.

Figure 4.55 The duplicate master clip appears in the Browser.

Figure 4.56 Choose Make Master Clip from the clip's shortcut menu.

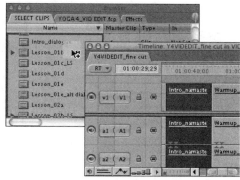

Figure 4.57 A special pointer (with an *M* for master) appears when both the Command and Option keys are held down, alerting you that you're creating a duplicate master clip.

To duplicate a Browser clip as a new master clip:

Select the clip in the Browser, and then *do one of the following:*

◆ Control-click the clip, and then choose Duplicate as New Master Clip from the shortcut menu (**Figure 4.54**).

◆ Choose Modify > Duplicate as New Master Clip.

The duplicate of the clip appears as a new master clip in the Browser (**Figure 4.55**).

To convert an independent or affiliate clip into a master clip:

Select the clip in the Browser, and then *do one of the following:*

◆ Control-click the clip, then choose Make Master Clip from the shortcut menu (**Figure 4.56**).

◆ Choose Modify > Make Master Clip.

✔ Tips

■ After you're done hacking, renaming, and subdividing, and the independent clips in your sequence finally settle down enough to get hitched, you can create master clips for every sequence clip simply by selecting the sequence icon in the Browser and choosing Tools > Create Master Clips. FCP will create a new Browser bin of master clips and your independent sequence clips become affiliates of those newly created master clips.

■ Create a duplicate master clip for a sequence clip by pressing Option as you drag the sequence clip out of the Timeline, and then adding the Command key as you drop the clip in the Browser (**Figure 4.57**). "Voilà!" is so overused these days, but still....

To locate an affiliate clip's master clip:

◆ Select the affiliate clip in the Timeline or Browser, then choose View > Reveal Master Clip.

The master clip is revealed in the Browser.

To make a sequence clip independent:

◆ In the Timeline, Control-click the sequence clip, then choose Make Independent Clip from the shortcut menu (**Figure 4.58**).

The affiliate sequence clip is converted to an independent-type clip.

To make all clips in a sequence independent:

◆ Select the sequence icon in the Browser, then choose Make Sequence Clips Independent from the shortcut menu (**Figure 4.59**).

To break an affiliate clip's relationship with its master:

Do one of the following:

◆ In the Browser, delete the master clip associated with that affiliate clip.

◆ Copy the sequence containing the affiliate clip into another project.

◆ In the Timeline, use the Make Independent Clip command to convert the affiliate clip into an independent clip.

To rename a clip to match its media file:

1. Select the clip in the Browser.

2. Choose Modify > Rename > Clip to Match File.

To rename a media file to match its clip name:

1. Select the clip in the Browser.

2. Choose Modify > Rename > File to Match Clip.

Figure 4.58 Choosing Make Independent Clip from the sequence clip's shortcut menu converts an affiliate-type clip to an independent-type clip.

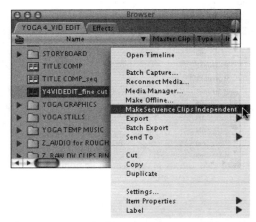

Figure 4.59 Control-click a sequence's icon in the Browser and choose Make Sequence Clips Independent, and you convert all the clips in that sequence to independent clips with a single command.

Figure 4.60 Choose an Item Properties window tab from the clip's shortcut menu.

Viewing and Setting Item Properties

The Item Properties window is the central location for information about an individual clip. The settings on four tabs in the Item Properties window allow you to view or change the properties of a clip. Besides the general clip information column in the far left of the window, you'll see a column for the clip's video track, and separate columns for each audio track in the clip. This expansion of the Item Properties window makes it possible to combine one video track with up to 24 tracks of audio from different sources and track each audio channel separately.

To open a clip's Item Properties window:

1. Select the clip in the Browser or Timeline, or open it in the Viewer.

2. *Do one of the following:*
   - Choose Edit > Item Properties; then choose one of the four Item Properties window tabs—Format, Timing, Logging Info, or Film—from the submenu.
   - Control-click the item; then choose an Item Properties window tab from the shortcut menu (**Figure 4.60**).
   - Press Command-9.

✔ Tips

- Want to view item properties for multiple clips in a single window? Just select the clips in the Browser or Timeline before you use the Edit > Item Properties command.

- What if you have renamed a clip and the new name no longer matches the name of the source media file it references? You can consult the Source property in the Item Properties window for the renamed clip to trace the underlying source media filename and location.

To get information about the format of a clip:

1. In the clip's Item Properties window, click the Format tab (**Figure 4.61**) to open it. This tab displays data on the location of the source media file, file size, and format characteristics for each track of the clip.

2. Control-click on the item's setting in the Clip column to modify the following Format properties:

   ◆ **Name:** Enter a new name for the clip.

   ◆ **Pixel Aspect Ratio:** Select a pixel aspect ratio for the clip.

   ◆ **Anamorphic:** If your clip's source media is 16:9, enabling this option ensures that FCP will interpret and display the clip's pixel aspect ratio properly.

◆ **Field Dominance:** Specify the dominant field by making a selection from the shortcut menu.

◆ **Alpha Type:** Select an alpha channel type for the video clip.

◆ **Reverse Alpha:** Reverse the alpha channel of the video clip.

◆ **Composite Mode:** Select the mode to be used when compositing the video clip.

3. You can view and modify a variety of other clip information; the data displayed is also displayed in Browser columns using the same names.

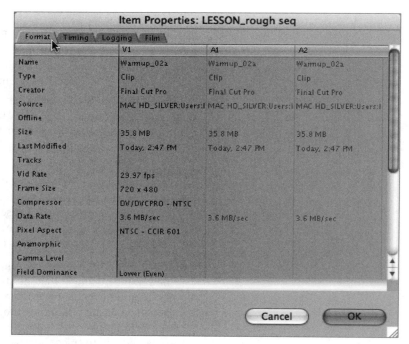

Figure 4.61 The Format tab of the Item Properties window displays format information about an individual clip or sequence.

To get information about the timing of a clip:

1. In the clip's Item Properties window, click the Timing tab to open it.

2. On the Timing tab (**Figure 4.62**), you can modify the following Timing properties (on Browser clips only):

   ◆ **Name:** Enter a new name for this clip.

   ◆ **In:** Enter or modify the In point of a clip.

   ◆ **Out:** Enter or modify the Out point of a clip.

   ◆ **Duration:** Enter or modify the duration of a clip.

3. You can view and modify a variety of other clip information; the data displayed is also displayed in Browser columns using the same names.

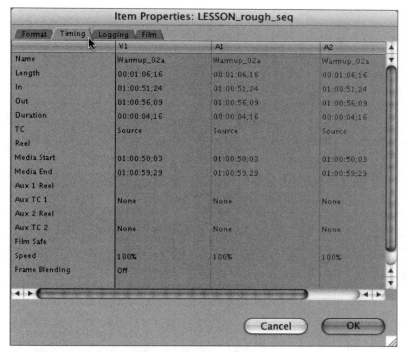

Figure 4.62 The Timing tab of the Item Properties window.

To get logging information for a clip:

1. In the clip's Item Properties window, click the Logging tab (**Figure 4.63**).

   This tab provides logging information for a clip.

2. You can modify the following properties:

   ◆ **Name:** Enter a new name for this clip.

   ◆ **Reel:** Enter or modify the name of the clip's source tape.

   ◆ **Description:** Enter or modify descriptive details for a clip.

   ◆ **Scene:** Enter or modify tracking information for a clip.

   ◆ **Shot/Take:** Enter or modify tracking information.

   ◆ **Capture:** Specify the status of a clip as Not Yet, OK, or Queued.

   ◆ **Log Note:** Enter or modify a log note.

   ◆ **Label:** Organize clips by preset classifications.

   ◆ **Label 2:** Organize clips by entering user-set classifications.

   ◆ **Good:** Click the Good check box to mark the clip for any sorting purposes.

   ◆ **Master Comments 1–4:** Enter or modify additional comments for the clip in these fields. Master comments are reflected in all affiliated clips.

   ◆ **Comment A, B:** Comments that apply to this clip only.

3. You can view and modify a variety of other clip information; the data displayed is also displayed in Browser columns using the same names.

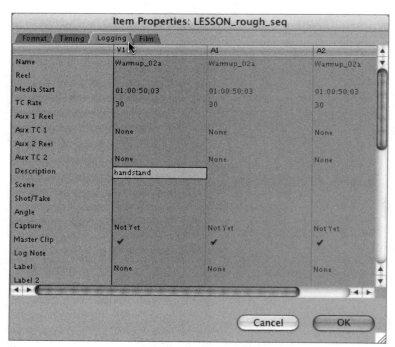

Figure 4.63 The Logging tab of the Item Properties window.

About Timecode Viewing Options

Driven by HD, 24P, and variable-frame-rate video cameras, video frame rates are now multiplying in the brave new world of digital post-production, and FCP is boldly going. So brew up another pot of coffee, and let's talk about FCP's timecode viewing options.

A clip's frame rate, as defined by FCP, expresses how many unique frames are displayed in one second. A speed-modified clip adjusted to playback at 50 percent displays 15 unique frames per second (fps). Timecode numbers are unique identifying numbers assigned per frame, whether that frame is unique or not.

New post-production pathways take advantage of FCP's flexibility and computational speed to support projects with native frame rates and timecode rates that don't match. Editing 60-fps HD using 30-fps timecode (or cutting 23.98 fps 24P-format video using 29.97 fps timecode) is becoming more common in professional editing suites. FCP offers newly configured timecode viewing options to assist editors working with projects where source media frame rates differ from the timecode rate of the project video.

If you're working with media whose source media frame rates and timecode rates match (and that's most of you), just leave your timecode viewing options set to FCP's default: Source Time, Native Speed mode enabled.

You can view and modify FCP's Timecode viewing and display modes in the Timeline, Canvas, and Viewer Current Timecode fields (**Figure 4.64**).

continues on next page

Figure 4.64 Control-click the Viewer's Current Timecode field to access FCP's timecode viewing options.

Time Display Modes
Time display modes offer time view options but don't alter timecode playback speed. For more information, see "Timecode navigation and display" in Chapter 8.

View Source or Auxiliary Timecode
FCP displays the clip's original source timecode by default. If you have assigned auxiliary timecodes, you can select one to display here. For more information, see "Changing Your Source Timecode," later in this chapter.

View Native Speed Mode
With View Native Speed enabled, FCP displays the native timecode number for each source media frame.

Timecode Viewing Modes
Clip Time is the clip's timecode based on its native frame rate.

Source Time is the clip's timecode based on the timecode track of the captured media source file.

About Timecode Viewing Options *continued*

Timecode Viewing Modes

Source Time: The timecode track of the captured media source file. This is the default Time display mode for projects with matching timecode and native frame rates.

Clip Time: FCP calculates and displays the clip's timecode based on the clip's native frame rate. When a clip's TC rate and frame rate match, Source Time and Clip Time are identical.

View Native Speed: In default mode (with View Native Speed enabled), FCP displays the native timecode number for each source media frame. With View Native Speed disabled, FCP adjusts each frame's native timecode number to reflect the speed change and displays the adjusted timecode. For example, enable View Native Speed on a 30-fps clip that you have speed-modified to play back at 25 percent normal speed, and then note the timecode display as you advance the clip by single frames. In View Native speed mode, the same timecode number appears four times before incrementing because FCP repeats each frame four times to create the slow motion playback. VNS mode applies to both source time and clip time modes.

Time Display Modes

While the timecode viewing modes detailed above can actually adjust the rate of timecode playback, time display offers elapsed time view options but doesn't change timecode playback speed. Time display options available depend on the frame and timecode rate of your source media file. For more information, see "Timecode navigation and display" in Chapter 8.

Figure 4.65 Control-click the Viewer's Current Timecode field to see your clip's currently selected timecode viewing options. You can switch between Source, Aux TC 1, or Aux TC 2 timecode views on the Timing tab of the clip's Item Properties window.

Changing Your Source Timecode

You can modify the source timecode of any clip in Final Cut Pro. When you use the Modify Timecode feature to modify a clip's source timecode, the change is written as a permanent change in the clip's source media file on disk. The source timecode modification will be reflected in every use of that clip in all projects.

Auxiliary timecodes allow you to assign an additional timecode reference to a clip without modifying its source timecode. Final Cut Pro clips have two auxiliary timecode fields. You can view a clip using the Source, Aux TC 1, or Aux TC 2 timecode (**Figure 4.65**).

There are no hard and fast rules about when to modify timecodes and when to reference auxiliary timecode fields. Generally speaking, modifying is an appropriate choice if your Final Cut Pro source timecodes need to be adjusted to conform to the timecode of your master tapes—the ones you're going to use to cut the finished version of the program. For example, you would modify the source timecode of your Final Cut Pro files to conform to master tapes if you needed to create an EDL whose timecode values would reference your master tapes, rather than the Final Cut Pro files.

Auxiliary timecodes are useful for synchronizing material from a variety of sources to a master timecode without modifying any clip's source timecode (synchronizing multiple shots to a music track in a music video, for example).

To change a clip's timecode:

1. Double-click a clip in the Browser (**Figure 4.66**) or in the Timeline to open it in the Viewer.

2. Move the playhead to the frame where you want to establish the new timecode.

3. Choose Modify > Timecode.

4. In the Frame to Set pop-up menu at the top of the Timecode dialog box, *do one of the following:*

   ◆ Choose Current to set the currently displayed frame to the timecode value you enter in the Source field.

   ◆ Choose First to set the first frame of the clip's underlying media file to the timecode value you enter in the Source TC field (**Figure 4.67**).

5. Enter a new timecode value in the Source TC field, and click OK.

   The timecode value of the media file on disk is modified to reflect the change.

To change a clip's auxiliary timecode:

1. Double-click a clip in the Browser or Timeline to open it in the Viewer.

2. Move the playhead to the frame where you want to establish the new timecode (**Figure 4.68**).

3. Choose Modify > Timecode.

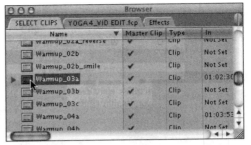

Figure 4.66 Double-click the clip in the Browser to open it in the Viewer window.

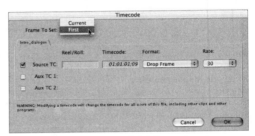

Figure 4.67 Select First, and the timecode value you enter in the Source TC Timecode field will be applied to the first frame of the clip's underlying media file.

Figure 4.68 Position the playhead on the frame where you want to establish the new timecode.

Figure 4.69 After you've entered a new timecode value in the Aux TC 1 Timecode field, click OK.

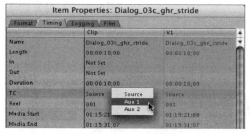

Figure 4.70 To display a clip's auxiliary timecode, open the Timing tab of the clip's Item properties window, Control-click next to the clip's TC property, and then select Aux TC 1 from the shortcut menu. You may need to close and then reopen the clip in the Viewer before the Viewer's Current timecode field display will switch to Aux TC timecode display.

4. In the Frame to Set pop-up menu at the top of the Timecode dialog box, *do one of the following:*

   ◆ Choose Current to set the timecode value at the currently displayed frame.

   ◆ Choose First to set the timecode value at the first frame of the clip.

5. Check the box next to the Aux TC you want to set, then enter a new timecode value in the Aux TC 1 or Aux TC 2 field and click OK (**Figure 4.69**).

To view a clip's auxiliary timecode:

◆ On the Timing tab of the clip's Item Properties window, Control-click in the column next to the TC property, then choose Aux TC 1 (or Aux TC 2) from the shortcut menu (**Figure 4.70**). Aux TC options will not appear in the shortcut menu unless you have modified an auxiliary timecode.

✔ Tip

■ Merged clips display a separate TC tab for each item in the clip that's linked to separate source media, so you can modify each element's timecode independently.

FCP 6 Update: Importing Audio-Only Files with Timecode

Importers of BWF format audio files will be pleased to know that QuickTime and FCP 6 will now import Broadcast Wave Format (BWF) files with their timestamps intact. No more Sebsky Tools.

Those of you importing BWF files recorded with NTSC timecode will need to visit the Editing tab of the User Preferences window and specify Drop or Non-Drop as your NTSC default timecode. For more information, see page I-325 of the *Final Cut Pro User Manual* PDF.

Working with Merged Clips

Merged clips are composed of video and/or audio from separate sources combined into a single clip. The most common use of merged clips is to sync video with production audio tracks that were recorded separately, or to sync up multiple audio tracks to create a single multichannel audio clip. Final Cut Pro's merged clips can preserve and track separate audio timecode for up to 12 stereo or 24 mono audio tracks, plus one video track. Merged clips are always created as master-type clips.

Open the Item Properties window on a merged clip, and you'll find a data column for each audio channel. The original time-code for each channel is tracked in the Media Start row (**Figure 4.71**).

This section explains how to create a merged clip in the Browser and in the Timeline. For information on audio editing protocols that apply to merged clips, see "Editing Clips with Multiple Audio Channels" in Chapter 12, or "Merging Clips from Dual System Video and Audio" on page 380 of *Apple's Final Cut Pro User Manual* PDF.

WORKING WITH MERGED CLIPS

Item Properties: Lesson_01e_alt dialog				
Format Timing Logging Film				
	A1	A2	A3	A4
Name	alog Lesson_01e_alt dialo	Lesson_01e_alt dialo	Lesson_01e_alt dialo	Lesson_01e_alt dialo
Length	00:00:10;00	00:00:10;00	00:00:05;02	00:00:05;02
In	01:08:40;16	01:08:40;16	01:08:41;11	01:08:41;11
Out	01:08:50;15	01:08:50;15	01:08:45;17	01:08:45;17
Duration	00:00:10;00	00:00:10;00	00:00:04;07	00:00:04;07
TC	Source	Source	Source	Source
Reel				
Media Start	01:08:40;16	01:08:40;16	01:08:31;11	01:08:31;11
Media End	01:08:50;15	01:08:50;15	01:08:35;17	01:08:35;17
Aux 1 Reel				
Aux TC 1	None	None	None	None
Aux 2 Reel				
Aux TC 2	None	None	None	None
Film Safe				
Speed	100%	100%	100%	100%
Frame Blending				

Cancel   OK

Figure 4.71 The Media Start row in the merged clip's Item Properties window tracks separate source timecode data for each audio channel.

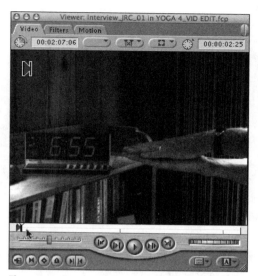

Figure 4.72 Open each Browser clip in the Viewer, and set the sync point. If you're shooting "run and gun" style, even a handclap slate mark with voice slate can still do the job. Throwing a digital clock in the shot can help you sort your takes out later.

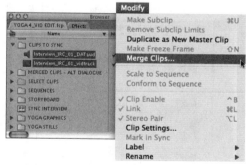

Figure 4.73 Select the clips you want to merge, and then choose Modify > Merge Clips.

Syncing up clips before merging

FCP can synchronize merged clip tracks based on In or Out points, or based on any of the three available timecode tracks: Timecode, Aux Timecode 1, or Aux Timecode 2.

If you're merging clips that don't have matching timecode, open each Browser clip in the Viewer and set In or Out points as sync markers (this is much easier if you used a slate to ID your takes during production). You can choose either In or Out points as your sync method, but you must use a single marker type (all In points or all Out points) for all the clips you're combining into a single merged clip. If your clips have matching timecode, you can sync up your merged clip just by matching the timecode numbers of video and audio clips.

You can also sync up by aligning multiple clips in the Timeline—definitely the way to go if your footage lacks slates or other formal synchronization aids, and you're syncing your footage "by eye."

✔ Tip

■ You can combine multiple audio tracks to create an audio-only merged clip.

To create a merged clip in the Browser:

1. Choose a synchronization method for the elements you are combining into the merged clip. If you use In or Out points to establish sync, open each Browser clip in the Viewer, and set the sync point (**Figure 4.72**).

2. In the Browser, select the clips you're merging, and then choose Modify > Merge Clips (**Figure 4.73**).

continues on next page

WORKING WITH MERGED CLIPS

3. In the Merge Clips dialog box, choose a sync method; then click OK (**Figure 4.74**).

FCP generates a new merged clip. If you open it in the Viewer, the merged clip's additional audio tracks appear on extra tabs in the Viewer window (**Figure 4.75**).

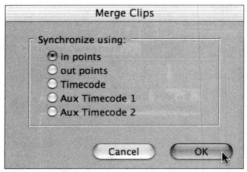

Figure 4.74 In the Merge Clips dialog box, choose a sync method by clicking its button; then click OK.

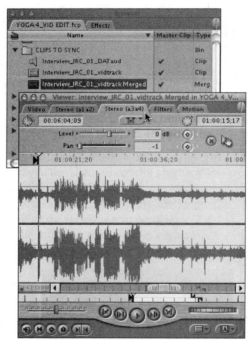

Figure 4.75 A new, merged clip appears in the Browser. If you open the merged clip in the Viewer, you'll see the additional audio tracks on extra tabs.

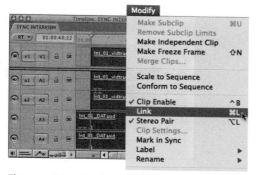

Figure 4.76 Synchronize your clip elements by positioning them on adjacent Timeline tracks. Next, link all the clips by selecting them and then choosing Modify > Link. You must link the clips before you can merge them.

Figure 4.77 Drag the linked sequence clips from the Timeline to the Browser.

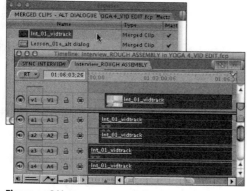

Figure 4.78 Your new, merged clip appears in the Browser. If you open the merged clip in the Timeline, you'll see that all the elements in the merged clip have been renamed to match the original video clip's name.

To create a merged clip in the Timeline:

1. In the Timeline, synchronize the elements you are combining into a merged clip by lining them up on adjacent Timeline tracks.

2. Select all the sequence clips you're merging, and then link them by choosing Modify > Link (**Figure 4.76**). You must link all the clip elements together first, or you won't be able to merge them.

3. Drag the selected, linked sequence clips from the Timeline to the Browser (**Figure 4.77**).

   FCP generates a new, merged clip, which appears in the Browser (**Figure 4.78**).

✔ Tip

■ Once you've created a merged clip, the only way to make multiframe adjustments to the sync relationship of its clip elements is to open the merged clip in the Timeline, and then delete its master clip from the Browser. Unlink the clip elements, adjust the sync, and then remake the merged clip using the steps described above. Be warned, however, that your sync adjustments won't be reflected in any previously used instances of the merged clip.

CAPTURING VIDEO

This chapter explains how to use Final Cut Pro's input features. The logging and capture functions have been designed to facilitate some common post-production strategies.

Logging and capturing are independent operations in Final Cut Pro. You can use the logging process to assess all your material for the entire project when you are getting under way. Your logged, offline clips are ready to be captured when you're ready for them, and they won't be taking up space on your hard drives.

You can use the Log and Capture window to review and log the media on an entire source tape and then capture all the clips that you want from that tape in one operation, called a *batch capture*.

Recapturing media is another vital process in most desktop video editing post-production plans. For more information, see the sidebar "The Wonders of Batch Recapture," later in this chapter.

You will not be able to use FCP's automated capture and output features unless your external video hardware supports device control. You still can capture clips that are logged and manually captured while the tape is playing, but you won't be able to perform automated batch capture and recapture or assemble segments of your project using the Edit to Tape feature when you're ready to output your final product to tape.

Anatomy of the Log and Capture Window

Use the Log and Capture window to capture video and audio media in Final Cut Pro. Log and Capture supports a range of capture options, from live video capture on the fly to automated batch capture with full device control.

Final Cut Pro logs shots by creating offline clips that it stores in a Browser bin of your choice.

Logging and capturing are independent operations in Final Cut Pro, so you can log all the footage for your entire program before you capture a single clip. When your disk storage space is tight (and disk storage space is *always* tight), having a detailed inventory of your material online means you can make use of the Browser's powerful database features to sort out your source material and develop a game plan before you start capturing media. For more information on the Browser's capabilities, see Chapter 7, "Organizing Clips in the Browser."

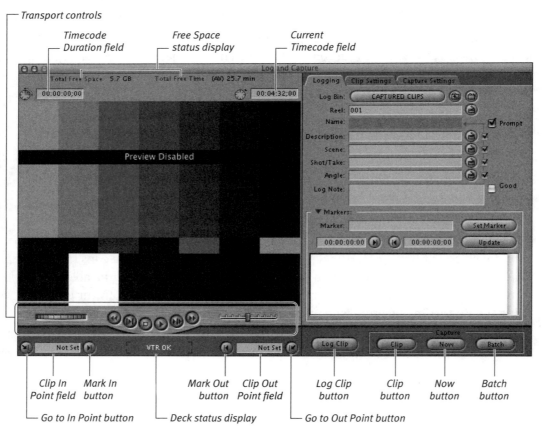

Figure 5.1 An overview of the Log and Capture window. Press Command-B to open the Log and Capture window.

Preview section

Many of the controls in the Preview section of the Log and Capture window also appear in the Viewer window. For more information, review "Anatomy of the Viewer" in Chapter 8.

Figure 5.1 shows an overview of the Log and Capture window.

◆ **Timecode Duration field:** This field displays the duration of the currently marked clip.

◆ **Current Timecode field:** This field displays the current timecode location of your source tape. Enter a timecode number in this field to shuttle the source tape to that timecode location.

◆ **Free Space status display:** This display shows the amount of available hard disk space remaining.

◆ **Transport controls:** Use these buttons to control your deck or camcorder transport if you have device control enabled. Transport control operation is described in more detail in Chapter 8, "Working with Clips in the Viewer."

◆ **Deck status display:** This display shows the status of communication between your deck or camcorder and Final Cut Pro.

◆ **Go to In Point button:** Click to shuttle tape to the currently marked clip's In point.

◆ **Clip In Point field:** This field displays the timecode location of the currently marked clip's In point.

◆ **Mark In button:** Click to mark an In point for your capture.

◆ **Mark Out button:** Click to mark an Out point for your capture.

◆ **Clip Out Point field:** This field displays the timecode location of the currently marked clip's Out point.

◆ **Go to Out Point button:** Click to shuttle tape to the currently marked clip's Out point.

Log and Capture controls

The Log and Capture control buttons appear below the tabbed portion of the window. The Log Clip button is used to log a clip without capturing it, and each of the other three buttons performs a different kind of capture operation.

◆ **Log Clip button:** Click to log the current clip in the log bin.

◆ **Clip button:** Click to capture a single clip immediately. This kind of captured clip can be saved directly to your Capture Scratch folder and need not be associated with a specific project. For more information, see "Capture Clip: Capturing Video with Device Control," later in this chapter.

◆ **Now button:** Click to capture without setting In or Out points. Capture Now is useful if your camcorder or deck doesn't have device control, or if you want to capture long clips without setting the Out point in advance. For more information, see "Capture Now: Capturing Video without Device Control," later in this chapter.

◆ **Batch button:** Click to batch capture a group of previously logged clips. For more information on batch capturing, see "Batch Capturing Clips," later in this chapter.

ANATOMY OF THE LOG AND CAPTURE WINDOW

Logging tab

The Logging tab (**Figure 5.2**) contains fields and shortcut tools you use to enter the information you need to log a clip.

◆ **Log Bin button:** Click to open the current log bin (the Browser bin where offline clips are stored during logging).

◆ **Up button:** Click to move the log bin selection up a level from the currently selected log bin.

◆ **New Bin button:** Click to create a new log bin inside the currently selected log bin.

◆ **Reel field:** Enter the name of your current source tape. Control-click the field to select from a list of recent reel names.

◆ **Reel Slate button:** Click to add a number at the end of the name for incremental labeling. Click again to increment the number by one. Option-click to clear the contents of the field. All the Slate buttons on the Logging tab perform the same functions for their respective fields.

◆ **Name display:** The name in this field is compiled from information entered in the Description, Scene, and Shot/Take fields. This is the name that appears in the Browser's Name column.

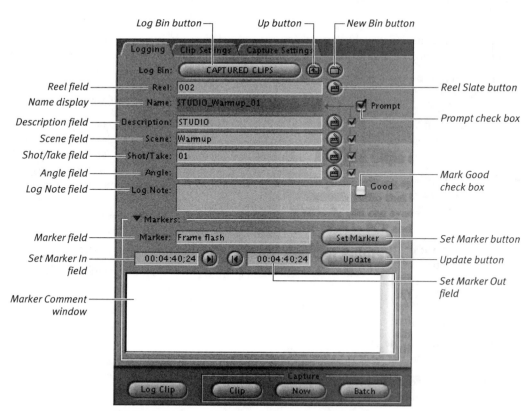

Figure 5.2 The Log and Capture window's Logging tab.

- **Prompt check box:** Check this box for a prompt to name a clip when you click the Log Clip button at the bottom of this tabbed window.

- **Description field:** Enter descriptive text in this field. Check the box at the right to include this description in the Name display.

- **Scene field:** Enter descriptive text in this field. Check the box at the right to include this description in the Name display.

- **Shot/Take field:** Enter descriptive text in this field. Check the box at the right to include this description in the Name display.

- **Angle field:** If you are capturing footage from a multicamera shoot, you can enter an angle number in this field. Check the box at the right to include this description in the Name display.

- **Log Note field:** Enter descriptive text in this field. Control-click the field to select from a list of recent log notes.

- **Mark Good check box:** Check this box to place a marker in the Browser's Good column. When you're done logging, you can use the Browser's sort function to group all the clips you've marked "Good."

- **Marker field:** Enter a marker name or remarks in this field. For more information, see "Using Markers" in Chapter 8.

- **Set Marker In field:** Click to set a marker In point, or enter a timecode in the field.

- **Set Marker Out field:** Click to set a marker Out point, or enter a timecode in the field.

- **Set Marker button:** Click to log the marker.

- **Update button:** Click to modify a previously entered marker.

- **Marker Comment window:** This window displays marker information for the current clip.

Capture Settings tab

The Capture Settings tab (**Figure 5.3**) provides shortcut access to the Device Control, Capture/Input, and Scratch Disk settings. The Free Space status display shows the amount of space currently available on designated scratch disks. The Capture Now limit indicates the time limit currently specified in the Scratch Disks tab of the System Settings window.

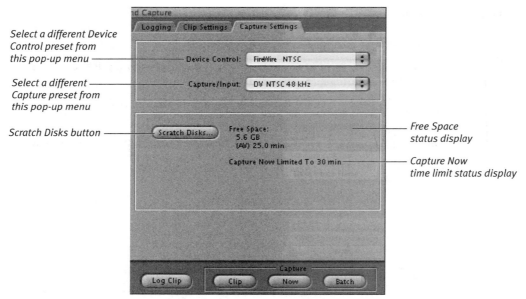

Select a different Device Control preset from this pop-up menu

Select a different Capture preset from this pop-up menu

Scratch Disks button

Free Space status display

Capture Now time limit status display

Figure 5.3 The Log and Capture window's Capture Settings tab.

Clip Settings tab

The Clip Settings tab (**Figure 5.4**) contains controls for calibrating and formatting your input. Once you've configured clip settings, the same settings will apply to subsequent captured clips until you change the settings again.

◆ **Include Video:** Check the box to include the video in the capture. Uncheck to capture audio only.

◆ **Image quality controls for video:** Use the sliders to adjust the image quality settings for video you are digitizing (not applicable for DV capture).

◆ **Video Scopes button:** Click to access the waveform monitor and vectorscope. Use the waveform monitor and vectorscope to calibrate input settings for video you are digitizing.

◆ **Use Digitizer's Default Settings button:** Click to restore the manufacturer's default audio/video settings for your capture card.

◆ **Include Audio:** Check the box to include audio in the capture. Uncheck to capture video only.

◆ **Master Gain control:** Adjust the slider to set incoming audio levels. (The Master Gain slider has no effect on audio levels for DV capture.)

◆ **Audio Input Format controls:** Select an audio input channel configuration for capture. Use the channel buttons to enable/disable individual audio channels.

◆ **Audio Preview Option:** Check the box to enable audio monitoring through your computer's speakers during log and capture operations.

ANATOMY OF THE LOG AND CAPTURE WINDOW

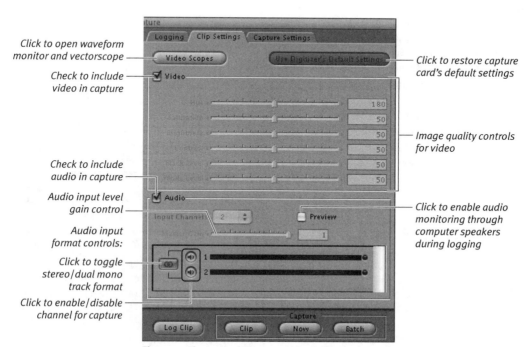

Click to open waveform monitor and vectorscope

Check to include video in capture

Check to include audio in capture

Audio input level gain control

Audio input format controls:

Click to toggle stereo/dual mono track format

Click to enable/disable channel for capture

Click to restore capture card's default settings

Image quality controls for video

Click to enable audio monitoring through computer speakers during logging

Figure 5.4 The Log and Capture window's Clip Settings tab.

To open the Log and Capture window:

◆ Choose File > Log and Capture (**Figure 5.5**); or press Command-8.

✔ Tips

■ When you open the Log and Capture window for the first time after launching FCP, the screen reads, "Preview Disabled." Don't freak out. That's standard operating procedure—the warning disappears when you click Play.

■ For best performance, the Log and Capture window should be completely visible on your computer monitor, with nothing overlapping the window, not even the pointer.

■ If you have been capturing clips, FCP will not play back clips in your external monitor until you close the Log and Capture window.

■ The size of your Log and Capture window is determined by the zoom level of the Canvas and Viewer windows in your workspace arrangement. If you're using large Canvas and Viewer windows, your Log and Capture window will be large as well. Small Canvas and Viewer windows will result in a small Log and Capture window. If you're using different sizes in the Viewer and Canvas windows, the Log and Capture window appears at the size of the smaller one.

Figure 5.5 To open the Log and Capture window, choose File > Log and Capture.

FCP 6 Update: Log and Transfer for Post-Tape Post-Production

Final Cut Pro, always running to keep pace with digital industry developments, has added the Log and Transfer window. Use the Log and Transfer window to import footage from non-tape based video formats, such as P2 cards, Advanced Video Codec High Definition (AVCHD), and Sony Video Disk Units (VDUs). Gosh, I guess "footage" is an anachronistic term in a post-tape world.

Setting Up for Capture

If you are new to Final Cut Pro, take a moment to read Chapters 7 and 8, which contain details on Browser and Viewer operations, before you start a capture process. You'll need to use both of these windows in the capture operation. Capturing video is probably the first thing you're going to want to do, but a little general knowledge of the FCP interface will make your first captures go more smoothly.

You may also need to review Chapter 3 for details on User Preferences and preset settings.

Capturing is important, and you should set up for it correctly. Here's an overview of the setup procedure and your objectives in each step:

◆ **Review your selected Easy Setup.** You want to be sure that you've selected an Easy Setup that uses the proper combination of presets for this capture operation. Select an Easy Setup that uses the correct audio sample rate to match the media you want to capture. Your capture settings should match the video hardware and tape format you're using. Your Device Control settings should be compatible with your camcorder or deck.

◆ **Check scratch disk preferences.** You want to ensure that any media you capture will be written to the correct hard disk or folder, that your designated scratch disk is fast enough to handle the data transfer, and that you have enough space to accommodate the media files you want to capture.

◆ **Test Device Control settings.** You want to ensure that your video, audio, timecode, and device control connections between your deck or camcorder and Final Cut Pro are operational.

◆ **Review capture-related options in the General tab of the User Preferences window.** These options directly affect FCP's behavior during capture. If your system and source tapes are in perfect condition, you should leave these options checked. However, if you're unable to complete a capture because FCP is reporting trouble (and you're willing to risk some uncertainty about timecode or frame integrity), you should uncheck the safeguard preference that's aborting your capture attempts:

  ◆ The On Timecode Break pop-up menu allows you to specify FCP's behavior when it encounters a timecode break during a capture operation. You can choose to make a new clip, abort the capture, or get a warning about the timecode break after the capture is complete.

  ◆ Abort Capture on Dropped Frames automatically stops the capture process if dropped frames are detected.

  ◆ Abort Capture on Timecode Break automatically stops the capture process if FCP detects a timecode break during the capture process.

  ◆ Sync Audio Capture to Video Source if Present locks any genlocked audio deck to the timecode of the genlocked video source during audio capture. This ensures sync accuracy during long sync audio captures.

continues on next page

◆ **Checking capture settings.** You want to be sure that you've selected the proper Capture preset. Your capture settings should match the video hardware and tape format you're using. Select the correct audio channels and sample rate to match the media you want to capture.

◆ **Calibrate the timecode signal input.** You want to compensate for any offset between the timecode of your source video and your captured video.

◆ **Calibrate input signals (for non-DV systems only).** You want to adjust the incoming video signal to ensure the best image quality or to match the quality of media you've already captured.

◆ **Check clip settings.** Clip settings are just customized capture settings that you can adjust for an individual clip only. In a DV system, even though you can't make adjustments to a clip's video or audio (DV capturing is a straight transfer of digital information), you can adjust the audio channel settings for an individual clip. In a non-DV system, you can adjust the clip's hue, saturation, brightness, contrast, sharpness, black level, white level, and gain settings.

✔ Tips

■ If you want to capture video by using a non-controllable device such as an analog-to-DV converter, switch to the non-controllable device Easy Setup that supports capture from converter boxes.

■ Before you start capturing footage, you should use color bars to check the image quality on your external video monitor as well. Your monitor is a critical tool for evaluating your footage, so set it up right—once you've calibrated it, leave the monitor's image settings alone. See page III-541 of Apple's *Final Cut Pro User Manual* PDF for instructions.

■ If your DV clips need image-quality adjustments, you can fix them post-capture by applying the appropriate image control filters. To learn how to use FCP's filters, see Chapter 14, "Compositing and Effects Overview."

■ Capturing video puts your entire FCP system—including external hardware—to the test. Any conditions that impair its performance can show up as dropped frames, audio sync drift, or error messages—not a good start for your project. Apple Support has a good article on the subject: "Final Cut Pro: Dropped Frames and Loss of Audio Sync" (article ID 58640).

 On Peachpit.com

"Calibrating the timecode signal output" and "Calibrating capture settings with color bars and audio tone" are available as PDFs at:
www.peachpit.com/finalcutpro6vqp

Capture Settings: Try These First

Final Cut Pro provides a variety of ways to adjust your capture settings and clip settings. But do you really need to make adjustments to the default settings? Which settings apply to your capture system?

For FCP users with DV/FireWire systems that use common external video devices, perfecting your preference settings should be as easy as selecting DV-NTSC or DV-PAL from the Easy Setup window's pop-up menu.

For users running more complex systems including third-party capture cards, getting the perfect configuration could take more effort. Check to see if your card's manufacturer offers a custom FCP Easy Setup, or configure your own using the documentation that comes with the hardware. Don't forget to check the manufacturer's Web site for the latest instructions or driver updates.

Once you have perfected your settings, you should save your settings configuration as a custom Easy Setup to protect your work. To learn how to save a custom Easy Setup, see "Using Easy Setups" in Chapter 3.

Here's a suggested configuration for DV/FireWire systems:

◆ **Capture preset:** DV-NTSC or DV-PAL.

◆ **Clip settings:** The only clip settings controls that have any effect on DV capture are Include Video and Include Audio check boxes, and the Audio Input Format controls. You can monitor, but not adjust, your audio input levels. You can adjust your DV audio levels in Final Cut Pro after you have captured the files. (If your DV audio levels are too high, you won't be able to fix clipping and distortion after capture.)

◆ **Audio sample rate:** The sample rate should match the sample rate of your recorded tape.

◆ **Sequence preset:** DV-NTSC or DV-PAL.

If you specified a DV Easy Setup when you installed the Final Cut Pro software, the correct capture settings (except the audio sample rate) were configured automatically.

SETTING UP FOR CAPTURE

Logging Clips

This section explains how to use all the logging features on the Log and Capture window's Logging tab. You use these features the same way in all three types of video capture. You'll also learn how to select a *logging bin*—the bin your clips will be stored in after capture.

Logging is the process of reviewing your source videotapes, and labeling and marking the In and Out points of usable clips. Other logging data could include shot and take numbers, added markers at specific points in the action, and production notes. You can also mark clips as "Good," so that you can easily sort out the most promising takes.

When you log a shot, Final Cut Pro creates an *offline clip*, which is stored in a logging bin you select (**Figure 5.6**).

This offline clip (**Figure 5.7**) specifies logging data and capture preferences for video or audio you haven't captured to disk yet.

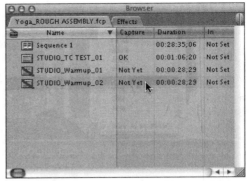

Figure 5.6 Offline clips in a Browser bin. Note the Capture status column, which shows that these clips haven't been captured yet.

Figure 5.7 An offline clip displayed in the Viewer. Note that the timecode and duration can be displayed for the offline clip.

Remember, when you specify a logging bin for your logged clips, you're making an entry in a database; you aren't specifying a hard disk location for the actual media file. You specify disk location for captured media files in the Scratch Disk preferences.

When you complete logging, you can select the offline clips you want to capture and then digitize them in a batch. (Clips logged from different tapes cannot be captured unattended.)

✔ Tip

- To use all the logging options in Final Cut Pro, you need device control over your video deck or camcorder. If you don't have a controllable video deck, you can log only the duration and In and Out points for individual clips, and you must enter the data manually.

FCP Protocol: What Are Offline Clips?

An *offline clip* is a clip reference to a media file that has been deleted, moved, or renamed. If you log and capture a clip and then delete the clip's media file from disk, the clip "goes offline" and a red slash appears through the clip icon.

The offline clips appear in the Browser; you can even edit them, but you won't see or hear anything on the screen while you're editing. The only difference is that online clips are linked to captured media files on disk.

You can restore offline clips referencing deleted media by using the Batch Capture feature, detailed later in this chapter, to recapture the media from tape.

You can use the Reconnect Media command to restore an offline clip's link to a moved or renamed media file.

Or you can delete a clip's media file deliberately to recapture some disk space, and recapture the clip's media only when you want to use it.

The Art of File Naming

When you capture or import media into Final Cut Pro, you name each file as a part of the process. You'll be living with these filenames for a long time. Since it's not a trivial matter to change filenames once you've assigned them, you should develop a file naming system before you start your project. Write it down, distribute it to your production team, and stick to it.

Much of the logic behind file naming schemes involves constructing filenames in a way that allows you to make use of FCP's Sort and Find functions and to identify the file's content, file type, and version number. In Final Cut Pro, an added level of flexibility is available because clips and their underlying media files do not need to have the same name.

A directory structure is the planned organization of folders you use to store your project's media elements. A complete file naming system should also be extended to the naming and organization of your files into folders. If you can, create your folder structure before you start acquiring your media elements. This will make it easier to file your elements correctly after the pace of production heats up.

Final Cut Pro imposes an automated directory structure for captured media files, automatically generating folders named after your current project inside the Capture Scratch folder. This complicates the process of filing media elements according to your own system, but if you're organized, you can work around it. After you capture, you can move your captured clips into your own folder system and then import them into a project before you start assembling sequences.

Here are a few guidelines to help you develop filenames that will remain useful throughout the life of your project:

◆ Incorporate filenames into your shooting scripts, voiceover scripts, and storyboards early in production. Some projects actually enter the entire script into a database and use that script/database to track media elements.

◆ Filenames should contain the shots' scene and take numbers, if appropriate.

◆ Avoid duplicate filenames.

◆ File suffixes are traditionally used as file type indicators. There are some standard file suffixes in use, but don't be shy about making up your own system of file type abbreviations. Be sure to document them.

◆ Audio filenames should incorporate a code that indicates sample rate, file format, and whether the files are stereo or mono.

◆ Your file naming system should include a code for version control. Don't rely on a file's creation or modification date as your only means of identifying the latest version of a file.

◆ If you're planning on exporting an Edit Decision List (EDL) of your Final Cut Pro project, make sure the filenames for your reels are consistent with the EDL format you're using. EDL naming restrictions differ, so check out the naming requirements before you start, or use a conservative naming scheme if you don't know your destination format.

LOGGING CLIPS

Figure 5.8 Click the New Bin button on the Logging tab to create a new bin inside the current logging bin, and select it as the current logging bin.

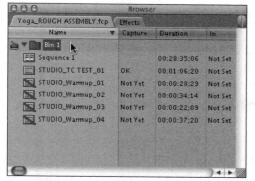

Figure 5.9 The new logging bin in the Browser. The clapboard icon indicates the current logging bin.

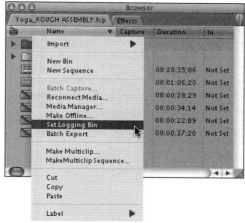

Figure 5.10 Control-click the bin; then from the bin's shortcut menu select Set Logging Bin.

Selecting a logging bin

A logging bin is the Browser bin where your offline clips are stored during logging. The default location for a new logging bin is the top level of a project tab in the Browser window. You can set a logging bin in the Log and Capture window or in the Browser window.

To set a logging bin in the Log and Capture window:

1. On the Logging tab of the Log and Capture window, *do one of the following*:
   - Click the New Bin button (**Figure 5.8**) to create a new bin inside the current logging bin, and select it as the current logging bin (**Figure 5.9**).
   - Click the Up button to set the bin hierarchically above the current logging bin as the new logging bin.

2. Click the Logging Bin button to switch to the Browser and open the new logging bin you created.

   A little clapboard icon appears in the Browser next to the current logging bin.

To set a logging bin in the Browser:

1. In the Browser, select the bin that you want to set as the logging bin.

2. *Do one of the following:*
   - Control-click the bin; then select Set Logging Bin from the bin's shortcut menu (**Figure 5.10**).
   - Choose File > Set Logging Bin.

   A little clapboard icon appears next to the current logging bin.

Speed Logging Tips

Each time you log a clip, Final Cut Pro resets several fields on the Logging tab to prepare for your next logging operation:

◆ The Out point from your last logged clip is assigned as the new In point.

◆ The Reel, Description, and Shot/Take fields that make up the clip's name will be updated automatically. Only the last field with the Use This Field check box checked will be incremented.

◆ When you log a clip by pressing F2, Final Cut Pro will automatically reset the Out point to the current tape position.

With automatic updating of the name fields and In and Out points, you can log your tape simply by pressing F2 whenever you want to log a new clip. With your source tape rolling, press F2 whenever you want to end a shot and begin a new one.

If you want to trim your logged shots a little more tightly, you can adapt this technique: Press the I key to mark the clip's In point; then press F2 to mark the Out point and capture the clip in one keystroke.

Here are a few more tricks that can make logging easier:

◆ Click the Bin button to display the selected logging bin on the front tab of the Browser.

◆ Control-click the Reel field to access a pop-up menu displaying all the reel names you've used in the current project. Selecting your reel name from the pop-up list helps you ensure you're entering exactly the same name each time. That's critical to successful batch capture.

◆ Clear text from a field by Option-clicking the Slate button next to it.

◆ Use the Mark Good check box to mark your best stuff. You can use the Find feature to search the Browser's Good column and select only the clips you've marked "Good" for your first rough cut.

◆ Not only can you copy and paste timecodes from one field to another, but you can also Option-click and then drag and drop a timecode to copy it into another timecode field—a useful procedure while you're logging.

Figure 5.11 Choose File > Log and Capture.

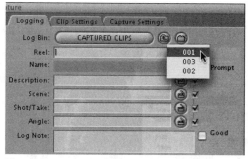

Figure 5.12 Control-click the Reel field; then select from a list of recent reel names.

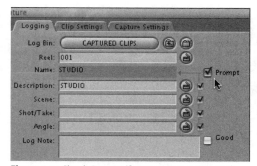

Figure 5.13 Check Prompt if you want to name each clip as you log it.

Logging

Before you begin logging, make sure your video deck is connected properly and device control is operational. If you're capturing with an analog capture card, calibrate your image and audio quality before you start capturing. Your clip settings will be saved with the logged takes. And don't forget: The best time to check the timecode calibration for your deck or camcorder is before you start logging.

To log footage:

1. Load the source tape you want to log into your deck.

2. Choose File > Log and Capture (**Figure 5.11**); or press Command-8.

3. In the Log and Capture window, specify a logging bin using one of the methods described in the previous task.

4. In the Reel field, *do one of the following:*
   - Enter a name for the reel (the tape or other video source you are currently logging).
   - Click the Reel Slate button to add a numeric reel name.
   - Control-click the Reel field; then choose from a pop-up list of recent reel names (**Figure 5.12**).

5. In the Description field, *do one of the following:*
   - Enter a name for the clip.
   - Select the Prompt check box if you want to name each clip as you log it (**Figure 5.13**).

continues on next page

LOGGING CLIPS

6. In the Description, Scene, and Shot/Take fields, *do any of the following:*

- ◆ Click the check boxes next to the fields you want to incorporate into the clip's name.

- ◆ Enter any identifying text you want to use in the text field.

- ◆ Click a Slate button to increment the corresponding text field automatically (**Figure 5.14**).

Final Cut Pro's automatic naming function creates clip names by combining the fields you selected, such as Description_Scene01_Take01, into the Name field. This is the name that appears in the Browser's Name column, and it is the name of your source media file on disk.

Figure 5.14 Click a Slate button to add an incremented numeral to any of the text fields.

FCP Protocol: Auto-Incrementing on the Logging Tab

There's not enough room here to list all the rules governing the behavior of the Description, Scene, and Shot/Take fields on the Logging tab. A few handy rules, however, should help you get more efficiency out of the auto-entry features built into the tab:

- ◆ The check box to the right of a field's name controls whether the field will be included in the clip's name.

- ◆ The last-checked field is the one that will increment automatically. Here are some examples:

  - ◆ If you check only the Description field, just the Description field will increment.

  - ◆ If Scene is the last-checked field, the scene number increments automatically, even if you entered a number in the Shot/Take field but left it unchecked.

  - ◆ If Shot/Take is the last-checked field, the Shot/Take field increments, and the scene number remains unchanged until you click its Slate button to increment it. Clicking the Scene field's Slate button resets the Shot/Take field to 01 (FCP assumes that your new scenes start with Take 01).

- ◆ You can include a Shot/Take number only if you include a scene number.

LOGGING CLIPS

Figure 5.15 Click the Mark Out button to set an Out point for the capture.

Figure 5.16 Click Log Clip to create an offline clip.

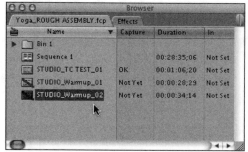

Figure 5.17 Your new offline clip appears in the selected logging bin.

7. Use the transport controls in the Log and Capture window to control your source deck and locate the footage that you want to log. If you have full device control enabled, you can also navigate to a specific timecode location on your source tape by entering a timecode value in the Current Timecode field.

8. Mark media In and Out points for a clip by *doing one of the following*:

◆ Click the Mark In and Mark Out buttons (**Figure 5.15**); or press the I key to set the In point and press the O key to set the Out point.

◆ Enter specific timecodes in the timecode fields at the bottom of the Log and Capture window. Enter the In point in the left timecode field and the Out point in the right timecode field.

9. To log a clip, *do one of the following*:

◆ If the Prompt option is on, click Log Clip, and then enter your clip's name.

◆ If the Prompt option is off, click the Slate button next to the fields you want to increment, and then click Log Clip (**Figure 5.16**) or press F2.

An offline clip appears in your selected logging bin (**Figure 5.17**). After you log your first clip, the Name fields will be incremented automatically.

✔ Tip

■ When you mark In and Out points for a clip during logging, the points you specify will appear in the captured clip as the Media Start and Media End frames. However, if you add handles to your logged clip before capture, the Media Start and End frames will reflect the addition of the handles. When you open the captured clip, the Viewer's playhead will be located at the media In point you logged before you added the handles, but you won't see any In and Out point icons in the Scrubber bar.

To add a marker to a clip while logging:

1. To access the marking controls, click the triangle indicator next to Markers at the bottom of the Logging tab.

2. Enter a marker name or comment in the Marker field.

3. To set the In and Out points of the marker, *do one of the following:*

   ◆ Enter timecode values in the In and Out timecode fields. You can Option-drag values from any timecode fields in the Log and Capture window to copy them into these fields.

   ◆ Click the Mark In and Mark Out buttons.

4. Click Set Marker (**Figure 5.18**).

   The Marker In and Out points and any information entered in the Marker field appear in the Marker Comment window (**Figure 5.19**).

   These markers appear as subclips in the Browser once a clip is captured.

✔ Tip

■ If you need to modify your marker data after you've set the marker, you can enter the revisions in the Marker fields and then click the Update button to save your changes.

Figure 5.18 Click Set Marker to enter the marker In and Out points as well as any information entered in the Marker field in the Marker Comment window.

Figure 5.19 The logged information appears in the Marker Comment field. When the clip is captured, this information will be used to create subclips within the master clip.

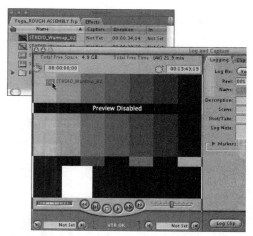

Figure 5.20 Drag the clip from the Browser and drop it on the Preview area of the Log and Capture window.

Figure 5.21 The clip's current data settings load into the Log and Capture window.

Figure 5.22 Modify the logged clip data on the Logging tab or by setting new media start and end points, as shown here.

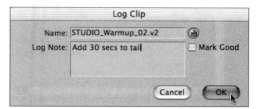

Figure 5.23 Give the clip a new name and description if you'd like; then click OK.

Modifying logged clip data

Even if you've organized your logging operation to a fare-thee-well, you'll probably need to go back and modify clip data on your logged clips before your project is complete. One common relogging operation is changing the tracks that are specified for capture. You may have a number of clips you're using as video-only inserts, or you might want to go back and capture just the audio from an interview because you find you're going to use it as voiceover. Final Cut Pro offers a couple of different ways to make it easy to change your mind.

To modify logged clip data:

1. Drag the clip you want to relog from the Browser and drop it on the Preview area of the Log and Capture window (**Figure 5.20**).

   The clip's current data loads into the Log and Capture window (**Figure 5.21**).

2. Modify the logged clip data as outlined in the task "To log footage," earlier in this chapter (**Figure 5.22**); then press F2 to relog the clip.

3. In the Log Clip dialog box, give the clip a new name and description, if desired; then click OK (**Figure 5.23**).

   The relogged clip appears as a new offline clip in the Browser (**Figure 5.24**).

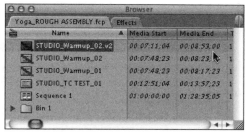

Figure 5.24 The relogged clip appears as a new offline clip in the Browser.

To modify logged clip track settings:

1. In the Browser, select the offline clips whose track settings you want to modify. Command-click to select multiple clips (**Figure 5.25**).

2. Choose Modify > Clip Settings.

3. In the Modify Clip Settings window, select tracks you want to add to your captured clip, or deselect tracks you want to exclude from the capture (**Figure 5.26**).

   All the offline clips you selected will be switched to the new setting (**Figure 5.27**).

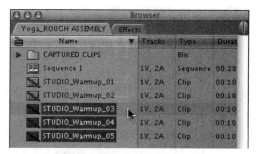

Figure 5.25 Command-click to select multiple offline clips.

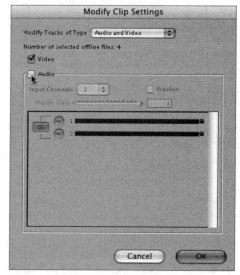

Figure 5.26 Disabling audio capture in the Modify Clip Settings window. In the Modify Clip Settings window you can choose to enable or disable video or audio capture, or you can choose different audio channels to capture from.

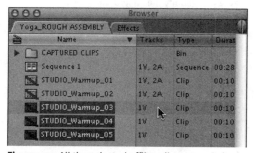

Figure 5.27 All the selected offline clips are switched to the new setting.

LOGGING CLIPS

Figure 5.28 Choose File > Log and Capture.

Capture Clip: Capturing Video with Device Control

Capturing a clip with device control combines logging tasks (marking In and Out points, naming the clip, entering comments) and the specification of the clip's settings for this capture on the Clip Settings tab.

When you capture a single clip by clicking the Clip button at the bottom of the Log and Capture window, Final Cut Pro runs a batch capture procedure with a single clip as the batch list, and the captured clip is saved in your Capture Scratch folder but outside the current project.

Unless you're picking up very few shots scattered about on different reels, it will be quicker to log your shots and capture them as a batch. Batch capture is easier on your video deck, camcorder, and source tapes as well.

For more information on logging clips for batch capture, see "Logging Clips," earlier in this chapter.

For more information on batch capture, see "Batch Capturing Clips," later in this chapter.

To capture a clip with device control:

1. Make sure your video device is properly connected and device control is operational. If you're using a camcorder, make sure it's switched to Play (VCR) mode; similarly, if you're using a deck with a Local/Remote switch, make sure the switch is set to Remote.

2. Choose File > Log and Capture (**Figure 5.28**).

continues on next page

3. Use the transport controls in the Log and Capture window to control the source device and locate the footage that you want to capture (**Figure 5.29**). If you have full device control enabled, you can also navigate to a specific timecode location on your source tape by entering a timecode value in the Current Timecode field.

4. In the Log and Capture window, click the Logging tab; then specify a logging bin using one of the methods described in "Selecting a logging bin," earlier in this chapter.

5. Enter logging information for your clip (follow steps 4 through 6 in "To log footage," earlier in this chapter).

6. Click the Clip Settings tab; then follow steps 4 through 7 (detailing clip settings procedures) in the task in the next section, "To capture a clip without device control."

7. To mark a clip, *do one of the following:*

   ◆ Click the Mark In and Mark Out buttons (**Figure 5.30**); or press I to set the In point and press O to set the Out point.

   ◆ Enter specific timecodes in the timecode fields at the bottom of the Log and Capture window. Enter the In point in the left timecode field and the Out point in the right timecode field.

8. Click the Clip button located at the bottom of the window (**Figure 5.31**).

   Final Cut Pro captures the clip, and the captured clip appears in a new Viewer window. Your captured clip is saved in the current project's designated logging bin.

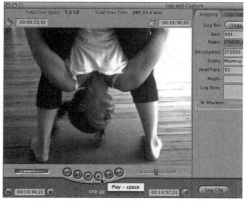

Figure 5.29 Use the transport controls in the Log and Capture window to control your video deck and locate the footage that you want to capture.

Figure 5.30 Click the Mark Out button to set an Out point for the capture. You could also enter a timecode value in the Out point timecode field.

Figure 5.31 Click the Clip button located at the bottom of the Log and Capture window.

Capture Now: Capturing Video without Device Control

If you don't have a video device that your computer can control, you can still capture video in Final Cut Pro by using the controls on your video deck or camcorder to search and play your source tape.

To log clips without the benefits of device control, you need to manually enter each clip's starting and ending timecodes and other information in the appropriate fields in the Log and Capture window. That clip information is used to identify the clip when you save it.

If you enter log information before a Capture Now operation, the captured clip will be saved along with that log information in your designated logging bin.

If you do not enter log information, the captured clip will be saved as an untitled clip in your designated logging bin.

✔ Tip

■ Before you start capturing, check your Capture Now time-limit setting on the Capture Settings tab of the Log and Capture window. The default limit is 30 minutes. Very long Capture Now time limits can increase the lag between the time you click the Capture Now button and the time that capture begins, so specify a time limit not much longer than the length of the longest clip you're planning to capture.

FCP Alert: Audio Format Changes

Because QuickTime is the media-handling engine that drives Final Cut Pro, FCP's capture capabilities are determined by QuickTime's media-handling capabilities. QuickTime 7 has expanded audio formatting options—supporting capture of mono audio tracks as discrete tracks and handling up to 24 tracks of audio in a QuickTime media file. Previous versions of QuickTime were limited to capturing one two-channel stereo pair to a single interleaved track.

The bottom line? FCP (and QuickTime 7) can recognize media files with audio captured as two separate mono tracks, but earlier versions of Final Cut Pro can only handle audio captured in the older QuickTime format: a single stereo pair audio track.

To capture a clip without device control:

1. Make sure your DV camcorder or deck is properly connected.

2. Choose File > Log and Capture; or press Command-8.

3. In the Log and Capture window, specify a logging bin and enter a name for your clip by one of the methods described earlier, then click the Clip Settings tab (**Figure 5.32**).

4. On the Clip Settings tab, use the Enable Video and Enable Audio check boxes to specify which tracks you want to include in this capture (**Figure 5.33**). Unchecking an option excludes that track from the capture.

Figure 5.32 Click the Clip Settings tab in the Log and Capture window.

Figure 5.33 If you want to capture both audio and video, leave the Enable Video and Enable Audio check boxes checked.

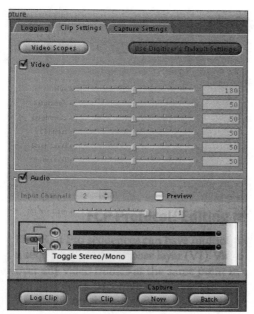

Figure 5.34 The audio control settings configuration determines the audio capture format. In this example, both audio channel controls are enabled and the Stereo/Mono control toggled to Mono. Final Cut Pro will capture both tracks, but configure them as separate channels that can be adjusted independently of one another.

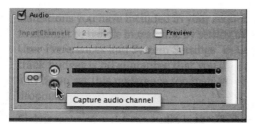

Figure 5.35 Toggling the Stereo/Mono control to Mono first allows separate control over the two audio input channels. Now you can disable Channel 2 and capture the audio from Ch 1 only.

5. If you are including audio in your capture, use the controls in the audio section to select a number of audio channels to capture and specify an audio capture format (**Figure 5.34**). Following are common audio formats and the audio control settings that specify them:

   ◆ **Ch 1 + Ch 2 (Dual mono):** Capture both tracks, but configure them as separate channels that can be adjusted independently of one another. Enable both audio channel controls, and toggle the Stereo/Mono control to Mono.

   ◆ **Ch 1 (L):** Capture only the left audio channel from the tape (Ch 1), with pan centered. (See Chapter 12 for information on pan settings.) Toggle the Stereo/Mono control to Mono, then disable the Ch 2 (bottom) audio channel control (**Figure 5.35**).

   ◆ **Ch 2 (R):** Capture only the right audio channel from the tape (Ch 2), with pan centered. Toggle the Stereo/Mono control to Mono, then disable the Ch 1 (top) audio channel control

   ◆ **Stereo:** Capture both channels as a stereo pair. Stereo pairs are always linked, and anything that is applied to one track is applied to both. Enable both audio channel controls, and toggle the Stereo/Mono control to Stereo.

6. If you are digitizing an analog video source, you can use the image quality slider controls to calibrate the incoming signal.

7. If you are digitizing an analog video source, you can use the Gain slider control to adjust your audio input levels.

8. To enter log information for your clip, follow steps 4 through 6 in "To log footage," earlier in this chapter.

continues on next page

9. Use your device's controls to locate the footage you want to capture; rewind 7 to 10 seconds; then press the device's Play button.

10. Click the Capture Now button at the bottom of the Log and Capture window 1 to 5 seconds before the device reaches the first frame in your clip (**Figure 5.36**).

There's a slight delay after you click the button before capture begins—the length of the delay depends on your Capture Now time limit and the number of scratch disks you have assigned to FCP.

11. To stop capturing, press the Escape key; then stop playback on your device.

The captured clip appears in the designated logging bin on the project's tab in the Browser (**Figure 5.37**).

12. Play the clip to make sure it contains the video you want. You may need to close the Log and Capture window—some video capture hardware won't play the captured clip while this window is open.

✔ Tips

- If you're using a camcorder, you can use Capture Now to capture live footage. On most consumer DV models, your camcorder must be recording to tape as you capture the live footage in Final Cut Pro.

- If you have a device-controllable deck or camcorder, you can use Capture Now to log and capture footage on the fly. As the tape plays, enter your log information and click the Capture Now button. FCP will capture the footage and its timecode.

- Analog-to-digital video converter boxes are handy for resurrecting treasured analog video footage, but if you're using a converter box with FCP to capture video, you must switch your Device Control preset to Non-Controllable Device to capture successfully.

Figure 5.36 Click the Capture Now button (at the bottom of the Log and Capture window) 1 to 5 seconds before the first frame in your clip appears.

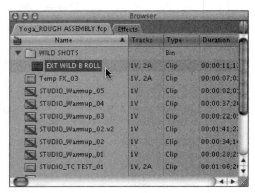

Figure 5.37 The captured clip appears in the logging bin on the project's tab in the Browser.

Figure 5.38 On the Clip Settings tab of the Log and Capture window, uncheck the Enable Video checkbox.

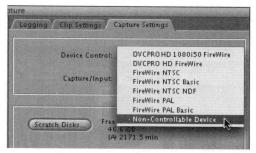

Figure 5.39 Choosing Non-Controllable Device from the Device Control pop-up menu allows FCP to capture without detecting timecode from an input device—you'll be able to capture live audio from your DV camcorder microphone without rolling tape.

Capturing audio

Final Cut Pro's basic capture procedures work the same for audio and video, but you may need to modify your Capture or Device Control presets, depending on the source device you're capturing from and the sample rate of any digital audio you're capturing. Here are some examples:

- **Capture audio only from DV source:** The only change required is to uncheck the Enable Video checkbox on the Log and Capture window's Clip Settings tab (**Figure 5.38**).

- **Capture live audio from your DV camcorder or deck:** Use your camcorder's microphone to record some quick rough narration or sound effects without the extra step of recording to DV tape first. On the Log and Capture window's Capture Settings tab, choose Non-Controllable Device from the Device Control pop-up menu (**Figure 5.39**); then follow the steps for performing a Capture Now operation described earlier in this chapter. Use FCP's audio meter to monitor your DV camcorder audio levels as you capture (**Figure 5.40**).

continues on next page

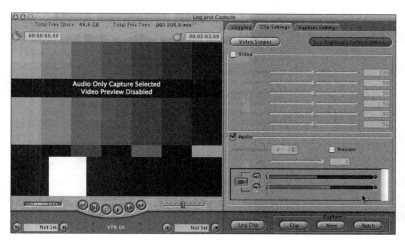

Figure 5.40 Use the audio meters on the Clip Settings tab to monitor audio input levels from your camcorder.

175

◆ **Capture analog audio with the Voice Over tool:** You can also use FCP's Voice Over tool to digitize analog audio from a cassette player, TV, or other source and capture it in Final Cut Pro. This can be a great convenience if you want to capture temporary rough voiceover or music. For more information, see "Recording Audio with the Voice Over Tool" in Chapter 12.

◆ **Digitize and capture analog audio using audio interface hardware:** If you're using FCP-compatible audio capture hardware, you must modify your Capture preset, selecting that hardware as the input device for capture (**Figure 5.41**).

◆ **Capture digital audio and timecode from a DAT using audio interface hardware:** With the right setup, you can configure FCP to capture "dual-system" production audio. See page I-198 of Apple's *Final Cut Pro User Manual* PDF for configuration details.

Create custom Easy Setups for your audio capture configurations, and you'll be able to switch quickly and reliably into audio capture mode. For more information on Easy Setups and Audio/Video settings, see Chapter 3, "Presets and Preferences."

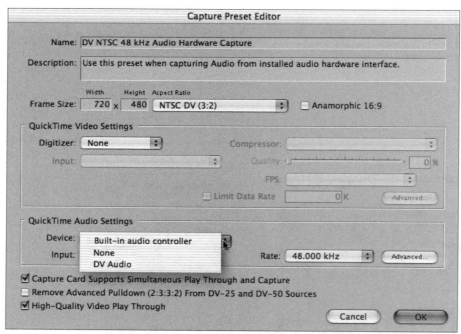

Figure 5.41 Modify the QuickTime Audio Settings of your Capture preset to select your audio hardware as the input device. If you have compatible audio capture hardware in your FCP system, it will appear in the Device pop-up menu.

Capturing HDV Video

HDV format video uses MPEG-2—that's the same compression used in iDVD—to squeeze the extra-large HD datastream down to a size that can be handled without an additional video card. MPEG-2 compression reduces the size of the HDV datastream by reducing the number of frames that contain complete picture information. One of these complete frames (called I-frames) is followed by a sequence of reduced-image-data frames (called B-frames and P-frames).

FCP offers a choice of two HDV capture schemes:

HDV Native: The HDV native option captures HDV in its compressed MPEG-2 GOP structure and relies on FCP's dazzling real-time performance to construct editable video on the fly. Working in native HDV means your source media files will have the same low data rates and modest file sizes as DV media files, but your computer is working harder to construct in real time everything you see whenever you're working with HDV.

FCP's HDV native capture interface appears only when FCP detects an HDV deck or camcorder. The interface artwork may look a little different (**Figure 5.42**), but HDV capture works just like the Log and Capture window you use in other capturing operations. FCP's native HDV capture does include one significant improvement over the standard capture interface: a scene detection feature that works just like iMovie's. During capture, FCP automatically creates a separate clip (and a separate media file on disk) each time it detects a Start/Stop (Record/Pause) signal in the captured HDV datastream.

Apple Intermediate Codec: FCP's other HDV capture option converts your HDV compressed format video to Apple Intermediate Codec (AIC) format as you capture. AIC's larger files take up more space and require higher data rates to play back, but don't require real-time image processing like HDV native files.

The AIC capture operation works a little differently from the DV format capture options. As you capture, FCP converts the HDV footage to Apple Intermediate Codec (AIC) format. AIC generates complete image and audio information for each frame. The HDV capture process is similar to Capture Now—you must manually cue up the footage you want to capture using your HDV camcorder's controls. For more information on both HDV capture schemes, see Apple's *Working With High Definition and Broadcast Formats* PDF, available from FCP's Help Menu.

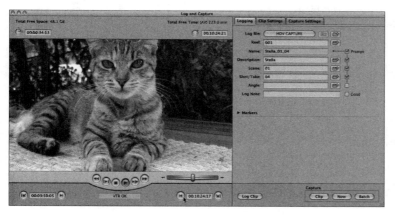

Figure 5.42 FCP's HDV native Log and Capture window offers a new look but operates just like the Log and Capture window you use for everything else.

177

Batch Capturing Clips

You can use the Log and Capture window to review and log the media on an entire source tape and then capture all the clips that you want from that tape in one operation, in a batch capture. Final Cut Pro uses the clip log you've created and automatically captures only the clips you select. You don't need to capture every clip you have logged.

You want to minimize the amount of wear and tear you put on your video source tapes, particularly if you won't be capturing the final versions of your media files until late in the editing process. Logging and batch capture are important tools for minimizing the amount of time your precious original tapes spend shuttling back and forth in your tape deck.

You can design an automated batch recapture process to restore a project you've removed from your hard disk. If you've accidentally deleted a few media files in the course of a project, you can use the Select Offline Items Only option to recapture just the footage you deleted.

You can batch capture clips from these sources:

◆ Clips you've logged with Final Cut Pro.

◆ Clips in a text log you've imported from another program or another Final Cut Pro project.

◆ Clips from an imported EDL file.

If you need to interrupt a batch capture, you can use the Batch Capture command to automatically redigitize all clips not captured previously by choosing the Aborted Clips option from the Capture pop-up menu.

Automated, unattended batch capture is limited to clips from one tape. You can set up an automated batch capture that involves clips from several reels, but you'll have to hang around and feed new tapes to your video deck during the process.

✔ Tip

■ Is there anything you can do to salvage a tape with timecode breaks? Certainly. Final Cut Pro can detect interrupted timecode during capture, automatically creating a new clip that starts after the break (choose the Make New Clip option from the On Timecode Break pop-up menu on the User Preferences window's General tab). If you're relying on batch recapture as part of your post-production plan and you'd rather work with unbroken timecode on your source tape, here's a workaround: You can dub the entire tape onto a tape with continuous timecode and start your logging and capturing process with the dubbed copy. If dubbing is not an option, you can assign separate reel numbers to each section and use those reel numbers as you log, but you won't be able to batch capture reliably on a tape with timecode breaks.

BATCH CAPTURING CLIPS

The Wonders of Batch Recapture

Final Cut Pro's basic design assumes that you will at some point want to use the Media Manager to analyze your edited project and batch recapture your source clips. The Media Manager offers several options for trimming your project files (you can read about them in detail in Chapter 20, "Managing Complex Projects"), but batch recapture is one of the most commonly used. The Media Manager constructs a trimmed, offline sequence that includes just the media you are actually using in your final product. Your next step would be to select the trimmed offline sequence and batch recapture just that footage from your original source tapes, restoring the trimmed, recaptured media files to your existing project.

Batch recapturing can increase your post-production efficiency in a number of other ways:

♦ You can capture your footage and then convert it to a low-resolution codec like Photo-JPEG (used in the Offline RT format). Photo-JPEG not only saves disk space but also renders faster while you're editing. When you've settled on a final version of your edited sequence, you can batch recapture at high resolution only the clips you're using in the final version.

♦ Some editors capture entire tapes and then select and log their shots by marking subclips within the long master. Then they export their logged subclips as a batch list and use it to recapture their selected material as individual online clips. This process allows random access to locations throughout the long master—you'll log faster because you won't be waiting for your video deck's transport mechanism to move the tape around. Your capture process is streamlined, too, saving wear and tear on your gear and your tapes.

♦ You use batch recapture when you are moving a production from another editing system to Final Cut Pro. You import your production's EDL (or any tab-delimited file with the right data) as a batch list and then use it to recapture your footage.

♦ If you lose your media files, batch recapture can speed reconstruction of your project—a good reason to back up your project files and store them outside your computer.

Preparing for a batch capture

Batch capture is an automated process. It's worthwhile to prepare carefully before you kick off an automated capture because, well, things can happen while your back is turned. Here are some suggestions:

Total Media Time: 00:03:47:03

Total Disk Space: 867.0 MB needed / 5.0 GB available

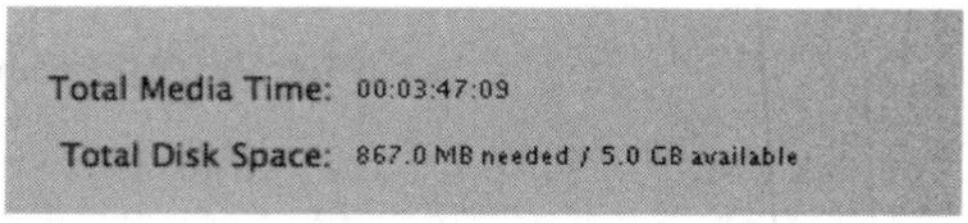

Figure 5.43 A comparison of available storage space and an estimate of the space needed for this batch capture appears in the Batch Capture dialog box.

◆ Check your currently selected Capture preset and Scratch Disk preferences. Make any changes you want applied to this batch capture; you won't be able to change these settings after you open the Batch Capture dialog box.

◆ Answer these questions: Are your capture settings correct for this batch capture, or are you capturing tapes in a different format? Is the estimated space available on your designated scratch disk sufficient to contain your incoming media files?

◆ Make a note of the Total Media Time and Total Disk Space estimate in the Batch Capture dialog box (**Figure 5.43**). This estimate can yield clues that can help you debug your batch capture list. For example, a 10-second subclip from a 20-minute master clip can throw your whole capture scheme out of whack; Final Cut Pro would capture the entire 20-minute master clip.

◆ If you suspect that your tape contains timecode breaks, you should enable Abort Capture on Timecode Break in the General tab of the User Preferences window before batch capturing clips. If you attempt to batch capture across a timecode break, Final Cut Pro won't be able to accurately locate your offline clips, which can cause your batch capture to go seriously haywire. (Timecode breaks can be caused by shutting down the camera or ejecting your tape in mid-reel and not re-cueing on the last bit of previously recorded timecode.)

"Additional Items Found"—What Are Your Options?

Many clips, one source media file: That's a common situation in FCP projects.

Both the Browser version of a clip and the copy you place in a sequence refer to the same source media file. And if you use subclips in your projects, divide clips with the razor blade, or simply use a number of different sections from the same clip, you end up with many, many clips in a project all referring to the same source media file.

You're most likely to encounter the "Additional Items Found (AIF)" dialog box when you batch recapture the media for a trimmed sequence because the trimmed "sequence" versions of the clips reference the same media files as the full-length Browser versions of those clips. The Additional Items Found dialog box is FCP's means of saying, "Hey! What do you want me to do about the Browser versions of these clips?"

You'll also see the AIF dialog box if you specify a Media Manager operation that trims or deletes media files referenced by unaffiliated clips in this or another open project. The dialog box appears before your media file processing operation proceeds.

This dialog box is a little vague, and your options are not always obvious. What are your options? Here's a translation:

Click Continue to proceed with your original item selection. Any additional clips that reference media files you're recapturing will be made offline (meaning the additional clips' links to these media files will be broken) if the new trimmed media file is written to the same folder location on disk as the original media file

Click Add to include the additional clips in this batch recapturing operation. If the "additional items found" are the untrimmed Browser versions of your clips, clicking Add will cause the full length of the clip's media files to be recaptured and then relinked.

Click Abort to abort this Media Manager operation. Your project and media files remain untouched.

To batch capture clips:

1. To select which clips to capture, *do one of the following:*

    ◆ To capture clips you've just logged, click Batch in the Log and Capture window (**Figure 5.44**). This captures clips in the selected logging bin.

    ◆ To capture all offline clips in a project, set the project tab as the logging bin, make sure nothing is selected in the Browser, and choose File > Batch Capture.

    ◆ To capture selected clips in your project, select the clips you want to batch capture in the Browser window (**Figure 5.45**); then choose File > Batch Capture.

    Your selection can include both offline clips and online clips, but all clips must be within a single project.

2. *Do one of the following:*

    ◆ Check the Use Logged Clip Settings check box if you want Final Cut Pro to capture all clips using the customized clip settings you have saved with individual clips.

    ◆ Uncheck the Use Logged Clip Settings check box if you want Final Cut Pro to bypass your individual clip settings (**Figure 5.46**). Disk space calculations are based on the data rate settings specified in the current Capture preset.

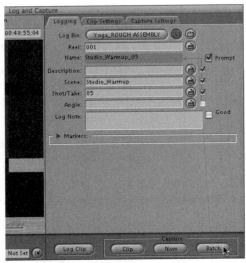

Figure 5.44 Click the Batch button in the Log and Capture window to capture clips in the currently selected logging bin.

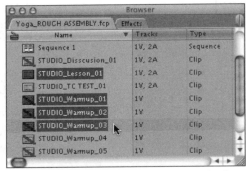

Figure 5.45 You can also batch capture multiple clips by selecting them in the Browser. You can select a combination of offline and online clips.

Figure 5.46 Uncheck the Use Logged Clip Settings box if you want Final Cut Pro to bypass your individual clip settings.

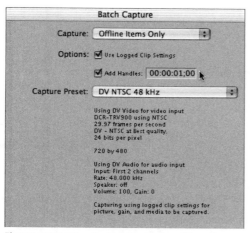

Figure 5.47 Setting the handle size for offline clips.

Figure 5.48 If your batch includes clips with duplicate filenames, you'll see this warning dialog box.

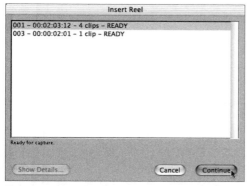

Figure 5.49 Load the reel you want to capture into your deck, select it from the list, and click Continue. When FCP has finished capturing all the clips from that reel, it will prompt you to select the next reel.

3. Enter a duration to set the handle size of offline clips (**Figure 5.47**). (This is optional.)

Handles add extra frames beyond the In and Out points of a captured clip.

4. Select a Capture preset option from the Capture Preset pop-up menu. This setting should match the video format and audio sample rate of the source tape you are recapturing.

5. Click OK.

6. If your selection includes clips with duplicate filenames, you'll see a warning dialog box (**Figure 5.48**). Click Continue to proceed with the recapture. If you need to reexamine settings or filenames for DV clips you're planning to recapture, click Abort to interrupt the recapture operation.

The Insert Reel dialog box appears, displaying a list of all the reels (tapes) required for this batch capture operation.

7. Load the first tape you want to capture into your camcorder or deck, select it from the list, and click Continue (**Figure 5.49**).

Final Cut Pro captures all clips in the first reel, then prompts you to load the next reel required until selected clips on all reels have been captured.

To interrupt batch capture:

1. Press Escape or click the mouse anytime during the batch capture operation.

   If you interrupt batch capture, Final Cut Pro displays the Insert Reel dialog box again with a count of "aborted" clips—project clips that remain uncaptured (**Figure 5.50**).

2. Click Cancel to abort the batch capture, or click Continue to resume capturing the remaining clips. If you cancel the process, the clips you selected for capture are still highlighted in the Browser; you can restart your batch capture from scratch.

✔ Tip

■ If you recapture online clips into the same scratch disk folder where the original clips' media files are stored, the original media files are overwritten. If you recapture into a different folder, the original media files are preserved.

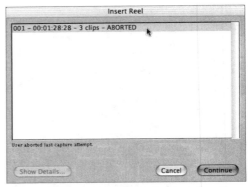

Figure 5.50 When you interrupt a batch capture, the Insert Reel dialog box appears, displaying a count of "aborted" clips—project clips that remain uncaptured.

Figure 5.51 Choose Mark > DV Start/Stop Detect.

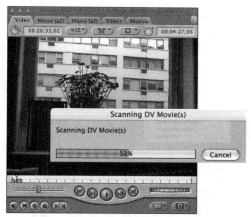

Figure 5.52 Final Cut Pro places a marker at every point where it detects a Start/Stop signal in your clip's media file.

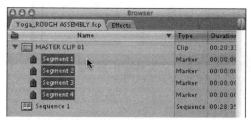

Figure 5.53 Click the expansion triangle next to the clip to view the new markers. Select the markers you want to convert to subclips.

Using DV Start/Stop Detection

The DV Start/Stop Detection feature automatically sets markers in a previously captured DV clip each time it detects a Start/Stop (Record/Pause) signal in that clip. Because FCP can use markers to break a clip into individual subclips, you can use the technique outlined here to capture long sections of DV tape and break them into usable subclip chunks. After you've "subclipped" your long captured clip, you can use the Media Manager to delete the unused master clip footage from your subclips.

As you might guess from its name, DV Start/Stop Detection works on DV format source media only.

For more information, see "About Subclips" in Chapter 8.

To divide a captured DV clip into subclips based on starts and stops:

1. Open your previously captured DV clip in the Viewer.

2. With the Viewer active, choose Mark > DV Start/Stop Detect (**Figure 5.51**).

    Final Cut Pro places a marker at every point where it detects a Start/Stop signal in the clip's media file (**Figure 5.52**).

3. If you want, add more markers at any point in the clip where you want to create a subclip.

4. Locate your clip's icon in the Browser; then click its expansion triangle to view the markers you just added to the clip (**Figure 5.53**).

    continues on next page

5. If you want, rename markers with the names you want your subclips to have.

6. Select all the markers; then choose Modify > Make Subclip.

   New subclips, derived from your marked clip, appear in the Browser (**Figure 5.54**). If you've renamed your markers, your new subclips use those names.

7. Review your new subclips and delete any with material you don't need.

✔ Tip

■ This DV Start/Stop technique is handy for converting a long clip into a group of smaller subclips, but when you're done, you still have a batch of subclips on your hands, and all of those subclips are still referencing the full length of your original media file. You can use the Media Manager to convert your subclips into full-fledged clips that reference discrete media files and then delete your unwanted extra footage. See "Trimming unused media from subclips" in Chapter 20.

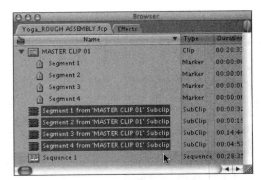

Figure 5.54 New subclips, derived from the markers in your marked clip, appear in the Browser.

What Is Offline RT?

Offline RT, a compressed video format, is a variation of Photo JPEG with a 320-by-240-pixel frame size that's been optimized to compress and compute quickly. Final Cut Pro offers Easy Setups you can use if you are capturing or working with Offline RT format. The DV and PAL Offline RT Easy Setups are loaded in FCP's default Easy Setup menu, along with setups for other FC-supported formats such as HD and 16:9. Because Offline RT has a different frame size, you'll need to switch to the appropriate Easy Setup to capture, create, and edit sequences in this format. See Chapter 3, "Presets and Preferences," for more information on switching Easy Setups.

There are two ways to create Offline RT files:

◆ Capture in Offline RT format directly from your source media; then use the Media Manager to create an offline sequence to recapture at full resolution after you've trimmed down your sequence.

◆ Use the Media Manager to convert or copy your source media files to Offline RT format.

continues on next page

What Is Offline RT? *continued*

Advantages of Offline RT

Depending on your needs, Offline RT's high compression ratio could offer significant advantages:

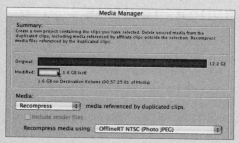

Figure 5.55 You can save a lot of disk space by using the Media Manager to convert your DV media files to Offline RT format. This Media Manager bar graph compares the disk space requirement for one hour of DV files and that same hour converted to Offline RT format.

◆ Offline RT media files are much smaller than DV format files. One hour of video in Offline RT format requires 1.7 GB of hard disk space. That same hour in DV format requires 12.7 GB (**Figure 5.55**).

◆ If you are working on a project with miles of footage, you could increase your media file storage capacity by 700 to 800 percent over DV media file requirements.

◆ MacBook and PowerBook users should also rejoice; now you can take your FCP project to bed with you without that pesky external hard drive. This video format is compact enough to allow good FCP performance even if your media files are located on the same internal drive as the FCP application.

◆ Offline RT maintains the same frame rate as your original footage, so your Offline RT timecode numbers will match those in your original footage.

◆ Offline RT format renders very quickly, even on a base-case G4 1.25 GHz machine.

The only disadvantage of Offline RT? When you've finished editing, you'll still need to recapture your sequence in full resolution and do all that final rendering you've been avoiding by using the Offline RT format.

System Requirements

Capturing your video in Offline RT format directly from a DV source via FireWire requires FCP to perform the format conversion on the fly during capture, so the minimum system requirements for capturing Offline RT format directly from DV via FireWire are stiffer than FCP's minimum.

If your Mac is fast enough to support real-time effects, you'll preview more effects using compressed Offline RT than you would if you were editing with full-resolution DV format media files.

Troubleshooting Capture Problems

If you experience problems during video capture, you may see an error message. Final Cut Pro monitors the state of controlled devices and reports an error if the problem is due to a camcorder or deck malfunction. Cancel the operation before proceeding and consult your camcorder or deck manual for troubleshooting information. Here are some basic troubleshooting tips that may help you get back on the road.

If "No Communication" appears in the Log and Capture window's Deck Status area (Figure 5.56):

◆ Check that your device is plugged in, switched on, and properly connected to your computer.

◆ Perform a quick check of the Audio/Video Settings window's Summary tab to see if an external device is considered missing (**Figure 5.57**).

◆ Turn on the device and restart the computer. If your device's power was not switched on when you started your computer, the device may not have been recognized.

◆ Reconnect the FireWire cable and restart the computer. If the cable was not connected properly when you started your computer, the device may not have been recognized.

Figure 5.56 The "No Communication" message appears in the Deck Status area of the Log and Capture window if device control is disabled.

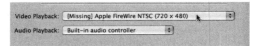

Figure 5.57 The Summary tab of the Audio/Video Settings window indicates that the selected external video device is considered missing.

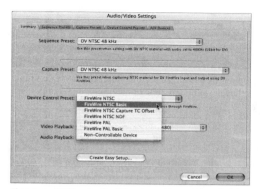

Figure 5.58 If Apple FireWire doesn't provide reliable device control, switch to the Apple FireWire Basic protocol by switching your Device Control preset.

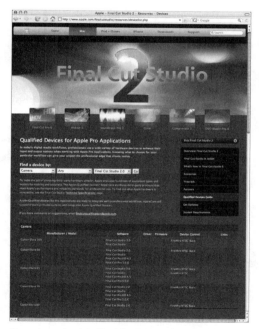

Figure 5.59 Apple's Final Cut Pro Device Qualifications page lists cameras qualified for use with Final Cut Pro, along with recommended device control settings and other bits of helpful data.

If you experience problems controlling your camcorder or deck:

◆ If your deck has a Local/Remote switch, be sure it's set to Remote.

◆ If you're using the Apple FireWire protocol, try Apple FireWire Basic instead. Edit the FireWire (NTSC or PAL) Device Control preset. In the Summary tab of the Audio/Video Settings window, choose the Apple FireWire Basic protocol from the Device Control Preset menu (**Figure 5.58**).

◆ Check that you're using the device control protocol specified for your deck or camcorder. Device control protocols are listed in the Device Control Preset Editor window.

◆ Not all decks and camcorders support all functions, such as hard recording, high-speed searching, insert editing, assemble editing, preview editing, and accurate movement to timecodes entered. You may need to use a different protocol. Apple's Final Cut Pro Device Qualifications page, available on the Apple Final Cut Pro Support Web site, lists all qualified cameras, decks, and capture interfaces (**Figure 5.59**).

Here's the URL for the Final Cut Pro Support page: http://www.apple.com/ support/ finalcutpro/.

TROUBLESHOOTING CAPTURE PROBLEMS

If you encounter a "Bus error" message when you try to capture:

◆ Something went wrong when your captured data crossed the bus, the data delivery interface between your computer and the outside world. Bus errors can be caused by a number of things, but you can try making sure that your cables are hooked up completely and that any hardware cards in your computer are seated properly.

If you encounter a "Batch Capture: Unable to lock deck servo" error message when you try to capture:

◆ Your camcorder or deck needs more pre-roll time before capture starts. Increase the pre-roll capture setting in the Device Control Preset Editor window (**Figure 5.60**).

If your captured audio and video play back out of sync:

◆ The video displayed in the Viewer and the Canvas will not appear to play back in sync if you are monitoring your audio through external speakers connected to your camcorder or deck. The audio from the external speakers will be synchronized with video displayed on the video monitor.

◆ The audio sample rate of your original source tape must match the audio sample rate of your capture settings. Check the source tape's audio sample rate against your capture settings.

◆ Your FCP system may be dropping frames during capture or playback. See the Apple Support article "Final Cut Pro: Dropped Frames and Loss of Audio Sync" (article ID 58640) for a list of possible causes of dropped frames.

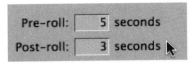

Figure 5.60 Increase the pre-roll capture setting in your Device Control Preset.

IMPORTING DIGITAL MEDIA

One of the most enchanting aspects of the DV revolution is the world of digital media elements that you can mix, match, and manipulate freely to spice up your video. Final Cut Pro is exceptional in the wide latitude of digital file formats it accepts. You can import most types of QuickTime-compatible files into an FCP project, including video clips, still images, and sound files.

Apple's QuickTime Web site contains a complete list of supported file formats at `http://www.apple.com/quicktime/pro/specs.html`.

Here's a list of common FCP-supported QuickTime formats:

- **Graphics:** Photoshop (PSD), JPEG/JFIF, TIFF, BMP, FlashPix, GIF, PICS, PICT, PNG, QuickTime Image File (QTIF), SGI, and TARGA (TGA).

- **Video:** H.264, MPEG-4, AVI, QuickTime Movie, Macromedia Flash (video only).

- **Audio:** AIFF/AIFC, Audio CD Data (.cdda), Sound Designer II, System 7 Sound, uLaw (AU), WAVE, and MPEG-4.

- **Other:** Numbered image sequences.

You can import an entire folder or an organization of multiple folders in a single operation. When you import a folder, Final Cut Pro imports all files it recognizes in the folder, as well as all recognized files in any subfolders. Folders are imported with their internal hierarchies intact.

To import files or a folder:

1. Copy or move the appropriate file (or folder) into the desired media folder in your project (**Figure 6.1**).

2. In the Browser, select a destination for your incoming file by *doing one of the following*:

   ◆ To import files or folders into the top level of a project, click the project's Browser tab.

   ◆ To import files into a bin within a project, double-click the bin to open it.

3. *Do one of the following:*

   ◆ Choose File > Import; then choose Files (or Folder) from the submenu, select the items, and click Open.

   ◆ In the Browser or any Browser bin window, Control-click and then choose Import File (or Import Folder) from the shortcut menu.

   ◆ Drag the desired files or folders directly from your Desktop (**Figure 6.2**) to a project tab or a bin within the Browser (**Figure 6.3**).

   ◆ Drag the desired files or folders from your Desktop to an open sequence in the Timeline. This places a clip reference to the media in the Timeline but does not place a reference in the Browser.

✔ Tip

■ FCP 6 can automatically adjust the gamma of imported video and still media files on import. The Imported Still/Video Gamma pop-up menu on the Editing tab of the User Preferences window offers a choice of gamma settings. For more information, see "Setting Editing Preferences" in Chapter 3.

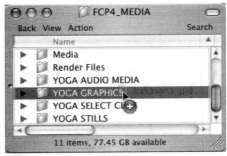

Figure 6.1 Before you import a file, copy or move it into the correct asset folder in your project.

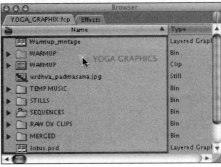

Figure 6.2 Drag the desired files or folders directly from your Desktop into Final Cut Pro.

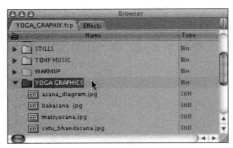

Figure 6.3 Drop the files or folder on a project tab or in a bin within the Browser.

IMPORTING DIGITAL MEDIA

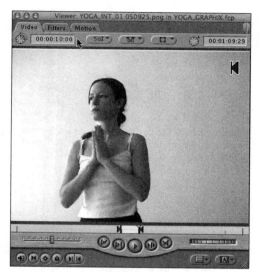

Figure 6.4 Imported still images have a default length of 2 minutes of identical video frames, with a duration of 10 seconds between In and Out points. The source media files for still image clips don't occupy 2 minutes' worth of drive space; you generate media only for the portions you render.

Importing Still Images

The default format for imported still images is a clip containing 2 minutes of identical video frames, with a duration of 10 seconds between In and Out points (**Figure 6.4**). If you edit still images into a sequence, they won't be visible on your NTSC external monitor until they are rendered.

Final Cut Pro supports all QuickTime-compatible graphics file formats. Check the QuickTime read-me file or Apple's QuickTime Web site for a complete list of compatible file formats.

✔ Tip

- Final Cut Pro does not import EPS files.

- Large size images take longer to insert and longer to open in projects because FCP must scale them before displaying them. Really large images should be scaled in a graphics program prior to importing.

FCP Protocol: File Location Is Critical

When you import a file into a Final Cut Pro project, that file is not copied into the FCP project file. Importing a file places a clip in your Browser, but that clip is a reference to the current hard disk location of your imported media file at the time you import it.

In Final Cut Pro, any clip's link to its underlying media file is entirely location based. If you move media files to another disk location after you've used them in a project, you break their links to the clip references in your FCP projects. You can use the Reconnect Media command to restore those clip-to-media file links, but a little forethought before you import files can save you a lot of hassle later. (The Reconnect Media function is discussed in Chapter 20, "Managing Complex Media.")

Before you import a file into FCP, be sure to copy it to its permanent folder location in your project's media assets directory structure. Importing files directly from a removable media storage device (such as a Zip disk) will cause your file to be marked "Offline" in your project once you remove that disk from your system. The same principle applies to audio imported from a CD.

Setting the default duration for stills

Still images and generators are assigned a duration at the time they're imported into Final Cut Pro. You specify the default duration for still images on the Editing tab of the User Preferences window.

No matter what duration you set, your Final Cut Pro clip references a single still image, so you won't create large, full-length video files until you render or export your stills at their edited lengths.

The default still duration is applied at the time you import the still into Final Cut Pro. If you have imported a still image and want the duration to be longer, you must modify the preference setting and then re-import the still.

To change the default still duration:

1. Choose Final Cut Pro > User Preferences; or press Option-Q.

2. On the Editing tab of the User Preferences window, enter a new default duration in the Still/Freeze Duration field (**Figure 6.5**).

3. Click OK.

✔ Tip

■ Modify the default still duration any time you're importing a large number of stills that you plan to cut to the same length. The stills will be imported at the final edited length, and you can drop them directly into your sequence. *Molto bene.*

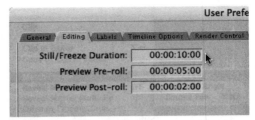

Figure 6.5 On the Editing tab of the User Preferences window, type a new default duration in the Still/Freeze Duration field.

Working with Adobe Photoshop Files

Adobe Photoshop is the industry-standard tool for creating graphics elements for use in Final Cut Pro. Its file format compatibility with Final Cut Pro makes importing your artwork's layers and alpha channels easy.

When you're creating graphics for use in a video program, keep your final format's requirements in mind. Remember that video has title-safe requirements, a different pixel aspect ratio, and a different tolerance for color and contrast levels than still graphics do.

Images that look beautiful in print or on a computer screen may not display well on a television monitor. The NTSC broadcast video standard cannot tolerate extreme contrast shifts on many of the colors that you can create and display in Photoshop.

Photoshop comes with an NTSC Colors filter that you can apply to your artwork to make it color safe for TV sets, and FCP has a Broadcast Safe filter that performs a similar function.

✔ Tip

- Photoshop's NTSC Colors filter is a fine tool, but it's easier to use the Broadcast Safe filter in Final Cut Pro once you've incorporated the Photoshop files into your sequence. For more information, see Chapter 16, "Filters and Compositing."

Preparing a Photoshop file for use in FCP

The best way to preserve image quality in digital image formats is to maintain the same frame size and resolution from beginning to end. You will get best results by creating your art with the required pixel dimensions in mind, but if you create artwork on a computer for display on broadcast television, you'll find that you must jump through a few hoops.

Computer monitors use square pixels, where each pixel's height equals its width. NTSC and PAL television monitors use a system that has a nonsquare pixel aspect ratio of 1.33:1, where each pixel's height is just a little bit greater than its width.

Because pixel aspect ratios in the computer world and the broadcast television world are different, if you create your artwork in Photoshop in a square-pixel format, your image looks squeezed when it displays on a TV monitor after printing to video.

To maintain the original appearance of your graphics when they are displayed on a broadcast monitor you must accommodate the difference between these two pixel shapes. You have a couple of options; both options are detailed in the following section.

- ◆ The easiest route is to use a recent version of Photoshop that allows you to create artwork in a variety of non-square pixel aspect ratios. You can create your artwork using the correct pixel shape and frame size, and skip the resizing hassle.

- ◆ If you're working with legacy square-pixel graphics, or an older version of Photoshop, you must create your full-frame graphics elements at a slightly larger size than your target resolution, and then size them down to the target resolution in Photoshop before you import them into Final Cut Pro. (*Target resolution* refers to the actual pixel count of an image's frame size in its final delivery, or target, format.)

✔ Tip

- High definition video displays in square pixels, so if your project format is entirely HD video, you should create square-pixel graphics.

To create a Photoshop file in a non-square pixel format:

1. In Photoshop CS or later, choose File > New; or press Command-N.

2. In the New file window's Preset pop-up menu, choose the preset file size that matched your video format (**Figure 6.6**), then click OK.

   Photoshop creates a new file at the correct frame size and pixel aspect ratio for the video format you selected.

To create a Photoshop file at DV-NTSC target resolution:

1. In Photoshop, choose File > New; or press Command-N.

2. Enter a width of 720 pixels, a height of 534 pixels, and a resolution of 72 pixels per inch (**Figure 6.7**).

   This ratio of 720:534, or 1.33:1, is the proper proportion for creating text and graphics that will look the same on your NTSC monitor as on your computer monitor.

3. Create your image file (**Figure 6.8**).

4. Save the file as your original image file. Use this original graphics file to make any subsequent changes to the artwork.

5. Choose Image > Image Size.

6. In the Image Size dialog box, uncheck Constrain Proportions.

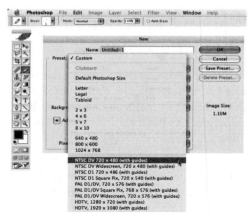

Figure 6.6 In the Preset pop-up menu, select a preset file size that matches your video format. The newly created Photoshop file will automatically display guides set at Title Safe and Action Safe boundaries. Deluxe.

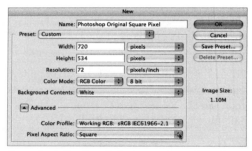

Figure 6.7 In the New dialog box, enter a width of 720 pixels, a height of 534 pixels, and a resolution of 72 pixels per inch.

Figure 6.8 The original Photoshop image before resizing, at 720-by-534 pixels.

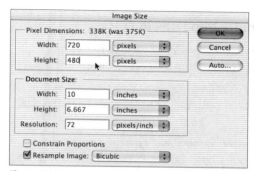

Figure 6.9 In the Image Size dialog box, specify a width of 720 pixels and a height of 480 pixels.

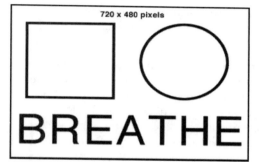

Figure 6.10 The "squashed" Photoshop image after resizing, at 720-by-480 pixels.

7. In the Pixel Dimensions section, enter a width of 720 pixels and a height of 480 pixels (**Figure 6.9**).

8. Click OK.

The vertical aspect of the image shrinks, which makes it look squashed (**Figure 6.10**).

9. Save the file as your production graphics file. Use this production graphics file in your project.

10. If you need to make changes to the artwork, use the original graphics file, which has the unaltered aspect ratio; then, when you're ready to save, repeat steps 4 through 9.

✔ Tips

- If you're planning to zoom in on the image you're preparing, you should import a file with pixel dimensions that will allow the tightest framing to fill the entire video frame without scaling the image above 100 percent.

- You don't have to import an entire full-screen image if your image uses only a small portion of the frame. Position your elements in full-screen format, resize for the pixel aspect ratio difference, and then crop down the artwork.

- You can import a variety of file formats, but the most common are the native Photoshop format (for images with multiple layers) and the standard PICT format (for single-layer images with alpha channels).

- You can also resize imported graphics clips and sequences in Final Cut Pro, but you'll get better results using Photoshop's bicubic scaling for resizing because it uses a better resampling algorithm.

WORKING WITH ADOBE PHOTOSHOP FILES

FCP Protocol: Updating Photoshop Files in FCP

It's easy to import Adobe Photoshop files into FCP, but if you need to change to a Photoshop file you've already used in a sequence, there are some hoops to jump through. Get ready to jump....

When you import a multi-layer Photoshop file into your project for the first time, Final Cut Pro constructs a description of this file that includes the number of layers and the frame size of each layer.

First hoop: If you want to revise a Photoshop file after you've already used it in FCP, select the Photoshop clip in the Timeline and choose View > Clip in Editor. FCP will open the file in Photoshop. Using the View > Clip in Editor method is the only reliable way to ensure that FCP will refresh its memory and update your Photoshop file's description to reflect your revisions. If you open and revise your existing image in Photoshop and save changes in the original file without using View > Clip in Editor, you'll return to Final Cut Pro and see that your Photoshop file is now offline. View > Clip in Editor is also available from the Timeline clip shortcut menu, but the command is called Open in Editor there, because I guess you can't have too many names for a good thing.

Second hoop: FCP uses the frame size data it recorded when you first imported your Photoshop file in all effect calculations that use x, y coordinates—motion paths, scaling, warp filters, and so on. However (get ready to jump...), FCP does not include transparent pixels when it calculates a Photoshop layer's frame size. Say you've created text on a transparent background in Photoshop, imported your file into FCP, and then applied effects. Should you need to revise your text, when you return to it, you'll find that the frame size of your text layer has changed. Even if you successfully reconnect your revised Photoshop file to your FCP sequence, FCP will use the data description from the original import (with the old frame size) to calculate your effects. The result? Your text effects will look distorted, and you'll briefly consider quitting the business.

There's a workaround for this dilemma. It's not pretty, but you can save yourself some headaches down the road by anticipating changes to your text. Again, get ready to jump....

◆ When you build your original Photoshop file, place a single nontransparent pixel in each corner of the frame (**Figure 6.11**). You'll need to do this for each and every layer. FCP will use the rectangle created by those four placeholder pixels to calculate the frame size. You can change text to your heart's content inside the bounding box created by the four corner pixels, and your FCP frame size will not change. So if you can reconnect your Photoshop file, your effects will be calculated with the correct frame size data.

continues on next page

FCP Protocol: Updating Photoshop Files in FCP *continued*

Final Warning: Once you've imported a layered Photoshop file into FCP, you should avoid adding or subtracting layers in the file.

FCP identifies a Photoshop layer by its position relative to the file's bottom layer. Increase the total number of layers in the Photoshop file, and FCP will ignore any layers numbered above the previously topmost layer. Deleting a layer from a Photoshop file that you've already imported could yield a variety of unpleasant results, so you should re-import any file with changes to the layer count.

The best workaround? Once you've imported your Photoshop graphics, don't change your mind. Or get ready to jump....

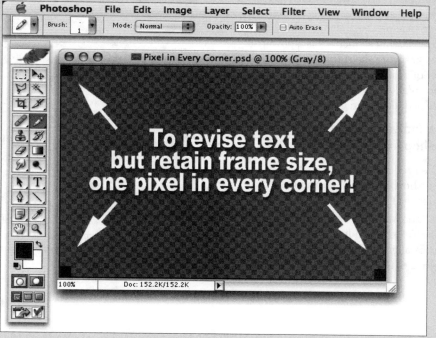

Figure 6.11 Place a single nontransparent pixel in each corner of each layer of your Photoshop composition. If you revise your Photoshop text later, those corner pixels will maintain a constant frame size, and when you re-import or reconnect your revised Photoshop file, FCP will recalculate your previously applied effects with the correct frame size. Hey—it's a workaround.

Importing a layered Photoshop file into Final Cut Pro

Final Cut Pro preserves the layers in a layered Photoshop file, importing the file as a special type of sequence, known as a *layered graphic* sequence. Each Photoshop layer is represented by a clip on a track in that sequence.

Double-click a Photoshop file sequence to open it in the Timeline, where you can choose individual layers to manipulate. Each layer is found on its own video track.

When you place a layered Photoshop file into your FCP sequence, you're actually *nesting* it: placing a sequence within another sequence. Nesting sequences is a powerful tool, and knowing the rules that govern the behavior of nested sequences will help you plan your work better. See "Working with Multiple Sequences" in Chapter 4.

To view individual layers in imported Photoshop files:

◆ In the Browser, double-click the Photoshop file, which appears as a sequence (**Figure 6.12**).

The Photoshop file opens as a sequence in the Timeline. Individual layers appear as clips aligned on separate video tracks (**Figure 6.13**).

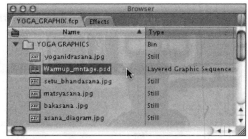

Figure 6.12 A layered Photoshop file appears as a sequence when it's imported into Final Cut Pro. Double-click the sequence icon to open it.

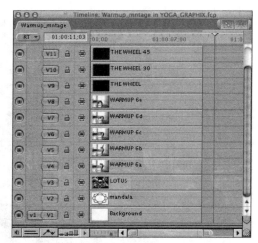

Figure 6.13 The Photoshop file opens in the Timeline as a sequence. Individual layers appear as clips.

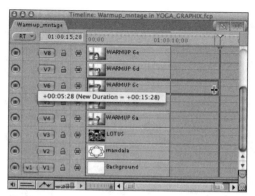

Figure 6.14 To extend the total duration of a layered Photoshop file, open it as a sequence in the Timeline and adjust the length of the individual layers.

✔ Tips

■ Once you've opened your multi-layer Photoshop file as an FCP sequence, you can drag individual layer "clips" out of the sequence and drop them in the Browser. You can then use the individual layers as independent graphics clips.

■ To import a layered Photoshop file as a clip instead of a sequence, flatten the image in Photoshop before importing it.

■ Because imported layered Photoshop files appear in FCP as sequences, your Still/Freeze Image Duration preference will set the total length of the imported file, with no allowance for handles. If you want to increase its length after you import, you'll have to open the Photoshop file sequence and extend the length of the individual layers inside (**Figure 6.14**). Extending the length of multiple layer clips in one operation is a terrific use for the Extend edit. See "To perform an Extend edit in the Timeline" in Chapter 11.

WORKING WITH ADOBE PHOTOSHOP FILES

Really LiveType

Fans of LiveType, FCP's insanely great titling helper application, will be happy to hear that LiveType project files can be imported directly into FCP. No need to render and export LiveType files—once you've imported your LiveType project, you can edit, trim, copy, paste and manipulate the project file within FCP just like other FCP clips. If you're using FCP 6 and LiveType 2 on a fast Mac, LiveType projects can be previewed in real time without rendering. For more information, see page 29 of Apple's *Final Cut Studio Workflows* PDF, "Using LiveType 2 With Final Cut Pro."

FCP Protocol: Layered Photoshop Files

◆ A layered Adobe Photoshop file imported into a Final Cut Pro project retains its transparency information, visibility, and composite mode.

◆ Layer opacity settings and layer modes are preserved, but layer masks and layer effects are not.

◆ If a Photoshop layer mode has no corresponding compositing mode in Final Cut Pro, the layer mode is ignored.

Importing Audio Files

You import digital audio files into Final Cut Pro just as you do any other digital media. You can import files in any QuickTime-supported audio format.

You can capture audio at its originally recorded sample rate and use it in the same sequence with audio recorded at other sample rates. When you play back the sequence, Final Cut Pro converts the sample rate in real time for any audio clips whose sample rates do not match the sequence settings.

Letting Final Cut Pro convert the sample rates in real time is not always the best solution, however, as real-time sample-rate conversion is optimized for speed, not audio quality. You can convert the sample rate of your nonconforming audio by using the Export feature in Final Cut Pro to make a copy of your audio file at the correct sample rate, or you can wait until you're ready to export your final product. FCP will sample-rate-convert your nonconforming audio tracks using a higher quality, non-real-time conversion during the audio mixdown rendering process. See Chapter 19, "Creating Final Output."

To import an audio CD track into an FCP project:

1. In the Finder, double-click the audio CD icon to open it; then select and drag the desired .cdda audio files into your project's media folder (**Figure 6.15**).

2. Rename the files so you can remember where they came from.

3. Follow the steps outlined in "To import files or a folder," earlier in this chapter (**Figure 6.16**).

Figure 6.15 Select and drag the .cdda audio files you want to import into your project's media folder.

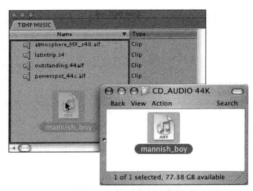

Figure 6.16 Rename the file; then drag it directly into your FCP project.

✔ Tip

■ FCP does not support playback of compressed audio formats (such as MP3 or AAC) in the Timeline, and rendering will not make them compatible. Convert your compressed audio files to AIFF before import.

■ FCP will import a Broadcast Wave Format (BWF) digital audio file and its timestamp—at long last. For the necessary details, see "Importing Broadcast Wave Files" on page I-325 of the *Apple Final Cut Pro User Manual.*

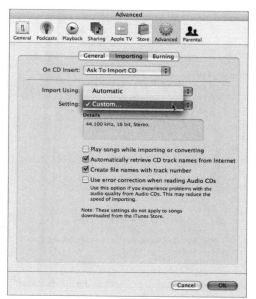

Figure 6.17 Set your file conversion settings in the Importing pane of the iTunes Preferences window.

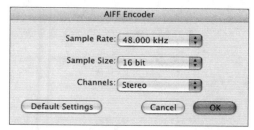

Figure 6.18 In the AIFF Encoder window, make your settings match these.

Convert Audio to 48 kHz on Import with iTunes

If you are using a lot of material from audio CDs in your FCP projects, consider using Apple's iTunes to import the CD tracks.. Here's how to set your preferences in iTunes to convert 44.1 kHz audio to 48 kHz as the application imports the CD audio track directly to your project's media folder.

To convert audio in iTunes:

1. Open iTunes, then choose iTunes > Preferences and click the Advanced icon, then click Importing.

2. In the Importing pane, choose AIFF Encoder from the Import Using pop-up menu and Custom from the Setting pop-up menu (**Figure 6.17**).

3. In the AIFF Encoder window, specify the following (**Figure 6.18**); then click OK.

   ◆ Sample Rate: 48.000 kHz

   ◆ Sample Size: 16 bit

   ◆ Channels: Stereo (or Auto)

4. Back in the Advanced pane of the Preferences window, click the General icon.

continues on next page

5. In the General pane, the iTunes Music Folder Location field shows the currently selected destination folder for the CD audio you're about to import. Click the Change button (**Figure 6.19**), and navigate to your project's audio media folder. Click Choose, and then click OK.

6. In the iTunes playlist window, choose the tracks you want to import by ensuring their check boxes are marked; then click the Import CD button (**Figure 6.20**). The CD audio tracks are converted into 48 kHz AIFF files and appear in the destination folder you specified in step 5, ready to import into your FCP project (**Figure 6.21**).

✔ Tip

- It is not recommended that you import audio tracks by dragging directly from an audio CD to the Browser window in Final Cut Pro because once you remove the CD from your computer, your project will no longer have access to the audio file.

Figure 6.19 Select your project's audio media folder as the destination folder for your sample-rate-converted audio files.

Figure 6.20 In the iTunes playlist window, check the tracks you want, and click the Import button.

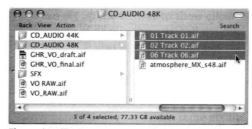

Figure 6.21 iTunes converts your CD audio tracks into 48 kHz AIFF files and places them in the specified folder.

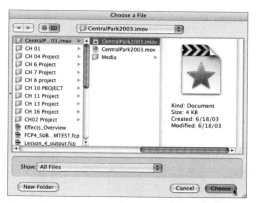

Figure 6.22 Choose File > Open, then select the imovie project file you want to open.

Importing an iMovie Project

Final Cut Pro can import, open, and edit movies created in iMovie. When you import an iMovie project, the clips in the Browser are linked to the original source media files you captured in iMovie.

iMovie uses a different DV encoding method, which produces files in DV Stream format. DV Stream differs from FCP's DV-NTSC (or DV-PAL) format, so you'll encounter a little extra work and a couple of limitations as you continue to work on a project that originated in iMovie:

◆ Once you've imported it, you must render all the media in your project to convert it to an FCP-compatible DV format.

◆ Your DV Stream iMovie files do not have timecode tracks, so you cannot recapture any media that originated in iMovie. Don't throw away your iMovie media files once you've rendered; you'll need them if you plan to continue editing.

◆ Final Cut Pro may not play back your iMovie DV files in real time unless you render them first.

◆ Your imported iMovie project won't include any iMovie sound effects, titles, transitions, effects, or iDVD chapter markers.

To open an iMovie project:

1. Choose File > Open.

2. Select the iMovie project you want to open (**Figure 6.22**).

The iMovie project appears on a project tab in the Browser. The project contains the iMovie sequence plus the individual clips from iMovie's clips shelf.

continues on next page

3. Double-click the sequence to open the iMovie project sequence in the Timeline.

4. Choose File > Save Project As, and save your imported iMovie project as a Final Cut Pro project (**Figure 6.23**).

5. Render the sequence if necessary.

Figure 6.23 Once you've opened your iMovie project in FCP and checked that your media and sequence information have imported successfully, choose File > Save Project As and save a new version of the project as a Final Cut Pro project.

ORGANIZING CLIPS IN THE BROWSER

The Browser is the window you use to organize and access clips, audio files, graphics, and offline clips—all the media elements you use in your project. It also includes the project's sequences—FCP objects that contain your edits. The Browser performs these organizing tasks on your project's virtual clips and sequences—although Browser items look like files on your computer Desktop, Browser items are *references* to media files, not the files themselves. It's very important to remember that copying, moving, or deleting a clip in the Browser does not affect that clip's source media file on disk. Moving a batch of clips from one bin to another in the Browser does not change the location of the clips' corresponding files on your hard drive. File storage is independent of Browser organization, so you can place the same clip in several Browser projects, and each instance of the clip will include a reference to the same media file on your hard drive.

See "What Is Nonlinear, Nondestructive Editing?" in Chapter 1, for more background on nonlinear editing technology.

Anatomy of the Browser

When you open Final Cut Pro for the first time, the Browser contains just two tabs:

◆ A new, Untitled Project tab with a single empty sequence.

◆ The Effects tab, which contains default copies of FCP's effects, filters, and generators, including the text generators.

For information on using FCP's effects features, see Chapter 14, "Compositing and Effects Overview." If you have multiple projects open, the Browser will display a tab for each open project. You can also open a Browser bin in a separate window, and then drag the bin's tab from the Bin window into the main Browser window to display the bin as a tab.

Figure 7.1 shows the Browser window in List view. Note that FCP opens projects with the Browser in List view by default. Icon view is useful for organizing a storyboard, but doesn't provide the wealth of clip data available from the Browser columns in List view. To learn how to switch between List and Icon views, see "Customizing the Browser Display," later in this chapter.

Browser columns

The Browser window can display over 60 columns of data, but you can customize the Browser to display only the columns you are using and hide the rest. Some columns accommodate remarks and other types of information that help you track and sort information about your clips.

Table 7.1 contains a complete list of the columns available for use in the Browser.

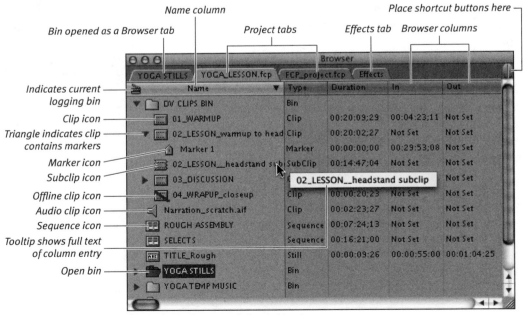

Figure 7.1 The Browser window in List view.

Table 7.1

Browser Columns and Functions

COLUMN	FUNCTION	COLUMN	FUNCTION
Alpha	Alpha channel present	Master	A checkmark indicates that this clip is a master clip
Anamorphic	Indicates whether clip is flagged to be displayed in anamorphic (16:9) aspect ratio	Master Comment 1-4	Four columns for displaying clip comments; column names can be edited
Angle	Displays a clip's angle number. Use to identify clips for multiclip/multicamera editing	Media Start	Starting timecode number of clip's source media
Aud Format	File format of audio clip	Media End	Ending TC number of clip's source media
Aud Rate	Frequency and bit rate of audio clip	Name	Name of the media element; rename clips and sequences here
Audio	Indicates the number of audio channels for clips that include audio	Offline	Indicates that the clip's source media has not yet been captured, is missing, or has been deleted from disk
Aux Reel 1-2	Lists Reel numbers for Aux TC 1 and 2	Out	Out point specified on a clip
Aux TC 1-2	Additional reference timecode numbers for use in synchronizing clips	Pixel Aspect	Pixel aspect ratio
Capture	Capture state of a clip in the Batch Capture list	Reel	Lists the reel number entered at time of capture; changing the Reel number in the Browser changes the identifying reel number of clip's source media file on disk
Cinema Tools Columns	These columns display information for clips imported from Cinema Tools		
Comment A-B	Used for logging information	Reverse Alpha	Choose Yes to reverse opaque and transparent area interpretation in clip's alpha channel
Composite	Composite mode this clip uses		
Compressor	Indicates the compression codec this clip uses	Scene	Displays information entered in Logging window's Scene field
Creator	Application used to create the media file referenced by this clip	Shot/Take	Displays information entered in Logging window's Shot/Take field
Data Rate	Rate of data flow per second	Size	Source media file size, in megabytes
Description	Displays information entered in Logging window's Description field	Source	Directory path name of the media file on disk
Duration	Duration between a clip's In and Out points	Speed	Displays adjusted speed of speed-modified clips as a percentage
Film Safe	Media Manager operations that trim clips marked "Film Safe" will be restricted on frame boundaries to ensure that whole frames are preserved for film negative matchback	TC	Timecode currently displayed in the Viewer, which can be the source timecode or an auxiliary timecode; the TC value displayed will be used for EDL export
Frame Blending	Indicates whether a speed-modified clip has frame blending enabled	TC Rate	Timecode rate of a source media file or sequence
Frame Size	Video frame size, in pixels	Thumbnail	Displays poster (or first) frame of the clip; click and drag a thumbnail to scrub through the clip
Good	Indicates whether a clip was marked "Good" in Log and Capture window, Browser, or Item Properties		
In	In point specified on a clip	Tracks	Number of video and audio tracks in the item
Label, Label 2	Displays sortable, color-coded label info	Type	The type of each item; possible types: sequence, clip, subclip, bin, effect
Last Modified	Displays the time and date of an item's last modification	Vid Rate	Video frame rate; the clip frame rate is written to source media file, and the sequence frame rate is based on that sequence's settings
Length	Length of the source media file on disk		
Log Note	Displays notes entered in Log and Capture window's Log Note field		

Browser window icons

Along the left side of the window, you'll notice icons that accompany each item listed in the Browser. These icons represent file types in Final Cut Pro.

 Sequence: An edited assembly of video and audio clips; open sequences are displayed in the Timeline.

 Bin: A folder used to organize groups of clips, sequences, or other Browser items. A bin can also contain other bins.

 Open Bin: A bin that is currently opened in a separate Browser window.

 Clip: A media file; can represent audio, video, graphics, or other media imported into Final Cut Pro.

 Subclip: A portion of a clip defined by In and Out points; any number of subclips can be created from a single master clip.

 Offline Clip: Placeholder clip referencing media not currently on the local hard drive.

 Audio Clip: Media clip composed of audio samples.

 Graphic: A clip in a single-layer graphic file format (multilayer Photoshop files appear with a sequence icon).

 Layered Graphic Sequence: A multi-layer graphic clip (such as a layered Photoshop file) appears with a sequence icon.

 Multiclip: A clip type that organizes multiple clips into a single structure. You can switch and cut between multiclip angles in real time.

 Marker: Reference point in a clip.

 Video Transition: Transition effect; can be applied to a video track.

 Audio Transition: Transition effect; can be applied to an audio track.

 Video Filter: Effects filter; can be applied to a video clip.

 Audio Filter: Effects filter; can be applied to an audio clip.

 Generator: Effects utility; generates screens, tones, and text for program transitions.

What Does "Not Set" Mean?

When you see "Not Set" displayed in the In (or Out) Browser column, it simply means that you haven't set an In (or Out) point in that clip. For instance, you could have inserted the full length of your clip into a sequence and then set In and Out points in the sequence version of the clip, or you could be using every captured frame of your clip in the sequence.

"Not Set" does not mean that you've somehow lost your source media file or that the clip has lost its timecode.

ANATOMY OF THE BROWSER

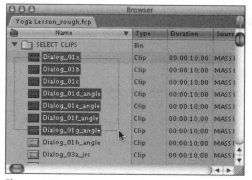

Figure 7.2 You can select a group of items by dragging a bounding box around them.

Using the Browser to Organize Your Project

The Browser is a powerful tool for organizing all your program elements in a way that makes sense to you. You could construct a multi-level folders-within-folders structure by organizing your material in multiple bins, or you could use one long list containing every element in the same display. You might want to keep separate bins for your live-action footage, graphics, and music files; or you might use bins to organize stock footage from multiple sources. You can search for your clips based on any clip property and sort from most Browser columns. Any markers you've placed in a clip will be noted in the Browser. You can use the Browser shortcut menu to modify some clip and sequence properties, or you can add or modify most clip information directly by double-clicking a Browser column entry.

To select an item in the Browser:

Do one of the following:

◆ Click the item you want to select.

◆ Use the arrow keys to step through the item list until you arrive at the item you want.

◆ Use the Tab key to move between items alphabetically from A to Z.

◆ Type the first few letters of an item's name, and the corresponding item will be highlighted.

✔ Tip

■ Multiple item selection in FCP's Browser works in the same way as it does in the Mac OS X Finder: Command-click to select multiple items individually; Shift-click to select a range of items; or drag a bounding box around a group of list items or icons (**Figure 7.2**).

Sorting items

Final Cut Pro allows you to sort by almost every column you see in the Browser. You can use a series of secondary sorts (up to eight) to further refine your list order.

To sort items in the Browser:

1. Click a column header to select the primary sort column (**Figure 7.3**). The primary sort column is indicated by a black arrow in the column header.

2. Click again to reverse the sort order (**Figure 7.4**).

3. Shift-click additional headers to select secondary sort columns (**Figure 7.5**).

4. A secondary sort column is indicated by a light grey arrow in the column header. Shift-click again to reverse the sort order.

✔ Tip

■ If you've defined secondary sort columns by Shift-clicking, you'll need to click a deselected column to clear the current sort before you can select a new primary sort column.

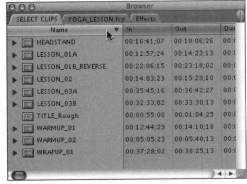

Figure 7.3 Click in the column header to sort by name; the direction of the tiny arrow to the right of the column name here indicates ascending order.

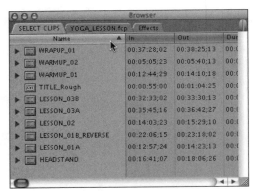

Figure 7.4 Click again to reverse the sort order; the arrow's direction now indicates a descending order.

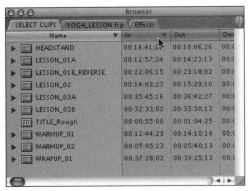

Figure 7.5 Shift-click in another column header to select a secondary sort column.

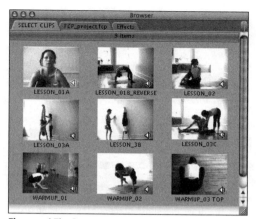

Figure 7.6 The Browser in Large Icon display mode. You can also select Medium Icon, Small Icon, or List view.

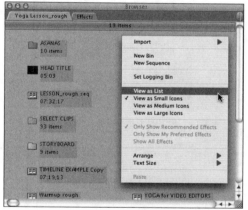

Figure 7.7 Control-click inside the Browser window and choose a display option from the shortcut menu.

Customizing the Browser Display

Different Browser display modes offer different functionality. List view, for example, offers a multitude of data, arranged in sortable columns, plus sexy scrubbable Thumbnail clips. Large Icon view allows you to drag your clips into any order you choose. Final Cut Pro will save your custom Browser arrangement between sessions, and you can save multiple custom Browser layouts with the Save Column Layout feature described later in this chapter. You can customize the Browser in the following ways:

◆ Make items appear as icons (**Figure 7.6**) or as a text list.

◆ In List view, rearrange, resize, hide, or show as many columns as you like. (Note: You can't hide the Name column.)

◆ Sort by most columns.

◆ Set a standard arrangement of columns and switch between that preset and another preset column arrangement for logging clips. Both presets are selectable from the column header's shortcut menu.

◆ Change the Comment column headers.

To display items as a list or as icons:

Do one of the following:

◆ If you're in Icon view, Control-click the Browser window; if you're in List view, Control-click the Name column. Then choose a display option from the shortcut menu (**Figure 7.7**).

◆ Choose View > Browser Items and select a display option from the submenu: As List, As Small Icons, As Medium Icons, or As Large Icons.

To change text display size in List view:

◆ In the Browser window, Control-click the Name column, then choose Text Size from the shortcut menu and select a text size display option (**Figure 7.8**).

To display thumbnails in List view:

1. In the Browser window, Control-click any Browser column except Name.

2. From the shortcut menu, choose Show Thumbnail (**Figure 7.9**).

✔ Tip

■ You can scrub a clip's thumbnail in the Browser by clicking the thumbnail and then dragging in the direction you want to scrub (**Figure 7.10**). Initially, your thumbnail will display the clip's first frame, but you can select another poster frame by scrubbing through the clip until you locate the frame you want and then pressing the Control key before you release the mouse button. Very slick.

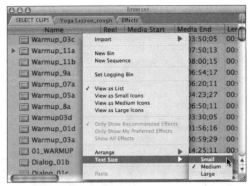

Figure 7.8 You can choose a larger text display size from the Browser's shortcut menu. The selected text size will also appear on Timeline clips.

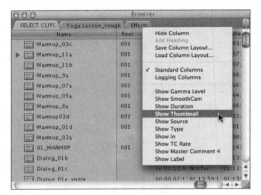

Figure 7.9 Choose Show Thumbnail from the shortcut menu.

Figure 7.10 Drag your pointer across a thumbnail in the Browser; the thumbnail scrubs through the action in that clip.

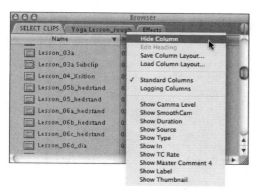

Figure 7.11 Choose Hide Column from the shortcut menu.

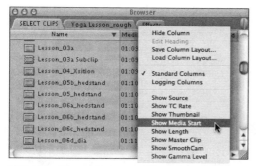

Figure 7.12 Choose the name of the column from the shortcut menu.

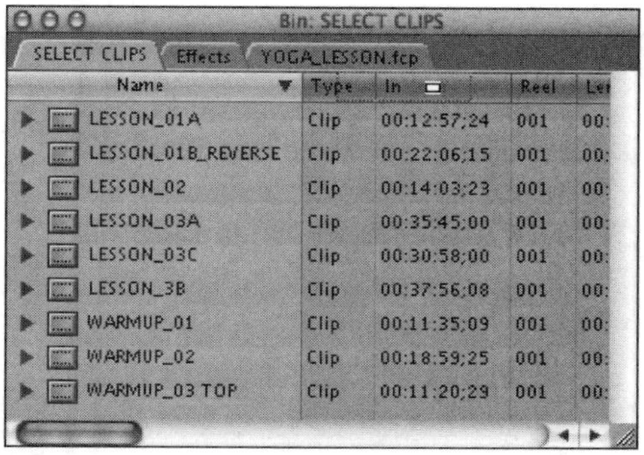

Figure 7.13 Drag a column to its new location.

To hide a column:

1. In the Browser window, Control-click the column header.

2. From the shortcut menu, choose Hide Column (**Figure 7.11**).

To display a hidden column:

1. In the Browser window, Control-click the column header to the right of the place you want the hidden column to be displayed.

2. From the shortcut menu, choose the name of the column you want to display (**Figure 7.12**).

✔ Tips

- Final Cut Pro initially hides some Browser columns by default. Check the shortcut menu in the Browser's column header for a complete list of available columns.

- You can keep your Browser columns narrow and still see a full-length entry in every column. Pause your pointer over a column entry to view a tooltip displaying the complete contents of the column.

To rearrange columns:

- ◆ Drag the column header to the new location (**Figure 7.13**).

To resize columns:

- ◆ Drag the right edge of the column header to the new width.

To save a custom Browser layout:

1. In the Browser, select and arrange the columns you want to include in your custom Browser layout.

2. In the Browser window, Control-click the column heading; then choose Save Column Layout from the shortcut menu (**Figure 7.14**).

   The Save dialog box opens with the Column Layouts folder selected.

3. Enter a name for your new custom layout; then click Save.

   Custom Browser layouts are stored in the Column Layouts folder, located inside the Final Cut Pro User Data folder, which is in your Preferences folder. You can copy layout files from here, or install layouts from another FCP system by copying them to this folder (**Figure 7.15**).

To load a custom Browser layout:

◆ In the Browser window, Control-click the column header; then choose a previously saved custom layout from the shortcut menu (**Figure 7.16**).

   Your custom Browser layout will be applied to the active tab in the Browser.

✔ Tip

■ You can save all the custom Browser column layouts you want, but FCP won't display more than 25 in the shortcut menu.

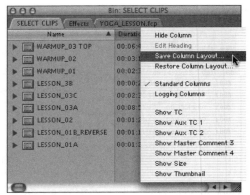

Figure 7.14 Control-click the column heading and choose Save Column Layout from the shortcut menu.

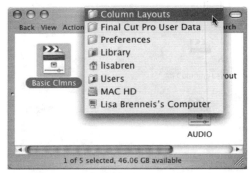

Figure 7.15 Here's the folder location of your Custom Browser layouts. You can copy layout files from here, or install layouts from another FCP system by copying them to this folder.

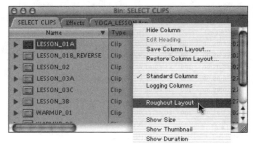

Figure 7.16 Control-click the column heading, and choose the custom layout you want to load from the shortcut menu.

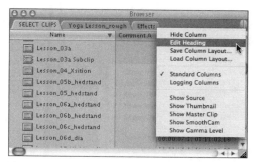

Figure 7.17 Control-click the Comment A or Comment B column heading and choose Edit Heading from the shortcut menu.

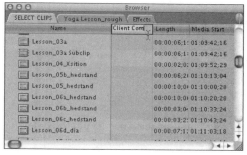

Figure 7.18 Type the new column header name and press Enter.

Figure 7.19 Control-click the clip's icon; then choose a label from the shortcut menu. Note the Label column; you can sort your clips by label.

To edit the Comment column name:

1. In the Browser window, Control-click the Comment A or Comment B column heading.

2. From the shortcut menu, choose Edit Heading (**Figure 7.17**).

3. Type the new column name (**Figure 7.18**).

4. Press Enter.

Or do this:

1. Choose Edit > Project Properties.

2. Type the new column name in the Comment text box, and then click OK.

✔ Tip

■ Try double-clicking or Control-clicking clip information right in its Browser column. You will find that you can modify lots of clip settings without bothering to open the clip's Item Properties window. You can also modify clip settings for multiple clips in a single operation: Select the clips, and then adjust the settings of just one of the selected clips.

To apply a label to a clip:

1. In the Browser window, Control-click the clip's icon.

2. From the shortcut menu, choose Label; then select a label from the submenu. (**Figure 7.19**).

✔ Tips

■ When you apply a label to a bin, all the previously labeled items contained in the bin should adopt the same label.

■ FCP has a keyboard shortcut for everything. You'll find shortcut keys for applying labels in Appendix A.

CUSTOMIZING THE BROWSER DISPLAY

Searching for Items in the Browser

Final Cut Pro has a powerful search engine in its Find function. You can perform a simple name search, but you can also search for single or multiple items by timecode, by file type, or by comment, or you can search your project for unused clips—clips you have not yet used in any sequence. Take a moment to explore the search options available in the Browser and imagine how you might plan your project to make use of them.

To search for a single item:

1. Start in the Browser window. Choose Edit > Find (**Figure 7.20**); or press Command-F.

2. In the Find dialog box, type your search criteria or choose from the search criteria options available from the pop-up menus along the bottom of the dialog box (**Figure 7.21**).

3. Click Find Next. Final Cut Pro highlights the found item in the Browser (**Figure 7.22**).

Figure 7.20 Choose Find from the Edit menu.

Figure 7.21 You can search for a clip by timecode number.

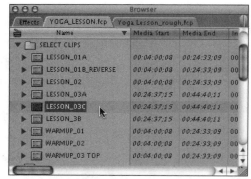

Figure 7.22 The clip with matching timecode highlights in the Browser.

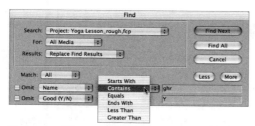

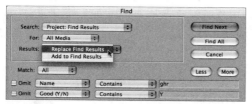

Figure 7.23 This example searches for all clips with names that contain "ghr" and that have a checkmark in the Good column.

Figure 7.24 You can set the Results option to Replace Find Results.

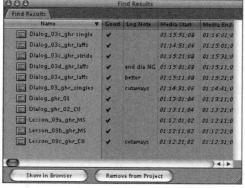

Figure 7.25 The Find Results window with the list of clips that match your search criteria; note the two shortcut buttons at the bottom of the window.

To search for multiple items:

1. Start in the Browser window. Choose Edit > Find; or press Command-F.

2. In the Find dialog box, type your search criteria, or select from the search criteria options available from the pop-up menus near the bottom of the dialog box (**Figure 7.23**).

3. Select an option from the Results pop-up menu. You can choose to replace the results of your previous Find or add the new results to your previous list of found items (**Figure 7.24**).

4. Click Find All. The list of found items that match your search criteria appears in the Find Results window (**Figure 7.25**).

✔ Tips

- Searching by the Name column in the Browser will return clips whose current name matches the search. But if you renamed your clips after capture, searching by both the Source and the Name columns will track down all the clips (including those pesky renamed clips) associated with a source media file.

- Here's a find feature FCP users have been requesting for a long time: now you can Control-click a clip in the Browser and select Reveal in Finder from the shortcut menu. FCP will obligingly switch over to the Finder and highlight your source media file wherever it may be.

Using the Find Results window

The Find Results window displays a list of found items that match your search criteria (**Figure 7.26**). This window displays the same clip information as the Browser, and it offers the same flexible sorting and display options, including custom column layouts. You can perform multiple searches in the Find dialog box and assemble a collection of items in the Find Results window to *do any of the following:*

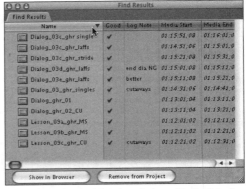

Figure 7.26 The Find Results window with the list of found clips; columns can be sorted just like in the Browser window.

◆ Copy or move found items to a single bin for assembly into an edited sequence.

◆ Delete found items from a project.

✔ Tips

■ You can search within the Find Results window. If you've assembled a large group of items in the Find Results window and you want to refine your list or perform an additional search, you can choose Project: Find Results from the Search pop-up menu (**Figure 7.27**).

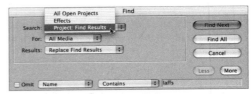

Figure 7.27 Performing a search of the Find Results window.

■ Can't remember the name of a clip, but you know what it looks like? The Find Results window displays thumbnail images in Icon mode, just like the Browser. What a relief.

Search the Project or Search the Sequence?

You can perform two types of searches in Final Cut Pro:

◆ Choose Edit > Find with the Browser window selected, and Final Cut Pro will search all open projects for clips, sequences, graphics, and effects, but will not search for items located inside sequences.

◆ Choose Edit > Find with the Timeline selected, and your search will be limited to the currently open sequence. You'll want to search in the sequence if you are looking for the sequence version of a particular clip—a clip you applied effects to after you inserted it into a sequence, for example. Searching for items in the Timeline is discussed in Chapter 10, "Editing in the Timeline and the Canvas."

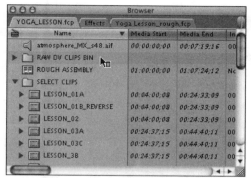

Figure 7.28 Control-click to bring up the shortcut menu.

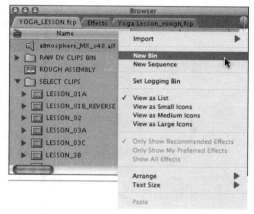

Figure 7.29 Select New Bin from the shortcut menu.

Figure 7.30 The current logging bin indicator is located at the left edge of the bin's Name column.

Working with Bins

Final Cut Pro's Browser bins are similar to the folders you use to organize your Mac Desktop—with one crucial difference. When you make changes to the contents of a bin, such as moving, renaming, or deleting clips, the changes will not affect the disk files or the folders in which your source material is stored. If you delete a clip from the bin, it is not deleted from the disk. Creating a new bin does not create a corresponding folder on your hard drive. The bin exists only within your project file. (See "What Is Nonlinear, Nondestructive Editing?" in Chapter 1 for more information.)

To add a new bin to a project:

1. In the Browser window, Control-click an empty portion of the Name column (**Figure 7.28**).

2. From the shortcut menu, choose New Bin (**Figure 7.29**).

Or do this:

◆ Choose File > New > Bin.

What's That Little Doodad?

The tiny clapboard icon (**Figure 7.30**) indicates that the current bin is set as the *logging bin*, the Browser bin where your captured clips will be stored. For details, see "Selecting a log bin" in Chapter 5.

To open a bin and create a Browser tab for it:

1. In the Browser window, double-click a bin name.

2. In the newly opened Bin window, drag the tab from the bin header into the area above the Name column in the Browser window (**Figure 7.31**).

   The bin appears as a tab in the Browser window (**Figure 7.32**).

To move items between bins in List view:

◆ Drag the items you want to move onto your destination bin; then drop the items into the bin.

✔ Tip

■ To move any item to the top level of a project, drag the item to the Name column header in the Browser window (**Figure 7.33**).

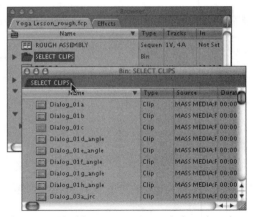

Figure 7.31 The bin opens as a new window; drag the tab to the Browser window.

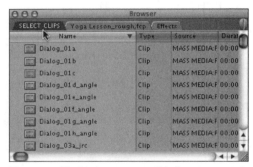

Figure 7.32 The bin is now accessible from its own tab in the Browser window.

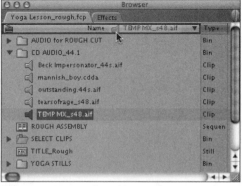

Figure 7.33 Drag a selected item to the Name column header to move it to the top level of a project.

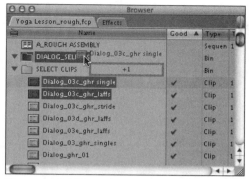

Figure 7.34 Hold down the Option key as you drag a selection to copy it to a new location.

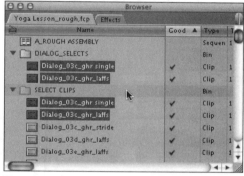

Figure 7.35 The item is copied and appears in both locations.

Working with Browser Items

Copying, pasting, and moving items in FCP's Browser is very much like working with items in the Mac Finder, with one important exception: When you delete a Browser clip, you're not actually deleting its underlying source media file, just the clip reference. Delete a sequence, though, and your edits are really gone for good.

To make a copy of a Browser item:

1. Hold down the Option key as you drag the item (or items) you want to copy (**Figure 7.34**).

2. In the new location, release the mouse button.

   The item is copied and appears in both locations (**Figure 7.35**).

Mouseless Browser Navigation

You can use this list of keyboard commands to move around the Browser without touching the mouse:

◆ Cmd-4 key to select the Browser window.

◆ Up and Down arrow keys to navigate to a bin.

◆ Right Arrow key to open a bin.

◆ Right Arrow key again to select a clip inside that bin.

◆ Up and Down arrows keys to navigate to a clip inside the bin.

◆ Return key to load the clip into the Viewer.

To remove a Browser item from a project:

1. Select the item.

2. Press Delete.

Or do this:

1. Control-click the item you want to delete.

2. From the shortcut menu, choose Cut (**Figure 7.36**).

✔ Tip

■ Remember—when you cut a clip from the Browser, you're not deleting the media file on disk, just the virtual reference that points to the file on disk. See Chapter 4, "Projects, Sequences, and Clips," for details on how to delete media files on disk.

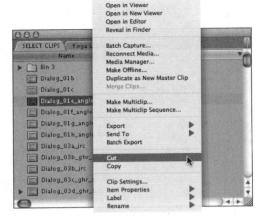

Figure 7.36 Control-click the item you want to delete; then choose Cut from the shortcut menu.

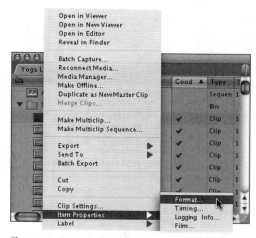

Figure 7.37 Control-clicking an item is the quickest way to access a specified tab in the Item Properties window.

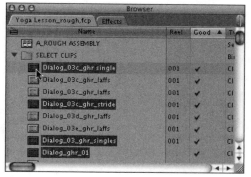

Figure 7.38 Command-click to select multiple items to modify.

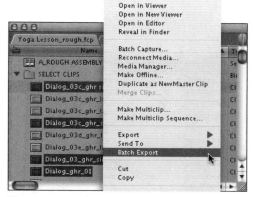

Figure 7.39 Specify a change in the shortcut menu.

To modify clip properties in the Browser:

1. Control-click the clip you want to modify.

2. From the shortcut menu, choose Item Properties, and then select the tab you want to open from the submenu (**Figure 7.37**).

   The Item Properties window opens with the clip's name highlighted.

✔ Tip

- Try selecting the clip and pressing Command-9—that's the keyboard shortcut you use to open the Item Properties window.

To make changes to multiple Browser items or entries:

1. Command-click to select the items or entries you want to modify (**Figure 7.38**).

2. Control-click one of the selected items.

3. From the shortcut menu, specify the change you want to make (**Figure 7.39**).

WORKING WITH BROWSER ITEMS

225

To rename clips, sequences, and bins:

1. Click to select the item you want to rename (**Figure 7.40**).

2. Click again on the item's name.

3. Type a new name (**Figure 7.41**).

✔ Tip

■ Heads up: If you rename a master clip after multiple sections have been edited into the Timeline, those Timeline clips will be renamed as well, unless you change the sequence clips to independent-type.

■ To meet the whole family of FCP clip types and learn about their quaint customs, see "About Clips" in Chapter 4.

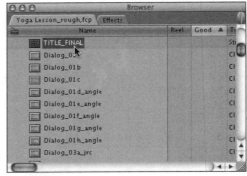

Figure 7.40 First, select the item you want to rename.

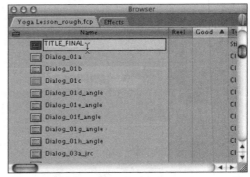

Figure 7.41 Click again on the item's name to open the field; then type a new name.

WORKING WITH CLIPS IN THE VIEWER

You'll be spending a lot of time in the Viewer window. Not only do you use the Viewer to play clips and mark edit points and keyframes, you also work in the Viewer to sculpt audio and video with effects and filters.

The Viewer window interface uses tabs to organize and display the clip controls. You'll see only the tabs that are relevant to the clip that's currently open; not all tabs are open by default. Following are summaries of the functions available on each tab:

◆ **Video tab:** View video frames and set In and Out points and keyframes. This is the default playback window for a video clip.

◆ **Audio tab:** Audition and mark edit points in audio-only clips. This is where you can set level and pan or spread settings. The Audio tab will display the audio portion of an audio+video clip. Clips with two channels of audio will display two Audio tabs: one for each audio channel. To learn more about working in the Audio tab, see Chapter 12, "Audio Tools and Techniques."

◆ **Filters tab:** Adjust the settings for any video or audio filter effects you have applied to a clip.

◆ **Motion tab:** Apply and modify motion effects. You can create animated effects by using a combination of keyframes and changes to motion settings. For more on creating motion effects, see Chapter 15, "Motion."

◆ **Controls tab:** Adjust the settings for a generator you have opened. A text entry field for a text generator appears on this tab.

◆ **Color Corrector tab:** Use the onscreen controls for FCP's color correction filters. The Color Corrector tab appears only on clips with a color correction filter applied. To learn about applying filters and effects, see Chapter 16, "Filters and Compositing."

Anatomy of the Viewer

The Final Cut Pro Viewer has a wide variety of tools for navigating and marking your clips: transport controls, clip-marking controls, pop-up selectors, view selectors, and timecode navigation displays (**Figure 8.1**).

All the Viewer controls listed here, except the pop-up selectors, appear in the Canvas window as well. The controls operate in the same way in the Canvas window that they do in the Viewer.

The next few sections discuss the onscreen controls you'll encounter in the Viewer.

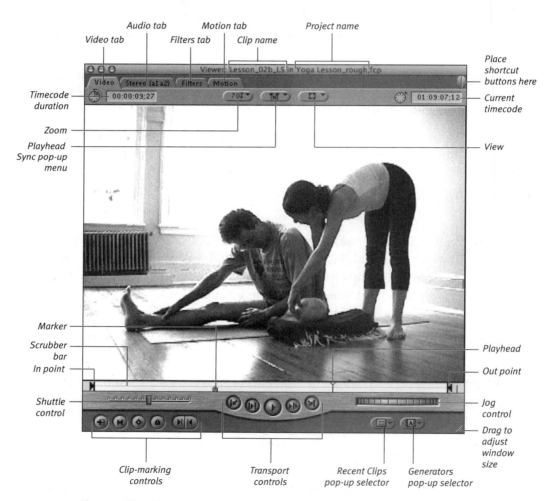

Figure 8.1 The Video tab. Note the location of the other tabs in the Viewer.

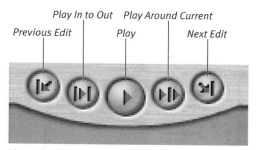

Previous Edit
Play In to Out   Play Around Current
Play   Next Edit

Figure 8.2 The Viewer's transport control buttons.

Figure 8.3 The Shuttle control.

Figure 8.4 The Jog control.

Figure 8.5 The Scrubber and playhead.

Transport controls

Figure 8.2 shows the transport controls, which are located in the middle of the bottom section of the Viewer:

◆ **Previous Edit button:** Click to jump the playhead back to the previous edit (if the open clip is a sequence clip).

◆ **Play In to Out button:** Click to play the clip from the In point to the Out point.

◆ **Play button:** Click to play the clip from the current position of the playhead. Click again to stop playback.

◆ **Play Around Current button:** Click to play the part of the clip immediately before and after the current position of the playhead. The pre-roll and post-roll settings (in the Preferences window) determine the duration of the playback.

◆ **Next Edit button:** Click to move the playhead to the next edit in a sequence clip.

◆ **Shuttle control:** Drag the control tab away from the center to fast forward or rewind (**Figure 8.3**). Speeds vary depending on the control tab's distance from the center. A green control tab indicates normal playback speed.

◆ **Jog control:** Drag to the left or right (**Figure 8.4**) to step through your clip one frame at a time.

◆ **Scrubber and playhead:** The Scrubber is the strip that stretches horizontally below the image window. Move through a clip by dragging the playhead, or click on the Scrubber to jump the playhead to a new location (**Figure 8.5**).

✔ Tip

■ The Viewer's transport and clip-marking controls all have keyboard shortcut equivalents. Use the Tooltips feature to learn keyboard shortcuts for onscreen controls you use regularly.

ANATOMY OF THE VIEWER

Clip-marking controls

All the onscreen controls you use to mark clips are grouped in the lower-left corner of the Viewer (**Figure 8.6**):

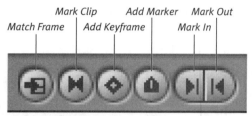

Figure 8.6 The Viewer's clip-marking controls.

◆ **Match Frame:** Click to match the frame currently showing in the Viewer with the same frame as it appears in your sequence. The sequence frame appears in the Canvas window. Match Frame is useful for synchronizing action.

◆ **Mark Clip:** Click to set In and Out points in the sequence. Edit points will be set at the outer boundaries of the clip at the current playhead position in the lowest-numbered auto-selected track.

◆ **Add Keyframe:** Click to add a keyframe to the clip at the current playhead position.

◆ **Add Marker:** Click to add a marker to the clip at the current playhead position.

◆ **Mark In (left) and Mark Out (right):** Click to set the In point or the Out point for the clip at the current playhead position.

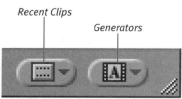

Figure 8.7 Pop-up selectors.

Pop-up selectors

Two buttons at the lower right of the Viewer window provide convenient access to source materials (**Figure 8.7**):

◆ **Recent Clips:** Select recently used clips directly from this pop-up menu.

◆ **Generators:** Select a generator effect from this pop-up menu. (To read about generators, see Chapter 17, "Titles and Generators.")

Figure 8.8 The Zoom selector.

Figure 8.9 The View selector.

Figure 8.10 The Playhead Sync pop-up menu.

View selectors

The selectors directly above the Viewer's image area allow you to adjust the window's view.

◆ **Zoom:** Adjust the Viewer's image display size (**Figure 8.8**). This pop-up selector does not affect the actual frame size of the image.

◆ **View:** Select a viewing format (**Figure 8.9**). Title Safe and Wireframe modes are accessible from this pop-up menu. (For more information, see "Viewing Overlays" later in this chapter.)

Playhead Sync pop-up menu

◆ Select a ganging mode from this pop-up menu (**Figure 8.10**). *Ganging* locks the Viewer and Canvas playheads together so that they move in sync as you step through a sequence. (For more information, see "Ganging Viewer and Canvas" in Chapter 11.)

Timecode navigation and display

Two timecode displays appear in the upper corners of the Viewer window. They are useful for precisely navigating to specific timecode locations.

Figure 8.11 The Timecode Duration display.

- **Timecode Duration:** This displays the elapsed time between the In and Out points of a clip. If no edit points are set, the beginning and end of the clip serve as the In and Out points (**Figure 8.11**). Control-click the Timecode Duration display to switch the elapsed time view among Drop Frame, Non-drop Frame, and Frames views.

- **Current Timecode:** This displays the timecode at the current position of the playhead. You can enter a time in the display to jump the playhead to that point in the clip.

Figure 8.12 The Current Timecode display and shortcut menu. The shortcut menu offers a variety of ways to view the clip's timecode, and lists any markers you've placed in a clip. Choose a marker from the menu to jump the playhead to that marker's location.

- **Current Timecode display shortcut menu:** Control-click the display to switch the elapsed time view among Drop (or Non-Drop) Frame, Feet + Frames, and Frames views (**Figure 8.12**). This shortcut menu also offers the option to switch the clip's timecode reference from Source timecode to an Auxiliary timecode you've assigned to your clip. You can view timecode for the current frame in Source Time (which displays the source media file timecode for the frame currently displayed) or Clip Time (which calculates timecode based on the source media file's native frame rate). Choose View Native Speed, and FCP displays the native timecode number for each source media frame. Disable this option, and FCP adjusts each frame's native timecode number to reflect the speed change, and then displays the adjusted timecode.

Figure 8.13 Control-click the clip's icon and choose Open in Viewer from the shortcut menu.

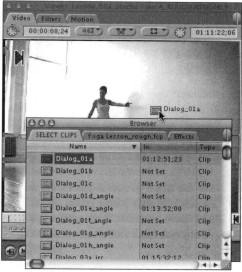

Figure 8.14 Open a clip by dragging it from the Browser and dropping it in the image area of the Viewer.

Working with Clips in the Viewer

You can open clips from the Browser or from the Timeline. You can open single and multiple clips, or clips you have viewed recently. You can also open clips from outside an open project.

When you open an audio+video clip, it appears in a Viewer window with the Video tab selected.

To open a clip in the Viewer:

Do one of the following:

◆ Double-click the clip's icon in the Browser or Timeline.

◆ Control-click the clip's icon and choose Open in Viewer from the shortcut menu (**Figure 8.13**).

◆ Select the clip's icon and press Enter.

◆ Drag a clip's icon from the Browser and drop it in the image area of the Viewer (**Figure 8.14**).

To open a clip in a new window:

1. Select the clip in the Browser or Timeline.

2. Choose View > Clip in New Window.

✔ Tips

- It's common practice in Final Cut Pro to load an entire sequence into the Viewer and edit it into another sequence, just as if it were a clip. To do this, select the sequence in the Browser; then choose View > Sequence, or drag the sequence's icon from the Browser and drop it in the image area of the Viewer.

- If loading a sequence into the Viewer causes the Canvas and Timeline to disappear, that means you loaded a sequence that was currently open in the Timeline. The Timeline closes because FCP protocol dictates that you cannot edit a sequence into itself.

To open multiple clips:

1. Command-click to select multiple clips in the Browser.

2. Drag the clips to the Viewer (**Figure 8.15**). The first clip opens in the Viewer, and the other selected clips are listed in the Recent Clips control (**Figure 8.16**).

Figure 8.15 Drag the clips to the Viewer, and then drop them on the image area.

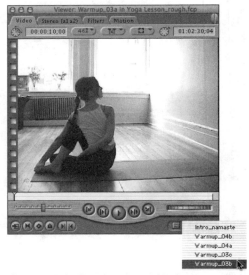

Figure 8.16 The first clip is opened in the Viewer; the rest are listed in the Recent Clips pop-up list.

Figure 8.17 Select a clip from the Recent Clips control's pop-up list.

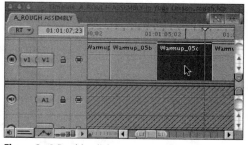

Figure 8.18 Double-click a sequence clip in the Timeline to open it in the Viewer.

Figure 8.19 The clip opens with the Viewer's playhead located at the same frame. Two lines of dots in the Scrubber indicate that you've opened a sequence clip.

To open a recently viewed clip:

◆ Select the clip name from the Recent Clips control's pop-up list (**Figure 8.17**).

✔ Tip

■ You can load an entire Browser bin of clips into the Viewer in one move by dragging the bin from the Browser and dropping it in the image area of the Viewer. The clips in the bin will show up in the Recent Clips control (as long as your List Recent Clips preference is set high enough to cover the folder's item count).

To open a clip from the Timeline or Canvas:

◆ Double-click the clip in the Timeline (**Figure 8.18**).

The clip opens in the Viewer. If you positioned the Timeline's playhead over a frame in the clip, the clip opens with the Viewer's playhead located at the same frame (**Figure 8.19**). The two lines of dots in the Scrubber indicate that you've opened a sequence clip.

To open an imported clip in its original application:

1. Open the clip in the Viewer or Canvas window.

2. Choose View > Clip in Editor (**Figure 8.20**).

   Clips created in an application other than Final Cut Pro will open in that application (**Figure 8.21**). If the application used to create the clip is not installed on your computer, a dialog box opens that allows you to choose an application in which to edit the clip.

✔ Tip

■ You can specify default applications for editing imported graphics, video, and audio files on the External Editors tab of the System Settings window. For more information, see "Setting External Editors Preferences" in Chapter 3.

Figure 8.20 Choose View > Clip in Editor to open a clip in the application you used to create it.

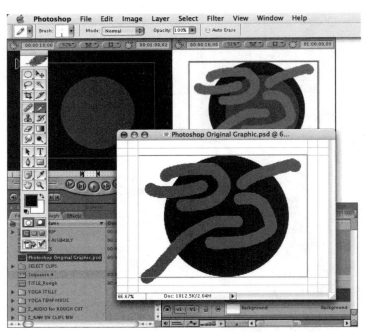

Figure 8.21 This clip, created in Photoshop, has opened in Photoshop, the application that was specified in the External Editors preference tab.

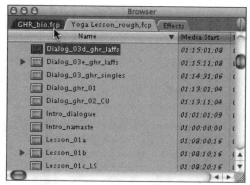

Figure 8.22 Click a project's tab to bring that project to the front of the Browser window.

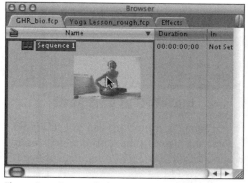

Figure 8.23 Drag a clip into a project in the Browser window. Clip changes will be saved with the project.

To open a clip outside the current project:

1. Choose File > Open.

2. Locate the clip's media file on disk.

3. Select the file and click Choose.

To save changes in a clip outside the current project:

1. In the Browser window, select a project in which to save your modified clip by clicking the tab of that project.

   This brings your selected project to the front of the Browser window (**Figure 8.22**).

2. Click and drag from the image area in the Viewer to the project's tab in the Browser.

   Your clip is now inserted in that project, and your changes will be saved with that project (**Figure 8.23**).

FCP Protocol: Saving Clip Changes

Say you have marked edit points and placed some other markers in a clip you opened outside of your project. To save the changes you made to that clip, you'll need to do the following:

◆ Insert the modified clip into a project that's currently open.

or

◆ Export the clip.

Remember that FCP will save the changes you make only if the clip has been placed in a project or exported as a new file. If you mark changes and close the Viewer window without taking the steps listed here...bye-bye changes. There's no warning dialog box, so take care. One exception to this rule: Any modification of a clip's reel number will be written to the clip's media file immediately.

To open a generator effect in the Viewer:

1. Start in the Browser window with the Effects tab selected.

2. *Do one of the following:*
   - ◆ Double-click the generator icon in the Browser (**Figure 8.24**) or Timeline.
   - ◆ Select a generator icon and press Enter.

✔ Tip

- ■ You can select generator effects directly from the Generators pop-up menu in the Viewer window (**Figure 8.25**).

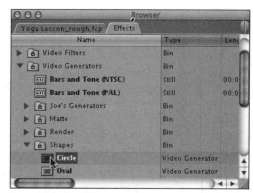

Figure 8.24 Double-click a generator icon to open the generator effect in the Viewer.

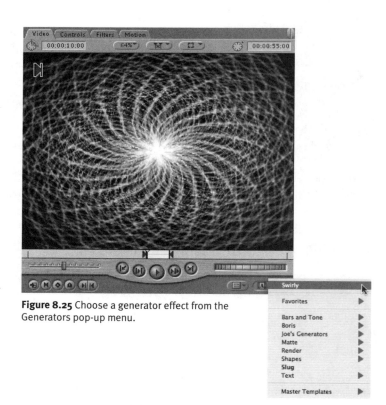

Figure 8.25 Choose a generator effect from the Generators pop-up menu.

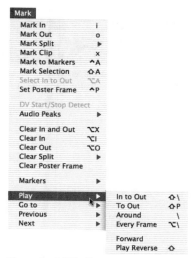

Mark

Mark In	i
Mark Out	o
Mark Split	▶
Mark Clip	x
Mark to Markers	^A
Mark Selection	⇧A
Select In to Out	⌥A
Set Poster Frame	^P
DV Start/Stop Detect	
Audio Peaks	▶
Clear In and Out	⌥X
Clear In	⌥I
Clear Out	⌥O
Clear Split	▶
Clear Poster Frame	
Markers	▶
Play	▶
Go to	▶
Previous	▶
Next	▶

In to Out	⇧\
To Out	⇧P
Around	\
Every Frame	⌥\
Forward	
Play Reverse	⇧

Figure 8.26 FCP offers so many ways to play.

Playing clips

Check out the Play submenu of the Mark menu (**Figure 8.26**), and you'll see a cadre of playback options. You can also select a playback option from the Viewer's transport controls (see Figure 8.2 earlier in this chapter), or use one of the keyboard shortcuts that control playback.

For all the play operations described in this section, start with an open clip and the Viewer window active.

To play a clip in the Viewer:

1. Click the Play button (**Figure 8.27**); or press the spacebar; or press L.

2. To stop playback, click the Play button; or press the spacebar; or press K.

To play a clip in reverse:

◆ Shift-click the Play button; or press Shift-spacebar; or press J.

To play a clip between In and Out points:

◆ Click the Play In to Out button (**Figure 8.28**); or press Shift-\ (backslash).

To play a clip from the current playhead position to the Out point:

◆ Command-click the Play button.

Figure 8.27 Click the Play button to start clip play. Click Play again to stop play.

Figure 8.28 Click the Play In to Out button to play the section of the clip between the In and Out points.

To play a clip before and after the current playhead position:

◆ Click the Play Around Current button (**Figure 8.29**); or press the backslash (\) key.

The clip plays back the specified pre-roll duration before the playhead location, and it plays back the post-roll duration after the playhead location.

Figure 8.29 Click the Play Around Current button to play a section of the clip before and after the current playhead position.

✔ Tip

■ You can set the duration of video playback using the pre-roll and post-roll settings in the Editing tab of FCP's User Preferences window.

JKL Keys: The Way to Move

"JKL Keys," a swift and efficient system for controlling variable-speed playback from your keyboard, is an import from expensive, pro digital editing systems. Learn it, and you'll be whipping through your footage like the pros do. Here's how it works.

The J, K, and L keys are in a row on your keyboard, and you use them to control playback speed and direction. The I and O keys, which you use for setting In and Out points, are located just above JKL. The comma (,) and period (.) keys, which you can use to trim edits, are located below JKL. The semicolon (;) and apostrophe (') keys control Previous and Next Edit. This arrangement makes it easy to edit because it places the most commonly used keyboard shortcuts under one hand. It's easy to see how editors get attached to this system.

Here's the rundown on J, K, and L keyboard command functions:

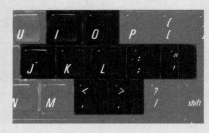

Press J to play in reverse. Tap J twice to double the reverse shuttle speed. Tap J three times for 4x reverse shuttle speed. Tap J four times for 8x reverse shuttle speed.

Press K to stop or pause.

Press L to play forward. Tap L twice to double the forward shuttle speed. Tap L three times for 4x forward shuttle speed. Tap L four times for 8x forward shuttle speed.

Hold down K and tap J or L to get slow-motion shuttling in either direction. A single J or L tap, with K held down, steps you forward or backward one frame at a time.

Figure 8.30 Choose View > Loop Playback to loop clip playback. Choose View > Loop Playback again to toggle looping off.

To play every frame:

◆ Choose Mark > Play > Every Frame; or press Option-P.

✔ Tip

■ If you've applied complex effects to a clip, use the Play Every Frame command to preview the clip without rendering it first. Playback is slower than normal, but you'll get a rough idea.

To loop playback in all playback modes:

1. Choose View > Loop Playback (**Figure 8.30**).

2. Choose View > Loop Playback again to turn off looping.

✔ Tip

■ You can toggle looped playback on and off from your keyboard by pressing Control-L.

Other ways to move: jogging, scrubbing, and shuttling

While editing, you may find yourself spending more time playing your material at fast and slow speeds than at normal speed. Use the following tools for high- and low-speed navigation:

◆ To scrub through a clip, drag the playhead along the Scrubber bar above the transport controls (**Figure 8.31**).

◆ To jump the playhead to a location within the clip, click in the Scrubber bar.

◆ To move the playhead frame by frame, use the arrow keys.

◆ To jump the playhead in one-second increments, press Shift as you use the arrow keys.

◆ To jog one frame at a time, drag the Jog control (**Figure 8.32**). You can drag off the control area if you continue to hold down the mouse button.

◆ To play a clip at various speeds, drag the Shuttle control (**Figure 8.33**). Drag farther from the center to increase the playback speed. Drag right to play forward; drag left to play in reverse.

Figure 8.31 Drag the playhead across the Scrubber to scrub through a clip.

Figure 8.32 Drag the Jog control to step through a clip one frame at a time.

Figure 8.33 Drag the Shuttle control to scan a clip in either direction at a range of speeds from slow to fast.

Figure 8.34 Current Timecode display in the Viewer window.

Figure 8.35 Adding 1 second, 15 frames (45 frames) to the current timecode position using a timecode entry shortcut.

Figure 8.36 The playhead is repositioned 1 second, 15 frames later, and the Current Timecode display is updated.

Figure 8.37 Timecode Duration display in the Viewer window. The current clip duration is 10 seconds.

Figure 8.38 Adding 1 second (30 frames) to the current clip duration using a timecode entry shortcut.

Figure 8.39 The Out point is extended by 1 second, and the Timecode Duration display is updated.

Navigating with Timecode

Moving around using timecode values can be the most efficient way to work, especially if your sense of timing is tuned to "frames per second." Final Cut Pro's timecode input functionality is quite flexible. If you know exactly where you want to go, this is the way to get there. Timecode navigation works the same way in both the Viewer and Canvas.

To navigate using timecode values:

1. Start with your clip open and the Viewer window selected. **Figure 8.34** shows the timecode location before repositioning.

2. Enter a new timecode number (or use the shorthand methods detailed in the nearby Tips and sidebar). You don't need to click in the field to begin entering a new timecode—just type the numbers (**Figure 8.35**) and then press Enter.

   The playhead moves to the location that matches the new timecode value, and the new timecode position displays in the Current Timecode field in the upper-right corner of the Viewer (**Figure 8.36**).

To change the Out point using timecode:

◆ To change the Out point for a clip or sequence, enter a new timecode value in the Duration field, in the upper-left corner of the Viewer; then press Enter. (See **Figures 8.37–8.39**.)

✔ Tips

■ In the Viewer or Canvas, press Tab once to select the Duration field or twice to select the Current Timecode field.

■ You can copy the timecode from one field and paste it into another if the timecode is valid in the location where it is being pasted. You can also drag a timecode from one field to another by pressing Option while dragging.

FCP Protocol: Entering Timecode Numbers

Final Cut Pro uses the standard timecode format of Hours:Minutes:Seconds:Frames, and employs a number of convenient shortcuts for timecode navigation.

For example, typing 01241315 sets the timecode to 01:24:13:15. You don't need to include the colons when you type.

You need to type only the numbers that change. Numbers that don't change, such as the hour or minute, don't need to be entered. Let's look at some examples.

Example 1

1. Start at timecode location 01:24:13:15.

2. To jump to timecode 01:24:18:25, type 1825 (for 18 seconds, 25 frames) and press Enter.

The playhead jumps to timecode location 01:24:18:25. The hour and minute don't change for the new timecode location, so you don't need to reenter the hour or minute.

Example 2

The same idea applies to a new timecode minutes away from your current location.

1. Again start at timecode location 01:24:13:15.

2. To jump to timecode 01:27:18:25, type 271825 (for 27 minutes, 18 seconds, 25 frames) and press Enter.

The playhead jumps to timecode location 01:27:18:25.

Entering Durations

Say you want to move 12 seconds, 27 frames back in your clip. You don't need to calculate the new timecode number yourself.

Type –1227, and your clip jumps back 12 seconds and 27 frames. You can enter the timecode value preceded by a plus (+) or minus (–) sign, and FCP will change the current time by that amount.

You can jump to a new location using the plus (+) and minus (–) keys in two ways: using time (Hours:Minutes:Seconds:Frames) or using the total number of frames, which Final Cut Pro converts into time plus frames. Here are some examples using time:

◆ Typing –3723 jumps back 37 seconds and 23 frames.

◆ Typing +161408 moves ahead 16 minutes, 14 seconds, and 8 frames.

In the Frames position in the timecode, any two-digit value between 30 and 99 is converted to the correct number of seconds (30 frames = 1 second). Here are some examples using the frame count:

◆ Entering –69 frames jumps back 69 frames, which is 2 seconds and 9 frames.

◆ Entering +36 frames jumps ahead 36 frames, which is 1 second and 6 frames.

One More Shortcut

There's one other keyboard shortcut: You can substitute a period (.) for zeros in a timecode value. Each period replaces a pair of zeros in a timecode number. Here's an example:

◆ To jump to timecode location 00:07:00:00, type 7.. (7 and two periods). The periods insert 00 in the Frames and Seconds fields.

◆ Type 11... to move to 11:00:00:00.

Sure beats typing all those colons, huh?

Figure 8.40 Set an In point by clicking the Mark In button.

Figure 8.41 Set an Out point by clicking the Mark Out button.

Figure 8.42 Click the Play In to Out button to review the edit points you have marked.

Working with In and Out Points

The In and Out points determine the start and end frames of the clip portion that is used when the clip is edited into a sequence. Determining the usable part of a clip and setting In and Out points is the first step in assembling your edit. Many editing functions are performed by adjusting these points, either within the clip itself or from within a sequence.

To set In and Out points for a clip in the Viewer:

1. In the Browser, double-click the clip to open it in the Viewer.

2. Press the Home key to position the playhead at the beginning of the clip.

3. Use the Play button or the spacebar to start playing the clip from the beginning.

4. Click the Mark In button (**Figure 8.40**), or press I, when you see (or hear) the beginning of the part you want to use.

5. Click the Mark Out button (**Figure 8.41**), or press O, when you see (or hear) the end of the part you want to use.

6. To check your In and Out points, click the Play In to Out button, or press the vertical bar key (|, or Shift-\) (**Figure 8.42**).

✔ Tips

■ You don't need to have the clip playing to set its In and Out points. You can drag the playhead to locate a particular frame and then set the edit point.

■ Ever heard of a split edit? How about an L-cut? Both terms refer to an edit where audio and video don't cut at the same frame. The split edit is Professional Editing Secret #1. For more information, see "Performing Split Edits" in Chapter 9.

To change In and Out points in the Viewer:

Do one of the following:

◆ Play the clip again and click Mark In or Mark Out at the new spot.

◆ Drag the In or Out point icon along the Scrubber bar to change the point's location.

◆ Press Option-I to remove an In point; Option-O to remove an Out point.

✔ Tip

■ You can use the shortcut menu to set and clear edit points. Control-click in the Scrubber and choose an option from the shortcut menu (**Figure 8.43**).

To move the In and Out points simultaneously:

1. Start in the Viewer.

2. Press and hold Shift while dragging either edit point indicator (**Figure 8.44**) with the pointer.

   The marked duration of the clip does not change, but the frames included in the marked clip shift forward or backward. Modifying an edit in this way is called *slipping*.

Figure 8.43 Use the Scrubber bar's shortcut menu to set and clear edit points.

Figure 8.44 Pressing Shift while dragging an edit point slides both the In and Out points.

Other Ways to Set In and Out Points

If you open FCP's Mark menu, you'll see a number of additional ways to set and clear In and Out points. Most of the marking shortcuts work only in the Timeline, but they'll come in handy after your sequence is assembled.

◆ **Mark Clip:** Sets In and Out points at the boundaries of a selected Timeline clip. You can also use Mark Clip to mark a Timeline gap. Place the Timeline playhead over the gap; then press X.

◆ **Mark to Markers:** Place your Timeline playhead between two markers, and FCP will use the markers' locations to set In and Out points.

◆ **Mark Selection:** Sets In and Out points at the boundaries of a selected area of the Timeline.

About Subclips

Subclips are shorter clips you create from a longer master clip. You can create multiple subclips from a single master clip. For example, you can open a 15-minute clip in the Viewer and subdivide it into as many subclips as you need. As you create subclips, the master clip remains open in the Viewer.

Once you've created a subclip, you can open it in the Viewer and work with it in the same way as any other clip. Changes you make to a subclip won't affect the master clip.

Final Cut Pro places new subclips in the same project bin as the master clip, automatically naming each clip as you create it. For example, if the master clip is named "Whole Thing," the first subclip is named "Whole Thing Subclip," the second is "Whole Thing Subclip 2," and so on.

Once you create a subclip, you can rename it and trim the edit points, but you cannot extend the subclip's In and Out points beyond the In and Out points of its master clip.

If you need to extend a subclip's edit points beyond its current duration, you must remove the subclip's limits, restoring your subclip to the full length of the master clip, and then set new In and Out points.

✔ Tip

- You can use subclips to mark selected portions of a long clip (you can even rename them) and then export all those subclips as a batch list. Use that batch list to recapture just the bits of the longer clip you really want to keep. They'll be captured as full-fledged, individual master clips.

Marking Shortcuts

FCP offers lots of ways to mark In and Out points. This is something editors do all day long, so it may be worthwhile to try these shortcuts and see which ones work best for you.

To mark the In point:

Do one of the following:

- Press I on the keyboard.
- Click the Mark In button in the Viewer.
- Press slash (/) on the keypad.
- From the Mark menu, choose Mark In.

To mark the Out point:

Do one of the following:

- Press O on the keyboard.
- Click the Mark Out button in the Viewer.
- Press the asterisk (*) on the keypad.
- From the Mark menu, choose Mark Out.

To delete edit points:

Do one of the following:

- To clear both In and Out points, press Option-X; or Option-click the Mark Clip button.
- To clear an In point, press Option-I; or Option-click the Mark In button.
- To clear an Out point, press Option-O; or Option-click the Mark Out button.

To jump the playhead to edit points:

Do one of the following:

- To go to the In point, press Shift-I; or Shift-click the Mark In button.
- To go to the Out point, press Shift-O; or Shift-click the Mark Out button.

To create a subclip:

1. Double-click a clip in the Browser or Timeline to open it in the Viewer window.

2. Mark the clip's In and Out points (**Figure 8.45**).

3. Choose Modify > Make Subclip (**Figure 8.46**); or press Command-U.

   A new, automatically named subclip appears in the Browser, below the master clip (**Figure 8.47**).

Figure 8.45 Mark an Out point for your subclip.

Figure 8.46 Choose Modify > Make Subclip.

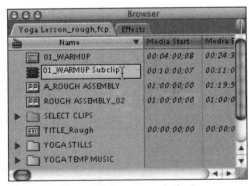

Figure 8.47 A new subclip appears in the Browser, below the master clip. The subclip's Name field is already highlighted; to rename the subclip, just start typing the new name.

FCP Protocol: Subclips Are Master Clips, Too

Final Cut Pro 4 introduced new clip-handling behavior, classifying clips as Master, Affiliate, or Independent. Each clip type has protocols that govern its actions. You can get the gory details on FCP's clip-handling behavior in Chapter 4, "Projects, Sequences, and Clips."

What's important to note here is that any new subclip you create starts out life as a separate master clip, with no affiliate ties to the master clip you created it from.

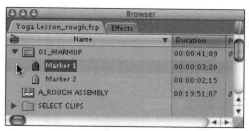

Figure 8.48 Click the clip's expansion triangle; then select the desired marker from the list.

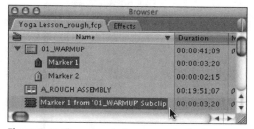

Figure 8.49 The new subclip appears in the Browser. Note that the subclip's duration is equal to the extended marker's duration.

✔ Tips

■ A word of caution: If you choose to recapture a project containing a subclip, Final Cut Pro will recapture the entire length of the master media file containing the subclip. For tips on project recapture, see Chapter 20, "Managing Complex Projects."

■ One more cautionary word: Test ahead of time if you are exporting an EDL of a sequence that includes subclips.

To create a subclip from a marker:

1. In the Browser, click the marked clip's expansion triangle to reveal a list of its markers; then select the marker you want (**Figure 8.48**).

2. Choose Modify > Make Subclip; or press Command-U.

   The new subclip appears in the Browser. The subclip has a duration equal to the extended marker's duration (**Figure 8.49**). If the marker has no extended duration, the subclip will extend to the next marker in the clip.

✔ Tip

■ DV Start/Stop Detection is akin to the popular "scene detection" feature in iMovie. FCP will automatically set markers in your captured clip each time it detects a Start/Stop (Record/Pause). Because FCP can use markers to break a clip into individual subclips, you can use the technique outlined here to capture long sections of DV tape and break them into usable subclip chunks. To learn how, see "Using DV Start/Stop Detection" in Chapter 5.

To adjust a subclip's length:

1. Select a subclip in the Browser or a sequence subclip in the Timeline.

2. Choose Modify > Remove Subclip Limits.

3. Open the subclip in the Viewer.

   The full length of the master clip appears. If you have selected a Timeline subclip, the current In and Out points will still be displayed.

4. Set new In and Out points for the subclip.

Using Markers

Markers are reference pointers in a clip or sequence, and they have a variety of uses. You can:

◆ Quickly jump the playhead to markers in clips or sequences.

◆ Align the clip marker to a marker in the sequence.

◆ Align a filter or motion keyframe to the marker.

◆ Mark a range of the clip to use as you might a subclip.

◆ Align other clip markers, clip boundaries, or transition boundaries to a marker in the Timeline.

FCP's special marker types—chapter, compression, and scoring markers—are used on FCP sequences to indicate to other applications (such as DVD Studio Pro or Compressor) a point where a change takes place. All special marker types are intended for use as sequence markers only, so make sure you apply all special markers to your sequence and not to an individual Timeline clip.

To learn more about using markers in sequences see Chapter 10, "Editing in the Timeline and the Canvas."

To add markers to a clip or sequence in the Viewer:

1. Open the clip in the Viewer.

2. Play the clip or sequence.

3. When playback reaches the place where you want to set a marker, click the Add Marker button (**Figure 8.50**); or press M.

4. To add a custom label or comments to the marker, click Add Marker (or press M) a second time to display the Edit Marker dialog box (**Figure 8.51**).

Figure 8.50 Click the Add Marker button to set a marker in your clip.

Figure 8.51 Click Add Marker again to call up the Edit Marker dialog box.

USING MARKERS

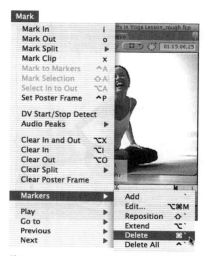

Figure 8.52 Choose Mark > Markers > Delete to remove a marker from your clip.

Figure 8.53 Choosing a marker from the shortcut menu. Control-click the Current Timecode display to see the shortcut menu listing of all markers in a clip.

Figure 8.54 Rename a marker or add comments in the Edit Marker dialog box; then click OK.

To delete a marker:

1. Move the playhead to the marker.

2. *Do one of the following:*
   - Choose Mark > Markers > Delete (**Figure 8.52**).
   - Press Command-` (accent grave, which shares a key with the tilde [~]).
   - Option-click the Marker button.
   - Select the marker's icon in the Browser and press the Delete key. You can select and delete multiple clip markers in a single operation.

To move the playhead to a marker:

Do one of the following:

- Press Shift-M to jump to the next marker, or Option-M to jump to the previous marker.

- Drag the playhead in the Scrubber bar to the marker location.

- Control-click the Current Timecode field in the Viewer and choose a marker from the shortcut menu (**Figure 8.53**).

- Choose Mark > Previous > Marker (or Mark > Next > Marker).

To rename a marker or add comments:

1. Move the playhead to the marker.

2. Press M to open the Edit Marker dialog box.

3. Type a new name or comment in the corresponding text box (**Figure 8.54**); then click OK.

To extend the duration of a marker:

1. Move the playhead to the marker.

2. Press M to open the Edit Marker dialog box.

3. Now, extend the marker's duration by entering a duration value (**Figure 8.55**).

   An extended duration marker appears as a marker icon with a bar extending along the Scrubber bar (**Figure 8.56**).

✔ Tip

■ You can place extended duration markers on audio tracks to visually mark the location and duration of key dialogue or a specific passage in a music track.

To extend the marker duration to the playhead location:

1. Position the playhead where you want the endpoint of your extended marker to go.

2. Choose Mark > Markers > Extend (**Figure 8.57**); or press Option-` (accent grave, which shares a key with the tilde [~]).

   The marker's duration will extend from the original location of the marker to the location of the playhead (**Figure 8.58**).

✔ Tip

■ You can double-click a marker icon in the Browser window to open it as a subclip in the Viewer.

Figure 8.55 Extend a marker's duration by entering a value in the Duration field of the Edit Marker dialog box.

Figure 8.56 The marker icon displays its duration on the Scrubber bar.

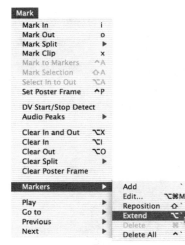

Figure 8.57 Choose Mark > Markers > Extend.

Figure 8.58 The marker's duration now extends to the playhead position.

Figure 8.59 Move the playhead to the new desired location for your marker.

To move a marker forward in time:

1. Move the playhead to where you want to reposition the marker (**Figure 8.59**).

You can move a marker only forward.

2. Choose Mark > Markers > Reposition; or press Shift-` (accent grave).

✔ Tip

■ To extend or reposition a marker on the fly during playback, use the keyboard shortcuts listed in the previous sections. Tap the keys when you see the frame you want to make your new marker location.

Adjusting the Viewer Display

You can set up the Viewer to show your clips in a variety of display formats and magnifications. Final Cut Pro can also overlay an array of useful information on your clip image, but you can turn off the overlay. View settings are clip-specific and are stored with each clip.

Figure 8.60 Choose a magnification level from the Zoom pop-up menu.

Changing magnification and window size in the Viewer or Canvas

Final Cut Pro has an ambitious interface. Unless you work with a dual monitor setup, you'll occasionally want to juggle window sizes in order to get a closer look at your work.

To zoom in:

Do one of the following:

◆ Choose a higher magnification level from the Zoom pop-up menu at the top of the Viewer or Canvas (**Figure 8.60**).

◆ Select the Zoom In tool from the Tool palette and click inside the Viewer or Canvas.

◆ From the View menu, choose a zoom-in amount from the Level submenu.

◆ Select the Zoom In tool from the Tool palette (**Figure 8.61**). Click the image area and drag a marquee to zoom in on the desired area of the image (**Figure 8.62**).

Note that clips will not play smoothly when you have zoomed in on a clip in the Viewer.

Figure 8.61 Select the Zoom In tool from the Tool palette.

Figure 8.62 Drag a marquee around the area you want to zoom in on.

Figure 8.63 Drag the Hand tool over a magnified image to move it in the Viewer window.

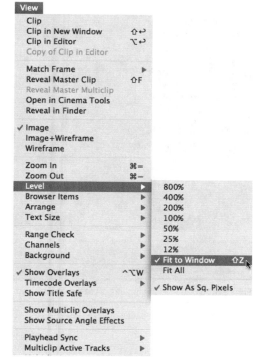

Figure 8.64 Choose View > Level and select a zoom-out level.

To view different parts of a magnified image:

Do one of the following:

◆ Select the Hand tool from the Tool palette and drag it over the image to move the view (**Figure 8.63**).

◆ Use the scroll bars to move around the image.

To zoom out:

Do one of the following:

◆ Choose a lower magnification level from the Zoom pop-up menu at the top of the Viewer.

◆ Select the Zoom Out tool from the Tool palette and click inside the Viewer or Canvas.

◆ From the View menu, select a zoom-out amount from the Level submenu (**Figure 8.64**).

To fit a clip into the window size:

◆ From the Zoom pop-up menu at the top of the Viewer, choose Fit to Window; or press Shift-Z.

✔ Tip

■ Shift-Z is one of FCP's most-beloved keyboard shortcuts. In the Viewer's video tab, Shift-Z zooms your image to fit the window size. In the Viewer's audio tabs, the same shortcut scales the clip's waveform to fit into the window. In the Timeline, Shift-Z scales your sequence view to fit the entire sequence inside the Timeline window.

To fit all items into the view plus a 10 percent margin:

Do one of the following:

◆ From the Zoom pop-up menu at the top of the Viewer, choose Fit All (**Figure 8.65**).

◆ Choose View > Level > Fit All.

✔ Tip

■ Choosing Fit All causes FCP to zoom out enough to show all objects in a multi-layered composited sequence, including those outside the screen area (**Figure 8.66**).

To view at actual size:

◆ From the Zoom pop-up menu at the top of the Viewer, choose 100%.

Figure 8.65 Select Fit All from the Zoom pop-up menu.

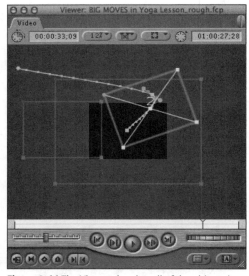

Figure 8.66 The Viewer showing all of the objects in a multi-layered composited sequence. Selecting Fit All is the only way to get the Viewer zoom level to go below 12.5 percent.

Wireframes in the Viewer

Wireframe and Image+Wireframe modes let you view schematic diagrams of the motion effects you apply to a clip or sequence. Wireframe modes are available in both the Canvas and Viewer. You can use the Viewer's View pop-up menu to switch on Wireframe mode, but you're more likely to use Wireframe mode in the Canvas. For details on Wireframe mode operation, see Chapter 14, "Compositing and Effects Overview."

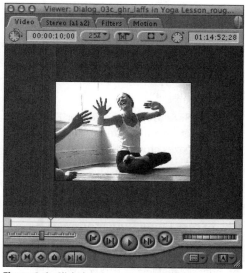

Figure 8.67 Click the Viewer to make it active.

To fit the window to the current clip size:

1. Make the Viewer active (**Figure 8.67**).

2. Double-click the Zoom In tool in the Tool palette (**Figure 8.68**).

   The Viewer window will adjust to fit the current clip size (**Figure 8.69**).

Figure 8.68 Double-click the Zoom In tool in the Tool palette.

Figure 8.69 The Viewer adjusts to fit the current clip image size.

Viewing overlays

Overlays are icons or text displayed on top of the video when the playhead is parked on a particular frame. Overlays indicate significant points, such as In and Out points, in a clip or sequence. Overlays appear only when the Viewer and Canvas are in Pause mode and are not rendered to output. Final Cut Pro displays the following overlays by default (**Figure 8.70**):

◆ **In and Out Points:** These icons appear when the playhead is positioned on the In or Out point frame.

◆ **Start and End of Media (not shown):** The filmstrip symbol along the left or right side of the video frame indicates the start or end of the video media.

◆ **Start and End of Edits (not shown):** An L shape at the lower left indicates the start of an edit, and a backward L shape at the lower right indicates the end of an edit. These icons appear only in the Canvas.

◆ **Marker:** A marker overlay appears as a translucent box displaying the marker's name and comment text.

The Title Safe, Action Safe, and Timecode overlays do not display by default, and they have their own display controls in the View menu:

◆ **Title Safe and Action Safe:** Title Safe and Action Safe boundaries are rectangular boxes around the edges of the video.

◆ **Timecode overlay:** The Timecode overlay displays the timecode locations for clips on all tracks at the playhead position.

The **Excess Luma indicator** overlays diagonal "zebra" striping on the areas of your image where luma values exceed the broadcast-legal level of 100 percent. The Excess Luma overlay is part of FCP's Range Check feature. For more information, see "About image quality measurement tools" in Chapter 16.

Figure 8.70 Viewer overlays.

Figure 8.71 Turn off all overlay displays in the Viewer by unchecking Show Overlays in the View pop-up menu.

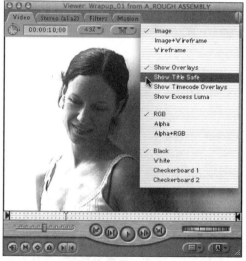

Figure 8.72 Choose Show Title Safe from the View pop-up menu to display the Title Safe overlay.

To view or hide overlays:

◆ Choose Show Overlays from the View pop-up menu at the top of the Viewer or Canvas to toggle the display of all overlays (**Figure 8.71**).

Viewing Title Safe and Action Safe boundaries

Most NTSC (National Television Standards Committee) television sets don't display the full video image on their screens. Use the Title Safe and Action Safe overlays to be sure that crucial parts of your composition or titles are not cut off at the edges when displayed on a television screen.

✔ Tip

■ Consumer TV sets may trim the edges of your video, but video for the Web displays the whole frame—so if you are aiming your show at both the Web and TV, you'll need to watch the edges of your frame.

To view or hide Title Safe and Action Safe boundaries:

Do one of the following:

◆ Choose View > Show Title Safe.

◆ From the View pop-up menu at the top of the Viewer, choose Show Title Safe (**Figure 8.72**).

◆ Choose Show Title Safe again to toggle the overlay.

ADJUSTING THE VIEWER DISPLAY

Viewing Timecode overlays

The Timecode overlay feature displays the timecode locations for clips on all tracks at the playhead position. All tracks containing clips with matching timecode are color-coded the same. You can display Timecode overlays in the Canvas or in the Viewer.

To view or hide Timecode overlays:

Do one of the following:

◆ Choose View > Timecode Overlays > Show (or Hide).

◆ From the View pop-up menu at the top of the Viewer, choose Show Timecode Overlays.

◆ Choose Show Timecode Overlays again to switch off the overlay (**Figure 8.73**).

Viewing with different backgrounds

If you are working with a clip that has an alpha channel—say some black generated text that you want to superimpose over video—you can change the default black background of your black text to white, in order to make the text more visible while you work with it. Translucent clips will be more visible if you choose a background that emphasizes them. When a clip is rendered, the background is always set to black.

To choose a background for viewing a clip:

◆ From the View menu, select a background from the Background submenu (**Figure 8.74**).

Figure 8.73 Choose Show Timecode Overlays again to toggle the Timecode overlay off.

Figure 8.74 Select a black background by choosing View > Background > Black.

BASIC EDITING

In this chapter, you'll learn not only basic procedures for performing edits in Final Cut Pro, including how to use the seven edit types available, but also the underlying concepts and protocols that govern editing: sequences, three-point editing, and multiple media tracks.

You assemble an edited sequence in the Timeline window, which displays a chronological view of a sequence. All the media elements you've assembled to create a sequence appear in the Timeline as elements that diagram the sequencing and layering of audio and video tracks. As you drag the playhead along the Timeline ruler, the current frame of the sequence updates in the Canvas window. The Canvas window is the viewer you use to play back the edited sequence you've assembled in the Timeline. (A more detailed discussion of Timeline and Canvas window operations appears in Chapter 10, "Editing in the Timeline and the Canvas.")

Once you've assembled a first draft of an edited sequence, known as a *rough cut* (isn't that a great expression?), you'll probably want to go back and *trim* (fine-tune) your edits. Final Cut Pro's edit trimming tools and techniques are outlined in Chapter 11, "Fine Cut: Trimming Edits."

If you need a review of FCP's project structure and media elements basics before the clips start flying, see Chapter 4, "Projects, Sequences, and Clips."

Basic Editing Overview

Figure 9.1 summarizes steps for performing a drag-and-drop-style edit that uses the Canvas overlay. The next section offers a step-by-step breakdown of the same edit.

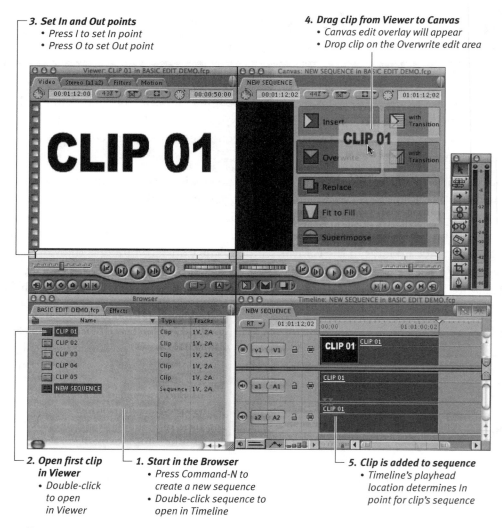

3. Set In and Out points
- *Press I to set In point*
- *Press O to set Out point*

4. Drag clip from Viewer to Canvas
- *Canvas edit overlay will appear*
- *Drop clip on the Overwrite edit area*

2. Open first clip in Viewer
- *Double-click to open in Viewer*

1. Start in the Browser
- *Press Command-N to create a new sequence*
- *Double-click sequence to open in Timeline*

5. Clip is added to sequence
- *Timeline's playhead location determines In point for clip's sequence*

Figure 9.1

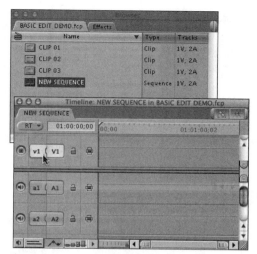

Figure 9.2 Double-click the new sequence's icon in the Browser to open it for editing. Examine the open sequence in the Timeline to check that destination tracks are assigned correctly and that the playhead is positioned at the beginning of the sequence.

Figure 9.3 Double-click the clip to open it in the Viewer; then mark In and Out points to specify which portion of the source clip you want to use.

Basic Editing Step-by-Step

Here's a step-by-step breakdown of a simple rough-assembly-style edit in Final Cut Pro. After you've reviewed this basic editing procedure, find out how to perform more specific types of edits in the sections that follow.

To add the first clip to your sequence:

1. In the Browser, press Command-N to create a new sequence.

2. Double-click the new sequence to open it in the Canvas and the Timeline (**Figure 9.2**).

   The new, empty sequence opens in the Timeline window. The Timeline's playhead is positioned at the beginning of the sequence.

   Before you insert a clip in a sequence, you need to check the target tracks (the destination tracks for your clip in the sequence).

3. In the Timeline, check the destination track assignment for your first clip. In a new sequence, default destination tracks will already be assigned to V1, A1, and A2. If necessary, you can target different destination tracks by clicking the target track controls.

4. In the Browser, double-click the first clip you want to insert in your new sequence; that clip opens in the Viewer.

5. In the Viewer, select the portion of the clip you want to use in the sequence by setting In and Out points (**Figure 9.3**). (See "Working with In and Out Points" in Chapter 8.)

continues on next page

6. Click the Viewer's image area and drag the clip to the Canvas window.

The Canvas edit overlay menu appears.

7. Drop the clip on the Overwrite edit area (**Figure 9.4**). (Overwrite is the default edit type in FCP unless you specify another type.)

The clip will be inserted at the beginning of your new sequence (**Figure 9.5**).

Figure 9.4 Drag the source clip from the Viewer to the Canvas edit overlay; then drop the clip on the Overwrite edit area.

Figure 9.5 The source clip has been added to the sequence. The Timeline playhead's position was used as the sequence In point, so the clip's In point has been placed at the beginning of the sequence.

Many Ways to Make an Edit

Dragging your source clip to the Canvas edit overlay is just one way to execute an edit. Once you have defined your edit points, you can also do the following:

◆ Drag the clip directly from the Viewer to the Timeline (**Figure 9.6**).

◆ Drag one or more clips directly from the Browser to the Timeline (now *that's* a rough edit).

◆ Use a keyboard shortcut to perform the edit. The keyboard shortcut for each edit type is listed in Appendix A.

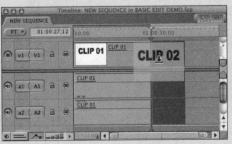

Figure 9.6 You can edit by dragging a clip directly from the Viewer or Browser and dropping it into a sequence in the Timeline.

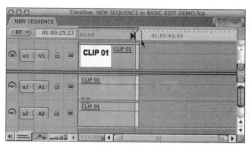

Figure 9.7 Position the Timeline playhead where you want your second clip to start, then press I to set a sequence In point.

Figure 9.8 The second source clip, displayed in the Viewer with In and Out points set.

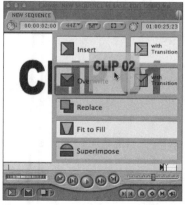

Figure 9.9 Drag the second source clip to the Canvas edit overlay; then drop the clip on the Overwrite edit area.

To insert additional clips:

1. In the Timeline, park the playhead on the frame where you want your new clip to start. You can press I to set a sequence In point on that frame, but it's not required (**Figure 9.7**).

2. In the Viewer, set In and Out points on your second clip (**Figure 9.8**).

3. Drag the clip from the image area of the Viewer to the Canvas window.

   The Canvas edit overlay menu will appear.

4. Drop the clip on the Overwrite edit area (**Figure 9.9**).

   The second clip will be inserted starting where you set the sequence In point (**Figure 9.10**).

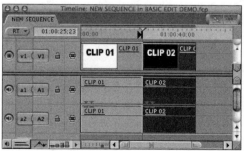

Figure 9.10 The sequence displayed in the Timeline, with the second clip inserted at the sequence In point.

FCP Protocol: Three-Point Editing

In a three-point edit, you can define any three points of an edit, and Final Cut Pro will calculate the fourth point for you. Here's an example:

1. Specify In and Out points for your source clip.

2. Park the playhead in the Canvas at the sequence In point (the point where you want your new clip to start).

When you insert the new clip into your sequence, Final Cut Pro uses the duration of the new clip insert to calculate the sequence Out point.

At least three edit points must be set in the Viewer and Canvas to complete an edit. But if you specify fewer than three points and begin an edit, FCP will calculate your edit based on the following protocols:

◆ If no In or Out point is set in the Canvas, the Canvas playhead location is used as the sequence In point.

◆ If no In or Out point is set in the source, FCP assumes that you want to use the entire source clip. The playhead's location in the sequence (Timeline and Canvas) is used as the sequence In point. FCP calculates the Out point for the sequence.

◆ If one edit point (In or Out) is set in a source clip, the second point is the beginning or the end of the media (depending on whether the user-defined point is an In or an Out point). The Canvas playhead is used as the sequence In point, and FCP calculates the Out point.

There are three exceptions to the three-point editing rules:

◆ Fit to Fill editing requires four user-specified points because FCP adjusts the speed of the specified source clip to fill a specified sequence duration.

◆ Replace editing ignores the In and Out points set in the source clip and uses the boundaries of the clip under the Canvas playhead as sequence In and Out points. Replace edits affect the target track media. To replace an audio track, turn off targeting for all video tracks.

◆ If In and Out points are set for both the source clip and the sequence, FCP ignores the source clip's Out point and uses the clip's In point and the sequence In and Out points.

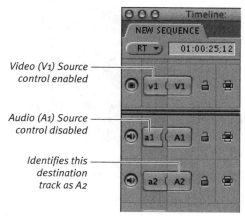

Video (V1) Source control enabled

Audio (A1) Source control disabled

Identifies this destination track as A2

Figure 9.11 The target track controls in the Timeline. A control's left side identifies which source clip track is assigned to this destination track; the right side identifies the destination track by number. Timeline base tracks are enabled by default; you can click either side of the control to *disconnect* (disable) a track.

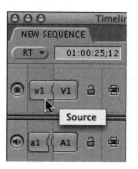

Figure 9.12 Set a target track by connecting a video Source control. The Source control is connected to the destination indicator when the track is targeted.

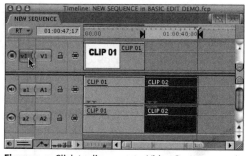

Figure 9.13 Click to disconnect a Video Source control. Audio tracks remain targeted.

Specifying target tracks

Each time you add clips to a sequence, you can specify which tracks the media will occupy. You specify target tracks using the Timeline's target track controls (**Figure 9.11**): the lozenge-shaped icons located on the left in the Timeline. The Destination (right) side of the control identifies the track. Set the Source control (the left side of the control) to specify which source track is assigned to that destination track and whether the track is enabled to receive a source clip. You can target one video target track plus one audio target track for each audio track in your source clip.

For more information on targeting and mapping track assignments, see "Mapping Timeline target track assignments" in Chapter 10.

To select target tracks in the Timeline:

◆ In the Timeline, click the target track control on the left side of the track you want to use.

The Source control is connected to the Destination track indicator when a track is targeted (**Figure 9.12**).

To use audio only from an audio+video clip:

◆ Click the left (Source) side to disconnect the target indicator of the video track before you perform your edit (**Figure 9.13**).

To use one channel of two-channel audio from the source clip:

◆ Click the left (Source) side to disconnect the target indicator of the track you want to exclude (**Figure 9.14**).

✔ Tips

■ Once you've used the target track controls to route your source clips to their proper tracks, you might want to lock the tracks to prevent further changes to edited clips on those tracks. See "Lock vs. Target" in Chapter 10 to learn the hows and whys of track locking.

■ When you are ready for big-time multi-track editing, be aware that FCP offers a raft of keyboard shortcuts for target track selection. Check them out in Appendix A, "Keyboard Shortcuts."

Moving the playhead

You can jump the playhead to the edit point of your choice with a single keystroke or mouse click. Most of these shortcuts work in the Viewer as well.

To move the playhead to the In point:

◆ Press Shift-I; or Shift-click the Mark In button.

To move the playhead to the Out point:

◆ Press Shift-O; or Shift-click the Mark Out button.

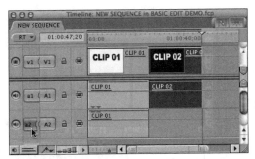

Figure 9.14 With A2 targeting turned off, channel 2 audio is excluded from the sequence.

✔ Tips

■ If you've been wishing that FCP would automatically activate the Timeline window whenever you perform an edit, wish no more. Use a keyboard shortcut to perform your edit, and FCP automatically highlights the Timeline after completing the edit. If you want the Viewer to stay activated at the end of an edit, drag the clip to the Canvas overlay or directly to the Timeline to perform your edit.

■ Next obvious question: Now that Apple's default keyboard shortcuts for their Expose feature override FCP's keyboard shortcuts for the three most common edits (F9 for Insert, F10 for Overwrite, F11 for Replace), how do you restore editing shortcuts in FCP? You have a choice: You can reassign Expose keys in the Expose pane of System Preferences, or you can reassign the edit keys. Choose Tools > Keyboard Layout > Customize to open FCP's Keyboard Layout window.

To jump the playhead to an adjacent edit point:

Do one of the following:

◆ Click the Previous Edit or the Next Edit button in the transport controls.

◆ Press the Up or the Down Arrow key.

◆ Open the Mark menu and choose from the Next or Previous submenu.

◆ Press Option-E (to go to the previous edit point) or Shift-E (to go to the next edit point).

✔ Tip

■ If you need to define the edit points for a clip, you'll find information on marking In and Out points on a source clip in Chapter 8, "Working with Clips in the Viewer."

FCP Protocol: Editing Multiple Tracks in Final Cut Pro

Final Cut Pro sequences can have multiple video and audio tracks. The first video clip you add to a sequence will be the base layer (V1). Video frames you place on track 2 (V2) are superimposed over any video frames at the same point in time on track 1. In a sequence with multiple layers, the base track becomes the background, and media on each higher-numbered track obscures the media on tracks below it. The result appears in the Canvas (after a little rendering).

Audio tracks A1 and A2 are the designated base tracks for stereo audio. Final Cut Pro can mix and play back several audio tracks in a sequence in real time.

How Many Audio Tracks?

The number of audio tracks you may mix in real time depends on your Macintosh's configuration (available RAM, processor speed, hard drive data transfer rate, and so on), the number of audio files requiring real-time sample rate conversion or filtering, and how many simultaneous audio transitions you have included in your sequence. You can specify how many tracks you want FCP to attempt to handle in real time by setting the Real-Time Audio Mixing preference (see "Specifying User Preferences and System Settings" in Chapter 3). However, increasing your real-time audio track budget is no guarantee that you'll be able to play back the number of tracks you specify, and if you set this preference too high, you could trigger dropped frames during playback or dropouts in audio.

Eight tracks of real-time audio is the FCP default setup, but you can have up to 99 tracks in a sequence.

In calculating the number of audio tracks you need for a sequence, note that each simultaneous audio crossfade or transition increases the track count by one. So if your sequence requires seven audio tracks, adding a pair of crossfades increases the count to nine tracks. It may also require rendering to preview.

You can reduce your audio track overhead by choosing Sequence > Render Only > Mixdown. Mixdown renders all the audio tracks in a sequence along with their transitions, and it filters and consolidates them into one render file. For more information on working with audio in FCP, see Chapter 12, "Audio Tools and Techniques."

Using FCP's Many Edit Types

One powerful editing option unique to Final Cut Pro is the Canvas edit overlay. When you drag a clip directly into the Canvas image area, the Canvas edit overlay appears with fields for each type of edit (**Figure 9.15**). Select the type of edit you want to perform by dropping your clip on the corresponding overlay area. The default type is an Overwrite edit.

You can also perform edits in the Canvas by dragging your source clip to one of the edit buttons at the bottom of the Canvas window.

Final Cut Pro offers many types of edits and many ways to perform those edits. Keep reading to find a rundown of the types of edits you can perform in FCP, along with variations they impose on the basic editing procedure.

Figure 9.15 The Canvas edit overlay allows drag-and-drop editing for seven types of edits.

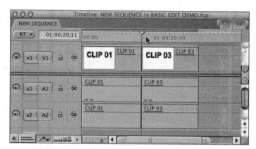

Figure 9.16 Position the Timeline playhead to set your sequence In point.

Figure 9.17 Drag the source clip from the Viewer to the Canvas edit overlay; then drop the clip on the Insert edit area.

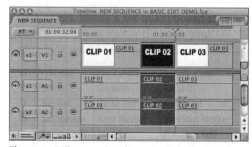

Figure 9.18 The completed Insert edit in the Timeline. Clip 02, inserted between Clip 01 and Clip 03, pushes Clip 03 to the right.

Insert edit

When you perform an Insert edit, the sequence clips at the In point move to the right to make room for the new source clip.

✔ Tips

- Insert edits can also be performed by dragging the source clip directly to the Timeline. See "Performing Edits in the Timeline," later in this chapter.

- Heads up! When you perform an insert edit, any sequence clips that span the In point are automatically split to accommodate the new clip.

To perform an Insert edit:

1. Set the sequence In point by positioning the Timeline (or Canvas) playhead where you want the edit to occur (**Figure 9.16**).

2. Drag the source clip from the Viewer to the Insert edit area in the Canvas overlay (**Figure 9.17**).

   The source clip is inserted into the sequence (**Figure 9.18**).

Overwrite edit

In an Overwrite edit, the source clip over-writes sequence clips past the sequence In point. Overwrite edits use the source In and Out points to calculate the edit duration, replacing sequence material with the incoming source clip, with no time shift in the existing sequence.

✔ Tip

■ You can also perform Overwrite edits by dragging the source clip directly to the Timeline. See "Performing Edits in the Timeline," later in this chapter.

To perform an Overwrite edit:

1. Set the sequence In point by positioning the Timeline (or Canvas) playhead where you want the edit to occur (**Figure 9.19**).

2. Drag the source clip from the Viewer to the Overwrite edit area in the Canvas overlay (**Figure 9.20**).

   The source clip is added to the sequence, overwriting any existing sequence material on the targeted tracks that falls between the sequence In and Out points (**Figure 9.21**).

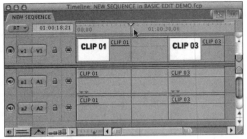

Figure 9.19 Position the Timeline playhead to set your sequence In point.

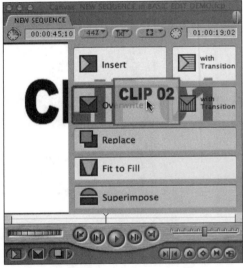

Figure 9.20 Drag the source clip from the Viewer to the Canvas edit overlay; then drop the clip on the Overwrite edit area.

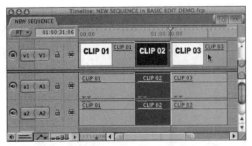

Figure 9.21 The completed Overwrite edit in the Timeline. Clip 02 overwrites the portion of Clip 01 that extends beyond the sequence In point, without moving Clip 03.

Replace edit

A Replace edit replaces the contents of a sequence clip with source clip material.

The Replace edit uses the playhead position in the Viewer, not the source In and Out points, to calculate the Replace edit; your source In and Out points will be ignored. If you don't set sequence In and Out points, FCP uses the boundaries of the clip under the Timeline playhead.

You can use a Replace edit to simply replace a shot in a sequence with footage from another shot with the same duration. Replace editing can also be a powerful tool for matching action; for example, when you're cutting between multiple-camera coverage of different angles on the same action (in your big-budget dreams). Park the Canvas playhead at the point in the action that you want to match in your source clip. Find the source clip frame that matches the action in the sequence frame. Mark In and Out points in the Canvas to select the section of the sequence you want to replace with the new material. The material between the sequence In and Out points is replaced by corresponding material from the source clip on either side of the frame that was matched.

Hate Your Edit? Do Undo

Undo is one of the great technological contributions to civilization. Especially when you're editing.

As you build your edited sequence, keep in mind that the fastest way to repair your sequence after you've done something brilliant but basically bad is to use the Undo feature. You can set your FCP user preferences to allow up to 99 Undos—10 is the default.

Undo is particularly useful when you've just performed an unsuccessful (or accidental) Overwrite edit and replaced some clips in your sequence. Deleting the clips that wiped out part of your sequence won't restore your original footage, but if you Undo (Command-Z) your Overwrite edit, your sequence footage will be restored.

So, go forth and be bold. Experiment with your edit. You can always Undo.

To perform a Replace edit:

1. Position the Viewer playhead on the frame you want to match with a frame in the Canvas (**Figure 9.22**).

2. Position the Canvas playhead on the frame you want to match with the one selected in the Viewer. If you want to specify the duration of the replacement clip, set sequence In and Out points (**Figure 9.23**).

Figure 9.22 Position the Viewer playhead on the frame you want to match with a frame in the Canvas.

Figure 9.23 Position the Canvas playhead on the frame you want to match with a frame in the Viewer.

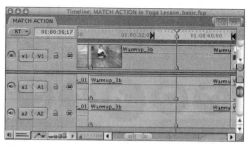

Figure 9.24 The sequence before the Replace edit in the Timeline.

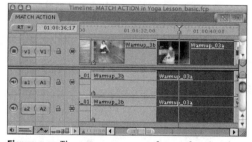

Figure 9.25 The same sequence after performing the Replace edit. The new clip replaces the old, using the match frame you selected as the sync point.

3. Drag the source clip from the Viewer to the Replace edit area in the Canvas overlay.

Figure 9.24 shows the Timeline before the Replace edit; **Figure 9.25** shows the Timeline after the Replace edit.

✔ Tip

■ Use the Replace edit technique to replace a clip with an offset copy of itself. This is a shortcut to adjust the timing of action in a clip or to sync action to music.

What's a Backtime Edit?

Say you're filling a gap in your edited music video sequence. The In point of the clip you want to use is not critical, but you know exactly where you want this clip to end—and you want the clip to fit your gap exactly. In this case, set up a *backtime* edit by marking the gap as your sequence In and Out points, along with the source Out point you identified in your source clip. FCP will calculate the other In point and back your clip in so it fits the gap perfectly.

Fit to Fill edit

In a Fit to Fill edit, the speed of the source clip adjusts to fill the duration specified by the sequence In and Out points; you must render the clip before you can play it back.

To perform a Fit to Fill edit:

1. In the Timeline, set sequence In and Out points to define the sequence section you want to fill (**Figure 9.26**).

2. In the Viewer, set source In and Out points to define the part of the source clip you want to speed-modify so it fits between your edit points in the sequence (**Figure 9.27**).

3. Drag the source clip in the Viewer to the Fit to Fill edit area in the Canvas overlay; or press Shift-F11.

   The source clip is speed-modified to fit between the sequence In and Out points (**Figure 9.28**).

✔ Tip

■ You've just added a clip to your sequence—but it's too short to fill the gap you're trying to fill. Here's a slick trick: Perform Fit to Fill on a clip that's already edited into your sequence by double-clicking the clip to open it in the Viewer, then dragging it to the Fit to Fill edit area. Voilà! Perfect fit.

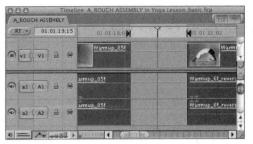

Figure 9.26 Setting the sequence In and Out points defines the section you want to fill.

Figure 9.27 Marking a source Out point in the Viewer. Setting source In and Out points defines the section you want to fit into the sequence.

Figure 9.28 The source clip is speed-modified to fit between the sequence In and Out points. Note that the speed change is indicated on the clip.

Figure 9.29 Using the Mark Clip keyboard shortcut (X) is a fast way to mark In and Out points at the clip boundaries of a clip you want to superimpose over.

Figure 9.30 In the Viewer, set a source In or Out point to specify the part of the source clip that you want to superimpose on the sequence.

Figure 9.31 Drag the source clip from the Viewer to the Canvas edit overlay; then drop the clip on the Superimpose edit area.

Superimpose edit

In a Superimpose edit, the source clip is placed on a new track above the target track, starting at the sequence In point. The target track does not change. If the clip has audio, the source audio is added to new tracks below the target audio track.

To perform a Superimpose edit:

1. Position the Canvas playhead or set a sequence In point where you want the source clip to start (**Figure 9.29**).

2. In the Viewer, set a source In or Out point to define the part of the source clip you want to add to the sequence (**Figure 9.30**).

3. Drag the source clip from the Viewer to the Superimpose edit area in the Canvas overlay (**Figure 9.31**); or press F12.

   The source clip is placed on a new track above the target track, starting at the sequence In point (**Figure 9.32**).

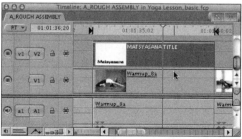

Figure 9.32 The source clip is placed on a new track above the target track, starting at the sequence In point.

Transition edits

FCP offers two types of edits that incorporate transitions: Insert with Transition and Overwrite with Transition. A transition edit automatically places your default transition at the head of the edit. When using either of the transition edit types, you'll need enough extra frames in each clip at the edit point where the transition is applied so that you can create the transition. (Each clip requires additional frames equal to half of the default transition's duration; see Chapter 13, "Creating Transitions," for more on using transitions.)

To perform a Transition edit:

1. Set the sequence In point by positioning the Timeline (or Canvas) playhead where you want the edit to occur (**Figure 9.33**).

2. In the Viewer, set source In and Out points to define the part of the source clip you want to add to the sequence (**Figure 9.34**).

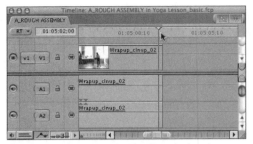

Figure 9.33 Positioning the Timeline playhead to set a sequence In point.

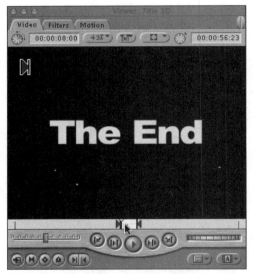

Figure 9.34 In the Viewer, set source In and Out points to specify the part of the source clip that you want to use.

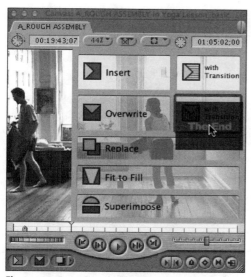

Figure 9.35 Drag the source clip from the Viewer to the Canvas edit overlay; then drop it on either of the Transition edit areas.

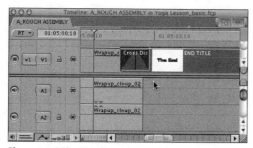

Figure 9.36 The Timeline, showing the source clip inserted into the sequence with the default transition at the head.

3. Drag the source clip from the Viewer to either the Insert with Transition or the Overwrite with Transition edit area in the Canvas overlay (**Figure 9.35**).

The source clip is inserted in the sequence with your default transition applied at the sequence In point (**Figure 9.36**).

✔ Tip

■ Once you've customized a transition in your sequence, you can select it in the Timeline, drag it to your Favorites folder in the Browser, and then set it as the default transition. It's so easy to set up a customized default transition that it's worth doing so even if you're building a fairly short sequence. Learn how to set a custom default transition in Chapter 13, "Creating Transitions."

Deleting clips from a sequence

Two types of edits can be used to remove material from a sequence:

◆ **Lift** removes the selected material, leaving a gap.

◆ **Ripple Delete** removes the selected material and closes the gap.

To perform a Lift edit:

Do one of the following:

◆ Select the clip in the Timeline and press Delete.

◆ Select the clip in the Timeline; then choose Sequence > Lift.

◆ Select the clip in the Timeline and press Command-X (Cut).

◆ Control-click the selected clip in the Timeline; then choose Cut from the shortcut menu. (Cut also lets you paste the deleted clip in another location in the sequence.)

Figure 9.37 shows a sequence in the Timeline before a Lift edit; **Figure 9.38** shows the same sequence after a Lift edit.

Figure 9.37 A clip selected in the Timeline. Press Delete to perform a Lift edit by deleting the clip from the sequence; or press Command-X to cut the clip for pasting elsewhere.

Figure 9.38 The sequence after a Lift edit. The rest of the sequence clips hold their positions.

Figure 9.39 Control-click the selected sequence clip to access the shortcut menu.

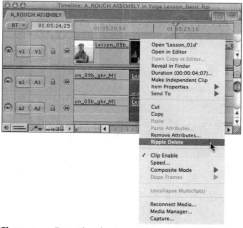

Figure 9.40 From the shortcut menu, choose Ripple Delete.

Figure 9.41 The sequence after a Ripple Delete edit. Material to the right of the deleted clip has been pulled up to close the gap.

To perform a Ripple Delete edit:

Do one of the following:

◆ Select the clip in the Timeline and press Shift-Delete.

◆ Select the clip in the Timeline; then choose Sequence > Ripple Delete.

◆ Control-click the selected clip in the Timeline (**Figure 9.39**); then choose Ripple Delete from the shortcut menu (**Figure 9.40**).

The clip is deleted from the sequence, and the material on all unlocked tracks to the right of the sequence pulls up to close the gap (**Figure 9.41**).

✔ Tip

■ You can delete a precisely defined section of a sequence by setting sequence In and Out points to mark the section you want to remove, and then pressing Delete to lift the section, or pressing Shift-Delete to ripple delete it.

USING FCP'S MANY EDIT TYPES

Performing Edits in the Timeline

Editing in the Timeline can be a faster way to go, particularly when you're in the early stages of assembly.

You have a number of ways to control the size and time scale of the Timeline window. You need the Timeline's big picture view when you deploy multiple tracks of visual or sound effects, but you can also zoom way in when performing precise work. See Chapter 10, "Editing in the Timeline and the Canvas," for details.

◆ You can assemble a sequence by dragging clips directly to the Timeline from the Browser or Viewer.

◆ You can use the Browser Sort function to sort your takes by timecode or by shot number, and then drag a whole group of clips from the Browser directly to the Timeline. FCP will place the clips in the Timeline based on your Browser sort order.

◆ You can construct a storyboard in the Browser's Large Icon view (**Figure 9.42**), and then drag all the clips into the Timeline (**Figure 9.43**). If the Browser tab from which you drag the clips is in Icon mode, the clips are placed in storyboard order, from left to right and top to bottom (**Figure 9.44**).

◆ You can designate target tracks in an edit just by dragging a source clip directly to the destination track.

◆ Drag a source clip to the space above your existing tracks, and FCP will automatically create a new track.

Figure 9.42 Using Large Icon view in the Browser, arrange clip icons in storyboard order.

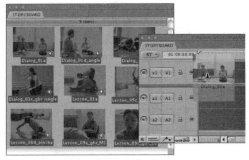

Figure 9.43 Select all clips in the Browser and drag them to the Timeline.

Figure 9.44 The sequence assembles clips in storyboard order.

Figure 9.45 Dragging a clip to the upper third of the Timeline track performs an Insert edit.

Figure 9.46 Dragging a clip to the lower two-thirds of the Timeline track performs an Overwrite edit.

Figure 9.47 When you drop a clip directly onto the Timeline, the Canvas displays details about the two clips adjacent to your edit point.

To perform an Insert edit:

◆ Drag the source clip from the Viewer or Browser to the upper third of the Timeline track (**Figure 9.45**).

The pointer changes to indicate the type of edit.

To perform an Overwrite edit:

◆ Drag the source clip from the Viewer or Browser to the lower two-thirds of the Timeline track (**Figure 9.46**).

✔ Tips

■ If you drag a clip to the Timeline when it is set to the smallest Timeline track size, you'll perform an Overwrite edit. Hold down the Option key to perform an Insert edit.

■ When you drag a clip from the Browser onto a clip or transition in the Timeline, a two-up display appears in the Canvas. This two-up display shows the frame just before your insert on the left, and it shows the frame just after your insert on the right. The names of the sequence clips adjacent to your edit point appear at the top of each display, and the timecode of the displayed frames appears at the bottom (**Figure 9.47**).

Performing split edits

A split edit sets different In and Out points for video and audio in a single clip (**Figure 9.48**). Split edits are commonly used in cutting synchronized dialogue scenes.

To mark a split edit:

1. With the clip open in the Viewer, position the playhead where you want the video to begin.

2. Control-click the Scrubber bar; then choose Mark Split > Video In from the shortcut menu (**Figure 9.49**).

3. Reposition the playhead at your desired Out point and choose Mark Split > Video Out from the shortcut menu.

4. Repeat the process to set your Audio In and Out points (**Figure 9.50**). You could also switch to your clip's Audio tab and mark the audio there.

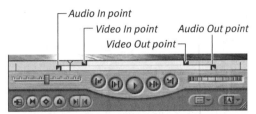

Audio In point
Video In point   Audio Out point
Video Out point

Figure 9.48 Split edit points as they appear in the Viewer's Scrubber bar.

Figure 9.49 Control-click anywhere on the Scrubber bar to call up the shortcut menu; then choose Mark Split > Video In.

Figure 9.50 Using the Scrubber shortcut menu to mark the Audio Out point. (Alternatively, you can switch to the clip's Audio tab to do this.)

Figure 9.51 Moving split In points by dragging them in the Scrubber. The Audio and Video In points will shift in tandem. Video edit points appear in the top half of the Scrubber; audio points appear in the bottom half.

Figure 9.52 Shift-dragging moves all four points at once. The timecode readout in the Viewer displays the current In point location of the point that you drag.

To move split edit points:

◆ Open the clip in the Viewer. In the Scrubber bar, click and drag either the In points or the Out points to a new position.

   The video and audio edit points move in tandem in a split edit (**Figure 9.51**).

To slip all split edit points at once:

◆ In the Scrubber bar, press Shift while dragging any of the edit points.

   All the edit points *slip*, or move in unison (**Figure 9.52**).

   The respective video and audio durations specified in the split edit don't change, but the frames that are included in the marked clip shift.

✔ Tip

■ As you slip a split edit, the updated In point frame with the timecode for the edit point you selected displays on the Viewer image, and the edit's Out point frame with timecode displays on the Canvas. Awesome.

Tips for Quicker Split Edits

Split edits are commonly used in cutting synchronized dialogue scenes. You can mark a split edit before you insert a clip into a sequence for the first time (as shown here), but a common split edit approach to a dialogue sequence starts by making straight cuts of both video and audio tracks based on the rhythm of the dialogue and then going back and using the Roll tool to adjust the edit points on the video track only. Hold down the Option key as you click the edit point to select only the video track of your clip. Check out "Tips on Tools" in Chapter 11 for more info.

Another approach is to include only video or only audio in your edit by targeting only the video or audio track in the Timeline.

As you play back your footage, you can use one of these keyboard shortcuts to mark a split edit on the fly:

◆ **Mark Video In:** Control-I

◆ **Mark Video Out:** Control-O

◆ **Mark Audio In:** Command-Option-I

◆ **Mark Audio Out:** Command-Option-O

To move only one edit point in a split edit:

◆ In the Scrubber bar, press Option while dragging the edit point you want to modify (**Figure 9.53**).

A display pops up as you drag to indicate the duration of the offset between Video In and Audio In, or Video Out and Audio Out. The Scrubber bar in the Viewer updates to reflect the new edit points.

To remove a split edit point:

Do one of the following:

◆ In the Scrubber bar, Control-click; then choose Clear Split and, from the shortcut submenu, select the point you want to clear (**Figure 9.54**).

◆ Press Option I to remove both Audio and Video In points; press Option-O to remove both Audio and Video Out points.

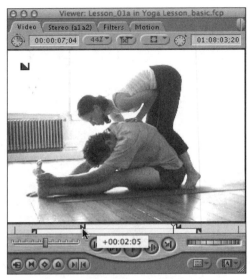

Figure 9.53 Option-click and drag to shift only one edit point in a split edit. The pop-up display shows the offset duration between Video and Audio In points.

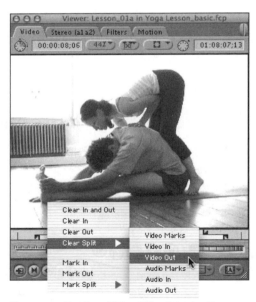

Figure 9.54 Clearing a Video Out point using the Scrubber shortcut menu. Control-click the Scrubber bar to access this menu.

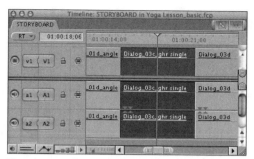

Figure 9.55 In the Timeline, place the playhead over the clip that you want to use to mark the sequence.

Figure 9.56 Check that the selected clip is on the lowest-numbered Auto Select–enabled track.

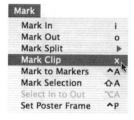

Figure 9.57 Choose Mark > Mark Clip.

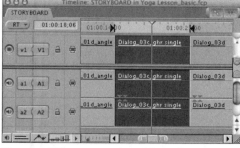

Figure 9.58 The sequence In and Out points are set to match the boundaries of the clip.

Shortcuts for Marking Sequence Edit Points

Use the same commands and keyboard shortcuts that you use to mark In and Out points in the Viewer to mark your sequence In and Out points in the Timeline and the Canvas.

FCP also offers a couple of handy commands specifically for marking edit points in a sequence:

◆ Use the Mark Clip command to set the sequence In and Out points to match the edit points of a particular clip in the sequence.

◆ Use Mark Selection to set the sequence In and Out points to match a multiple-clip selection or a selection that includes only part of a clip.

To use the Mark Clip command:

1. Place the playhead over a clip in the Timeline (**Figure 9.55**).

2. Check that your selected clip's track is the lowest-numbered Auto Select–enabled track (**Figure 9.56**).

3. Choose Mark > Mark Clip (**Figure 9.57**); or press X.

   The sequence In and Out points are set to match the boundaries of the clip (**Figure 9.58**).

   continues on next page

✔ Tips

- Mark Clip is a quick way to mark sequence In and Out points if you want to super-impose something over a particular clip.

- FCP automatically selects sequence material between sequence In and Out points on all tracks with Auto Select controls enabled. For more information, see "To use Auto Select to select items between In and Out points" in Chapter 10.

To use the Mark Selection command:

1. Make a selection in the Timeline. The selection can range from an entire sequence to a part of a single clip (**Figure 9.59**). See Chapter 10, "Editing in the Timeline and the Canvas," for information on using the Tool palette's selection tools.

2. Choose Mark > Mark Selection (**Figure 9.60**).

   The sequence In and Out points are set to the boundaries of the selection (**Figure 9.61**).

Figure 9.59 Selecting a region of the sequence. Use Range Select from the toolbar if you want to include just part of a clip.

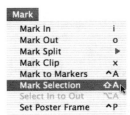

Figure 9.60 Choose Mark > Mark Selection.

Figure 9.61 Sequence In and Out points are set to match the boundaries of the selected region.

Figure 9.62 Park the Canvas playhead on the frame that you want to match in the source clip.

Figure 9.63 FCP displays the match frame for the frame at the playhead position on the lowest-numbered Auto Select–enabled track.

Locating a Match Frame

Final Cut Pro offers two commands you can use to locate the source clip for any frame in your sequence. Match Frame quickly locates the source for a clip you've used, which is convenient when you'd like to select another part of that clip for use elsewhere in your sequence.

◆ View > Match Frame > Master Clip locates the master clip affiliated with your sequence clip in the Browser and opens it in the Viewer. The playhead is positioned on the frame matching the sequence frame, and the master clip's In and Out points are matched to those in the sequence copy of the clip.

◆ View > Match Frame > Source File locates the original source clip in the Browser and opens it in the Viewer, but does not set matching In and Out points. Use Match Frame > Source File when you're looking for footage that's located in the original source file on disk, but outside the boundaries of your master clip.

To find a source frame of video matching a sequence clip frame:

1. In the Canvas or the Timeline, park the playhead on the frame for which you want to locate the source clip (**Figure 9.62**).

2. Set the track containing the clip to be the lowest-numbered Auto Select–enabled track (**Figure 9.63**).

continues on next page

3. *Do one of the following:*

◆ Choose View > Match Frame > Master Clip (**Figure 9.64**); or press F to locate the master clip affiliated with your sequence clip.

◆ Choose View > Match Frame > Source File; or press Command-Option-F to locate the original source clip for your sequence clip.

The matching clip opens in the Viewer. The current frame in the Viewer matches the current frame on the target track in the Canvas (**Figure 9.65**).

Figure 9.64 Choose View > Match Frame > Master Clip.

Figure 9.65 The master clip that matches the sequence clip opens in the Viewer. The frame displayed in the Viewer matches the current frame displayed in the Canvas.

Basic Multiclip Editing

Final Cut Pro's multiclip editing system inaugurates a whole new style of cutting designed to make it easy to organize and edit footage derived from multiple camera shoots. FCP's multiclip structuring offers enormous flexibility—powerful automated multiclip sequencing for multicamera footage synchronized to a single master timecode source during shooting, plus a variety of manual synchronizing methods. FCP's manual methods allow you to synchronize multiple camera footage shot without the benefit of master timecode.

Once your material has been organized into a multiclip file structure, it's possible to load that multiclip into the Viewer and edit it into a sequence in much the same way as you would a regular clip, but you also have the option of using FCP's Multiclip Playback editing mode to cut between multiclip angles on the fly (**Figure 9.66**). FCP's multiclip editing system has a lot of depth; you can add, subtract, or replace angles, resynchronize angles, cut audio and video separately, trim edits, and apply effects. For more information, see "Working With Multiclips" on page II-241 of Apple's *Final Cut Pro User Manual* PDF.

 On Peachpit.com

"Basic Multiclip Editing," a 12-page PDF, is available at:
www.peachpit.com/finalcutpro6vqp

Figure 9.66 Final Cut Pro's Multiclip Playback editing mode brings real-time multiclip editing, a new editing methodology, and a new look to the interface.

Editing in the Timeline and the Canvas 10

The previous chapter introduced basic editing procedures in Final Cut Pro; this chapter outlines your display, navigation, and editing options in the Timeline and the Canvas windows. You'll also learn about the Tool palette, a deceptively tiny floating toolbar that's packed with editing, selection, and display tools. The Tool palette is key to efficient workflow in the Timeline.

The Timeline and the Canvas work together, but they present two different views of your edited sequence. The Timeline displays a chronological diagram of all the clips in your sequence; the Canvas is a monitor where you view playback of an edited sequence. That's why the Canvas and Timeline playheads are locked together. The Canvas always displays the frame at the current position of the Timeline's playhead.

When you open a sequence, it appears in the Timeline and the Canvas simultaneously. Any changes you make to the sequence in the Timeline reflect in the Canvas playback, and any changes you make in the Canvas reflect in the Timeline display.

Double-clicking a sequence clip in the Timeline opens it in the Viewer; sequence clips are identified in the Viewer by two lines of dots in the Scrubber bar. Why the identification? Remember that when you insert a clip into a sequence, you are inserting a copy of the clip from the Browser. If you change the sequence version of the clip, your changes will be reflected in the sequence only. Opening the same clip directly from the Browser in a Viewer window opens a different copy of the clip. If you change the Browser copy (for example, by making audio-level adjustments or adding motion effects), those changes will not affect the copy of the clip in the sequence. It's important to understand the difference between working with clips that you have opened from the Browser and clips that you have opened from the Timeline. (For more information, see "FCP Protocol: Clips and Sequences" in Chapter 4.)

Anatomy of the Canvas

The Canvas window (**Figure 10.1**) looks like the Viewer and has many of the same controls. You can use the controls in the Canvas window to play edited sequences, mark sequence In and Out points, add sequence markers, and set keyframes. See "Anatomy of the Viewer" in Chapter 8 for a detailed description of Canvas tools and interface elements. In addition to the Viewer-like marking controls, the Canvas features a pop-up overlay where you can perform various types of drag-and-drop edits. The Canvas edit overlay appears only when you drag a clip from the Browser or the Viewer to the Canvas.

You can also use the Canvas window to plot out effects. Learn about applying filters and effects in Chapter 14, "Compositing and Effects Overview."

✔ Tips

- You can use tooltips to identify most of the control buttons in the window. Place your pointer over a button and then wait a moment, and a name label will appear. (Enable tooltips in the User Preferences window if they're not showing up.)

- Two playback options don't have interface controls: Play Every Frame (Option-P) and Loop Playback (Control-L).

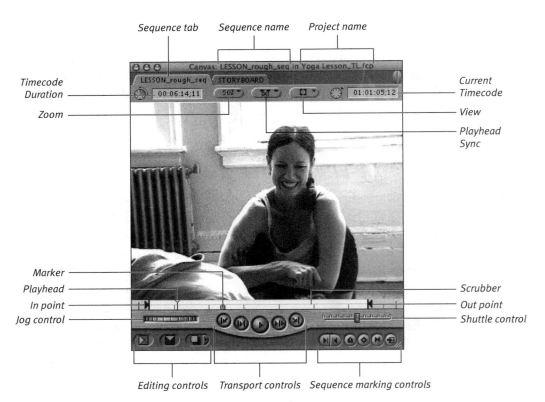

Figure 10.1 An overview of the Canvas window. Use the Canvas to play sequences, perform edits, and set keyframes.

Figure 10.2 The Timecode Duration display.

Figure 10.3 The Current Timecode display.

Figure 10.4 The Current Timecode pop-up menu. Select a sequence marker from the list to jump to that marker's location.

Timecode navigation and display

Two timecode displays, located in the upper corners of the Canvas window, are useful for precisely navigating to specific timecode locations.

◆ **Timecode Duration:** This display shows the elapsed time between the In and Out points of a clip. If no edit points are set, the beginning and the end of the sequence serve as the In and the Out points (**Figure 10.2**).

◆ **Current Timecode:** This display shows the timecode at the current position of the playhead. You can enter a timecode in this display to jump the playhead to that point in the sequence (**Figure 10.3**).

✔ Tips

■ Control-click the Current Timecode field to see a pop-up menu of sequence markers in the current sequence (**Figure 10.4**). Select one to jump the playhead to that marker's location. The same list of sequence markers is available from the Timeline ruler's shortcut menu.

■ You can use keyboard shortcuts to step through both sequence and clip markers in the Timeline, but you must open a clip in the Viewer to make changes to that clip's markers. For details, see "Using Markers in the Timeline and the Canvas," later in this chapter.

Editing controls

Seven buttons in the lower-left corner of the Canvas (**Figure 10.5**) allow you to insert a clip displayed in the Viewer into your sequence by clicking the appropriate editing control button.

All the edit types available from the editing control buttons are also available in the Canvas edit overlay.

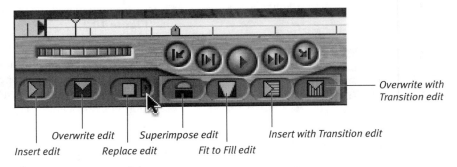

Overwrite with
Transition edit

Overwrite edit   Superimpose edit   Insert with Transition edit

Insert edit   Replace edit   Fit to Fill edit

Figure 10.5 The Canvas edit buttons.

Anatomy of the Canvas edit overlay

When you drag clips from the Viewer and drop them on the Canvas, the edit overlay appears (**Figure 10.6**). The edit overlay and its related edit procedures are detailed in Chapter 9, "Basic Editing." You can perform the following types of edits:

◆ **Insert edit:** This type of edit inserts a source clip into a sequence by pushing back the part of the sequence that's past the sequence In point, making room for the new source clip.

◆ **Overwrite edit:** The source clip overwrites sequence clips past the sequence In point. Overwrite uses the source In and Out points to calculate the edit duration. The incoming source material replaces the sequence material; there is no time shift in the existing sequence.

◆ **Replace edit:** This edit type replaces the contents of a sequence clip with the source clip material. It allows you to specifically align single frames in the source clip and sequence. The material between the sequence In and Out points is replaced by corresponding material from the source clip on either side of the frame that was matched.

◆ **Superimpose edit:** The source clip is placed on a new track above the target track, starting at the sequence In point. The target track is not changed. If the clip has audio, the source audio is added to new tracks below the target audio track.

◆ **Fit to Fill edit:** The speed of the source clip will be modified to fill the duration specified by the sequence In and Out points; the clip must be rendered before the edit can be played back.

◆ **Transition edits:** The source clip is inserted into the sequence with the default transition at the source clip's head.

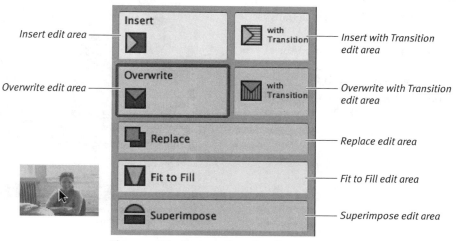

Figure 10.6 The Canvas edit overlay allows drag-and-drop editing for seven types of edits.

Using the Canvas Window

The Canvas and the Viewer windows operate in much the same way. If you review the sections in Chapter 8, "Working with Clips in the Viewer," that detail operating the Viewer window, you'll know how to use the Canvas window as well.

Editing in the Canvas is detailed in Chapter 9, "Basic Editing."

So what does that leave for this section? Just a few odds and ends.

To open a sequence in the Canvas:

◆ Start in the Browser. Double-click the sequence icon. The sequence opens in the Canvas and the Timeline.

To composite or add effects to a sequence in the Canvas:

1. Start in the Canvas with your sequence cued to the location to which you want to add effects.

2. Choose Wireframe or Image+Wireframe from the View selector in the Canvas (**Figure 10.7**).

   The Canvas acts as your monitor as you compose and review effects or create motion paths (**Figure 10.8**). Learn more about creating effects in Chapter 14, "Compositing and Effects Overview."

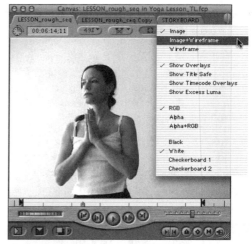

Figure 10.7 Selecting Image+Wireframe from the View pop-up selector.

Figure 10.8 Motion paths, filters, and scaling can be directly applied in the Canvas window.

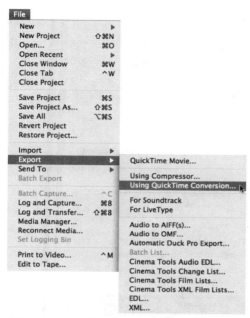

Figure 10.9 Locate the frame, then choose File > Export > Using QuickTime Conversion to export a still image directly from the Canvas or Viewer.

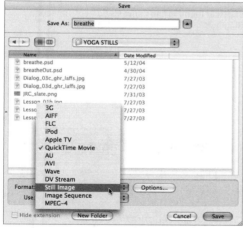

Figure 10.10 Select Still Image from the Format pop-up menu.

Creating and exporting still frames

It's easy to turn a single video frame into a freeze-frame image and use it in a sequence. If you want to convert this image into a graphics file and work with it outside of FCP, you'll need to export it using the Export command on the File menu.

To create a still image from a Canvas frame:

1. In the Canvas, position the playhead on the desired frame.

2. Choose Modify > Make Freeze Frame; or press Shift-N.

   The new freeze-frame image opens in the Viewer window as a clip. It has the default duration for stills, as specified on the Editing tab of the User Preferences window. You can modify the freeze-frame clip's duration by setting In and Out points before you edit it into your sequence.

To export a still image from a Canvas frame:

1. In the Canvas, position the playhead on the desired frame.

2. Choose File > Export > Using QuickTime Conversion (**Figure 10.9**).

3. In the dialog box, type a new name for your exported still image in the Save As field and select a destination folder.

4. Select Still Image from the Format pop-up menu (**Figure 10.10**).

   continues on next page

5. To set export format options, click the Options button.

6. In the Export Image Sequence Settings dialog box, select an export format from the Format pop-up menu at the top (**Figure 10.11**); click OK. You can ignore the frame rate settings because you are exporting a single frame.

7. Back in the Save dialog box, click Save.

To set the time display view:

◆ In the Canvas, Control-click either of the timecode display fields; then select a time display option from the shortcut menu (**Figure 10.12**).

✔ Tips

■ Check the time display mode to quickly determine which type of timecode is currently specified in your sequence settings. The timecode type specified in your sequence settings appears in bold.

■ Changing the timecode display in the Canvas won't alter your sequence's timecode settings; you're just selecting a different display mode.

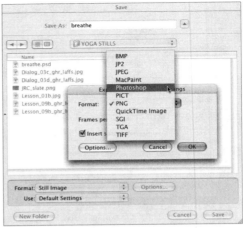

Figure 10.11 Select an export format for your still image from the pop-up menu.

Figure 10.12 Select a time display option from the shortcut menu in the Canvas's Current Timecode display.

Adjusting the Canvas Display

You can set up the Canvas to show clips in a variety of display formats and magnifications. FCP also lets you overlay an array of useful information on your clip image, or you can turn off everything.

Display options operate the same way in the Canvas and the Viewer. Learn more about Canvas display options by reading "Adjusting the Viewer Display" in Chapter 8.

Figure 10.13 The Tool palette as a compact floating toolbar.

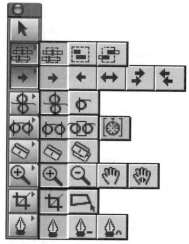

Figure 10.14 The Tool palette with every pop-up selector displayed. You'll see only one of these bars at a time when you select a tool.

Anatomy of the Tool Palette

The Tool palette contains tools for selecting and manipulating items in the Timeline, Canvas, and Viewer. As you work in the Timeline with an assembly of clips in a rough sequence, you use the tools in the palette to do the following:

◆ Select anything, from a sliver of a single clip to all the tracks in your sequence.

◆ Select and adjust edit points in your sequence.

◆ Adjust the scale of the Timeline so you can see what you are doing.

◆ Crop or distort an image.

◆ Add and edit keyframes in the Timeline.

◆ Modify a clip's playback speed.

Figure 10.13 shows the Tool palette as it appears in the program.

Figure 10.14 shows the Tool palette with all its pop-up selectors fully extended. When you actually use the Tool palette to select a tool, you will see only one of these selectors at a time, but they are assembled in this illustration to show the location of every available tool.

ANATOMY OF THE TOOL PALETTE

Here's a complete rundown of the tools you'll find in the Tool palette.

Selection tools

 Selection: Selects individual items.

 Edit Selection: Selects just the edit points inside your selection.

 Group Selection: Selects whole clips or groups of whole clips.

 Range Selection: Selects the area inside the selection marquee you draw. Select partial clips with this tool.

 Select Track Forward: Selects all the contents of the track after the selection point.

 Select Track Backward: Selects all the contents of the track before the selection point.

 Track Selection: Selects the entire contents of a single track.

 Select All Tracks Forward: Selects the contents of all tracks after the selection point.

 Select All Tracks Backward: Selects the contents of all tracks before the selection point.

Edit tools

 Roll: Rolls edit points.

 Ripple: Ripples edit points.

 Slip: Slips a clip's In and Out points.

 Slide: Slides a clip in a sequence.

 Time Remap: Modifies a clip's playback speed. Speed modification can be constant or variable speed.

 Razor Blade: Cuts a single clip into two sections.

 Razor Blade All: Cuts clips on all tracks at the selection point into two sections.

Learn more about performing these edits in Chapter 11, "Fine Cut: Trimming Edits."

View tools

 Zoom In: Zooms in on an image or within the Timeline.

 Zoom Out: Zooms out from an image or within the Timeline.

 Hand: Moves the Timeline or image view from side to side.

 Video Scrub Hand: Scrubs the thumbnail image displayed on Timeline clips.

Image modifiers

 Crop: Crops the edges of an image in the Viewer or the Canvas (in Wireframe mode).

 Distort: Distorts a selection by click-dragging corner points.

Keyframe tools

 Pen: Adds a keyframe.

 Delete Point Tool: Deletes a keyframe.

 Smooth Point Tool: Smoothes a curve by adding Bézier handles to the selected keyframe.

You can use the Pen tools in keyframe graphs on the Viewer effects tabs, in keyframe overlays in the Timeline, and on a motion path in the Canvas or the Viewer.

Figure 10.15 Click a tool to select it from the Tool palette.

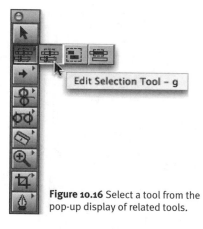

Figure 10.16 Select a tool from the pop-up display of related tools.

Figure 10.17 Rest the pointer over a tool to display its tooltip.

Using the Tool Palette

When you click and hold the mouse on a tool in the palette, the Tool palette extends to display multiple tools on pop-up selectors. Each pop-up displays all the tools available from its palette button. After you've made a selection from the pop-up, your selected tool will display on the palette.

✔ Tip

■ See Appendix A for a complete list of keyboard shortcuts for tool selection. Shortcuts are also listed in tooltips and on FCP menus.

To select a tool from the palette:

Do one of the following:

◆ Click the tool to select it (**Figure 10.15**).

◆ Click and hold on the tool icon; then make a selection from the pop-up display of related tools (**Figure 10.16**).

◆ Use a keyboard shortcut. To quickly see the proper key, rest the pointer over the tool icon in the palette. A tooltip displaying the name of the tool and its shortcut will appear (**Figure 10.17**).

Anatomy of the Timeline

The Timeline displays multiple video and audio tracks along a time axis (**Figure 10.18**). The base layers of video (V1) and audio (A1 and A2) appear toward the center of the Timeline window. Additional audio tracks extend below the base layer; additional video tracks stack above the base layer.

If you have multiple sequences open, the Timeline and the Canvas display a tab for each sequence.

Advanced display options, like individually resizable track heights, and tools like editable keyframe graphs built right into the Timeline, make it easier to tweak edits and effects without leaving the Timeline window.

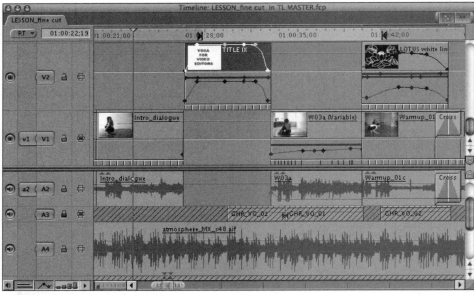

Figure 10.18 An overview of the Timeline.

Onscreen controls and displays

Use the controls in the Timeline window to move the playhead, view the tracks in your edited sequence, and perform edits and keyframe adjustments. Timeline controls and displays include track icons, sequence edit points, and clip and sequence markers (**Figures 10.19, 10.20, 10.21,** and **10.22**).

Sequence controls and displays
(**Figure 10.19**)

◆ **Sequence tabs:** Each open sequence in the Timeline has its own sequence tab. To make a sequence active, click its tab.

◆ **Real-Time Effects (RT) pop-up menu:** Select a level of playback quality for real-time effects. Your trade-off is the number of effects you can see in real time versus the visual quality of the playback. For more details, see Chapter 18, "Real Time and Rendering."

◆ **Current Timecode field:** This field displays the timecode at the current position of the playhead. You can enter a time in the display to jump the playhead to that point in the clip. This display/control operates like the Current Timecode fields in the Viewer and the Canvas.

continues on next page

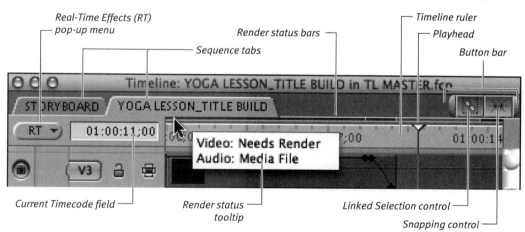

Figure 10.19 Sequence controls and displays in the Timeline.

ANATOMY OF THE TIMELINE

◆ **Render status bars:** Two render status bars indicate which parts of the sequence have been rendered. The upper bar is for video tracks, and the lower bar is for audio tracks. Red bars indicate material that requires rendering before playback. Gray bars indicate material that does not require rendering. A blue-gray bar indicates material that has already been rendered. On real-time–capable systems, a green status bar indicates that the material can be played back in real time, dark green indicates an effect that can be played back and output to video at full quality in real time, orange indicates an effect that probably exceeds the real-time capabilities of the system and could result in dropped frames during playback, and yellow indicates real-time playback with a proxy (lower-quality) version of the material.

◆ **Timeline ruler:** This displays the timecode for the current sequence and sequence In and Out points. Edit-point overlays are displayed along the ruler. Adjust the ruler's time scale with the Zoom slider or the Zoom control.

◆ **Playhead:** The playhead reflects the chronological position in the sequence of the frame displayed in the Canvas. The playhead in the Timeline always moves in tandem with the Canvas playhead.

◆ **Button bar:** The Timeline button bar has two buttons that are displayed by default, but you can add other buttons and customize to your taste. See "Customizing Final Cut Pro" in Chapter 3.

　◆ **Linked Selection control:** The Linked Selection indicator controls whether linked selection is active or disabled. Note: This control toggles the Linked Selection feature, not Link/Unlink. One click on this tiny icon does not permanently unlink the linked clips in your sequence. You typically disable linked selection to select just the audio or video track of a linked AV clip—to adjust a split edit in a sync sequence, for example.

　◆ **Snapping control:** Click to toggle snapping on and off.

Timeline Track controls (Figure 10.20)

◆ **Track Visibility control:** Click to make a track invisible. When the track is invisible, the contents remain in the Timeline but are not played or rendered with the sequence. Invisible tracks appear dimmed in the Timeline. Caution: Video render files can be lost if the track is made invisible.

◆ **Lock Track control:** Lock a track to prevent any changes to its contents. Locked tracks are crosshatched in the Timeline.

◆ **Auto Select control:** Use sequence In and Out points to define a selected area; then disable any tracks you want to exclude from your selection. You can cut, copy, search, delete, or ripple delete an auto-selected area. You can also apply copies of a filter to all the clips in an auto-selected area in a single operation.

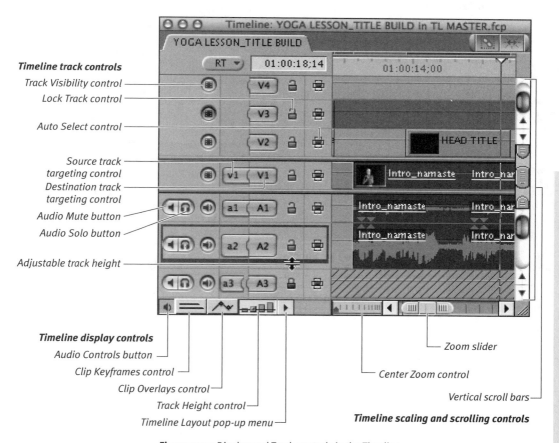

Figure 10.20 Display and Track controls in the Timeline.

ANATOMY OF THE TIMELINE

◆ **Source and Destination controls for targeting tracks:** Set the Source control to specify which source track is assigned to a destination track and whether the track is enabled to receive a source clip. The Destination control identifies the track. You can target one video target track plus one audio target track for each audio track in the source clip.

◆ **Audio Solo button:** Click to mute playback of any other audio tracks, except those tracks where Solo is enabled.

◆ **Audio Mute button:** Click to mute a track's audio playback.

◆ **Adjustable track height:** Drag the lower border of any individual track to adjust its height.

Timeline display controls (**Figure 10.20**)

◆ **Audio Controls button:** Click to toggle the display of Mute and Solo buttons. Controls are hidden by default.

◆ **Clip Keyframes control:** Click to toggle the display of the Timeline's keyframe editor, Filter and Motion bars, and clip speed indicator bar underneath tracks.

◆ **Clip Overlays control:** Click to toggle the display of Audio Level line graphs over audio clips and Opacity Level line graphs in video clips.

◆ **Track Height control:** Click to switch among the four track display sizes in the Timeline.

◆ **Timeline Layout pop-up menu:** Click the triangle to display a pop-up menu containing Timeline display options, and to access saved custom track layouts.

Timeline scaling and scrolling controls (**Figure 10.20**)

◆ **Center Zoom control:** Click to jump between different time scale views.

◆ **Zoom slider:** Use this slider to scroll through your sequence and to adjust the time scale of your view.

◆ **Vertical scroll bars:** This two-part scroll bar allows the video and audio tracks to scroll independently. Adjust the thumb tabs between the scroll controls to create a static area in the center of the Timeline.

Clip controls and displays (Figure 10.21)

◆ **Link indicators:** Linked clips display in the Timeline with their names underlined. When a linked clip is selected, moved, or trimmed, items linked to it are affected in the same way. Linked selections can be switched on and off as a sequence preference.

◆ **Out-of-Sync indicators:** This display indicates the number of frames by which a clip's video and audio tracks are out of sync.

◆ **Clips:** You can display clips as solid bars or as video frames. Clips that have been disabled appear dimmed in the Timeline. Clips on locked tracks are crosshatched in the Timeline. Clips with a speed change applied display the current speed setting.

◆ **Stereo Pair indicators:** These indicators appear as two triangles. These two audio clips are linked as a stereo pair.

◆ **Item Level Render Status indicator:** Audio clips that require rendering display this render status indicator. The indicator's color coding is the same as the render indicators above the Timeline ruler. Audio clips rendered at item level can be moved or edited without losing their render files.

◆ **Through edit indicator:** This indicates an edit point joining two clips with the same reel number and contiguous timecode (such as a clip divided in two with the Razor Blade tool).

◆ **Transition:** An effect applied at the edit point between two clips. See Chapter 13, "Creating Transitions."

◆ **Locked track:** A track whose contents cannot be moved or edited.

◆ **Opacity Level line graph:** Adjust and apply keyframes to this editable overlay to set the opacity level of a video clip.

◆ **Audio Level line graph:** Adjust and apply keyframes to this editable overlay to set the level of an audio clip.

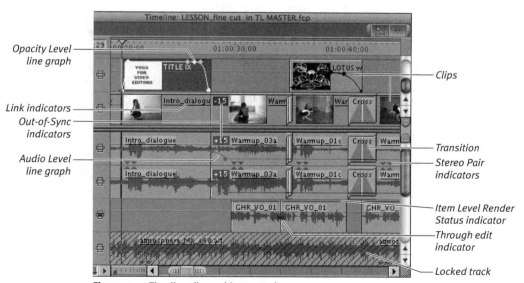

Figure 10.21 Timeline clip marking controls.

ANATOMY OF THE TIMELINE

Keyframe controls and displays
(**Figure 10.22**)

◆ **Speed indicator:** Indicates the frame rate for clips whose playback speeds have been modified to variable speed (with the Time Remap tool), or to another constant speed.

◆ **Keyframe editor:** Timeline keyframe editors are adjustable in height, but can only display keyframe values for one effect parameter at a time. Keyframe editors are hidden by default. Use the Clip Keyframes button to hide or show Timeline keyframe editors.

◆ **Keyframe Editor shortcut menu:** Control-click and select which effect parameter you want to display in the Keyframe editor.

◆ **Filter and Motion bars:** This bar displays keyframes for any filters or motion effects applied to a clip. Double-click the bar to open the settings in the Viewer window.

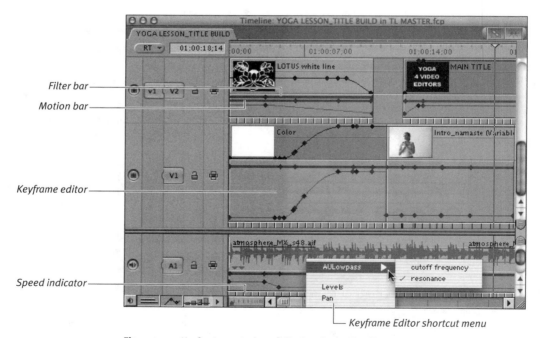

Figure 10.22 Keyframe controls and displays in the Timeline.

Table 10.1

Color Coding in the Timeline

COLOR	ITEM
Purple	Video sequences
Cyan	Video clips
Aquamarine	Video graphics
Green	Audio clips
Light green	Audio sequences
White	Offline video or audio clips

Table 10.2

Clip/Bin Labels and Colors

COLOR	LABEL
Orange	Good Take
Red	Best Take
Blue	Alternate Shots
Purple	Interviews
Green	B-Roll

Color coding in the Timeline

Final Cut Pro uses two types of color coding:

◆ Final Cut Pro uses a color-coding system to identify the various clip and sequence types found in the Timeline. **Table 10.1** lists the file types and their colors.

◆ Mac Finder–style labels provide an additional sorting option. Labeled clips and bins appear in the Timeline with the item's name highlighted in the label color. You can customize the label text; the default labels and label colors are listed in **Table 10.2**.

Customizing Timeline Display Options

Every sequence is different, which is why you can customize Timeline display options for each one—perhaps you don't need to see thumbnails in a complicated sequence, or maybe it's easier to edit a short montage using larger tracks. These display settings are modified in the Sequence Settings window. Your custom display settings will apply only to the sequence that's open on the top tab of the Timeline; if you want the same appearance every time you create a new sequence, you can specify your preferred Timeline display setup on the Timeline Options tab of the User Preferences window. This section details your choices for the Timeline display options you're most likely to adjust often; for complete preferences setting details, see "Customizing the Timeline Display" in Chapter 3.

To set clip display mode on video tracks for the current sequence:

1. Make the Timeline active; then choose Sequence > Settings; or press Command-0 (zero).

2. When the Sequence Settings window appears, click the Timeline Options tab.

3. From the Thumbnail Display pop-up menu, select from three thumbnail display options (**Figure 10.23**):

   ◆ Name displays the name of the clip with no thumbnail images.

   ◆ Name Plus Thumbnail displays the first frame of every clip as a thumbnail image and then the name of the clip.

   ◆ Filmstrip displays as many successive thumbnail images as possible for the current zoom level of the Timeline.

4. Click OK.

Figure 10.23 Select a name display option from the Thumbnail Display pop-up menu.

✔ Tip

■ If you are editing a long program in multiple-sequence segments, you might want to set the starting timecode to reflect each sequence's start time in the master program. You can do that by entering the start time in the Starting Timecode field on the Timeline Options tab.

Figure 10.24 The Timeline Layout pop-up menu speeds access to frequently used display options and any customized Timeline layouts you have saved.

Figure 10.25 Check Show Audio Waveforms to toggle the display of waveforms in the Timeline.

Figure 10.26 Select from the four track display sizes by clicking one of the icons in the Track Height control.

To show or hide audio waveforms for the current sequence:

◆ Click the triangle next to the Track Height display to open the Timeline Layout pop-up menu (**Figure 10.24**); then select Show Audio Waveforms to toggle the display of waveforms in the Timeline (**Figure 10.25**).

✔ Tip

■ The Timeline's audio waveform display is really useful for tweaking your audio edits, but Timeline display performance suffers when waveforms are visible. If you want to quickly look at the waveforms without taking a trip to the Timeline Layout pop-up, press Command-Option-W.

To set the track display size:

Do one of the following:

◆ Click one of the four icons in the Track Height control (**Figure 10.26**).

◆ Press Shift-T to toggle through the four track display sizes.

◆ Select a track display size from the Timeline Layout pop-up menu.

To adjust Timeline display text size:

◆ Click the Browser window to select it, then choose View > Text Size and choose a size option from the submenu.

To resize track height:

Do any of the following:

◆ In the Timeline control area, drag the upper boundary of a single video track, or the lower boundary of an audio track (**Figures 10.27** and **10.28**).

◆ Hold the Shift key while dragging to resize all video and all audio Timeline tracks.

◆ Hold the Option key while dragging to resize all the video or all the audio Timeline tracks.

◆ Click a Track Height control to reset all the Timeline tracks to one of the four default display settings.

✔ Tip

■ If you hold the Option key while clicking a Track Height control, you can resize your variously sized Timeline tracks relative to one of the four default display settings.

To show or hide the Timeline's keyframing tools:

◆ Click the Clip Keyframes button to toggle the display of the Timeline's keyframe editor, Filter and Motion bars, and clip speed indicator bar (**Figure 10.29**). For more information about using these keyframing tools, see "Working with Keyframes in the Timeline" in Chapter 14.

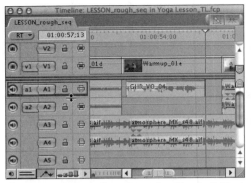

Figure 10.27 Drag the lower boundary of an individual Timeline audio track.

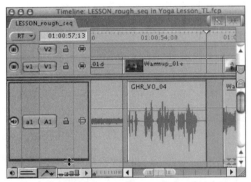

Figure 10.28 The audio track resized. Stretching the height of the waveform display makes it much easier to cut dialogue tracks right in the Timeline.

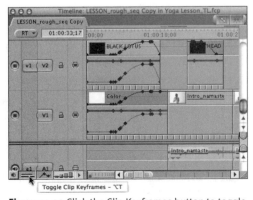

Figure 10.29 Click the Clip Keyframes button to toggle the display of the Timeline's keyframe editor, Filter and Motion bars, and clip speed indicator bar.

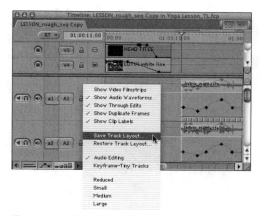

Figure 10.30 Choose Save Track Layout from the Timeline Layout pop-up menu.

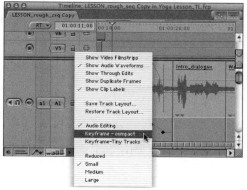

Figure 10.31 You can load a previously saved custom layout from the Timeline Layout pop-up menu.

✔ Tip

■ Don't forget—if you're thrilled with your customized Timeline display and want to make your current settings the defaults for all subsequent new sequences, go to the Timeline Options tab of User Preferences and tweak your settings there.

Custom track layouts

The Timeline is an extremely flexible workspace; your display choices are many and varied. Custom track layouts allow you to tweak a setup for cutting dialogue or for keyframing a motion graphics title sequence— any layout that's helpful—and then save it as a custom track layout.

✔ Tip

■ Any custom screen layouts you save will include not just the program window size and arrangement, but also the customized track layouts and Browser column layouts you've used. All will be saved as one big, perfect picture you can recall with a single command. Such power and grace—must be time to raise your rates!

To save a custom track layout:

1. In the Timeline, select and arrange the columns you want to include in your custom track layout.

2. Click the triangle next to the Track Height display; then choose Save Track Layout from the Timeline Layout pop-up menu (**Figure 10.30**).

   The Save dialog box opens to the default location for custom track layouts: Home/Library/Preferences/Final Cut Pro User Data/Track Layouts.

3. Enter a name for your new custom layout; then click Save.

To load a custom track layout:

◆ Choose a previously saved custom layout from the Timeline Layout pop-up menu (**Figure 10.31**).

   Your custom track layout will be applied to the active tab in the Timeline.

Timeline scaling and scrolling

Final Cut Pro has state-of-the-art zoom features and scroll bars. The time scale in the Timeline is continuously variable; you can transition smoothly from viewing several minutes of your sequence down to a single frame. The horizontal scroll bar—the Zoom slider—is a combination zoom and scroll control. The Zoom control is handy—you can jump to any time scale with a single mouse click.

The vertical scroll bar separating the video and audio tracks allows you to set a static area in the center of the Timeline window, so your base tracks are always in view.

To adjust the time scale of the Timeline display:

Do one of the following:

◆ Click either thumb control and drag it to adjust the time scale, keeping the selected clip (or the playhead, if no clip is selected) centered in the Timeline as it scales (**Figure 10.32**). (The thumb controls are the ribbed-looking ends of the Zoom slider.)

◆ Shift-click and drag a thumb control to lock the position of the thumb control on the other end of the Zoom slider and to make the zoom adjustment only to the side you're dragging.

◆ Click the Zoom control to the left of the Zoom slider to jump to a different time scale (**Figure 10.33**). This Zoom control keeps the playhead or selected clip centered in view as you change zoom levels.

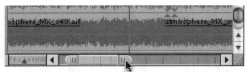

Figure 10.32 Drag a thumb control of the Zoom slider to adjust the scale of your Timeline view.

Figure 10.33 Click the Zoom control to jump to a new time scale. This control keeps the playhead or selected clip centered in view as you change zoom levels.

Figure 10.34
Click the Zoom In tool to select it from the Tool palette.

Figure 10.35 Drag a marquee around the section you want to zoom in on.

To zoom the view of the Timeline:

1. From the Tool palette, select the Zoom In or the Zoom Out tool (**Figure 10.34**); or press Z.

2. Click in the Timeline or drag a marquee around the section you want to display (**Figure 10.35**).

Or do one of the following:

◆ Use a keyboard shortcut. (See Appendix A for a complete list of shortcuts.)

◆ Choose View > Zoom In (or Zoom Out).

✔ Tips

■ When the Timeline is zoomed in or out to the maximum, the plus sign (+) or minus sign (–) disappears from the Zoom tool's pointer.

■ Pressing Option while using the Zoom In tool toggles it to Zoom Out.

■ When you're zoomed in on the Timeline but your playhead is located elsewhere in the sequence, you can quickly jump the Timeline view to your playhead location by tapping the Left or Right Arrow key.

Best Zoom Shortcuts

Final Cut Pro has a jillion ways to zoom and scroll program windows. Which shortcuts are most useful in the Timeline?

◆ **Option-+ (plus) / Option- – (minus):** This keyboard combo zooms the Timeline even if the Canvas or the Viewer is currently selected, and it keeps the selected clip (or the playhead, if no clip is selected) centered in the Timeline as it scales. This shortcut is the best way to zoom in and out of the Timeline.

◆ **Command-+ (plus) / Command- – (minus):** This shortcut works like Option plus and minus, but it zooms the selected program window.

◆ **Shift-Z:** When the Timeline is selected, this key combination adjusts the time scale to fit the entire sequence in the Timeline window.

◆ **Shift-Page Up / Shift-Page Down:** This shortcut scrolls the Timeline one full length of the Timeline window at the current scale.

To scroll through your sequence:

◆ Drag the Zoom slider across the scroll bar.

To set up the vertical scroll bars:

1. In the Timeline, click and hold the uppermost thumb tab near the center of the vertical scroll bar. Drag the thumb tab up the scroll bar to create a static area for as many video tracks as you want to keep in constant view (**Figure 10.36**).

   You can use the upper scroll bar to scroll through higher video tracks in the upper portion of the Timeline.

2. Click and hold the lowest thumb tab in the vertical scroll bar. Drag the thumb tab down the scroll bar, creating a static area for as many audio tracks as you want to keep in constant view (**Figure 10.37**).

   You can use the lower scroll bar to scroll through additional audio tracks in the lower portion of the Timeline window.

3. Once you have set up your static view area, use the center tab on the scroll bar to move the static area up or down in the window (**Figure 10.38**).

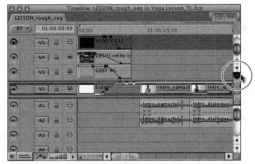

Figure 10.36 Drag the thumb tab up the scroll bar to create a static display area for a video track in the Timeline.

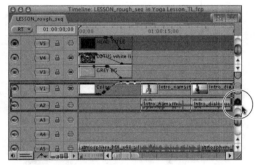

Figure 10.37 Drag the thumb tab down the scroll bar to create a static display area for an audio track in the Timeline.

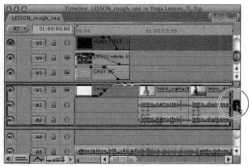

Figure 10.38 Use the center tab in the scroll bar to move the static display area up or down the Timeline display.

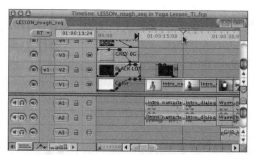

Figure 10.39 Click a point in the Timeline ruler to jump the playhead to that location.

Navigating in the Timeline

Many of the tasks described here can be accomplished with the help of keyboard shortcuts. Final Cut Pro has an army of key commands; many professional editors prefer a keyboard-intensive working style. This section demonstrates some other ways to approach the Timeline interface because, frankly, keystrokes don't make good illustrations. Check out the keyboard shortcuts in Appendix A. Before you flip to the back of the book, though, consider the alternatives in this section. You keyboard diehards might find something here you actually like.

✔ Tip

■ You can use the playhead's locator line to help identify the exact timecode location of an item way down at the bottom of the Timeline window. Set the playhead's locator line on the point you want to identify, and the Current Timecode display will give you its exact timecode location.

Positioning the playhead in a sequence

The playhead in the Timeline can be positioned by the same methods as those used for the Canvas and the Viewer playheads.

The playhead sits on the Timeline ruler and has a vertical locator line that extends down through the Timeline track display.

To scrub through a sequence in the Timeline:

◆ Drag the playhead along the Timeline ruler.

To jump the playhead to a new location:

◆ Click the location on the Timeline ruler to move the playhead to that location (**Figure 10.39**).

To jump the playhead from edit to edit:

Do one of the following:

◆ Press the Up Arrow key (for the previous edit) or the Down Arrow key (for the next edit).

◆ Press ; (semicolon) for the previous edit, or ' (apostrophe) for the next edit. (These are the most convenient alternatives if you use J K L keys for navigation.)

◆ In the Canvas, click the Previous Edit button or the Next Edit button.

◆ Choose Mark > Previous (or Next) > Edit.

◆ Press Option-E (for the previous edit) or Shift-E (for the next edit).

◆ Press Home to jump to the beginning of the sequence, and the playhead jumps to the first frame of the clip. If you've enabled Show Overlays on the View menu, an L-shaped icon appears in the lower left or right of the Canvas window, indicating that you are on the first or last frame of the sequence clip (**Figure 10.40**).

◆ Press End to jump to the end of the sequence.

Figure 10.40 An L-shaped icon in the lower left of the Canvas indicates the first frame of a clip after an edit point.

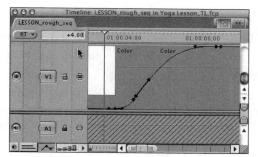

Figure 10.41 Type +4.00 to move the playhead 4 seconds later in the sequence.

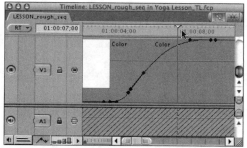

Figure 10.42 The playhead is repositioned 4 seconds later in the sequence.

Navigating with timecode in the Timeline

Just as in the Viewer, using timecode values to position the playhead in the Timeline and the Canvas will result in frame-accurate positioning. Final Cut Pro's timecode input function is very flexible (see "FCP Protocol: Entering Timecode Numbers" in Chapter 8 for protocol and entry shortcuts).

To navigate using timecode values:

1. Start in the Timeline. Make sure all clips are deselected, or you'll move the selected clip and not the playhead.

2. Enter a new timecode number, or use the shorthand methods noted in Chapter 8. You don't need to click in the field to begin entering a new timecode; just type the numbers (**Figure 10.41**).

3. Press Enter.

   The playhead moves to the new timecode value, and the new timecode position displays in the Current Timecode field in the upper left of the Timeline (**Figure 10.42**).

✔ Tip

- Deselecting everything in the Timeline can be tricky—unless you know the keyboard shortcut. Press Shift-Command-A and you're completely deselected.

About snapping in the Timeline

Snapping is an interface state that makes certain points in the Timeline "sticky." With snapping turned on, the edges of clips will snap together, or a clip will snap to an edit point on an adjacent track when dragged close to it. The playhead snaps to edits, clip and sequence markers, and keyframes (if displayed) on all visible tracks. If you drag the playhead across the Timeline ruler, it snaps to items in the Timeline when it encounters them. Small triangles flanking the playhead locator line appear above or below the edit, marker, or keyframe, showing you what the playhead has snapped to (**Figure 10.43**).

To turn snapping on or off:

Do one of the following:

◆ Choose View > Snapping.

◆ Click the Snapping control located in the upper-right corner of the Timeline window (**Figure 10.44**).

To toggle snapping on or off on the fly:

◆ Press N; then drag the playhead, or your selected clip, to the new location (**Figure 10.45**).

Snapping remains in the toggled state until you press the N key again. Snapping can be toggled at any time, even in mid-edit.

✔ Tip

■ Use the "gear-down dragging" option to make precision adjustments to clips, levels, or edits in the Timeline—hold down the Command key while dragging an item.

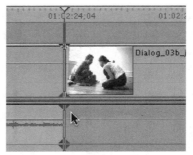

Figure 10.43 The Timeline with snapping turned on. The playhead's locator line displays small triangles to show that it has snapped to an edit.

Figure 10.44 You can activate Timeline snapping by clicking the Snapping control on the right side of the Timeline. The control turns green when snapping is enabled.

Figure 10.45 Snapping a clip to an edit point. You can toggle Timeline snapping even in mid-edit by pressing N at any time.

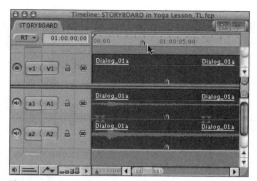

Figure 10.46 Clip markers appear on individual clips, and clip marker information is stored with the clip. Sequence markers appear on the Timeline's ruler; sequence marker data is stored with the sequence.

Using markers in the Timeline and the Canvas

Final Cut Pro has two types of markers (**Figure 10.46**):

- Clip markers appear on individual clips in the Timeline.

- Sequence markers appear on the Timeline ruler.

If you open a Timeline clip in the Viewer, the clip markers appear in the Viewer Scrubber bar.

You can learn more about working with markers in Chapter 8, "Working with Clips in the Viewer."

To set a sequence marker:

1. In the Timeline, position the playhead at the point where you want to set the marker. Make sure no clips are selected at the playhead's location.

2. Press M.

   A sequence marker appears in the Canvas Scrubber and on the Timeline ruler. Press M a second time to open the Edit Marker dialog box.

✔ Tips

- You can set a sequence marker only if no clips are selected at the playhead position in the Timeline. With a selected Timeline clip under the playhead, your marker will be set as a clip marker on that clip.

- You can delete sequence markers only if no clips are selected in the Timeline.

- Any two adjacent sequence markers can be used to locate sequence In and Out points. Just position your Timeline playhead anywhere between the two markers you want to use, and choose Mark > Mark to Markers; or press Control-A.

To position the playhead on a specific sequence marker:

◆ Control-click the Timeline ruler; then choose a marker from the list of sequence markers in the shortcut menu (**Figure 10.47**).

The playhead jumps to the selected marker's position (**Figure 10.48**).

To jump the playhead to the next or the previous sequence marker:

Do one of the following:

◆ Choose Mark > Previous (or Next) > Marker.

◆ Press Option-M for the previous marker.

◆ Press Shift-M for the next marker.

These are the same commands you use to locate clip markers in the Viewer; when you use them in the Canvas or the Timeline, FCP looks for sequence markers only, unless you have selected a Timeline clip. With a Timeline clip selected, these commands will locate both sequence and clip markers in the selected clip.

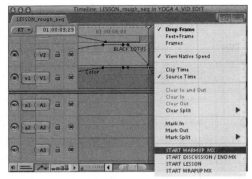

Figure 10.47 Choosing a marker from the Timeline ruler's shortcut menu.

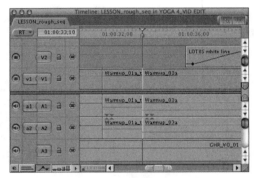

Figure 10.48 Selecting the marker jumps the playhead to that marker's location.

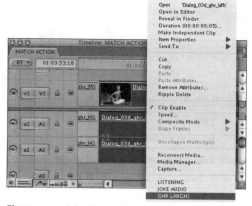

Figure 10.49 Selecting a clip marker from a Timeline clip's shortcut menu jumps the playhead to that marker's location.

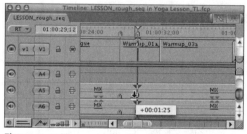

Figure 10.50 You can grab a Timeline clip by its marker and drag it to align it to another marker or to an edit point.

To position the playhead on a specific Timeline clip marker:

◆ In the Timeline, Control-click the clip; then choose a marker from the list of clip markers in the shortcut menu (**Figure 10.49**).

The playhead jumps to the selected marker's position.

✔ Tip

■ Say you have a specific phrase in the middle of a narration track that you'd like to align with an action in your video track. You can place a clip marker in the audio track and a sequence marker in the video clip at a key point; then grab the audio clip by its marker and drag it to align it to your video clip marker (**Figure 10.50**). This procedure works best with snapping enabled.

Working with Timeline Tracks

Editing operations in Final Cut Pro frequently involve configuring tracks. Timeline tracks can be locked, unlocked, targeted, added, deleted, and made visible or invisible. There is a difference between tracks and the contents of tracks. The procedures described in this section affect whole tracks. To learn about editing procedures that affect individual sequence clips, edit points, and keyframes, see "Working with Items in the Timeline," later in this chapter.

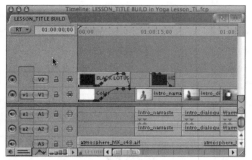

Figure 10.51 A sequence in the Timeline. Note the open space above the last video track.

To add tracks to a sequence:

1. Open the sequence in the Timeline (**Figure 10.51**).

2. Choose Sequence > Insert Tracks.

3. In the Insert Tracks dialog box, select the appropriate check box if the Insert field is inactive, then enter the number of new video or audio tracks you want to add. Final Cut Pro supports up to 99 tracks for video and 99 tracks for audio.

4. Select from options for inserting tracks:
   - Choose Before Base Track to insert your tracks before the first track in the Timeline.
   - Choose After Last Track to insert your tracks after the last track in the Timeline (**Figure 10.52**).

5. Click OK to insert the tracks.

   The new tracks are added at the specified location (**Figure 10.53**).

Figure 10.52 Adding new video tracks to the sequence. The location specified is after the last track.

Figure 10.53 Two new video tracks (V3 and V4) have been added at the specified location above V2.

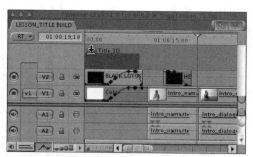

Figure 10.54 Drag and drop a clip in the area above the top video track.

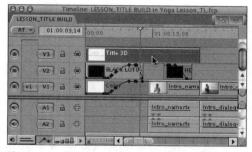

Figure 10.55 A new track is created automatically, and the clip is added to the sequence.

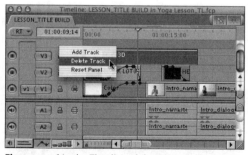

Figure 10.56 In the Timeline, delete a track by Control-clicking the track's header and then choosing Delete Track from the shortcut menu.

To add a track to a sequence quickly:

Do one of the following:

◆ Drag a clip to the area above the top video track or below the bottom audio track (**Figure 10.54**).

 A new track will be added to the sequence automatically (**Figure 10.55**).

◆ Control-click anywhere on the track header; then choose Add Track from the shortcut menu.

To delete a single track from a sequence:

◆ Control-click anywhere on the track header; then choose Delete Track from the shortcut menu (**Figure 10.56**).

To delete empty tracks from a sequence:

1. Open the sequence in the Timeline (**Figure 10.57**).

2. Choose Sequence > Delete Tracks.

3. In the Delete Tracks dialog box, select from the options for deleting tracks:

   ◆ Click the Video Tracks and/or Audio Tracks check boxes to select track types.

   ◆ Choose All Empty Tracks to delete every empty track in the Timeline (**Figure 10.58**).

   ◆ Choose All Empty Tracks at End of Sequence to delete all empty tracks above (or below) the highest-numbered track used in the Timeline.

4. Click OK to delete the tracks.

   The selected tracks are deleted from the sequence; remaining tracks are renumbered consecutively (**Figure 10.59**).

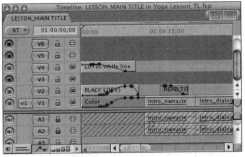

Figure 10.57 Open the sequence in the Timeline; then choose Sequence > Delete Tracks.

Figure 10.58 Click the appropriate check box to specify the track type you're deleting.

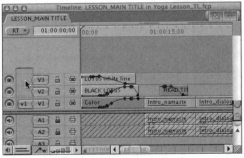

Figure 10.59 All the empty tracks are deleted from the sequence, and the remaining tracks are renumbered.

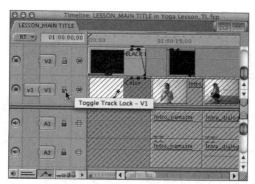

Figure 10.60 Lock a Timeline track by clicking the Track Lock control. Click again to unlock the track.

To lock a Timeline track:

Do one of the following:

◆ In the Timeline, click the Track Lock control on the left side of the track. Click again to unlock the track (**Figure 10.60**).

◆ To lock a video track, press F4 plus the track number of the track you are locking.

◆ To lock an audio track, press F5 plus the track number of the track you are locking.

To lock all Timeline video tracks:

◆ To lock all video tracks in the sequence, press Shift-F4.

To lock all Timeline audio tracks:

◆ To lock all audio tracks in the sequence, press Shift-F5.

✔ Tip

■ Option-click a Track Lock control to toggle locking on all other audio or video tracks except the selected track.

FCP Protocol: Lock vs. Target

One of the tasks when learning a new program is getting in sync with the logic behind the program design. If you are coming to Final Cut Pro from another editing system, you'll probably notice a few things that FCP does differently. Understanding the differences between locking and targeting is important to your editing happiness, so let's get them straight.

Locking a track keeps it out of trouble. So unless you're working on a particular track, you might as well keep it locked so that your editing operations don't have unforeseen consequences, like trimming or moving tracks that are stacked above or below the base tracks, out of your Timeline view (spooky music here). You have to take the responsibility for locking tracks because FCP defaults to unlocked tracks (unlike other editing systems, which may disable tracks by default until you enable them).

Here are the keyboard shortcuts for locking tracks:

◆ Shift-F4 locks all video tracks.

◆ F4 plus the track number locks that video track.

◆ Shift-F5 locks all audio tracks.

◆ F5 plus the track number locks that audio track.

Lock 'em. Just do it. You're welcome.

Even if you've selected a specific edit on one track with the Selection tool, any unlocked track is capable of responding to changes you make to that edit. If you have locked all the tracks that you don't want cut or moved, this capability is a great thing. For example, you can make multi-track cuts, moves, and lifts to dialogue tracks or multicamera sync setups and leave your locked music track right where it is.

Target track controls are a scheme for mapping each source clip to its proper Timeline track. Even though you don't always need to specify a target track to perform an edit, it's a good habit to check your target assignments whenever you perform an edit.

FCP also uses targeting as a way to specify the track when you perform a specific operation. For example, you target a track when you are getting ready to delete it.

Figure 10.61 Choose a new destination track from the Source control shortcut menu.

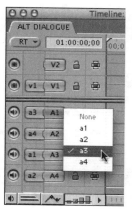

Figure 10.62 Drag a Source control to your desired destination track.

Figure 10.63 Select a source track from the Destination control shortcut menu.

Mapping Timeline target track assignments

Final Cut Pro's track-targeting scheme has been adapted to accommodate multichannel audio source clips. Targeting Timeline tracks to receive source clips is now a two-step process: first you map which source tracks are going to what destination tracks. Once your source clip's audio and video are mapped to the proper destination tracks, you have the option of disabling track targeting when you want to exclude selected source tracks from a pending edit. For information on simple track targeting, see "Specifying target tracks" in Chapter 9. To learn how to operate the Timeline's track-targeting controls, and the protocols that govern target track behavior, read on.

To map a source clip's destination tracks in the Timeline:

Do one of the following:

◆ Control-click the Source control, then choose a new destination track from the shortcut menu (**Figure 10.61**).

◆ Drag a Source control to your desired destination track (**Figure 10.62**).

◆ Control-click the Destination control of the track you want to target, then select a source track from the shortcut menu (**Figure 10.63**).

✔ Tips

■ When you load a clip into the Viewer, the number of Source controls available in the Timeline automatically updates to match the number of tracks in that source clip.

■ You can click the Destination control on a track you want to target, and the closest Source control will be assigned. Video targeting is limited to one track, so this is a quick way to target any video track with a single click.

To return destination track mapping to default settings:

◆ Control-click in the Timeline track control area, then choose Reset Panel from the shortcut menu (**Figure 10.64**).

✔ Tip

■ When you open that shortcut menu, you'll see a menu item that allows you to assign your audio tracks to audio output channels. Assigning output channels is independent of destination track mapping. Unless your FCP system has additional audio hardware that supports multiple audio output channels, you're limited to two channels of audio output: A1 and A2. For more information on FCP audio, see Chapter 12, "Audio Tools and Techniques."

To disable a targeted track:

◆ Click the Source control to disconnect the target indicator of the track before you perform your edit (**Figure 10.65**).

Figure 10.64 Choose Reset Panel from the track control area shortcut menu to reset the Timeline patch panel.

Figure 10.65 To disable a track, click the Source control to disconnect the target indicator of the track before you perform your edit.

FCP Protocol: Target Tracks

◆ Once you specify target tracks, your edits will use the same target tracks until you change your target selection.

◆ If the target track is locked, it will not accept any additional audio or video.

Making a Timeline track invisible

You can temporarily hide a track by making it invisible so that the contents of that track do not appear in the sequence when you play it back. This is useful when you tweak multi-layered composited sequences.

You can also single out a track by making all the other tracks in the sequence invisible. This lets you focus on the contents of a single track temporarily. You can single out video and audio tracks independently.

Audio render files are protected from loss, but note that changing the visibility of a video track will cause a loss of any render files associated with the track. A warning dialog box appears when you attempt to change visibility on a track.

If you've invested a lot of rendering in a sequence, you can use a couple of work-arounds to avoid re-rendering just because you turned a track off for a moment:

◆ You don't need to turn off the entire track. You can disable an individual clip by Control-clicking the clip in the Timeline and unchecking Clip Enable in the shortcut menu. If you are interested in a short section of your sequence, you can disable just the clips you want to hide, and you'll sacrifice only the render file for that clip, preserving your render files for the rest of the sequence.

◆ Undo and Redo might work. FCP has many layers of undo, and if you haven't been messing around too much in the interim, you can revert to the state before the render file loss.

Dragging Is Different

Final Cut Pro has the common sense to allow drag-and-drop edits to override track target assignments. When you insert a clip into a sequence by dragging it to a specific track in the Timeline, the clip will be placed on that track even if you did not target it previously.

If you've disabled a targeted track by disconnecting its Source control, things work a little differently.

If you disable the *video* target and then drag an audio+video clip to an *audio* track, the video will be excluded from the edit. With disabled *audio* target tracks, dragging an audio+video clip to a *video* track will exclude the audio from the edit.

Drag audio into target-disabled audio tracks (or video to disabled video tracks) and the drag-and-drop edit *will* override your disabled target controls.

To make a track invisible:

1. In the Timeline, click the Track Visibility control at the far left of the track you want to affect (**Figure 10.66**).

2. If the sequence has been rendered, a dialog box will appear warning you about the impending loss of render files. If you don't need your render files, click Continue (**Figure 10.67**).

3. The track is made invisible. The render status bar updates to show which sections of your sequence have been altered and may require re-rendering (**Figure 10.68**).

✔ Tips

- You can still edit invisible tracks. Lock invisible tracks if you don't want them to respond to edits.

- Next time you build a sequence involving multiple takes or a multicamera shoot, try loading your synchronized clips into tracks above and below the base layer (V1 and A1 to A2), keeping the base layer clear to assemble your cut. You can turn on single tracks for viewing and then copy and paste your selections into the base layers.

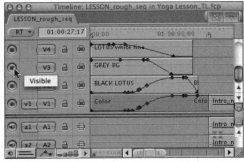

Figure 10.66 Click the Track Visibility control to make a track invisible.

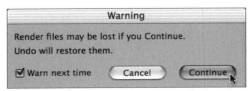

Figure 10.67 If making a track invisible will cause a loss of render files, you'll see this warning. You can turn off the warning on the Editing tab of User Preferences.

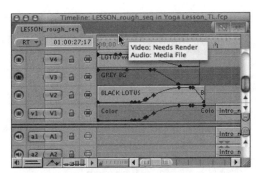

Figure 10.68 The invisible track will be excluded from playback, and the render status bar updates to remind you about your lost render files.

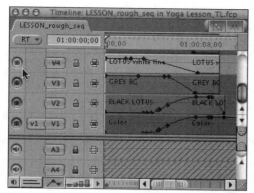

Figure 10.69 Video track V4 will play back alone. All other tracks are made invisible.

Figure 10.70 Click the Audio Controls button in the lower-left corner of the Timeline window to reveal the Solo and Mute buttons.

To single out a track for visibility:

Do one of the following:

◆ Option-click the Track Visibility icon.

◆ Select items in the track, then choose Sequence > Solo Item(s); or press Control-S.

The contents of all the video or audio tracks except the selected one are dimmed in the Timeline, and are hidden from view in the Canvas (**Figure 10.69**). All audio tracks except the selected track are muted.

✔ Tip

■ In addition to the Track Visibility control, each Timeline audio track has its own Solo and Mute buttons. These controls are hidden by default, but you can unearth them by clicking the Audio Controls button at the extreme lower left of the Timeline window (**Figure 10.70**).

Working with Items in the Timeline

This section covers Timeline editing procedures that affect individual sequence clips, edit points, and keyframes. Manipulating Timeline items requires extensive use of the tools in the Tool palette (**Figure 10.71**). Final Cut Pro boasts some great selection tools but very few keyboard equivalents. If you haven't used the Tool palette yet, review "Anatomy of the Tool Palette," earlier in this chapter.

Selecting items in the Timeline

All the selection tasks described here use tools from the Tool palette.

Items you can select in the Timeline:

◆ **Clips**, including multiple clips or ranges of clips.

◆ **Transitions**, which can be trimmed or deleted.

◆ **Edits**, which can be modified in several ways.

◆ **Gaps**, which can be closed or filled with media.

◆ **Keyframes**, which can be moved in the Timeline keyframe editor, and when they're displayed over the Timeline clip.

Items you cannot select in the Timeline:

◆ **Tracks:** You can't select a track, but you can select the contents of a track.

◆ **Filter and Motion bars and their keyframes:** You can't select the keyframes, but you can move them by dragging them.

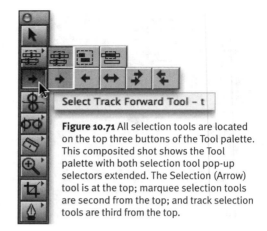

Select Track Forward Tool – t

Figure 10.71 All selection tools are located on the top three buttons of the Tool palette. This composited shot shows the Tool palette with both selection tool pop-up selectors extended. The Selection (Arrow) tool is at the top; marquee selection tools are second from the top; and track selection tools are third from the top.

Figure 10.72 Choose the Select Track Forward tool from the Tool Palette.

Figure 10.73 Using the Select Forward tool to click the first clip on any track to be included in the selection.

To select the entire contents of the Timeline:

◆ Press Command-A.

To deselect the entire contents of the Timeline:

◆ Press Shift-Command-A.

Selecting items with the track selection tools

The track selection tools offer a variety of ways to select the contents of one or more tracks. Don't forget: If you select an item that you've included in a linked selection, all the items involved in that linked selection will be affected by whatever operation you're about to perform.

✔ Tip

■ Deselect an individual Timeline item from a group selection by Command-clicking the item.

To select all items on a single track:

◆ From the Tool palette, choose the Select Track tool and click anywhere in the track.

To select all items on a single track forward or backward from the selected point:

1. From the Tool palette, choose the Select Track Forward or the Select Track Backward tool (**Figure 10.72**).

2. In the Timeline track, click the first clip to include in the selection.

   That entire clip is selected, plus all the items in front of or behind it (**Figure 10.73**).

To select all items on all tracks forward or backward from the selected point:

1. From the Tool palette, choose the All Tracks Forward or the All Tracks Backward tool (**Figure 10.74**).

2. In the Timeline, click the first clip on any track that should be included in the selection.

   The contents of all tracks from that point forward or backward are selected.

✔ Tips

- The Track Forward and Track Backward tools select entire clips only; they do not make range selections.

- When one of the Select All Tracks tools is active, you can quickly switch to the corresponding Select Track tool by holding down the Shift key.

To select an entire clip:

1. From the Tool palette, choose the Selection tool; or press A.

2. In the Timeline, use the Selection tool to click the clip you want to select.

   The Canvas indicates the selection by displaying a cyan border around the video of the selected clip.

To select part of a clip or a larger selection including partial clips:

1. From the Tool palette, choose the Range Selection tool (**Figure 10.75**).

2. In the Timeline, click at the point in the clip where you want to start your selection and then drag a marquee around the range to select it (**Figure 10.76**).

   A two-up display in the Canvas shows the first and last frames of your selection.

Figure 10.74 Choose the All Tracks Forward tool from the Tool Palette to select clips on all tracks forward from the selection point.

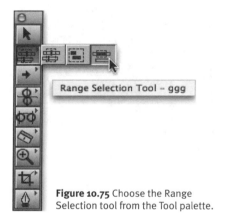

Figure 10.75 Choose the Range Selection tool from the Tool palette.

Figure 10.76 Drag the tool across a Timeline clip to define the range you want to select. You can select partial clips with this tool.

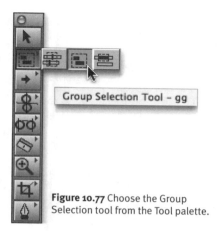

Group Selection Tool - gg

Figure 10.77 Choose the Group Selection tool from the Tool palette.

Figure 10.78 Command-click to select discontinuous clips in the Timeline or to deselect an individual clip from a group selection.

To select multiple whole clips:

1. From the Tool palette, choose the Group Selection tool (**Figure 10.77**).

2. In the Timeline, drag a marquee around all the clips you want to select. You don't need to include the entire clip; any clip you touch will be included in its entirety.

To select multiple noncontiguous clips:

1. From the Tool palette, choose the appropriate selection tool.

2. In the Timeline, Command-click the items you want to select (**Figure 10.78**). Command-click again on a selected item to deselect it.

To select all items between the In and Out points:

1. Set the sequence In and Out points in the Timeline or in the Canvas.

2. In the Timeline Track control area, click to enable the Auto Select controls on tracks you want to include in your selection.

3. Choose Mark > Select In to Out; or press Option-A.

   All items between the In and Out points on tracks with Auto Select enabled are selected.

To use Auto Select to select items between In and Out points:

1. In the Timeline Track control area, click to enable the Auto Select controls on tracks you want to include in your selection (**Figure 10.79**).

2. Set In and Out points to define the part of the sequence you want to select (**Figure 10.80**).

   You can cut, copy, delete, ripple delete, or search the auto-selected area. These operations will include only the selected sequence section (defined by In and Out points) and only tracks with Auto Select enabled.

✔ Tips

- Option-click an Auto Select control to select just that track and deselect all others.

- Auto-selected areas are automatically highlighted, so it's easy to see what's included in your auto-selection.

- See "To use Auto Select to apply a filter to multiple clips" in Chapter 16 to learn another slick Auto Select move.

Figure 10.79 Click to enable the Auto Select controls on tracks you want to include in your selection. Enabled controls are dark.

Figure 10.80 Set In and Out points to define the portion of the sequence you'd like to select.

FCP Protocol: Cut, Copy and Paste, and Auto-Select

- When you paste cut or copied clips into a sequence, the clips will be pasted into the same tracks you cut them from *unless you make a change to the Auto Select controls after you cut (or copy) but before you paste.* If you do, then the Auto Select controls determine the track destination of pasted tracks. Clips will be pasted starting at the lowest-numbered Auto Select–enabled track.

- Audio and video paste destinations are tracked separately. For example, if you enable a video Auto Select control between cutting and pasting but leave the audio Auto Select controls untouched, the video portion will be pasted according to your Auto Select setting, but the audio portion will be pasted into the same tracks you cut them from.

- Copying and pasting between sequences is governed by the same rules that govern copying and pasting within the same sequence.

FCP Protocol: Auto-Select Protocol Summary

The Timeline's Auto Select controls affect a wide variety of Timeline operations. Auto Select is meant to make the editor's life easier, and it would make your life easier—if only you could remember how Auto Select works for each edit operation. FCP designers decided to optimize Auto Select behavior for each type of editing operation, and that's why we have all these special rules. Here's a summary of the current protocols:

◆ **Cut, Copy, and Paste:** FCP will paste to the same tracks you copied from unless you change the Auto Select controls between copy and paste. If you do, clips will be pasted starting at the lowest-numbered Auto Select–enabled track.

◆ **Mark Clip and Select In to Out:** FCP selects clips on all Auto Select–enabled tracks.

◆ **Match Frame:** FCP displays the match frame for the frame at the playhead position on the lowest-numbered Auto Select–enabled track.

◆ **Add Edit:** FCP adds an edit on all Auto Select–enabled tracks.

◆ **Select Closest Edit:** FCP jumps to the closest edit point on the lowest-numbered Auto Select–enabled track (most of the time).

◆ **Apply Filter:** FCP applies a copy of the filter to clips between the Timeline In and Out points on all Auto Select–enabled tracks.

◆ **Previous and Next Keyframe Commands:** FCP navigates to the next (or previous) keyframe on an Auto Select–enabled track.

◆ **Playhead Sync in Open Mode:** FCP automatically opens in the Viewer the Timeline clip at playhead position on the highest-numbered Auto Select–enabled track.

◆ **Search Timeline:** FCP searches only Auto Select–enabled tracks if the Auto Select option is selected in the Find Dialog box.

◆ **Selection Tools Override Auto-Select:** The Tool palette's Selection, Range Selection, and Edit Selection tools can override the Auto Select feature. No need to click those teeny control buttons: Select a selection tool and then just—select. One exception here: The Add Edit Command ignores selected clips and observes Auto Select controls only.

To set In and Out points around a selected part of a sequence:

1. From the Tool palette, choose the Range Selection tool. If your desired selection is composed of whole clips, use the Group Selection tool.

2. In the Timeline, drag a marquee around the range you want to select.

3. Choose Mark > Mark Selection; or press Shift-A.

   The bounds of the selection become the sequence In and Out points (**Figure 10.81**).

Figure 10.81 The boundaries of your selection become the sequence In and Out points.

To set In and Out points at two markers:

1. Position the Timeline playhead anywhere between the two markers you want to use.

2. Choose Mark > Mark to Markers; or press Control-A.

   Sequence In and Out points are now set at the markers' Timeline locations.

Figure 10.82 Select the sequence clips you want to link in the Timeline.

Linking clips

Linking clips is Final Cut Pro's scheme for grouping clips. When clips are linked, any action performed on one clip affects the other clips as well. Check out the sidebar, "FCP Protocol: Linked Clips," later in this chapter, for the rules governing linked clips and the operation of linked selections.

To link a group of unrelated clips:

1. In the Timeline, select the clips you want to link (**Figure 10.82**).

   You can select one video and up to two audio clips from different tracks.

2. Choose Modify > Link; or press Command-L.

   In the Timeline, an underline appears beneath the linked clips' names, indicating their linked status.

> ## Merged Clips and Linking
>
> When you're editing sync video with production audio that has been recorded separately, you can sync up your audio and video takes in FCP and use the Modify > Link command to create linked audio+ video clips. Select your newly linked Timeline clips and drag them back into the Browser to create merged clips. Merged clips will load into the Viewer as if they were a single clip. Audio and video will reference each other, keeping track of changes in sync, but original audio and video timecode data is preserved; it's stored with the merged clip. For more information, see "Working with Merged Clips" in Chapter 4.

Figure 10.83 Activate linked selection by clicking the Linked Selection control. The control is enabled when the shading moves to the top half of the button.

FCP Protocol: Linked Clips

Here's how Final Cut Pro handles linked clips:

- Video and audio clips that originated from the same media file are linked automatically.

- You can set up multiple linked clip groups.

- You can switch linked selection on or off.

- When linked selection is turned on, FCP treats your linked items as a single entity for most operations.

- If you switch linked selection off, all your linked items will be treated as if they were unlinked, with the following exception: Audio and video clips that were captured in sync continue to reference each other even when linked selection is disabled, and will display out-of-sync indicators if moved out of sync with each other.

- Locking a track overrides a linked selection. If a linked item is on a locked track, it won't be modified, even if you modify an item it's linked to.

- Moving a linked clip's video to a higher track (for example, from track V1 to track V2) will automatically move the clip's audio to higher-numbered audio tracks (for example, from tracks A1 and A2 to tracks A3 and A4).

To permanently unlink a group of linked clips:

1. Select the linked items.

2. Choose Modify > Link; or press Command-L.

   In the Timeline, the underline beneath the linked clips' names disappears, indicating their unlinked status.

✔ Tip

- You can unlink a group of linked clips in a single operation, but linking operations must be performed one at a time.

Using linked selection

You can temporarily override the rules that govern a linked clip's selection. Editors frequently disable linked selection to select just the video (or audio) track of a linked clip, in order to create a *split edit* (that's an edit where a clip's audio and video tracks have different lengths).

You can disable linked selection for the entire sequence or for a single selection operation.

To turn linked selection on or off:

Do one of the following:

- Click the Linked Selection control on the right side of the Timeline window. (**Figure 10.83**).

- Choose Edit > Linked Selection.

- Press Shift-L to toggle linked selection on and off.

To select an item without selecting any items that are linked to it:

- Hold down the Option key when you select the item.

Moving Timeline clips

As with most things in Final Cut Pro, you have a choice of methods for moving clips within and between sequences. There are a variety of drag-and-drop methods, plus the timecode entry method, which offers greater precision but a little less flexibility.

To drag a clip to a new position:

1. In the Timeline, select the clip and drag it to a new position (**Figure 10.84**).

2. In the new position, *do one of the following:*
   - ◆ Drop the clip to perform an Overwrite edit (**Figure 10.85**).
   - ◆ Drop the clip while holding the Option key to perform an Insert edit.

To shift a clip to another track at the same timecode location:

1. In the Timeline, select the clip you want to move.

2. Hold down the Shift key while dragging the clip vertically to another track (**Figure 10.86**).

   The clip maintains its timecode position at the new track location.

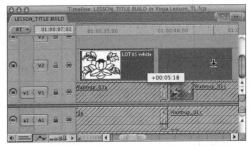

Figure 10.84 Dragging a clip to a new location. The pop-up indicator shows the offset from the clip's original location.

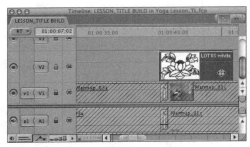

Figure 10.85 Dropping the clip performs an Overwrite edit in the new location.

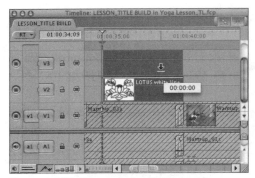

Figure 10.86 Holding down the Shift key while dragging the clip to a higher track.

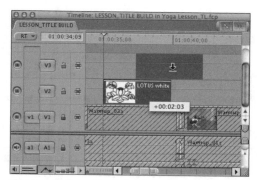

Figure 10.87 Press the Option key as you start to drag to copy the clip. Continue pressing Option as you drop the clip copy to perform an Insert edit; or release the key before you drop to perform an Overwrite edit.

To copy a clip to a new location:

1. In the Timeline, select the clip you want to move.

2. Hold down the Option key while dragging the clip to another location (**Figure 10.87**).

   A copy of the selected clip is edited into the new location.

✔ Tips

- You can make copies of sequence clips by dragging them from the Timeline into the Browser. Select, then drag multiple clips to make a copy of each clip in a single operation. Remember that this clip copy will include any changes you have made to the clip in the sequence.

- A quick way to make a Browser copy of every clip you've used in a sequence is to select the entire sequence in the Timeline (Command-A), and then drag the clips over to a Browser bin. Don't worry about wiping out your sequence—remember, you're making copies.

To copy and paste a clip into the Timeline:

1. Working in the Timeline, select the clip (**Figure 10.88**); or, use the Group Selection tool from the Tool palette to select clips from multiple tracks.

2. Cut or copy the selected material to the clipboard, *then do one of the following:*

   ◆ To paste the material into the same tracks you cut or copied from, position the playhead where you want to paste the clip.

   ◆ To assign different destination tracks for your pasted material, set the destination track by enabling its Auto Select control (and ensuring that all Auto Select controls on lower-numbered tracks are disabled), and then position the playhead where you want to paste the clip (**Figure 10.89**).

3. Choose Edit > Paste; or press Command-V. The pasted material overwrites the sequence clips, starting at the playhead location in the destination track and extending for the duration of the pasted material (**Figure 10.90**).

✔ Tip

■ Press Shift-V to insert-edit the pasted material in the new sequence location.

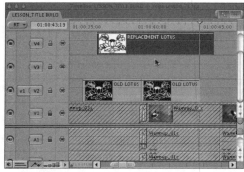
Figure 10.88 Select the clip you want to copy and paste.

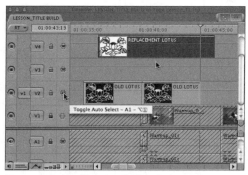
Figure 10.89 Position the playhead where you want the pasted clip to start; then target the track you want to paste into by ensuring that it's the lowest-numbered track with Auto Select enabled.

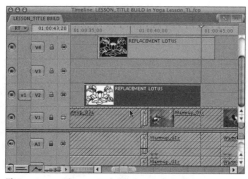
Figure 10.90 The pasted clip overwrites the contents of the lowest-numbered Auto-selected track.

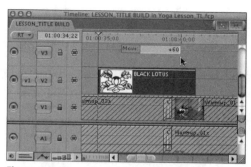

Figure 10.91 Type +60 and then press Enter to position the clip 60 frames (2 seconds) later in the sequence.

To reposition an item in the Timeline by entering a timecode:

1. In the Timeline, select the clip you want to move.

2. Enter a new timecode number; or use the shorthand methods detailed in Chapter 8, "Working with Clips in the Viewer."

   As you type, a text entry window appears below the Timeline ruler (**Figure 10.91**).

3. Press Enter.

   The clip is repositioned, if there is space at the new timecode location.

   If you had selected an edit tool from the Tool palette before making the timecode entry, an edit of that type is performed in the direction indicated by the timecode.

✔ Tip

■ Moving clips around via timecode entry is wonderfully mouse-less and precise, but there are limitations: When you're repositioning a clip by entering a timecode, FCP won't allow you move the clip so it overwrites another clip. Your clip will move as far as possible without overwriting, and you'll see a "clip collision" error message.

Finding and closing gaps

As you assemble a sequence, all that cutting and pasting and slipping and sliding may create gaps in your sequence tracks. Sometimes the gaps are too small to see in the Timeline, but a gap of even a single frame is easily detectable in Canvas playback.

This section contains a repertoire of techniques for detecting and closing gaps and explains FCP protocol for defining gaps.

To find gaps in a sequence:

1. Make the sequence active; then press the Home key to position the playhead at the beginning of the sequence (**Figure 10.92**).

2. Choose Mark > Next > Gap; or press Shift-G.

   The playhead moves to the beginning of the first gap found (**Figure 10.93**).

3. If you want to close the gap, use one of the procedures described in the next section, "To close a gap."

4. Repeat steps 2 and 3 until you reach the end of the sequence.

✔ Tip

■ Press Option-G to jump the playhead back to the previous gap.

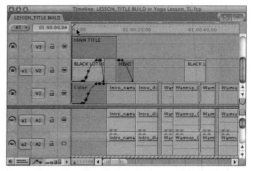

Figure 10.92 Pressing the Home key positions the playhead at the beginning of the sequence.

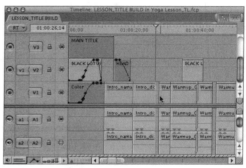

Figure 10.93 The playhead jumps to the start of the first gap found.

FCP Protocol: Gaps and Track Gaps

Final Cut Pro defines two classes of gaps: gaps and track gaps.

◆ A gap is any empty spot across all unlocked video or audio tracks.

◆ A track gap is any empty spot on an individual track in a sequence; if you have a gap on one track, but a clip bridges the gap on a higher or lower track, FCP defines that as a track gap.

Some gap-closing techniques, such as Ripple Delete, work only with gaps, not track gaps. To close track gaps, lock all other tracks, leaving the gapped tracks as the only unlocked tracks in your sequence.

Figure 10.94 Control-click the gap; then choose Close Gap from the shortcut menu.

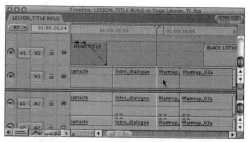

Figure 10.95 Clips to the right of the gap shift left to close the gap.

To close a gap:

1. Make the sequence active; then position the playhead anywhere in the gap.

2. *Do one of the following:*
   - ◆ Select the gap and press Delete.
   - ◆ Control-click the gap; then select Close Gap from the shortcut menu (**Figure 10.94**).
   - ◆ Choose Sequence > Close Gap.

   Clips to the right of the gap will shift left to close the gap. These clips adjust their timecode location to occur earlier, and the sequence duration may change (**Figure 10.95**).

To find track gaps in a Timeline track:

1. In the Timeline, target the track you want to search (**Figure 10.96**).

2. Press the Home key to position the playhead at the beginning of the sequence.

3. Choose Mark > Next > Track Gap.

   The playhead moves to the beginning of the first track gap found (**Figure 10.97**).

To close a track gap:

Do one of the following:

◆ Open the shortcut menu over the gap and choose Close Gap.

◆ Select the gap and press the Delete key.

◆ Position the playhead anywhere within the gap; then choose Sequence > Close Gap.

✔ Tip

■ Sometimes a gap can't be closed because clips don't have space to shift back. If the command can't be completed, the Close Gap command will appear dimmed (**Figure 10.98**). Try the track-locking technique discussed next.

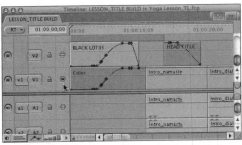

Figure 10.96 To select a track to search for track gaps, target the track and enable the Auto Select control.

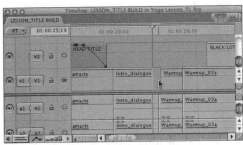

Figure 10.97 The playhead jumps to the start of the first track gap found.

Figure 10.98 The Close Gap command is dimmed when a gap can't be closed because clips don't have space to shift back. Resizing one of the adjacent clips to fill the gap looks like a better option here.

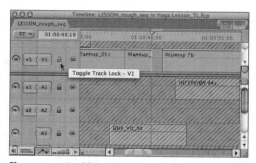

Figure 10.99 Locking every track but the gapped track allows you to close the gap by shifting material on the unlocked track only.

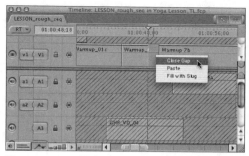

Figure 10.100 Control-click the gap; then choose Close Gap from the shortcut menu.

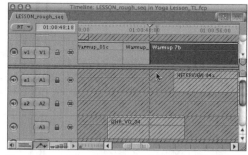

Figure 10.101 Clips to the right of the gap shift left to close the track gap. Clips on the locked tracks have not moved.

To close a track gap without affecting other tracks in a sequence:

1. Press Shift-F4 to lock all video tracks in your sequence.

2. Press Shift-F5 to lock all audio tracks in your sequence.

3. Click the Track Lock control of the gapped track.

   Your selected track is now the only unlocked track in the sequence (**Figure 10.99**).

4. *Do one of the following:*
   - Select the gap and press Delete.
   - Control-click the gap; then select Close Gap from the shortcut menu (**Figure 10.100**).
   - Choose Sequence > Close Gap.

   Clips to the right of the gap will shift left to close the gap. These clips adjust their timecode locations to occur earlier, and the sequence duration may change (**Figure 10.101**).

5. If you want to unlock your sequence tracks after closing the gap, press Shift-F4 and Shift-F5 again to toggle track locking off.

To close a track gap with the Select Forward tool:

1. Snapping must be on; if necessary, choose View > Snapping to turn it on.

2. From the Tool palette, choose the Select Track Forward tool; then click the first clip to the right of the track gap (**Figure 10.102**).

    The clips to the right of the sequence are selected, and the pointer changes to a four-headed arrow.

3. Drag the selected clips to the left until they snap to close the gap; then drop them as an Overwrite edit (**Figure 10.103**).

To close a gap by extending an adjacent clip (an Extend edit):

◆ In some cases, you may prefer to close a gap in a sequence by extending the duration of a clip that's adjacent to the gap. One advantage of an Extend edit is that all the clips in your sequence can stay put, and you won't develop sync problems. To learn how to perform an Extend edit, see Chapter 11, "Fine Cut: Trimming Edits."

✔ Tips

■ When you fine-tune gaps in sequences, take advantage of the Zoom tools to scale your view so you can see what you're doing. You may also find that turning on snapping will simplify selection and manipulation of gaps and track gaps.

■ Here's a quick way to read a gap's duration: Select the gap in the Timeline and then press Shift-A. The Mark Selection command sets sequence In and Out points, and your gap's duration appears in the Timecode Duration field in the Canvas. Wow—it actually takes longer to describe it than to do it.

Figure 10.102 Use the Select Track Forward tool to click the first clip to the right of the track gap.

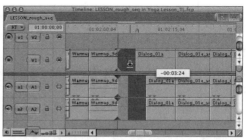

Figure 10.103 Drag the selected clips to the left until they snap to close the gap; then drop them as an Overwrite edit.

FCP Protocol: Deleting Items in the Timeline

You can delete items in the Timeline simply by selecting them and then pressing Delete. But if the Timeline window is active and you press Delete with no items selected in the Timeline, FCP protocol dictates that all material between the Timeline and Canvas In and Out points is deleted on all unlocked tracks.

Learn more about performing Delete edits in Chapter 9, "Basic Editing."

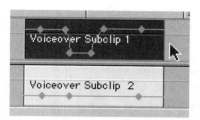

Figure 10.104 Select the clip whose attributes you want to copy; then press Command-C.

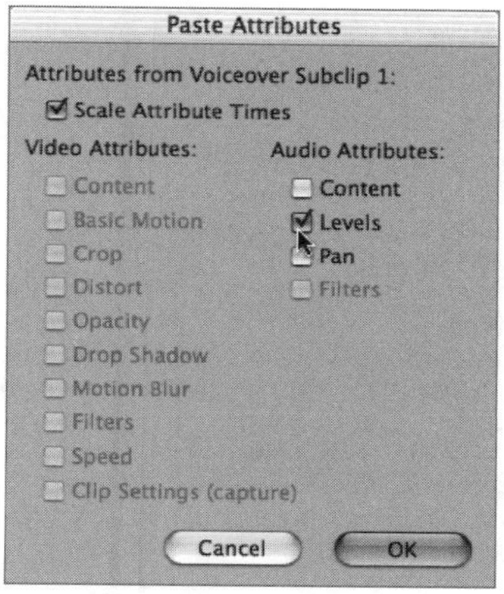

Paste Attributes

Attributes from Voiceover Subclip 1:

☑ Scale Attribute Times

Video Attributes:
- ☐ Content
- ☐ Basic Motion
- ☐ Crop
- ☐ Distort
- ☐ Opacity
- ☐ Drop Shadow
- ☐ Motion Blur
- ☐ Filters
- ☐ Speed
- ☐ Clip Settings (capture)

Audio Attributes:
- ☐ Content
- ☑ Levels
- ☐ Pan
- ☐ Filters

Cancel   OK

Figure 10.105 Selecting audio levels in the Paste Attributes dialog box.

✔ Tip

- Pasting audio levels can be a quick way to add an audio element—say, another sound effects track—to a scene you have already mixed. You can "borrow" the mix levels from a track that has already been adjusted to match action and paste those levels onto your new effects track. You can apply the same idea to video compositing: Paste the motion path from one video layer to another that you want to track the same path; or, paste and then offset the timing of the motion path.

Copying and pasting clip attributes

A clip's *attributes* comprise the settings applied to a particular media file in Final Cut Pro. You can paste all the attributes of one clip onto another clip, or you can select and paste some of a clip's settings onto another clip without affecting other attributes. For example, you can apply just the filter settings from clip A to clip B without changing the video frames of clip B. Conversely, you can replace the video frames of clip B without disturbing the filters that have been applied to it by pasting only the video frames from another clip. If you just paste into a sequence without selecting a clip in the Timeline or the Canvas, the clip's media contents and selected attributes are included.

The Remove Attributes command is an easy way to strip selected settings from a clip or to remove selected settings from multiple clips in a single operation.

To paste the attributes of a copied clip into another clip:

1. In the Timeline or the Browser, select a clip whose attributes you want to copy (**Figure 10.104**); then press Command-C to copy it to the clipboard.

2. Select the clip that will inherit the attributes; then choose Edit > Paste Attributes; or press Option-V.

3. In the Paste Attributes dialog box, select the attributes that you want to transfer to the selected clip (**Figure 10.105**).
   - ◆ **Scale Attribute Times:** Check this box to adjust the timing of the incoming keyframes to fit the duration of the clip inheriting the attributes. If this option is not selected, leftover keyframes will be cropped off the end.

continues on next page

Video Attributes:

◆ **Content:** Paste the video frames only. If the receiving clip is a different length, incoming video frames are cropped or lengthened to match the duration of the receiving clip. The clip speed is not affected.

◆ **Basic Motion, Crop, Distort, Opacity, Drop Shadow, Motion Blur,** and **Filters:** You can pick and choose among these options to apply the parameter values and keyframes you have set for each attribute.

◆ **Speed:** Apply the same speed settings.

◆ **Clip Settings:** Paste all capture settings that are logged with a clip. (You can review these settings on the Clip Settings tab of the Log and Capture window.)

Audio Attributes:

◆ **Content:** Paste the audio waveform only. If the receiving clip is a different length, the incoming audio file is cropped or lengthened to match the duration of the receiving clip. The clip speed is not affected.

◆ **Levels, Pan,** and **Filters:** Apply the parameter values and keyframes you have set for each attribute.

4. Click OK.

The selected attributes are pasted into the receiving clip (**Figure 10.106**).

To remove attributes from a clip:

1. In the Timeline, select the clip or clips whose attributes you want to remove.

2. Choose Edit > Remove Attributes.

3. In the Remove Attributes dialog box, check the attributes you want to remove (**Figure 10.107**); then click OK.

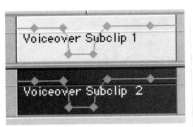

Figure 10.106 The audio levels from Voiceover Subclip 1 have been copied and pasted into Voiceover Subclip 2.

Figure 10.107 Check the attributes you want to remove; then click OK.

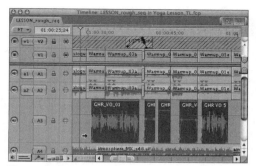

Figure 10.108 Selecting multiple audio clips with the Select Track Forward tool.

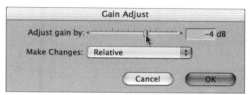

Figure 10.109 Adjusting the audio levels relative to their current levels.

✔ Tips

■ Use FCP's audio level meters to check your audio level adjustments. Choose Window > Audio Meters to display the meters.

■ Are you ear-wrestling with audio tracks that have been recorded just a little too hot for comfort? FCP's Audio Peak Detection feature will scan your tracks and drop markers to identify those hot spots. For more information, see "Using Audio Peak Detection" in Chapter 12.

■ *Normalizing* is a fast, automated way to adjust the gain of an entire audio track. Select the audio clip(s), then choose Modify > Audio > Apply Normalization Gain. FCP will scan your track, identify its loudest point, and adjust the overall level so that peak is at the dB level you specify.

Adjusting levels or opacity of multiple clips

Use the Modify > Levels command to adjust multiple clips in a single operation:

◆ Use Modify > Levels to adjust levels for a group of audio clips.

◆ Use Modify > Opacity to adjust opacity levels for a group of video clips.

To adjust audio levels for a group of clips:

1. In the Timeline, select a group of audio clips whose levels you want to adjust (**Figure 10.108**).

2. Choose Modify > Levels.

3. In the Gain Adjust dialog box, *do one of the following:*

◆ Choose Relative from the pop-up menu; then use the slider to adjust each clip's volume relative to its current level by the dB value indicated next to the slider (**Figure 10.109**).

◆ Choose Absolute from the pop-up menu; then use the slider to set each clip's volume to the dB value indicated next to the slider.

4. Click OK.

To adjust opacity levels on a group of clips:

1. In the Timeline, select just the video portion of a group of clips whose levels you want to adjust.

2. Choose Modify > Levels.

3. In the Opacity Adjust dialog box, *do one of the following:*

   ◆ Choose Relative from the pop-up menu; then use the slider to adjust each clip's opacity relative to its current level by the percentage value indicated next to the slider.

   ◆ Choose Absolute from the pop-up menu; then use the slider to set each clip's opacity to the percentage value indicated next to the slider (**Figure 10.110**).

4. Click OK.

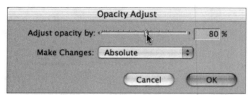

Figure 10.110 Setting opacity levels to 80 percent for all selected clips.

Changing the playback speed of a clip

Changing the playback speed of a clip adjusts its duration by duplicating or skipping clip frames and creates either a slow-motion or a fast-motion effect. For example, if you start with a 1-minute clip and set the playback speed to 50 percent, Final Cut Pro will duplicate each frame, doubling the clip length to 2 minutes. Your adjusted 2-minute clip will appear to play back at half speed. If you start with the same 1-minute clip and increase the playback speed to 200 percent, the adjusted clip will skip every other frame and appear to play back at double speed in 30 seconds. You can specify frame blending when modifying a clip's speed to smooth out the slow-motion or fast-motion effect.

✔ Tips

■ You wanted it, you got it—the Time Remap tool (available in the Tool palette) and the Timeline's Speed Indicator display (available in the Clip Keyframes menu). Now you too can create all that wild time-bending you see in every other ad on ESPN2. For more information, see "Time Remapping" in Chapter 15.

■ When a clip is simply too short to fit that gap in your montage, the Fit to Fill edit is a one-step solution that automatically speed-modifies the clip so it fills that gap perfectly. See "Fit to Fill edit" in Chapter 9.

■ The View Native Speed timecode viewing option displays each frame's native timecode number instead of timecode derived from the clip's original timecode rate (**Figure 10.111**). You'll see the difference only when viewing timecode for a speed-modified clip. For example, if you view the native speed of a 30-fps clip speed-modified to play back at 50 percent normal speed, you'll note that the same timecode number appears on two consecutive frames before incrementing because FCP repeats each frame twice to create the slow-motion playback.

Figure 10.111 In the Viewer's Current Timecode field, timecode appears italicized when the View Native Speed timecode viewing option is enabled. View Native Speed displays the native timecode number for each frame, which can be a help when you're trying to finesse a variable speed effect.

To change the playback speed of a clip:

1. Select the clip in the Timeline (**Figure 10.112**).

2. Choose Modify > Speed; or press Command-J.

3. Choose from the options in the Speed dialog box (**Figure 10.113**):

   ◆ Choose Constant Speed or Variable Speed from the pop-up menu. (For information on working with variable speed-modified clips, see "Time Remapping" in Chapter 15.)

   ◆ You can modify the clip speed by a percentage or specify a duration for the adjusted clip. Changing the clip speed or duration automatically adjusts the other value.

   ◆ The Reverse check box renders the clip's frames in reverse order; the adjusted clip plays in reverse.

   ◆ The Frame Blending option smoothes motion at slow or fast speeds.

4. Click OK.

   The adjusted duration of the modified clip will be calculated based on the clip's original In and Out points (**Figure 10.114**).

✔ Tip

■ Speed effects can be applied only to whole clips, but if you want to speed-modify only a portion of a clip, you can use the Time Remap feature, or use the Razor Blade tool to break out the portion of the clip that you want to process.

■ You can also make constant and variable speed changes to generator clips.

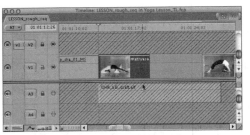

Figure 10.112 Select the clip in the Timeline.

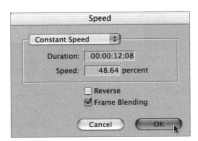

Figure 10.113 Choose Constant Speed, then modify your entire clip's speed by a percentage or specify a duration; or choose Variable speed and use the Time Remap tool.

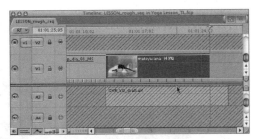

Figure 10.114 The size of the clip's icon increases to reflect the duration change caused by modifying the playback speed, and the adjusted speed appears next to the clip's name.

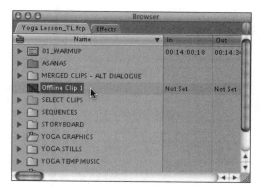

Figure 10.115 A new offline clip appears in the Browser. You can insert an offline clip into a sequence and edit it, but you will not see it.

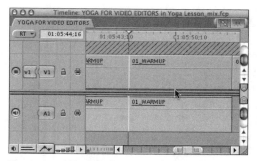

Figure 10.116 Final Cut Pro uses color-coded lines at the bottom of sequence clips to indicate frames that are duplicated elsewhere in the sequence. The color indicates how many times the frames have been re-used.

Using offline clips

An offline clip is defined as a placeholder for an actual media file. An offline clip could be:

◆ Logged but not yet captured

◆ A stand-in for the actual media file, which has been moved or deleted

◆ A stand-in for media that is not yet available

You can treat offline clips just like regular clips: You can set In and Out points, add transitions and filters, rename the clips, and so on. Later, you can replace an offline clip by recapturing it or reconnecting to the original source media.

To create an offline clip:

◆ Choose File > New > Offline Clip.

An offline clip is inserted into the Browser (**Figure 10.115**).

See "Reconnecting Offline Files" in Chapter 20 for more information on offline clips.

Using duplicate frame detection

Final Cut Pro's dupe detection uses a color-coded overlay that appears at the bottom of Timeline clips containing frames that are duplicated elsewhere in the sequence (**Figure 10.116**). Enable duplicate frame overlays by selecting them in the Timeline's Layout popup menu. For more information, see "Options for Displaying Duplicate Frames" on page I-130 of Apple's *Final Cut Pro User Manual* PDF.

To see a clip's list of frames duplicated elsewhere in the sequence:

◆ Control-click the clip, then choose Dupe Frames from the shortcut menu.

The Dupe Frames submenu lists the clips containing frames also used in this clip, and the number of duplicate frames in each instance (**Figure 10.117**). Select a clip from the submenu to jump to the first duplicated frame in that clip.

Working with keyframes in the Timeline

Final Cut Pro has two types of keyframes:

◆ **Keyframe overlays** indicate clip opacity for video clips and volume level for audio clips. Keyframe overlays are displayed as line graphs right on top of the track display in the Timeline (**Figure 10.118**).

◆ **Keyframes** appear in the keyframe editor and the Filter and Motion bars beneath sequence clips that have filter and motion effects applied to them (**Figure 10.119**). Keyframes indicate where parameters change for filter and motion effects. You can select the parameter keyframes you want to display in a particular Filter or Motion bar. Working with keyframes to create motion effects is covered in Chapter 15, "Motion."

For more information about using these keyframing tools, see "Working with Keyframes in the Timeline" in Chapter 14.

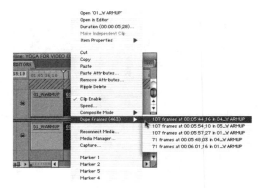

Figure 10.117 Choose Dupe Frames from the clip's shortcut menu to see a list of clips containing the duplicated frames. Select a clip to jump to the first duped frame in that clip.

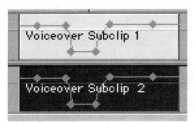

Figure 10.118 Keyframe overlays allow you to sculpt audio levels right in the Timeline.

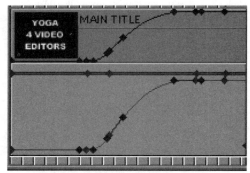

Figure 10.119 Keyframes also appear on the keyframe editor in the Timeline. The same Opacity keyframes are shown here in two places; on the clip's overlay and in the clip's keyframe editor.

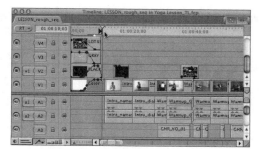

Figure 10.120 Position the playhead at the beginning of the section you want to search.

Searching for Items in the Timeline

The Final Cut Pro search engine is built to search for other items beyond clips and sequences. Use FCP's Find command to search the Timeline for clip names, marker text, and clip timecodes. You can search for items forward or backward. You can also search for and close gaps in all tracks in a sequence or in individual tracks.

✔ Tip

■ This might be a good time to mention that when you place a clip in a sequence, the new sequence clip is a separate version from the one that stays in the Browser, even though the two clips may have the same name. So if you are searching for the sequence version of a clip, you need to search in that sequence.

To search for items in the sequence:

1. Open the sequence in the Timeline.

2. *Do one of the following:*

 ◆ To search the entire sequence, position the playhead at the start of the sequence.

 ◆ To search a selected portion of the sequence, set the sequence In and Out points to specify the search area; or position the playhead at the beginning of the section you want to search (**Figure 10.120**).

3. Choose Edit > Find; or press Command-F.

continues on next page

4. From the Search pop-up menu, choose the type of item to search for (**Figure 10.121**):

- ◆ **Names/Markers:** Search for the text in clip names, marker names, and marker comments.

- ◆ **Timecode Options:** Search for any source or auxiliary timecode in a clip.

5. Choose which tracks to search from the Where pop-up menu:

- ◆ **All Tracks:** Search all tracks in the sequence.

- ◆ **Auto Select Tracks:** Search only tracks with Auto Select controls enabled.

- ◆ **From In to Out:** Search between the sequence In and Out points on all tracks (**Figure 10.122**).

6. To perform the search, *do one of the following:*

- ◆ Click Find to find the item.

- ◆ Click Find All to find all occurrences of clips that match the search criteria (**Figure 10.123**).

Clips matching the search criteria are selected in the Timeline (**Figure 10.124**). If the search returns a marker, the playhead is positioned on the marker.

To cycle through items in the Timeline that match the criteria:

- ◆ Follow the search procedure outlined in the preceding steps; then press F3.

To search for an item backward from the position of the playhead:

- ◆ Follow the search procedure outlined in the preceding steps; then press Shift-F3.

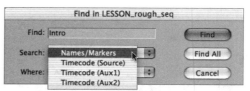

Figure 10.121 Specifying a search for clips or markers with "Intro" in their names.

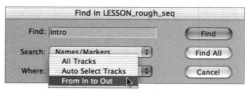

Figure 10.122 Specifying a search of the sequence from the sequence In to the sequence Out point.

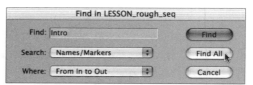

Figure 10.123 Clicking Find All causes FCP to highlight all clips in the sequence that match the search criteria.

Figure 10.124 Two clips whose names contain the phrase "Intro" are highlighted in the Timeline. Only the section between the sequence In and Out points has been searched.

FINE CUT: TRIMMING EDITS

What's the difference between performing an edit and trimming an edit? An edit adds new material to a sequence; a trim adjusts previously assembled sequence material. The development of nonlinear editing has expanded the repertoire of trim edit types. Some trim edit types (like Ripple and Roll) date back to the tape-to-tape days of video editing; others (like the Slide edit) could not have existed before the advent of nonlinear systems.

In this chapter, you'll learn about the types of trim edits available in Final Cut Pro. Each can be performed in a variety of ways (with tools, with timecode entry, and with keystrokes) and in a few different locations (the Timeline, the Trim Edit window, and the Viewer), so you'll learn how and where you can perform each type. This chapter also introduces the Trim Edit window, a specialized work environment for making fine adjustments to your edits.

Types of Trimming Operations

Each trim edit type can solve a particular editing problem, so it's a good idea to become familiar with the whole palette—maybe even try them all in advance. (If you would like to review FCP's basic editing types, return to Chapter 9, "Basic Editing.")

Figure 11.1 A Ripple Left edit, as performed in the Timeline.

◆ **Ripple:** A Ripple edit adjusts the length of one clip in a sequence by changing either the In or the Out point of that clip. A Ripple edit accommodates the change by rippling (or shifting) the timecode location of the clips that come after the adjusted edit, without affecting their duration. Use a Ripple edit if you want to adjust the length of a clip in a sequence without losing sync or creating a gap. Locked tracks will not be rippled. As an example, the Close Gap command in the Timeline performs a Ripple Delete edit.

Figure 11.1 shows a Ripple Left edit, in contrast to **Figure 11.2**, which shows a Ripple Right edit. Note the differences in the pointer and in the selected edit points.

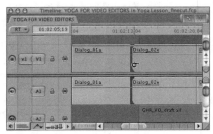

Figure 11.2 A Ripple Right edit, as performed in the Timeline.

◆ **Roll:** A Roll edit (**Figure 11.3**) adjusts the location of an edit point shared by two clips. A rolling edit makes the change by subtracting frames from clip A on one side of the edit to compensate for the frames added to clip B on the other side of the edit. The overall duration of the sequence remains unchanged, but the location of the edit in the sequence is changed.

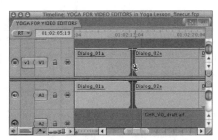

Figure 11.3 A Roll edit, as performed in the Timeline.

◆ **Slip:** A Slip edit (**Figure 11.4**) is an adjustment made within a single clip. When you slip a clip, you select a different part of that clip to include in the sequence, while maintaining the same clip duration and timecode location in the sequence. Surrounding clips are not affected, and the sequence duration does not change.

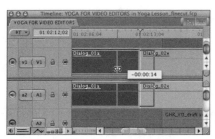

Figure 11.4 A Slip edit, as performed in the Timeline. The selected portion of the clip has shifted –14 frames.

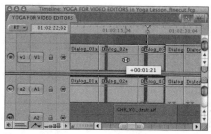

Figure 11.5 A Slide edit, as performed in the Timeline. The selected clip has slid 1 second, 21 frames later in the sequence.

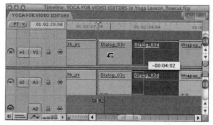

Figure 11.6 A Swap edit, as performed in the Timeline. The two clips will swap positions.

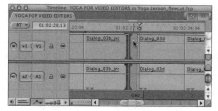

Figure 11.7 An Extend edit. Select the edit point of the clip you want to extend to the playhead position.

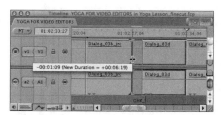

Figure 11.8 Resizing a clip in the Timeline. Drag an edit point with the Selection tool to adjust the clip's duration.

◆ **Slide:** A Slide edit (**Figure 11.5**) moves a single clip in relation to those before and after it, so that the durations of the clips on either side change, but the In and Out points of the clip you're sliding remain the same. The clips immediately adjacent to the sliding clip accommodate the change; the overall sequence duration does not change.

◆ **Swap:** A Swap edit (**Figure 11.6**) doesn't alter any sequence clips, but it does change the order in which they appear in the sequence. Perform a Swap edit in the Timeline by selecting a clip, dragging it to a new location, and placing it into the sequence using an Insert edit.

◆ **Extend:** An Extend edit (**Figure 11.7**) moves a selected edit point to the playhead position by extending the clip's duration, rolling over any gaps or clips that are encountered. You can extend an edit only to the maximum length of that clip's media. An Extend edit is a useful way to fill sequence gaps without affecting the sequence duration.

◆ **Resize:** The Selection (or Arrow) tool can be used to resize a clip in the Timeline by dragging an edit point (**Figure 11.8**). You can drag the edit point to create a gap (by making the duration of the clip smaller); or to cover an existing gap.

TYPES OF TRIMMING OPERATIONS

Selecting an Edit for Trimming

The first step in trimming an edit in the Trim Edit window or the Timeline is selecting the edit. If you use a trimming tool from the Tool palette to select the edit, you can select and define the type of trim to perform at the same time. You can select only one edit per track.

If an edit point you select for trimming has been linked to others, the edit points of the linked items are also selected. Any adjustments you make will be applied to all clips in the linked selection, so if you find that you can't trim an edit point, the conflict may be with one of the linked items. You can toggle linked selection off by holding down the Option key as you select the edit.

With snapping turned on, edit points will stick to markers, keyframes, the playhead, and edit points on other tracks. Snapping can simplify alignment of edits in the Timeline. To toggle snapping on the fly, press the N key while dragging edit points.

✔ Tips

■ Many trim operations will ripple all of your unlocked tracks as part of the trim process. If you don't want your tracks taking unplanned trips when you are trimming, lock all tracks except the ones you want to adjust.

■ If FCP refuses to execute a trim edit that would ripple your unlocked tracks backward, check to see if clips on other tracks in your sequence can't move back in time without bumping into other clips.

Tips on Tools

FCP's edit tools get a heavy workout when you transform your rough assembly into a fine cut. You can review the contents of the Tool palette's selection and edit tools in "Anatomy of the Tool Palette" in Chapter 10, but here are some other ideas for making efficient use of these tools:

◆ Use the keyboard shortcuts to call up an edit tool. See **Table 11.1** for a list of basic selection shortcuts. Check out Appendix A for more shortcuts.

◆ Once you've selected an edit tool, press U to cycle through the three principal trim types: Roll, Ripple Left, and Ripple Right.

◆ You can use the Ripple and Roll tools to directly select the edit you're adjusting. With one click, you've selected the edit and specified the edit type.

◆ After you've selected your first Timeline edit point, use the Up and Down Arrow keys to jump to your next or previous edit. FCP automatically selects each edit point as you jump to it.

◆ Pressing the Option key to override linked selection works on all edit tools, not just the Selection arrow.

◆ Pressing the Command key while dragging an edit tool on a selected edit in the Timeline will "gear down" the tool and allow you to make fine adjustments.

◆ Turn off snapping to make fine adjustments that don't align with an existing edit point, marker, or clip boundary.

◆ Turn on snapping to align an edit to another existing edit point or marker.

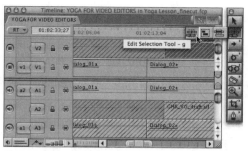

Figure 11.9 Choose the Edit Selection tool from the Tool palette. This tool is designed to detect and select edits only.

Table 11.1

Tool Selection Shortcuts

Tool	Shortcut
Roll	R
Ripple	R+R
Slip	S
Slide	S+S
Razor Blade	B
Razor Blade All	B+B
Selection	A
Edit Selection	G

To select an edit in the Timeline:

Do one of the following:

◆ From the Tool palette, choose the Edit Selection tool (**Figure 11.9**); or press G. Then click an edit point in the Timeline. The Trim Edit window opens.

◆ From the Tool palette, choose the Selection tool; then click the edge of the clip in the Timeline. Double-click the edit if you want the Trim Edit window to open as well.

◆ From the Tool palette, choose the Ripple tool or the Roll tool; then click the edge of the clip in the Timeline.

◆ Press V to select the edit point nearest the playhead's location.

✔ Tips

■ If you are having trouble selecting Timeline edit points, use the Zoom slider to magnify your view, or try again with the Ripple tool or the Roll tool; they're designed to select edit points only, so you can't accidentally select a clip.

■ Using the Option key to override linked selection works with any edit tool, just as it does with the Selection tool.

Quick Navigation Keys

Option and Shift modifier keys are used throughout FCP's keyboard shortcuts for navigation. Here's a set of keyboard shortcuts to help you motor through your sequence while you fine-tune your edit.

Key	Function	Shift + key	Option + key
I	Set In	Go to In	Clear In
O	Set Out	Go to Out	Clear Out
M	Set Marker	Next Marker	Previous Marker
E	Extend Edit	Next Edit	Previous Edit
G		Next Gap	Previous Gap
K		Next Keyframe	Previous Keyframe

To select multiple edits in the Timeline:

Do one of the following:

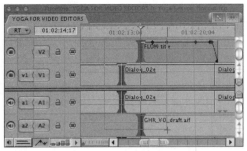

Figure 11.10 Draw a marquee around the edit points you want to select.

◆ From the Tool palette, choose the Edit Selection tool; then draw a marquee around the edit points of one or more Timeline tracks (**Figure 11.10**). You can select one edit per track; the selected edits don't have to be aligned in time.

The Trim Edit window opens as you release the mouse button.

◆ From the Tool palette, choose the Selection tool; then Command-click the edge of the clips in the Timeline. Double-click any selected edit if you want the Trim Edit window to open as well.

◆ From the Tool palette, choose the Ripple tool or the Roll tool; then Command-click the edge of the clips in the Timeline.

All Keys: Mouseless Trimming in FCP

You can work your way through your edit without touching the mouse. Here's one possible scenario:

1. Press Shift-E to jump the playhead to the next edit in the Timeline.

2. Press V to select the nearest edit.

3. Press \ (backslash) to play the sequence before and after the selected edit point.

4. Press R to select the Roll tool.

5. Press + (plus) or – (minus), and then enter a number of frames to roll the edit. So many keyboard shortcuts in FCP—and so many ways to speed your work while you give your mouse hand a rest. To learn more, check out the keyboard shortcuts in Appendix A.

Anatomy of the Trim Edit Window

The Trim Edit window is a work environment optimized for making fine adjustments to a single edit point. You can trim the selected edit by one frame or several frames, quickly switch between Ripple and Roll edits, and play back the edit to review your trim adjustments. The Play Around Edit button is designed to loop playback of your edit while you fine-tune it. The looping is not seamless, though; a slight interruption occurs in the playback when you nudge the edit point.

Figure 11.11 shows an overview of the Trim Edit window.

- **Outgoing clip name:** Displays the name of the outgoing clip.

- **Outgoing clip duration:** Displays the elapsed time between the In and Out points of the outgoing clip. This value updates to reflect trim adjustments.

- **Outgoing clip current timecode:** Displays the clip's source timecode at the current position of the playhead.

continues on next page

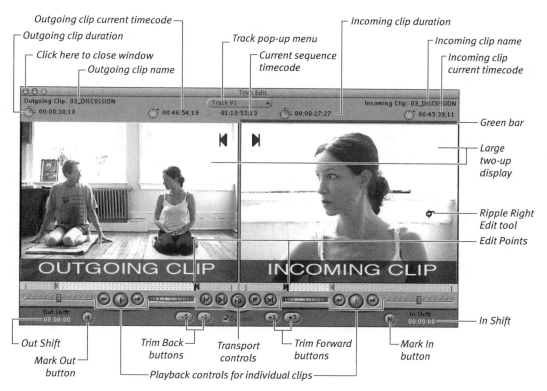

Figure 11.11 Use the Trim Edit window to make fine adjustments to a selected edit point.

◆ **Track pop-up menu:** Displays a list if multiple edits have been selected. Select the track you want to edit in the Trim Edit window.

◆ **Current sequence timecode:** Displays the sequence timecode location of the edit point. Enter + or – and a duration to roll the edit point. You don't need to click in the field; just start typing.

◆ **Incoming clip current timecode:** Displays the clip's source timecode at the current position of the playhead.

◆ **Incoming clip duration:** Displays the elapsed time between the In and Out points of the incoming clip. This value updates to reflect trim adjustments.

◆ **Incoming clip name:** Displays the name of the incoming clip.

◆ **Large two-up display:** The left screen displays the last frame before the edit. The right screen displays the first frame after the edit.

◆ **Green bar:** Indicates which side of the edit you are trimming.

◆ **Edit points:** Indicate the current Out and In points for the two clips in the Trim edit window. You can trim by dragging the outgoing clip's Out point or the incoming clip's In point with an edit tool.

◆ **Playback controls for individual clips:** The outgoing and incoming clips have separate playback controls. Use these controls to play only that clip without changing the current edit point location.

◆ **Out Shift:** Indicates the number of frames that the Out point has been adjusted.

◆ **Mark Out button:** Click to set a new Out point for the outgoing clip at the current playhead position.

◆ **Trim Back buttons:** Nudge the selected edit point to the left. Trim by single-frame increments or by another frame increment you specify on the General tab of FCP's Preferences window.

◆ **Dynamic Trim check box:** Check to enable dynamic trimming mode. See "To use dynamic trim mode to adjust an edit point," later in this chapter.

◆ **Trim Forward buttons:** Nudge the selected edit point to the right.

◆ **Mark In button:** Click to set a new In point for the incoming clip at the current playhead position.

◆ **In Shift:** Indicates the number of frames that the In point has been adjusted.

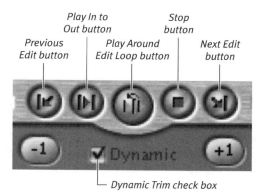

Play In to
Out button

Stop
button

Previous
Edit button

Play Around
Edit Loop button

Next Edit
button

Dynamic Trim check box

Figure 11.12 Trim Edit window transport controls detail. The Dynamic Trim check box is located beneath the transport controls.

Figure 11.12 shows the Trim Edit window's transport controls.

◆ **Previous Edit button:** Click to move the previous edit into the active area of the Trim Edit window.

◆ **Play In to Out button:** Click to play from the start of the first clip to the end of the second clip.

◆ **Play Around Edit Loop button:** Click to loop playback of the edit point plus the specified pre-roll and post-roll. Playback loops until you click Stop. You can continue trimming the edit while playback is looping.

◆ **Stop button:** Click to stop playback and position the playhead on the edit point.

◆ **Next Edit button:** Click to move the next edit into the active area of the Trim Edit window.

Audio Monitoring Options in the Trim Edit Window

FCP's Trim Edit window offers audio monitoring flexibility during trimming but the implementation of this feature is a little tricky, so prick up your ears:

Two audio monitoring preferences appear on the Editing tab of the User Preferences window. You can enable and disable either monitoring option without leaving the Trim Edit window by using a keyboard shortcut.

Trim with Sequence Audio (Command-Option-A) allows you to monitor all audio tracks at the playhead position when trimming an edit in the Trim Edit window. Disable this preference to confine Trim Edit audio monitoring to the selected clip's audio.

Trim with Edit Selection Audio (Mute Others) (Command-Option-Z) limits audio monitoring in the Trim Edit window to just the audio tracks included in the edit you selected for trimming in the Trim Edit window. With this preference enabled, you'll hear all selected audio, whether or not it is linked to the selected edit point. Disable this preference to confine Trim Edit audio monitoring to audio that's linked to the edit point you selected for trimming.

Here comes the tricky part: These audio monitoring configurations are in effect *only* when you use the JKL keys to play back incoming or outgoing clips. If you use the spacebar to play through your edit point, you'll hear all the sequence audio tracks regardless of your audio monitoring preference settings. Also remember—the Trim Edit window's Dynamic Trim mode uses JKL keys to perform trim edits; if you just want to review your audio without adjusting the edit point when you hit the K key, be sure to disable Dynamic Trim mode first.

Using the Trim Edit Window

The Trim Edit window offers plenty of flexibility to accommodate your editing style; you can mix and match trimming methods in a single trim operation. This window features two good-sized screens displaying the clips on either side of the edit you are adjusting, as well as Duration and Current Timecode displays for each side.

✔ Tip

■ If you're using Timecode entry in the Trim Edit window, you can cancel an edit by pressing the Esc key while the Timecode field is still active. You can also undo an edit at any time by pressing Command-Z.

FCP Protocol: Trimming Error Messages

When you attempt a trim operation that can't be executed, Final Cut Pro will warn you by displaying one of the following error messages:

◆ **You cannot set the In point later than a disabled Out point:** When you're adjusting an In or Out point in the Trim Edit window, you can't position your clip's In point later than its Out point. Likewise, Out points cannot be placed before In points. The word *disabled* in the message refers to Trim Edit window protocol. Only the outgoing clip's Out point and the incoming clip's In point are active while you're in the Trim Edit window.

◆ **Clip collision:** A trimming operation would cause clips to collide or one clip to overwrite another. Specifies the track number where the error occurred.

◆ **Transition conflict:** A transition duration adjustment would be required to accommodate the trimming change. Specifies the track number where the error occurred.

◆ **Insufficient content:** The source clip does not contain sufficient media to complete the edit.

◆ **Media limit:** Similar to the "Insufficient content" error; one of the items in your edit selection does not include sufficient media to complete the edit as specified. Specifies the track number location of the item that ran out of media.

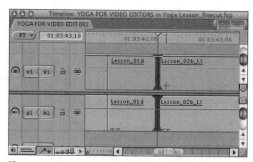

Figure 11.13 Click an edit point in the Timeline with the Edit Selection tool.

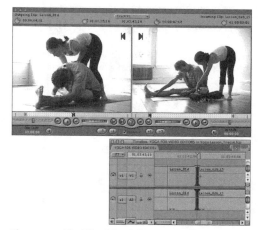

Figure 11.14 The Trim Edit window opens automatically.

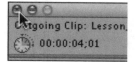

Figure 11.15 Close the Trim Edit window by clicking the close button in the upper-left corner.

To open the Trim Edit window:

Do one of the following:

◆ Press Command-7.

The playhead jumps to the closest edit on the target track, and the Trim Edit window opens with a Roll edit selected.

◆ In the Timeline, click an edit with the Edit Selection tool (**Figure 11.13**).

The edit is selected, and the Trim Edit window opens automatically (**Figure 11.14**).

◆ Double-click an edit with the Ripple or Roll tool, and the Trim Edit window opens with that edit type already selected.

◆ Choose Sequence > Trim Edit.

◆ In the Timeline, double-click an edit.

To close the Trim Edit window:

Do one of the following:

◆ Move the Timeline or the Canvas playhead away from the edit.

◆ Click anywhere in the Timeline away from an edit to deselect all edits in the Timeline.

◆ Click the close button in the upper-left corner of the Trim Edit window (**Figure 11.15**).

✔ Tip

■ All the plus and minus adjustments you make in the Trim Edit window refer to the location of the edit point, not the duration of either clip. That's especially important to remember when you're making adjustments on the right side of the edit point.

To trim an edit in the Trim Edit window:

1. Select one or more edit points to trim, using any of the methods described earlier in this section. Then, if the Trim Edit window has not opened automatically, press Command-7 to open the Trim Edit window.

2. In the Trim Edit window, select the type of trim operation by clicking in the appropriate image area (the pointer changes to indicate whether you've selected Ripple Left, Roll, or Ripple Right):

    ◆ Click the left image to trim the outgoing clip with a Ripple Left edit.

    ◆ Click the right image to trim the incoming clip with a Ripple Right edit (**Figure 11.16**).

    ◆ Click the area between the images to select a Roll edit.

    A green bar appears above the clip image, indicating the side of the edit that is selected for trimming.

3. Trim the edit using *one of the following methods:*

    ◆ Use the trim buttons to move the edit point to the left or right by frame increments (**Figure 11.17**).

    ◆ Trim the edit point by typing + or – and a duration to add or subtract. You don't need to click in the field—just start typing and then press Enter. The type of trim performed depends on the edit selection you made in step 2.

    ◆ Click and drag an edit point in the Scrubber bar.

    ◆ Use the individual playback controls under either clip to play the clip; then mark a new Out point for the outgoing clip or a new In point for the incoming clip.

Figure 11.16 Click the image on the right in the Trim Edit window to select a Ripple Right edit.

Figure 11.17 Clicking this Trim Forward button moves the edit point to the right by single-frame increments.

Figure 11.18 Review your trim by clicking the Play In to Out button to play from the beginning of the incoming clip to the end of the outgoing clip.

Figure 11.19 Use the Track pop-up menu to choose another selected edit point for trimming. Even when you're trimming an audio clip, you'll still see video playback in preview mode, and you'll be able to hear all the audio tracks at that edit point in your sequence.

The In Shift and Out Shift fields update to show the total cumulative shift in the edit point. These fields will track the shift, even if you perform the trim as several small adjustments. The Timeline display updates to reflect your trim.

4. Use the transport controls to review your edit.

- ◆ Click the Play In to Out button to play from the start of the first clip to the end of the second clip (**Figure 11.18**).

- ◆ Click the Play Around Edit Loop button to loop playback of the edit point plus the specified pre-roll and post-roll.

- ◆ Click the Stop button to stop playback and position the playhead on the edit point.

5. When you finish trimming, close the Trim Edit window.

✔ Tips

- You can use the Previous Edit and Next Edit buttons in the Trim Edit window to move to the next edit on the current track without leaving the Trim Edit window.

- If you have selected multiple edits to trim, use the Track pop-up menu to select the track to view in the Trim Edit window (**Figure 11.19**).

USING THE TRIM EDIT WINDOW

375

To adjust an edit point on the fly:

1. In the Trim Edit window, select the type of trim operation by one of the methods described in the previous task.

   A green bar appears above the clip image, indicating the side of the edit that is selected for trimming.

2. Click the Play Around Edit Loop button (or press the spacebar) to loop playback of the edit point (**Figure 11.20**).

3. As the preview loop plays, tap the I key to set a new In point on the incoming clip, or tap the O key to set a new Out point on the outgoing clip (**Figure 11.21**).

   The corresponding In or Out edit point is adjusted accordingly. The looped playback hesitates briefly, then resumes.

✔ Tip

■ The right amount of pre- and post-roll can establish a perfect rhythm and pace that helps you nail a tricky edit. You can adjust the default pre-roll and post-roll settings on the Editing tab of the User Preferences window.

Figure 11.20 Click the Play Around Edit Loop button to loop the playback of your edit point plus the specified pre-roll and post-roll.

Figure 11.21 As the playback loops in preview mode, you can use the I and O keys or the Mark buttons to adjust the edit point on the fly.

USING THE TRIM EDIT WINDOW

Figure 11.22 Dynamic Trim mode uses the mouse pointer's location to determine which side of the edit you're trimming, and lets you use the JKL keys to control playback and mark edit points.

Figure 11.23 Shift-dragging an active edit point in the Trim Edit window slips the selected clip. During the slip, the display changes to show the new In and Out points.

To use dynamic trim mode to adjust an edit point:

1. Position the mouse pointer in the image area of the clip you want to trim.

The pointer changes to the Ripple Left, Ripple Right, or Roll tool depending on the pointer's location; the Play control on the affected clip highlights (**Figure 11.22**).

2. Use the JKL keyboard transport commands to play the clip you're adjusting.

3. Click the K key to stop the playhead at the point you want to set as your new edit point.

The edit point adjusts to the playhead position automatically.

✔ Tip

■ For more information on using the JKL keys for transport control, see "JKL Keys: The Way to Move" in Chapter 8.

To slip an edit in the Trim Edit window:

1. In the Trim Edit window, Shift-drag the active edit point on either Scrubber bar to slip that clip (**Figure 11.23**); or drag the edit point with the Slip tool.

The Current Time display switches to show the adjusted timecode location for the edit point you are slipping.

2. Release the mouse button to complete the Slip edit.

The Current Time display reverts to displaying the timecode location at the clip's current playhead position.

Trimming Edits in the Timeline

The Timeline can be a good place to trim your sequence if you need to keep tabs on multiple tracks in relation to one another. You can perform all types of trim edits in the Timeline: Ripple, Roll, Slip, Slide, Extend, Swap, and Resize.

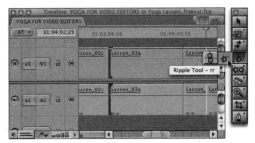

Figure 11.24 Choose the Ripple tool from the Tool palette.

✔ Tip

■ Set up your Timeline display to optimize the efficiency of your trim operation. Things to check include the time scale, track size, snapping, and vertical scroll bar setup. You'll find details on Timeline display options in Chapter 10, "Editing in the Timeline and the Canvas."

To perform a Ripple edit in the Timeline:

1. From the Tool palette, choose the Ripple tool (**Figure 11.24**).

2. In the Timeline, select the edit by clicking near the edge of the clip.

   The selected side of the edit will be highlighted.

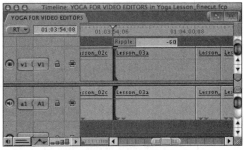

Figure 11.25 After selecting the edit you want to ripple, type + or – followed by the number of frames to add or subtract from the edit point.

3. Ripple the edit using *one of the following methods:*

   ◆ Click and drag the edit to adjust the duration of the clip in the sequence.

   ◆ Type + or – followed by the number of frames to add or subtract from the current edit point (**Figure 11.25**); then press Enter.

To perform a Ripple edit on multiple tracks simultaneously:

   ◆ Command-click to select multiple edit points; then use the Ripple tool to perform the Ripple edit across all the tracks (**Figure 11.26**).

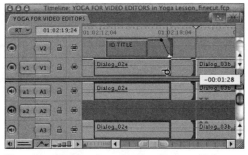

Figure 11.26 Performing a Ripple edit on multiple tracks in the Timeline.

✔ Tip

■ Holding down the Shift key while you perform a trim toggles the pointer between the Ripple and Roll tools.

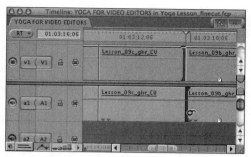

Figure 11.27 Command-clicking the right side of this edit with the Ripple tool selects just the audio edit point of this linked clip to ripple right.

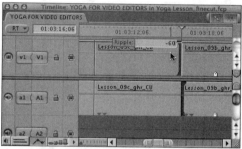

Figure 11.28 Use timecode entry to adjust the edit point. In this example, typing -60 trims 60 frames off the end of the V1 track of the left-hand clip and 60 frames off the head of the A1 track of the right-hand clip.

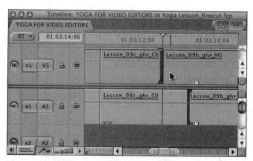

Figure 11.29 The completed asymmetric ripple edit produces a split edit. Both clips were rippled by the same number of frames without affecting the sync of the downstream clips—note that the position of the clip markers is unchanged.

To perform an asymmetric Ripple trim in the Timeline:

1. Make a Ripple Left edit selection on the video track clip by clicking the left side of the edit point with the Ripple tool. If the clip is linked, you must Option-click to override linked selection.

2. On the audio track clip, use the Ripple tool again to make a Ripple Right edit selection on the other side of the audio track's edit point. If you're working on a linked clip, Command-click to select just the right side of the edit point with the Ripple tool (**Figure 11.27**).

3. Type + or – followed by the number of frames to add or subtract from the current edit points (**Figure 11.28**); then press Enter.

   The video track edit point shifts back, while the audio track edit point shifts ahead by the same amount (**Figure 11.29**).

✔ Tip

- Use asymmetric trimming to create a split edit without changing the sync relationship of your sequence clips.

To perform a Roll edit in the Timeline:

1. From the Tool palette, choose the Roll tool (**Figure 11.30**).

2. In the Timeline, select the edit point.

3. Roll the edit *using one of the following methods:*

   ◆ Click and drag in either direction. As you drag, the Canvas display changes to two smaller screens, which show the Out point of the outgoing clip on the left and the In point of the incoming clip on the right (**Figure 11.31**).

   ◆ Type + or – followed by the number of frames to add or subtract from the current edit point; then press Enter.

To roll multiple tracks simultaneously:

◆ Command-click to select multiple edit points; then use the Roll tool to perform the Roll edit across all the tracks (**Figure 11.32**).

✔ Tip

■ If you're still dragging but your Roll edit stops rolling, your clip has reached the end of the media.

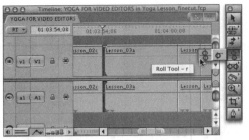

Figure 11.30 Choose the Roll tool from the Tool palette.

Figure 11.31 During a Roll edit, the Canvas window converts to dual-screen mode, displaying the outgoing Out point on the left and the incoming In point on the right.

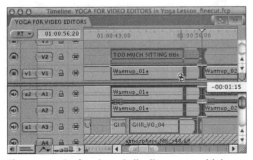

Figure 11.32 Performing a Roll edit across multiple tracks in the Timeline.

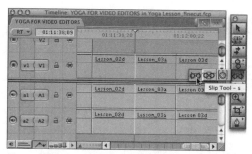

Figure 11.33 Choose the Slip tool from the Tool palette.

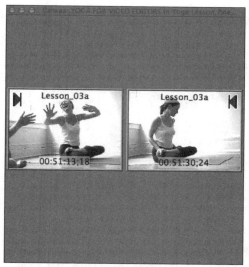

Figure 11.34 During the Slip edit, the Canvas window converts to dual-screen mode, displaying the In point frame on the left and the Out point frame on the right.

To slip a clip in the Timeline:

1. In the Tool palette, choose the Slip tool (**Figure 11.33**).

2. In the Timeline, select the clip and drag it left or right. As you drag:
   - ◆ An outline of the complete clip appears, indicating the amount of media available.
   - ◆ The Canvas display changes to two smaller screens, which show the In point frame on the left and the Out point frame on the right (**Figure 11.34**).

3. Release the mouse button when you have positioned the clip at its new location.

✔ Tip

- ■ Try turning off snapping in the Timeline before you slip your clip. Your clip will slip more smoothly.

To slip a clip in the Timeline using numerical timecode entry:

1. Select the clip in the Timeline.

2. In the Tool palette, choose the Slip tool.

3. Type + or − and the number of frames to slip; then press Enter.

TRIMMING EDITS IN THE TIMELINE

To slide a clip in the Timeline:

1. In the Tool palette, choose the Slide tool.

2. In the Timeline, select the entire clip (**Figure 11.35**) and drag it left or right. As you drag:
   - ◆ An outline of the complete clip appears, indicating the amount of media available (**Figure 11.36**).
   - ◆ The Canvas display changes to two smaller screens, which show the Out point frame of the clip to the left of the sliding clip and the In point frame of the clip to the right of the sliding clip.

3. Release the mouse button when you have positioned the clip at its new location (**Figure 11.37**).

To slide a clip in the Timeline using numerical timecode entry:

1. In the Tool palette, choose the Slide tool.

2. Select the clip in the Timeline.

3. Type + or – and the number of frames to slide; then press Enter.

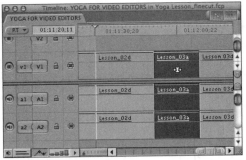

Figure 11.35 Select the clip with the Slide tool.

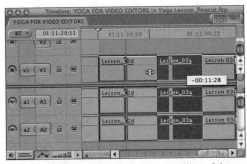

Figure 11.36 During the Slide edit, an outline of the complete clip appears in the Timeline, indicating the amount of media available outside the clip's edit points.

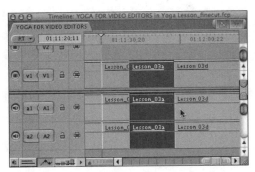

Figure 11.37 The clip in its new sequence location.

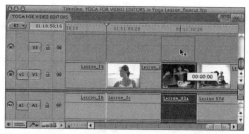

Figure 11.38 Drag the clip out of its sequence location.

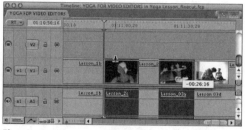

Figure 11.39 Use snapping to help you line up the head of the clip you are moving with the edit point where you want to insert the clip.

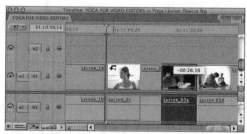

Figure 11.40 When you press Option as you drop the clip into the Timeline, the pointer changes to a curved arrow. Drop the clip at the insertion point.

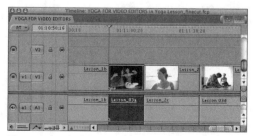

Figure 11.41 The inserted clip pushes the rest of the sequence clips down without altering any sequence durations.

To perform a Swap edit in the Timeline:

1. In the Timeline, select the clip you want to move.

2. Drag the clip out of the Timeline track (**Figure 11.38**).

3. Align the head of the selected clip with the head of the clip in the Timeline at the insert location (**Figure 11.39**); then press Option without releasing the mouse button.

   The pointer becomes a curved arrow.

4. Drop the selected clip at the insertion point you selected (**Figure 11.40**).

   The inserted clip swaps out with the sequence clip's position; no sequence clip durations are altered (**Figure 11.41**), but the order in which they appear has changed.

✔ Tips

- The Swap edit is one way to go if you want to preserve render files you've already created. The swapped clips don't change duration, and they maintain the linkage to their previously rendered files.

- You can perform Swap edits only with single clips.

To perform an Extend edit in the Timeline:

1. Check the Snapping control to make sure snapping is on. (An Extend edit is a little easier with snapping turned on.)

2. From the Tool palette, choose the Selection tool or the Edit Selection tool.

3. In the Timeline, click the edit of the clip you want to extend (**Figure 11.42**).

4. Move the playhead to the position that the edit will extend to (**Figure 11.43**); then press the E key.

   The clip with the selected edit extends to the playhead position. An Extend edit will overwrite any gaps or clips it encounters, up to the position of the playhead (**Figure 11.44**).

   If there is not enough media to reach your selected playhead position, an "insufficient content for edit" error message appears, and the edit is canceled.

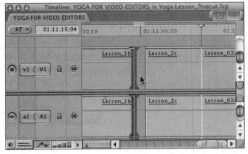

Figure 11.42 Use the Selection (or the Edit Selection) tool to select the edit of the clip you want to extend.

Figure 11.43 Position the playhead to mark the new edit point for the edit; then press E.

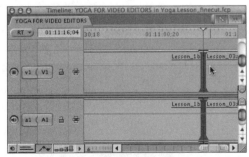

Figure 11.44 The clip on the left lengthens, extending to the playhead position, overwriting any gaps or clips.

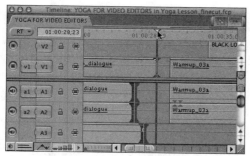

Figure 11.45 Select the edit points of the shorter clips; position the playhead at the end of the longest clip; then press E.

Figure 11.46 The edit extends the duration of all the selected clips to match that of the longest clip.

✔ Tips

- Use an Extend edit to create a split edit on the fly. In the Timeline, select the edit you want to adjust by Option-clicking it; then, play back your sequence and press the E key when you see your new edit location. The edit point will move to the playhead's position at the moment you press E—if you have enough media in your clip to extend it to that point.

- Extend edits are also a neat way to clean up the tail ends of a stack of clips with different durations. Select the edit points of the shorter clips, position the playhead at the end of the longest clip, and press E (**Figure 11.45**). If you've got enough media available, all the clips will align their durations to match that of your longest clip (**Figure 11.46**).

To resize the duration of a clip in the Timeline:

1. In the Tool palette, choose the Selection tool (**Figure 11.47**).

2. In the Timeline, select an edit point and drag it (**Figure 11.48**).

   You can drag the edit point to create a gap (by making the duration of the clip shorter; **Figure 11.49**) or cover an existing gap (by making the duration of the clip longer).

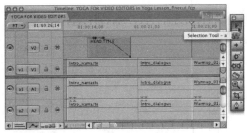

Figure 11.47 Choose the Selection tool from the Tool palette. The Selection arrow changes to a Resize pointer when you position it near an edit point.

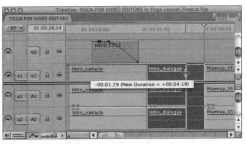

Figure 11.48 Dragging the edit point of the selected clip in the Timeline resizes the clip.

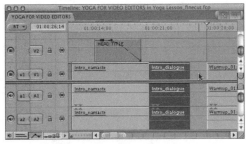

Figure 11.49 The clip, resized to a shorter duration, leaves a gap in its Timeline track.

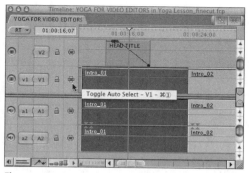

Figure 11.50 Enable the Auto Select controls on tracks that contain the clip before you select its division point.

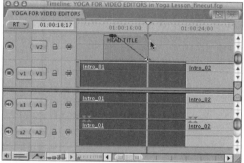

Figure 11.51 Position the playhead at the point where you want to divide the clip.

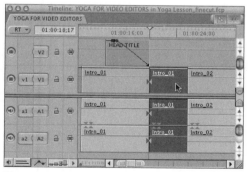

Figure 11.52 The clip divides at the playhead position. The added edit point creates an additional clip that starts at the playhead position.

To divide (razor-blade) a clip in the Timeline:

1. Enable the Auto Select controls on the tracks that contain the clip you want to divide (**Figure 11.50**).

2. In the Timeline, position the playhead at the point where you want to divide the clip (**Figure 11.51**); then press Control-V to add an edit point.

   The added edit point will create an additional clip that starts at the playhead position (**Figure 11.52**).

   Or do this:

   Press B to select the Razor Blade tool; then click at the point where you want to divide the clip.

✔ Tips

- Both halves of a divided clip will have the same name as the original, so if you plan on keeping both of them around, you may want to give them new names that reflect their history as two halves of a bladed clip—for instance, intro_01.1 and intro_01.2. Remember, though, that renaming an affiliate clip causes all other affiliates and the master clip they reference to be renamed as well. If you've bladed an affiliate clip, you'll need to change the status of each additional piece to Independent or Master in order to give it a unique name. Learn more about FCP's clip-handling grammar in Chapter 4.

- Use the Razor Blade All tool to divide clips on all Timeline tracks at the same point.

TRIMMING EDITS IN THE TIMELINE

About through edits

FCP defines a through edit as an edit point joining two clips with the same reel number and contiguous timecode (such as a clip you've divided in two with the Razor Blade tool). You can choose to display a Through edit indicator on through edit points in the Timeline, or turn off the indicator display on the Timeline Options tab of the User Preferences window. You also have the option of removing the through edit and merging the two adjacent clips into one continuous clip.

To remove a through edit:

Do one of the following:

◆ In the Timeline, select the Through edit indicator and press Delete.

◆ Control-click the Through edit indicator in the Timeline; then choose Join Through Edit from the shortcut menu (**Figure 11.53**).

The edit point disappears, and the divided clip is rejoined. The newly merged clip adopts the properties (filters, opacity, audio levels, and so on) of the first (left) clip.

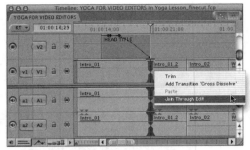

Figure 11.53 Control-click the Through edit indicator; then choose Join Through Edit from the shortcut menu.

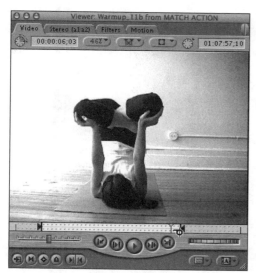

Figure 11.54 Dragging the Out point with the Ripple tool. The edit point will be rippled to the left.

Trimming Edits in the Viewer

You can perform four types of trim operations in the Viewer: Ripple, Roll, Slip, and Resize. Remember that you can perform trim operations only on sequence clips, so all these trim operations require you to open the sequence clip in the Viewer by double-clicking it in the Timeline.

To perform a Ripple edit in the Viewer:

1. From the Tool palette, choose the Ripple tool.

2. In the Timeline, double-click the clip to open it in the Viewer.

3. In the Viewer's Scrubber bar, drag either the In or the Out point to ripple the clip (**Figure 11.54**).

To perform a Roll edit in the Viewer:

1. From the Tool palette, choose the Roll tool.

2. In the Timeline, double-click the clip to open it in the Viewer.

3. In the Viewer's Scrubber bar, drag either the In or the Out point to roll the edit.

   If you run out of media to accommodate the shift in your edit point, an overlay appears on the image in the Viewer warning you of a "Media limit" error on the track that's run out of frames.

To slip a clip in the Viewer:

1. From the Tool palette, choose the Slip tool.

2. In the Timeline, double-click the clip to open it in the Viewer.

3. In the Viewer's Scrubber bar, drag either the In or the Out point to slip the clip.

   As you slip, the Viewer displays the first frame of the clip; the Canvas displays the last frame of the clip (**Figure 11.55**).

✔ Tip

■ You can also slip a clip in the Viewer by Shift-dragging either the In or the Out point with the Selection tool.

To resize a clip in the Viewer:

1. In the Tool palette, choose the Selection tool.

2. In the Timeline, double-click the clip to open it in the Viewer.

3. In the Viewer's Scrubber bar, drag either the In or the Out point to resize the clip (**Figure 11.56**).

   You can drag the edit point to create a gap (by decreasing the duration of the clip) or cover an existing gap (by increasing the duration of the clip).

Figure 11.55 As you slip the edit, the Viewer displays the first frame of the clip, and the Canvas displays the last frame.

Figure 11.56 Dragging the edit point in the Viewer's Scrubber bar resizes the selected clip.

Ganging Viewer and Canvas

Ganging locks the Viewer playhead to the Canvas and Timeline playheads. Once the playheads are locked together, they will move together until you disable the gang mode. FCP offers three gang modes:

- **Open:** Open mode's distinctive (and quite useful) feature is that FCP automatically opens the sequence clip at the Timeline's playhead position in the Viewer as you scrub through your sequence. Because FCP is designed to display the same Viewer tab as each successive clip opens, Open mode is great for color correction and effects tweaking. You can use Open mode to step through a series of clips and access each clip's Filters tab with no extra effort.

- **Gang:** Use Gang mode when you want to lock the Viewer and Canvas together with a specific synchronization. You can use Gang mode to do a frame-by-frame comparison of two sequences by opening one sequence in the Timeline and loading the other in the Viewer. Once you've established a sync point, set the gang mode to Gang, and the two sequences will remain in that sync relationship as you examine them.

- **Off:** Choose Off to disable all gang modes.

FCP Protocol: Auto Select Behavior with Ganged Playheads

When Viewer and Canvas playheads are locked together in Open mode, FCP automatically opens the Timeline clip at the playhead position into the Viewer.

While many FCP operations default to the lowest-numbered track with Auto Select enabled, track selection in Open mode is governed by a special Auto Select protocol: FCP will open the clip on the *highest*-numbered video track with Auto Select enabled. If no video clips are present on auto-selected tracks, FCP defaults to the *highest*-numbered audio track with Auto Select enabled.

Selecting a gang mode

Because you're locking the three playheads so they move together, the Viewer, Canvas, and Timeline will always be in the same gang mode. You'll find Playhead Sync pop-up menus in both the Viewer and the Canvas windows. You can select a gang mode from either pop-up menu.

To select a gang mode:

◆ In the Viewer or Canvas, select a gang mode from the Playhead Sync pop-up menu (**Figure 11.57**).

The Canvas and Viewer playheads are locked together in the selected gang mode (**Figure 11.58**).

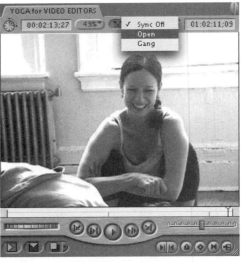

Figure 11.57 You'll find Playhead Sync pop-up menus in both the Viewer and the Canvas. You can select the gang mode from either menu.

Figure 11.58 With Open gang mode selected, the sequence clip currently at the Timeline playhead position opens in the Viewer automatically as you play through the sequence in the Timeline and Canvas.

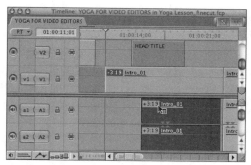

Figure 11.59 Control-click the out-of-sync indicator on the part of the clip you wish to reposition.

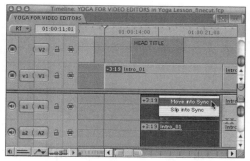

Figure 11.60 Choose Move into Sync from the shortcut menu.

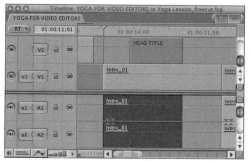

Figure 11.61 The portion of the clip you selected is repositioned in the Timeline so the sync is corrected. Note that you can move a clip into sync only if there is a gap in the track to accommodate the move.

Correcting Out-of-Sync Clips

When you insert a sync clip into a sequence, the audio and video are automatically linked. That means you'll have to go out of your way to knock them out of sync, because linked items are selected and moved together. However, if you have turned linked selection off, it's possible to knock a sync clip out of sync.

Boxes appear on the clips that are out of sync. These indicators display the number of frames that the audio and video portions of the clip are out of sync in relation to each other.

Final Cut Pro offers two options for correcting a sync problem:

◆ You can move a clip into sync, which repositions the selected portion of the clip so that the sync is corrected.

◆ You can slip a clip into sync, which corrects the sync problem by performing a Slip edit on the selected portion of the clip (keeping the clip in the same position and shifting the contents of the clip).

Occasionally, you'll want to move a clip out of sync intentionally—for example, when you combine the video from one take with substitute audio from another take.

In that case, you might want to mark the video and the substitute audio as being in sync if you don't want to be warned of a sync problem.

To move a clip into sync:

◆ In the Timeline, Control-click the out-of-sync indicator (the red box on the clip; **Figure 11.59**); then choose Move into Sync from the shortcut menu (**Figure 11.60**).

The portion of the clip you selected is repositioned to correct the sync (**Figure 11.61**).

To slip a clip into sync:

◆ In the Timeline, Control-click the out-of-sync indicator (the red box) on the clip portion you want to slip into sync; then choose Slip into Sync from the shortcut menu.

To mark clips as in sync:

◆ In the Timeline, select the audio and video clips you want to mark as in sync (**Figure 11.62**); then choose Modify > Mark in Sync.

The two selected clips are marked as in sync, without shifting their positions in the Timeline (**Figure 11.63**).

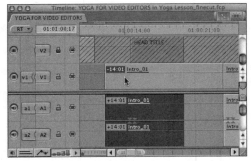

Figure 11.62 Select the audio and video clips you want to mark as in sync.

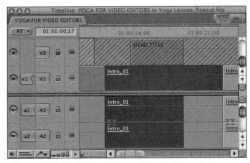

Figure 11.63 The clips do not shift position, but are marked as in sync.

CORRECTING OUT-OF-SYNC CLIPS

AUDIO TOOLS AND TECHNIQUES

12

The basic editing and finishing features in Final Cut Pro operate in the same way for video and audio clips. This chapter covers the few tools and techniques unique to audio editing, audio effects, and mixing.

You can learn about other aspects of audio elsewhere in this book. Capturing audio is covered in Chapter 5, "Capturing Video." Steps for importing digital audio from CDs or other digital sources appear in Chapter 6, "Importing Digital Media," and exporting audio back to tape or to another digital format is covered in Chapter 19, "Creating Final Output." Also, audio transitions are covered in Chapter 13, "Creating Transitions," and rendering audio is explained in Chapter 18, "Real Time and Rendering."

The FCP interface has six areas where you edit and finish audio.

◆ **The Audio tab in the Viewer:** The Audio tab displays audio-only clips, as well as the audio portion of audio+video clips. This is where you can audition and mark edit points in audio clips, and use keyframes to set audio level and pan settings. The Audio tab is the only place in FCP where you can get a large view of your audio clip's waveforms and make subframe adjustments to edit points.

◆ **The Audio tracks in the Timeline:** The Timeline is the only place where you can view all audio tracks at once. Turn on the Timeline's audio waveform display (it's off by default) and you can edit audio quite nicely; you can do everything from basic assembly to fine trimming. Track height is completely adjustable, so, when you need to concentrate on fine-tuning an edit, you can expand the track until the waveform display is a healthy size. You can use keyframes to set and sculpt audio levels using the Timeline's clip overlays. Playback in the Audio tab and the Trim Edit window is independent of Timeline/ Canvas playback, so the Timeline is the only place you can trim audio on the fly as you watch your sequence play back.

◆ **The Voice Over tool:** FCP's audio recording tool can record multiple tracks of sync audio as FCP plays back a selected portion of your sequence. Sounds complicated, but it's easy to use and very useful.

◆ **The Filters tab in the Viewer:** Apply and adjust audio filters and effects in the Filters tab of the Viewer.

◆ **The Audio Mixer:** The audio mixing window has virtual tracks and faders. You can use the mixer to record audio mix moves in real time; FCP records your fader moves as audio level or pan keyframes.

◆ **The Trim Edit window:** The latest edition of the Trim Edit window is the best yet (dynamic trimming, improved performance), and if the Trim Edit window displayed large-size waveforms as you fine-tuned your audio edits, it would be a great place to do fine cutting of dialogue or music. Unfortunately, you can't see waveforms in this window, so it's not a top choice for tight audio editing.

Audio Tracks vs. Timeline Tracks

One small clarification: *Audio track* is an old expression describing an audio recording, such as a soundtrack or an album track.

In Final Cut Pro, *track* refers to an empty layer in the Timeline where you assemble video and audio clips, but not the clips themselves.

In an attempt to avoid confusion, this book uses the term *CD track* to refer to an audio recording on CD, *audio tracks* to refer to Timeline tracks that hold audio clips, *audio clips* to refer to the individual items you manipulate in FCP, and *audio files* to refer to the source media files those audio clips reference.

So—are we avoiding confusion yet?

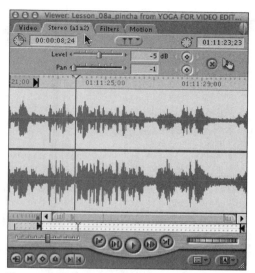

Figure 12.1 The two audio channels that make up a stereo pair appear in a single Audio tab. Any adjustments made to one channel are automatically applied to both channels.

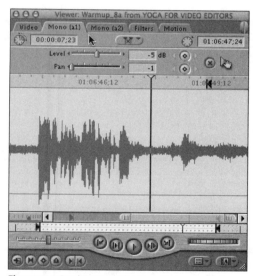

Figure 12.2 Dual mono audio format appears in the Viewer with two Audio tabs. Each channel is distinct and can be adjusted independently.

FCP's Audio Formats

In the audio world, "format" has entirely too many meanings.

There are media formats, such as DV, CD, and DAT, which describe the media used to record the original audio. There are also digital audio file formats, such as AIF, MP3, and WAV.

And then there are the audio formats discussed here, which describe the structure of multiple-channel audio recordings such as stereo or mono. These audio formats apply to audio captured with video, as well as to imported clips or audio-only clips captured with the Voice Over tool:

♦ **Stereo:** Both channels have been captured as a stereo pair. Stereo pairs are always linked, so anything applied to one track applies to both. Waveforms for the two channels that make up the stereo pair appear in a single Audio tab (**Figure 12.1**).

♦ **Dual mono (2 Mono):** Both channels have been captured but are distinct and can be adjusted independently of one another. Two Mono Audio tabs appear in the Viewer (**Figure 12.2**).

♦ **Single mono (1 Mono):** The audio consists of a single mono channel. A single Audio tab appears in the Viewer. The source track designation (a1, a2, and so on) refers to the audio format of these tracks' source media at the time of capture.

Modifying audio channel formats

Two linked audio clips behave differently than two linked audio clips defined as a stereo pair.

◆ Two linked audio clips will be selected together, but their levels and filters must be controlled separately. Two linked audio clips can appear on two separate Audio tabs in the Viewer.

◆ Two audio clips defined as a stereo pair share everything except their audio content and their Timeline tracks. The two stereo channels appear on a single Audio tab in the Viewer, and they are always selected together. Any filter, panning, or level modification applied to one stereo channel is automatically applied to the other.

You can modify the audio format of captured audio using the Modify > Stereo Pair and Modify > Link commands. For example, toggling Stereo Pair off will convert a pair of clips captured as a stereo pair to two linked clips in dual mono format.

✔ Tip

■ Converting two single audio clips to form a stereo pair is a quick way to apply identical level changes to a couple of clips. You can always toggle stereo off after you have made your level adjustments.

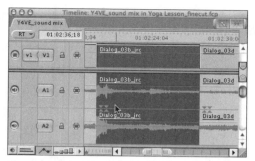

Figure 12.3 Select the stereo audio clip in the Timeline; then choose Modify > Stereo Pair (or press Option-L) to toggle stereo off.

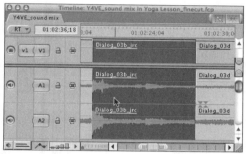

Figure 12.4 The stereo audio clip converted to dual mono format. Note that the small triangles indicating a stereo pair are gone, but the clip names remain underlined because the two audio channels remained linked.

To convert a stereo pair to dual mono format:

◆ Select the stereo audio clip in the Timeline (**Figure 12.3**), then choose Modify > Stereo Pair to toggle stereo off.

The stereo audio clip is converted to dual mono format, but the two audio channels remained linked (**Figure 12.4**). If you want to convert these to two completely independent audio clips, select the linked audio clips in the Timeline, then choose Modify > Link to toggle linking off.

✔ Tip

■ Toggling stereo off will automatically unlink audio-only clips.

To convert two audio clips to stereo pair format:

◆ Select the two audio clips in the Timeline, then choose Modify > Stereo Pair to toggle stereo on.

The Browser's audio format columns

You'll find four Browser columns devoted to info about the formatting of your audio clips (**Figure 12.5**); this summary will help you decode what each column is telling you about your audio files.

◆ **Tracks:** The number of audio and video tracks used in a clip or sequence. Note the higher total number of tracks in the sequences.

◆ **Audio:** The audio clip's format as defined inside FCP. "2 Mono" indicates the dual mono format, FCP's default DV capture format.

◆ **Aud Format:** The audio format of the audio's source media file. The number (8, 12, 16, or 24) indicates the audio's bit depth. Note the 32-bit floating-point bit depth listed for sequences.

◆ **Aud Rate:** The sample rate of the audio's source media file.

✔ Tip

■ Unlike previous versions, QuickTime 7 supports capture of single or multiple mono audio tracks as discrete tracks. New audio format terminology in the Browser's Audio column reflects these new audio capabilities. Dual mono format audio tracks that were called "A1 + A2" or "Ch 1 + Ch 2" in previous versions of FCP now appear as "2 Mono."

FCP's Audio Formats

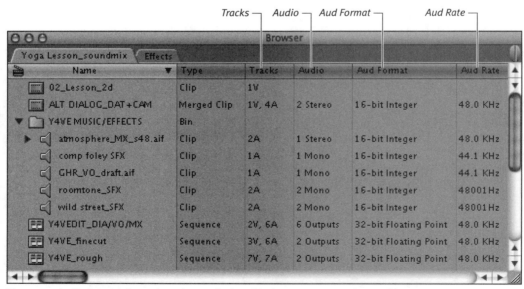

Figure 12.5 Audio format information columns displayed in the Browser. Note the new format names used in the Audio column.

About 16-bit, 24-bit, and 32-bit Resolution

DV cameras usually offer a choice between 12-bit/32 kHz and 16-bit/48 kHz audio recording resolution; 16 bits is the highest bit depth available. Meanwhile, the latest pro digital audio hardware records and outputs 24-bit audio. Final Cut Pro can capture 24-bit audio, or you can import 24-bit audio files captured in another program. Final Cut Pro will preserve their 24-bit quality because in FCP, audio mixing is calculated at a 32-bit floating-point resolution. Mixing audio in the digital domain is a mathematical process; the added accuracy of floating-point calculation plus the extra dynamic range resolution provided by 32 bits ensures that your 24-bit audio preserves its original quality. You can then output 24-bit audio AIFF files from FCP.

✔ Tip

- Final Cut Pro allows you to mix audio tracks with different sample rates within the same sequence. The program can convert the sample rate of nonconforming audio on the fly as you play back a sequence. Real-time sample-rate conversion does take processor power, however, and can occasionally produce nasty audible artifacts; so, for best results, you should convert the sample rates of all your audio tracks to match the sequence settings. For more information, see "To export audio only from a clip or sequence" in Chapter 19.

FCP's Audio Formats

What's Bit Depth and Sampling Rate Got to Do with My Audio Quality?

Digital audio is recorded at a bit depth and a sampling rate.

The bit depth indicates the fidelity of the recording's dynamics (volume levels), and the sample rate determines the fidelity of the recording's frequency response.

The bit depth defines the resolution of the dynamic range—the number of possible steps between the softest and loudest sound—of the recording.

An 8-bit digital audio recording uses 256 levels to represent the possible dynamic range. A 16-bit digital recording has a range of 65,536 levels.

The recording's sampling rate tells you how many times per second audio samples are saved to memory or disk. A 22 kHz sample rate means 22,000 audio samples would be recorded each second; in contrast, a 48 kHz sample rate recording would take 48,000 audio samples each second.

Remember: Your audio recording's fidelity is set at the time you record the original. You can't improve a recording by choosing a higher sample rate later; you can, however, convert an audio file to a lower bit depth and sample rate.

If you're looking for audio fidelity, more is better, so go for the highest possible bit depth and sampling rate when you record original audio.

For more information on measuring dynamic range, see "FCP Protocol: Measuring Digital Audio in Decibels (dB)," later in this chapter.

Anatomy of the Viewer's Audio Tab

The Audio tab in the Viewer window is where you review, mark, and edit single audio clips opened from the Browser or the Timeline. You can see the audio waveforms of audio clips, and in addition to the editing functions, you can use onscreen controls to adjust the level and stereo pan settings (**Figure 12.6**).

Before you start marking up audio clips, make sure you understand how and where FCP saves your changes. See the sidebar "FCP Protocol: Clips and Sequences" in Chapter 4.

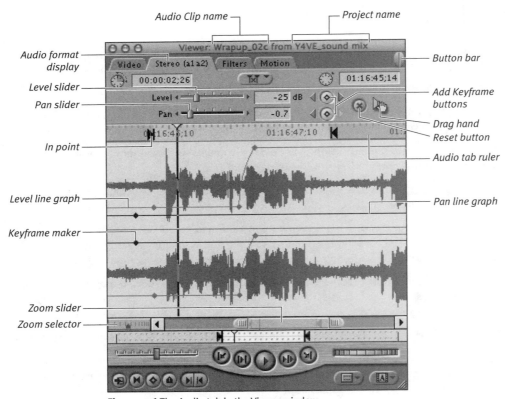

Figure 12.6 The Audio tab in the Viewer window.

Onscreen controls and displays

Editing digital audio requires different interface tools than editing digital video. When you open an audio clip in the Viewer, a graph of the audio waveform appears in the Audio tab, and the playhead travels across a stationary waveform image.

The Audio tab retains the transport controls from the Video tab interface in the lower part of the tab, but it has its own set of onscreen controls in the upper part.

Here's a brief rundown of the onscreen controls unique to the Audio tab (**Figures 12.7** and **12.8**):

◆ **Level slider:** Use to adjust the amplitude or volume of the audio clip.

◆ **Pan slider:** Use to adjust stereo panning or swapping of the left and right channels. Single channel (mono) clips use the Pan slider for left/right positioning of mono audio.

◆ **Reset (X) button:** Use to delete all marked points in the audio timeline and reset the level and pan values to their original settings.

◆ **Drag hand:** This is your handle for drag-and-drop editing. Drag to move the audio clip with edits to another window, such as the Browser or the Timeline.

◆ **Audio tab ruler:** This shows the timecode for the audio displayed. Edit point overlays appear along the ruler. You can adjust the time scale with any Zoom tool, selector, or slider.

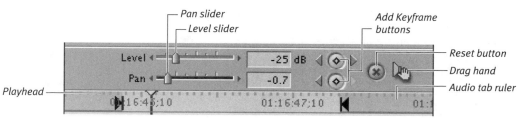

Figure 12.7 Controls displayed in the upper half of the Audio tab.

ANATOMY OF THE VIEWER'S AUDIO TAB

- **In and Out points:** These appear in both the Scrubber bar and the ruler.

- **Level line graph:** Both a tool and an indicator, it graphs level changes by indicating the amplitude of the audio. You can also click and drag the Level line graph to adjust the overall level of your audio clip, or you can click and drag keyframes to create dynamic volume effects.

- **Pan line graph:** This has the same basic operation as the Level line graph. Click and drag to adjust the stereo spread (for stereo clips) or pan (for mono clips).

- **Zoom selector:** Click to jump between different time scale views. The Zoom selector keeps your playhead centered as you change time scales.

- **Zoom slider:** Use to scroll through an audio file and to adjust the time scale of your view.

✔ Tip

- You can link two single audio clips to form a stereo pair. This is a quick way to apply identical level changes to a couple of clips. You can always unlink them after you have made your level adjustments. For more information, see "Modifying audio channel formats," earlier in this chapter.

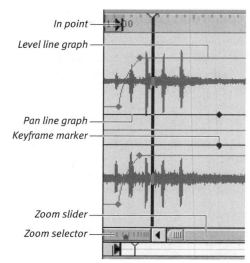

Figure 12.8 Controls displayed in the lower half of the Audio tab.

Figure 12.9 When you review a long, unedited audio recording, the wide Viewer window is a great place to set markers in preparation for breaking the clip into subclips.

Figure 12.10 Click the Audio tab to access the audio portion of an audio+video clip.

Using the Audio Tab

The capture settings for a clip determine how its audio appears in the Viewer. Stereo clips are panned full left and full right by default, and clips with one or two channels of discrete audio are panned center.

To open an audio clip:

Do one of the following:

◆ Double-click the clip icon in the Browser or the Timeline.

◆ Select a clip icon and choose View > Clip; or press Return.

◆ Select the clip in the Browser or the Timeline and choose View > Clip in New Window.

✔ Tip

■ Don't forget: You can stretch the Viewer window across your monitor to make a wide view—great when you're working with audio. You can see more of the clip, which makes marking and level adjustments easier (**Figure 12.9**). Resize it manually or click the green zoom button in the upper-left corner of the window.

To access the audio channel for an audio+video clip:

◆ Open the clip in the Viewer and click the Audio tab (**Figure 12.10**).

Scaling and scrolling an audio file

The Zoom slider is located along the bottom of the Audio tab. You use it to scroll through an audio file and to adjust the time scale of your view. You can view several minutes of audio in the window or focus on a fraction of a frame. The Zoom slider also appears on the Filters tab, the Motion tab, and the Timeline.

To scroll through your file:

◆ Drag the Zoom slider across the scroll bar (**Figure 12.11**).

To adjust the time scale:

Do one of the following:

◆ Press Command-+ (plus) to zoom in, expanding the time scale, and Command-− (minus) to zoom out, shrinking the time scale. These zoom keyboard shortcuts are useful in the Audio tab because your view stays centered on the current playhead position.

◆ The thumb controls are the ribbed-looking ends of the Zoom slider (**Figure 12.12**). Click a thumb control and drag it to shrink the time scale and expose more of your audio file (**Figure 12.13**).

◆ Click the Zoom selector to the left of the Zoom slider to jump to a different time scale (**Figure 12.14**); the current playhead position stays centered in the view area.

Figure 12.11 Drag the Zoom slider across the scroll bar to navigate through an audio file. This control doesn't move the playhead, just the view.

Figure 12.12 Use the thumb controls to vary time scaling. A smaller Zoom slider indicates an expanded time scale.

Figure 12.13 Drag the thumb control. A longer Zoom slider indicates a more compressed time scale.

Figure 12.14 Jump to a different time scale with one click using the Zoom selector.

Setting edit points in the Audio tab

You set In and Out points and markers in the Audio tab in the same way you do in the Viewer's Video tab. The overlays for these markers show in the Audio tab ruler at the top of the waveform display.

Because video is captured and stored as frames, the smallest adjustment you can make to a video edit point is a single frame. Digital audio, however, is captured in sub-frames as samples forming a continuous waveform. In FCP, audio edit points can be set to an accuracy of 1/100 frame. The Audio tab is the only place you can make subframe adjustments to an audio clip's In and Out points. Most likely, you'll need this kind of fine-tuning when you are finessing a music edit.

You can also place keyframes with the same precision—a lifesaver when you are working your way through a really good dialogue take with a couple of bad clicks or pops. The sub-frame precision allows you to use audio level keyframes to silence that audio just for the few milliseconds it takes to mute the click.

Lost in the Waveforms? Audio Tab Editing Tips

When you're trying to fine-tune an audio edit point in the Audio tab, it's easy to lose track of your location as you zoom and scroll through your audio clip's waveforms. Here's a navigation method to try while editing in the Audio tab:

- Start by playing back the clip.

- When you hear the spot where you think your edit point should be, tap the spacebar to pause the playhead at that spot.

- Use the marquee selection feature of the Zoom tool to draw a narrow selection box around the playhead. You won't lose track of the playhead this way.

- While you're zoomed in, take advantage of the detailed waveform display to get a precise edit. Press I or O to mark your edit point at the current playhead position.

- When you finish tweaking, press Shift-Z to zoom out and fit the clip to the window with a single keystroke.

To make subframe adjustments to an audio clip's edit points:

1. Open the audio clip in the Audio tab; then jump the playhead to the edit point you want to adjust.

2. Use the marquee selection feature of the Zoom tool (**Figure 12.15**) to zoom in until the playhead looks like a bar.

3. Hold down the Shift key; then click the Audio tab playhead and drag it to the subframe location of the new In or Out point (**Figure 12.16**).

4. Press I (or O) to stamp a new In (or Out) point (**Figure 12.17**).

✔ Tip

■ To add an audio keyframe in a location that's not on a frame line, you don't need to adjust the playhead; just zoom way in and use the Pen tool to add the keyframe.

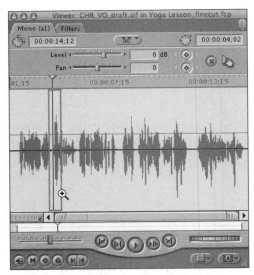

Figure 12.15 Use the Zoom tool to drag a marquee around the playhead. When the view zooms in, the playhead will still be in view.

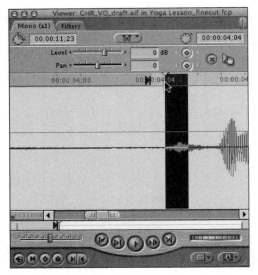

Figure 12.16 Hold down the Shift key; then drag the Audio tab playhead to the exact location of the new In or Out point.

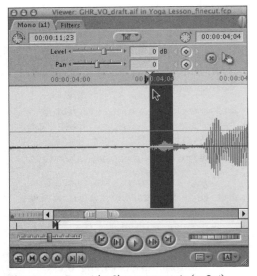

Figure 12.17 Press I (or O) to set a new In (or Out) point. This In point has been adjusted to trim out a small pop at the beginning of a word.

USING THE AUDIO TAB

Figure 12.18 Click and hold to grab the drag hand.

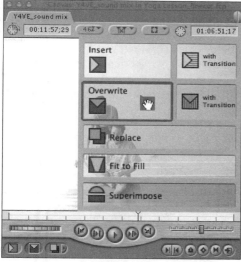

Figure 12.19 Drag and drop to insert a clip into a sequence in the Canvas window.

To drag an audio clip into the Timeline or the Canvas window:

1. Start with an open clip and the Viewer window selected.

2. Position the pointer over the drag hand. When the pointer changes to a hand shape, you're in the right spot (**Figure 12.18**).

3. Drag from that spot to the Canvas or the Timeline. This inserts your audio clip into the open sequence (**Figure 12.19**).

USING THE AUDIO TAB

Sounds Good: Scrubbing Audio with JKL Keys

Use JKL keys to get a better low- and high-speed playback; dragging the playhead across the Scrubber produces ghastly chopped-up–sounding playback that's not useful for much. (Toggle audio scrubbing off and on by pressing Shift-S; you'll still be able to use the JKL key method.) Here's how to use JKL to zero in on a precise point:

◆ Press L and K together for slow forward playback, J and K together for slow reverse playback.

◆ Release the L (or J) as you keep the K key depressed for precision playhead parking on any frame.

Editing Audio in the Timeline

Editing in the Viewer is fine, but here are a few compelling reasons to do your audio editing right in the Timeline:

◆ Timeline tracks are the only place where you can view all your audio tracks at once.

◆ You can set audio level or filter keyframes and sculpt audio levels right in the Timeline.

◆ Canvas and Timeline playback are locked together, so the Timeline is a good place to trim audio on the fly as you watch your sequence play back.

Most of the tools and techniques collected here are discussed in Chapter 10, "Editing in the Timeline and the Canvas." These techniques can give you more control when you need to fine-tune a particular bit of dialogue or a sound effect in a busy soundtrack (**Figure 12.20**).

◆ **Track Height:** Use the largest track size for fine-tuning and close work; use the smallest size for a multi-track overview. Press Shift-T to cycle through the track sizes. If you're using the waveform display to fine-tune an edit, you can stretch just the track you're focusing on.

◆ **Turn on Audio Waveforms:** Displaying audio waveforms in the Timeline can be a big help when you edit audio, but displaying waveforms slows the Timeline's performance. Toggle audio waveforms off and on by pressing Command-Option-W.

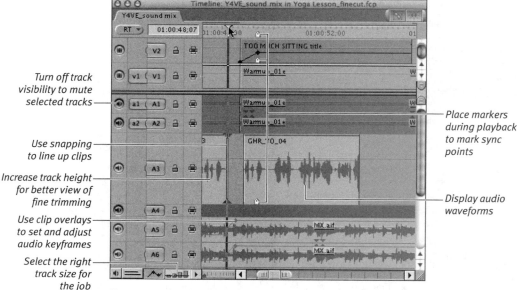

Turn off track visibility to mute selected tracks

Use snapping to line up clips

Increase track height for better view of fine trimming

Use clip overlays to set and adjust audio keyframes

Select the right track size for the job

Place markers during playback to mark sync points

Display audio waveforms

Figure 12.20 Use these tools to gain more control over audio editing in the Timeline.

- **Markers:** When you're trying to hit the perfect spot for a sound effect or music cue, you can set a Timeline marker right at the sweet spot by tapping the M key as you watch your sequence play back.

- **Soloing and Muting Tracks:** As you build up your audio tracks, *track soloing*—silencing all but one audio track so you can concentrate on one sound—makes it much easier to trim precisely or isolate problem sounds in a busy track. Click the Solo button on the track you want to hear. The Mute button offers another route to selective monitoring: Just mute the tracks you want to silence.

- **Snapping:** Snapping makes certain points in the Timeline "sticky." With snapping on, the edges of clips snap together, or a clip will snap to an edit point on an adjacent track when dragged close to it. When you're making fine adjustments to your audio, snapping can be a help (like when you're trying to line up a stack of audio clips to a marker or the playhead position) or a hindrance (when you're trying to drag a sound effect to the perfect location and snapping jerks your clip to the nearest edit point). Remember, you can toggle snapping on or off *at any time*—even midmove—by pressing the N key.

EDITING AUDIO IN THE TIMELINE

Editing Clips with Multiple Audio Channels

Final Cut Pro 4 introduced official support for *merged clips*—a type of clip created in FCP by permanently linking up to 24 audio clips with a single video clip. Earlier versions of the program used workarounds to support clips composed of audio and video linked inside Final Cut Pro, but "official" merged clips make it possible to reliably sync video with production audio recorded separately, while preserving separate audio timecode. Open the Item Properties window on any audio+video clip, and you'll see that each audio channel has its own data column (**Figure 12.21**).

Merged clips appear in the Viewer with multiple Audio tabs sufficient to accommodate the number of audio channels in the clip (**Figure 12.22**). When you open a merged clip in the Viewer, additional source track-targeting controls automatically appear in the Timeline—one for each audio channel in the merged clip (**Figure 12.23**).

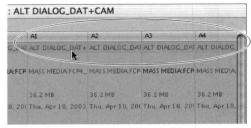

Figure 12.21 The Item Properties window displays separate tracking data for each audio channel.

Figure 12.22 This merged clip contains four channels of stereo audio, so two Audio tabs appear in the clip's Viewer—one tab for each of the two stereo audio pairs.

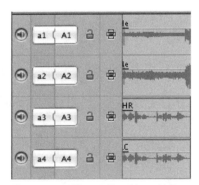

Figure 12.23 When a clip with multiple audio channels is opened in the Viewer, additional source track-targeting controls automatically appear in the Timeline.

You can set separate source In and Out points for video and audio (**Figure 12.24**), but you can mark only a single set of audio edit points. Those audio edit points will be used on all audio channels when you perform the edit (**Figure 12.25**).

You can trim edit points on individual tracks in the Timeline by overriding linked selection (**Figure 12.26**). You can also exclude selected audio channels from an edit by disconnecting source track-targeting controls on the tracks you wish to exclude before you perform the edit (**Figure 12.27**). For more information on merged clips, see Chapter 4, "Projects, Sequences, and Clips."

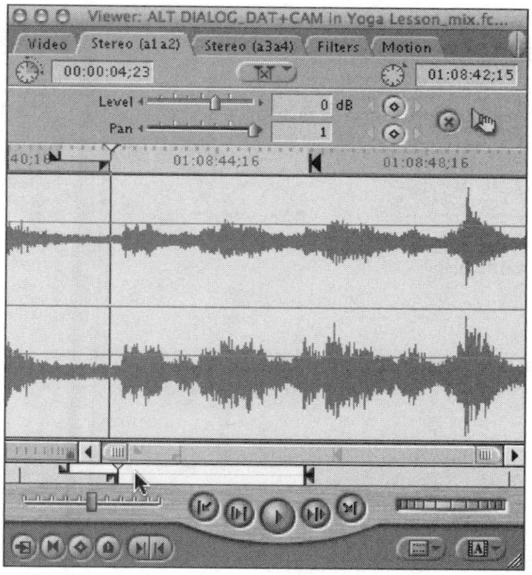

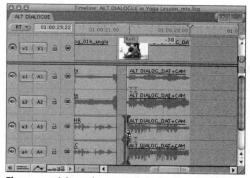

Figure 12.26 Once the merged clip has been edited into the Timeline, you're free to trim the individual audio channels.

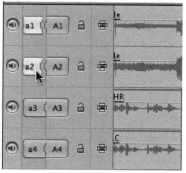

Figure 12.27 Disconnect the source targeting controls on tracks you want to exclude from a multichannel audio edit.

Figure 12.24 You can mark split video and audio edit points in a merged clip, but you can mark only a single set of audio edit points.

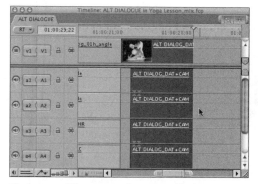

Figure 12.25 When you perform the edit, the same audio edit points will be used on all audio channels.

Recording Audio with the Voice Over Tool

The Voice Over tool is a nifty gadget designed to record synchronous audio as FCP plays back a selected portion of your sequence. Here's a brief rundown of its features:

◆ You can monitor your existing tracks through headphones as you record.

◆ Each completed audio take is automatically placed on a new Timeline track in the portion of the sequence you specified.

◆ When you record multiple takes, FCP automatically creates a new Timeline track for each take's clip.

◆ The Voice Over tool automatically records before and after your Mark In and Mark Out points, so your recorded track won't be cut off if your voiceover runs over.

◆ Once you complete your recording, you are free to reposition, trim, and polish your new voiceover tracks just as you would any other FCP clip.

Anatomy of the Voice Over tool

The Voice Over tool is a self-contained audio recording interface within FCP. When you set up for your recording session, use the Input controls to configure your audio input hardware settings and set audio recording levels, and the Headphones controls to set monitoring levels. When you're ready to record, use the transport controls for preview and capture. The status display helps you keep in step with FCP's playback without having to watch the picture.

To open the Voice Over tool:

◆ Choose Tools > Voice Over.
The Tool Bench appears with the Voice Over tool displayed (**Figure 12.28**).

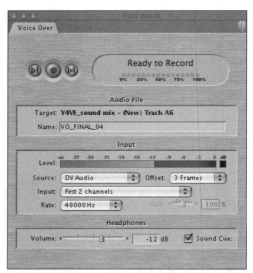

Figure 12.28 An overview of the Voice Over tool controls.

 On Peachpit.com

"Recording Audio with the Voice Over Tool," a 7-page PDF, is available at:
www.peachpit.com/finalcutpro6vqp

Mixing and Finishing Audio

This section covers all the ways you can adjust your audio clips' volume (levels), stereo pan position, and sound quality. You'll get a basic orientation to FCP's Audio Mixer window, plus a few tips on mixing. You'll learn how to use the Audio Peak detection feature, and how to apply and tweak FCP's audio filters.

Setting audio levels

A sequence clip's levels and pan position are adjustable from several locations (**Figure 12.29**):

◆ In the Viewer's Audio tab, set levels and pan by visually editing the line graph that appears as an overlay on your audio waveform, or by adjusting the Level and Pan sliders. See "Adjusting levels and pan in the Audio tab," later in this chapter.

continues on next page

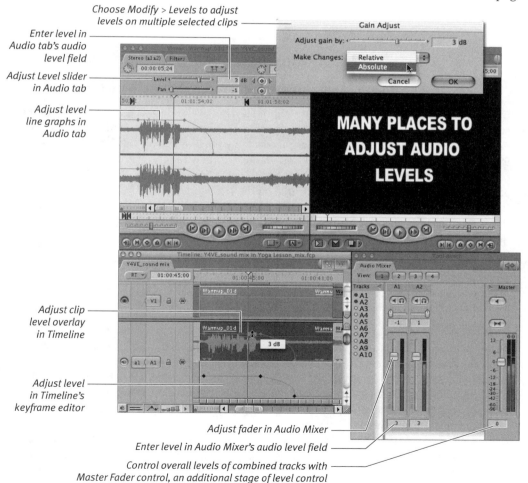

Choose Modify > Levels to adjust levels on multiple selected clips

Enter level in Audio tab's audio level field

Adjust Level slider in Audio tab

Adjust level line graphs in Audio tab

Adjust clip level overlay in Timeline

Adjust level in Timeline's keyframe editor

Adjust fader in Audio Mixer

Enter level in Audio Mixer's audio level field

Control overall levels of combined tracks with Master Fader control, an additional stage of level control

Figure 12.29 You can adjust a clip's audio level from any of the locations illustrated here.

MIXING AND FINISHING AUDIO

415

◆ In the Timeline, adjust a clip's audio levels with the Audio Level line clip overlay or in the clip's keyframe editor. For more information about using these keyframing tools, see "Working with Keyframes in the Timeline" in Chapter 14.

◆ You can use the Modify > Levels command to set levels for multiple audio clips in a single operation. See "Making multiclip adjustments" in Chapter 10.

◆ In the Audio Mixer, record level and pan keyframes in real time as your clip plays back, or adjust levels or pan for each clip by positioning the Timeline playhead at the point you want to adjust. For more information, see "Using the Audio Mixer," later in this chapter.

Remember, adjusting a sequence clip's levels or pan position in *any* of these locations will be reflected in the other locations.

FCP Protocol: Measuring Digital Audio in Decibels (dB)

Decibels (dB) is a unit of measurement for audio levels. Several decibel scales are used in the audio/video world (and some excellent technical articles on the Web explain them in detail). All of these scales describe amplitude as perceived by the human ear, but they measure different amplitude-tracking indicators. The scales all express amplitude in relationship to a fixed reference point, but different scales use different reference points. Professional analog audio uses a reference point of 0 dBVU, and expresses dynamic range by adding *headroom* (range above 0 dBVU) plus *signal to noise* (the range from 0 dBVU down to the device's *noise floor*). For instance, an analog audio device with a "signal to noise ratio" of 76dB, and 22dB of headroom, has a total dynamic range of 98dB.

Digital audio behaves differently and therefore requires a different structure for expressing dynamic range. There's no such thing as headroom in audio that's stored as binary numbers. Digital audio signal quality improves as levels approach 0 dBfs, but exceed the maximum level allowed by even a hair, and the audio levels are clipped.

That's why the *dBfs scale,* the standard decibel scale used for digital audio, uses a reference point that corresponds to the *highest* value that can be expressed in a particular bit depth, and calls that value 0 dBfs. The amplitude measurement of dBfs scales down from 0 dBfs to the lowest level that can be expressed at that bit depth. For example, 16-bit digital audio has a dynamic range of 0 dBfs (the maximum) to −96 dBfs (the smallest value). Greater bit depth increases digital signal processing resolution; FCP uses 32-bit floating-point resolution to compute audio mixes. Even with this increased accuracy, the dBfs scale still maintains the same maximum allowable level; the extra dynamic resolution accommodates the intermediate bit values generated by blending and processing multiple digital audio streams during the mixing process. The extended dynamic range (−177 dBfs) of 32-bit resolution seems enormous, but it's necessary for accurate processing of 24-bit digital audio.

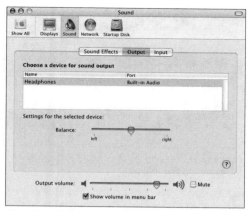

Figure 12.30 The Macintosh's Sound preferences pane.

Monitor levels and mixing

It's important to keep your speaker levels constant when you adjust audio levels for a sequence. There's more than one place to adjust your monitoring level. Take a moment before you start working to set up everything, and note your settings so that you can recalibrate if necessary.

If you'll be recording out to an external video deck or camera, check the audio output levels on the recording device's meters. Play the loudest section of your program. If your recording device has no meters, record a test of the loudest section and review the audio quality.

Check your Macintosh's Sound preferences pane to make sure your computer's sound output level is set high enough (**Figure 12.30**). Next, set a comfortable listening level on the amplifier that drives your external speakers. Now you are in a position to make consistent volume adjustments to the audio in your sequence.

✔ Tip

- There's no way to adjust computer audio levels within Final Cut Pro. Instead, adjust your levels from your Mac's Sound preferences pane (Figure 12.30).

Adjusting levels and pan in the Audio tab

To set audio clip levels in the Audio tab:

1. Start with an open clip and the Viewer window selected.

2. *Do one of the following:*

   ◆ Drag the Level slider to the right to increase clip volume, or to the left to lower clip volume (**Figure 12.31**).

   ◆ Drag the pink Level line graph displayed over the audio waveform: Higher increases volume, lower decreases volume (**Figure 12.32**).

   ◆ Press Control-+ (plus) or Control-– (minus) to adjust audio levels by single-decibel increments.

   ◆ Choose Modify > Audio, and make a gain selection from the submenu (**Figure 12.33**). Note that the submenu lists keyboard shortcuts for nudging audio levels.

✔ Tip

■ *Normalizing* is a fast, automated way to adjust the gain of an entire audio track. Select the audio clip(s), then choose Modify > Audio > Apply Normalization Gain and FCP will scan your track, identify the loudest point in the track and adjust the overall level so that peak is at the dB level you specify.

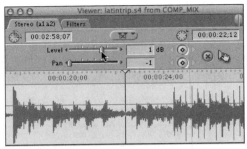

Figure 12.31 Dragging the Level slider to the right increases the clip volume.

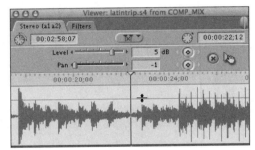

Figure 12.32 Dragging the Level line graph higher increases the volume.

Figure 12.33 Choose Modify > Audio and make a gain selection from the submenu. Note the keyboard shortcuts listed to the right of the submenu choices.

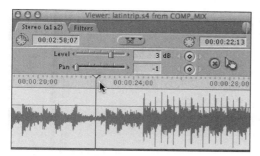

Figure 12.34 Move the playhead to the location where you want the level change to start.

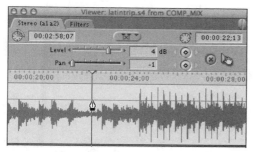

Figure 12.35 Adjust the level with the Level slider, and click the level line with the Pen tool to set a keyframe.

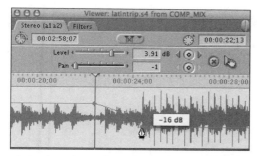

Figure 12.36 At the next location where you want a level change, use the Pen tool to drag the level line to the new level setting.

To create dynamic level changes within a clip:

1. Start with an open clip and the Viewer window selected.

2. Park the playhead where you want to start the level change (**Figure 12.34**).

3. Adjust the level using the Level slider.

4. Select the Pen tool from the Tool palette, then set a keyframe by clicking on the level line with the Pen tool (**Figure 12.35**).

5. Move the playhead to the next location where you want a change in the level.

6. With the Pen tool, drag the level line to the new audio level (**Figure 12.36**).

   Another keyframe is set automatically as you drag the level line with the Pen tool.

✔ Tip

- Click the Add Audio Keyframe button in the lower part of the window to set a keyframe on both the Level and Pan line graphs at the current playhead position.

- To make the most common kind of dynamic audio level adjustment—moving from one constant level to another constant level—requires that two keyframes be set for each level shift; one at the start of the level shift and the other at the new volume level. Here's the fastest, easiest way to set a pair of audio keyframes: With the Timeline or Viewer playhead positioned at the point you want to start the level change, press Cmd-Option-K—that's the keyboard shortcut to set an audio keyframe. Press the right arrow button to advance the playhead one frame and then press Cmd-Option-K again. Drag that second keyframe to set the incoming audio level; you won't affect the levels set to the left of the keyframe. Try it.

Adjusting the pan position

The pan position is the left/right placement of sound for single audio channels. Clips with one or two channels of discrete audio will initially open with pan set to the center.

To set a pan position:

1. Start with an open clip and the Viewer window selected.

2. *Do one of the following:*

   ◆ Drag the Pan slider to the right to pan toward the right; drag the slider to the left to pan toward the left (**Figure 12.37**).

   ◆ Drag the purple Pan line graph displayed over the audio waveform. Drag higher to pan right; drag lower to pan left (**Figure 12.38**).

   ◆ Choose Modify > Audio and make a pan selection from the submenu.

Figure 12.37 Dragging the Pan slider to the left pans your track toward the left channel.

Figure 12.38 Dragging the Pan line graph lower pans your track toward the left channel.

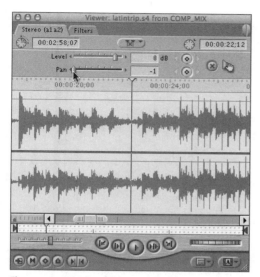

Figure 12.39 The Pan slider at its base setting of –1. This setting replicates the original mix of a stereo source track.

Adjusting stereo spread

On stereo audio clips, the Pan control adjusts the *spread* (the degree of stereo separation), and it adjusts left and right channels simultaneously and equally.

You can use the Pan slider or line graph to adjust the stereo spread. The setting options on the Pan slider are as follows:

◆ The base setting of –1 outputs the left audio channel to the left and the right audio channel to the right. This setting accurately reproduces the stereo mix of a track from a music CD.

◆ A setting of 0 outputs the left and right audio channels equally to both sides.

◆ A setting of +1 swaps the channels, outputting the left audio channel to the right and the right audio channel to the left.

To adjust the pan on a stereo audio clip:

1. Start with an open clip and the Viewer window selected.

2. *Do one of the following:*

◆ Drag the Pan slider to adjust the stereo pan positioning (see **Figure 12.39**).

◆ Drag the purple Pan level line graph displayed over the audio waveform at the center line between the two stereo channels. Drag away from the center line for a +1 setting; drag toward the center for a –1 setting.

Using Audio Peak Detection

When you record audio (or capture prerecorded audio), you need to be especially careful about audio levels. Digital audio does not allow levels that exceed its maximum amplitude of 0 dBfs; any part of the recording that exceeds 0 dB is clipped off. Clipped digital audio sounds nasty—snapping and crackling. If you're unlucky enough to have clipped audio in parts of your tracks and you're unable to recapture the audio at a lower level, you'll need to cut around it somehow.

The Audio Peak Detection feature is an analysis tool that scans an audio file you select and places a marker in the clip at each location where the audio exceeds 0 dB. Armed with this information, you can evaluate your over-crisp audio track and plan your recovery strategy.

To detect audio peaks:

1. To select the clips you want to analyze, *do one of the following:*
   - Select clips from the Browser, or select sequence clips in the open sequence in the Timeline.
   - Select an entire sequence for analysis by opening it in the Timeline or clicking an open sequence's Timeline tab to make it active, making sure no individual clips are selected.

2. Choose Mark > Audio Peaks > Mark (**Figure 12.40**).

   Final Cut Pro places a numbered marker, labeled Audio Peak *n*, each time it detects an audio level of 0 dB (Figure **12.41**).

To clear audio peak markers:

- In the Browser or Timeline, select the clips that you want to clear, then choose Mark > Audio Peaks > Clear (**Figure 12.42**).

   Final Cut Pro deletes all audio peak markers from the selected clips.

Figure 12.40 Choose Mark > Audio Peaks > Mark to identify points where your audio levels exceed 0 dB.

Figure 12.41 FCP places a marker at each audio peak it detects.

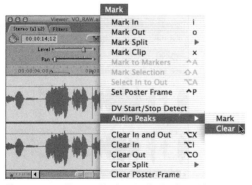

Figure 12.42 Choose Mark > Audio Peaks > Clear to remove audio peak markers from an audio clip.

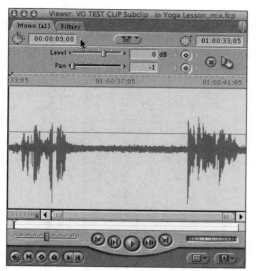

Figure 12.43 Create a test subclip using a representative section of your audio track.

Adjusting Audio Filters

Final Cut Pro's suite of audio filters is geared toward repairing problems in production audio. That's good, because production audio frequently has problems—problems that don't come to light until you review your footage in the editing room. FCP's equalization, compression, and noise reduction filters are tools you can use to reduce rumble in an exterior street recording or improve the crispness in a dialogue track. (Before you ask, there is no filter that will strip background music out of dialogue.)

You apply FCP's audio filters in the same way that you apply video filters.

FCP has improved the real-time previewing of audio filters considerably, but some audio filters have to be rendered before you can hear the results of your settings adjustment. Lack of real-time feedback can make adjusting audio filters in FCP more challenging. Try the method described here to reduce the lag time between adjusting an audio filter's setting and hearing the results. If the filter you're adjusting plays back without rendering, so much the better—you get to skip the rendering step.

To adjust an audio filter's settings:

1. Make a short test subclip from a representative section of your audio track (**Figure 12.43**). If you're trying to fix a problem, pick out a worst-case section and then maybe an average-case section to try your worst-case settings on. Make the test subclip long enough so you can evaluate your work, say 5 to 10 seconds.

continues on next page

ADJUSTING AUDIO FILTERS

2. Open your test clip in the Viewer, apply the filter, and start tweaking the filter settings. If you like, you can pull the Filters tab completely out of the Viewer window so you can view your subclip playing back in the Audio tab as you adjust filter settings.

3. You'll hear a series of beeps (FCP's rendering indicator for audio) if your test clip requires rendering. In that case, you'll need to render the audio before you can hear the effect of the audio filter you've applied. Your short test clip should render quickly.

4. Enable looped playback, and then try to get into a rhythm of adjusting and listening. When you think you've zeroed in on your filter settings, copy and paste the filter (and its settings) from the test clip to your full-length audio track in the sequence (**Figure 12.44**). Use the Paste Attributes command to paste just the filters (**Figure 12.45**).

✔ Tips

- Audio filters applied to audio that is formatted as a stereo pair are applied to both channels equally, and only one set of controls appears on the Viewer's Filters tab.

- You can copy an audio filter with all its current settings and paste it onto other clips or onto an entire nested sequence. If you perfect the EQ setting that cancels out the sound of your camera, you can easily apply the same filter setting wherever it's needed. See "Copying and pasting clip attributes" in Chapter 10.

- "Using Audio Filters" which starts on page III-153 of Apple's *Final Cut Pro User Manual* PDF contains 23 pages on working with FCP's audio filters.

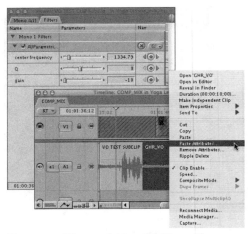

Figure 12.44 When you've tuned in filter settings, copy them and then use the Paste Attributes command to paste the filter and its settings from the test clip to your full-length audio track in the sequence.

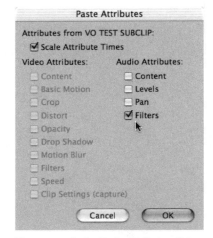

Figure 12.45 In the Paste Attributes dialog box, paste just the filters from your test audio clip onto the longer audio clip you're filtering.

Adjusting Audio Filters

To record audio filter keyframes in real time:

1. In the Audio Mixer, make sure that the Record Audio Keyframes button is on.

2. Open the audio clip in the Viewer, then select the Filters tab.

3. Locate the point where you want to start recording filter control keyframes, and position the playhead a few seconds before your first planned move. You might want to loop playback of the section you're working on.

4. Start playback.

5. Position the pointer over the first filter control you want to adjust in real time, then press the mouse button to start recording keyframes. Keep the mouse button held down until you've completed your move, then release the mouse to stop recording keyframes.

Smart Filter Tweaking Tips

The best way to pinpoint the frequency of a problem sound in your production audio is to apply an EQ filter that's set to a narrow bandwidth, and then boost the filter gain. Sweep that narrow bandwidth slowly across the frequency spectrum until the problem sound is the *most* noticeable. Now that you've identified the problem frequency, attenuate the filter gain and widen the filter's bandwidth until the problem sound is minimized.

Overprocessing your audio to eliminate acoustic deficiencies or noise can actually hurt your overall sound quality. Consider your soundtrack as a whole—is the noise really noticeable, or is it buried in the mix? Audiences are accustomed to ambient noise; we're surrounded by it and are already trained to listen selectively. Sometimes adding a little more ambient noise to a mix creates a constant field that's less noticeable.

This last tip is the most important: If the program you're editing is going to be handed over to a post-production sound crew for finishing, *don't* try to fix your production audio with filters and processing beforehand. Audio specialists can do their best work when you give them unprocessed tracks to work with.

ADJUSTING AUDIO FILTERS

Anatomy of the Audio Mixer

The Audio Mixer's interface (**Figure 12.46**) is a virtual representation of an automated mixing board. The mixer is designed to offer you a lot of display flexibility. The mixer window is organized into four areas. You can hide or show panes, and set up customized views that display just the track strips of audio tracks you want to focus on. For more information, see "Overview of the Audio Mixer" on page III-69 of Apple's *Final Cut Pro User Manual* PDF. Here's a rundown of the Audio Mixer interface features and functions:

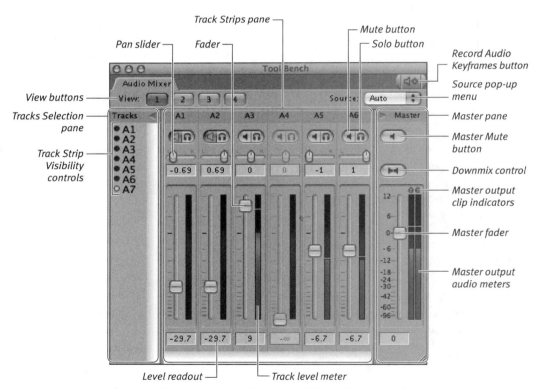

Figure 12.46 Choose Tools > Audio Mixer, and the Audio Mixer window appears as a tab in the Tool Bench.

ANATOMY OF THE AUDIO MIXER

✔ Tips

- Editing with compressed audio will cause Final Cut Pro to lose sync, and it could cause a crash. Don't do it.

- Compressing audio should be the very last step in your post-production process. Trying to mix or filter compressed audio can produce distorted tracks. Don't compress your final audio unless you absolutely have to.

- The Tool Bench window is FCP's catchall drawer—in addition to showing the Audio Mixer and the Voice Over tool, the Tool Bench is the display window for a wide variety of other FCP features. All tools appearing on a tab in the Tool Bench share a single button bar, so you may see buttons appearing at the top of the Tool Bench that don't apply to the tool you're using at the moment.

Figure 12.47 Clicking a Track Strip Visibility control hides a track strip but doesn't disable the track.

Figure 12.48 Control-click a Track Strip Visibility control to assign the track to an audio output channel.

At the top of the mixer window, you'll find a couple of general controls:

- ◆ **View buttons:** Click one of the four buttons to recall a previously saved Audio Mixer track layout. Command-click a View button to save the current mixer layout as a customized view.

- ◆ **Record Audio Keyframes button:** Enables real-time recording of level and pan keyframes during playback. (Record Audio Keyframes can also be enabled on the Editing tab of the User Preferences window.) With Record Audio Keyframes disabled, adjusting the Audio Mixer controls will make overall adjustments to clips' level and pan settings but won't record any new keyframes; instead, it will raise or lower the entire clip's level if no keyframes are present or adjust all existing keyframe values by the same amount without recording any new keyframes.

Tracks Selection pane

- ◆ **Track Strip Visibility controls:** Click the control to the left of the track's name to toggle visibility of that track strip in the Audio Mixer (**Figure 12.47**). These controls are independent of the Track Visibility controls in the Timeline and do not mute audio playback of hidden tracks; only the visibility of the track strip is affected. Use these controls to create customized track strip layouts; one layout could show just your sound effects tracks, another could include just sync dialogue. Custom mixer views can be saved to one of the four View buttons at the top of the mixer. Control-click a Track Strip Visibility control to assign it to an audio output channel (**Figure 12.48**).

Track Strips pane

◆ **Solo button:** Click to mute playback of all audio tracks except this one. Enable multiple solo buttons to audition a selected group of tracks. This button duplicates the function of the track's Solo button in the Timeline.

◆ **Mute button:** Click to mute playback of this track. Mute multiple tracks to limit monitoring to the tracks that remain unmuted. The Audio Mixer's mute control duplicates the function of that track's Mute button in the Timeline.

◆ **Pan slider:** Adjust the slider to set a clip's pan position. Pan slider information entered here is directly reflected in that individual clip's Audio tab and Timeline pan settings. Note that if you assign a track to a single mono output, any clips on that track will be panned center and can't be pan-adjusted.

◆ **Fader:** Use the track strip's fader to set and manipulate audio levels for the clip at the playhead position on that track. Fader moves are recorded as audio level keyframes and are stored with the individual clip.

◆ **Level readout:** Displays the current level of a track in dBfs. You can set a precise level by entering a dB value in the Level readout field.

◆ **Track level meter:** While your sequence plays, the track level meters respond dynamically, constantly updating to reflect the current clip amplitude. When sequence playback is paused, each track level meter displays the audio level of the clip at the current playhead position on that track.

✔ Tips

■ Solo and Mute buttons affect monitoring during playback, but they don't disable audio output during Print to Video, Edit to Tape, or file export operations. If you want to exclude a track from any of these output operations, you must disable the track in the Timeline by turning off its Track Visibility control.

■ If you're using an aftermarket, multibutton mouse that's equipped with a scroll wheel, lucky you! You'll find that scrolling will adjust the Audio Mixer's faders when the pointer is positioned directly over the fader.

Master pane

The track faders in the Master section of the mixer offer an additional stage of level control that affects all audio tracks. Mastering allows you to adjust the overall level of your output without modifying individual clip level and pan settings. You'll see a master fader for each audio output you're using in the current sequence. Master control settings aren't designed to be manipulated during a mix, so you can't record automated mix moves, but your Master control settings are saved with each sequence.

◆ **Source pop-up menu:** Choose Viewer from the Source pop-up menu to assign Audio Mixer controls to record audio keyframes for clips played back in the Viewer. Choose Canvas to record keyframes for clips played back in the Canvas. Choose Auto to switch automatically to the active window.

◆ **Master Mute button:** Click to mute playback of all tracks. This master mute control overrides the track-level Mute and Solo buttons in the mixer's track strips and in the Timeline, but doesn't disable audio output during Print to Video, Edit to Tape, or file export operations.

◆ **Downmix control:** Click to mix all master output channels to two stereo output channels. When the mixer is configured to output audio to more than two channels, the Downmix control is a fast way to convert your output to stereo so you can monitor, make a work dub, or export your sequence as a digital file. Downmixing routes odd-numbered audio outputs to the left channel, and even-numbered audio outputs to the right channel. The process of combining multiple audio tracks can easily over-modulate the downmixed stereo output, so you'll need to reduce each audio output channel's level before downmixing. Choose an attenuation level for each output from the Downmix pop-up menu, in the Audio Outputs tab of the current sequence's settings.

◆ **Master fader:** Use the master fader to set and manipulate audio levels for all the tracks assigned to that audio output. Master fader levels give you an additional stage of level control, letting you adjust the overall mix levels without changing individual clip level and pan settings. Master fader levels are used for playback, printing the sequence to tape, and exporting the sequence in a digital file format.

continues on next page

ANATOMY OF THE AUDIO MIXER

◆ **Master output audio meters:** These meters display combined output amplitude for all the tracks assigned to that master output channel.

The upper limits of digital audio levels are unforgiving, so it's essential that you do not overload your final output levels, or your final mix will be unusable. Master output meters feature clip indicators, which light up whenever total levels exceed 0 dBfs and stay lit until you pause and then restart playback. Even though your output levels should never exceed 0 dBfs, the Master output meter's range extends to +12 dB. That extra 12 dB of readout on the meter makes it much easier for you to tell exactly how many decibels your clipped audio has pushed over the 0 dBfs limit (**Figure 12.49**). Remember: Clip lights mean danger!

Figure 12.49 The Master fader's clip indicators have been triggered; the meter's readout shows that the current output levels are about 10 dB over the 0 dBfs limit.

✔ Tip

■ Need more precision in your mix moves? You can increase the throw of the track strip's faders by stretching the Audio Mixer window in the Tool Bench (**Figure 12.50**). Taller faders give you more room to make your moves. You can also Command-click the faders to gear down their response.

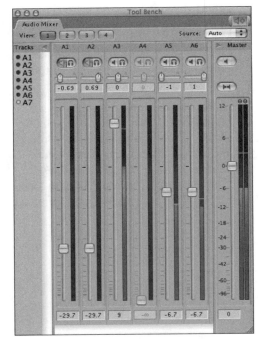

Figure 12.50 Stretch the Audio Mixer window to lengthen the throw of the track strip faders.

Figure 12.51 Choose Tools > Audio Mixer to open the Audio Mixer window.

About Soundtrack Pro

From its humble roots as an FCP 4 helper application, Soundtrack Pro 2 has developed into an ambitious audio post-production tool.

STP (as it's known in the FCP user community) features a powerful waveform editor you can use to manipulate audio non-destructively. The STP waveform editor tracks your editing and effects settings in a kind of History list; you can freely backtrack and reorder or temporarily disable any step in your process. Once you've perfected it, you can save a multi-step processing operation as an Applescript batch process and apply it to other audio files in a single operation. Soundtrack Pro comes with a suite of 50 Logic Pro effect plug-ins and a library of sound effects in addition to the original Soundtrack music loops.

Soundtrack Pro 2 is substantially improved from its 1.0 release. Apple has listened to user feedback and made the interface, JKL keys, and editing tools operate much more like Final Cut Pro. Plugin effect interfaces have been simplified and OMF/AAF import/export has been beefed up.

STP's integration with other Final Cut Studio applications has been significantly refined. Just keep one eye on Apple's online Support site to keep you apprised of the latest conditions. For information on exporting FCP audio files to STP, see Chapter 19, "Creating Final Output."

Using the Audio Mixer

The Audio Mixer is patterned after a hardware audio mixing console. Each Timeline audio track in your sequence is represented by a track strip with mixer-like level faders and pan controls. Here the hardware mixer analogy gets a bit blurry; the mixer's Solo and Mute buttons affect the entire Timeline track, but when you manipulate a track strip fader or pan slider, you're adjusting levels or pan for the *individual sequence clip at the current playhead position on that track*. You could think of the Audio Mixer as a method of recording the audio clip level and pan keyframes in real time.

You can freely mix and match real-time mixing with manual tweaking of level and pan keyframes in the Timeline or Audio tab; they're just two means of achieving the same end: fine-tuning the dynamic level and pan information stored with each individual clip. What you cannot do is set one level for all the clips on a track simply by setting the track strip fader on one clip. If you set a track fader and then play your sequence back, you'll see the faders move in response to the level settings of each individual clip. In areas where no clip is present on a track, the track fader jumps to −∞ dB and cannot be adjusted.

To open the Audio Mixer window:

Do one of the following:

◆ Choose Tools > Audio Mixer (**Figure 12.51**); or press Option-6.

◆ Choose Window > Arrange > Audio Mixing to select the custom screen layout for audio.

To adjust clip audio levels in the Audio Mixer:

1. Open the sequence in the Timeline.

2. In the Audio Mixer, make sure that the Record Audio Keyframes button is toggled off (**Figure 12.52**).

3. In the Timeline, position the playhead over the first clip requiring level adjustment (**Figure 12.53**).

4. Position the pointer over the track strip fader for the track where the level adjustment is required, *then do one of the following:*

   ◆ Click and drag the fader to the desired level (**Figure 12.54**).

   ◆ Set a precise level by entering a dB value in the Level readout field.

   ◆ Start playback, then use the faders to adjust clip audio levels in real time as the sequence plays back. You must set a level for each clip individually.

   If no keyframes are present on the clip you're adjusting, the clip level adjusts to the new level you selected.

   If you have already applied keyframes to the clip's audio levels, the dB value of your level adjustment is applied to the area between the two keyframes on either side of the current playhead position.

Figure 12.52 Toggle the Record Audio Keyframes button off.

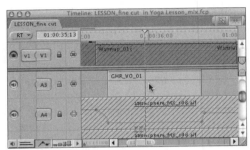

Figure 12.53 Position the Timeline playhead over the clip you want to adjust.

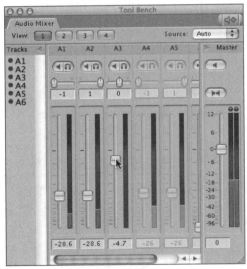

Figure 12.54 Click and drag the track strip fader to the new level.

Audio Mixer Tip: Setting Levels Across Edit Points

Most audio levels in mixed video soundtracks move from one constant level to another constant level; that is, music fades up, holds at –4 dB, fades to –10 dB under narration, holds at –10 dB, and so on. To make this kind of a level change requires that two keyframes be set for each level shift; one at the start of the level shift and the other at the new volume level—the characteristic "plateaus" we see in audio clip overlays.

To record this type of level change in the Audio Mixer, you've got to:

1. Click, make the fade-up move, and release.

2. Click again, make your fade-under move, and release.

If you happen to cross an edit point between the fade-under and fade-up, you need to hold the mouse down through the edit point, or your levels jump to incoming clip levels.

Here's a workaround that can simplify automated mixing of tracks composed of many, many short clips: You can select the clips in the Timeline and then nest them in a sub-sequence. The sub-sequence will be treated as a single clip when you're recording mix moves in real time.

Other Ways to Set Levels

These two methods can speed up level tweaking:

- If you want to use the Audio Mixer to make quick level or pan adjustments to an entire group of clips, here's an alternate method to try: Press the Down Arrow key to skip the playhead to the first frame of each successive clip; then use the mixer controls to make the level or pan change.

- If you just want to make quick level adjustments to an entire group of clips, it's faster to select the clips in the Timeline and then use the Modify > Levels command to adjust all levels in the selected clips in a single operation. For more information, see "Making multi-clip adjustments" in Chapter 10.

Why Are My Track Strip Faders Disabled?

You're ready to mix, but a track fader is grayed out or doesn't respond. Here are a few possible reasons:

- The track is locked.

- There's no clip present on that track at the current playhead position.

- The clip has been disabled in the Timeline. Make sure Clip Enable is checked in the clip's shortcut menu.

- The entire track has been disabled and appears dimmed in the Timeline. You can't make any changes to a disabled Timeline track, but all of its settings were preserved at the time the track was disabled.

To record audio level or pan keyframes in real time:

1. In the Audio Mixer, make sure that the Record Audio Keyframes button is toggled on (**Figure 12.55**).

2. In the Timeline, locate the point where you want to start recording audio keyframes, and position the playhead a few seconds before your first planned move (**Figure 12.56**). You might want to loop playback of the section you're working on.

3. Start playback.

4. Position the pointer over the track strip fader for the track where the level adjustments are required, and then press the mouse button to start recording keyframes (**Figure 12.57**). Drag the fader to the desired level, keeping the mouse button held down until you've completed your move, then release the mouse to stop recording keyframes.

Final Cut Pro sets audio level keyframes that track your mixer moves. These keyframed audio levels appear in the clip's audio level overlays in the Timeline (**Figure 12.58**) and in the Audio tab of the Viewer.

Figure 12.55 Toggle the Record Audio Keyframes button on.

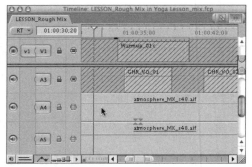

Figure 12.56 Position the Timeline playhead a few seconds before your first planned fader move.

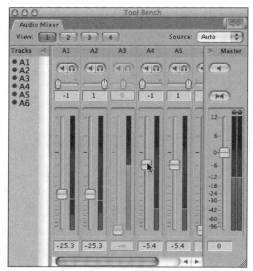

Figure 12.57 Drag the fader to the desired level, holding down the mouse button until you complete your move. If you want to maintain a steady audio level at the end of a move, release the mouse at the end of the move, and then press and drag the mouse again when you want to perform your next move.

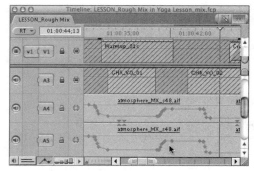

Figure 12.58 Audio level keyframes that track your mixer moves appear on the clip's audio level overlays in the Timeline.

✔ Tips

- If you have already applied keyframes to sculpt a clip's audio levels, the new keyframes you just recorded will overwrite any previously applied keyframes.

- During real-time automation recording, fader movements on one channel of a stereo pair control the level of the other channel. Note that keyframes appear on both stereo channels of a clip *after* you stop recording automation.

- Big news! You can use FCP's real-time automation to record filter control keyframes in the Filters tab of the Viewer. See "To record audio filter keyframes in real time," earlier in this chapter.

How Many Keyframes Do You Want to Record?

FCP offers you a choice of three different levels of detail in your automated audio keyframe recording:

- **All:** Records the maximum number of keyframes possible and tracks your moves very precisely, but produces dense clusters of many keyframes.

- **Reduced:** Tracks your moves but records fewer keyframes.

- **Peaks Only:** Sets keyframes only at the highest and lowest levels in each mixer move.

You can select an audio keyframe recording level preference on the Editing tab of the User Preferences window (**Figure 12.59**).

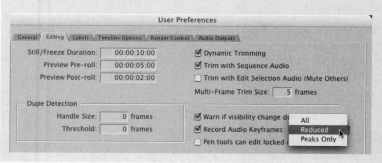

Figure 12.59 Select a level of detail for audio keyframe recording on the Editing tab of the User Preferences window.

To delete all audio keyframes from a clip:

1. In the Timeline, select the clip.

2. Choose Edit > Remove Attributes; or press Command-Option-V.

3. In the Remove Attributes dialog box, check Levels and/or Pan; then click OK.

Or do this:

1. In the Timeline, select the clip.

2. Choose Modify > Levels; or press Command-Option-L.

3. In the Gain Adjust dialog box, choose Absolute from the pop-up menu; then use the slider to set a clip volume, or enter a dB value indicated next to the slider (**Figure 12.60**).

   The clip's level is set to the dB value you entered, and all level keyframes are removed from the clip.

✔ Tip

■ Both of these methods for resetting audio clip levels can be used on multi-clip selections. Quick level resetting will surely save your sanity as you're trying to master the art of real-time automated audio mixing.

To reset a fader to 0 dB:

Do one of the following:

◆ Option-click the fader you want to reset.

◆ To reset all faders in the mixer, Control-click the top of any track strip, and then choose Reset All from the shortcut menu.

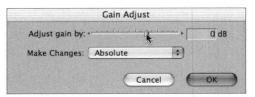

Figure 12.60 Use the Modify > Levels command to reset all selected clip levels to a specific decibel level in a single operation.

CREATING TRANSITIONS

Transitions are a small but essential part of film grammar. Over the years, transitions have developed an important role in film story language. Filmmakers rely on the audience's knowledge of the transition "code." This grammar of transitions and what they signify in movie language has grown up with the movies. These days, viewers are hardly aware of the translations that they make while watching film: Fade-out/fade-in means the passage of time; a ripple dissolve means "it was all a dream"; and a heart-shaped iris wipe means you're watching reruns of *The Dating Game*.

Final Cut Pro offers a library of more than 50 transition effects, which range from simple dissolves to complex 3D transitions. This chapter introduces the procedures for working with transitions in an editing context. For information on modifying effects settings to sculpt transitions, see Chapter 14, "Compositing and Effects Overview."

Adding Transition Effects

You can add transitions along with clips as you assemble your sequence by performing one of the two transition edit types available in the Canvas edit overlay, or you can apply transitions to edit points after you have assembled your sequence. Once you've applied transitions, you can go back and modify them as you refine your cut.

Final Cut Pro displays transitions as overlays within a single Timeline track—an efficient use of screen real estate (**Figure 13.1**). You can adjust a transition directly in the Timeline window, or you can make more complex adjustments in the Transition Editor. The following procedures for adding a transition to a sequence are performed in the Timeline.

Figure 13.1 Transitions appear as overlays within a single Timeline track. The dark gray diagonal shading on the transition's Timeline icon indicates the transition's direction, alignment, and speed.

FCP Protocol: Transitions

◆ Because transitions are created by overlapping material from two adjacent clips, each source clip must have enough additional frames to span half of the transition's duration. If a source clip is too short to create the transition at your specified duration, Final Cut Pro will calculate and apply the transition with a shorter duration, or not apply it at all if you have no additional frames.

◆ You can add transition effects as you edit a clip into a sequence, or you can add transitions to a previously edited sequence.

◆ You can place a transition so that it is centered on the cut, starts at the cut, or ends at the cut.

◆ When you use the Transition edit in the Canvas overlay to add a clip to your sequence, FCP always centers the transition on the cut between the two clips. If you want to add a transition that either starts or ends at the cut, add the transition after the clips are placed in the sequence.

◆ If you plan to export an Edit Decision List (EDL) from your FCP project so that you can finish the project on another editing system, you should keep in mind that EDL formats don't support transitions in any tracks other than V1. Transitions in other tracks won't appear in the EDL. Cross dissolves and simple wipes are supported, but it's probably best to apply more complex transition effects after you've migrated to your destination system. See Chapter 19, "Creating Final Output," for more information on EDLs and FCP.

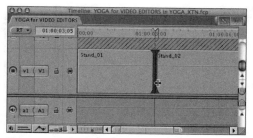

Figure 13.2 Selecting an edit point in the Timeline.

Figure 13.3 Choosing Cross Dissolve from the Effects menu.

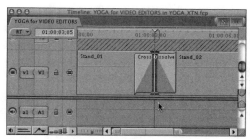

Figure 13.4 The Cross Dissolve transition is applied to the selected edit point in the Timeline.

To add a transition effect that's centered on a cut:

1. In the Timeline, select the edit point between two clips on the same Timeline track (**Figure 13.2**).

2. To add the transition effect, *do one of the following:*

   ◆ Choose Effects > Video Transitions; then select from the submenu's list of effects (**Figure 13.3**).

   ◆ Drag a transition effect from the Effects tab in the Browser onto the cut, centering it over the cut.

   ◆ To add the default transition, Control-click the edit point; then choose Add Transition from the shortcut menu.

The transition is applied to the selected edit point (**Figure 13.4**).

✔ Tip

■ You can change the alignment of an existing transition by Control-clicking the selected transition in the Timeline and then choosing a different alignment from the shortcut menu.

ADDING TRANSITION EFFECTS

To add a transition effect that starts or ends at a cut:

◆ Drag a transition effect from the Effects tab in the Browser onto the edit point in the Timeline, aligning it so that it starts or ends at the cut (**Figure 13.5**).

✔ Tips

■ Create a fade-to-black transition by dragging the Cross Dissolve transition from the Effects tab of the Browser to the final clip in your sequence, aligning it so that it ends at the cut.

■ To fade up from black, drag the Cross Dissolve transition onto the beginning of the first clip in your sequence, aligning it to start at the first frame of the sequence.

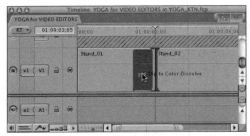

Figure 13.5 Dragging the transition from the Effects tab of the Browser to the edit point in the Timeline. This Dip to Color transition is aligned to end at the cut, creating a fade-out.

FCP Protocol: Saving Changes to Modified Transitions

When saving changes to a transition, remember that transitions follow the same protocols as clips and sequences. (For more information, review "FCP Protocol: Clips and Sequences" in Chapter 4.) Here's a summary of the main points:

◆ When you add a transition to a sequence by dragging it from the Browser to the Timeline, a copy of the transition is inserted into the sequence.

◆ You can open a transition from the Browser (outside a sequence) or from the Timeline (within a sequence).

◆ If you modify a transition from the Browser before you insert the transition into a sequence, the transition that is placed in the sequence includes the changes made in the Browser.

◆ Any changes you make to a transition from within a sequence are not made to the transition in the Browser. If you want to reuse a transition you've designed within a sequence, drag a copy of your revised transition from the Timeline back to the Browser.

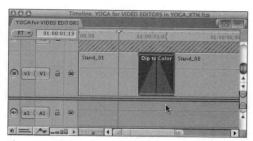

Figure 13.6 Select the transition you want to replace.

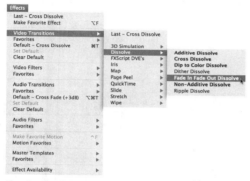

Figure 13.7 Choose a replacement transition from the Effects menu.

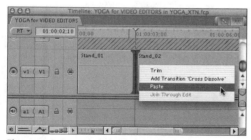

Figure 13.8 Control-click the edit point; then choose Paste from the shortcut menu.

To delete a transition from a sequence:

◆ In the Timeline, select the transition; then press the Delete key.

To replace one transition with another:

1. In the Timeline, select the transition you are replacing (**Figure 13.6**).

2. Choose Effects > Video (or Audio) Transitions; then select a replacement transition from a submenu (**Figure 13.7**).

To copy a transition and paste it in another location:

1. In the Timeline, select the transition you want to copy; then press Command-C.

2. Control-click the edit point where you want to paste the transition; then choose Paste from the shortcut menu (**Figure 13.8**).

✔ Tip

■ You can copy and apply a transition to another edit point in one stylish move. Press the Option key, then click your desired transition, and then hold down Option while dragging the transition to another edit point in the Timeline. This technique works with clips, too.

ADDING TRANSITION EFFECTS

Working with Default and Favorite Transitions

You can specify one video and one audio transition to be used as default transitions. The default transitions are available from the Effects menu, from the edit point's shortcut menu, and as keyboard commands. A transition edit, available in the Canvas edit overlay, automatically includes your default transition at the time you perform the edit. A default transition can be a transition you have already modified within a sequence.

You can also designate a transition (or any other type of effect) as a Favorite. Favorite effects appear in the Favorites bin on the Effects tab in the Browser and are available from the Effects menu. Using Favorites is an easy way to save a transition's settings so you can reproduce the effect later. You can build up a small group of favorite transitions for a particular project. When you're ready to bang out a string of identical transitions, you can promote one of your Favorites to a default transition and get busy.

Defaults and Favorites can speed up the work of constructing those quick-cut montages your producer is so fond of.

To set the default transition:

◆ On the Effects tab of the Browser, Control-click the effect you want to designate as your default transition; then choose Set Default Transition from the shortcut menu (**Figure 13.9**).

The default transition appears on the Effects tab with a line under its name (**Figure 13.10**).

✔ Tip

■ Any customized transition in your Favorites bin can be set as the default transition.

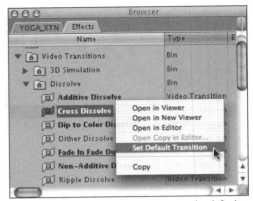

Figure 13.9 Use the shortcut menu to set the default transition. FCP's default video transition is a 1-second cross dissolve, but you can select your own default.

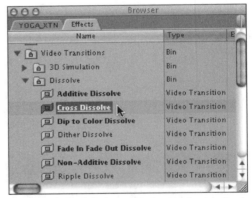

Figure 13.10 The default transition's name is underlined.

Figure 13.11 Choose Effects > Clear Default.

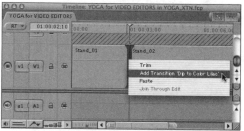

Figure 13.12 Control-click the edit point; then choose Add Transition *'name of the current default transition'* from the shortcut menu.

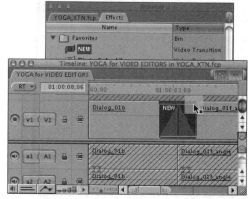

Figure 13.13 Dragging a modified transition from the Timeline to the Favorites bin, located on the Effects tab of the Browser.

To clear the default transition:

◆ Choose Effects > Clear Default (**Figure 13.11**).

To apply the default transition:

Do one of the following:

◆ Select the edit point where you want to place the transition; then choose Effects > Default *'name of the current default transition.'*

◆ Control-click the edit point; then choose Add Transition *'name of the current default transition'* from the shortcut menu (**Figure 13.12**).

◆ Select the edit point; then press Command-T.

To create a Favorite transition by saving its settings:

◆ In the Transition Editor or the Timeline, click and drag the transition icon to the Favorites bin on the Effects tab in the Browser (**Figure 13.13**).

Or do the following:

1. In the Timeline, double-click the transition you want to make a Favorite.

   The transition opens in the Transition Editor window.

2. Choose Effects > Make Favorite Effect; or press Option-F.

To create a Favorite transition before changing its settings:

1. On the Effects tab in the Browser, double-click the transition (**Figure 13.14**).

   The transition opens in the Transition Editor.

2. Adjust the transition's settings in the Transition Editor; then use the drag handle to drag the modified transition into the Favorites bin (**Figure 13.15**).

3. In the Favorites bin, rename the new transition (**Figure 13.16**).

✔ Tip

■ You can also select a transition in the Browser and choose Duplicate from the Edit menu. A copy of the transition appears in the Favorites folder and the appropriate Favorites submenu of the Effects menu (you'll find separate Favorites submenus for each class of audio and video effects).

To delete a Favorite transition from the Favorites bin:

◆ In the Favorites bin, select the transition you want to delete; then press Delete.

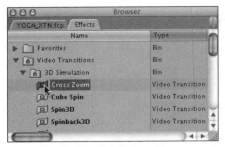

Figure 13.14 Double-click the transition you want to customize to open it in the Transition Editor.

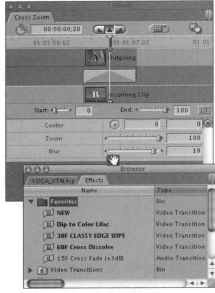

Figure 13.15 Adjust the transition settings in the Transition Editor, and then drag the customized transition into the Favorites bin.

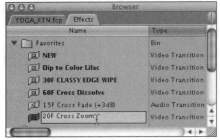

Figure 13.16 Rename your modified transition in the Favorites bin.

Figure 13.17 The Timeline playhead is positioned at the selected edit point; the playhead position will be used as the sequence In point.

Figure 13.18 Set Source In and Out points in the Viewer. If you're using a 1-second dissolve, be sure to leave at least 15 extra frames at the beginning of your clip to accommodate the transition.

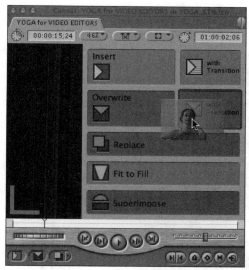

Figure 13.19 Drag the source clip from the Viewer to the Canvas edit overlay; then drop the clip on the Overwrite with Transition edit area.

About transition edits

There are two types of transition edits: Insert with Transition and Overwrite with Transition. A transition edit automatically places your default transition at the head of the edit. When using either of the transition edit types, you'll need enough footage in your source clip to create the transition. Each source clip will need enough additional frames to span half of the transition's duration.

To perform a transition edit:

1. Set the sequence In point by positioning the Timeline playhead where you want the edit to occur (**Figure 13.17**).

2. In the Viewer, set source In and Out points to define the part of the source clip you want to add to the sequence (**Figure 13.18**).

3. Drag the clip from the Viewer to either the Insert with Transition or the Overwrite with Transition edit overlay in the Canvas (**Figure 13.19**).

✔ Tip

- Scenario: You need to apply the same 1-second dissolve to 101 sequence clips before your client arrives for a screening, and she just pulled into the parking lot. Don't panic. Here's a slick trick: Set the transition you want to use as the default transition. Use the Group Select tool to select all 101 sequence clips, then drag the whole group of clips from the Timeline to the Canvas edit overlay and drop them on the Overwrite with Transition area. Final Cut Pro will apply your default transition to all 101 clips in a glorious display of computer automation—that is, if you remembered to allow handles on your clips. Try it sometime.

Editing Video Transitions

You can make dramatic changes to a video transition even after you have added it to your sequence. You can adjust its duration and placement and customize its appearance. Opening your transition in the Transition Editor will give you maximum access to the transition's settings, but you can perform many adjustments directly in the Timeline.

Figure 13.20 shows an overview of the Transition Editor interface.

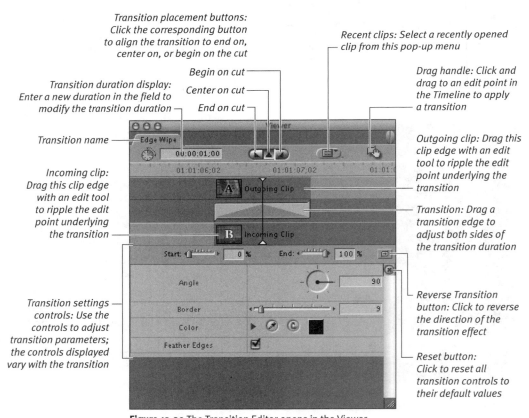

Transition placement buttons: Click the corresponding button to align the transition to end on, center on, or begin on the cut

Recent clips: Select a recently opened clip from this pop-up menu

Begin on cut

Transition duration display: Enter a new duration in the field to modify the transition duration

Center on cut

End on cut

Drag handle: Click and drag to an edit point in the Timeline to apply a transition

Transition name

Outgoing clip: Drag this clip edge with an edit tool to ripple the edit point underlying the transition

Incoming clip: Drag this clip edge with an edit tool to ripple the edit point underlying the transition

Transition: Drag a transition edge to adjust both sides of the transition duration

Transition settings controls: Use the controls to adjust transition parameters; the controls displayed vary with the transition

Reverse Transition button: Click to reverse the direction of the transition effect

Reset button: Click to reset all transition controls to their default values

Figure 13.20 The Transition Editor opens in the Viewer window.

Figure 13.21 The Transition Editor with Thumbnail Display set to Filmstrip.

Using the Transition Editor

The Transition Editor (sometimes called the Transition Viewer) is a special version of the Viewer window that you use to make detailed adjustments to transition settings. Use the Transition Editor to do the following:

◆ Adjust the duration of the transition.

◆ Reverse the direction of the transition.

◆ Trim the edit point underlying the transition.

◆ Adjust the placement of the transition relative to the edit point. You can set a transition to end on the cut, center on the cut, begin on the cut, or occur anywhere in between.

◆ Adjust the starting and ending effect percentages. The default settings of a simple cross dissolve would range from 0 to 100 percent. However, in a transition effect that incorporates a motion path, effect percentages specify the portion of the full path that will be included in the transition.

The Timeline's Thumbnail Display option controls the way clips appear in the Transition Editor (**Figure 13.21**). You can adjust the thumbnail display on the Timeline Options tab of the Sequence Settings window.

EDITING VIDEO TRANSITIONS

447

To open a transition in the Transition Editor:

Do one of the following:

◆ Control-click the transition; then choose Open *'name of the transition'* from the shortcut menu (**Figure 13.22**).

◆ In the Timeline, double-click the transition to open it in the Transition Editor.

◆ Select the transition's icon in the Timeline; then choose View > Transition Editor.

To change the duration of a transition in the Transition Editor:

Do one of the following:

◆ Type a new duration in the Duration field; then press Enter (**Figure 13.23**).

◆ Drag either end of the transition.
The change in duration applies equally to both sides of the transition (**Figure 13.24**).

✔ Tip

■ FCP transitions apply equally to both sides of an edit point, so if you need an asymmetrical effect—where the transition effect is not applied to an equal number of frames on either side of the edit point—you must build it yourself. Here's how to build an asymmetrical dissolve. Place the incoming and outgoing clips on separate Timeline tracks, and allow the areas you want to include in the dissolve to overlap. Then ramp the opacity levels to cross dissolve from one clip to the other.

Figure 13.22 Control-click the transition; then choose Open *'name of the transition'* from the shortcut menu.

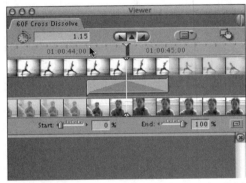

Figure 13.23 Type a new duration in the Duration field of the Transition Editor.

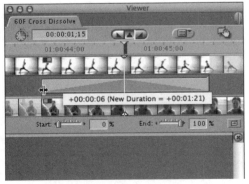

Figure 13.24 Dragging the edge of a transition to adjust its duration.

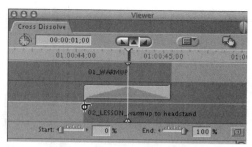

Figure 13.25 Positioning the pointer on the incoming clip's In point in the Transition Editor.

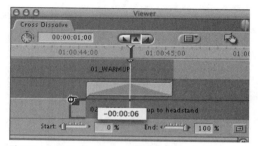

Figure 13.26 Performing a Ripple edit on the incoming clip's In point. Drag the edge of the clip to ripple the edit point underlying the transition.

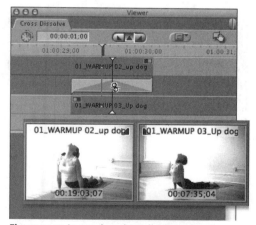

Figure 13.27 As you drag the Roll Edit tool on the transition, a two-up display in the Canvas shows the frames adjacent to the new edit point.

To perform a Ripple edit on a transition in the Transition Editor:

1. Position the pointer on the edit point you want to trim (**Figure 13.25**).

   In the Transition Editor, the edit points appear on the clip icons displayed in the tracks above and below the transition icon.

   The pointer changes to the Ripple Edit tool.

2. Drag the edit point (**Figure 13.26**).

   A Ripple edit is performed on the edit point underlying the transition as the Canvas display changes to show your new In point.

To perform a Roll edit on a transition in the Transition Editor:

◆ Place the pointer anywhere on the transition. When the pointer changes to the Roll Edit tool, drag it on the transition to perform a Roll edit on the edit point underlying the transition.

   As the Roll edit is performed, a two-up display in the Canvas changes to show the two frames adjacent to your new edit point (**Figure 13.27**).

EDITING VIDEO TRANSITIONS

To change the settings for a transition:

Do one or more of the following:

◆ To change the starting and ending effect percentages, drag the Start and End sliders (**Figure 13.28**) or type percentage values in the text boxes.

◆ To change the direction of the effect, click the Reverse button.

◆ To have the transition center on, begin on, or end on the edit, click the corresponding placement button at the top center of the Transition Editor. Once you've changed the center point of a transition, these controls won't remember the original edit point.

◆ Make other settings as desired for the transition. For more information on modifying effects settings, see Chapter 14, "Compositing and Effects Overview."

To preview a transition in the Canvas:

1. Open the transition in the Transition Editor.

2. Position the Transition Editor's playhead at any point in the transition (**Figure 13.29**).

Figure 13.28 Using the slider to adjust end position settings for a wipe transition.

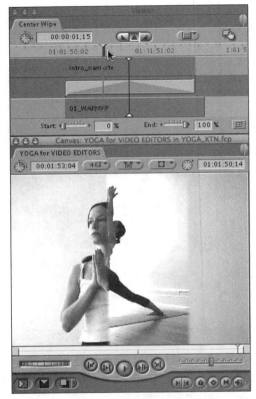

Figure 13.29 Position the Transition Editor's playhead at any point in the transition. The Canvas displays a preview of the transition at the selected playhead location.

3. Adjust the transition settings.

The Canvas display updates to reflect any adjustments made to the transition settings (**Figure 13.30**).

4. To preview a frame at another point in the transition, reposition the Transition Editor playhead (**Figure 13.31**).

✔ **Tip**

■ Hold down the Option key as you scrub the Canvas's Scrubber bar to preview your transition. You can also step through a transition one frame at a time by pressing the Right Arrow key to advance the transition by single frames. Press the Left Arrow key to step backward. A slow-motion view of the transition appears in the Canvas.

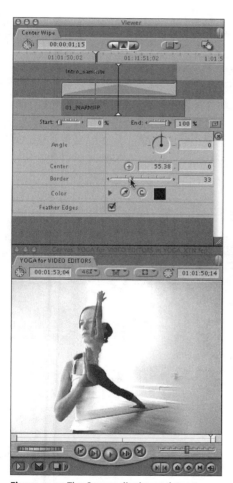

Figure 13.30 The Canvas display updates to reflect an adjustment to the transition's border width settings. A Center Wipe with wide, transparent border settings and soft edges can make a subtle replacement for yet another cross dissolve.

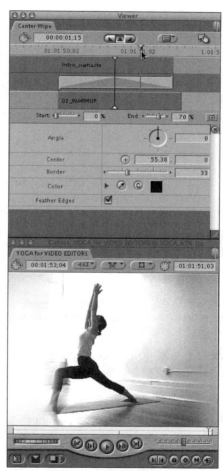

Figure 13.31 Reposition the Transition Editor's playhead, and the Canvas displays a preview of a frame later in the transition.

EDITING VIDEO TRANSITIONS

Editing transitions in the Timeline

You can streamline transition editing in the Timeline by using the shortcut menus. Control-clicking the transition itself opens one of the shortcut menus. A different shortcut menu is available for the edit point underlying the transition. Edit points that have transitions applied to them can still be trimmed in the same way as other edits; you can use the Trim Edit or Viewer windows or drag directly in the Timeline. For more information about trimming operations, see Chapter 11, "Fine Cut: Trimming Edits."

To adjust the duration of a transition in the Timeline:

◆ With the Selection tool, drag one edge of the transition to adjust its length.

Or do this:

1. Control-click the transition; then choose Duration from the shortcut menu (**Figure 13.32**).

2. In the Duration dialog box, enter a new duration (**Figure 13.33**); then click OK.

✔ Tip

■ Control-D is the keyboard shortcut to open the Duration dialog box for a selected clip or transition.

To trim an edit point underlying a transition:

Do one of the following:

◆ From the Tool palette, select the appropriate edit tool; then drag the edit point underlying the transition (**Figure 13.34**).

◆ Control-click an edit point with any edit tool to open the Trim Edit window.

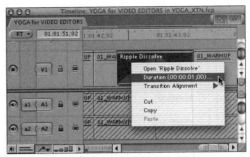

Figure 13.32 Control-click the transition; then choose Duration from the shortcut menu.

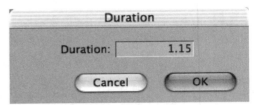

Figure 13.33 Enter a new duration for your transition.

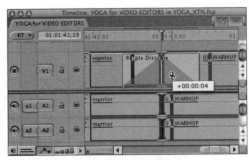

Figure 13.34 Trim an edit point underlying a transition by dragging the edit point with an edit tool. This Roll edit will shift the edit point downstream by 4 frames.

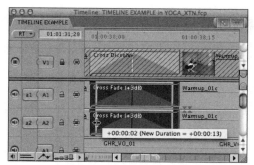

Figure 13.35 Adjusting the duration of an audio transition in the Timeline. Dragging a transition's edge affects the length of the transition but does not alter any underlying edit points.

Modifying Audio Transitions

Final Cut Pro offers only two audio transitions; both are cross-fades. One is a 0 dB (decibel) cross-fade. The standard default is a +3 dB cross-fade. The +3 dB amplitude increase of the default cross-fade is designed to compensate for any perceived volume drop during the transition, but the only way to decide which cross-fade works best to finesse your audio edit is to try them both and trust your ears. You can adjust only the duration of audio transitions.

To modify the duration of an audio transition:

◆ With the Selection tool, drag one edge of the transition to adjust its length (**Figure 13.35**).

Or do this:

1. Control-click the transition; then choose Duration from the shortcut menu.

2. In the Duration dialog box, enter a new duration.

3. Click OK.

✔ Tip

■ Duration is the only adjustable parameter for the audio cross-fade transitions in Final Cut Pro, but you can build your own cross-fades. Set up the audio clips you want to transition between on adjacent tracks. You can adjust the clips' overlap and then set Level keyframes to sculpt your special-purpose cross-fade.

FCP Protocol: r u YUV?

When you use a transition between two shots, you're likely to be looking for a way to blend the two shots more seamlessly. Because you're trying to create that seamless illusion, rendered transitions are where most people notice the effects of RGB color space versus YUV (aka YCrCb) color space. Most computers store image data in RGB color space, but many digital video formats (including DV) use the YUV color space. If you render your transition and then notice color and luminance shifts during the rendered transition, you probably haven't selected the correct color space to render in. See "RGB or YCrCb: Choosing a Color Space" in Chapter 17 for information on how to select the correct color space for your project format.

Rendering Transitions

If you are using a real-time FCP system, you can preview many transitions without rendering, but you'll also find many transitions you must render before you can play them back. With the advent of FCP's scalable Real Time architecture, your rendering options have become a bit more complex: Before you can render, you must specify which of the six video and two audio Timeline playback states you want to include in the render operation (**Figure 13.36**). Thank goodness for real-time preview, eh? For more information, see Chapter 18, "Real Time and Rendering."

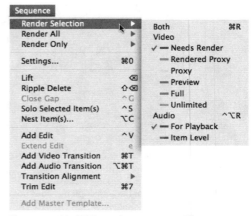

Figure 13.36 In FCP's render menus, you'll encounter six video and two audio render categories. You can specify which render categories you want to include in your render operations.

RENDERING TRANSITIONS

Real-Time Transitions

If your Final Cut Pro system supports real-time effects, you can play certain transitions without rendering them first. The real-time transitions available on your particular system appear in bold type in the Effects menu and on the Browser's Effects tab (**Figure 13.37**). For more information on real-time systems and rendering, see Chapter 18, "Real Time and Rendering."

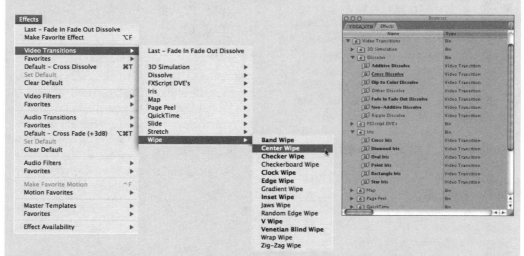

Figure 13.37 Transitions supported by your real-time system appear in bold type in the Effects menu and on the Browser's Effects tab.

COMPOSITING AND EFFECTS OVERVIEW

Creating visual effects in the pre-digital era was expensive, time-consuming, and required technical expertise to be successful. Twenty years into the digital media era, it's hard to find a snippet of film or video that hasn't been digitally massaged—even on YouTube. Modern mass media relies heavily on the same techniques you'll be introduced to in this chapter. Once you understand the role of each basic building block of effects creation, you'll never look at movies and TV in the same way again because you'll be able to see how complex visuals are constructed. The effects creation tools found in Final Cut Pro are designed to be easy to use, but effects tools are the most challenging part of the FCP interface to master.

This chapter offers an overview of the basic elements you combine and sculpt to create effects, provides details on how to apply effects to your sequence, and shows where you can modify those effects.

As you start to apply effects, it's important to keep this in mind: Adding a clip from the Browser to a sequence in the Timeline places a copy of the clip in the sequence. By placing a clip in a sequence, you create a new instance of the clip. Before you modify a clip with effects, be sure you have selected the correct copy of the clip you want to change. This rule is central to understanding editing in Final Cut Pro. For more information, see "FCP Protocol: Clips and Sequences" in Chapter 4.

You can use Final Cut Pro's fine tools for motion graphics, compositing, filtering, color correction, and generating titles without ever leaving the application, however Final Cut Studio offers much more complex and powerful effects tools in FCP's sister applications: Motion 3 for 2D and 3D motion graphics, effects and titles; LiveType for animated titles; and Color for color correction and finishing. Incredible applications, powerful features—but outside the scope of this Final Cut Pro compact reference guide.

Basic Building Blocks of Effects Creation

The basic building blocks you use to create video effects are fairly simple. You can generate complex effects by combining and then animating images using the processes described here.

◆ **Layering** is an arrangement of multiple clips at one point in time, each clip in its own track. Superimposing a title over a video clip is a simple example of layering, with the video clip forming the background layer and the title forming the foreground layer. Other layering arrangements require making the upper layers semitransparent, so you can see the image in the background layer.

◆ **Compositing** can be any process that combines two or more image layers to create an effect. Compositing techniques can include the adjustment of one or more image layers' transparency and the selection of a Composite mode, which is the algorithm that controls the way the image layers are combined.

◆ **Motion properties** are image modification tools that control a clip's size and shape, its position in the frame, and its designated center point, among other characteristics. The tools that are grouped together on the Motion tab don't always have an obvious connection to image movement; for example, the Opacity controls are located there. However, making incremental adjustments to a clip's size, position, and angle of rotation are basic steps in animating a static element—that's when things start to move.

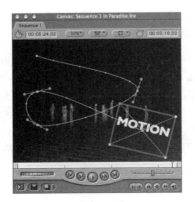

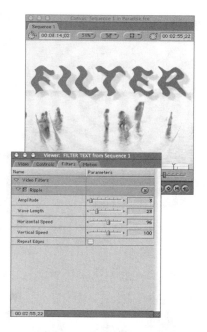

◆ **Filters** are image modifiers that process the image data in a clip. Over time, filters have developed into a diverse effects category that includes everything from basic tools, such as brightness, contrast, and color controls, to complex 3D simulators.

◆ **Opacity** refers to a clip's level of transparency. A clip with an opacity level of 100 percent is completely opaque; one with an opacity level of 0 percent is completely transparent. Adjusting opacity is a basic procedure in compositing layers of images. Alpha channels and mattes are a means of adjusting opacity in selected portions of an image. You can adjust a clip's opacity on the Viewer's Motion tab or by using the opacity clip overlay in the Timeline.

◆ **Generators** are effects that create (or generate) new video information rather than modify existing video. Generators are useful for producing utility items such as black frames (known as slugs), a plain-colored background, or text titles.

BASIC BUILDING BLOCKS OF EFFECTS CREATION

Locating and Applying Effects

You can access Final Cut Pro's effects features in a variety of places:

◆ The Browser's Effects tab (**Figure 14.1**) displays bins containing all the types of effects available in Final Cut Pro except motion properties.

◆ The same effects found on the Browser's Effects tab are also available from the Effects menu (**Figure 14.2**).

◆ Motion properties are applied to every clip automatically. Open a clip in the Viewer and click the Motion tab to access a clip's motion controls.

You can apply effects to clips and sequences in the following ways:

◆ Select a clip in the Timeline, and then choose an effect from the Effects menu.

◆ Select an effect from a bin on the Effects tab of the Browser, and drag it onto the clip.

◆ Select a customized effect or motion from the Favorites bin on the Effects tab of the Browser, and drag it to the clip to apply it.

◆ Choose a generator from the Generators pop-up menu in the lower-right corner of the Viewer.

◆ Open a Timeline or a Browser clip in the Viewer; then use the controls on the clip's Motion tab to apply motion effects.

◆ Open a Timeline clip in the Canvas; then use the Canvas's Wireframe mode overlay to animate a motion path.

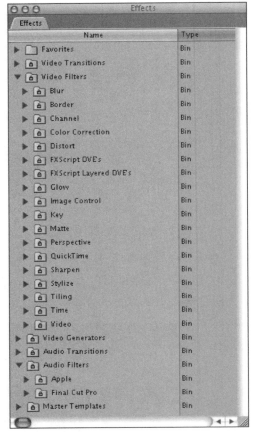

Figure 14.1 The Browser's Effects tab organizes available effects in bins.

Figure 14.2 The same library of effects is available from the Effects menu.

Onscreen effects controls

You can make adjustments to effects you've already applied in the following ways:

◆ Double-click the clip in the Timeline; then select the Audio, Filters, or Motion tab in the Viewer and use the controls to make your adjustments. **Figure 14.3** illustrates the operation of the controls found on the Filters, Motion, and Controls tabs. **Figure 14.4** highlights the keyframing controls found on these tabs.

◆ In the Timeline, you can add, edit, adjust, or delete keyframes by using the tools in the Clip Keyframes area. **Figure 14.5** shows an overview of the keyframing tools available in the Timeline window.

◆ In the Canvas, turn on Wireframe mode and adjust a clip's motion properties (motion properties also include a static clip's size, position, and opacity) or use motion keyframes to animate a motion path. For more information, see Chapter 15, "Motion."

Effects Production Shortcuts

Creating effects can be time-consuming and repetitive. Here are a few production shortcuts.

Copying and pasting clip attributes: Clip attributes are settings applied to a particular media file in Final Cut Pro. You can copy and paste selected settings from one clip to another clip in the Timeline or in the Canvas, or use the Remove Attributes command to restore a clip's default settings. For more information, see Chapter 10, "Editing in the Timeline and the Canvas."

Nesting sequences: When you place, or create, a Final Cut Pro sequence within another sequence, it's called *nesting* a sequence. Nested sequences can streamline and enhance your effects work in a variety of ways. You can use nested sequences to protect render files, to force effects to render in a different order, or to group clips so you can apply a single filter or motion path to all of them in one operation. Nested sequences are discussed in Chapter 4, "Projects, Sequences, and Clips."

"Effecting" multiple clips: FCP allows you to adjust opacity levels for a group of clips. You can also adjust audio levels for multiple clips in a single operation. See "Setting a clip's opacity in the Timeline" in Chapter 15.

Favorites: Favorites are customized effects presets. For example, if you need to apply the same color correction to a large group of clips, you can tweak the settings once, save that filter configuration as a Favorite, and then apply it to the whole group without having to make individual adjustments. Favorites are discussed in the next section.

Frame Viewer tab: The Frame Viewer is a new addition to FCP's Tool Bench. Open multiple Frame Viewers to compare multiple frames from your sequence (handy for scene-to-scene color correction adjustments), or use the Frame Viewer's split-screen feature to compare two frames within a single viewer (wonderful when you're trying to match compositional elements or horizon lines from two different shots to establish a beautiful cut point). You can split the viewer horizontally or vertically, or carve out a rectangle to display your comparison frame in a picture-in-picture configuration.

LOCATING AND APPLYING EFFECTS

Effects tabs: *Click to access a tab containing effects controls and keyframe graphs*

Adjustable column width: *Drag separator lines*

Color controls:
- *Click the triangle to open HSB controls*
- *Use the eyedropper to pick colors from Video windows*
- *Click the arrow to perform color cycling for sweep direction*
- *Click the square to bring up the Apple Color Picker*

Expansion triangle: *Click to show or hide controls*

Toggle switch: *Check box to turn effect on or off*

Current Timecode field: *Shows playhead's timecode location; enter time to move keyframe graph playhead*

Reset button: *Click to reset all controls to default values*

Slider controls: *Drag the slider to set a value*

Incremental controls: *Click tiny arrows to change value by one*

Clip control: *Drop other clips here to affect the filtering of this clip*

Text field: *Enter exact parameter values*

Dial controls: *Drag the needle to set a value*

Point control: *Set point values, such as x,y positions, by clicking the image area*

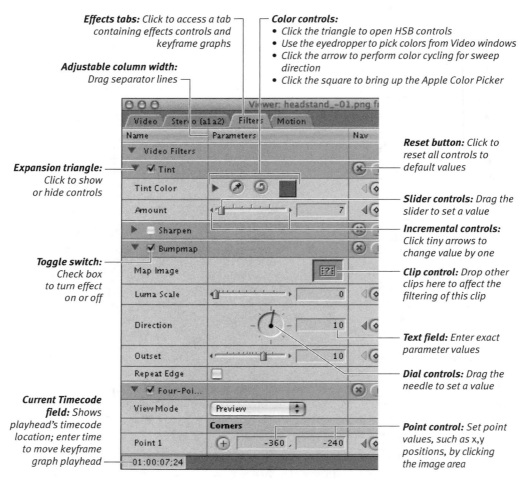

Figure 14.3 Overview of the effects controls found on the Filters, Motion, and Controls tabs in the Viewer window.

Sequence marker: *Sequence markers placed in the Timeline also appear here; use them to align keyframes over multiple tracks*

Playhead: *Shows current frame location; linked to Timeline playhead*

Filter In point: *Drag to adjust filter duration*

Filter Out point: *Drag to adjust filter duration*

Keyframe ruler: *Displays the timecode for the current sequence*

Keyframe graph: *Displays keyframe information for this parameter*

Graph expander: *Drag down to increase size of 2D keyframe areas*

Keyframe line graph: *Smooth styled Bézier curves for easy in or easy out*

Keyframe line graph: *Corner styled*

Keyframe view: *Pop-up menu toggles the keyframe overview*

Point keyframes: *Describe point values, such as x,y positions*

Drag this corner to resize the Viewer

Next Keyframe button: *Click to jump playhead to the next keyframe*

Previous Keyframe button: *Click to jump the playhead to the previous keyframe*

Insert/Delete Keyframe button: *Toggle to set (or delete) a keyframe at the current location of the playhead*

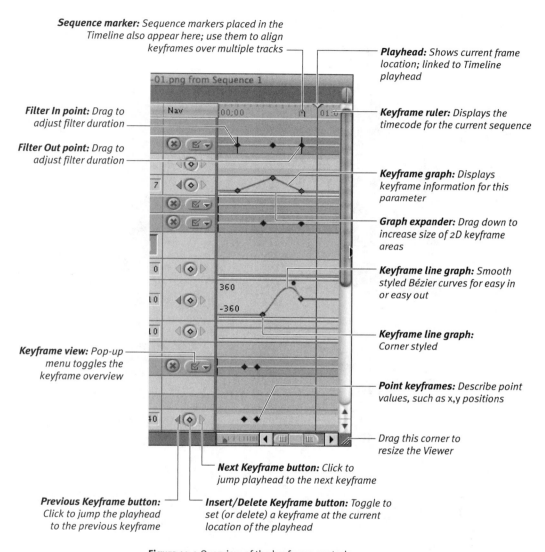

Figure 14.4 Overview of the keyframe controls found on the Filters, Motion, and Controls tabs in the Viewer window.

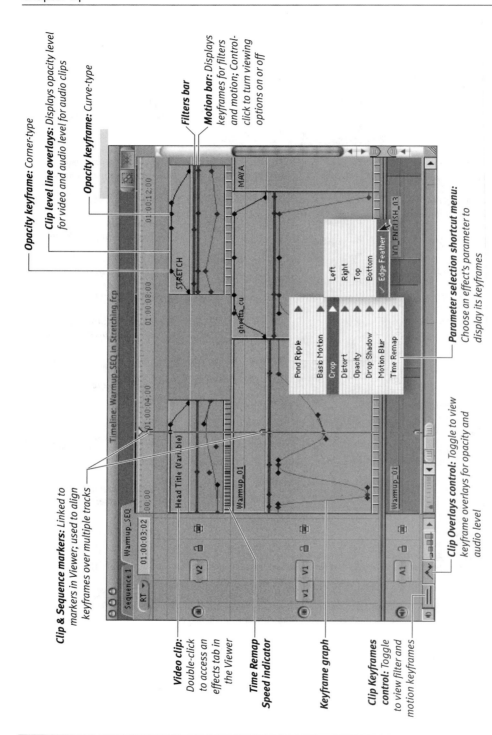

Opacity keyframe: Corner-type

Clip level line overlays: Displays opacity level for video and audio level for audio clips

Opacity keyframe: Curve-type

Filters bar

Motion bar: Displays keyframes for filters and motion; Control-click to turn viewing options on or off

Clip & Sequence markers: Linked to markers in Viewer; used to align keyframes over multiple tracks

Parameter selection shortcut menu: Choose an effect's parameter to display its keyframes

Video clip: Double-click to access an effects tab in the Viewer

Time Remap Speed indicator

Keyframe graph

Clip Keyframes control: Toggle to view filter and motion keyframes

Clip Overlays control: Toggle to view keyframe overlays for opacity and audio level

Figure 14.5 Overview of effects tools in the Timeline.

Tuning in Effects: Using Dial, Slider, and Point Controls

Here are some keyboard/mouse combos you can use to enhance your control over any effect parameter with a dial interface:

◆ Hold down the Shift key to constrain the dial to 45-degree increments.

◆ Hold down the Command key to gear down the dial's movement and make precise adjustments.

◆ Drag way, way out of the dial to reset the effect to the previous value.

◆ Scroll-wheel mouse users can make precise dial adjustments by positioning the pointer over the dial and nudging the scroll wheel.

Here are a few tips for effect parameters with slider interfaces:

◆ Expand the horizontal throw of any slider by widening the Parameters column in the column title bar. A longer slider makes it easier to adjust values.

◆ Hold down the Command key to gear down the slider's movement and make precise adjustments.

◆ Scroll-wheel mouse users can nudge the scroll wheel to make single-digit adjustments to slider values.

◆ Hold down the Shift key to add two decimal places of accuracy to a slider's value. (This command could be more useful if it incorporated gearing down as well.) You need to expand the horizontal throw of the slider by widening the Parameters column on the Filters or Controls tab before the double-digit accuracy becomes useful.

◆ The Point control is that little crosshairs button you use to select location coordinates for a clip's center point. You can select the Point control and then click the Canvas to specify a center point. That's very handy, but here's a way to use the Point control that's even better: Once you've clicked, keep the mouse button pressed, and you can drag the center point location around the canvas until you find a position you like. The Canvas will update even while you hold down the mouse button.

LOCATING AND APPLYING EFFECTS

Using Keyframes

Whenever you create motion paths, change filters over time, sculpt audio levels, or just fade to black, you need to use keyframes. Think of a keyframe as a kind of edit point—you set a keyframe at the point at which you want to change the value of an effect's parameter. Keyframes work the same way wherever they are applied.

You don't need keyframes to set a single level or value that applies to an entire clip; keyframes are required only if you want to change the value at some point within the clip. After you have added the first keyframe to a clip, Final Cut Pro adds a new keyframe automatically whenever you change an effect setting for that clip at a different point in time.

You can edit and adjust keyframes in a variety of places (**Figure 14.6**). Final Cut Pro has a few different types of keyframe graphs; basic keyframe commands work the same in all the graphs, but each graph type can offer unique advantages. Choose the keyframe graph that works best for the task at hand. Here's a quick rundown on keyframe graph locations and features.

◆ **The Viewer's Filters, Motion, and Controls tabs:** Keyframe graphs on the various effects tabs in the Viewer are located to the right of the controls for each effect parameter. The Viewer's keyframe graphs provide a detailed view of all the parameter controls for a single effect. Here's an example: If you need to nudge multiple parameters to sculpt a filter, the keyframe graph of the Filters tab is the only place where you can see the filter's parameter controls in relationship to one another, or coordinate the keyframe positions of multiple filters.

◆ **The Timeline's Clip Keyframes area:** These keyframing tools are hidden by default, but click the Timeline's Clip Keyframes control and each audio and video track expands to reveal mini keyframe editors beneath each clip. These keyframe graphs are limited to the display of a single parameter at a time. The beauty of these graphs is that you can view and adjust keyframes across multiple tracks. If you're synchronizing stacks of animated text layers, or timing your effects to a music track, this is the way to go.

◆ **The Timeline's Keyframe overlay:** Keyframe overlay graphs are displayed as line graphs right on top of the track display in the Timeline. These overlays are designed to offer easy access to clip properties you tweak frequently: clip opacity (for video clips) and volume level and stereo pan position (for audio clips).

◆ **The Canvas or Viewer's Wireframe mode:** Motion keyframes can be set and sculpted in the Wireframe display in the Canvas or in the Viewer. Enable Wireframe or Image+Wireframe mode, and a wireframe overlay appears on your clip image. This wireframe overlay features controls you can use to graphically manipulate the size, shape, and position of your clip's image. Wireframe mode is the best place to manipulate a clip's motion properties and create motion paths.

✔ Tip

■ Audio keyframe overlays also appear over the waveform display on the Viewer's Audio tab.

Filters, Motion, and Controls tabs:
Edit and adjust keyframes in these keyframe graphs if you need a detailed view of all the parameter controls for a single effect.

The Canvas or Viewer's Wireframe mode:
Set and sculpt motion keyframes to animate motion paths; graphically manipulating your clip's size, shape, and movement—sure beats entering x, y coordinates to plot each move.

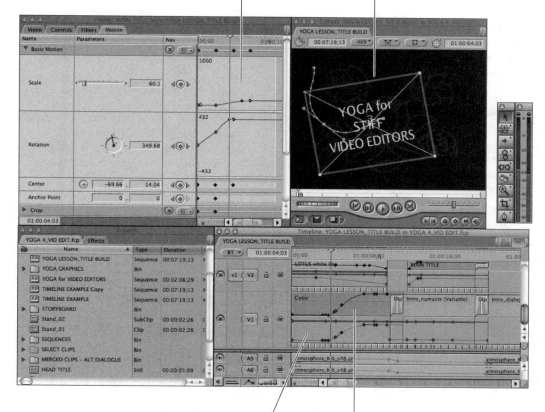

Clip Keyframes area:
Use these mini keyframe editors to view and adjust keyframes across multiple tracks. These graphs can display keyframes only for a single parameter at a time.

Keyframe overlay: *These graphs are displayed right on top of the Timeline's track display, offering easy access to clip opacity levels (for video clips) and volume level and stereo pan position (for audio clips).*

Figure 14.6 FCP's keyframe graphs are available in multiple locations.

Working with Keyframes in the Viewer's Effects Tabs

This section describes how to set and adjust keyframes in the keyframe graphs on the Viewer's Filters, Motion, and Controls tabs.

The Viewer's effects tabs display the keyframes on a keyframe graph (**Figure 14.7**), which extends to the right of each effect parameter control. Each effect parameter has its own set of keyframes, so you have individual control of every parameter and the way that parameter changes over time.

After you have added the first keyframe to a clip, Final Cut Pro adds a new keyframe automatically whenever you change an effect setting for that clip at a different point in time.

You use the keyframe navigation controls in the Nav column on the Viewer's Filters and Motion tabs to navigate through, add, or delete keyframes.

Motion keyframes can also be set and sculpted in the wireframe display in the Canvas or in the Viewer. For information about working in wireframe mode, see Chapter 15, "Motion Effects."

✔ Tip

- For a wider view of your effects controls tab, try dragging the tab out of the Viewer and then stretching the display. When you're done, drag the tab back to the Viewer.

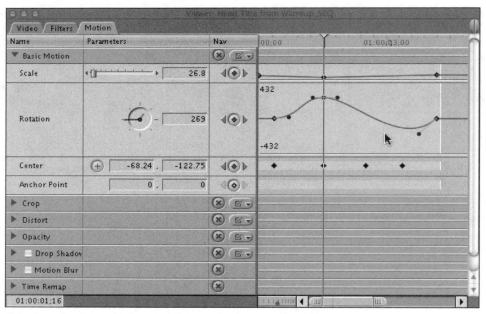

Figure 14.7 The Viewer's keyframe graphs extend to the right of each effect parameter control.

Figure 14.8 To set a keyframe, click the Insert/Delete Keyframe button in the Nav column to the left of the keyframe graph.

Working with basic keyframe commands

The Nav bar and keyframe graphs (to the right of the effects controls on the Viewer's Filters, Motion, and Controls tabs) offer the most detailed control over individual keyframes. Here's a rundown of basic keyframe commands.

To set a keyframe:

1. On the Motion tab of the Viewer, position the playhead at the point in the keyframe graph where you want to set the keyframe.

2. Click the Insert/Delete Keyframe button (**Figure 14.8**).

3. To set additional keyframes, move the playhead to the next location where you want to set a keyframe; then *do one of the following:*
   - Click the Insert/Delete Keyframe button.
   - Click the Add Keyframe button in the Canvas or in the Viewer.
   - Click the keyframe graph with the Arrow or Pen tool.
   - Make an adjustment to an effects tab parameter control.

   Final Cut Pro adjusts the values and then automatically adds the keyframe.

✔ Tip

■ Click the Add Keyframe button in the Canvas or in the Viewer window to set a motion keyframe across all motion parameters for the current frame.

Keyframing Cheatsheet

Here's a quick summary of the basic keyframing steps, in order:

1. Open the selected clip or sequence in the Viewer.

2. In the keyframe graph on the clip's Motion, Filters, or Controls tab, move the playhead to location A.

3. Enter value A for the parameter.

4. Click the Insert/Delete Keyframe button.

5. Move the playhead to location B.

6. Enter value B.

   The second keyframe is added automatically.

KEYFRAMES IN THE VIEWER'S EFFECTS TABS

To move a keyframe:

1. Click the keyframe graph with the Arrow or Pen tool.

2. *Do one of the following:*

   ◆ Drag the keyframe up or down to adjust the value (**Figure 14.9**).

   ◆ Drag the keyframe left or right to adjust the timing.

To navigate between keyframes:

◆ Click the Previous or Next Keyframe button (**Figure 14.10**).

   The playhead will move to the next keyframe in either direction. The arrows are dimmed if no other keyframes are in the clip.

✔ Tip

■ If you've opened a sequence clip, the keyframe graph's playhead is locked to the Timeline playhead and the keyframe ruler shows that portion of the sequence where the clip is located.

To delete a keyframe:

Do one of the following:

◆ In the keyframe graph, position the playhead on the keyframe you want to remove; then click the Insert/Delete Keyframe button (the button is green when it's on a keyframe).

◆ In the keyframe graph, Option-click the keyframe with the Arrow or Pen tool and choose Clear.

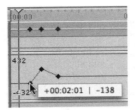

Figure 14.9 Drag a keyframe up or down the keyframe graph to adjust its value, or left and right to adjust its position. Hold down the Shift key as you drag, and you'll be able to adjust both parameters at the same time. Your adjustments are aided by this tooltip readout of the keyframe's current position.

Figure 14.10 To move the playhead to the next keyframe in either direction, click the Previous or Next Keyframe button.

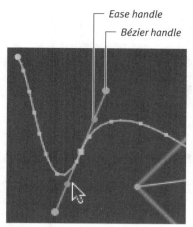

Ease handle

Bézier handle

Figure 14.11 A curve-type keyframe's Bézier handle shapes the clip's motion path. The ease handles control the speed of the effect change immediately before and after the keyframe.

Figure 14.12 To smooth a corner-type keyframe to a Bézier curve type, Control-click the keyframe and choose Smooth from the shortcut menu.

Figure 14.13 Drag the small blue circle at the end of the Bézier handle to adjust the motion path leading away from the keyframe.

Smoothing keyframes

When you use a keyframe to change a parameter, you have the option of making that keyframe a *curve type*. Curve-type keyframes have two added controls: *Bézier handles*, which you can use to fine-tune the shape of the motion path's curve, and *ease handles*, which you can use to fine-tune a clip's speed immediately before and after the keyframe location (**Figure 14.11**). You can also use curve-type keyframes to fine-tune the rate of change in an effect parameter's level. Converting a keyframe from a corner-type to a curve-type is sometimes called *smoothing* a keyframe. For more information on keyframe types, see "Adjusting motion path curves and corners" in Chapter 15.

To smooth a keyframe:

1. Control-click the keyframe, and choose Smooth from the shortcut menu (**Figure 14.12**).

   The keyframe will change into a curve type, and Bézier handles appear.

2. Drag the small blue circle at the end of the Bézier handle to adjust the motion path leading up to (or away from) the keyframe (**Figure 14.13**).

Using keyframes to set a single parameter

This task explains how to set keyframes for a single parameter on the Motion tab. As an example, we'll control the opacity of a clip to create a fade-out effect.

To use keyframes to set a single parameter:

1. In the Timeline, double-click the clip that you want to fade out.

   The clip opens in the Viewer window.

2. In the Viewer, click the Motion tab; then click the Opacity control's expansion triangle to reveal the Opacity settings controls (**Figure 14.14**).

3. In the keyframe ruler, drag the playhead to the point in the clip where you want to start the fade out.

4. Verify that the clip's Opacity level is set to 100 percent; then click the Insert/Delete Keyframe button in the Nav column to the left of the keyframe graph (**Figure 14.15**).

   The first keyframe is set with a value of 100 percent.

5. Press End to jump the playhead to the end of your clip.

6. To set a second keyframe with an Opacity level of 0 percent, *do one of the following:*

   ◆ On the keyframe ruler, click in the keyframe graph and drag down to set the keyframe value to 0 percent.

   ◆ In the Opacity settings, drag the slider to the left to set the keyframe value to 0 percent.

   ◆ Enter 0 in the Opacity text field.

   The second keyframe is set automatically. You can see a graphical representation of your fade-out as a diagonal line in the keyframe graph (**Figure 14.16**).

7. Play back your fade-out effect.

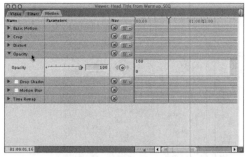

Figure 14.14 The Opacity control is located on the Motion tab of the Viewer. Click the control's expansion triangle to reveal the Opacity settings controls.

Figure 14.15 Position the playhead where you want the fade-out to start, and then set the first keyframe by clicking the Insert/Delete Keyframe button in the Nav column to the left of the keyframe graph.

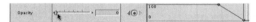

Figure 14.16 Your fade-out is represented by a diagonal line in the keyframe graph. The second keyframe appeared automatically when you set the Opacity level to 0 percent.

Figure 14.17 Click the Insert/Delete Keyframe button, located to the right of the Rotation parameter control.

Figure 14.18 Click the Current Timecode field at the bottom left of the Motion tab; then type +30 to add 30 frames to the playhead location.

Setting keyframes with timecode entry

Evenly spaced keyframes are essential for smooth, even changes in your effects and for precision synchronization to music or other effects. This is especially true for motion effects. When you animate a program element, using timecode ensures that your keyframes will be set at precise intervals. This task shows you how to rotate a clip using timecode entry to set keyframes.

To set keyframes using timecode entry:

1. In the Timeline, double-click the clip you want to rotate to open it in the Viewer.

2. In the Viewer, click the Motion tab; then press Home to set the playhead in the keyframe graph to the first frame of your clip.

3. Click the Insert/Delete Keyframe button located to the right of the Rotation control (**Figure 14.17**).

   The clip's first Rotation keyframe is set on the first frame.

4. Verify that the Rotation control is set to zero.

   This establishes the clip's orientation at the beginning of the rotation.

5. Click the Current Timecode field at the bottom left of the Motion tab; then type +30 to move the playhead 30 frames forward (**Figure 14.18**).

   The playhead advances 30 frames in the keyframe graph.

   continues on next page

6. Click the Insert/Delete Keyframe button again; then *do one of the following*:

  ◆ In the Rotation control dial, drag the needle clockwise to set the keyframe value to 180 (**Figure 14.19**).

  ◆ Click in the keyframe graph and drag up to set the keyframe value to 180.

  ◆ Enter 180 in the Rotation text field.

7. Repeat steps 5 and 6, increasing the keyframe value to 360.

  You have set three keyframes, exactly 30 frames apart, causing your clip to complete one full 360-degree rotation in 2 seconds (**Figure 14.20**).

8. Press Option-K to step backward through your three keyframes, noting that the clip flips and the Rotation value updates at each keyframe. Press Shift-K to step forward through the keyframes.

9. If you need to render your rotating clip before you can play it back, select the clip; then choose Sequence > Render Selection.

10. Play back your rotation effect.

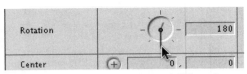

Figure 14.19 Drag the Rotation control dial needle clockwise to set the keyframe value to 180.

Figure 14.20 You have set three keyframes, exactly 30 frames apart, that program your clip to complete one full 360-degree rotation in 2 seconds.

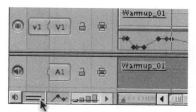

Figure 14.21 Click the Clip Keyframes control, and the Timeline tracks expand to display the Timeline keyframe area.

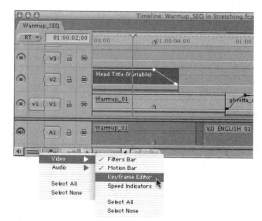

Figure 14.22 Control-click the Clip Keyframes control to access the Clip Keyframes display shortcut menu. Use the shortcut menu selections to show or hide keyframe area elements.

Working with Keyframes in the Timeline

You can edit and adjust keyframes in two areas of the Timeline:

- **Clip Keyframes area:** The Timeline keyframe area can display any or all of these four effects tools: The Filters bar, the Motion bar, a compact keyframe graph, and the clip speed indicator. These keyframing tools are hidden by default.

- **Keyframe overlay:** These graphs are overlaid on top of the track display in the Timeline. Video clips display clip opacity levels; audio clips display volume level and stereo pan position.

To show or hide the Timeline Clip Keyframes area:

- In the Timeline, click the Clip Keyframes control (located in the lower-left corner) to display the Timeline keyframe area (**Figure 14.21**).

  Keyframes are displayed in a clip's keyframe graph and on the Filters and Motion bars.

To customize the Clip Keyframes area display:

1. Control-click the Clip Keyframes control.

   The Clip Keyframes display shortcut menu appears (**Figure 14.22**).

2. Choose Audio or Video, then from the Audio or Video submenu, *choose one of the following:*

   - Select an area to toggle its visibility: Checked areas are visible; unchecked areas are hidden.

   - Choose Select All to show all four areas.

   - Choose Select None to hide all four areas.

To display keyframes for a selected effect's parameter in the keyframe graph:

1. In the Timeline, Control-click a clip's keyframe graph to access its shortcut menu (**Figure 14.23**).

2. From the list of all the parameters for each effect currently applied to the clip, choose the name of an effect parameter to display its keyframes in the clip's keyframe graph.

To display keyframes for a selected effect's parameter in a Filters bar or Motion bar:

1. In the Timeline, Control-click the Filters or Motion bar to access its shortcut menu (**Figure 14.24**).

2. From the list of all the parameters for each filter currently applied to the clip:

   - Choose the name of a parameter to display its keyframes in the Timeline.

   - Choose a filter name to display all the parameters for that filter.

✔ Tips

- Double-click a Filters bar or a Motion bar with a Selection tool to open that effect in the Viewer, with the correct tab already displayed.

- You can slide a whole set of keyframes in a clip's Filters and Motion bars. Use the Selection tool to drag the bar, and the keyframes will slide left or right (**Figure 14.25**).

- Any time you're working with the Selection tool, the fastest way to a Pen tool is to press Option. The Selection tool switches to Pen tool mode as long as you're holding down the Option key.

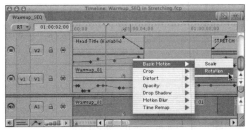

Figure 14.23 Control-click a clip's keyframe graph to access its shortcut menu, and then choose the name of an effect parameter to display its keyframes in the clip's keyframe graph.

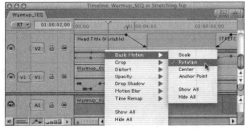

Figure 14.24 Control-click a clip's Filters or Motion bar to access and choose from a list of parameters to display.

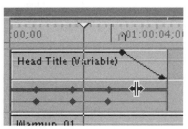

Figure 14.25 Slide a whole set of keyframes in a clip's Filters and Motion bars by dragging the bar with the Selection tool.

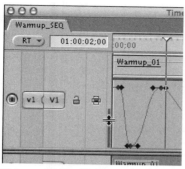

Figure 14.26 To adjust graph height, drag the Resize pointer up or down in this narrow column on the right edge of the Track control area.

Figure 14.27 Click the Clip Overlays control in the Timeline window to toggle the display of keyframe overlays.

Figure 14.28 Use the Pen tool to add a keyframe to a clip's keyframe overlay graph.

To adjust keyframe graph height:

1. Position the Selection tool over the right edge of the Timeline track control area.

   The Selection tool turns into the Resize pointer when it's in position.

2. Drag the Resize pointer up or down to adjust graph height (**Figure 14.26**).

To move keyframes in the Timeline:

◆ In the sequence clip's Filters and Motion bars, click and drag the effect keyframe left or right to adjust its timecode location.

   If snapping is on, the keyframe snaps to other keyframes and markers to help you align keyframes to particular points in the sequence.

To display keyframe overlays in the Timeline:

◆ In the Timeline, click the Clip Overlays control in the lower-left corner (**Figure 14.27**).

To add an overlay keyframe to a track:

1. From the Tool palette, select the Pen tool.

2. On the selected clip's overlay keyframe graph, click where you want to place the keyframe (**Figure 14.28**).

   A new keyframe is added to the overlay.

✔ Tip

■ Did you just add one keyframe too many? Press Option, and your Pen tool toggles to Pen Delete mode. Click on that extra keyframe to delete it; then release the Option key.

To adjust the values of individual overlay keyframes:

Do one of the following:

◆ Using the Pen tool or the Selection tool, drag overlay keyframes vertically to adjust their values. As you drag, a tooltip appears, displaying the parameter's value (**Figure 14.29**).

◆ Using the Selection tool, drag the level line between two overlay keyframes to adjust its position.

◆ Using the Pen tool, Shift-drag the level line between two overlay keyframes to adjust its position.

To delete overlay keyframes:

Do one of the following:

◆ Drag keyframes off the track completely to delete them.

◆ With the Pen tool selected, press the Option key to toggle to the Pen's Delete mode. Click the keyframe you want to delete.

The keyframes (except for the last one) are removed, and the keyframe path adjusts to reflect the change.

Precision control of a keyframe's positioning

Even in a compact screen layout, FCP offers a variety of techniques to help you get a grip on your keyframe's positioning:

◆ You can expand the vertical scale of most keyframe line graph displays on the Viewer's effects tabs. Drag the separator bar at the bottom of a keyframe line graph to make a roomier keyframe graph (**Figure 14.30**).

Figure 14.29 A tooltip displaying the current level updates as you adjust the keyframe.

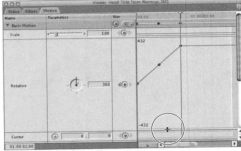

Figure 14.30 Drag the separator bar at the bottom of a keyframe line graph to expand the vertical scale.

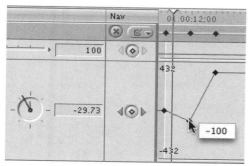

Figure 14.31 Adjust a keyframe while the playhead is located on a different frame, and the text field in the parameter controls will show the value at the playhead position.

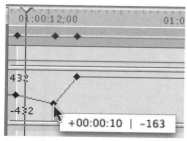

Figure 14.32 Shift-drag the keyframe to change both the value and the keyframe's point in time simultaneously.

Table 14.1

Keyboard Shortcuts for Keyframes	
Go to Next Keyframe	Shift-K
Go to Previous Keyframe	Option-K
Add Motion Keyframe	Control-K
Add Audio Keyframe	Cmd-Option-K

◆ Here's another keyframe graph trick: You can adjust a keyframe while the playhead is located at a particular target frame, and the text field in that parameter's controls will show the value *at the playhead position*, so you can set a keyframe that results in a position or size at that target frame (**Figure 14.31**).

◆ In the effect's Viewer tab, use the incremental controls (the tiny arrows at either end of the effect parameter control sliders) to nudge values by +1 or by –1, or enter an exact numeric value in the parameter's text field.

◆ In the Timeline or the Viewer, hold down the Command key while you drag a keyframe. This enables "gear-down" dragging, which allows you to move the keyframe in precise increments.

◆ Shift-drag to change both the value and the keyframe's point in time simultaneously (**Figure 14.32**).

Keyframe navigation shortcuts

Table 14.1 shows keyboard shortcuts for jumping forward and backward through a series of keyframes, and for adding a motion keyframe. These keyboard shortcuts work for the Timeline's level line overlays and the Canvas's wireframe overlay. These shortcuts will boost your speed and accuracy, and are highly recommended.

✔ Tip

■ If you're using the Next Keyframe and Previous Keyframe commands to navigate through keyframes in the Timeline, note that FCP ignores keyframes on tracks with Auto Select disabled.

Saving Effects Settings as Favorites

You can designate an effect, transition, or generator as a Favorite. Favorite effects are placed in the Favorites bin on the Browser's Effects tab and are also available from the Effects menu. Favorites provide an easy way to save an effect that you want to reproduce later. Favorite motions are particularly useful for streamlining animation. For more information on creating and using Favorites, see "Working with Default and Favorite Transitions" in Chapter 13.

To create a Favorite effect by saving its settings:

1. In the Timeline, double-click the clip with the effect you want to make a Favorite.

   The clip opens in the Viewer.

2. Select the Filters, Motion, or Controls tab to access the selected effect's controls.

3. Select the effect in the Name column; then *do one of the following:*

   ◆ Choose Effects > Make Favorite Effect (**Figure 14.33**).

   ◆ Choose Effects > Make Favorite Motion to save motion properties settings.

   ◆ Drag the effect's name from its control bar to the Favorites bin on the Browser's Effects tab.

✔ Tip

■ If you've created a set of Favorite effects for use in a particular project, you can archive those effects by dragging the Favorites folder (or selected Favorite effects) from the Browser's Effects tab onto your project tab. Your project's Favorite effects are saved with the project file.

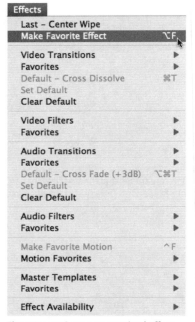

Figure 14.33 Save a customized effect setting by selecting an effect in the Name column and choosing Effects > Make Favorite Effect.

Customizing the Effects Menu Display

The Preferred Effects scheme allows you to edit the list of effects that appear in FCP's Effects tab and Effects menu. If you're like most editors, you rarely use most of the effects FCP offers. Using the Preferred Effects scheme should save you the time of wading through that Candyland of FCP effects in search of your old standbys. If it's Candyland you seek, simply choose All Effects from the Effects Availability submenu, and FCP will display them all. Preferred Effects settings are not affected if you delete your Final Cut Pro preferences file.

To specify which effects are displayed in the Effects tab and the Effects menu:

1. In the Browser's Effects tab, click in the Preferred column next to the effects you wish to display (**Figure 14.34**).

2. Choose Effects > Effect Availability (**Figure 14.35**), then choose one of the following options from the shortcut menu:

   ◆ **Only Recommended Effects:** Restricts effects listed in the Effects Menu and Effects tab to effects recommended by Apple. Minimizes display of duplicate FXScript and FxPlug filters.

   ◆ **Only My Preferred Effects:** Restricts effects listed in the Effects Menu and Effects tab to effects with a checkmark in the Preferred column.

   ◆ **All Effects:** Displays all installed plug-ins.

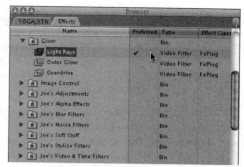

Figure 14.34 In the Browser's Effects tab, click in the Preferred column next to the effects you wish to display.

Figure 14.35 Choose Effects > Effect Availability, then select Only my Preferred Effects from the submenu to restrict the effects displayed in the Effects tab and Effects menu to those you have checked as Preferred.

Independent Developers of Final Cut Pro Plug-ins

Final Cut Pro's open architecture has attracted a small group of independent plug-in designers. Please explore and patronize these folks; they make an important contribution to the FCP world. Perhaps you'll be inspired to join in and start building your own effects.

Joe's Filters

www.joesfilters.com

www.fxscriptreference.org

New York City resident Joe Maller brings his expertise as a graphic designer to his creations—a set of 43 beautiful FX-scripted FCP plug-ins known as Joe's Filters. Back in the early days of Final Cut Pro, Joe taught himself FXScript in order to improve on the existing filters, and he has generously documented his FXScript knowledge (and created a public clearinghouse) on his FX Script Reference Web site.

CHV Plug-ins for Final Cut Pro/Express

www.chv-plugins.com

German designer Christopher Vorhein was one of the first to design plug-ins specifically for FCP, and he's assembled a nice library of reasonably-priced effects. The collection includes generators, transitions, and filters.

Nattress

www.nattress.com

British ex-patriate Graeme Nattress operates his plug-in empire out of Canada. Nattress features a real showstopper: Standards Conversion, an NTSC-PAL/PAL-NTSC conversion filter that produces good results. Graeme also features extensive film-look filter packages and image-control filters.

Digital Heaven

www.digital-heaven.co.uk

London-based Digital Heaven has a tidy collection of useful FCP plug-ins. The main focus here is on problem solving and productivity: bad-pixel and drop-out repair, grids and guides, and a subtitling plug-in.

stib's free Final Cut Pro plug-ins page

www.fxscript.org

This site offers a listing of free FCP plug-ins available from good-hearted folks all over the globe.

MOTION EFFECTS

Unlike filters or generators, motion properties are already present on every clip. You can access them by loading a clip or sequence into the Viewer and then selecting the Motion tab.

A few of the controls you find on the Motion tab, such as Opacity, Crop, Distort, and Drop Shadow, don't have any obvious connection to movement.

The first part of this chapter introduces motion properties as static image modification tools, which can be used in either static or animated compositions. The second part of the chapter, "Animating Clip Motion with Keyframes," discusses motion paths: the time-based uses of motion properties.

Setting Motion Properties

The motion properties listed below are present automatically on every clip, and their controls can be adjusted on the clip's Motion tab in the Viewer (**Figure 15.1**), or on the clip's Image+Wireframe mode overlay in the Canvas (**Figure 15.2**).

◆ **Scale:** Adjusts the size of the clip to make it smaller or larger than the sequence frame size.

◆ **Rotation:** Rotates the clip around its anchor point without changing its shape.

◆ **Center:** *x, y* coordinates specify the center point of the clip.

◆ **Anchor Point:** *x, y* coordinates specify another point relative to the clip's center point to use as a pivot point for rotating, scaling, or animating the motion path of the clip.

◆ **Crop:** Crops (removes) a portion of the clip from the side you specify.

◆ **Distort:** Changes the shape of the clip by adjusting its corners. The Aspect Ratio parameter sets the clip's height:width proportions.

◆ **Opacity:** Makes a clip opaque or translucent; 100 percent is completely opaque, and 0 percent is completely transparent.

◆ **Drop Shadow:** Places a drop shadow behind the selected clip, with a color, softness, and opacity you specify.

◆ **Motion Blur:** Blurs moving images by a specified percentage, by combining the images of adjacent frames to create the effect.

◆ **Time Remap:** Modifies a clip's playback speed. You can set a clip's speed to a constant frame rate, or keyframe the Time Remap motion property to produce variable playback speed.

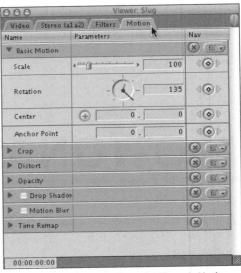

Figure 15.1 Use the controls on the Viewer's Motion tab to adjust motion properties.

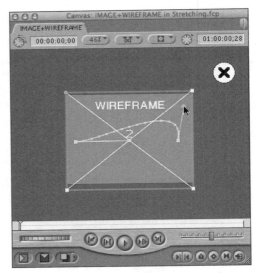

Figure 15.2 You can also adjust motion properties graphically, using the Canvas wireframe overlay.

Locating x, y coordinates

Final Cut Pro uses *x, y* coordinates to specify a clip's position in the frame. For example, in the DV-NTSC frame size (720 by 480 pixels), you can specify locations outside the visible frame by using coordinate values greater than plus or minus 360 on the x-axis, or plus or minus 240 on the y-axis. You'll often see *x, y* coordinates specified like this: (50,25). The first number (50) is the *x*-coordinate; the second number (25) is the *y*-coordinate. **Figure 15.3** is a diagram of *x, y* coordinate locations in a DV-NTSC frame (720 by 480 pixels).

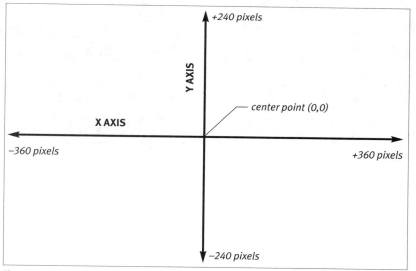

Figure 15.3 The *x, y* coordinates for a DV-NTSC frame size (720 by 480 pixels).

Motion Properties Modify an Image or Make it Move

Motion properties perform basic image modifications when used as static composition tools, but they can also create motion effects when you adjust their values over time. For example, you might use the Rotation control as a static composition tool to display a title at a 90-degree angle (**Figure 15.4**) or animate rotation by setting incrementally increasing values over time (**Figure 15.5**).

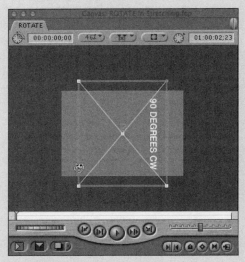

Figure 15.4 Use the Rotation control as a static composition tool to set a title clip at a 90-degree angle.

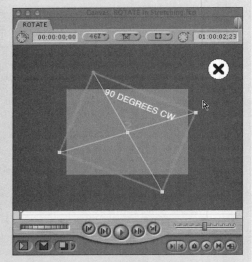

Figure 15.5 Use the Rotation control to animate the title clip's rotation by setting incrementally increasing values over time.

SETTING MOTION PROPERTIES

Using Wireframes

Enabling Image+Wireframe mode in the Canvas or the Viewer activates a wireframe overlay that appears on your clip image. You must be in Image+Wireframe mode in order to graphically manipulate a clip's motion properties in the Canvas or the Viewer.

The elements of the wireframe aren't just indicators; they're also controls you can use to manipulate the size, shape, and position of your clip's image. Select the appropriate

tool from the Tool palette; then drag a handle on the clip's wireframe. **Figure 15.6** offers a key to wireframe handles and tools.

✔ Tip

■ While you work in Wireframe mode, note that the selected track's number appears just above the clip's center point. The track number helps you remember which layer you've selected. If you're working on an effects sequence with many layered elements, that's a big help.

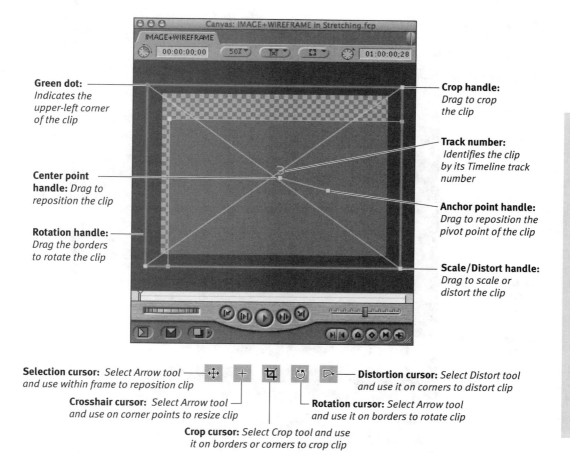

Green dot: *Indicates the upper-left corner of the clip*

Crop handle: *Drag to crop the clip*

Track number: *Identifies the clip by its Timeline track number*

Center point handle: *Drag to reposition the clip*

Anchor point handle: *Drag to reposition the pivot point of the clip*

Rotation handle: *Drag the borders to rotate the clip*

Scale/Distort handle: *Drag to scale or distort the clip*

Selection cursor: *Select Arrow tool and use within frame to reposition clip*

Distortion cursor: *Select Distort tool and use it on corners to distort clip*

Crosshair cursor: *Select Arrow tool and use on corner points to resize clip*

Rotation cursor: *Select Arrow tool and use it on borders to rotate clip*

Crop cursor: *Select Crop tool and use it on borders or corners to crop clip*

Figure 15.6 To manipulate motion properties in Image+Wireframe mode, select a tool; then click and drag the appropriate handle on the clip's wireframe.

Wireframe keyframe indicators

Wireframe mode uses green highlighting to indicate whether a keyframe is present on a frame and what type of keyframe it is (**Figure 15.7**).

To enable Wireframe mode:

Do one of the following:

◆ Press W once to put the Viewer or the Canvas in Image+Wireframe mode. Press W a second time to toggle to Wireframe mode. Press W again to return to Image mode.

◆ Choose Image+Wireframe or Wireframe from the View pop-up menu at the top of the Viewer or the Canvas (**Figure 15.8**).

◆ Choose View > Image+Wireframe.

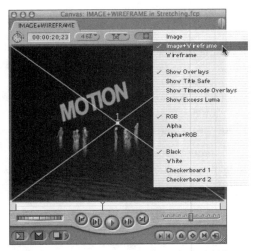

Figure 15.8 Choose Image+Wireframe from the View pop-up menu at the top of the Viewer or Canvas.

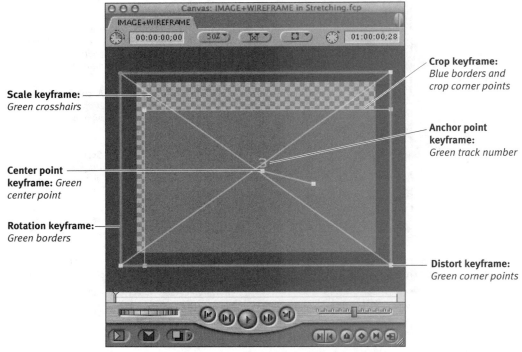

Scale keyframe: *Green crosshairs*

Center point keyframe: *Green center point*

Rotation keyframe: *Green borders*

Crop keyframe: *Blue borders and crop corner points*

Anchor point keyframe: *Green track number*

Distort keyframe: *Green corner points*

Figure 15.7 Wireframe mode uses highlighting to indicate the presence of keyframes.

USING WIREFRAMES

Using Motion Properties to Change a Clip's Appearance

In Final Cut Pro, when you want to make a clip's image larger or smaller, tilted or skewed, opaque or transparent, you adjust the clip's motion properties—even if the clip's not moving. Not very intuitive, is it?

As long as you're not animating the clip (changing the size and shape of the clip's image over time), you don't need to add any motion keyframes. Simply open the clip and adjust the clip's default motion properties settings. FCP offers two ways to modify a clip's motion properties—by adjusting the controls and entering numerical values on the clip's Motion tab in the Viewer, or by using the Tool palette's image modification tools to manipulate the clip's image directly in the Canvas wireframe overlay. When you're going for precision and consistency, you'll probably end up working both numerically and graphically.

All operations described in this section can be performed in both places. Start each operation by following the general setup procedure for each respective mode; the setup tasks are described in the sections that follow.

Using Keyboard Shortcuts with Wireframes

Many of the scaling and positioning tools have keyboard modifiers—keys you press as you drag the tool on the wireframe handles in the Canvas or in the Viewer—that you can use to create complex alterations to a clip.

◆ **Option:** Use this key to force automatic rendering while you drag the clip.

◆ **Shift:** Use this key to enable nonproportional scaling (modification of a clip's aspect ratio while scaling). You can use the Shift and Option keys together.

◆ **Command:** Use this key to rotate and scale the clip simultaneously. You can use the Command and Option keys together.

To set up for motion properties adjustment in the Canvas's Wireframe mode:

1. In the Timeline, select the clip you want to reposition (**Figure 15.9**). If you are working with a layered composition, be sure to choose the layer you want to affect.

2. From the Tool palette, choose the appropriate image modification tool for the motion property you want to adjust. Refer to the key to wireframe handles and tools in Figure 15.6.

3. If it's not already activated, press W to turn on the Canvas's Image+Wireframe mode.

   The outline of the wireframe overlay appears on the selected clip's image (**Figure 15.10**).

To set up for motion properties adjustment on the Viewer's Motion tab:

1. Double-click the clip in the Timeline or the Browser to open it in the Viewer.

2. In the Viewer, click the Motion tab.

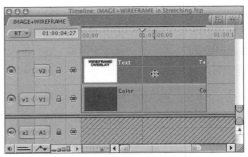

Figure 15.9 In the Timeline, select the clip you want to reposition.

Figure 15.10 Press W to activate Image+Wireframe mode, and the wireframe overlay appears on the selected clip's image.

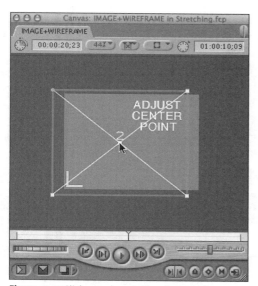

Figure 15.11 Click anywhere in the clip's wireframe, and then drag it to a new position.

Figure 15.12 Click the Point Select button, which is located to the left of the Center value field.

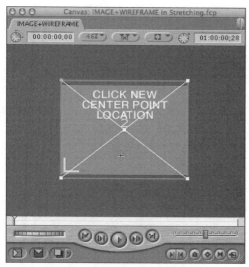

Figure 15.13 Click a new center location in the Canvas to specify new center coordinates.

Positioning clips

Clips start out positioned at the center of the Canvas or the Viewer. You can reposition a clip's center point by dragging it to a new position in the Canvas or in the Viewer, or you can specify new center point coordinates on the clip's Motion tab. You can position a clip partially or completely outside the sequence frame.

To adjust a clip's center point using Wireframe mode:

◆ Follow the setup steps for Wireframe mode presented earlier; then click anywhere inside the clip's wireframe and drag it to a new position (**Figure 15.11**).

To adjust a clip's center point on the Viewer's Motion tab:

Follow the setup steps for the Motion tab mode described earlier; then *do one of the following:*

◆ Enter new *x, y* coordinates for the clip's center location. Enter the *x*-coordinate in the left value field and the *y*-coordinate in the right value field.

◆ Click the Point Select (+) button (**Figure 15.12**) (located to the left of the Center value field) and then specify new center coordinates by clicking the new center location in the Canvas (**Figure 15.13**) or on the Video tab of the Viewer.

Scaling clips

A clip placed in a Final Cut Pro sequence plays at the same frame size at which it was captured, regardless of the sequence frame size. A clip whose native size is smaller than the sequence frame size appears in the center of the sequence frame; a clip whose native size is larger than the sequence frame size shows only the portion of the clip that fits inside the sequence frame dimensions.

You can adjust the scale of a clip to change its frame size (for the current sequence only). If you want to create a media file of your clip at a different size that does not need to be rendered before it can be played back, you should export a copy of the clip at the frame size you need.

To scale a clip in Wireframe mode:

1. Follow the setup steps for Wireframe mode presented earlier.

2. Drag a corner handle to scale a clip while maintaining its proportions (**Figure 15.14**).

✔ Tips

■ Smooth your keyframes with Bézier curves when you animate scale. Curve-type keyframes produce a change in the rate of scale at the beginning and the end of the scaling animation, making the movement less mechanical. To learn how to convert a keyframe to a Bézier curve type, see "To refine a motion keyframe," later in this chapter.

■ When you're scaling a clip, it's easy to drift away from the clip's original aspect ratio, but not easy to find the control that resets your clip to its native proportions. Go to the clip's Motion tab and scroll down to the Distort controls. That's where you'll find the Aspect Ratio parameter. Reset the value to 0, and you'll restore height:width sanity to your scaled clip.

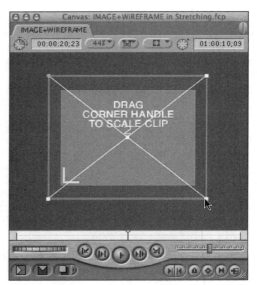

Figure 15.14 Dragging a corner handle scales a clip while maintaining its proportions.

FCP Protocol: Center Point vs. Anchor Point vs. Origin Point

All three types of points—the center point, anchor point, and origin point—are used to define position, but each serves a different purpose:

Center point: Establishes the clip's position inside the Canvas area. The center point's default position (0,0) is the same as the anchor point's.

Anchor point: Establishes the pivot point for a clip's movement inside the Canvas area. Rotation and Scale properties and motion paths are all based on the anchor point. The anchor point's default position (0,0) is the same as the center point's.

Origin point: Origin appears on the Motion tab for text generators and establishes the positioning of text elements placed inside the clip.

Figure 15.15 Adjust the Scale slider on the Motion tab to scale the clip.

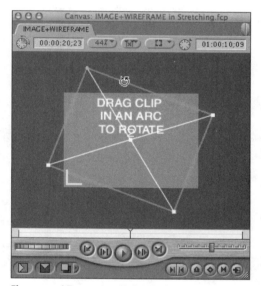

Figure 15.16 To rotate a clip in Wireframe mode, drag in an arc around the clip's center point.

To scale a clip on the Viewer's Motion tab:

Follow the setup steps for Motion tab mode presented earlier; then *do one of the following*:

◆ Adjust the Scale slider (**Figure 15.15**).

◆ Enter a percentage in the text field located to the right of the slider; 100 percent is equal to the clip's native size.

Rotating clips

Rotation is an important part of modern video effects (as you know if you've watched a TV commercial break recently).

A clip rotates around its anchor point. The default anchor point location matches the clip's center point, but you can rotate a clip around a different pivot point by changing the location of the anchor point. You can position a clip at the edge of your sequence frame and rotate your clip partially or completely outside the Canvas, so it appears on the screen for only a portion of its rotation. You can also rotate a clip up to 24 revolutions in either direction or use the Rotation control to angle a clip as part of a static composition.

To adjust a clip's rotation angle in Wireframe mode:

Follow the setup steps for Wireframe mode presented earlier; then *do one of the following*:

◆ Click an edge of the border and drag in an arc around the clip's center point (**Figure 15.16**).

◆ Click a border edge, and then drag farther away from the clip's center point to get more precise control over the rotation.

◆ Hold down the Shift key while dragging to constrain the rotation positions to 45-degree increments.

◆ Drag around the clip multiple times without releasing the mouse to specify a number of rotations.

To adjust a clip's rotation angle on the Viewer's Motion tab:

Follow the setup steps for the Motion tab mode described earlier; then *do one of the following:*

◆ Drag the black rotation needle around the dial to set a rotation position (**Figure 15.17**); the red needle indicates the number of complete revolutions.

◆ Enter a new value in the text box.

The clip realigns at the new rotation angle for the selected frame.

✔ Tip

■ To create an animated rotation effect on the Motion tab, you must set individual keyframes for each rotation angle value. (See "Animating Clip Motion with Keyframes," later in this chapter.)

Cropping clips

You can crop a clip either by dragging with the Crop tool or by specifying the number of pixels to crop from the borders. Use the Edge Feather option to create a soft border at the crop line.

When you use the Crop tool to remove part of a clip's image, the selected parts are hidden, not deleted. You can restore the cropped sections to view by clicking the Reset button next to the Crop controls on the Viewer's Motion tab.

Figure 15.17 Drag the rotation control dial needle to set a rotation position. The black hand indicates the current angle of the clip, and the small red hand indicates how many total rotations forward or backward have been specified.

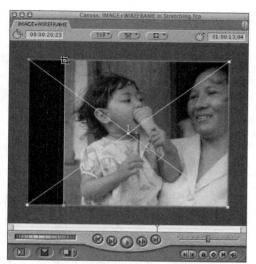

Figure 15.18 Drag from the edges of the clip to crop out elements in the image.

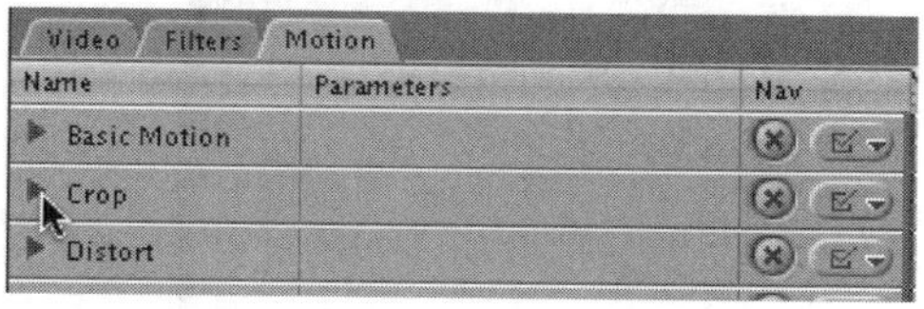

Figure 15.19 Open the Crop controls by clicking the Crop expansion triangle.

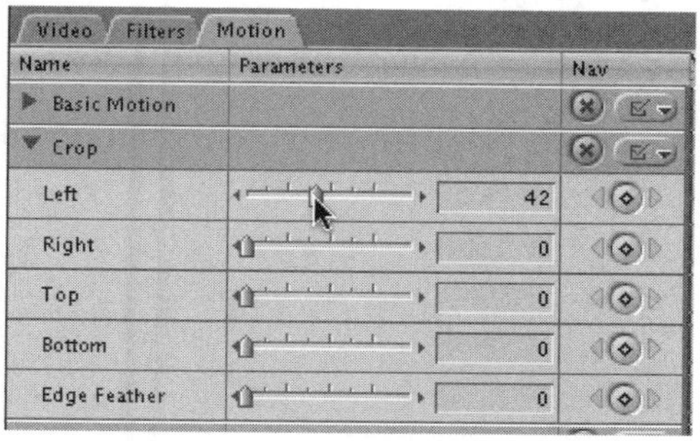

Figure 15.20 Crop a clip by dragging the slider for the side you want to crop and setting it to a new value.

To crop a clip in Wireframe mode:

1. Follow the setup steps for the Wireframe mode presented earlier; then select the Crop tool from the Tool palette.

2. *Do one of the following:*
   - Drag from the edges of the clip to hide elements in the image (**Figure 15.18**).
   - Shift-drag to constrain the clip's aspect ratio as you crop.
   - Command-drag to trim both horizontal edges or both vertical edges simultaneously.
   - Use Option in combination with Shift and Command to force rendering while you perform a crop operation.

To crop a clip on the Motion tab:

1. Follow the setup steps for the Motion tab mode described earlier; then open the Crop control bar by clicking the expansion triangle on the left (**Figure 15.19**).

2. To crop the clip from a specific side, *do one of the following:*
   - Drag the slider for that edge to a new value (**Figure 15.20**).
   - Enter a new value in the corresponding text field.

3. To soften the cropped edges of the clip, *do one of the following:*
   - Adjust the Edge Feather slider to specify the width of the feathered edge.
   - Specify a value in the Edge Feather text field.

Distorting a clip's shape

Use the Distort tool to make independent adjustments to each corner point of a clip's wireframe, or use the Viewer's Motion tab to numerically specify *x, y* coordinates for the location of each corner point.

To distort the shape of a clip in Wireframe mode:

1. Follow the setup steps for the Wireframe mode presented earlier; then select the Distort tool from the Tool palette (**Figure 15.21**).

2. To distort the clip's image, *do one of the following:*
   - Drag a corner handle of the clip's wireframe (**Figure 15.22**).
   - Shift-drag to change the perspective of the image.

To distort a clip on the Viewer's Motion tab:

1. Follow the setup steps for the Motion tab mode presented earlier; then open the Distort control bar by clicking the expansion triangle.

2. To specify new locations for the corner points, *do one of the following:*
   - Enter new values for the corner points you want to move.
   - Adjust the Aspect Ratio parameter to change the clip's height:width ratio, relocating all four corner points. A clip's original aspect ratio has a value of zero.

Figure 15.21 Select the Distort tool from the Tool palette.

Figure 15.22 Drag a corner handle of the clip's wireframe to distort it.

Figure 15.23 The title is 100 percent opaque and completely obscures the background.

Figure 15.24 The superimposed title with opacity set to less than 100 percent appears semitransparent.

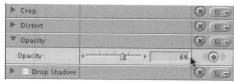

Figure 15.25 Type a value between 0 and 100 in the Opacity text field.

Adjusting opacity

Final Cut Pro clips start out 100 percent opaque (**Figure 15.23**). If you superimpose a clip over another clip in the base track of your sequence, the background image will be completely hidden until you adjust the opacity of the superimposed clip to less than 100 percent, making it semitransparent (**Figure 15.24**).

Layering multiple, semitransparent images is a basic compositing technique, and one you may be familiar with if you have ever worked with Adobe Photoshop.

You can adjust a clip's opacity on the Viewer's Motion tab or with the opacity clip overlay in the Timeline.

To set a clip's opacity on the Viewer's Motion tab:

1. Follow the setup steps for the Motion tab mode described earlier; then open the Opacity control bar by clicking the triangle.

2. To set the opacity level, *do one of the following:*
   - Use the slider control.
   - Enter a value between 0 and 100 in the Opacity text field (**Figure 15.25**).

Setting a clip's opacity in the Timeline

A clip's opacity can be adjusted directly in the Timeline using the clip overlay for opacity, a level line graph that appears over the clip icon in the Timeline. To display clip overlays, click the Clip Overlays control in the lower-left corner of the Timeline.

For information on adjusting clip overlays in the Timeline, see "Working with Keyframes in the Timeline" in Chapter 14.

Use the Modify > Levels command to adjust opacity levels for a group of Timeline clips in a single operation.

To adjust opacity levels on a group of clips:

1. In the Timeline, select a group of clips whose levels you want to adjust (**Figure 15.26**).

2. Choose Modify > Levels.

3. In the Opacity Adjust dialog box, *do one of the following*:

   ◆ Choose Relative from the pop-up menu. Adjust each clip's opacity relative to its current level by specifying a percentage value (**Figure 15.27**).

   ◆ Choose Absolute from the pop-up menu; then set an absolute value for all clips' opacity by specifying a percentage value.

4. Click OK.

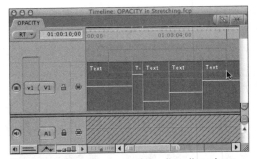

Figure 15.26 Select a group of Timeline clips whose opacity levels you want to adjust.

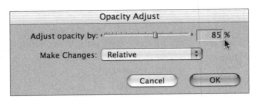

Figure 15.27 Choose Relative in the Opacity Adjust dialog box to adjust the opacity of all the selected clips by the percentage you specify.

Figure 15.28 Drop shadows add depth to a superimposed title.

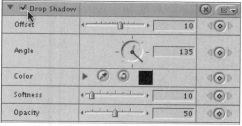

Figure 15.29 Check the box to enable the Drop Shadow option.

Adding a drop shadow to a clip

Drop shadows add the illusion of dimensional depth to the 2D television screen (**Figure 15.28**). Titles pop out from the backgrounds, or clips softly float over other clips; complex silhouettes can add a special depth to your sequences. You can add a drop shadow to any clip whose display size is smaller than the sequence frame size.

You can apply drop shadows to clips that were captured at a smaller frame size and to clips that have been scaled, cropped, moved, or distorted. You can also add a drop shadow to a full-size clip with an alpha channel.

To add a drop shadow to a clip:

1. Double-click the clip in the Timeline or the Browser to open it in the Viewer.

2. In the Viewer, click the Motion tab; then check the Drop Shadow check box (**Figure 15.29**).

3. To adjust your drop shadow settings, *do any of the following:*

   ◆ Enter Offset settings to specify the shadow's distance from the clip.

   ◆ Enter Angle settings to specify the position of the shadow relative to the clip edge.

   ◆ Enter Softness settings to specify the degree of blending in the shadow's edge.

   ◆ Enter Opacity settings to specify the shadow's degree of transparency.

continues on next page

4. In the Color control bar, click the expansion triangle; then pick a color by *doing one of the following:*

- ◆ Drag the hue, saturation, and brightness sliders to new values.

- ◆ Enter numeric color values in the text fields.

- ◆ Click the eyedropper and click in the Canvas to sample a color.

- ◆ Click the color swatch and use one of the color pickers to choose the desired color (**Figure 15.30**).

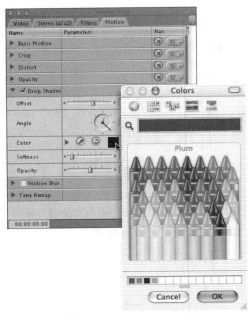

Figure 15.30 Click the color swatch; then choose a color from one of the color pickers.

Figure 15.31 Motion blur produces soft-focus effects based on movement within your video image.

Figure 15.32 You can apply motion blur to a static graphic as well, but you must animate the graphic with a motion path first.

Adding a motion blur effect

The motion blur effect enhances the illusion of movement by compositing the images of adjacent frames (**Figure 15.31**). This is definitely one control to experiment with, particularly for creating interesting, animated, soft-focus background textures. If you're using graphics or stills, you must combine motion blur with other motion effects—scaling, rotation, or motion paths, for example—to see the motion blur effect, but you can use it to create a lot of action in your composition, even with static elements (**Figure 15.32**).

✔ Tip

■ Nest a clip containing an element you want to blur. By increasing the frame size when you nest, you can create a roomier bounding box that will accommodate the larger size of your blurred element.

To add motion blur to a clip:

1. Double-click the clip in the Timeline or the Browser to open it in the Viewer.

2. In the Viewer, click the Motion tab; then check the Motion Blur check box near the bottom of the tab (**Figure 15.33**).

3. Click the Motion Blur expansion triangle to reveal the controls for blurring motion.

4. Use the % Blur slider, or enter a value in the text field. Values range from 1000%, which blurs a frame's image across 10 frames, to 100%, which blurs the image on a single frame.

5. To change the quality of the motion blur, adjust the sample rate by choosing a value from the Samples pop-up menu (**Figure 15.34**).

   The sample rate is the number of in-between images FCP calculates when it compares two adjacent frames to calculate motion blur. A low sample rate produces more visible intermediate steps; a high sample rate produces a smoother look but takes longer to render.

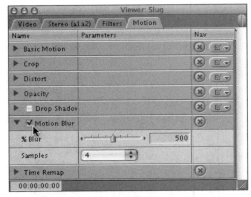

Figure 15.33 Check the Motion Blur check box to enable motion blurring.

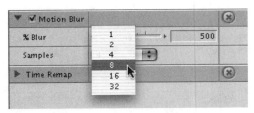

Figure 15.34 Specify a number of samples by selecting a value from the Samples pop-up menu. The sample rate changes the quality of the motion blur. Fewer samples create more visible intermediate steps.

Figure 15.35 Click the Add Motion Keyframe button on the Canvas to set a keyframe.

Animating Clip Motion with Keyframes

The previous section explained how to use motion properties to alter a clip's shape, size, and transparency in a static composition. In this section you'll finally learn how to use motion properties to actually move clips around.

Working with basic motion keyframe commands

The best place to use motion keyframes to animate a motion path is either the Canvas or the Viewer when it is in Image+Wireframe mode—all the operations described in this section are performed in Wireframe mode.

You can work with motion keyframes in both the Canvas and the Viewer, but because keyframing more commonly happens in the Canvas, the directions in this section mention only the Canvas.

To set a motion keyframe:

1. In the Canvas, position the playhead at the frame where you want to set the keyframe.

2. Click the Add Motion Keyframe button (**Figure 15.35**); or press Control-K.

continues on next page

The Best Way to Fine-Tune a Motion Sequence: Jump Around

Using the Shift-K and Option-K keyboard shortcuts to step through a series of keyframes, you can review your clip's settings at each keyframe. For best results, keep an eye on both the Canvas and the Motion tab—the Canvas wireframe overlay updates to show the way your composition looks, and the clip's Motion tab updates to show the precise value of each keyframe's settings.

3. To set an additional keyframe, move the
playhead to the next location where you
want to set a keyframe; then *do one of
the following:*

- ◆ Add another keyframe; then adjust
  the Motion tab parameter control or
  make a graphical adjustment to the
  clip's wireframe.

- ◆ Make an adjustment to a Motion tab
  parameter control or make a graphical
  adjustment to the clip's wireframe.

Final Cut Pro adjusts the values and
then automatically adds the keyframe
(**Figure 15.36**).

✔ Tip

- ■ Clicking the Add Motion Keyframe button
  in the Canvas sets a motion keyframe
  across all motion parameters for the
  current frame.

ANIMATING CLIP MOTION WITH KEYFRAMES

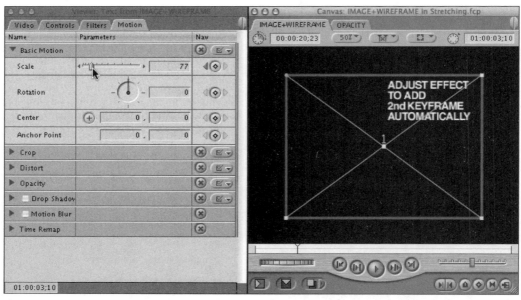

Figure 15.36 Move the playhead to the next location; then adjust a parameter control, and FCP adds the next
keyframe automatically.

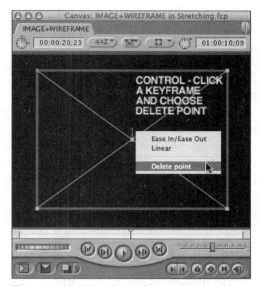

Figure 15.37 To delete the keyframe, Control-click it and choose Delete Point from the shortcut menu.

Figure 15.38 Another way to delete a motion keyframe is to Option-click it with the Selection tool or the Pen tool.

To navigate between motion keyframes:

◆ Press Shift-K to move to the next motion keyframe.

◆ Press Option-K to move to the previous keyframe.

The playhead moves to the next keyframe in the appropriate direction, and the Canvas updates to show the new position of the clip.

✔ Tip

■ Toggle the Auto Select control off for any track you want to exclude from your keyframe review. FCP will ignore the keyframes on that track.

To delete a motion keyframe:

In the Canvas wireframe overlay, *do one of the following:*

◆ Control-click the keyframe and choose Delete Point from the shortcut menu (**Figure 15.37**).

◆ Option-click the keyframe with the Selection tool or the Pen tool (**Figure 15.38**).

To refine a motion keyframe:

1. Control-click the keyframe and choose Ease In/Ease Out from the shortcut menu (**Figure 15.39**).

   The keyframe changes into a curve type, and Bézier handles appear.

2. Drag the small blue circle at the end of the Bézier handle to adjust the motion path leading up to (or away from) the keyframe (**Figure 15.40**).

✔ Tip

■ Refine opacity and audio level overlay keyframes in the Timeline by Control-clicking the overlay keyframe and selecting Smooth from the shortcut menu.

To move a motion keyframe:

◆ In the Canvas wireframe overlay, click the motion keyframe with the appropriate selection tool and drag it to a new location.

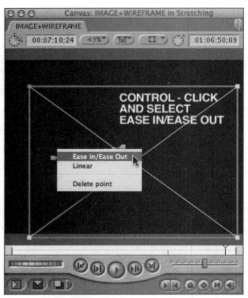

Figure 15.39 To smooth a corner-type keyframe to a Bézier curve type, Control-click the keyframe and choose Ease In/Ease Out from the shortcut menu.

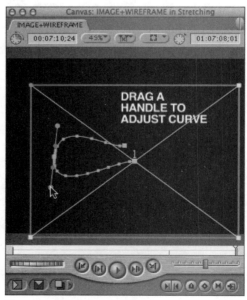

Figure 15.40 Drag the small blue circle at the end of the Bézier handle to adjust the motion path leading away from the keyframe.

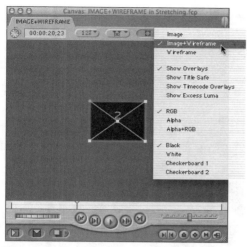

Figure 15.41 Choose Image+Wireframe from the View pop-up menu.

Creating Motion Paths

If you are new to motion paths, try one—if your FCP system is powerful enough to support real-time previewing, you can play back a moving clip without rendering, and you will get a feel for how the Canvas function changes when you are working in Wireframe mode. You can work in Wireframe mode in the Viewer as well.

When you animate the center point, you move the whole clip. The following section explains the basic steps for animating a simple motion path.

✔ Tip

- Motion paths are limited to single sequence clips; you must nest sequence clips if you want to create a motion path that includes two or more clips that have been edited together. For more information on nesting items, see Chapter 4, "Projects, Sequences, and Clips."

To create a motion path in the Canvas:

1. In the Timeline, select a sequence clip; then position the playhead on the first frame in your clip.

2. Make the Canvas active; then choose 12% from the Zoom pop-up menu and Image+Wireframe from the View pop-up menu (**Figure 15.41**).

3. To add the first keyframe, click the Add Motion Keyframe button in the Canvas. Final Cut Pro sets the first keyframe across all motion parameters for that sequence frame.

continues on next page

4. In the Canvas, drag the wireframe's center handle to the left until the right side of the wireframe aligns with the left edge of the black background. Hold down the Shift key while you drag to constrain the motion path. This makes it easier to drag in a straight line.

Your clip is now positioned just off the screen, at the left (**Figure 15.42**).

5. In the Timeline, position the playhead on the last frame in your sequence clip.

6. In the Canvas, click inside the wireframe and Shift-drag it to the right. Drag the wireframe across the black background until its left side aligns with the right edge of the black background.

As you drag, the motion path appears across the center of the screen. The white line indicates the motion path of your clip's center point (**Figure 15.43**).

7. To preview your motion path, hold down the Option key while you scrub the Canvas Scrubber bar from side to side.

8. If your computer supports real-time previewing, you can play your moving clip immediately. If not, you must render before playback. Select the clip; then choose Sequence > Render Selection.

✔ Tip

■ When your clips and motion paths are so spread out that you need to make the Canvas or the Viewer view smaller than the smallest level listed on the Zoom control (12%), choose Fit All, which will zoom the view out enough to fit all elements of your multi-layered composited sequence within the window.

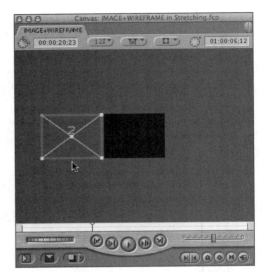

Figure 15.42 Your clip is positioned just off the screen, at the left.

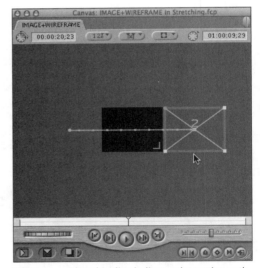

Figure 15.43 The white line indicates the motion path of your clip's center point.

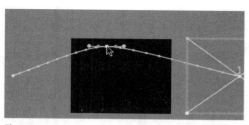

Figure 15.44 As you drag the motion path into a curve, additional keyframes appear with Bézier handles; drag the handles to sculpt the motion path's curves.

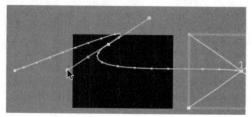

Figure 15.45 Rotate the handle to change the direction of the curve relative to that keyframe.

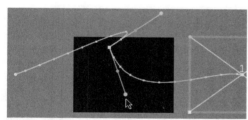

Figure 15.46 Command-drag to restrict rotation to one side of the curve.

To add curves to a motion path:

1. If you don't already have a sequence clip with a motion path applied, follow steps 1 through 6 in the previous task, "To create a motion path in the Canvas."

2. To create a curve in your straight motion path, click the motion path and drag in the direction you want the path to curve.

   As you drag the motion path into a curve, additional keyframes appear on the motion path automatically; the keyframes have little handles, called Bézier handles, which you use to sculpt the motion path's curves (**Figure 15.44**).

3. Click the Canvas Play button to play back the first draft of your edited motion path. Watching real-time playback in Wireframe mode is the best way to evaluate your clip's speed and movement.

4. To adjust the curve, click a keyframe's Bézier handle; then *do any of the following*:

   ◆ Drag the handle away from the keyframe to deepen the curve.

   ◆ Drag the handle toward the keyframe to reduce the curve.

   ◆ Rotate the handle to change the direction of the curve relative to that keyframe (**Figure 15.45**).

   ◆ Command-drag to restrict rotation to one side of the curve (**Figure 15.46**). Release the Command key to set the new relationship between the two curves.

To reposition an entire motion path:

1. Choose the Selection tool from the Tool palette.

2. In the Canvas, hold down the Command and Shift keys; then place the pointer near the motion path that you want to reposition.

   The Selection tool turns into a Hand pointer when you position it correctly (**Figure 15.47**).

3. Drag the motion path to a new position.

   The entire motion path repositions but does not change its shape or timing (**Figure 15.48**).

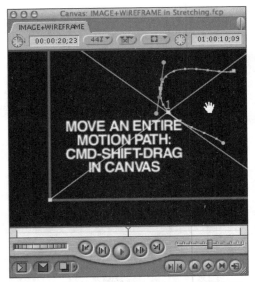

Figure 15.47 Hold down the Command and Shift keys; then place the Selection pointer near the motion path that you want to reposition. The pointer turns into a Hand pointer when you're in the right spot.

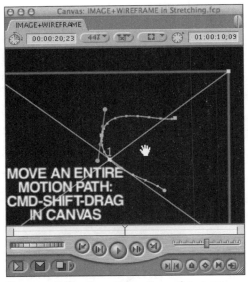

Figure 15.48 Drag the entire motion path to a new position without changing its shape or timing.

Editing a Motion Path

Once you have created it, you can adjust a motion path directly in the Canvas (or Viewer) by moving or deleting motion path keyframes. When you're working with a motion path in the Canvas, the playhead doesn't need to be over a keyframe for you to move or delete it, nor does the playhead location prohibit you from adding a motion path keyframe.

Remember that a keyframe is like an edit point: It signals a change in an effect. In a motion path, keyframes are placed automatically only when a motion path changes direction. A straight motion path requires only two keyframes: a start keyframe and an end keyframe.

The two motion path variables you are adjusting are your clip's speed of travel (determined by the ratio of duration to distance between keyframes) and the path's route (indicated by the shape of the white line that connects the start and end keyframes). The little dots that appear between the keyframes indicate the duration between path points.

Adjusting motion path curves and corners

Final Cut Pro features two types of motion path keyframes: corners and curves. The default motion path keyframe is a corner, which creates an instant change in direction. If you want a smoother motion effect, the curve keyframes have Bézier handles, which you can use to fine-tune the shape of the path's curve, as well as ease handles, which you can use to fine-tune your clip's speed immediately before and after the keyframe location.

You switch a corner-type motion path keyframe to a curve type as the first step in smoothing your motion path and finessing its timing.

✔ Tip

- You can use the Shift and Command keys while dragging a Bézier or ease handle to influence the connections between the angles of the curve.

To toggle a keyframe between corner and curve types in Wireframe mode:

With your clip displayed in Wireframe mode in the Canvas, Control-click a keyframe and *choose one of the following options:*

- Make Corner Point toggles the keyframe from a curve type to a corner type (**Figure 15.49**).

- Ease In/Ease Out accesses the ease handles, which are discussed later in this section.

- Linear applies a constant rate of speed to the path immediately before and after the keyframe location.

- Delete Point deletes the keyframe.

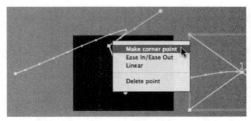

Figure 15.49 Control-click a keyframe on the Canvas; then choose Make Corner Point to toggle the keyframe from a curve type to a corner type.

Adjusting speed along a motion path

You can increase the speed of a clip's movement by shortening the timecode duration between two keyframes without changing their spatial coordinates. The clip's speed increases, since it takes less time to travel between the two locations on your motion path. Or, keep the time interval the same and move the keyframes farther apart on the motion path, so the clip travels farther in the same amount of time. Other timing factors in your sequence composition will dictate your choice.

Ease handles, located in the Canvas between the Bézier handles and the keyframe's position point (**Figure 15.50**), fine-tune the rate of speed at which a clip approaches and leaves a curve keyframe. The default Ease In and Out setting slows the speed on the motion path by 33 percent before and after the keyframe, but you can customize that setting. Drag both handles to set the clip's ease in and ease out to the same rate, or drag the handles separately to set different ease-in and ease-out rates.

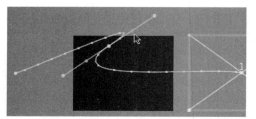

Figure 15.50 Ease handles are located about midway between the Bézier handles and the keyframe's position point.

Setting a Single Motion Path for Multiple Clips

How can you easily apply a single motion path to multiple clips? A couple of different techniques are available; your choice depends on whether you are dealing with a series of clips on a single track or with multiple clips stacked in layers on Timeline tracks.

One approach is to copy and paste just the series of clips into a separate sequence, which you edit back into your main sequence just as if it were a single clip. You can then apply a single motion path to the entire series, because it's contained in a single sub-sequence. You can use the same technique to convert multiple layers into a sub-sequence in order to apply a single motion path.

You also have the option of copying a clip and pasting only its motion path using the Paste Attributes function.

For more information on working with multiple sequences, see Chapter 4, "Projects, Sequences, and Clips."

For more information on the Paste Attributes feature, see Chapter 10, "Editing in the Timeline and the Canvas."

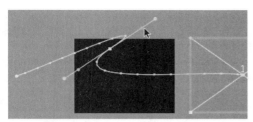

Figure 15.51 Drag the ease handle away from the keyframe to increase a clip's speed as it passes through the keyframe's location on the motion path.

Figure 15.52 Drag the ease handle toward the keyframe to decrease a clip's speed as it passes through the keyframe's location on the motion path.

To make a clip ease in and out of a keyframe:

1. With the Canvas in Wireframe mode, start with a curve motion path keyframe.

2. Choose the Selection tool.

3. Click the curve keyframe; then *do one of the following:*

   ◆ Drag the ease handle away from the keyframe to increase the clip's speed as it passes through the keyframe's location on the motion path (**Figure 15.51**).

   ◆ Drag the handle toward the keyframe to slow the clip's speed as it passes through the keyframe's location on the motion path (**Figure 15.52**).

   ◆ Drag either ease handle to adjust the path's timing on both sides of the keyframe equally.

   ◆ Shift-drag one ease handle to adjust the path's timing only on the selected side.

4. Play back in Wireframe mode to see your results.

✔ Tip

■ You can copy and paste motion paths between clips or sequences by using the Paste Attributes command on the Edit menu. Check the Scale Attributes box when you paste attributes onto your destination clip, and you can reuse a motion path on a different clip that's shorter or longer than the original.

EDITING A MOTION PATH

Creating Variable Speed Playback Effects

You've been able to change a clip's playback speed to another constant speed since FCP 1.0. You could speed up, slow down, or reverse clips, but your adjustments were limited to one playback speed modification per clip. No more.

The Time Remap feature is a tool/interface combo that allows you to make complex variable speed adjustments directly in the Timeline—without math calculations, folks.

Time remapping is classified as a motion property, so when you open a Timeline clip in the Viewer, you'll find its Time Remap controls at the bottom of the Motion tab (**Figure 15.53**). Time remapping tools also appear in a clip's Timeline keyframe area.

"Creating Variable Speed Playback Effects," a 9-page PDF available online, will describe the time remapping tools and walk you through a couple of basic variable speed adjustments. For more information, see "Changing Clip Speed and Time Remapping" on page III-337 of Apple's *Final Cut Pro User Manual* PDF. To learn how to change a clip's playback speed to another constant speed, see "Changing the playback speed of a clip" in Chapter 10.

⊙ On Peachpit.com

"Creating Variable Speed Playback Effects," a 9-page PDF, is available at:
www.peachpit.com/finalcutpro6vqp

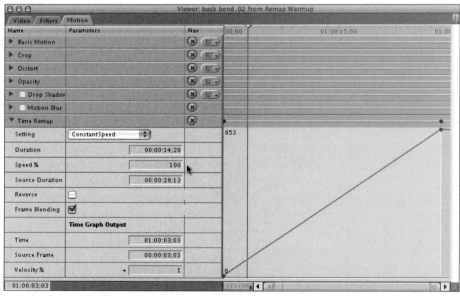

Figure 15.53 The Time Remap keyframe graph appears at the bottom of the Viewer's Motion tab. Parameter controls offer a detailed view of playback speed values and source frame relative to the current playhead position. See Apple's FCP manual for settings details.

FILTERS AND COMPOSITING

Just as the term *motion properties* is used to describe a collection of tools that do a lot more than move things, so the term *filters* applies to a lot more than just tools for tinting or texturing an image. Final Cut Pro comes with more than 70 video filters, with a wide variety of uses. In addition to a suite of image-control filters for color correction and tinting, Final Cut Pro provides filters you can use to blur, twirl, emboss, ripple, flip, mask, and key. When you're done, you can apply another filter to generate visible timecode over your final results! For a list of video filters, refer to page III-241 of Apple's *Final Cut Pro User Manual* PDF.

But wait—there's more. Final Cut Pro can also make use of the QuickTime effects that are installed with QuickTime, and the program is compatible with many of Adobe After Effects' third-party filters.

For more information about After Effects' third-party filters, see "Using Third-Party After Effects Filters," later in this chapter.

You'll find filters on the Browser's Effects tab or in the Effects menu. After installation, QuickTime effects and third-party After Effects filters are stored in separate bins within the main Video Filters bins.

For information on working with audio filters, see Chapter 12, "Audio Tools and Techniques."

To apply a filter to a clip:

1. *Do one of the following:*

- ◆ Drag the filter from the Browser's Effects tab and drop it on the clip in the Timeline (**Figure 16.1**).

- ◆ Select the clip in the Timeline, choose Effects > Video (or Audio) Filters, and make your filter selection from the submenu.

2. Position the playhead over a frame in the selected clip to see a preview of the effect in the Canvas (**Figure 16.2**).

✔ Tip

- ■ Many filters' default settings have no visible effect on a clip. You must make settings adjustments before you can detect a difference.

- ■ You must set your FCP real-time play-back setting to Unlimited RT to enable real-time playback of any third-party FXScript filters and transitions.

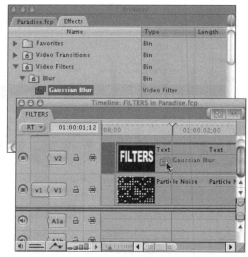

Figure 16.1 Drag the filter from the Effects tab and drop it on the clip in the Timeline.

Figure 16.2 Position the playhead over a frame in the filtered clip to see a preview of the effect in the Canvas.

Figure 16.3 Choose the Range Selection tool from the Tool palette.

Figure 16.4 Choose Effects > Video Filters; then select a filter from the submenu.

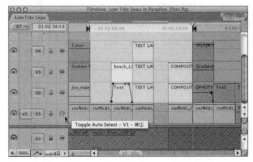

Figure 16.5 Auto-selected clips appear highlighted in the Timeline; In and Out points mark the boundaries of the selection. Disabling the Auto Select control on V1 will exclude V1 clips from the batch filter application. Make sure the Auto Select control is enabled on all tracks where you want the filter to be applied.

To apply a filter to a range of clips or part of a clip:

1. From the Tool palette, choose the Range Selection tool (**Figure 16.3**).

2. In the Timeline, drag to select whole or partial clips.

3. Choose Effects > Video (or Audio) Filters, and select a filter from the submenu (**Figure 16.4**).

   If you selected multiple clips, Final Cut Pro adds a separate copy of the filter to each clip.

4. Position the playhead over a frame in the selected clip range to see a preview of the effect in the Canvas.

To use Auto Select to apply a filter to multiple clips:

1. In the Timeline, set In and Out points at the boundaries of the section where you want to apply the filter.

2. Make sure the Auto Select control is enabled on all tracks where you want the filter to be applied; disable any tracks containing clips that you want to exclude from filtering (**Figure 16.5**).

3. Choose Effects > Video (or Audio) Filters and select a filter from the submenu. If you selected multiple clips, Final Cut Pro adds a separate copy of the filter to each clip between the In and Out points on tracks where Auto Select is enabled.

4. Position the playhead over a frame in the selected clip range to see a preview of the effect in the Canvas.

To adjust a filter:

1. In the Timeline, double-click a clip to which you've added a filter; it opens in the Viewer.

2. In the Viewer, click the Filters tab to access the filter's controls.

3. Configure the filter's settings (**Figure 16.6**). The items you can change vary according to the type of filter.

4. To see the changes you've made, use the arrow keys to move through the clip frame by frame, or try a low-quality real-time preview. To see the highest-quality playback, you must render the clip before you can play it with a video filter applied.

To disable a filter:

1. In the Timeline, double-click a clip to which you've added a filter; then select the clip's Filters tab.

2. Uncheck the box next to the filter's name on the Viewer's Filters tab.

   The filter is disabled but is still applied to the clip. To toggle it back on, recheck the box.

✔ Tips

- Final Cut Pro renders a clip's filters in the order they appear on the Filters tab. You can drag a filter up or down in the list to rearrange the filter order. Rendering order affects your final results.

- If you need more space to adjust sliders (or just to read the full name of a filter control), expand the width of the columns containing the effect controls on the Filters, Controls, and Motion tabs. Drag the column header separators to adjust column width (**Figure 16.7**).

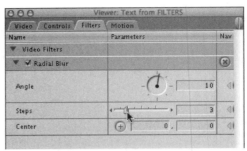

Figure 16.6 In the Viewer, adjust the filter's settings on the clip's Filters tab.

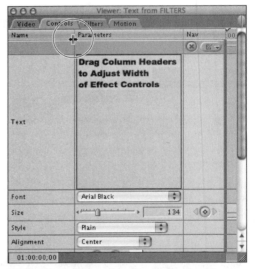

Figure 16.7 Drag the column headers on the Filters, Controls, and Motion tabs to adjust the width of the effect controls.

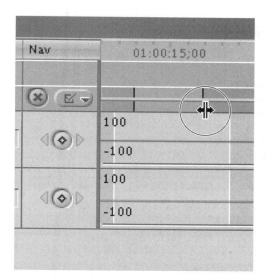

Figure 16.8 In the filter's keyframe graph, use the Arrow tool to drag the filter boundaries at set start and end points for a filter.

To adjust the position or duration of a filter in a clip:

Open the clip in the Viewer and click the Filters tab. In the filter's keyframe graph, locate the start and end points for the selected filter; then *do one of the following*:

◆ To set a filter's start and end points within a clip, use the Arrow tool to drag the filter boundaries (**Figure 16.8**). The default filter start and end points match the clip's In and Out points.

◆ Drag between the filter's start and end points to slip the position of the filter's duration within the clip.

To remove a filter:

To remove a filter from a clip, *do one of the following*:

◆ Select the filter in the Filters tab and press Delete.

◆ Control-click the filter and choose Cut from the shortcut menu.

◆ Select the filter and choose Edit > Clear.

Using keyframes to animate filters

You can use keyframes to animate filter settings over time. For more information, see "Using Keyframes" in Chapter 14.

Useful Filters

There's a boatload of filters in Final Cut Pro. Some of them do really useful and cool things that you might not normally associate with the idea of a filter.

Here's the rundown of a few interesting ones that you might have missed:

◆ **Flop:** This Perspective filter flip-flops the image horizontally, vertically, or in both directions at the same time. John Huston used this effect in his World War II documentary *The Battle of San Pietro* to keep the Allied forces heading right to left, and the Axis forces heading left to right, regardless of which direction they were actually moving during filming.

◆ **De-interlace:** This Video filter can improve the stability of still images by duplicating either of the two fields that make up a video frame. De-interlace is also useful for correcting jittery high-speed movement, if you can accept a slightly softened image quality. Try the Flicker options for the best control over the effect.

◆ **Timecode Print:** Two Video filters (Timecode Reader and Timecode Generator) that simplify making "window burns" (copies of your FCP sequence with visible timecode printed in the frame) for production outside of FCP or for client review copies. Nest a sequence, apply this effect, and render a quick dub for your music composer. If your Mac's processor is speedy enough, FCP's real-time previewing may allow you to make that dub without rendering the Timecode Print filter.

◆ **View Finder:** This Video filter simulates footage from security cameras, home cameras, or pre-production screen tests. Other filters in the Video group—**Blink, Strobe,** and **Image Stabilizer**—are also interesting and can be applied creatively. Check 'em out.

◆ **Sepia:** This Image Control filter tints the clip to an old-time, faded film color. Why use this filter when the Tint filter does that as well? Well, with Sepia, you can change the color in the same way as you can using the Tint filter, but you have the advantage of being able to tweak the contrast as well, which you can't do using the Tint filter.

◆ **Echo and Reverb:** These two Audio filters help make that pickup dialogue you recorded in your bedroom sound believable when you cut it into the scene you shot in the gymnasium.

◆ **Bad TV:** Horrible, degraded image quality you can control. Tons of fun.

◆ **Film Noise:** This QuickTime filter adds hair, scratches, dust, and the look of old film to your video. Lots of people skip the dust and scratches completely and use Film Noise just for a faded-color-film look that renders quickly. This is not, however, a filter that can be found on the Effects tab in the Browser. To use Film Noise, you have to export your clip as a QuickTime movie and access the filter as described in "To export a clip or sequence in another QuickTime format" in Chapter 19. Be sure to set your movie settings to match your audio and video sequence settings. Re-import your processed clip into your project and enjoy your film noise.

◆ **Joe's Filters:** Joe Maller's custom filters, originally written for Final Cut Pro, work just fine in Final Cut Pro 6. Demo versions of these filters are available online. Be sure to check out Joe's documentation for each filter, including the beautiful color illustrations of each filter at work; you can learn a lot about how filters work just by reading his descriptions. Highly recommended. www.joesfilters.com.

Figure 16.9 Select the clips you want to analyze, then Control-click in the Browser's SmoothCam column and choose Run Analysis from the shortcut menu.

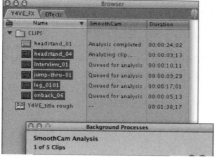

Figure 16.10 Final Cut Pro queues the selected clips, performing motion compensation analysis as a background process. FCP will analyze the entire length of the clip's media file.

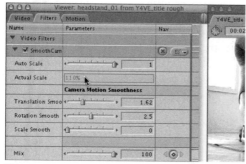

Figure 16.11 Once you've applied the SmoothCam filter, FCP uses the motion compensation analysis data to create a real-time preview of the corrected shot.

Using the SmoothCam Filter

The SmoothCam filter uses motion compensation to smooth out jerky jittery handheld shots and bumpy dolly moves. Unlike other FCP filters, the SmoothCam filter process has two parts. Clip analysis is a background process you can complete before you apply the SmoothCam filter. Final Cut Pro analyzes every pixel of every frame of your media file to calculate the motion compensation required. FCP will analyze the entire clip, not just the section marked by In and Out points—so shorter, discrete clips will be analyzed more quickly. Once clip analysis is complete, you can apply the SmoothCam filter and adjust the filter's parameters with real-time previewing.

To apply SmoothCam motion compensation to a clip:

1. In the Browser, select the clips you want to analyze, then Control-click in the SmoothCam column and choose Run Analysis from the shortcut menu (**Figure 16.9**).

   Final Cut Pro queues the selected clips and performs motion compensation analysis as a background process (**Figure 16.10**). You can continue to work in FCP during clip analysis.

2. When clip analysis is complete, select a clip and choose Effects > Video Filters > Video > SmoothCam to apply the filter.

   Using the clip's analysis data, Final Cut Pro creates a real-time preview of the smoothed shot using the filter's default settings (**Figure 16.11**). Review this real-time preview before making settings adjustments.

Using Color Correction Filters

Like editing, color correction is an invisible art. It's an essential part of post-production that can have a significant impact on a show, but it's not a high-profile part of the process. Final Cut Pro introduces an improved set of image-quality measurement and color correction tools that make it feasible to complete a broadcast-quality finished product without leaving the Desktop.

At the most basic level, you can use these tools to ensure that the video levels in your finished program don't exceed broadcast-legal limits. If the video in your program already looks good, careful color correction can make it look even better—if you have exposure problems or intercut shots that don't match, color correction can salvage your show. You can also use color correction tools to completely transform the look of your footage or to create an illusion—one example is "day for night," an old movie trick where scenes shot during the day are printed very dark to simulate night lighting.

This section serves as a brief overview of the tools and the basics of working with the Color Correction filter interface, but it does not delve into the complexities of color correction (there are entire books written on the subject). You should supplement your reading with "Color Correcting Clips" on page III-545 of Apple's *Final Cut Pro User Manual* PDF, a 69-page introduction to the principles of color correction and the full protocols governing the operation of Final Cut Pro's color correction tools. Be sure to use the full-color PDF version of the manual; any demonstration of color correction technique is severely handicapped when it's presented in grayscale. The PDF version of the manual is available from FCP's Help menu.

About Color: Final Cut Studio's Latest Addition

Color, the color grading application formerly known as Final Touch and recently acquired by Apple, is the most recent addition to Final Cut Studio's growing family of applications. Color combines more advanced and controllable color correction tools with compositing and motion tracking tools, offering greater bit depth, greater resolution, and integrated motion tracking mattes for specialized secondary color effects (now you can finally ace that magical purple horse galloping across the Highland moor). Like all applications in Final Cut Studio, Color is a power-hungry program: Apple recommends specific graphics cards, up to 4GB of RAM, and a couple of large displays for satisfactory Color performance.

A couple of caveats:

◆ Color's complex interface and operation requires some study and practice, so don't expect to be able to fire up the program at the last minute and get great-looking results.

◆ This is the first version of Color to be integrated into FCS, so you won't be surprised to find a few little glitches in the program. Check your favorite FCS message boards and Apple's online Support site for the latest gotchas and fixes.

Always Be Color Safe!

It's a fact of life: It's easy to produce video with colors and luminance levels that look great on your Macintosh, but look scary, overblown, and distorted on a home television set. With DV footage you shouldn't need to worry about color levels, but images created in the computer need to be created correctly. Many colors, including black, white, and quite a few reds, are considered to be outside the color-safe guidelines. While this may not matter so much if you are creating content for the Web, it will matter if you are intending your masterpiece to be premiered on broadcast or cable TV.

Although you can't adjust DV video levels as you're capturing, you can adjust your levels on previously captured video clips. Use the built-in vectorscope and waveform monitor (on the Video Scopes tab of the Tool Bench window) to check levels on your video output.

Marked on the waveform monitor are levels of IRE—a unit of luminance. DV video IRE levels can range from –10 to 110, but the NTSC legal limits (in the United States) are a strict 7.5 to 100 IRE.

It's easy to exceed NTSC broadcast limits for luminance and color intensity; Photoshop and other programs allow you to create images with colors and levels well outside the legal broadcast limits. You can use FCP's color correction tools to tone down your graphics after you import. See "Using the Broadcast Safe filter," later in this chapter.

Be sure to check your work on an external TV monitor as you proceed. The best way to get out of trouble is not to get in.

If your project is headed for national broadcast, you might want to re-create your edit at a professional post-production house for a proper online session, where all the technical demands of broadcast TV can be honored in style.

For more information on FCP's role in handling the conversion of digital video levels to analog video levels, see Apple's technical article "Final Cut Pro: About Luminance" (article 60864) at the Apple Web site: www.info.apple.com/kbnum/n60864.

About image-quality measurement tools

- **Video Scopes:** On the Video Scopes tab of the Tool Bench (**Figure 16.12**), you'll find FCP's four image-quality analysis tools: the Waveform Monitor, Vectorscope, Histogram, and Parade scope. You can use these tools to get objective numerical readings of the luminance and chrominance levels in your video. Use these readings to help fine-tune color match between clips. You can set the scope to display levels for the currently displayed frame in the Viewer or in the Canvas, or to switch automatically between the two. To learn more about using the video scopes, see Apple's FCP documentation.

- **Range Check feature:** The Range Check feature superimposes color-coded pulsating zebra stripes that flag those areas of your picture with luma or chroma values that approach or exceed broadcast-legal limits. Separate Range Check overlays are available for chroma and luma, and you can also choose to enable both. Range Check is very useful for making a quick assessment of the levels in your footage or for catching hot spots that are too small to be detected by the video scopes, which examine only 16 sampled lines from the video frame. As you color-correct your video, you can leave the Range Check overlay on to ensure that your color adjustments don't push your video levels over the legal limits.

✔ Tip

- Remember that the Range Check overlay status applies only to the single frame you're currently viewing. Luma and chroma levels vary from frame to frame. Spot-check multiple frames in clips you're concerned about, or apply the Broadcast Safe filter to control levels throughout the clip.

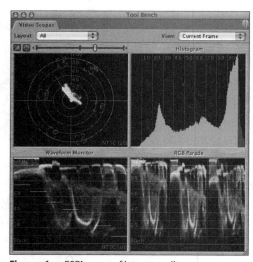

Figure 16.12 FCP's array of image-quality measurement tools are located in the Tool Bench window. Use these tools to get objective numerical readings of the luminance and chrominance levels in your video.

Figure 16.13 Choose View > Range Check; then make a submenu selection to check your clip for excess luma or chroma levels, or both.

USING COLOR CORRECTION FILTERS

Figure 16.14 Choose View > Range Check > Both, and the Range Check overlay will flag illegal-level areas for both luma and chroma with red zebra stripes. The yellow exclamation point icon indicates that the frame has illegal levels.

Figure 16.15 A green checkmark icon indicates that all luma and chroma levels in the frame are legal.

To turn on the Range Check overlay:

1. Select the Viewer or the Canvas.

2. Choose View > Range Check (**Figure 16.13**), and choose one of the following submenu items:

   ◆ **Excess Luma:** The Range Check overlay displays red zebra stripes on all areas with luminance levels above 100 percent, and green zebra stripes in areas with luminance levels from 90 to 100 percent. A yellow status icon is displayed on any clip with illegal luma levels. A green checkmark status icon displays on clips with legal levels. The in-range status icon appears when the clip's luma levels range from 90 to 100 percent but do not exceed 100 percent.

   ◆ **Excess Chroma:** The Range Check overlay displays red zebra stripes on all areas with illegal chroma levels. A yellow status icon is displayed on any clip with illegal chroma levels. A green checkmark indicates that all chroma in the picture is legal.

   ◆ **Both:** The Range Check overlay uses a yellow exclamation point status icon and flags illegal level areas for both luma and chroma with red zebra stripes (**Figure 16.14**). A green checkmark indicates that all luma and chroma levels in the frame are legal (**Figure 16.15**).

The Range Check overlay appears on the image area of the selected program window. Choose View > Range Check > Off to turn off the overlay.

The Color Correction filter suite

You'll find seven filters in FCP's Color Correction filter bin (**Figure 16.16**). Some of the filters are general-purpose color correction tools; others have special applications. It's common to use more than one filter type on a single color-corrected clip.

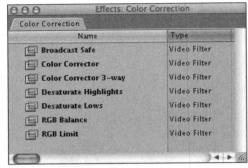

Figure 16.16 These seven filters make up FCP's color correction suite. Some, like the Color Corrector, are general-purpose color correction tools; others, like the Desaturate Highlights filter, have special uses.

- ◆ **Broadcast Safe:** This filter is designed to *clamp* (filter out) any illegal luma and chroma levels in your clip. See "Using the Broadcast Safe filter," later in this chapter.

- ◆ **Color Corrector:** This filter is for general-purpose color correction and offers both numerical controls and graphical onscreen controls. For more information, see "Anatomy of the Color Corrector tab," later in this chapter.

- ◆ **Color Corrector 3-way:** This filter is similar to the Color Corrector filter and has the same choice of controls. The 3-way filter features separate color balance adjustments for blacks, midtones, and whites, which makes precision color adjustments a bit easier.

- ◆ **Desaturate Highlights/Desaturate Lows:** These two filters (actually the same filter with two different default settings) are designed to solve a common color correction problem: altering or increasing the intensity of a color in your image without tinting the highlights or black areas of the image. These filters desaturate (reduce the chroma levels) in those areas of the image, keeping your whites and blacks pure.

- ◆ **RGB Balance:** This simple RGB color balance filter has separate highlight, midtone, and blacks controls for reds, greens, and blues.

- ◆ **RGB Limit:** Use this filter to set hard upper and lower limits for RGB values.

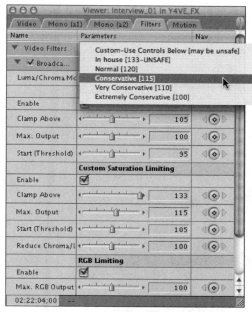

Figure 16.17 The Broadcast Safe filter offers a menu of presets designed to clamp illegal luma or chroma levels in your clip to broadcast-legal limits. The filter's default settings work fine in most cases.

Using the Broadcast Safe filter

The Broadcast Safe filter is a quick fix you can apply to any NTSC or PAL video in your program. The filter offers a menu of preset settings (**Figure 16.17**) designed to clamp any illegal luma or chroma levels in your clip to within legal limits. The default setting should work well for most clips, but if you want to tweak the settings yourself, you can choose the Custom setting, which enables the individual luma and chroma level controls. The filter displays NTSC or PAL broadcast-safe presets based on your sequence settings.

✔ Tips

- You can apply a single Broadcast Safe filter to your entire sequence by nesting the sequence inside a parent sequence before you apply the filter. To learn more about the care and feeding of nested sequences, see "Working with Multiple Sequences" in Chapter 4.

- Once you've applied the Broadcast Safe filter, your image may appear a little too dark and desaturated on your computer monitor; remember to reserve final judgment until you've scrutinized the picture on an external broadcast monitor.

Monitors and Color Correction

A properly calibrated broadcast video monitor is an essential tool for accurate color correction (and most other post-production tasks). Use the best broadcast video monitor you can afford. Follow the procedures outlined in "Using Color Bars for Video Calibration" (page III-540 of Apple's *Final Cut Pro User Manual* PDF) before you color-correct your first clip. You should not color-correct based on the color you see in the image areas of the Viewer or the Canvas.

Anatomy of the Color Corrector tab

The Color Corrector and Color Corrector 3-way filters—two of the six filters available in FCP's Color Correction filter bin—feature graphical onscreen controls in addition to the standard numeric controls found on the Filters tab of the Viewer. The visual controls appear on their own Viewer tab after you apply the Color Corrector filter (**Figure 16.18**).

✔ Tip

■ Position the pointer over a filter control in the interface to display a tooltip with the name of the control and its keyboard shortcut equivalent.

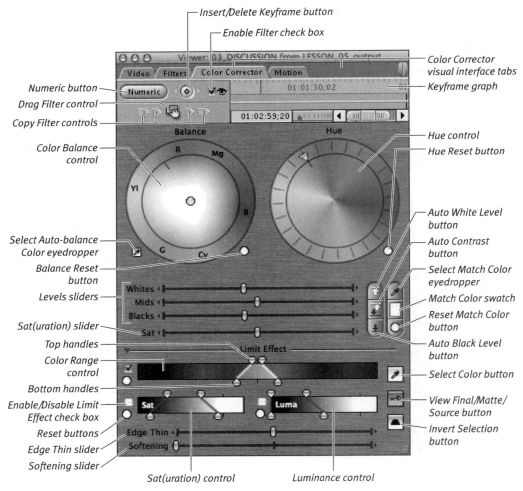

Figure 16.18 The Color Corrector filter's visual controls appear on their own tab in the Viewer.

The top section of the tab contains clip controls for keyframing the color correction filter and for copying the filter's settings to other clips in your sequence.

◆ **Color Corrector Viewer tabs:** The filter's visual controls appear on their own Viewer tab. If you have multiple copies of the Color Corrector filter applied to the clip, a separate numbered tab appears for each copy.

◆ **Numeric button:** Click this button to switch to the filter's numeric controls on the Filters tab.

◆ **Insert/Delete Keyframe button:** Click to insert a keyframe across all color correction settings. Individual settings can be keyframed only on the Filters tab, in the Color Corrector filter's standard control interface.

◆ **Enable Filter check box:** Check to enable this filter. Uncheck to disable the filter.

◆ **Keyframe graph:** Displays only the keyframes you set across all color correction settings.

◆ **Copy Filter controls:** The Copy Filter feature (**Figure 16.19**) is one of the secret weapons of the Color Corrector filter. Once you have color-corrected a representative shot in your sequence to your satisfaction, you can use the Copy Filter controls to copy your filter's settings to other clips in your sequence with a single mouse click.

◆ **Copy from 2nd Clip Back:** Copies settings from the Color Corrector filter that is applied two clips upstream from the currently selected clip, and pastes the settings into this copy of the Color Corrector filter, replacing any previously applied settings. If the source filter's settings have been keyframed, the pasted values are derived from the last keyframe. If the source clip has no color correction filter, this control is dimmed.

◆ **Copy from 1st Clip Back:** Copies settings from the Color Corrector filter that is applied to the first clip upstream from the currently selected clip, and pastes the settings into this copy of the Color Corrector filter, replacing any previously applied settings. If the source filter's settings have been keyframed, the pasted values are derived from the last keyframe. If the source clip has no color correction filter, this control is dimmed.

continues on next page

Figure 16.19 Use the Copy Filter controls to copy your filter settings to other clips in your sequence with a single mouse click.

◆ **Copy to 1st Clip Forward:** Copies the settings of this Color Corrector filter into the next clip downstream in your sequence. If this filter is keyframed, the pasted values are derived from the last keyframe. If no Color Corrector filter is present on the destination clip, FCP applies one automatically.

◆ **Copy to 2nd Clip Forward:** Copies the settings of this Color Corrector filter into the clip located two clips downstream in your sequence. If this filter is keyframed, the pasted values are derived from the last keyframe. If no Color Corrector filter is present on the destination clip, FCP applies one automatically.

◆ **Drag Filter control:** Drag this button to another Timeline clip to copy the current Color Corrector filter and its settings into that clip.

The tab's center section contains the filter's Color Balance controls and Level and Saturation controls, your everyday color balance tools.

◆ **Color Balance control:** Use the Balance control like a virtual trackball control. Click the dot at the center of the control and drag it across the circular face of the control to adjust the color balance of your clip. The center of the circle represents pure white; drag farther from the center to increase the saturation of your color shift.

The positioning of the color spectrum values around the circular face of the Color Balance control is mapped to correspond to each color's position (or angle) in the circular readout of the vectorscope, so that a move in any direction on the Color Balance control results in a corresponding shift in the vectorscope readout.

Hold down the Shift key while dragging to constrain the angle of the adjustment—a useful technique for adjusting the intensity of a color without shifting its hue.

Hold down the Command key while dragging to "gear up" the control, increasing the magnitude of the color balance adjustments in response to your mouse movements. (This is the opposite of the Command-drag "gear down" modifier implemented elsewhere in FCP, which enables precision adjustments.)

◆ **Select Auto-balance Color eyedropper:** Click the eyedropper icon; then click on a color in your image you'd like to match to the color you selected with the Hue Match controls. For more information, see "Hue Match controls," later in this section.

◆ **Balance Reset button:** Click to reset the Balance control to its default settings. Shift-click the button to reset the Levels and Sat(uration) sliders to their default values as well.

◆ **Hue control:** Click the outer edge of the Hue control's circular face and rotate the dial to make an overall adjustment to the clip's hue.

◆ **Hue Reset button:** Click to reset the Hue control to its default settings. Shift-click the button to reset the Levels and Sat(uration) sliders to their default values as well.

◆ **Levels sliders:** Use these sliders to make overall adjustments to the luminance levels in your clip. Click the tiny arrow at either end of a slider to nudge the value by a single increment.

   ◆ **Whites slider:** Use the slider to adjust the clip's maximum white level.

   ◆ **Mids slider:** Use the slider to adjust just the midtones in the clip, leaving any black or white areas untouched.

   ◆ **Blacks slider:** Use the slider to adjust the clip's minimum black level.

◆ **Sat(uration) slider:** Move this slider to make overall adjustments to the color saturation levels in your clip. Click the tiny arrow at either end of the slider to nudge the value by single increments. Moving the slider all the way to the left removes all color from the clip, leaving a grayscale image. Moving the slider all the way to the right will almost certainly push your color values into distortion, so use caution and check your work on your broadcast video monitor.

◆ **Auto White Level button:** Click to find the maximum white level in the current frame and automatically adjust the Whites slider to set the maximum white level.

◆ **Auto Contrast button:** Click to set Auto black and Auto white levels in a single operation.

◆ **Auto Black Level button:** Click to find the maximum black level in the current frame and automatically adjust the Blacks slider to set the maximum black level.

◆ **Hue Match controls:** Hue Match controls extend the function of the auto-white balance controls, allowing you to adjust any color in your image to match the color you've selected as the Match Color. For more information, see "Hue Matching Controls in the Color Corrector Filter" on page III-574 of Apple's *Final Cut Pro User Manual* PDF.

   ◆ **Select Match Color:** Use the eyedropper to select the color hue you want to match.

   ◆ **Match Color:** This swatch displays the color you've selected as the auto-balance target color.

   ◆ **Reset Match Color:** Click to set the Match Color to white, the default setting.

USING COLOR CORRECTION FILTERS

✔ Tip

■ To use Hue Match as an auto-white balance tool, click the Reset Match Color button to set the tool to white, its default setting. Next, use the Select Auto-balance Color eyedropper icon to click on a highlight in your image you'd like to match to white. The Hue Match control analyzes the hue value of the selected pixel, and then automatically adjusts the overall color balance of the image; for example, selecting a light-green highlight will result in an overall color shift toward magenta to correct the green highlight to neutral white.

The Limit Effect section at the bottom of the interface contains color key tools you can use to restrict your adjustments to a specified color, saturation, or luma range.

◆ **Enable/Disable Limit Effect check boxes:** Check the boxes to include the settings of the Color Range, Luma, or Saturation controls in the criteria used to calculate the color key matte that limits the effect of the filter's color adjustment. Uncheck to exclude a control from the calculation.

◆ **Reset buttons:** Click to restore a control's default values.

◆ **Color Range control:** Adjust the handles to define the target color range you want to adjust.

   ◆ **Top handles:** Define the size of the target color range.

   ◆ **Bottom handles:** Define the tolerance of the target color range.

   ◆ **Color Gradient:** Drag left or right on the Color Range control's gradient to shift the hue of the target color range by moving all four handles simultaneously.

◆ **Sat(uration) control:** Adjust the handles to define which color saturation levels fall within the target range.

◆ **Luminance control:** Adjust the handles to define which luminance levels fall within the target range.

◆ **Select Color button:** Click the Select Color eyedropper button; then click the color in your image that you want to include in your target range. Shift-click the image to add colors to your selection and widen the target range.

◆ **View Final/Matte/Source button:** Click to toggle through this button's three states:

   ◆ **Final:** The clip's image shows the final result of your color key effect. This is the button's default state.

   ◆ **Matte:** The clip's image area shows the image areas you've selected for your color key as a grayscale image.

   ◆ **Source:** The clip's image area shows the current frame before the effect is applied.

◆ **Invert Selection button:** Click to invert the areas selected for the color key.

◆ **Edge Thin slider:** Controls the size of the color key area selected by the Limit Effect controls. Move the slider to adjust the width of the selected area's border.

◆ **Softening slider:** Feather the edge of the color key selection to soften the transition between the selected area and the rest of the image.

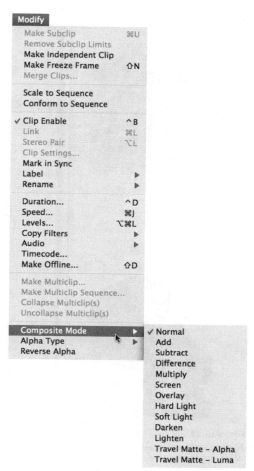

Figure 16.20 Choose Modify > Composite Mode, and then select a Composite mode from the submenu. You can also access Composite modes from a Timeline clip's shortcut menu.

Compositing

Compositing can be any process that combines two or more image layers to create an effect. A compositing process can also include filters and motion that have been applied to modify individual layers or to modify the composited image.

Setting Composite mode

A Composite mode is an algorithm, a mathematical formula that controls the way the colors in a clip combine with the clip colors in underlying video layers.

All compositing happens from the top down; the highest-numbered track's image sits on the front plane and obscures the image on a track beneath it, unless the foreground image is made transparent. Each clip's opacity setting influences the final effect of the Composite mode.

For a complete list of Final Cut Pro's Composite modes, see "Composite Modes in Final Cut Pro" on page III-396 of Apple's *Final Cut Pro User Manual* PDF.

To set the Composite mode for a clip:

◆ Select the clip in the Timeline, then *do one of the following:*

　◆ Choose Modify > Composite Mode; then select a Composite mode from the submenu (**Figure 16.20**).

　◆ Control-click the clip in the Timeline, and then select a Composite mode from the submenu.

COMPOSITING

531

Using alpha channels

An RGB image is composed of three 8-bit grayscale images—the red, green, and blue color channels—that express color information as a gray scale: 256 brightness values (ranging from 0 for black to 255 for white), plus an alpha channel. An alpha channel is a fourth 8-bit channel that can be assigned to an RGB image to track which areas of the image are transparent.

Figures 16.21, 16.22, and **16.23** illustrate how an alpha channel can be manipulated to mask selected areas in an image.

Figure 16.21 A still graphics image.

Figure 16.22 The image's alpha channel. With the alpha channel set to Straight, the white area will be interpreted as transparent.

Figure 16.23 The graphics frame superimposed over video. With the frame's alpha channel set to Straight, the white areas in the alpha channel shown in Figure 16.19 are made transparent here, allowing the video background to show through.

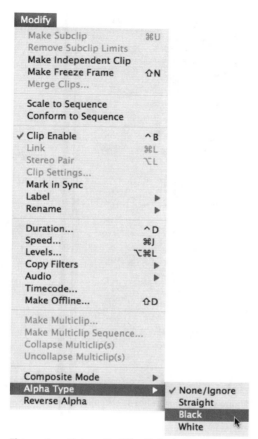

Figure 16.24 Choose Modify > Alpha Type; then select a different alpha channel type from the submenu.

Alpha channels are useful critters with a variety of applications in digital imaging. Final Cut Pro video clips automatically have alpha channels assigned to them; it's the alpha channel that's being manipulated when you adjust the opacity of a clip or apply a key or matte filter.

◆ When you import an image that has an alpha channel, Final Cut Pro interprets the clip's alpha channel and sets it to Straight, Black, or White (corresponding to the background setting for the clip at the time the clip was created).

◆ When you place a clip in a sequence, Final Cut Pro automatically makes the alpha channel area transparent. You can override the automatic setting by modifying the alpha channel type.

◆ You can reverse an alpha channel if you want to invert the transparency of an image, or you can choose to ignore the clip's alpha channel altogether.

To view or modify a clip's alpha channel type:

1. Select the clip.

2. Choose Modify > Alpha Type, and select a different alpha channel type from the submenu (**Figure 16.24**).

✔ Tip

■ DV clips do not retain their alpha channel information if you export them in a DV format. If you want to save a clip's alpha channel when you export, use the Animation codec, set to Millions of Colors+. If you're exporting FCP elements for processing in a digital effects creation program such as Adobe After Effects, this is the way to go. Use the Animation codec again when you export from After Effects.

Working with Mattes

Mattes are filters that you shape to define which areas of opaque video clips are to be made transparent during compositing. For example, you could use a circular matte to isolate a clock face from its background, or you could create a matte in the shape of a keyhole to simulate peeking through a key-hole in a door.

Final Cut Pro offers many types of matte filters (**Figure 16.25**). "Garbage mattes" are used to quickly rough out large areas of the frame. A *key* is a type of matte that uses a clip's color or luminance information to determine which opaque areas will be made transparent (bluescreen effects are created with color key mattes set to make blue areas transparent). You can combine layers of dif-ferent types of mattes to create very complex composite shapes.

To apply a matte:

1. *Do one of the following:*
   - ◆ Drag the Key or Matte filter from the Browser's Effects tab and drop it on the clip in the Timeline.
   - ◆ Select the clip in the Timeline, choose Effects > Video Filters; then select a filter from the Key or Matte submenu.

2. Position the playhead over a frame in the selected clip to see a preview of the effect in the Canvas.

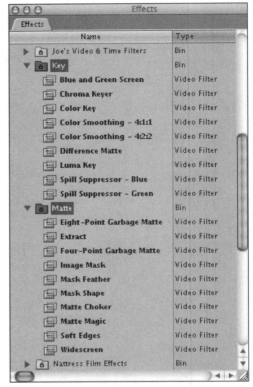

Figure 16.25 Final Cut Pro offers a toolbox full of special-purpose matte and key filters. When you create multi-layer compositions, use these filters to mask out portions of the frame.

Figure 16.26 Drag your background clip to track V1.

Figure 16.27 Drag your matte clip to track V2. The white areas in this clip will define the opaque areas of the foreground clip.

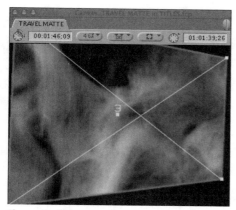

Figure 16.28 Place your foreground clip on track V3.

Travel mattes

A travel matte allows one video clip to play through another. The alpha information in a third clip is used as a matte that defines the transparent and opaque areas of the composited image.

When you create a travel matte effect, there are usually three video tracks involved; this is sometimes called a "matte sandwich." The background clip is placed on V1, or the lowest video track available. The matte clip, preferably a high-contrast, grayscale motion clip or still image, goes on the video track just above the background clip, on V2; and the foreground clip sits on V3, or the video track above the matte clip. A Composite mode specifically for creating travel mattes, called Travel Matte – Luma, is applied to the foreground clip. If the matte clip is placed on video track V1 without a background clip, then the background is automatically black.

To create a travel matte:

1. In the Timeline, drag your background clip (**Figure 16.26**) to V1.

2. Drag the clip selected to be the matte clip (**Figure 16.27**) to V2.

3. Drag your foreground clip (**Figure 16.28**) to V3.

4. To establish the travel matte, select the foreground clip on V3 (**Figure 16.29**) and choose Modify > Composite Mode > Travel Matte – Luma.

The completed travel matte effect (**Figure 16.30**) uses the matte clip's luminance (or grayscale) levels as the mask. The matte clip's black area creates the shape of the foreground clip's transparent areas, revealing the background clip video. The matte clip's white area creates the shape of the foreground clip's opaque areas—that's where you see the foreground clip's video.

✔ Tips

■ After you composite your travel matte, you can refine the effect by adjusting the matte clip's brightness and contrast.

■ You can apply animated filters and effects, as well as any other standard clip motion, to the travel matte in V2 for some very interesting looks.

■ Play with Edge Feather and Edge Thin to soften the halo effect you might find around your matted objects when working with color keys.

■ DV video is not the best video format for creating effects that require critical color key mattes, for example, blue or green-screen effects. DV compression throws out too much color information to give you the best control over edges.

Figure 16.29 To composite the travel matte, select the foreground clip on V3 and choose Modify > Composite Mode > Travel Matte – Luma. The foreground clip on V3 is now composited with the matte clip on V2.

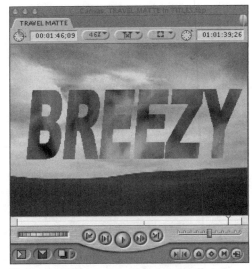

Figure 16.30 The completed travel matte effect.

Using Third-Party After Effects Filters

Final Cut Pro is compatible with many of the Adobe After Effects third-party image filter plugins. The standard plugins that come with After Effects, however, are not compatible with Final Cut Pro. Once you've installed them, After Effects–compatible plugins will appear in the Video Filters section of the Effects menu and can be used just like any other Final Cut Pro filter.

There may be some trial and error involved in determining which third-party filters will work and weeding out the ones that don't. Make sure you have the latest versions of the filters installed—check the Final Cut Pro Web site at www.apple.com/finalcutpro/ for a current list of compatible filters.

To install third-party video filters:

1. In the Finder, locate and open the After Effects Plugins folder; then *do one of the following:*

   ◆ Duplicate the third-party After Effects filters and then drag the copies to FCP's Plugins folder.

   ◆ Create aliases of your third-party filters' folders and then move the aliases to the Plugins folder.

   ◆ Create aliases of individual third-party filters and move them to the Plugins folder.

2. If any of your third-party filters requires a hardware key or dongle, refer to the filter's installation instructions.

3. Launch Final Cut Pro.

4. Choose Effects > Video Filters > AE Effects; then test your third-party filters.

5. Remove the individual files or aliases of any incompatible filters from your Plugins folder, and contact the manufacturer for details about compatibility with Final Cut Pro.

✔ Tip

■ Save your work before using a third-party filter for the first time. Some filters may surprise you with a system crash that will require you to restart Final Cut Pro.

FCP Protocol: Third-Party After Effects Filters

Your third-party After Effects filters may not operate in Final Cut Pro and After Effects in exactly the same way. It's important to note differences in how the two programs use the same filter plugin.

◆ Final Cut Pro assigns the (x,y) origin point of a filter to the center of a clip, whereas After Effects assigns the origin point to the upper-left corner.

◆ Custom interfaces for third-party filters are supported on the Filters tab of the Viewer.

◆ When you use After Effects filters in FCP, never forget that After Effects filters render only in RGB color space. FCP's default is to use the YUV (YCrCb) color space when rendering. What does this all mean? For more information, see "RGB or YcrCb: Choosing a Color Space" in Chapter 3.

TITLES AND GENERATORS

Generators are a class of effects that create (or *generate*) new video information rather than modify existing video. After you have generated it by rendering, a generated clip can be used just like any other clip; you can even adjust the playback speed of a generator clip. Text is a high-profile member of the generator class of effects; using the text generator to produce titles is covered later in this chapter.

Final Cut Pro's generators include the following:

◆ Bars and Tone, which generates HD, NTSC or PAL color bars and includes a 1 kHz audio tone with an adjustable level.

◆ More Bars & Signals, a suite of specialized color bar patterns and gradients.

◆ Matte, which generates solid, single-color clips.

◆ Render, a grab bag of customizable patterns, color gradients, and different types of "noise."

◆ Shape, which generates an opaque geometric shape on a black background. You can scale or color the shape.

◆ Slug, which generates solid black frames and silent audio. (There are no controls for this effect.)

◆ Text, which generates simple titles using TrueType fonts loaded in your system.

◆ Title 3D and Title Crawl, two text generators from third-party developer Boris, offer much more precise control over title text, such as individual letter control over kerning. See "Creating titles with Boris Calligraphy," later in this chapter.

◆ Vector Shape and Text Scrambler, two effect generators from Boris.

To add a generator to a sequence:

1. In the Viewer, choose an item from the Generators pop-up menu in the lower-right corner (**Figure 17.1**).

   The generator effect is loaded into the Viewer as an unrendered clip.

2. Click the Controls tab to access the generator controls.

3. Adjust the generator's controls (**Figure 17.2**); then click the Video tab to view the generator clip in the Viewer.

4. Edit the generator into your sequence just as you would a clip.

5. Render your generated clip. You may need to render it before you can play it back. Select the clip; then choose Sequence > Render Selection.

✔ Tips

■ A small but helpful shortcut: Hold down the Command and Option keys as you drag your generator clip into the Timeline. The sequence copy of the generator will open automatically in the Viewer with its Controls tab active. FYI: Don't press the keys until you've started the dragging or you'll drag the Viewer window instead of the generator clip.

■ When you are configuring settings for a generator clip, it's much easier to see what you're doing if you drag the generator clip's Controls tab out of the Viewer window first. Now you can view the generator image on the Viewer's Video tab as you configure the settings on the Controls tab.

To edit a generator in a sequence:

1. Double-click the generator clip in the Timeline to open it in the Viewer.

2. Click the Controls tab; then make your adjustments.

Figure 17.1 Choose a generator from the Generators pop-up menu in the lower-right corner of the Viewer window.

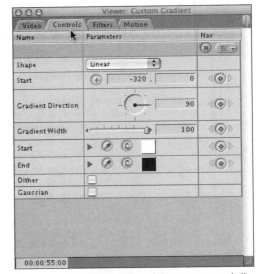

Figure 17.2 Adjust the settings for your generated clip on the clip's Controls tab.

Always Be Title Safe!

Every TV set is different: different colors, different screen geometries, different projection skews—never the same color, never the same combinations. Since even the middle area of the screen is not reliably centered (especially on home sets!), it's important to keep your text and graphic elements within a screen area that television engineers call *title safe*.

With the Title Safe overlay on, two boxes are superimposed on your clip—the inside border outlines the Title Safe boundary. Keep your graphic elements inside this box, and the edges won't get cropped off, even on consumer TVs. The slightly larger box surrounding the Title Safe boundary is known as the Action Safe boundary. Any visual elements critical to your project should occur within the Action Safe region. You should check Title Safe boundaries on all graphic elements before you invest too much time on a layout. For more information, see "Viewing Title Safe and Action Safe boundaries" in Chapter 8.

Title Safe and Action Safe areas apply only to program material displayed on a TV (both NTSC and PAL). If you plan to show your FCP project on the Web or via some other computer-based format, remember that Web-based video displays the entire frame, so check the edges for unexpected surprises—microphones, shadows, dolly grips, and so on. The same caveats apply if you're compositing a Picture in Picture (PiP) effect—every pixel in your frame is included.

Particle Noise = Generator Fun

When you're stuck for a way to add a little flash and color to a title sequence, load up Particle Noise. This generator is a ready source of animated textured backgrounds that range from serene (**Figure 17.3**) to trippy (**Figure 17.4**). Remember, you can stack multiple copies in layers, apply filters, and animate generators with motion keyframes. Now your only problem is how to stop fooling with Particle Noise and finish your title sequence.

Figure 17.3 The Particle Noise generator in a misty mood.

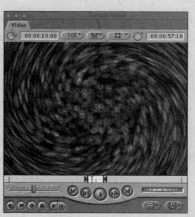

Figure 17.4 Make trippy animated backgrounds in seconds with the Particle Noise generator and the Whirlpool distortion filter.

About LiveType 2

Who says you can't get a free lunch? LiveType 2 (**Figure 17.5**) is an amazing animated title generator that's bundled into the FCP suite of applications.

◆ You can create customized animated fonts, objects, and textures for importing into your FCP project.

◆ LiveType offers a library of animated LiveFonts, along with hundreds of pre-set combinations of fonts and backgrounds.

LiveType 2, the latest version of LiveType, is tightly integrated with Final Cut Pro:

◆ You can drag a LiveType project directly into FCP's Browser, and work with it just as you would a clip.

◆ You can keep a LiveType project open in both FCP and LiveType at the same time.

◆ LiveType title settings can only be adjusted inside LiveType, but you can render your LiveType project file directly in Final Cut Pro; there's no need to render out a LiveType element before importing it into FCP.

It would take another Visual QuickPro Guide to explore all of LiveType's possibilities, so instead, head for the file called *LiveType User Manual* PDF found in the Documentation folder on your Final Cut Pro application DVD.

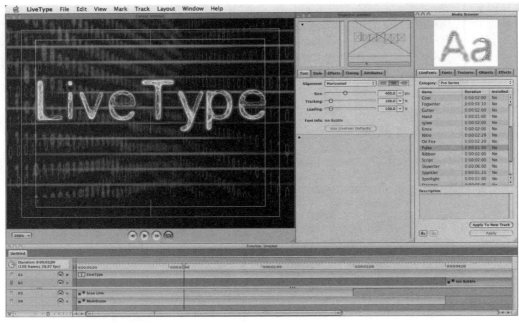

Figure 17.5 LiveType's main interface.

Figure 17.6 Six text generator options are available from the Generators pop-up menu's Text submenu in the Viewer window.

Complex Text: Other Options

If you need to build more complex text elements, your best bet, outside of LiveType, is to use Title 3D and Title Crawl, the (free) Boris Calligraphy text generator plugins that are included on your Final Cut Pro DVD. These third-party text generators offer a number of additional titling features you can use within FCP. For more information, see "Creating titles with Boris Calligraphy," later in this chapter.

Here's another option: Create your text outside of FCP in a professional graphics program, such as Adobe Photoshop, Illustrator, or After Effects, and then import the text elements as motion clips.

Advanced third-party plugins, such as Boris Red, or Graffiti, are all-in-one solutions that allow you to create complex elements while remaining within FCP.

Generating Text

Use text generators to create text elements and title screens in Final Cut Pro. A text generator can create titles using any TrueType font currently loaded in your System Folder. You can specify text size, style, color, tracking, and kerning.

Final Cut Pro offers six built-in text generators, which appear in the Text submenu of the Viewer's Generators pop-up menu (**Figure 17.6**):

- ◆ **Text:** Generates static text in a single size and style. This option allows carriage returns.

- ◆ **Lower 3rd:** Generates two lines of static text. Each line has separate controls for font, style, and size. The Lower 3rd generator is designed to create the standard titles used to identify interview subjects in news and documentary programs.

- ◆ **Crawl:** Generates a single line of animated text that scrolls across the screen horizontally. Crawl speed is determined by the duration of the clip—a longer clip duration results in a slower crawl speed.

- ◆ **Outline Text:** Generates static text with an adjustable outline stroke and background matte. You can also matte graphics into the text, outline, or background elements.

- ◆ **Scrolling Text:** Generates animated text that scrolls up or down the screen vertically. A longer clip duration results in a slower scrolling speed. Scrolling text allows carriage returns.

- ◆ **Typewriter:** Generates animated text that appears on the screen one letter at a time, as if typed.

These built-in generators are the simplest means of adding text to your sequences, but there are some limitations: Although text generators offer extensive control over the font, size, style, and positioning of text, with the exception of the Lower 3rd generator, you're limited to a single font per text generator.

Final Cut Pro also comes with two optional, third-party plugin text generators: Boris Title 3D and Title Crawl. These generators allow you to use as many fonts as you want (and probably more than you should); fancy text fanciers should read "Creating titles with Boris Calligraphy," later in this chapter, for more details.

You can edit a text generator clip into a sequence in the Timeline and apply effects, just as with other clips. You can also animate static text by using keyframes to make dynamic adjustments to a text generator clip's motion properties.

Your animation applies to all text in the generator—you cannot control individual letters, words, or sentences.

✔ Tip

- The simplest way to fade titles in and out is to keyframe opacity at the head and tail of the text generator clip. If you're building a title sequence, you can copy and paste just the opacity attribute to ensure a consistent look.

Using Generator Favorites

If you have a big stack of title or text screens to produce, this assembly-line production technique may help:

1. To produce a title template, create a standard text generator that specifies all basic formatting: font, size, color, position, and so on. Save it as a Favorite Effect. (Generator Favorites appear only in the Generators pop-up menu.)

2. Choose File > Open, and open a text document in a new window that contains all your title copy.

3. Select your template generator from the Favorites submenu of the Generators pop-up menu.

4. Copy and paste the copy for each title from the text window to the Text field in the template text generator, then add it to your sequence.

5. Repeat steps 3 and 4 until you've banged out all those titles.

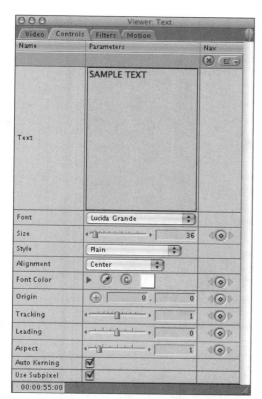

Figure 17.7 Style your text generator on the Viewer's Controls tab.

Text generator options checklist

On the Controls tab, you can specify the following text control settings (**Figure 17.7**):

◆ **Text:** Enter your text in this field, or cut and paste from a word-processing program.

◆ **Font:** Choose a font from this pop-up menu.

◆ **Size:** Use the slider or enter a point size for your type.

◆ **Style:** Choose a font style (Plain, Bold, Italic, and so on) from this pop-up menu.

◆ **Alignment:** Choose Center, Left, or Right alignment from this pop-up menu.

◆ **Font Color:** Click the expansion triangle to reveal the full set of color controls; then *do one of the following:*

　◆ Drag the hue, saturation, and brightness sliders to new values.

　◆ Enter color values numerically in the text fields.

　◆ Select the eyedropper and click the Canvas to sample a color.

　◆ Click the color swatch and use one of the color pickers to select a color.

◆ **Origin:** Click the Point Select (+) button (located to the left of the Origin value field), and then specify new coordinates for your text's origin point relative to the frame by clicking the new Origin location in the Canvas or on the Video tab of the Viewer. Animating the Origin point (rather than the Center point) of your text allows you to position your text at a starting point outside your frame.

◆ **Tracking:** Use the slider or enter a value to specify the spacing between letters.

continues on next page

FCP 3 Projects in FCP 6: Your Text May Vary

If you're working on a project that originated in Final Cut Pro 3, you may find that your text tracking has changed, and your titles appear narrower or wider than they did in FCP 3. Check your work before you output.

- **Leading:** Use the slider or enter a value to specify the spacing between lines of text.

- **Aspect:** Use the slider or enter a value to specify the height:width proportion of your selected font.

- **Auto Kerning:** Check the box to enable automatic adjustment of the spacing between individual letters.

- **Use Subpixel:** Check the box to enable subpixel accuracy in your rendered text generator. Subpixel rendering takes longer.

To generate a basic title screen:

1. To generate a title screen, *do one of the following:*

   - From the Generators pop-up menu in the lower right of the Viewer window, choose Text > Text.

   - On the Browser's Effects tab, choose Text from the Video Generators bin (**Figure 17.8**).

   The Text generator appears in the Viewer.

2. In the Viewer, click the Controls tab to access the generator's controls; then specify your text control settings as outlined in the previous section, "Text generator options checklist" (**Figure 17.9**).

   Although you can use keyframes to animate parameters such as size, origin point, colors, and tracking, you can specify only one font per text generator.

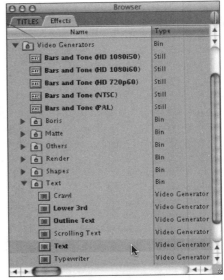

Figure 17.8 Choose the Text generator from the Video Generators bin in the Effects tab of the Browser window.

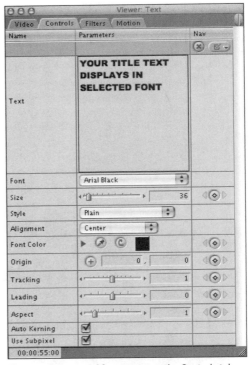

Figure 17.9 Enter and format text on the Controls tab.

Figure 17.10 Drop the text clip on the Superimpose area of the edit overlay. A Superimpose edit automatically places your text clip on a new Timeline track above the target track, starting at the sequence In point.

3. Click back to the Viewer's Video tab, and edit the text clip into your sequence in the Timeline. If you want to superimpose your text over video, choose the Superimpose edit type when you perform your edit (**Figure 17.10**).

You can edit, filter, and animate text clips as you would any other video element.

GENERATING TEXT

Tips for Better-Looking Titles

◆ Always check your type on an actual television monitor. (If you are outputting for home viewing on videotape, preferably test it on the absolute worst television set and VCR you can find in the nearest back-alley or junkyard.)

◆ Text should be larger than 24 points if you want it to be legible on TV.

◆ Black-and-white titles will never look their best if you use pure white and pure black; these extreme values exceed DV video's capacity to handle contrast. Try using a 10% gray over 90% black. (Compare the results on your video monitor with a title composed using pure white over pure black.) The same principle applies to color titles; using pure red, green, or blue will produce that "bad, late-night infomercial" look you are probably trying to avoid.

◆ When you superimpose a solid color title over production video, try setting the title's opacity to 90%.

◆ Don't forget the simple drop-shadow effect found on the Motion tab of any clip. With some tweaks, you can create a professional-quality drop shadow that really pops your title out from any background.

Using Animated Text Generators

Final Cut Pro offers three animated text generators: Scrolling Text, Crawl, and Typewriter. These generators offer the font styling and positioning controls of the static text generators, plus simple animation routines built into the generator. You set up the animation on the text generator's Controls tab.

Like the other parameters on the generator's Controls tab, the animation controls can be keyframed to change over time, but you don't need to use keyframes at all to throw together a simple scroll, crawl, or typewriter title effect.

Because these animated titles typically start offscreen, you will not see any text onscreen if your playhead is parked at the beginning or end of the clip. You have to scrub the playhead through the clip to see how your animated title is shaping up.

Creating scrolls

Scrolls are most often found as credit sequences at the end of a show (or at the beginning of *Star Wars* parodies). Scrolling text displays a lot of information in a little time, but take care not to roll your text too quickly. If you set your scroll speed too high, the titles will stutter (they won't appear to scroll smoothly), and no one will be able to read them.

There are several ways to create the scrolling graphic elements. The easiest is to use the Scrolling Text generator found in the Video Generator list, but if you plan to use multiple fonts or specialized tracking, sizing, and kerning, then your best bet is to use the free Boris Calligraphy Title Crawl text generator plugin found on your Final Cut Pro DVD. See "Creating titles with Boris Calligraphy," later in this chapter.

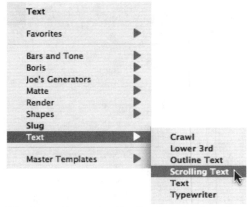

Figure 17.11 Choose Scrolling Text from the Viewer's Generators pop-up menu.

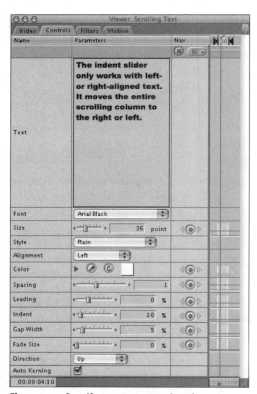

Figure 17.12 Specify your text control settings as outlined in the section "Text generator options checklist."

To generate a scrolling text title:

1. *Do one of the following:*

   ◆ From the Generators pop-up menu in the lower right of the Viewer window, choose Scrolling Text (**Figure 17.11**).

   ◆ On the Browser's Effects tab, choose Scrolling Text from the Video Generators bin.

   The Scrolling Text generator appears in the Viewer.

2. In the Viewer, click the Controls tab to access the generator's controls; then specify your text control settings as outlined earlier in this chapter, in the section "Text generator options checklist" (**Figure 17.12**).

3. You can also specify any of the following scrolling text parameters:

   ◆ **Spacing:** Use the slider or enter a value to specify the spacing between letters (as with Tracking).

   ◆ **Leading:** Use the slider or enter a value to specify the spacing between lines of text.

   ◆ **Indent:** Use the slider or enter a value to set the x-axis (left-right) positioning of the scroll's aligned edge, expressed as a percentage of the screen. Indent is enabled only for left- or right-aligned scrolls. The title-safe area begins inside 10% of the screen.

   ◆ **Gap Width:** Use the slider or enter a value to specify the width of the gap between any two text entries separated by an asterisk (*).

◆ **Fade Size:** Use the slider or enter a value to set the vertical display area of your scrolling text, expressed as a percentage of the screen. The scrolling text will fade in as it enters (and fade out as it exits) the vertical display area you specify.

◆ **Direction:** Choose Up or Down from this pop-up menu to specify the direction in which the generated text will scroll.

4. Click back to the Viewer's Video tab and edit the text clip into your sequence in the Timeline. If you want to superimpose your text over video, choose the Superimpose edit type when you perform your edit.

✔ Tip

■ Use the Gap Width setting to create a double-column credit scroll with a center gutter. Here's how: Set the Gap Width parameter to specify the width of the gap between any two text entries separated by an asterisk (*). When you assemble the text for your credit scroll, type Production Credit*Name, for example, Visual Effects*Xochi Studios, and the gutter in your credit scroll will be set to the Gap Width value. How*about*that?

Creating crawl titles

Like the stock market ticker tape creeping along the bottom of your TV screen, a text crawl is an animated title that scrolls horizontally. Text crawls can be useful for displaying short phrases—but keep them short, unless you are trying to annoy your audience.

To generate a crawl text title:

1. *Do one of the following:*
   - From the Generators pop-up menu in the lower right of the Viewer window, choose Crawl (**Figure 17.13**).
   - On the Browser's Effects tab, choose Crawl from the Video Generators bin.

   The Crawl text generator appears in the Viewer.

2. In the Viewer, click the Controls tab to access the generator's controls; then specify your text control settings as outlined earlier in this chapter, in the section "Text generator options checklist" (**Figure 17.14**).

3. You can also specify any of the following crawl text parameters:
   - **Spacing:** Use the slider or enter a value to specify the spacing between letters (as with Tracking).
   - **Location:** Use the slider or enter a value to specify the y-axis (top-bottom) positioning of your crawl.
   - **Direction:** Choose Left or Right from this pop-up menu to specify the direction in which the generated text will scroll.

4. Click back to the Viewer's Video tab and edit the text clip into your sequence in the Timeline. If you want to superimpose your text over video, choose the Superimpose edit type when you perform your edit.

Figure 17.13 Choose Crawl from the Viewer's Generators pop-up menu.

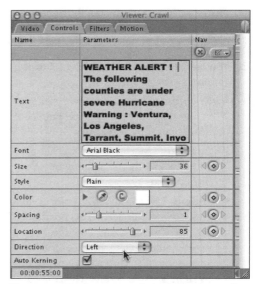

Figure 17.14 On the generator's Controls tab, specify your text control settings as outlined in the section "Text generator options checklist."

✔ Tip

- Stuttering is more pronounced during a text crawl than during any other type of text effect. Take care to test your crawl on an NTSC monitor, and watch for optical jumpiness. Possible remedies include using a wider-stroked font, a larger font size, a slower crawl speed, or a motion blur.

USING ANIMATED TEXT GENERATORS

Figure 17.15 Choose Typewriter from the Viewer's Generators pop-up menu.

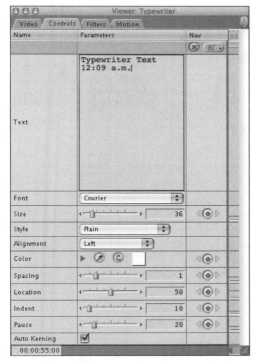

Figure 17.16 On the generator's Controls tab, specify your text control settings as outlined in the section "Text generator options checklist."

Creating animated typewriter text

The cute little Typewriter text generator automates the animation of single letters popping onto the screen; that's why it's called Typewriter. It's a real time-saver, as anybody who has manually animated simulated typing will tell you.

To generate a typewriter text title:

1. *Do one of the following:*
   - From the Generators pop-up menu in the lower right of the Viewer window, choose Typewriter (**Figure 17.15**).
   - On the Browser's Effects tab, choose Typewriter from the Video Generators bin.

   The Typewriter text generator appears in the Viewer.

2. In the Viewer, click the Controls tab to access the generator's controls; then specify your text control settings as outlined earlier in this chapter, in the section "Text generator options checklist" (**Figure 17.16**).

   continues on next page

3. You can also specify any of the following typewriter text parameters:

- ◆ **Spacing:** Use the slider or enter a value to specify the spacing between letters (as with Tracking).

- ◆ **Location:** Use the slider or enter a value to specify the y-axis (top-bottom) positioning of your text element.

- ◆ **Indent:** Use the slider or enter a value to specify the x-axis (left-right) positioning of your text element, expressed as a percentage of the screen.

- ◆ **Pause:** Use the slider or enter a value to specify the timing of your typewriter animation. A larger Pause value results in a longer hold at the end of the clip. The speed of the type-on effect is calculated based on the overall duration of the generator clip minus the pause value you set here.

4. Click back to the Viewer's Video tab and edit the text clip into your sequence in the Timeline. If you want to superimpose your text over video, choose the Superimpose edit type when you perform your edit.

✔ Tips

- ■ If you're looking for an old-fashioned typewriter font, try Courier.

- ■ Use a techno-style font like Andale Mono or VT 100 for simulating computer input (and don't forget to add the Blink filter!).

- ■ Keyframing the Pause value of your Typewriter text generator will vary the rate that the letters appear on the screen and give your typing a nice human touch.

- ■ Title 3D, the Boris Calligraphy text generator, also offers an animated Type On effect.

Creating titles with Boris Calligraphy

Two Boris Calligraphy text generators, Title 3D and Title Crawl, are available as an installation option in the Final Cut Pro installer. Once you install them, these third-party generators show up in the Viewer's Generators pop-up menu along with the standard FCP generators (**Figure 17.17**).

◆ Title 3D features vector-based text you can manipulate in 3D space with pivot control, animated tracking, and a host of text transformations.

◆ Title Crawl is an automated roll and crawl title generator.

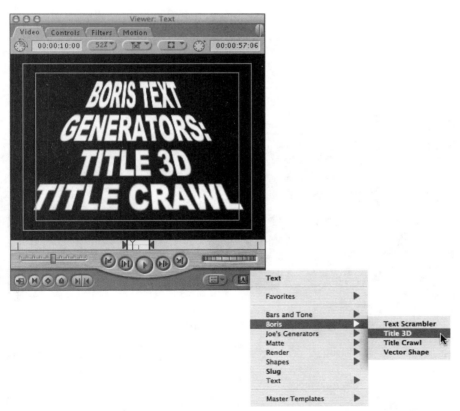

Figure 17.17 If you choose to install them, the Boris Text generators appear in the Generators pop-up menu along with the standard FCP generators.

553

In both generators, you can:

◆ Enter text in a larger, text-entry field (**Figure 17.18**).

◆ Create static titles.

◆ Use the Type On parameters to create a variety of animated type-on effects.

◆ Set font, size, style, and color properties for individual characters.

◆ Apply drop shadows and borders.

◆ Choose from other 2D title animation options.

◆ Copy and paste text from a word processor.

Note that you can set individual parameters such as font, size, color, and tracking for every character, but you cannot animate individual character properties over time. You can, however, keyframe changes in motion properties, roll, crawl, rotation, scale, and opacity for the entire text block.

Boris Calligraphy 2 includes two effects generators:

◆ Vector Shape generates simple but customizable geometric forms you can use as matte shapes behind your titles.

◆ Text Scrambler transforms text into textures by randomizing and repositioning text styles and characters. The Jitter feature offers controls that animate your jumping jittery text.

For more information, see the *Boris Calligraphy User Guide*, an 84-page, illustrated PDF file, located in the Documentation folder on the Final Cut Pro DVD.

Figure 17.18 Boris text generators feature a large text input window and myriad text styling options.

REAL TIME AND RENDERING

Final Cut Pro offers many, many ways to manipulate your raw media—a wild world of complex effects. We enjoy more real time and less rendering in each successive version of Final Cut Pro, but even FCP's impressive real time performance improvements can barely keep pace with increased performance demands as industry and consumer video standards move to higher-resolution HD formats.

Apple engineers persevere, however, and their efforts have brought us the Open Format Timeline feature, new in FCP 6. Now you can combine media with different formats, frame rates, and scanning methods in a single sequence and edit without rendering. In this mega-multi-format world, Open Format is a lifesaver.

This chapter outlines the workings of RT Extreme, FCP's software-only effects previewing feature. Real-time systems use the power of your Mac's CPU to process added effects on the fly, allowing you to play them back without rendering them first. For editors (and their clients) who work extensively with effects, these systems can dramatically improve efficiency and creativity.

Rendering is the process of combining your raw clip media with filters, transitions, and other adjustments to produce a new file. This new file, called the *render* file, can be played back in real time.

This is a chapter with more protocol than most. Understanding rendering protocols can be a big factor in making your post-production work efficient while producing high-quality results. This chapter lays out the rules governing video and audio render files and lays out some strategies for minimizing render time.

About Real-Time Playback

Real-time effects take advantage of the Mac's graphics handling power to compute and display previews of many effects in real time. Final Cut Pro's real-time effects come in two flavors: RT Extreme (RTE), a software-based effects previewing feature that doesn't require additional hardware; and hardware-assisted options for editors working with uncompressed video formats. RTE effects are computed on the fly and play back in the FCP program windows and on external TV monitors.

Real-time previewing handles much more than effects and transitions. RTE can preview freeze frames, blend multiple layers of semi-transparent video, display multiple angles of synchronized video in a multiclip, play back mixed formats and frame rates in a single sequence, or insert a pulldown pattern on the fly for real-time output of 24-frame video to a 25 fps PAL or 29.97 fps NTSC monitor.

RT Extreme: scalable software-based real time

Working with lower-resolution formats, you can enjoy a lot of real-time effects previewing without extra hardware. Basic Final Cut Pro 6 systems are qualified to handle at least some real-time playback in DV, DVCAM, DVCPRO, and DVCPRO 50, IMX, Offline RT, and 8- and 10-bit uncompressed 4:2:2 video formats.

RT Extreme also supports high-definition formats such as DVCPRO HD, HDV, and Apple Intermediate Codec, but requires additional RAM, at least 2 GB.

Check the Technical Specifications page of Apple's Final Cut Pro Web site at www.apple.com/finalcutstudio/specs.html for a list detailing which real-time effects are supported on which systems.

Real-Time Hardware Systems for FCP

Why would you want a hardware-assisted real-time system for Final Cut Pro when software-only RT Extreme effects are available? There are still some good reasons to consider a hardware assist for your effects-previewing ability:

RT Extreme effects don't work in all video formats; the power of your FCP system determines what formats are supported. If you are working in an unsupported format, you'll need a hardware helper to take advantage of real-time previewing. You can see a list of the real-time codecs supported on your FCP system by choosing Final Cut Pro > System Settings > Effect Handling. If you're working in any other format, such as SD or another HD format, you'll need a hardware helper.

Real-time hardware usually offers you more than just real-time effects previews. Both the AJA Kona 3 and Blackmagic Design DeckLink HD cards, for example, support uncompressed HD video capture and enhance your ability to mix material from different video formats in the same Timeline without requiring rendering.

Real-time hardware offers superior image quality as you preview your effects on your NTSC or PAL monitor—if you rely on your preview to make critical decisions, viewing your work on the TV is a must.

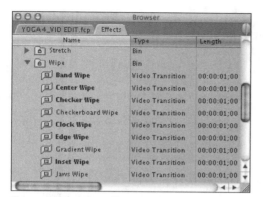

Figure 18.1 Real-time effects appear in boldface type on the Browser's Effects tab.

Figure 18.2 Real-time effects also appear in boldface in the Effects menu. Select Unlimited RT from the RT pop-up menu, and you'll enable additional real-time effects.

FCP will identify your Mac model and display the RTE effects it supports in boldface. If a real-time card is installed in your Mac's PCI slot, Final Cut Pro identifies that card and indicates which effects the card supports by displaying the available real-time effects in boldface type, both on the Browser's Effects tab (**Figure 18.1**) and in the Effects menu (**Figure 18.2**).

The Timeline's render status bars are color coded to let you know which sections of your sequence will play back in real time, and which sections still require rendering before you can play them. (See "Rendering indicators," later in this chapter.)

Hardware-assisted real time for uncompressed video

Final Cut Pro also supports hardware-assisted real-time video effects for HD formats other than HDV and DVCPRO HD, and additional uncompressed video formats. FCP's design allows video card developers to pick and choose which individual effects their real-time systems support. Effects that aren't programmed into that system's hardware are handled by FCP software, but won't play back without rendering. Users can match real-time previewing hardware and video formats on the Effect Handling tab of the System Settings window.

✔ Tips

■ RTE's real-time magic works on footage compressed in Offline RT, FCP's low-resolution draft-quality format. Offline RT files are smaller, so you can preview more complex real-time effects in Offline RT format than you can in a higher-resolution format. For more information, see "What is Offline RT?" in Chapter 5.

■ Remember that RTE previews are optimized for real-time processing, not resolution. They work great for judging timing and composition, but for critical judgment of color and detail, view them on your external NTSC or PAL monitor at final output resolution.

Controlling real-time playback quality

Final Cut Pro's real-time architecture offers flexibility far beyond the simple enabling or disabling of individual effects. Finding the right balance between image quality and system performance for each specific working situation involves some tweaking, but you have a couple of important tools to assist you.

Dynamic real-time playback is the most convenient option for configuring real-time playback for everyday use. Dynamic quality and frame rate settings analyze upcoming frames and then display the best real-time performance your system can produce based on the present real-time demands. You have the flexibility of choosing Dynamic image quality while maintaining a fixed frame display rate or opting for a fixed image quality with a Dynamic frame display rate. Combining Dynamic image quality and Dynamic frame rate should give you the greatest range of real-time playback and minimize the appearance of the blue "Unrendered" screen.

Setting up image quality of real-time playback

You use the settings on the RT pop-up menu to adjust the balance between image quality and playback performance.

Real-time playback quality settings can be adjusted in either of two locations: the Timeline's RT pop-up menu (**Figure 18.3**) and the Playback Control tab of the System Settings window. The RT pop-up menu is the more convenient route, but complete playback quality controls are available only on the Playback Control tab For details on Playback Control tab settings, see Chapter 3, "Presets and Preferences."

✔ Tips

- Real-time playback quality settings also control the image quality of FCP's Digital Cinema Desktop Preview mode.

- You must enable Unlimited RT to see any real-time playback of clips with 3rd party filters applied. Unlimited RT is also required for any real-time previewing of LiveType or Motion projects embedded in your FCP sequence.

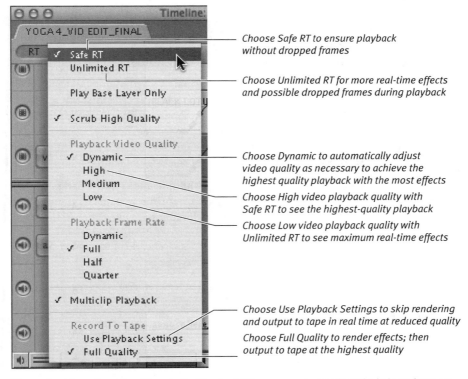

Choose Safe RT to ensure playback without dropped frames

Choose Unlimited RT for more real-time effects and possible dropped frames during playback

Choose Dynamic to automatically adjust video quality as necessary to achieve the highest quality playback with the most effects

Choose High video playback quality with Safe RT to see the highest-quality playback

Choose Low video playback quality with Unlimited RT to see maximum real-time effects

Choose Use Playback Settings to skip rendering and output to tape in real time at reduced quality

Choose Full Quality to render effects; then output to tape at the highest quality

Figure 18.3 Mix and match settings in the Timeline's RT pop-up menu to adjust the balance between playback quality and real-time performance.

Rendering

FCP 6 has made dramatic improvements in real-time effects performance, but when you finally run out of processing power, you must render.

This section outlines FCP's rendering quality settings and rendering protocols, and also explains how to navigate the Sequence menu's vast forest of Render commands.

For more information, see page III-645 of Apple's *Final Cut Pro User Manual* PDF.

Setting up image quality of rendered material

Use the settings on the Render Control tab of the Sequence Settings window to balance the image quality and rendering speed of rendered material in your current sequence. For more information, see "Changing the Settings of an Existing Sequence" in Chapter 4. For details on Render Control tab settings in your Sequence preset, see Chapter 3, "Presets and Preferences."

Use the Video Processing tab of the Sequence Settings window to specify the color space in which the rendered sections of your sequence will be processed. For more information, see "RGB or YCrCb: Choosing a Color Space" in Chapter 3.

Rendering Protocols

Here are some general guidelines to help you understand Final Cut Pro's rendering protocols.

What needs to be rendered

In general, you must render any transitions, effects, and composited layers that exceed the real-time capacity of your FCP system.

Also, before your sequence can be exported or printed to video, you have to render any source media with frame rate, frame size, or video or audio compression settings that differ from those settings in your sequence.

Audio tracks with transitions or filters, as well as multiple audio tracks over your real-time playback limit, have to be rendered before playback.

Clips whose speed has been changed must also be rendered before playback.

What doesn't need to be rendered

Final Cut Pro sequences that include real time–supported transitions, effects, and composited layers can be played back in real time without rendering, as long as the sequence size and frame rate match those of the original source material.

Multiple audio tracks can be played back in real time without rendering. (See "Rendering audio" later in this chapter, for more information.)

RENDERING

Figure 18.4 The "Unrendered" screen appears when you try to play back video that cannot be played back in real time without rendering.

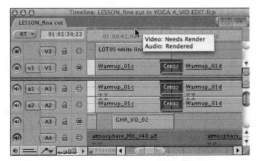

Figure 18.5 The rendering status bars are located above the Timeline ruler. The upper bar indicates the render status of video tracks. The lower bar shows the audio track status. Pause the pointer over the rendering indicator bars, and a tooltip displays render status details.

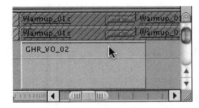

Figure 18.6 An audio clip requiring sample-rate conversion displays an item-level render status indicator overlay right on the clip in the Timeline.

Rendering indicators

As you build your sequence, you'll encounter the following indicators:

◆ When you try to play video material that requires rendering in the Viewer or the Canvas, a blue background with the word "Unrendered" appears (**Figure 18.4**), indicating that the video can't play in real time.

◆ When you try to play audio material that requires rendering in the Viewer or the Canvas, you'll hear a steady beeping sound, indicating that the audio can't play in real time. You can disable the render warning beeps on the Playback Control tab of the System Settings window.

◆ In the Timeline, the rendering indicator above the ruler (**Figure 18.5**) consists of two thin bars. These bars indicate which sections of the sequence currently require rendering to play back smoothly. The upper bar indicates the render status of video tracks; the lower bar shows the audio track status.

◆ A sequence audio clip requiring sample-rate conversion displays a render status indicator overlay right on the clip in the Timeline (**Figure 18.6**).

Non-real-time FCP systems use the following status codes in the rendering indicators:

◆ **Red (Needs Render):** The material needs to be rendered.

◆ **Gray:** No rendering is required.

◆ **Blue-gray:** The material has already been rendered.

continues on next page

Real-time effects previewing adds six (!) more color codes to the render status indicator:

- **Dark Green (Full):** The material can be played back and output at full quality in real time. No rendering is required.

- **Green (Preview):** No rendering is required for real-time playback in the Canvas or the Viewer. For playback on an external device, green indicates a lower-quality output of scaling and motion effects.

- **Yellow (Proxy):** Real-time playback is an approximation of the final effect. To get the true final effect, you still need to render the material. You'll see the final effect when playback is stopped or during scrubbing.

- **Dark Yellow:** The material has been rendered at a quality lower than that currently specified on your sequence's Render Control tab. FCP preserves these render files even if you modify the sequence's render quality settings later.

- **Orange (Unlimited):** Indicates effects enabled by selecting Unlimited RT in the Timeline's RT pop-up menu. These effects exceed your computer's "official" real-time playback capabilities and may drop frames during playback, but you can get a rough idea of how a complex effect is shaping up.

- **Blue:** FCP has detected unsupported real-time enabler files. This material may drop frames during playback.

FCP Protocol: Audio Rendering Options

Here's the rundown on the audio rendering options available in the Render submenus:

- **For Playback:** Only the portions of your sequence audio tracks that require rendering in order to play back in real time are processed.

- **Item Level:** This option renders individual audio clips that require sample-rate conversion to match the sequence sample rate, and clips with applied audio filters. Item-level processing generates item-level render cache files. Audio levels and multi-track playback are still processed in real time.

- **Mixdown Audio:** Your audio tracks, along with all applied filters, levels, and transitions, are processed into a set of render files, a single file for each audio output. This command is available only in the Render Only submenu.

Figure 18.7 Choose Sequence > Render Selection, and then specify which render types you want to include in this rendering operation by selecting those items from the submenu. Making a selection toggles the checked status on or off; you'll have to select multiple times if you want to include or exclude multiple render types.

Using Render Commands

Final Cut Pro's rendering commands are all about choices. At the top level of the Sequence menu, you'll find three Render commands:

◆ Render Selection processes only the material you select in the Timeline.

◆ Render All creates render files for the entire sequence.

◆ Use Render Only to process a single type of unrendered material. Render Only can process either the portion of the sequence you select, or the entire sequence if you don't mark a selection.

Each Render command has a submenu that offers a second tier of choices.

◆ In all three submenus, you can choose to render just video, just audio, or both.

◆ Both the Render Selection and Render All submenus allow you to pick and choose which types of render-eligible sections you want to process in this rendering operation. Check any or all of the render types before you kick off a render (**Figure 18.7**). The render options stay checked until you change them, so once you've set up a render specification, you can render with a simple keyboard command.

FCP Protocol: Estimating Render Processing Time

Render processing times can range from a couple of seconds to many hours. How do you know whether you've got just enough time for a quick break or enough for a two-hour lunch? Read on.

Final Cut Pro expresses the progress of your rendering operation as an estimate of the time remaining. Even so, the time displayed on the progress bar is based on how long the current frame takes multiplied by the number of remaining frames; so, if your effects differ drastically in complexity, predicting the time required to render is difficult—even for Final Cut Pro. Watch the progress bar for a few minutes and make a guess, based on the speed of the progress bar and your knowledge of the sequence.

To render a section of a sequence:

1. *Do one of the following:*
   - In the Timeline, select a portion of a clip or one or more clips or transitions.
   - In the Timeline or the Canvas, set the sequence In and Out points to mark the area that you want to render (**Figure 18.8**).

2. Choose Sequence > Render Selection, and then select which types of render-eligible material you want to include in this rendering operation by selecting those items from the submenu. Selected types are checked; making a selection toggles the checked status on or off.

3. Press Command-0 (zero) to open the sequence's Sequence Settings window. Verify (or adjust) the settings on the Render Control tab to specify the image quality of this render operation (**Figure 18.9**); then click OK.

4. *Do one of the following:*
   - Choose Sequence > Render Selection; or press Command-R to render both video and audio in the selected area.
   - Choose Sequence > Render Selection > Video (**Figure 18.10**) to render just video in the selected area.
   - Choose Sequence > Render Selection > Audio; or press Control-Option-R to render just the audio in the selected area.

   A progress bar displays the percentage of completed processing while the selected area is being rendered (**Figure 18.11**).

5. Click Cancel if you want to stop rendering. Final Cut Pro saves all the rendered frames it has processed, even if you cancel rendering.

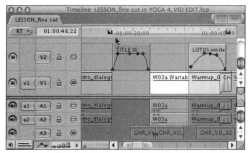

Figure 18.8 Set the Sequence In and Out points to select the area you want to render. (This figure shows split edit points, marking Video In and Video Out.)

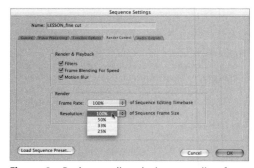

Figure 18.9 Review or adjust the image quality of your rendered material on the Render Control tab of the Sequence Settings window.

Figure 18.10 To start rendering, choose Sequence > Render Selection. Your submenu selection determines whether you render video only (pictured here), audio only, or both audio and video.

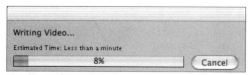

Figure 18.11 A progress bar tracks the speed of the rendering process. More complex effects will take more time to render than simple effects or audio processing.

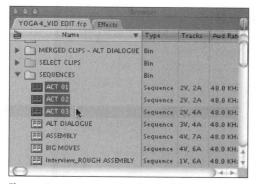

Figure 18.12 You can use the Render All command to render an entire sequence, but you can also use it to batch render multiple sequences. Select the sequences that you want to batch render in the Browser.

USING RENDER COMMANDS

To render an entire sequence or multiple sequences:

1. *Do one of the following:*
   - Open the sequence you want to render in the Timeline.
   - In the Browser, select the icon of the sequence you want to render (**Figure 18.12**). You can select multiple sequences in multiple projects.

2. Choose Sequence > Render All, and then select which types of render-eligible material you want to include in this rendering operation by selecting those items from the submenu. Selected types are checked; making a selection toggles the checked status on or off.

3. Choose Sequence > Render All.
   A progress bar displays the percentage of completed processing while the sequence is being rendered. Click Cancel if you want to stop rendering. Final Cut Pro saves all the rendered frames it has processed, even if you cancel rendering.

To render a single type of render-eligible material:

1. Select a portion of the sequence, or, to render the entire sequence, leave the entire sequence unselected.

2. Choose Sequence > Render Only, and select a type of render-eligible material to render from the submenu. Video render options are listed at the top of the submenu; the three options at the bottom are audio-only.

To disable rendering:

- Press the Caps Lock key to temporarily disable rendering. Press Caps Lock again to cancel.

Quick Preview Tips

The "instant preview" techniques listed here can show you a quick, temporary preview of an effect or transition before you commit to rendering it. Place the Timeline playhead at the section you want to preview, and then use one of these methods:

- Press Option-P (the Play Every Frame command) to force a frame-by-frame preview of your unrendered material. FCP displays the frames as fast as they can be processed.

- Use the Left and Right Arrow keys to step through your footage a frame at a time.

- Scrub the playhead across the Scrubber bar in the Canvas or the Timeline's ruler.

Rendering audio

FCP can mix and play back at least eight tracks of audio in real time, so audio rendering is often unnecessary.

The number of tracks you specify in the Real-Time Audio Mixing preference (located in the General tab of the User Preferences window) determines how many tracks Final Cut Pro attempts to play back before it asks for audio rendering.

There's an additional factor that determines whether you have maxed out your real-time audio playback capabilities: All audio tracks are not created equal. When you apply filters or transitions to an audio track, Final Cut Pro must allocate processing power to calculate those effects on the fly in order to play back the result in real time—which brings us to track costs. (See the sidebar "FCP Protocol: Track Costs" and **Table 18.1**.)

✔ Tips

- The Mixdown Audio command produces a render file with a computed mix. Even though the command is called "Mixdown," you still have individual control over all your audio tracks. Think of Mixdown Audio as a "temp mix" you can use while you're working.

- In addition to the Mixdown Audio command, FCP offers a couple of less drastic audio rendering alternatives. For details, see "FCP Protocol: Audio Rendering Options," earlier in this chapter.

Table 18.1

Final Cut Pro Audio Track Costs		
ITEM	TYPE	APPROX TRACK COST
Each mono track	Track	1
Each mono track with transitions applied	Transition	2
Pair of stereo tracks	Track	2
Sub-sequence containing one stereo track	Track	4
Each track referencing a sub-sequence	Track	Number of audio tracks in sub-sequence
Compressor/limiter	Filter	6
Expander/gate	Filter	6
Vocal de-esser	Filter	6
Vocal de-popper	Filter	6
Reverb/echo	Filter	6
All other filters	Filter	3

FCP Protocol: Track Costs

The concept of track equivalent costs, or *track costs*, can help you to estimate the total processing power needed to play back multiple audio channels. The track costs listed in Table 18.1 are approximate, but they do indicate the relative processing power required by FCP audio operations. Track costs can accumulate quickly when even a couple of unmixed tracks are combined, if you have used filters and transitions.

Depending on the speed of your system, you may be able to play back multiple audio tracks with filters or transitions applied. Choose Low Audio Quality playback from the General tab of the User Preferences window, and you'll pick up an extra track or two.

If you exceed your real-time playback capability, you'll hear beeps instead of your audio when you attempt playback. Before you can play back, you'll need to render by selecting Mixdown Audio from the Sequence menu.

Managing Render Files

Render files are valuable media elements, stored as actual media files on your hard disk like your original captured media files. Final Cut Pro names render files according to its own internal naming protocols. You won't be able to identify individual render files by their filenames, so planning your render file management strategy is a critical part of your post-production work. This will become clear the next time you invest considerable time in a single complex rendering process.

Specifying storage locations for render files

You can specify up to 12 disks for storing captured video, captured audio, or render files. As you create render files, Final Cut Pro stores them on the disk with the most available space. If you don't specify disk locations, Final Cut Pro saves video and audio render files in separate folders (called Render Files and Audio Render Files), which are located, along with your Capture Scratch folder, in the Final Cut Pro Documents folder. Render files are media files and should be stored on the same media drives as your captured media.

Specify storage locations for your render files on the Scratch Disks tab in the System Settings window. For more information, see Chapter 3, "Presets and Preferences."

Using the Render Manager to manage rendered files

When you work on multiple projects, each with multiple sequences, render files can accumulate quickly. You can use the Render Manager to delete render files for deleted or obsolete projects, or to remove obsolete render files from your current projects. The Render Manager finds and lists files from unopened projects as well as open projects.

The Render Manager window organizes files by project and sequence. The Last Modified column indicates the last time each render file was rewritten. Freeing up disk space by dumping old render files is an attractive proposition, but use caution if you delete render files for your current projects. Final Cut Pro uses render filenames that are useful to the program but unintelligible to you.

A word of caution: Do not dispose of render files by deleting them in the Finder. Use the Render Manager instead, so that FCP can track the status of the deleted files and update the affected projects and sequences.

FCP Protocol: Render Manager File Tracking

There are a couple of limitations to the Render Manager's ability to track render files in multiple FCP projects:

◆ The Render Manager will track only render files you've stored in folder locations currently specified for render file storage on the Scratch Disks tab in the System Settings window. If you have other render files stashed in scratch disk locations not currently selected on the Scratch Disks tab, they won't appear in the Render Manager list. To use the Render Manager to track (and manage) all your render files, simply include all render file folder locations when you specify storage locations for render files on the Scratch Disks tab. For more information on setting Scratch Disk preferences, see Chapter 3, "Presets and Preferences."

◆ The Render Manager can display time and date information only for render files in open projects. Time and date information for render files in closed projects is listed as "unknown."

To view or delete render files:

1. Choose Tools > Render Manager (**Figure 18.13**).

   The Render Manager lists all the Final Cut Pro render files on your designated scratch disks.

2. In the Remove column of the Render Manager, click next to the names of render files you want to delete (**Figure 18.14**).

   A checkmark appears in the column to indicate each selection.

3. Click OK.

4. A dialog box appears, warning you that deleting your render files will "flush your undo queue," meaning that you won't be able to undo this operation. If that's all right, click OK.

   All selected render files are deleted from your hard disk.

Figure 18.13 Choose Tools > Render Manager.

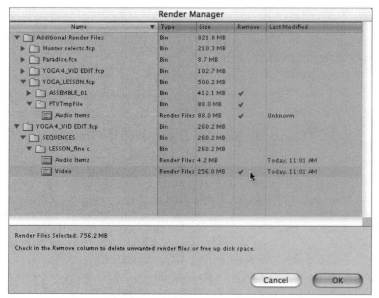

Figure 18.14 The Render Manager displays a list of folders containing all render files currently on your designated scratch disks. Click to place a checkmark next to a folder or render file you want to delete. Render files are named according to a program protocol; you cannot name them.

MANAGING RENDER FILES

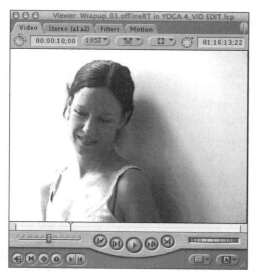

Figure 18.15 This clip looks normal when opened from the Browser.

Figure 18.16 The same clip as it appears in the Canvas. The mismatched sequence settings override the clip settings, causing the clip to appear distorted and to play back poorly.

Rendering Strategies

To take full advantage of the media manipulation techniques that are possible with Final Cut Pro, you will need to render to produce your finished results; you'll also need to render to review your sequence and evaluate any effects you've created. The rendering strategies in this section fall into three basic categories:

◆ Tips for avoiding unnecessary rendering

◆ Techniques for speeding up rendering times

◆ Schemes for preserving render files

Avoiding unnecessary rendering

Final Cut Pro allows you to add source material whose frame rate and compression settings do not match your sequence settings. However, if the frame rate, frame size, or video or audio compression settings in your source media are different from the settings in your sequence, those frames need to be rendered before the sequence can be exported or printed to video.

If a particular group of source clips looks normal when you open it from the Browser window (**Figure 18.15**) but requires rendering or changes size or shape when you add it to a sequence and view it in the Canvas window (**Figure 18.16**), you probably have a settings mismatch between your source clips and your sequence settings.

Important: To avoid rendering when creating a sequence with cuts only, make sure that the sequence's editing timebase, frame size, and compression settings are the same as the frame rate, frame size, and compression settings of your source media.

How do you compare source clip and sequence settings? Open the clip's Item Properties window and note the clip's video rate, frame rate, frame size, and compression settings. Then open the Sequence Settings window. Note the sequence's video rate (called the "Editing Timebase"), Frame Size, and Compressor settings; these should match the clip's video rate (called the "Vid Rate"), Frame Size, and Compressor settings (**Figure 18.17**). To learn more about specifying source clip settings, see Chapter 5, "Capturing Video." For information on specifying sequence settings, see Chapter 3, "Presets and Preferences."

✔ Tip

■ The Auto conform sequence feature can help avoid unnecessary rendering right from the start—by identifying the format settings of the first clip you add to a new sequence and automatically conforming the sequence settings to match. Enable Auto conform sequence on the Editing tab of the User Preferences window.

Disabling rendering

There are two ways to delay rendering your sequence until you have completed your desired adjustments: You can enable the Play Base Layer Only option in the RT pop-up menu, or you can press the Caps Lock key to temporarily disable rendering.

The Play Base Layer Only option allows playback with minimal rendering. With Play Base Layer Only enabled, Final Cut Pro will play the lowest opaque track in the sequence and all audio tracks rather than displaying the "Unrendered" message in areas that still require rendering. Cuts will be substituted for un-rendered transitions. Motion will not be applied to clips or sequences when played back in the Viewer.

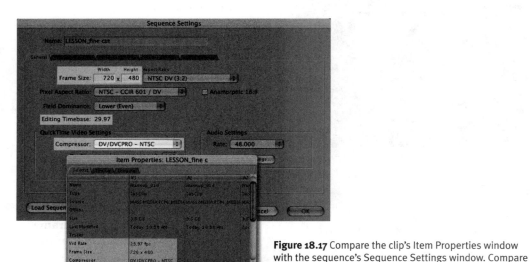

Figure 18.17 Compare the clip's Item Properties window with the sequence's Sequence Settings window. Compare the Frame Size and the Compressor settings in the two windows, and then check the sequence's Editing Timebase against the clip's Vid Rate. Highlighted settings must match for the sequence to play in real time.

Reducing Rendering Time

Following are a few strategies that can help you minimize your rendering time. Using a lower-resolution draft quality saves disk space as well as time, because lower-resolution render files are smaller.

Use draft mode

Use a low-resolution render quality to perfect element positioning, motion paths, scaling, and other basic design decisions. After you are satisfied with the timing and movement of your effects sequence, start including your most calculation-intensive effects. Render short test sections first, and then review them to evaluate your final image quality. If you are set up to use an external NTSC or PAL monitor, check your output on the monitor to see that your render quality is sufficient.

Render in stages

If you are building a highly complex effects sequence, you may want to render your elements in stages. For example, you might perfect just the motion paths and interactions of your composited layers, and then render just that portion of your sequence in high quality by exporting and re-importing your rendered elements. The export process creates a new piece of source media, and you can continue to sculpt your sequence using the new composited clip as a fully rendered base track. Exporting to preserve a render file is described later in this chapter.

Batch render

Use the batch render feature to render all your projects while you're busy elsewhere.

FCP Protocol: Nested Sequences and Rendering

When you nest, or place a sequence inside another sequence, render files for the nested sequence are saved separately, along with the nested sequence.

Nested sequences may require separate rendering in a parent sequence under the following circumstances:

- If a parent sequence modifies a nested sequence, the nested sequence must be re-rendered. Modifications include compositing, filters, transitions, speed changes, and so on.

- If movement, such as rotation, has been applied to a sequence and then rendered, the sequence needs to be re-rendered if it is nested inside another sequence.

- If a nested sequence is placed inside a parent sequence, its alpha channel type is set to Straight. If you set the alpha channel for that nested sequence to None, the clips it contains won't need to be re-rendered. Its rendered files will be retained as long as they do not need to be combined with other tracks in the sequence, but because you've turned off the alpha channel, the clip will be opaque.

Preserving render files

You can spend days creating a polished effects or title sequence in Final Cut Pro and wait hours for your final product to render. How can you protect your time investment?

Following are a few strategies to help you hold onto your render files.

Salvaging renders with Undo

Final Cut Pro allows multiple undos. If you just want to try a new idea on material you've already rendered, when you're done, you can undo (Command-Z) your experiment until you have reverted to your previously rendered file. Careful use of the Undo function can give you freedom to experiment without risking rendered sequence material.

FCP protocol dictates that when you invalidate a render file by changing a sequence, the invalid render file becomes unrecoverable either when you next save the project or when you are past the point where you can use Undo to make the render file valid again, whichever is later.

Export to preserve render files

Exporting creates a physical copy of your rendered file on your hard disk. Exporting is the safest way to preserve rendered material. Once you have exported render files, you can re-import and use them just as you would raw captured media. For your render file to be exported without re-rendering, the export settings must match the render file's settings.

Using nested sequences to preserve render files

You can select a group of sequence clips or a portion of a Final Cut Pro sequence and, by nesting it, convert that selection into a self-contained sub-sequence. As a sub-sequence inside a parent sequence, nested sequences are treated the same as other clips in a sequence. But unlike clips, nested sequences are actually pointers, or references, to the original sequence, not copies.

A nested sequence can help preserve your render files because even though it can be edited into another sequence in pieces just like a clip, the render files associated with the nested sequence are preserved within the nested sequence. Even if you make a change in the parent sequence that requires the nested sequence to re-render, when you open the nested sequence, your original render files created within the nested sequence will still be available.

However, like everything else associated with rendering, you need to be aware of particular protocols governing the preservation of render files when a sequence is nested as a sub-sequence in another, parent sequence.

To learn how to create nested sequences, see Chapter 4, "Projects, Sequences, and Clips."

✔ Tips

- Before rendering a sequence that you intend to nest in a parent sequence, make sure that the nested sequence has the same render settings (frame rate, frame size, and compression settings) as the parent sequence to avoid rendering the nested sequence again.

- Final Cut Pro cannot reliably track down all nested sub-sequence material that requires rendering when you perform a Render All process. If you have built multiple levels of nested, unrendered sub-sequences into your project, this tip's for you: Try rendering at least one element in each nested sequence to help FCP track down the nested rendering required. Double-check your rendered sequences before you invite your client in for a screening.

CREATING

You've come this far. Now it's time to send your masterpiece out into the world.

Final Cut Pro has a variety of output options. How do you choose the right one? The best output format for your Final Cut Pro project depends on where you plan to take it next.

◆ Will you distribute your program as a DVD?

◆ Do you need a broadcast-quality master?

◆ Do you need a VHS tape version so Grandpa can see your directorial debut?

◆ Are you preparing a webcast?

◆ How about "all of the above"?

This chapter walks you through Final Cut Pro's output options and helps you decide which one will deliver what you need.

In the first part of this chapter, you'll learn about three different methods for outputting your project to tape: recording Timeline playback, printing to video, and editing to tape.

The second part of the chapter is devoted to Final Cut Pro's file export options. You can export just the editing and clip information from a sequence as a formatted text file. You can also use the file export options to convert your FCP sequence or clip to another digital format for use in computer-based media.

One of the beautiful things about digital video is the wide variety of output options available to you—right at your desktop.

Using Tape Output Modes

Final Cut Pro is designed to support external video monitoring at any time using your deck or camcorder, so you can always record FCP's output. You don't need to process your FCP material unless you are exporting your sequence in a computer-compatible format.

Final Cut Pro offers three tape output modes:

◆ **Recording Timeline Playback:** One of the easiest ways to record Final Cut Pro's output to videotape is simply to start recording on your video deck or camcorder; then play your sequence in the Timeline. For more information, see "Recording Timeline Playback," later in this chapter.

◆ **Print to Video:** Use Print to Video to output a Final Cut Pro sequence or clip to videotape. The Print to Video function lets you configure pre- and post-program elements such as color bars and a 1 kHz tone, leader, slate, and countdown. Print to Video's Loop feature allows you to print your sequence multiple times automatically.

You don't need device control to use Print to Video. Use Print to Video if you want to make a videotape copy of your FCP sequence that includes customized pre-program elements, or if you want to loop your sequence.

 On Peachpit.com

"Editing to Tape," a 12-page PDF, is available at:
www.peachpit.com/finalcutpro6vqp

Output Options For HDV

Two years after Final Cut Pro 5 introduced HDV support, HDV is a consumer-level video format. Major manufacturers may offer HDV cameras priced well under $1000, but FCP users with HDV-format projects still face a lack of true HD distribution options. DVD burners and players that support DVD-HD and Blu-Ray—the two competing DVD formats that can handle HD video—are still rarer than hen's teeth. What are your options right now?

These are the best available options for HDV:

◆ You can use FCP's Print to Video function to record your HDV material back out to your HDV deck or camcorder. FCP will automatically render any footage requiring it, and then conform your HDV sequence as a properly formatted MPEG-2 output stream before recording the material back to video tape.

◆ You can export your HDV format material for use in DVD Studio Pro or iDVD. The export operation is the same for HDV and DV format material; both are converted to MPEG-2 for use in your DVD-authoring program.

◆ To get the best possible image quality on conversion, export a self-contained QuickTime Movie in HDV-native format, and then use Compressor to downconvert to MPEG-2. FCP users offer various recipes for the best Compressor settings to use when down coverting HDV to DVD. Consult your preferred FCP Internet oracle.

Figure 19.1 Set your camcorder or deck to VTR (or VCR) mode.

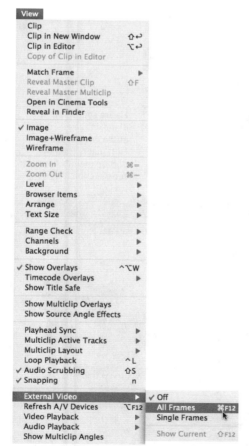

Figure 19.2 Enable the external video feed by choosing View > External Video > All Frames.

◆ **Edit to Tape:** If your external video hardware supports device control, you can use the Edit to Tape window to perform frame-accurate Insert and Assemble edits to videotape, using Final Cut Pro's output as source material.

The editing functions available in the Edit to Tape window depend entirely on the capabilities of your video hardware. The DV format has some significant limitations when it comes to editing to tape, so it's smart to investigate your equipment's capabilities before you make plans.

If you are using Final Cut Pro with a DV system, you can use Edit to Tape to assemble multiple sequences onto tape as a single, longer program or to place your sequence to start at a specific time-code, such as 01:00:00;00.

Setting up for recording to tape

Before you record FCP's output on video-tape, make sure that your recording device is connected and receiving Final Cut Pro's output, and that the sequence or clip you're outputting is set up correctly.

Use this setup checklist for all three tape output modes:

◆ Make sure your camcorder or deck is set to VTR (or VCR) mode (**Figure 19.1**). Final Cut Pro can't record to devices set to Camera mode.

◆ Make sure your video deck or camcorder is receiving output from Final Cut Pro. Check the external video settings for your current Easy Setup. Your external video settings should send FCP's video signal to the external video device you want to record to. Enable the video output feed to your camcorder or deck by choosing View > External Video > All Frames (**Figure 19.2**).

continues on next page

If you want to examine your external video settings in more detail, check the A/V Devices tab of the Audio/Video Settings window (**Figure 19.3**), particularly the Different Output for Edit to Tape/Print to Video setting. That's where you choose which video output routing to use when you're using Print to Video or Edit to Tape.

For more information, see "Using Video and Audio Playback Settings" in Chapter 3.

◆ All of FCP's tape output modes print your selected sequence or clip to tape at the playback quality currently selected in the Record to Tape section of the Timeline's RT pop-up menu. Open your selected sequence in the Timeline and check to see which playback quality is currently selected before you kick off the recording process. If you want to output at full video playback quality, select Full Quality from the pop-up menu's Record to Tape section (**Figure 19.4**). For more information, see "Controlling playback and rendering quality" in Chapter 18.

◆ If you want to print only a selected portion of a sequence or clip, open the clip or sequence and then set In and Out points to specify the portion you want to record (**Figure 19.5**).

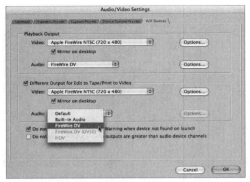

Figure 19.3 You can examine your external video settings in more detail on the A/V Devices tab of the Audio/Video Settings window.

Figure 19.4 To output at maximum video and audio quality, select Full Quality from the RT pop-up menu's Record to Tape section.

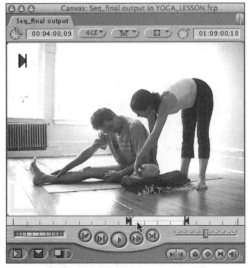

Figure 19.5 Set In and Out points to specify the portion you want to record.

◆ You should enable the Report Dropped Frames During Playback preference on the General tab of the User Preferences window. Feedback on dropped frames is especially critical during final output.

If you enable dropped-frames reporting and find you're dropping frames in your external output during playback, you might try this first: Disable the Mirror on Desktop option on the A/V Devices tab of the Audio/Video Settings window. You'll immediately free up some performance power for the Print to Video or Edit to Tape functions.

See "Optimizing Performance" in Chapter 2 for more tips on eliminating dropped frames by improving FCP's performance.

◆ Test your setup by recording a section of your show to tape. Play back the test recording and scrutinize the results in your external monitoring setup. Do the rendered sections of the program match quality with the rest of the footage? Are your titles crisp? Are your video levels within the recommended IRE range for your output format, or has your video image developed hot spots? Is the audio playback level healthy but not overmodulated? Are both stereo tracks balanced properly and panned correctly? A little extra care and patience now, when you're producing your final product, will protect all the care and patience you've lavished on your project so far.

Other Export Options

◆ **Audio export to OMF:** FCP can export your audio tracks as OMF-format files. That means you can export audio tracks with track separations, edit points, audio levels, crossfades, and video sync intact. You can add handles, too—if there's enough audio in your source file. Most audio post-production facilities use OMF-compatible digital audio workstations (DAWs), such as ProTools.

◆ **Third-party XML and OMF interchange applications:** Independent software developers have used FCP's XML and OMF "hooks" to develop custom interchange applications that make it possible to transfer a surprising amount of project data between FCP and other programs such as the Avid NLEs and After Effects. For more information, see the sidebar at the end of this chapter.

◆ **Cutting film on FCP:** You can use Cinema Tools to track the conversion of your film's edge code numbers through conversion to timecode for a video post-production process. Cinema Tools and your FCP project share an XML database that you can update from either application. You can keep track of Cinema Tools' data properties in FCP's Browser; you can even view your timecode display in feet and frames as you edit, making it easier to track changes in an FCP/Cinema Tools project that's destined for the negative cutter. Now that this post-production path has been cleared, expect more and more films to be edited in Final Cut Pro. Your best source of up-to-date information on using FCP for 24-frame editing is DigitalFilm Tree, pioneers of FCP 24-frame post-production (www.digitalfilmtree.com).

Recording Timeline Playback

If you are receiving Final Cut Pro's output in your video deck or camcorder, you don't need to use Print to Video or Edit to Tape to record your FCP sequence to tape. Print to Video and Edit to Tape provide mastering options (color bars, slate, and so on). Edit to Tape also lets you start your recording at a specified timecode location. Otherwise, recording Timeline playback directly provides exactly the same output quality, and you may find it more convenient.

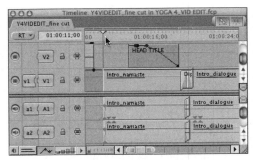

Figure 19.6 Cue your sequence in the Timeline. You don't need to set In and Out points unless you want to record less than the entire sequence.

To record Timeline playback onto tape:

1. Cue your videotape to the point where you want to start recording.

2. Cue your sequence in the Timeline (**Figure 19.6**).

3. Render any unrendered sections of your sequence. Unrendered material appears as blue, unrendered graphics when you record Timeline playback to tape.

4. Start recording on your video deck.

5. Choose Mark > Play, and then select a play option from the submenu (**Figure 19.7**). Final Cut Pro plays the contents of the Timeline as you specified and then holds on the final Timeline frame marked for playback. A freeze-frame is recorded on your tape until you stop recording.

6. Stop recording on your deck when Timeline playback is done.

Figure 19.7 Choose Mark > Play, and then select a play option from the submenu. In to Out plays only the portion of your sequence between the In and Out points.

Touching Up Your Timeline Playback

Recording your Timeline playback can be a real time-saver, but because you are making a live recording of Final Cut Pro's output, you need to do a few things differently to get smooth-looking results. Here are a few pointers:

◆ You don't have to use Print to Video just because you want to add pre-program elements to your tape output. Black leaders, color bars, and audio reference tones are available in the Viewer's Generators pop-up menu. You can edit your pre-program elements into the Timeline. For more information, read the introductory material in Chapter 17, "Titles and Generators."

◆ When you record Timeline playback, your camcorder or deck records whatever is sent to Final Cut Pro's external video output from the instant you press your deck's Record/Play button. If the Viewer or the Canvas is active, you'll record whatever is currently displayed until you start playback of your Final Cut Pro sequence. Even if you have positioned the Timeline playhead at the start of your sequence, you'll record a freeze-frame of the first frame of the sequence until you start Timeline playback. Make sure your external video output is displaying black by inserting a frame of black before the first frame in your sequence. Now the freeze-frame will appear as a solid black leader at the start of your recording.

◆ Place another frame of black at the end of your sequence, so when FCP reaches the end of the Timeline and freezes the final frame, that frame is black as well.

◆ Wait a few seconds after you start recording before you start the Timeline playback. You'll give your videotape time to get up to speed, and your picture will be rock solid from the first frame of your sequence.

Printing to Video

The Print to Video command is the correct choice when you want to make a videotape copy of a Final Cut Pro sequence or clip that includes pre-program elements, such as color bars, slate, and countdown. Print to Video is also your best choice if you want to loop playback and print multiple passes of your sequence on the same tape. If you have a controllable deck or camcorder, you can set up your Device Control preset so that FCP controls your deck during a Print to Video operation, but you don't need a deck that supports device control to use Print to Video. For information on hardware setup, see Chapter 2, "Installing and Setting Up."

If you don't need customized pre-program elements at the beginning of your dub, playing your sequence in the Timeline and recording the output directly may give you satisfactory results and save you some time as well. See "Recording Timeline Playback," earlier in this chapter.

Print to Video: Rendering Tips

◆ The quality of the render settings you specify before you use Print to Video is reflected in the quality and size of the playback window you see on your computer screen and on your videotape copy. In other words, what you see is what you get.

◆ If you have multiple layers of sub-sequences in your sequence (sub-sequences within sub-sequences inside the master sequence), it's a good idea to render things in the nested items at the lowest root, or sub-sequence, level first—at least for the first render. Subsequent adjustments and re-renders can be processed at the parent level, and Final Cut Pro will more reliably find all the nested sub-sequence material that requires re-rendering.

◆ The pre-program elements discussed in the section "Print to Video settings checklist" must be rendered before you can print to video.

◆ If you use the same pre-program sequence frequently, you might want to use the Print to Video function to assemble your color bars, leader, slate, and countdown in advance. After your pre-program sequence has been rendered, print it to video and then capture it as a clip. You can drop your prepared pre-program clip into sequences before you print, speeding up the final output process.

Print to Video settings checklist

The Print to Video dialog box (**Figure 19.8**) displays a list of formatting options. Select the elements you want to include in your videotape copy. You can specify durations for all options.

◆ **Leader:** Select the pre-program elements you want to include in your videotape copy. Your pre-program sequence will be assembled in the same order that the elements are listed in the dialog box, which is why there are two separate Black options. Check the elements you want to include, and then specify a duration (in whole seconds) for each option in the field next to the option. These elements must be rendered before printing to video can begin.

◆ **Color Bars:** Check this box to include color bars and a 1 kHz tone, preset to −12 dB, before the beginning of the sequence or clip.

◆ **Tone Level:** If necessary, adjust this slider to change the level of the preset −12 dB, 1 kHz audio reference tone. Note that this slider does not adjust the output level of your audio track, just the level of the reference tone.

◆ **Black:** Check this box to add black frames between the color bars and the slate.

◆ **Slate:** Check this box to include the slate information specified in the Slate Source pop-up menu in the adjoining field.

◆ **Slate Source pop-up menu:** Select a source for the information that appears on your slate. You can specify the sequence or clip name, a file on disk, or multiple lines of custom text.

◆ **Black:** Check this box to include black frames between a slate and a countdown (or before the beginning of the sequence or clip, if you aren't adding a slate and a countdown).

continues on next page

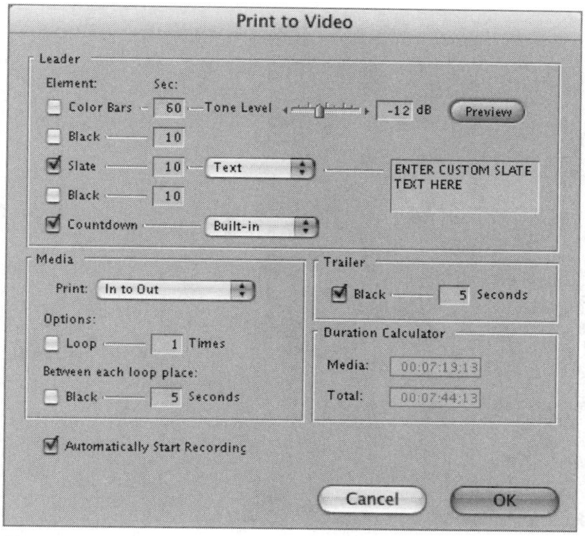

Figure 19.8 Select the pre-program elements you want to include in your videotape copy from the Print to Video dialog box.

- ◆ **Countdown:** Check this box to add a 10-second countdown before the sequence or clip (**Figure 19.9**). Choose FCP's built-in 10-second SMPTE standard countdown or use the corresponding pop-up menu and Browse button to specify your own custom countdown file.

- ◆ **Media:** Specify the material you want to include in the program section of your tape copy. You can print an entire sequence or clip, or only a marked portion. You can also loop the sequence or clip selection and insert black at the end of each loop.

  - ◆ **Print pop-up menu:** Choose Entire Media if you want to print the entire sequence or clip. Choose In to Out if you want to print a portion of the selected item. Specify the portion to be printed by setting In and Out points in the sequence or clip.

  - ◆ **Loop:** Check this box to print your selection multiple times.

- ◆ **Times:** Specify the number of repetitions for Loop.

- ◆ **Black:** Check this box to insert black frames between repetitions for the duration specified in the Black field.

- ◆ **Trailer:** Check the Black box to add a black trailer at the end of the printed sequence or clip; then specify the duration in the Seconds field. If you are looping the sequence or clip, the trailer appears after the last repetition.

- ◆ **Duration Calculator:** These fields display the total duration of all the media you selected to print, as you have specified it.

✔ Tip

- ■ Be sure your tape is long enough to record the entire program running time as calculated by the Duration Calculator. Most tape stock has a little extra capacity over the program length printed on the packaging, but it's a good idea to respect the official program length capacity.

Figure 19.9 Final Cut Pro's default countdown screen.

Figure 19.10 In the Browser, select the sequence you want to print to video.

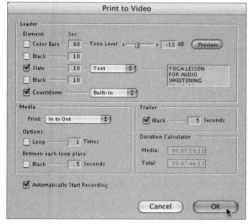

Figure 19.11 Select the pre-program elements you want to include in your videotape copy, and then click OK.

To print a sequence or clip to video without device control:

1. Read and follow the setup process described in "Setting up for recording to tape," earlier in this chapter.

2. In the Browser, select the sequence or clip you want to print (**Figure 19.10**). Open the sequence and make the Timeline active.

3. Choose File > Print to Video. The Print to Video dialog box will appear.

4. Select the program elements you want to include in your program. Refer to the "Print to Video settings checklist," earlier in this chapter, for explanations of your options. If you need to change any of the settings, do so now.

5. Click OK (**Figure 19.11**). If the sequence you select needs to be rendered before it can be printed, FCP automatically renders any unrendered sequence material, plus any additional program elements you've specified. When the rendering is complete, FCP displays a dialog box telling you to go ahead and start recording on your video deck.

PRINTING TO VIDEO

583

6. Start recording on your video deck or camcorder, and, when the device is up to speed, click OK to start playback of your Final Cut Pro sequence (**Figure 19.12**).

7. When your program material has finished printing, stop recording on your deck or camcorder. Final Cut Pro doesn't provide any end-of-process beep (the large black box disappears from the screen, and the interface returns), so check in at the scheduled end-of-program if you plan on recording unattended.

8. Play back your recorded sequence and check the quality.

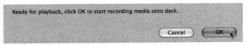

Figure 19.12 Click OK to start playback of your Final Cut Pro sequence.

✔ Tips

■ If you don't specify a post-program black trailer, Final Cut Pro will hold on the last frame of your sequence, creating a freeze-frame that will be recorded onto your tape until you stop recording.

■ Once the Print to Video process is complete, you'll have access to the render files created for Print to Video in your regular Timeline version of the sequence.

◆ If the Mirror on Desktop option is enabled (on the A/V Devices tab of the Audio/Video Settings window), you could experience dropped frames during your output to tape. You can disable mirroring by unchecking the box next to this setting.

To print a sequence or clip to video with device control:

1. Modify your Device Control preset to support device control during Print to Video operations (**Figure 19.13**) by following the instructions in "Specifying Device Control Settings" in Chapter 3.

2. Load the tape to which you want to record into your deck or camcorder, and cue the tape to the point where you want recording to start. If you are starting your recording at the beginning of a tape, be sure to record a few seconds of black at the very head of the tape.

3. Follow steps 1 through 4 in the preceding section, "To print a sequence or clip to video without device control"; then click OK.

   When the sequence rendering is complete, Final Cut Pro will automatically place your video deck in Record mode and then start playback. When the recording is complete, FCP will stop recording on your deck, the large black box will disappear from the screen, and the interface will return.

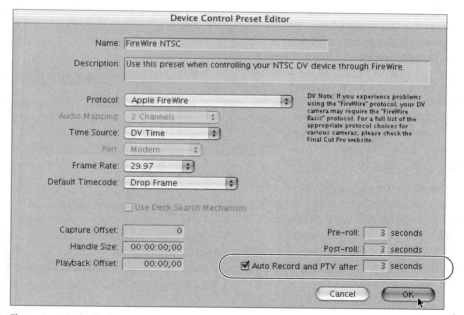

Figure 19.13 In the Device Control Preset Editor, check Auto Record and PTV After *x* Seconds to enable device control.

Editing to Tape

Use the Edit to Tape window to perform frame-accurate Insert and Assemble edits to videotape using Final Cut Pro's output as source material.

You must have device control over your video deck or camcorder to use Edit to Tape. The editing functions available to you depend on the capabilities of your external video hardware. If Final Cut Pro finds that your deck or camcorder is unable to perform certain functions, the Edit to Tape window will appear with those buttons or functions dimmed (**Figure 19.14**).

Edit to Tape offers three edit modes:

- **Insert edit:** An Insert edit overwrites media on the tape with the item you drag, using three-point editing rules. An Insert edit won't disturb the control track or timecode track. An Insert edit is the default edit type, if it is available on your deck. Note that Insert editing is not available for DV decks. For more information, see "FCP Protocol: Three-Point Editing" in Chapter 9.

- **Assemble edit:** An Assemble edit overwrites media on the tape, including the control and timecode tracks; this may cause a glitch at the beginning and end of the material being recorded. Note that Assemble editing is the only edit type available for DV decks.

- **Preview edit:** A Preview edit simulates an Insert edit without actually recording to tape. The preview includes all selected mastering options and plays back on your external monitor, if you have one. Note that Preview editing is not available for DV decks.

Figure 19.14 If your deck or camcorder is not equipped to perform Insert or Preview edits, the Edit to Tape window will appear with the Insert and Preview buttons dimmed.

On Peachpit.com

"Editing to Tape," a 12-page PDF, is available at:
www.peachpit.com/finalcutpro6vqp

Insert vs. Assemble Editing

Insert edits allow you to select which elements to include in the edit: video or audio, or both. An Insert edit begins and ends exactly at the specified timecode and leaves the timecode on your recording tape untouched.

Assemble edits overwrite the entire contents of the tape: video, audio, and timecode information. Modern assemble-only DV video decks are pretty good at performing accurate Assemble edits, because they generally extend the Out point of an edit operation a few frames to ensure that the deck can pick up the existing timecode when it performs the next edit. This guarantees a continuous timecode track, but it may not produce an Out point edit that's accurate enough to let you drop a shot into the middle of a finished program. Test the capabilities of your video equipment to see what kind of results you can expect.

EDITING TO TAPE

Exporting Sequences and Clips

If you want to convert a Final Cut Pro sequence to another digital format for use in computer-based media, exporting is the right choice. You can also export sound files, snippets of clips, or single-frame images. Final Cut Pro offers a variety of export formats.

When you export, Final Cut Pro uses QuickTime's compression codec and file format conversion features to generate a media file on your hard drive in the format you choose.

Here's how FCP's export options are organized:

When you choose File > Export, you'll see a list of QuickTime media export options: QuickTime Movie and Using QuickTime Conversion, plus a few special-purpose export options (**Figure 19.15**).

◆ The Export > QuickTime Movie command streamlines your export configuration chores by offering very limited settings options (**Figure 19.16**). Use Export > QuickTime Movie to export your sequence as a single movie using the same format settings as your sequence, or to export a reference movie for use in another compression program.

QuickTime Movie is also the correct export choice if your export destination is DVD Studio Pro or iDVD.

◆ The Export > Using QuickTime Conversion command gives you access to the full range of QuickTime-supported file formats. Export > Using QuickTime Conversion is your starting point when you want to export anything from still images to compressed audio files.

One of the QuickTime format options, QuickTime Movie format (**Figure 19.17**), is a good choice for producing highly compressed QuickTime movies or media files in full-resolution, uncompressed formats. QuickTime Movie format also offers video filters that you can apply as you export a sequence.

continues on next page

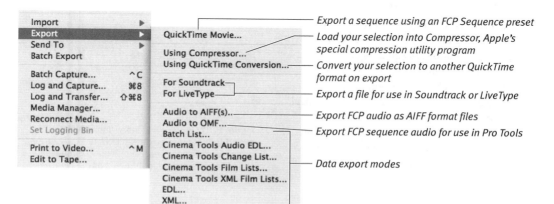

Figure 19.15 When you choose File > Export, you'll see FCP's palette of media export options.

EXPORTING SEQUENCES AND CLIPS

◆ These export options' settings are preset to offer streamlined export paths to FCP's family of special-purpose helper applications:

- ◆ Export > Using Compressor opens your selected clip or sequence in Compressor as a reference movie.

- ◆ Export > For Soundtrack generates a file optimized for use in Soundtrack by automatically including any scoring markers you've set in your sequence.

- ◆ Export > For LiveType creates a video element for use in LiveType, but the settings work just the same as Export > QuickTime Movie. Go figure.

◆ Two audio-only export options, Export > Audio to AIFF(s) and Export > Audio to OMF, offer an export path for project audio that's going to be finished in another digital audio editing environment. OMF format export is the right choice if your project audio is going to be finished in Pro Tools.

◆ Use Export > Batch List and Export > EDL to export just the editing and clip information from an FCP sequence as a formatted text file. Both types of edited text files can be used to re-create your FCP sequence on another editing system. A batch list is a tab-delimited text file containing the clip data listed in the Browser window. Batch lists can be used to recapture clip media, but you can't export a batch list of a sequence. If you need a text file that contains a sequential list of all the edits and all the individual clips used in your edited sequence, you should export your sequence as an EDL. For more information, see page IV-144 of Apple's *Final Cut Pro User Manual* PDF.

Figure 19.16 Use Export > QuickTime Movie to export your sequence as a single movie using one of your Sequence presets, or to export a reference movie for use with a third-party compression program.

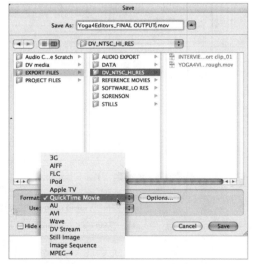

Figure 19.17 One of your QuickTime Conversion export format options, the QuickTime Movie format, is a good choice for producing highly compressed QuickTime movies for multimedia or the Web.

What's a Reference Movie?

The Export > QuickTime Movie feature offers the option of exporting your FCP clip or sequence as a reference movie. A reference movie is a bit of QuickTime media-handling wizardry. A small file that contains no media (except for a render file of your mixed sequence audio, plus video render files for parts of your exported sequence that haven't been rendered yet), a reference movie simply points to the original media files used in the exported sequence. Compressor, included with FCP, or third-party media compression programs, such as Cleaner, can use the reference movie pointer information from that small file to process the compressed version of your sequence using the larger original media files. DVD Studio Pro or iDVD can also use FCP reference movies to create a DVD disk image of your sequence.

Reference movies work with any QuickTime-compatible compression application that's installed on the same computer as your Final Cut Pro system. The compression program must have access to the original QuickTime source media files for your reference movie to work.

You won't see a "Make Reference Movie" option in the Save dialog box for the Export QuickTime Movie function. The only way to export your Final Cut Pro clip or sequence as a reference movie is to leave Make Movie Self-Contained unchecked. Pretty esoteric, huh?

✔ Tips

■ When you export a clip or sequence, Final Cut Pro includes only the material between the In and Out points. You can set In and Out points to select a portion of your clip or sequence, but be sure to clear In and Out points before you export if you want to export the entire clip.

■ The two tables that follow provide a sketch of the codecs and file formats you are most likely to use with Final Cut Pro and the way they're most commonly used. Note that these tables do not contain a complete list of QuickTime formats and codecs, and the summary of uses and characteristics is not comprehensive. **Table 19.1** lists the codecs most commonly used with Final Cut Pro. **Table 19.2** lists the most commonly used file formats. A complete list is available at the QuickTime Web site, at www.apple.com/quicktime/player/specs.html.

Table 19.1

FILE FORMAT	TYPE	USED FOR	ALPHA CHANNEL?
Some Useful QuickTime Codecs			
H.264	A/V	Scales from mobile devices to HD	No
Sorenson	A/V	CD-ROM	No
Cinepak	A/V	Older CD-ROM	No
QuickTime Fast Start	A/V	Web movies	No
QuickTime Streaming	A/V	Web movies	No
Animation	V	High-res digital export	Yes
M-JPEG A/M-JPEG B	V	Compressed files for editing	No
MPEG-4	A/V	Web streaming	No
DV-NTSC/DV-PAL	A/V	Importing DV into FCP	No
MPEG-2	V	DVD video	No
Apple ProRes 422	A/V	Compressed files for editing HD formats	Yes

Table 19.2

FILE FORMAT	TYPE	USED FOR	ALPHA CHANNEL?	COMPRESSION?
Some Useful QuickTime File Formats				
QuickTime Movie	A/V/Graphic/+	Cross-platform multimedia	Yes	Available
DV stream	A/V	iMovie DV media files	No	Yes
JPEG	Graphic	Graphics, video still frames	No	Available
Photoshop	Graphic	Multi-layered graphics	Yes	No
PICT	Graphic	Mac format	Yes	Available
PNG	Graphic	Graphics	Yes	No
TIFF	Graphic	Graphics	Yes	Available
AIFF	A	Common audio format	N/A	Available
WAVE	A	Windows audio format	N/A	No

EXPORTING SEQUENCES AND CLIPS

Codec vs. File Format

A codec is an algorithm, or mathematical formula, for compressing and decompressing digital media. The word *codec* is techie shorthand for COmpression/DECompression. Whenever you see compression options in the QuickTime interface, you're looking at a list of codecs.

A file format is one standardized way of organizing data so it can be recognized and used by an application or operating system. You could use the same compression codec in a variety of file formats, and vice versa. QuickTime Movie is an example of a file format that supports many, many codecs.

Figure 19.18 If you want to include the entire length of your sequence, be sure to clear any In and Out points before you export.

Exporting a QuickTime movie

The Export > QuickTime Movie command is the right choice when you want to export a sequence using the same sequence settings you used in the project, or the settings from another Sequence preset.

The Save dialog box for the Export QuickTime Movie function opens with your current Sequence preset settings already loaded, but you can select any other Sequence preset as an export format. Choose a render quality and specify whether to include audio or video, or both; specify your marker export preference; and you're done.

QuickTime Movie is the only export format that offers the option of exporting your sequence as a QuickTime reference movie.

Because the QuickTime Movie format supports the export of both chapter markers and reference movies, it's also the right export choice when you want to use DVD Studio Pro or iDVD to create a DVD of your FCP project.

To export a clip or sequence as a QuickTime movie:

1. *Do one of the following:*
   - Select a clip or sequence in the Browser.
   - In the Timeline, open the sequence you want to export.

2. Set In and Out points in your clip or sequence to mark the section you want to include in the exported file. If you want to export the entire item, clear any In and Out points from the item before export (**Figure 19.18**).

continues on next page

3. Choose File > Export > QuickTime Movie. The Save dialog box appears. This is your opportunity to review and confirm the export format settings.

4. From the Setting pop-up menu, use the default option—Current Settings—to use your current sequence preset as the export format, or select another sequence preset from the menu.

5. From the Include pop-up menu, choose Audio and Video, Audio Only, or Video Only (**Figure 19.19**).

6. If you want to export markers along with your file, select the type of markers you want to export from the Markers pop-up menu (**Figure 19.20**).

7. *Do one of the following:*

- ◆ Check Make Movie Self-Contained to export a QuickTime movie that duplicates all audio, video, and render files in one self-contained media file (**Figure 19.21**).

- ◆ Leave Make Movie Self-Contained unchecked to export a reference movie—a small movie file that contains only pointers to the original audio, video, and render files.

8. Type a name for your file in the Save As field and select a destination folder; then click Save.

✔ Tip

- ■ If your clip or sequence doesn't have an audio track, select Video Only from the Include pop-up menu. Even empty audio tracks will increase the file size of your exported clip.

Figure 19.19 Make a selection from the Include pop-up menu. You can export audio plus video, or audio or video only.

Figure 19.20 Choose Chapter Markers from the Markers pop-up menu to export chapter markers for use in iDVD or DVD SP.

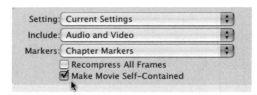

Figure 19.21 Check the Make Movie Self-Contained box to create a stand-alone movie.

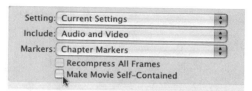

Figure 19.22 Uncheck the Make Movie Self-Contained box to create a compact reference movie you can use in another processing program like iDVD or DVD SP.

Figure 19.23 Open your exported reference movie in QuickTime Player, and you'll see a pop-up menu containing your exported chapter markers.

To export a Final Cut Pro movie for use in iDVD or DVD Studio Pro:

1. Follow steps 1 through 4 in the previous task, "To export a clip or sequence as a QuickTime movie."

2. If you want to export chapter markers along with your file, choose Chapter Markers from the Markers pop-up menu.

3. *Do one of the following:*

   ◆ Check Make Movie Self-Contained to make a stand-alone file that can be used with iDVD or DVD SP on this or another computer.

   ◆ Leave Make Movie Self-Contained unchecked to export a reference movie—a small movie file that contains only pointers to the original audio, video, and render files—which can be used only with a copy of iDVD or DVD SP that is located on the same computer as your Final Cut Pro project (**Figure 19.22**).

4. In the Save dialog box, type a name for your file in the Save As field and select a destination folder; then click Save.

   The exported movie contains any sequence markers you have designated as chapter markers (**Figure 19.23**).

FCP Protocol: DVD Chapter Markers

It's very simple to export a QuickTime Movie with chapter markers that you can import into iDVD or DVD Studio Pro, but you should be aware of a few rules governing the number and placement of chapter markers:

◆ Final Cut Pro chapter markers must be sequence markers, not clip markers.

◆ You can set a maximum of 99 chapter markers per video stream in a DVD SP project; iDVD allows no more than 36 chapter markers per project.

◆ Chapter markers must be set more than one second apart, and more than one second from the start or the end of a sequence.

Exporting Other QuickTime Formats

The Export > Using QuickTime Conversion option gives you access to the full range of QuickTime-supported file formats. Use this option to convert your FCP media to any of the following:

◆ Compressed QuickTime movies (use the QuickTime Movie format)

◆ Uncompressed, full-resolution file formats that include an alpha channel

◆ Still images in a variety of graphics file formats

◆ Audio tracks in a variety of compressed and uncompressed formats

To export a clip or sequence in another QuickTime format:

1. *Do one of the following:*

   ◆ Select a clip or sequence in the Browser (**Figure 19.24**).

   ◆ In the Timeline, open the sequence you want to export.

2. Set In and Out points in your clip or sequence to mark the section you want to include in the exported file. If you want to export the entire item, clear any In and Out points from the item before export.

3. Choose File > Export > Using QuickTime Conversion (**Figure 19.25**).

   The Save dialog box opens.

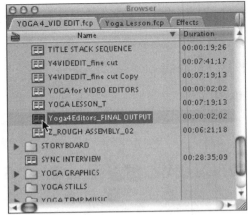

Figure 19.24 Select the sequence in the Browser.

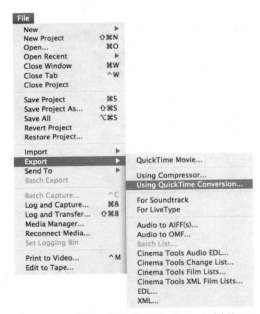

Figure 19.25 Choose File > Export > Using QuickTime Conversion. Choosing QuickTime gives you access to the full range of QuickTime's output formats.

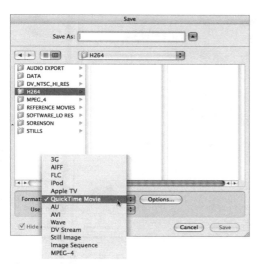

Figure 19.26 Choose an export file format from the Format pop-up menu.

Figure 19.27 Choose one of the Export Settings presets from the Use pop-up menu. These are the export presets available for the QuickTime Movie export format.

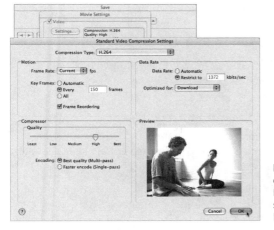

4. In the Save dialog box, choose an export file format from the Format pop-up menu (**Figure 19.26**); then *do one of the following:*

◆ Choose one of the Export Settings presets from the Use pop-up menu (**Figure 19.27**).

◆ Click the Options button to access the full QuickTime settings for the format you have selected. In the settings dialog box (or boxes) that follow, confirm or modify the export format settings, and then click OK. Export options will vary according to the format you have selected (**Figure 19.28**).

continues on next page

Figure 19.28 In the settings dialog boxes, confirm or modify the export format settings and click OK. Export options will vary according to the format you've selected. These are the settings dialog boxes for the H.264 codec.

EXPORTING OTHER QUICKTIME FORMATS

5. In the Save dialog box, name your file in the Save As field (**Figure 19.29**), and then select a destination folder.

6. Click Save.

✔ Tip

■ The QuickTime Movie format gives you the option of applying QuickTime's suite of video filters, and you can choose from a range of effects and image control filters (check out the Film Noise filter!). Select the filters as you configure your export options, and they will be processed as part of the export operation. You can access the filters by clicking the Filter button in the Movie Settings window (**Figure 19.30**).

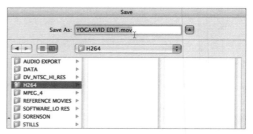

Figure 19.29 Type a name for your file in the Save dialog box's Save As field.

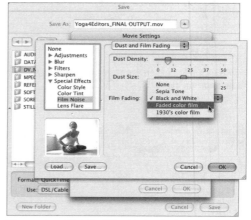

Figure 19.30 Click the Filter button in the Movie Settings window to access a palette of QuickTime filters you can apply as part of your export operation. QuickTime filters are available only in the QuickTime Movie format.

FCP Alert: Web Video Uses the Whole Video Frame

If you are converting your FCP sequence to a compressed format for Web or CD-ROM distribution, be aware that your exported file will show the entire video frame when viewed on a computer screen.

External video monitors typically don't display the edges of the video frame; that's why you're advised to keep your titles inside the "title safe" area. If you have unwanted elements, such as microphones, hovering about the edges of your video frame, you may never have seen them if you've been monitoring your framing only on an external video monitor.

So check your whole video frame by viewing it on your computer monitor. If you do find that your frame has unsightly edges, you can always crop your frame before you export.

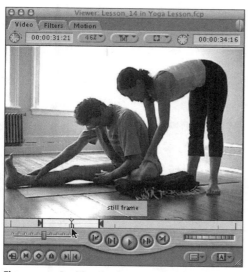

Figure 19.31 Position the Canvas or the Viewer playhead on the frame you want to export as a still frame.

To export a still image from a Canvas or a Viewer frame:

1. In the Canvas or the Viewer, position the playhead on the frame you want to export (**Figure 19.31**).

2. Choose File > Export > Using QuickTime Conversion.

3. In the Save dialog box, choose Still Image from the Format pop-up menu (**Figure 19.32**); then *do one of the following:*
   - Choose one of the Still Image settings presets from the Use pop-up menu.
   - Click the Options button to access a complete list of QuickTime still image formats and their settings. In the Export Image Sequence Settings dialog box, select an export format from the pop-up menu at the top of the dialog box (**Figure 19.33**), and then click OK.

continues on next page

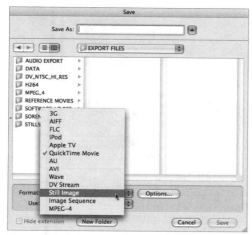

Figure 19.32 Select an export format from the Format pop-up menu.

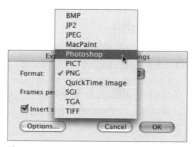

Figure 19.33 Selecting Photoshop as the export format from the pop-up menu in the Export Image Sequence Settings dialog box.

4. In the Save dialog box, type a name for your still frame in the Save As field and select a destination folder.

5. Click Save (**Figure 19.34**).

Final Cut Pro automatically adds the correct image file extension to the name you typed.

✔ Tips

■ If you want to export multiple still frames in a batch process rather than exporting them directly (as outlined in this task), you'll first need to use the Modify > Make Freeze Frame command to create FCP still clips. When you're done selecting your freeze-frames, you can use the batch-export feature to convert them all to graphics files in one operation.

■ When you export a still frame, ignore the frames-per-second settings—they don't apply to still-frame export.

To export an image sequence:

1. *Do one of the following:*

◆ Select a clip or sequence in the Browser.

◆ In the Timeline, open the sequence you want to export.

2. Set In and Out points in your clip or sequence to mark the section you want to export as a numbered image sequence (**Figure 19.35**). If you want to export the entire item, clear any In and Out points from the item before export.

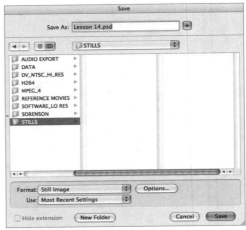

Figure 19.34 In the Save dialog box, type a name for your still frame in the Save As field; then select a destination folder and click Save.

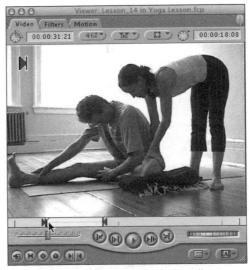

Figure 19.35 Set In and Out points in your clip or sequence to mark the section you want to include in the exported image sequence file.

Figure 19.36 Select Image Sequence from the Format pop-up menu.

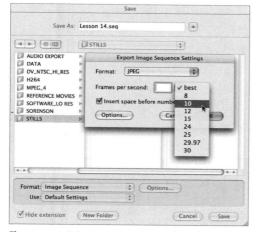

Figure 19.37 Select an export format from the pop-up menu at the top of the dialog box; select a frame rate for your image sequence; and then click OK.

3. Choose File > Export > Using QuickTime Conversion.

4. In the Save dialog box, choose Image Sequence from the Format pop-up menu (**Figure 19.36**); then *do one of the following:*

   ◆ Choose one of the Image Sequence settings presets from the Use pop-up menu.

   ◆ Click the Options button to access a complete list of QuickTime still image formats and their settings. In the Export Image Sequence Settings dialog box, select an export format from the Format pop-up menu; select a frame rate for your image sequence (**Figure 19.37**); and then click OK.

5. In the Save dialog box, type a name for your still frame in the Save As field, and then select a destination folder.

6. Click Save.

   Your image sequence is saved as a series of still graphics in the file format you selected.

Exporting Audio Files

If you need more control over your audio tracks than you can get inside FCP, or if you just got off the phone with the BBC and you have a sudden need for an audio-only excerpt from your movie, read on. This section describes three options for exporting audio from your Final Cut Pro project.

◆ If you'd like to export just the audio from your sequence, and you need access to export formats other than AIFF, you can use the Export > Using QuickTime Conversion command to convert and export your audio in a single operation.

If you plan to finish your audio in a dedicated audio editing workstation, you have a couple of options:

◆ Export your edited sequence audio tracks as individual AIFF files, and you can export up to 8 channels simultaneously, by mapping audio tracks to specific channels. Because each AIFF file exports as a single, continuous piece, you'll retain volume, pan, and filters settings but lose edit points.

◆ Export the audio tracks from an FCP sequence in Open Media Framework (OMF) format, and you can transport your edited audio to any OMF-compatible digital audio workstation.

To export audio only from a clip or sequence:

1. Select a clip or sequence in the Browser, or open the sequence in the Timeline.

2. Set In and Out points in your clip or sequence to mark the section you want to export as an audio file.

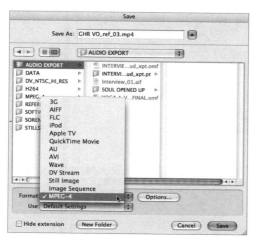

Figure 19.38 Choose File > Export > Using QuickTime Conversion, and then select an audio format from the Format pop-up menu. AIFF, AU, and Wave are all audio formats.

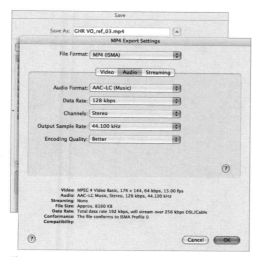

Figure 19.39 Select audio quality and compression settings from the Sound Settings dialog box, and then click OK.

3. Choose File > Export > Using QuickTime Conversion.

4. In the Save dialog box, choose an audio export file format from the Format pop-up menu (**Figure 19.38**); then *do one of the following:*

   ◆ Choose one of the audio export settings presets from the Use pop-up menu.

   ◆ Click the Options button to access the full QuickTime settings for the format you have selected. In the Sound Settings dialog box, select sample-rate (**Figure 19.39**) and compression settings, and then click OK.

5. In the Save dialog box, type a name for your audio file in the Save As field, select a destination folder, and then click Save.

✔ Tips

■ You can use the export method just described to convert the 44.1 kHz sample rate of a CD audio track. In the Sound Settings dialog box (see step 4 in the preceding procedure), choose 48 (or 32) kHz—the sample rate that matches your sequence audio's rate. Once you complete the export/sample-rate conversion, import the exported copy back into your project.

■ Final Cut Pro allows you to mix audio tracks with different sample rates in the same sequence. The program can convert the sample rate of nonconforming audio on the fly as you play back a sequence. Real-time sample-rate conversion does take processor power, however, and can occasionally produce nasty audible artifacts, so for best results, convert the sample rates of all your audio tracks to match the sequence settings.

To export audio in AIFF format:

1. Select a clip or sequence in the Browser, or open the sequence in the Timeline.

2. Set In and Out points in your clip or sequence to mark the section you want to export as an audio file.

3. If you want to map your sequence audio tracks to multiple audio output channels before export, follow the steps outlined in "To map sequence audio tracks to multiple audio output channels," later in this chapter.

4. Choose File > Export > Audio to AIFF(s).

5. In the Save dialog box, choose a sample rate, a bit depth, and an output channel configuration from the pop-up menus at the bottom of the box (**Figure 19.40**).

6. Type a name for your audio file in the Save As field; then select a destination folder and click Save.

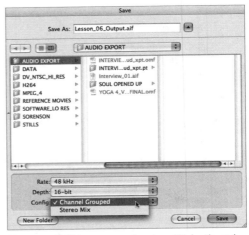

Figure 19.40 Choose a sample rate, a bit depth, and an output channel configuration from the pop-up menus at the bottom of the Save dialog box.

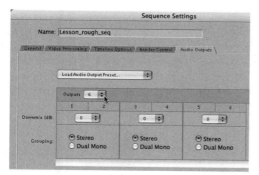

Figure 19.41 Before you can assign audio tracks to additional outputs, you must create those audio outputs in the sequence's Sequence Settings window. On the Audio Outputs tab, select output channels from the Outputs pop-up menu.

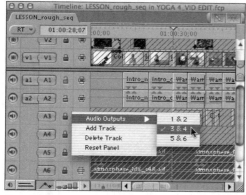

Figure 19.42 Once you've created the additional audio output channels, you can make output assignments by Control-clicking the track controls in the Timeline and choosing from the list of available output channels in the shortcut menu.

To map sequence audio tracks to multiple audio output channels:

1. On the Audio Outputs tab of the selected sequence's Sequence Settings window, select the number of output channels from the Outputs pop-up menu (**Figure 19.41**).

   If FCP doesn't detect compatible multi-channel audio hardware, you'll see a warning dialog box. You don't need the hardware to output multiple-channel AIFF files, so it's OK to dismiss the warning.

2. *Do one of the following:*
   - Control-click the track's targeting controls in the Timeline; then choose from the list of available output channels in the shortcut menu (**Figure 19.42**).
   - Control-click the track's name in the Track Selection pane in the Audio Mixer; then select outputs from the list of available output channels in the shortcut menu.

✔ Tip

- You can automatically configure sequence audio ouputs to match a selected sequence clip. Here's how: In the Timeline, select the sequence clip you want to match, then choose Sequence > Match Audio Outputs. Bingo. Audio output configuration is automatically set to match the selected clip's.

Exporting audio in OMF format

Final Cut Pro offers a powerful audio format conversion tool: the option to export the audio tracks from an FCP sequence in Open Media Framework (OMF) format. The exported OMF file contains the audio files, plus the audio edit information from your project file. That means you can export audio tracks with the original track separations, edit points, crossfades, and video sync intact.

Once your audio tracks are in an OMF-formatted file, you can import them into any OMF-compatible digital audio workstation (DAW) (**Figure 19.43**), the kind used at most professional audio post-production facilities. OMF export builds a much-needed bridge between FCP and professional audio post-production tools (and the audio professionals who use them).

Figure 19.43 Use Audio to OMF export to generate a file containing your audio tracks and edit information. You can then convert that file to a Pro Tools session file (see "Destination: Pro Tools?" later in this chapter).

FCP Protocol: OMF Audio Export

Here's a list of FCP's protocols governing the export of sequence audio to OMF format:

◆ Audio level and pan settings are included (FCP 6 only), however, audio filter settings from your sequence audio tracks are not included in the OMF export.

◆ Disabled sequence audio tracks (tracks with Track Visibility toggled off) are not included in the export.

◆ Any disabled individual audio clips are also excluded from export. To learn how to disable audio clips and tracks, see "Making a Timeline track invisible" in Chapter 10.

◆ All crossfades are exported as linear crossfades. Some OMF import utilities can't handle crossfade data at all, so perform a test conversion of your OMF file. If you can't test, configure your export OMF options to exclude crossfade data.

◆ Speed and Reverse effects that you have applied to your sequence audio clips will also be applied to the exported sound media.

◆ All the audio tracks contained within a nested sequence will be exported as a single, mixed audio item.

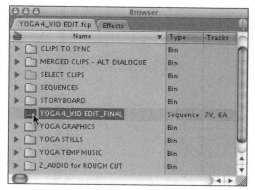

Figure 19.44 Select a clip or sequence in the Browser.

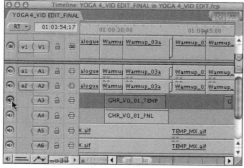

Figure 19.45 Click the Track Visibility button to turn off visibility of audio tracks you want to exclude from OMF export.

Figure 19.46 In the OMF Audio Export dialog box, specify sample-rate, handle duration, crossfade, audio level and pan options; then click OK.

To export audio from a clip or sequence in OMF format:

1. Select a clip or sequence in the Browser (**Figure 19.44**), or open the sequence in the Timeline.

2. In the Timeline, turn on track visibility for each audio track you want to export by clicking the track's Audible button. Turn off visibility on any audio tracks you want to exclude (**Figure 19.45**).

3. Choose File > Export > Audio to OMF.

4. In the OMF Audio Export dialog box, specify the following options; then click OK (**Figure 19.46**).

   ◆ **Sample Rate:** Choose a sample rate that matches your sequence audio sample rate. If your destination audio program can't work with files at that sample rate, choose the highest compatible rate. All sequence audio tracks will export at the sample rate you select. Sequence audio with different sample rates will be sample-rate-converted.

   ◆ **Sample Size:** Choose the highest bit depth supported by your Pro Tools system: 16- or 24-bit.

   ◆ **Handle Length:** Specify a duration for handles added to the audio clips. Clips used in their entirety will be exported without handles.

continues on next page

◆ **Include Crossfade Transitions:** Check this box to include crossfade transition data in your export file. Because crossfade transition data is incompatible with some OMF importing tools, you should test before you include transition data in your OMF export. When this option is disabled, extra source media is substituted for the duration of the crossfade. The source media added to cover the area of the crossfade will be in addition to extra source media added by the Handle Length option.

◆ **Include Levels:** Include sequence audio level settings and keyframes in the exported OMF file.

◆ **Include Pan:** Include sequence pan settings and keyframes in the exported OMF file.

5. In the Save dialog box, type a name for your OMF audio file in the Save As field, and then select a destination folder. Remember that the exported file contains the audio media as well as edit information, so it may be quite large.

6. Click Save (**Figure 19.47**).

Figure 19.47 Select a destination folder, type a name for your OMF file, and then click Save.

Destination: Pro Tools?

There's a good chance that your audio post-production facility will be using Digidesign's Pro Tools—the most widely used digital audio workstation program—to edit, sweeten, and mix your audio tracks.

The Export > Audio to OMF procedure itself is simple, but there are many versions of Pro Tools, each with different capabilities.

To make the OMF-to-Pro Tools conversion, you'll need one of the two helper applications available from Digidesign: OMF Tool or DigiTranslator. DigiTranslator is not free, but it's more reliable.

All the many specifics and "gotchas" are detailed in Apple's online technical article "Final Cut Pro 6: Limitations in exported OMF files:" http://docs.info.apple.com/article.html?artnum=305431

Batch Exporting

You can use the Batch Export feature to assemble groups of clips and sequences and then export them as QuickTime files in a single operation. You organize and specify export settings for your items in the export queue, which appears as a tab in the Export Queue window (**Figure 19.48**). Each top-level bin in the Export Queue window can contain multiple clips and sequences, individually or arranged in separate folders. All items and folders of items contained in a top-level bin in the Export Queue window will be exported with the same export settings, so you need a separate top-level export bin for each settings configuration you use. You don't need to export all the items in the export queue at once; you can select items and process only the items you select. The Status column in the Export Queue window tracks which items have been exported.

The batch export process exports only QuickTime files.

✔ Tip

■ Be sure to complete your batch export operations before you quit Final Cut Pro. All items will be deleted from the export queue when you quit.

◎ On Peachpit.com

"Batch Exporting," a 7-page PDF, is available at:
www.peachpit.com/finalcutpro6vqp

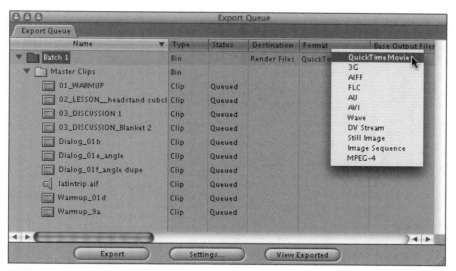

Figure 19.46 Organize and specify batch export settings in the Export Queue window. Columns in the Export Queue window display details about the batch export items and operate in the same way as Browser columns. Some export settings can be modified directly by Control-clicking in the data column.

Exporting for LiveType

LiveType accepts exported FCP reference movies in a variety of formats and resolutions. The Export > For LiveType menu command is an amenity, but you don't actually need to use it to export a movie you can use to position and time your titles.

If you aren't manipulating your exported sequence video as an object within LiveType, then it's best to place it as a background object so that it won't be rendered into the final title sequence.

To export a file for use in LiveType:

1. In the Browser, select the sequence that you want to export to LiveType, and then choose File > Export > For LiveType (**Figure 19.49**).

2. Name your exported file, and be sure to include markers if you are using them within your sequence.

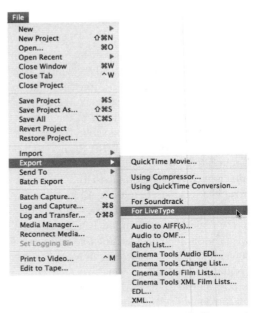

Figure 19.49 Choose File > Export > For LiveType to export a movie to use in LiveType.

3. In the Finder, launch LiveType and create a new project.

Do one of the following:

◆ Choose File > Place and select your exported FCP sequence movie file. Your file will be placed into a new, modifiable layer in LiveType.

◆ Choose File > Place as Background Movie and select your exported FCP movie. Your file will be placed into a protected layer in LiveType (**Figure 19.50**).

✔ Tips

■ You can open a LiveType project, place it into your FCP Timeline and manipulate it just as you would a clip. There's no need to export a rendered version of your LiveType element as you refine the placement and timing of your titles, but you'll still need to open your LiveType element in LiveType if you want to adjust title elements. You can save back and forth between FCP and LiveType as many times as you need.

■ If you brought your FCP movie into LiveType as an object but you want added flexibility once you reopen your LiveType project back in FCP, disable your imported FCP movie element and save your LiveType project before you open it. Your LiveType project file will display titles only.

Figure 19.50 To import your FCP movie as a protected layer in a LiveType project, launch LiveType, and then choose File > Place as Background Movie.

Exporting for Soundtrack Pro

Final Cut Pro offers multiple options for exporting material from FCP for use in Soundtrack Pro (STP).

◆ Send To > Soundtrack Pro Audio File Project creates a new STP project file containing just the selected clip.

◆ Send To > Soundtrack Pro Multitrack Project creates a new STP project file containing multiple selected clips or the entire contents of the selected sequence.

◆ Send To > Soundtrack Pro Script processes FCP audio using a script created in STP.

Get the full details on FCP-Soundtrack Pro interaction protocols in Apple's Soundtrack Pro manual.

✔ Tip

■ It's important to note that Send To > Soundtrack Pro Script processing is non-destructive *only* when the audio clips you select in FCP are already Soundtrack Pro projects. If you use this command to process FCP audio clips your original audio files will be processed in STP and then overwritten. Once you've processed it, you won't be able to revert to your original audio, so don't use the Send To > Soundtrack Pro Script command on FCP audio unless you know you want to make a permanent change to your audio media file.

Third-Party XML and OMF Interchange Applications

Final Cut Pro's designers built OMF and XML awareness into the program hoping that independent software developers would use these interchange formats to build custom interchange applications that make it easier to transfer work between FCP and other programs. Developers have fulfilled that promise. You can see Apple's list of approved developer/partners here: http://www.apple.com/finalcutstudio/partners/plugins.html

Automatic Duck, the first company to create XML and OMF interchange tools for FCP, has developed a suite of FCP plug-ins essential for editors working with FCP, Avid, Pro Tools, or After Effects.

◆ Export your FCP sequence as an XML file, then use Pro Import AE to import into After Effects with your Timeline reproduced—layers and clips, clip attributes such as scale and position, and even keyframes are ported into After Effects.

◆ Use the Pro Export plug-in to export your FCP sequence in an OMF format that Avid Media Composer or Symphony can read.

Contact Automatic Duck for details at www.automaticduck.com/products/ .

Figure 19.51 Control-click the audio clip you want to process in STP, then choose Send To > Soundtrack Pro Audio File Project from the shortcut menu.

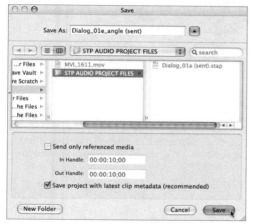

Figure 19.52 Enter a filename and choose a destination for the Soundtrack Pro audio project containing a copy of your clip. These STP project files contain copies of your media, so they can be quite large. Save them on your media drive.

To export an audio clip for use in Soundtrack Pro:

1. In the Timeline, Control-click the clip, then choose Send To > Soundtrack Pro Audio File Project from the shortcut menu (**Figure 19.51**).

2. In the Save dialog box, *do any of the following:*

   ◆ Check "Send only referenced media" if you want to copy into your new Soundtrack Pro audio project file only the portion of the media file between the clip's In and Out points. Ten second handles are added by default, but you can set a different handle size.

   ◆ Leave "Send only referenced media" unchecked, and the entire length of the selected clip's media file is copied.

   ◆ The "Save project with latest clip metadata (recommended)" checkbox is selected by default. With this option enabled, Final Cut Pro will automatically save the project immediately after the sequence is sent to Soundtrack Pro, making it easier to keep your FCP project and its related Soundtrack Pro projects in sync.

3. Enter a filename and choose a destination for the Soundtrack Pro audio project containing a copy of your clip (**Figure 19.52**).

continues on next page

EXPORTING FOR SOUNDTRACK PRO

The Send To Command: Final Cut Pro's Gateway to Final Cut Studio

Apple continues to tighten the integration between its suite of Final Cut Studio applications.

You can use the Send to command to save selected FCP project media and data as a Soundtrack Pro, Motion, or Shake project. Projects created with the Send to command maintain links with your original FCP project: modify the project file in one of FCP's sister applications and the FCP project it's linked to will automatically update to reflect the changes you made in the sister application. For more information, see Apple's *Final Cut Studio Workflows* PDF, available on the official Final Cut Pro Support Web site.

Soundtrack Pro creates a new project file containing a copy of the clip you selected.

4. Your new Soundtrack Pro audio project opens automatically in STP (**Figure 19.53**).

5. When you return to FCP, your audio clip has been relinked to a Soundtrack Pro render file of your processed audio (**Figure 19.54**).

Figure 19.53 The new Soundtrack Pro audio project automatically opens in STP.

Figure 19.54 When you return to FCP, you'll see that the audio in your Timeline clip has been relinked to a Soundtrack Pro render file of your processed audio.

MANAGING COMPLEX PROJECTS

Media management in a complex project requires creative solutions. Final Cut Pro has a few tools to help you keep your wig on straight as your current project snowballs toward the finish line, even as you're gearing up for the next one.

You'll be introduced to Final Cut Pro's media management tools: the Media Manager, the Reconnect Media feature, and the Make File Offline feature. You'll also find tips on how to delete files—and how to save them.

Final Cut Pro is a nondestructive, nonlinear editing system, and that design has an impact on the way it handles file management. You'll be much more effective as a media manager if you understand how Final Cut Pro tracks media files and project data before you use the media management tools described in this chapter.

Two sidebars in the book explain Final Cut Pro's file management protocols and how they affect the way the program operates. This information is key to understanding how Final Cut Pro works. If you haven't read them, see "What Is Nonlinear, Nondestructive Editing?" in Chapter 1, and "FCP Protocol: Clips and Sequences" in Chapter 4.

Using Media Management Tools

The amount of media you must handle seems to expand with your capacity to handle it. Digital video files are huge—you need more than 1 GB of disk space to store 5 minutes of full-resolution DV. Even a large disk array can be overwhelmed by the storage demands of a single digital video project.

Even if you have more than enough storage space to handle your project, you can reach a point where the number and complexity of sequence versions, clips, and render files in an open project can start to slow Final Cut Pro's performance. That's the time to think about shedding some excess baggage.

Final Cut Pro has powerful tools to help you manage your projects' media files: the Media Manager, the Render Manager, and the Reconnect Media and Make File Offline features.

◆ Like a Swiss Army knife, the **Media Manager** is a powerful, flexible tool for copying, moving, and recompressing your media files, and for trimming unused footage from media files. Spend some time exploring the Media Manager's capabilities early in your project—before you need them.

◆ Use the **Render Manager** to delete render files for obsolete projects or to remove obsolete render files from current projects. The Render Manager finds and lists files from unopened projects as well as from open projects. For more information, see "Using the Render Manager to manage rendered files" in Chapter 18.

◆ You can use the **Reconnect Media** feature to reestablish the links between the clips and sequences in your FCP project and their source media. If you accidentally break the link between a project, sequence, or clip and its underlying media files, you can use the Reconnect Media command to reestablish the connection. You can also use Reconnect Media to redirect online clips to use different source media.

◆ **Make File Offline** offers options for deleting media files, or just breaking the links between clips and sequences and their media files while leaving the media files on disk.

✔ Tips

■ Chapter 4, "Projects, Sequences, and Clips," outlines Final Cut Pro's organizing frameworks and the rules governing the behavior of projects, sequences, and clips. Before you try to manage your project media, read "About Clips," which describes FCP's clip types and clip handling behavior.

■ Please take time to read the excellent and informative "Overview of the Media Manager" starting on page IV-87 of Apple's *Final Cut Pro User Manual* PDF. This short chapter lays out the specifics of Media Manager protocols for processing media.

Using the Media Manager

The Media Manager is a multifunction tool for copying, moving, and deleting unused media from your Final Cut Pro projects, sequences, and clips. The flexibility of the Media Manager lets you customize media management operations for a wide variety of needs.

A media management operation involves your precious files, so you should plan your procedure before you proceed. Here's an overview of the process and recommended objectives; you'll find a few step-by-step examples later in this chapter.

This section includes:

◆ A setup checklist you can use when you're preparing your project for a Media Manager operation

◆ A step-by-step overview of a Media Manager operation

◆ A list of your options in the Media Manager window

◆ A description of the Media Manager operation processing order

◆ Step-by-step instructions for performing five common media management operations

 ◆ Copying or moving an entire project and its media

 ◆ Deleting media from a project

 ◆ Trimming unused media from a sequence.

 ◆ Creating an offline trimmed sequence

 ◆ Making a copy of a project and its media in a compressed file format

Setting up for a Media Manager procedure

Media management is a lot like house painting: You get the best results by investing most of your time in careful preparation. Here are some recommended prep steps:

◆ Figure out what you want to accomplish. Do you need a trimmed offline version of your sequence because you want to batch recapture your footage from the original tapes? Do you need to delete unused media from your project because you're running short on disk space? Develop a clear, detailed idea of the project and media that's going to best serve you as you move on to the next stage of your post-production work; then design a media management process that produces that project.

◆ Clean up before you operate. If you're processing all the elements in your project, follow the procedures recommended in "To streamline a project in progress," later in this chapter. If you are managing multiple projects that all reference the same media files, remember to include all relevant projects in your cleanup and inspection.

continues on next page

USING THE MEDIA MANAGER

◆ Give unique names to clips with duplicate names. If you've used a lot of subclips and *razor-bladed* (divided) clips in your sequences, consider renaming your subclips with a system of names that are brief, consistent, and easy to identify (**Figure 20.1**). Note that if your project requires a lot of subdividing and renaming, FCP's default clip-handing scheme is probably not the best setup for your project management; instead, you should convert your subdivided clips into subclips (which are master clips) so you can rename them individually. For more information, see "About Clips" in Chapter 4.

◆ Final Cut Pro will look in all projects open at the time you run your Media Manager operation. If you want Final Cut Pro to track items from other projects that might be affected by media files you're moving or deleting, open those projects before you proceed (**Figure 20.2**). You should also close any projects you want to exclude from item tracking.

✔ Tip

■ One final, important step: Before you proceed with your Media Manager operation, make a safety copy of your cleaned-up project files. If FCP should crash during Media Manager processing, your project files and/or media files could become damaged.

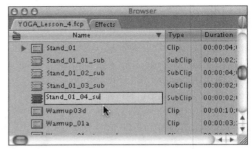

Figure 20.1 Give unique names to clips with duplicate names. Use names that are brief, consistent, and easy to identify.

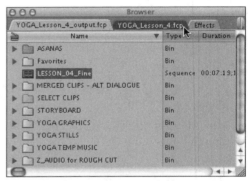

Figure 20.2 Final Cut Pro will look for additional items that reference your media files in all projects open at the time you run your Media Manager operation. Open all projects you want FCP to include in its scan.

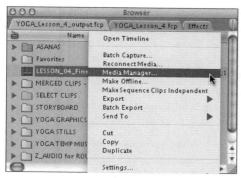

Figure 20.3 Select the clips and sequences you want to operate on; then Control-click a selected item and choose Media Manager from the shortcut menu. You can select items from the Timeline or, as pictured here, from the Browser.

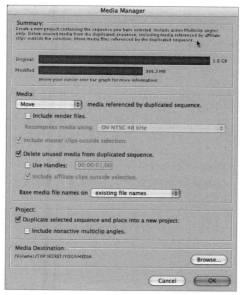

Figure 20.4 While you're setting options in the Media Manager window, keep checking the Summary feedback at the top of the window to see that you've designed your media management operation correctly.

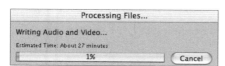

Figure 20.5 During Media Manager processing, a status window displays the progress of each stage in the operation.

To perform a Media Manager operation:

1. Select the clips and sequences you want to operate on. You can select a whole project by selecting every item on the project's tab in the Browser. You can even select a clip you've used in a sequence.

2. Choose File > Media Manager; or Control-click the item and choose Media Manager from the shortcut menu (**Figure 20.3**).

3. Configure your options in the Media Manager window, and keep checking the feedback in the Summary section at the top to see that you've designed your media management operation correctly, that you're getting the results you want, and that you have enough disk space to accommodate any new files you're creating (**Figure 20.4**).

4. When you click OK to start the process, Final Cut Pro examines the clips and sequences you've selected. Any requests for additional information or warnings will appear now.

5. After you've responded to any warnings or prompts, processing begins. A status window displays the progress of each stage in the operation (**Figure 20.5**). If the operation encounters an error, processing stops and Final Cut Pro displays an error message.

6. When the Media Manager operation is complete, go to the processed files' location on disk and check out the results. If the product of your media management procedure is a new project and a trimmed sequence, you should open the sequence, play it, and check your media thoroughly before you throw away your old files. Is it in sync? Are the handles you specified present? Are all your graphics and digital audio files present and intact?

Media Manager window options

After you've selected the items in your project that you want to process, open the Media Manager window to configure the media management procedure you want to perform.

The Summary section at the top of the window updates as you move down the options list, setting up your Media Manager operation. The upper feedback area displays a description for each process option you've specified. The lower feedback area displays a pair of bar graphs representing the total time and file size of the media you've selected—before and after processing. The upper bar (labeled Original) represents the size of your selected media files before processing. The lower bar (labeled Modified) shows the size of your files after processing. Moving your pointer over a bar graph reveals the hard disk location of the selected media files, pre- and post-processing.

The Media section lists your media file management options. In this section, you specify how you want to process the actual media files attached to the virtual clips and sequences in your project. Your choice of individual options determines how FCP will process the media files referenced by the clips and sequences you've selected. Media Manager options are context sensitive; options that aren't compatible with your currently selected settings are dimmed.

In the Project section, you specify how you want to process the selected items (the virtual clips and sequences) in your project file. This section doesn't create or destroy media files; it creates new project files that contain virtual clips and sequences that have been modified to reflect the changes you've specified in the Media section.

In the Media Destination section, you'll choose a folder location for any media files you're copying or moving.

You can fine-tune your media management process specifications by selecting and deselecting various combinations of options and then looking over the feedback in the Summary section to see whether you're getting the results you need. **Figure 20.6** shows an overview of the Media Manager window.

✔ Tip

- Understanding the distinction between modifying your project's virtual clip and sequence information in the Project section and modifying your actual media files with the file-processing options available in the Media section is key to using the Media Manager successfully. To learn more, see "FCP Protocol: Clips and Sequences" in Chapter 4.

Summary section: Get feedback on the results of your Media Manager settings

◆ The Summary section displays a description of the media management process specified by the current options settings. The status area updates every time you change your Media Manager window settings.

Media section: Choose settings for your project's media files

◆ **Process Mode:** Choose a process mode from this pop-up menu. This option specifies how you want to process the source media files on disk that are linked to your selected clips and sequences:

◆ **Copy:** Copies the source media files attached to the clips in your sequence. The original source media files are not touched. Make sure you have enough disk space available to use the Copy option.

◆ **Move:** Moves the source media files to the new location you specify and removes them from their current locations on disk. All projects that reference these media files must be open at the time you move the media, or they will lose their links to these media files.

continues on next page

As you select your options in the lower part of the window, the Summary updates to show you how your selection affects the process

The bar graphs represent the size of your media files before and after processing

Make a selection from the Media section's pop-up menu to specify how you want to process the source media files referenced by your selected FCP project

Check this box to delete unused portions of your selected media files

If you are adding handles, enter a duration to be added to the head and tail of each file

Check to create a new project containing your processed clips and sequences

Choose a destination for any new source media files you are creating

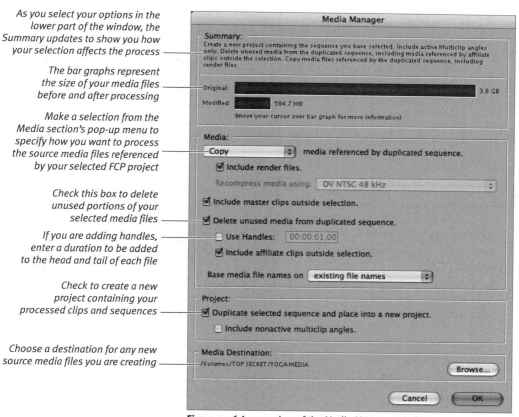

Figure 20.6 An overview of the Media Manager window.

◆ **Recompress:** Makes copies of the selected files using a different compression codec. Use Recompress when you want to make an Offline RT low-res copy of your project's media files.

◆ **Use Existing:** Creates a trimmed version of each clip by copying just the portion you've marked from the original file, and then deletes the full-length original. When you select a batch of clips or a sequence to trim, the Media Manager performs trim operations one clip at a time. Even though you are deleting unused media from existing clips, you will need enough extra drive space to accommodate the first trimmed media file copy. You can't undo this operation.

◆ **Create Offline:** Performs all project data processing as specified, and then produces offline copies of your selected clips and sequences that reflect your changes. The new offline clips and sequences have no links to existing media files and are ready to be used for batch recapturing.

◆ **Include Render Files:** Check the box to include render files in any Copy or Move operation.

◆ **Sequence Preset Options for Recompress and Offline Mode:** This pop-up menu contains a list of currently available Sequence presets. The pop-up menu's purpose (and its label) are context sensitive.

   ◆ **Recompress Media Using:** If you select Recompress as your Process Mode, you should select the Sequence preset whose settings you want to use to transcode the source media files on disk that are linked to your selected clips and sequences. For more information, see "To copy a project and its media in a compressed format," later in this chapter.

◆ **Set Sequences To:** If you select Offline as your Process Mode, you should select the Sequence preset you want to use for your new offline sequence. For more information, see "Creating an offline trimmed sequence," later in this chapter.

◆ **Include master clips outside selection:** Check the box to analyze any media files attached to the items you've selected for processing and to add to your selection any master clips that are referenced by the items you selected.

◆ **Delete Unused Media from Duplicated Items:** Check the box, and the Media Manager will analyze any media files attached to the items you've selected for processing and remove any media outside the In and Out points. If you're copying or moving your files, checking this option means that the unused media won't be included in the new copies. If you're trimming existing files, the unused media will be deleted from your hard disk. See "FCP Protocol: Deleting Unused Media in Projects Containing Affiliate Clips" for protocols governing the interaction of this option, the Include Affiliate Clips option, and the Duplicate and Place in New Project option.

◆ **Use Handles:** Check the box to add handles (extra frames beyond the In and Out points) to files that will have unused media removed. Use Handles is available only if you've checked the Delete Unused Media option. To set the handle duration, enter a value in the field. The default duration is one second. If your files have insufficient media to accommodate the handles, Final Cut Pro will make the handles as long as the existing media allows. If you have enough footage, and if your disk space allows it, it's a good idea to include handles when you trim media files. You'll be glad to have the flexibility later.

✔ Tip

■ The Delete Unused Media and Use Handles options won't affect AIFF- or WAV-format audio files. Final Cut Pro will copy the entire file.

◆ **Include Affiliate Clips Outside Selection:** Check the box to analyze any media files attached to the items you've selected for processing and to add to your selection any material that's referenced by other project clips affiliated to the items you selected.

◆ **Base Media File Names On:** Choose to base the filenames of any new media files created in your Media Manager operation on the filenames of existing media files or on clip names. If you've renamed your clips and want to generate media files with names that match the new names, choose clip names.

Project section: Choose settings for your project's virtual clips and sequences

◆ **Duplicate Selected Items and Place into a New Project:** Check the box to create a new project file that contains duplicates of the sequences and clips you've selected. The duplicate items in the new project will reflect any trimming you've specified. Any new media files you create will be linked to this new project. Creating a duplicate project that reflects your changes is generally a good idea. Because the duplicate you're creating is a project file containing edit information only, it's not very big. When the process is complete, you can compare the new project with the original to see whether your Media Manager process yielded the results you wanted.

◆ **Include nonactive multiclip angles:** Check the box to include the media for both active and nonactive multiclip angles. Uncheck the box to process only the media associated with active multiclip angles. For more information about multiclip editing, see Chapter 9, "Basic Multiclip Editing."

Media Destination section: Choose a storage location for your media files

◆ **Media Destination:** Click Browse, and then navigate to the drive location where you want to save any new project and media files created by a Copy or Move operation.

FCP Protocol: Deleting Unused Media in Projects Containing Affiliate Clips

Final Cut Pro's clip-handling behavior affects media management procedures that delete unused media from your project. When you edit a master clip from the Browser into a sequence, FCP's default behavior is to make an affiliated clip copy, which then appears in your sequence. Edit that same master clip into a different sequence, and you generate another affiliated sequence clip copy—and all three are taken into consideration when you make a selection in the Media Manager. Select a sequence in your project and choose to delete unused media, and FCP will examine the media files attached to those sequence clips and also preserve any media that's referenced by other project clips affiliated to the clips in the sequence you selected for processing. Which additional media is preserved depends on your configuration of the Include Affiliate Clips option, the Include Master clips option, and the Duplicate and Place in New Project option.

If you check the Include Master Clips option (or if this option is selected by default in the Media Manager operation you've configured), Media Manager adds any media in affiliated master clips that's been selected by In or Out points. This rule is the one that's the most likely to trip you up and add unexpected gigabytes of extra media to your trimmed project. Affiliated clips trigger this automatic behavior because the Media Manager is programmed to save enough media so that every clip included in your trimmed project can be reconnected automatically.

So, how can you limit your trimmed project to just the media you've actually used in a sequence? Here are a few options:

- Uncheck "Include master clips outside selection" and "Include affiliate clips outside selection" to restrict your selection to clips and sequences you've actually selected. The only Media manager modes that allow you to uncheck these options are Copy and Recompress, and only with the Duplicate and Place in New Project option checked.

- Convert the project clips in your Media Manager operation to independent type, breaking their connection to any affiliated clips.

- Delete any unnecessary affiliated clips from your project before you media-manage.

- Clear all unnecessary In and Out points from master clips affiliated with your sequence clips. See the tip later in this chapter that outlines an easy way to do this.

- Copy just your selected clips and sequences into a new project, and then close the original project; clip affiliations apply only within a single project.

On page IV-101 of Apple's *Final Pro User Manual* PDF, you'll find advice on using the Media Manager to delete unwanted media from your projects. Recommended reading for all aspiring media losers.

FCP Protocol: Media Manager Operation Processing Order

When you're planning (or troubleshooting) a media management operation, it can help to know the specific order of events in a Media Manager operation *after* you've selected your options and clicked OK.

Media Manager events are processed in the following order:

1. If you've chosen Duplicate Selected Items and Place in New Project, you're prompted for a name and location for the new project file containing your processed clip and sequence data.

2. If you've chosen to delete unused media from any existing media files, all items outside your current selection are scanned to see if they use those same media files. FCP will look in all projects open at the time you perform the Media Manager operation, but it will not check any closed projects.

3. If FCP detects other clips or sequences that refer to the media files you're about to alter, the Additional Items Found dialog box appears, asking if you want to add these items to the current selection, exclude them from your selection and risk making them offline, or cancel the operation. For more information, see "'Additional Items Found'—What Are Your Options?" in Chapter 5.

4. FCP checks your selected destination disk to see if there is enough available disk space to hold any new media files generated by the media processing options you've selected. If there's not enough available disk space, a dialog box appears, asking you to specify a new destination disk or cancel the operation.

5. If items outside your selection were found and you chose to exclude additional items, those items are taken offline now.

6. FCP copies or moves your specified media files to your selected destination. If you selected Delete Unused Media from Duplicated Items, the unused media is removed. If your selection includes multiple clips referencing the same media file, Final Cut Pro creates (and names) separate media files copied from the original clip. If any of the multiple clips have overlapping reference points, Final Cut Pro creates (and names) a single media file for use by those clips. See "FCP Protocol: Deleting Unused Media in Projects Containing Affiliate Clips," earlier in this chapter, for additional protocols governing this processing step.

7. If you included render files, they're copied or moved to the selected destination.

8. If you chose Duplicate Selected Items and Place in New Project, FCP creates a new project and copies all selected sequences and clips.

9. Sequence and clip items in your original or newly created project are relinked with any copied or moved media files.

Copying or moving an entire project and its media

If you have been working on a project with media files scattered across a number of different drives, you might want to copy your entire project and all the media files associated with it to a single drive as part of general project streamlining and maintenance. Or you might copy an entire project onto an external drive to hand off the project to another editor. **Figure 20.7** shows the Media Manager window settings for copying a project and its media. For more information on these settings, see "Media Manager window options," earlier in this chapter.

✔ Tip

■ Do you really need to preserve every scrap of media and every old duped sequence in your project? Redundant copies of project items may seem valuable now, but will you remember why you saved them when you return to this project in a year? Consider some project streamlining before you pack up and move. Check out the "Deleting Media" and "Project Maintenance Tips" sections later in this chapter for ideas.

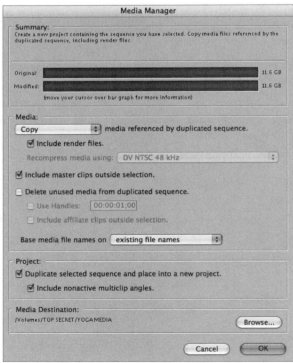

Figure 20.7 Setting Media Manager window options for copying an entire project and its media files to a new location.

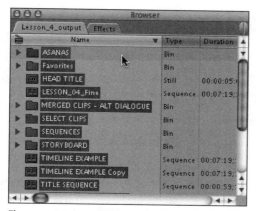

Figure 20.8 Select all the items on the project's tab in the Browser.

Figure 20.9 Control-click one of the selected items in the Browser; then choose Media Manager from the shortcut menu.

To move or copy a project and its media to another location:

1. In the Browser, select all the items on the project's tab (**Figure 20.8**); *then do one of the following:*
   - ◆ Choose File > Media Manager.
   - ◆ Control-click a selected item in the Browser; then choose Media Manager from the shortcut menu (**Figure 20.9**).

2. In the Media Manager's Media section, *do one of the following:*
   - ◆ Choose Copy from the Process Mode pop-up menu if you want the Media Manager to make a copy of your project and files in the new location and leave your original project and files untouched.
   - ◆ Choose Move from the Process Mode pop-up menu if you want the Media Manager to make a copy of your project and files in the new location and then delete your original project and files from their current locations.

3. Check Include Render Files to include any render files associated with your project.

4. Uncheck Delete Unused Media from Duplicated Clips to deselect it.

   The Use Handles, Include Master Clips, and Include Affiliate Clips Outside Selection check boxes are unavailable because you are copying the full length of all your clips.

continues on next page

USING THE MEDIA MANAGER

5. In the Project section, check Duplicate Selected Items and Place into a New Project to select it.

6. In the Media Destination section, click Browse; then navigate to the disk location where you want to copy or move the project's media files (**Figure 20.10**).

7. Check the Summary section at the top of the window to see that you've configured your settings correctly; then click OK.

8. In the dialog box, enter a name in the Save As field, choose a location to save your new project file, and then click Save (**Figure 20.11**).

   The Media Manager operation proceeds. A status window displays the progress of each stage in the operation. If the operation encounters an error, the processing stops and Final Cut Pro displays an error message. When the process is complete, your new project appears on the front tab of the Browser (**Figure 20.12**).

Figure 20.10 Select the disk location where you want to copy or move the project's media files.

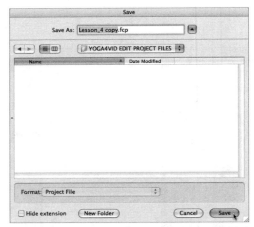

Figure 20.11 Enter a name for your new project file and choose a location in which to save it; then click Save.

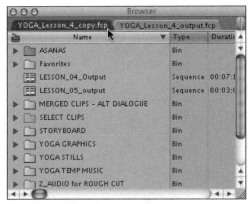

Figure 20.12 When the process is complete, your new project appears on the front tab of the Browser.

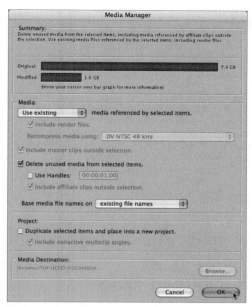

Figure 20.13 Media Manager window options configured to delete unused media from an existing project.

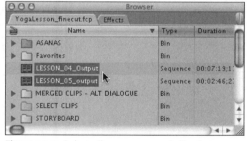

Figure 20.14 Select all sequences and clips from which you want to delete unused media.

Deleting media from a project

You can use the Media Manager to free up disk space by deleting just the parts of media files that you're not using in your project. When you delete unused portions of existing media files, the Media Manager creates the trimmed version of each media file by copying just the used portion from the original file, and then deletes the original. Even if you select a batch of clips or a sequence to trim, the Media Manager performs this trim operation one file at a time, so you need only enough drive space to accommodate a copy of your single largest trimmed media file. **Figure 20.13** shows the Media Manager window settings for deleting unused media from an existing project. For more information on these settings, see "Media Manager window options," earlier in this chapter.

To delete unused media from a project:

1. In the Browser, select all sequences and clips from which you want to delete unused media (**Figure 20.14**); *then do one of the following:*

   ◆ Choose File > Media Manager.

   ◆ Control-click a selected item in the Browser; then choose Media Manager from the shortcut menu.

2. In the Media Manager's Media section, choose Use Existing from the Process Mode pop-up menu.

3. Check Delete Unused Media from Selected Items to select it.

   If your selection includes affiliated clips, the Include Master Clips and Include Affiliate Clips Outside Selection options are enabled automatically. See "FCP Protocol: Deleting Unused Media in Projects Containing Affiliate Clips," earlier in this chapter, for details on your options.

continues on next page

4. If you want to maintain handles beyond the In and Out points of your media, check the Use Handles option; then enter a timecode duration.

5. In the Project section, uncheck Duplicate Selected Items and Place into a New Project to deselect it.

6. Check the Summary section at the top of the window to see that you've configured your settings correctly; then click OK.

7. If the files you've selected for trimming would delete media referenced by additional clips or sequences in this or another open project, the Media Manager displays the Additional Items Found dialog box (**Figure 20.15**) and offers you an opportunity to add those items to your selection. See "'Additional Items Found'—What Are Your Options?" in Chapter 5 for more information. Click Add or Continue to complete the operation.

If you choose to continue the process, the Media Manager operation proceeds. A status window (**Figure 20.16**) displays the progress of each stage in the operation. If the operation encounters an error, the processing stops and Final Cut Pro displays an error message. Your source media files are trimmed to include only the media actually used in your selected sequences and clips (plus handles, if specified) and remain in the same disk location.

Figure 20.15 If the trim operation you specified would delete media used by additional clips or sequences in this or another open project, the Media Manager displays the Additional Items Found dialog box.

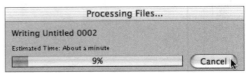

Figure 20.16 While the Media Manager is processing, a status window displays the progress of each stage in the operation.

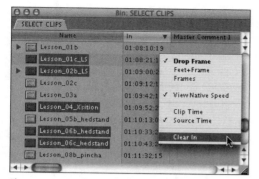

Figure 20.17 To clear In (or Out) points from multiple Browser clips in a single operation, Control-click the In (or Out) point column and choose Clear In from the shortcut menu.

✔ Tips

- Irrelevant In and Out points lingering in your master clips can cause the size of your trimmed project's media to swell unnecessarily, because FCP automatically preserves the media of any master clips affiliated with your selection that are marked with In or Out points. Here's an easy way to blow them away. In the Browser, select the master clips whose In and Out points you want to clear, then Control-click the In or Out column and choose Clear In (**Figure 20.17**). With the edit points removed, your trimmed project will retain less media. Be sure to leave In and Out points on master clip media you want to preserve in your trimmed project.

- If your Media Manager operation allows it, you could uncheck the Include Master Clips Outside Selection option, and then hand-select the additional master clips you want to preserve.

Trimming unused media from a sequence

This Media Manager operation is designed to copy one or more sequences into a new, trimmed project that contains just the footage you're using in your sequences. This technique can simplify your project management by removing the outtake footage from your drive. **Figure 20.18** shows the Media Manager window settings for trimming unused footage from sequences.

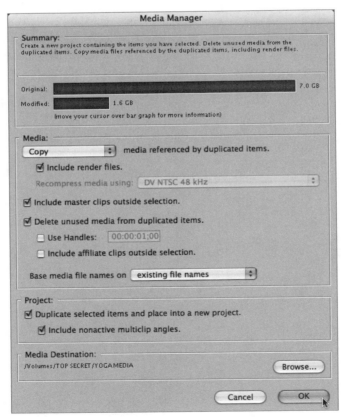

Figure 20.18 Media Manager window options configured to copy one or more sequences into a new, trimmed project that contains the sequence footage.

Figure 20.19 Select the disk location where you want to store the new, trimmed media files generated by the copy operation.

To trim unused media from a sequence:

1. In the Browser, select just the sequences from which you want to delete unused media, *then do one of the following:*

    ◆ Choose File > Media Manager.

    ◆ Control-click a selected item in the Browser; then choose Media Manager from the shortcut menu.

2. In the Media Manager's Media section, choose Copy from the Process Mode pop-up menu.

3. In the Project section, check Duplicate Selected Items and Place into a New Project.

    The Include Master Clips Outside Selection and Include Affiliate Clips Outside Selection options become available.

4. Check Delete Unused Media from Selected Items to select it.

5. Uncheck Include Master Clips Outside Selection and uncheck Include Affiliate Clips Outside Selection to ignore affiliated clips and include just the media you're using in your selected sequences.

6. If you want to maintain handles beyond the In and Out points of your media, check the Use Handles option; then enter a timecode duration.

7. If you've renamed your clips and you want your trimmed media files to use the new names, choose Clip Names from the Base Media File Names On pop-up menu.

8. In the Media Destination section, click Browse; then navigate to the disk location where you want to store the project's new, trimmed media files generated by the copy operation (**Figure 20.19**).

continues on next page

9. Check the Summary section at the top of the window to see that you've configured your settings correctly, then click OK.

10. In the dialog box, enter a name in the Save As field, choose a location to save your new project file, and then click Save (**Figure 20.20**).

11. If the media files you've selected for trimming are referenced by additional subclips, clips, or sequences you didn't select, the Media Manager displays the Additional Items Found dialog box and offers you an opportunity to add those items to your selection. Your objective is to trim unused media from your sequences, so if you're confident of your selection, click Continue to complete the operation. See " 'Additional Items Found'—What Are Your Options?" in Chapter 5 for more information.

The Media Manager operation proceeds. A status window displays the progress of each stage in the operation. If the operation encounters an error, the processing stops, and Final Cut Pro displays an error message. When the process is complete, your new project appears on the front tab of the Browser. The media bin you created in your new project contains clips referencing media files that match the selected clips you assembled in your sequence (**Figure 20.21**). These files are trimmed to include only the media actually used in the sequence.

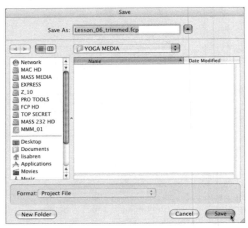

Figure 20.20 Enter a name and choose a location to save your new project file; then click Save.

Figure 20.21 The new project appears on the front tab of the Browser. The new project's media bin contains clips referencing media files that match your sequence's clips.

Creating an offline trimmed sequence

You can use the Media Manager to analyze a sequence and then create a new offline version of the sequence that includes only the clips you actually used in the sequence, plus handles (extra frames) of a length you specify. The new offline sequence also includes all your clip names, filter settings, transitions, keyframes, titles, generators, and so on.

Creating a trimmed offline sequence is the first step in a commonly used media management plan. The second step is to use the new, offline sequence as a batch list to batch recapture your source media from the original tapes. You recapture only the media you need for the trimmed sequence; then your sequence is re-created, and you're ready to perform the third step, which is to re-render and carefully check your re-created sequence. If you're satisfied, and if you are short of drive space, you can then delete the old version of your sequence and the old, untrimmed media files associated with it.

(Be careful that you don't toss your graphics and music files, though!)

Creating a trimmed offline sequence is also an important part of any media management plan that involves capturing and editing a project with lower-resolution media (such as the Offline RT format) and then recapturing the media at a higher resolution at the final output stage.

Any source media used in your sequence that doesn't have a timecode reference (such as Adobe Photoshop files or digital audio from a CD) is not trimmed. The sequence clips in the new, trimmed version of the sequence retain their links to those source media files in their present disk location.

Figure 20.22 shows the Media Manager window settings for creating a trimmed offline sequence. For more information on these settings, see "Media Manager window options," earlier in this chapter.

For more information on batch capturing, see "Batch Capturing Clips" in Chapter 5.

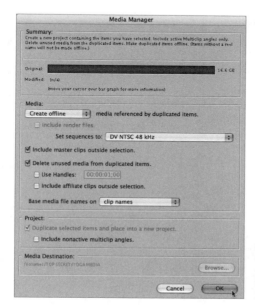

Figure 20.22 Media Manager window options configured to create an offline version of your sequence, ready for batch recapturing.

To create a trimmed offline sequence:

1. Select the sequence in the Browser, *then do one of the following:*

   ◆ Choose File > Media Manager.

   ◆ Control-click the selected sequence in the Browser, then choose Media Manager from the shortcut menu (**Figure 20.23**).

   The Media Manager opens.

2. In the Media Manager's Media section, choose Create Offline from the Process Mode pop-up menu.

   Because you're creating a duplicate offline sequence, the Check Duplicate Selected Items and Place into a New Project option is selected by default.

3. Select the Delete Unused Media from Duplicated Items check box.

4. If you want to add offline copies of affiliated project items to your project, check the Include Master Clips Outside Selection and Include Affiliate Clips Outside Selection options to add clips affiliated with the clips in your selected sequence. See "FCP Protocol: Deleting Unused Media in Projects Containing Affiliate Clips," earlier in this chapter, for details on your options.

5. If you want to maintain handles beyond the In and Out points of your sequence clips, check the Use Handles option, then enter a timecode duration.

6. Check the Summary section at the top of the window to see that you've configured your settings correctly, then click OK.

7. In the dialog box, enter a name for the project containing your new offline sequence, choose a location to save your new project file, and click Save (**Figure 20.24**).

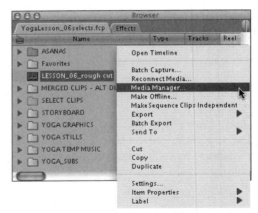

Figure 20.23 Control-click the selected sequence in the Browser; then choose Media Manager from the shortcut menu.

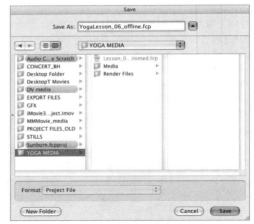

Figure 20.24 Enter a name for the project containing your new offline sequence; choose a location to save your new project file; and click Save.

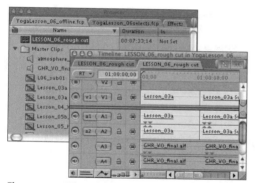

Figure 20.25 When the processing is complete, a new project file containing your offline sequence appears on the front tab of the Browser.

The Media Manager operation proceeds. A status window displays the progress of each stage in the operation. If the operation encounters an error, the processing stops, and Final Cut Pro displays an error message. When the processing is complete, a new project file containing your offline sequence appears on the front tab of the Browser (**Figure 20.25**). Clips with reel designations appear in the Timeline as offline clips, but items that do not have a reel name, such as graphics and digital audio files, are not taken offline, so your links to those elements remain intact.

Working with Graphics in Offline RT

If you're using FCP's low-resolution Offline RT format in the early stages of your edit, you might be wondering if you need to make two different-sized versions of your graphics. After all, Offline RT uses a frame size of 320 by 240 pixels, and your default DV-NTSC sequence frame size is 720 by 480, so won't you need to make a set of graphics in each frame size?

Nope. Final Cut Pro will resize your 720-by-480 graphics automatically to fit Offline RT's smaller frame size. Here's how it works:

When you edit graphics that are larger than the sequence frame size into an Offline RT sequence, Final Cut Pro automatically resizes the graphics by setting each graphical clip's Scale property to 50 percent to fit the sequence's 320-by-240 frame size.

Any generators you edit into an Offline RT sequence will be scaled in the same way.

When you're ready to convert your Offline RT sequence into a full, online-resolution sequence (such as DV-NTSC), use the Media Manager to create an offline trimmed duplicate of your Offline RT sequence in an online Sequence preset such as DV-NTSC. FCP will automatically reset the scale of any graphics you used so they fit the new, online frame size. Any generators you used in your sequence will also have their frame sizes reset to match the new online frame size.

Offline RT and media management

Offline RT, Final Cut Pro's low-resolution video format, is a lifesaver for editors with tons of raw footage and limited drive space because video captured in Offline RT requires only 1 GB of storage space for 45 minutes of captured footage. Compare that with captured DV format footage, which demands a gigabyte for every 5 minutes of captured footage. Offline RT's small file size speeds up rendering and file transfer and backup operations as well.

Using Offline RT in your post-production plan means that at some point you'll need to use the Media Manager to assist you in switching the format of your source media files while retaining the edit information contained in your edited sequences.

If you choose to capture your footage directly in Offline RT format, you'll want to *up-res* (that's editor slang for recapturing in a higher-resolution format) your edited sequence at some point in your editing process because you'll want to use the best image quality for final output.

To prepare your project for recapture at a higher resolution, use the Media Manager to create a new project containing all your edited sequences plus offline copies of any clips you'll need to complete your edit. See "To create a trimmed offline sequence," earlier in this chapter.

If you've captured your footage in a high-resolution format, you may want to recompress your footage in the Offline RT format because you're running out of drive space, or because you want to edit using only a PowerBook's internal drive. You might want to create a compressed version of an effects-heavy section of your program because Offline RT's faster rendering performance will save you time as you tweak your complex visual effects.

Offline RT format uses the same frame rate as your original footage (that means your timecode numbers will match as you switch back and forth between formats), but it has a smaller frame size and a different image format. One of the basic truths about Final Cut Pro is that your project's sequence settings must match your media format; to switch to Offline RT format, you'll need to create a copy of your project that uses Offline RT sequence settings. To create a copy of your project in a lower-resolution format, see "Recompressing a project in Offline RT format," next.

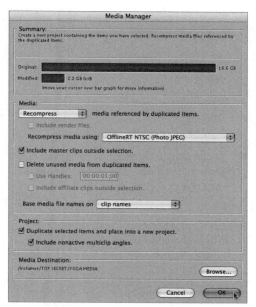

Figure 20.26 Media Manager window settings for copying an entire project and its media files in a compressed format.

Recompressing a project in Offline RT format

You can use the Media Manager to make a copy of your project and its media in the compressed Offline RT format or another format. You might make a compressed copy of an entire project to use on a PowerBook system or to take advantage of Offline RT's fast rendering to work out the timing of a complex effects sequence. **Figure 20.26** shows the Media Manager window settings for making an Offline RT format copy of your project and its media. For more information on these settings, see "Media Manager window options," earlier in this chapter.

✔ Tip

■ Desperate editors in search of a quick, cheap PAL version of their program have tried to use the Media Manager's Recompress option to convert their project and its media from NTSC to PAL. Unfortunately, you can't use the Recompress feature to convert NTSC to PAL, or PAL to NTSC. Compressor, FCP's file conversion helper application, does offer a transcoding feature.

To copy a project and its media in a compressed format:

1. In the Browser, select all the items on the project's tab, *then do one of the following:*
   ◆ Choose File > Media Manager.
   ◆ Control-click a selected item in the Browser; then choose Media Manager from the shortcut menu.

2. In the Media Manager's Media section, choose Recompress from the Process Mode pop-up menu.

   The Include Render Files option is unavailable; you'll need to re-render your sequence in your new project's compressed format.

continues on next page

3. Choose Offline RT NTSC (or Offline RT PAL) from the Recompress Media Using pop-up menu.

4. If you want to add compressed copies of affiliated project items to your project, check the Include Master Clips Outside Selection and Include Affiliate Clips Outside Selection options to add any clips affiliated with your selected sequences and clips. See "FCP Protocol: Deleting Unused Media in Projects Containing Affiliate Clips," earlier in this chapter, for details on your options.

5. *Do one of the following:*

◆ Check Delete Unused Media from Duplicated Items to select it if you want to exclude unused footage from the compressed-format copy of your project's media.

◆ Uncheck Delete Unused Media from Duplicated Items to deselect it if you want to copy the full length of all your media files in the compressed-format copy of your project's media.

The Use Handles option is unavailable because you are copying the full length of all your clips.

6. If you've renamed your subclips and you want your trimmed media files to use the new names, choose Clip Names from the Base Media File Names On pop-up menu.

7. In the Project section, check Duplicate Selected Items and Place into a New Project to select it.

8. In the Media Destination section, click Browse, then navigate to the disk location where you want to store the new project's media files.

9. Check the Summary section at the top of the window to see that you've configured your settings correctly, then click OK.

10. In the dialog box, enter an appropriate name, such as Project Name_RT, in the Save As field; choose a location to save your new project file; and then click Save (**Figure 20.27**).

Figure 20.27 Enter a name (you may want to add an identifying suffix, such as RT), choose a location to save your new project file, and then click Save.

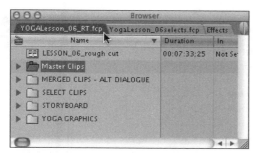

Figure 20.28 When the process is complete, your new Offline RT project appears on the front tab of the Browser.

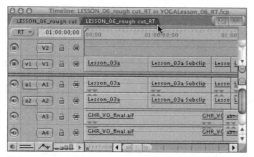

Figure 20.29 Add an identifying suffix to make it easier to tell your Offline RT sequence from your DV format sequence.

The Media Manager operation proceeds. A status window displays the progress of each stage in the operation. If the operation encounters an error, the processing stops, and Final Cut Pro displays an error message. When the process is complete, your new Offline RT format project appears on the front tab of the Browser (**Figure 20.28**).

✔ Tips

- When you view your new Offline RT project, note that the sequences keep their original names, so a sequence in your new Offline RT project has exactly the same name as its DV counterpart. If you plan on flipping back and forth between your Offline RT and DV format sequences in the course of your work, consider renaming your Offline RT sequences with an identifying suffix: for example, Montage_RT. You'll have an easier time distinguishing between them when both sequences are open in the Timeline (**Figure 20.29**).

- If the project you're recompressing contains still graphics, here's good news: As it creates the compressed-format copy of your project, FCP copies the graphics at full size and then automatically scales your graphics to 50 percent to fit the Offline RT sequence's 320-by-240 pixel frame size. For more information, see "Working with Graphics in Offline RT," earlier in this chapter.

Reconnecting Offline Files

In Final Cut Pro, the links between your clips and sequences in the Browser and the underlying media source files on disk are based on the media file's name and location. FCP relies on the file path described in a clip's Source property to maintain the link between that clip and its source media file. If you move or rename the source media files used in a project or sequence, the file path listed in the Source property becomes invalid and you'll be greeted with an Offline Files alert the next time you open your project. Don't panic. You can reconnect clips to media on your disk using the Reconnect Media command.

It's important to understand how Final Cut Pro's protocols governing clip versions affect the reconnection process. Starting in FCP 4, sequence clips by default are affiliated with a master clip in the Browser. The offline/online status of the master clip and all affiliated clips is linked; make any one affiliated clip offline, and all its affiliated clips are taken offline automatically.

Fortunately, the same principle applies to relinking. Remember, however, that any independent clips in your sequence are considered separate copies of the clips in the Browser. If an independent clip is used in a sequence, the sequence copy and the Browser copy must be reconnected separately. This is a little tricky, because the sequence icon in the Browser doesn't display the red diagonal offline indicator to warn you that it contains offline clips. Selecting the sequence when you are reconnecting allows you to locate files for all offline clips in the sequence.

✔ Tip

- You can use Final Cut Pro's Find function to search for all the offline clips and sequences in a project (search the Offline Yes/No column for Yes), and then select and reconnect the offline clips and sequences right in the Find Results window.

FCP Protocol: Broken Links

How did your clips get thrown offline? Here's a list of things you might have done that severed the link between your FCP project and its source media files:

- ◆ You renamed your source media files.

- ◆ You renamed the folder containing your source media files.

- ◆ You moved your source media files to another disk.

- ◆ You deleted your source media on disk.

RECONNECTING OFFLINE FILES

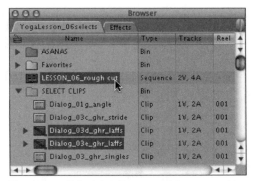

Figure 20.30 Select the clip you want to reconnect to its source media file.

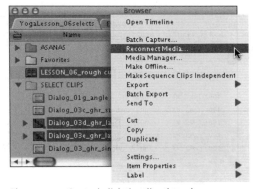

Figure 20.31 Control-click the clip; then choose Reconnect Media from the shortcut menu.

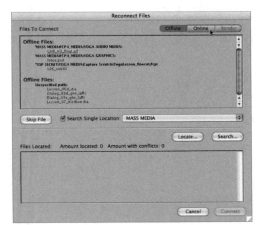

Figure 20.32 In the Reconnect Files window, enable the button for each type of file you want to reconnect. The Files to Connect list will filter out any clip types you deselect.

To reconnect offline files:

1. Select the file or files to be reconnected (**Figure 20.30**). You can select a clip or sequence in the Browser or clips in an open sequence in the Timeline.

2. *Do one of the following:*
   - ◆ Choose File > Reconnect Media.
   - ◆ Control-click the clip or sequence; then choose Reconnect Media from the shortcut menu (**Figure 20.31**).

   The Reconnect Files window opens.

3. In the Reconnect Files window, the Files to Connect list may display Offline, Online, or Render files, depending on your current file selection. Enable the button for each type of file you want to reconnect (**Figure 20.32**).

   The Files to Connect list updates to show only the type of files you have selected. Files with the same source media file location path are grouped together. The first file to locate is highlighted.

4. To specify how you want to locate the file, *do one of the following:*
   - ◆ Click Locate if you want to navigate manually to the source media file's location. If you know the location of the file and you have multiple files to reconnect in the same location, this can be the fastest way to go.
   - ◆ Click Search if you want Final Cut Pro to search for the file in all locations, or just in the locations you specify in the Search Folders pop-up menu.

   continues on next page

RECONNECTING OFFLINE FILES

Final Cut Pro searches the specified locations for the first file in your selection. If FCP successfully locates the source media file for your first offline clip, the Reconnect dialog box appears with that source file listed in the file window (**Figure 20.33**).

5. In the Reconnect dialog box, *do any of the following:*

- ◆ Select a file type from the Show pop-up menu to limit the file list display to the selected file type.
- ◆ Check Matched Name Only to restrict your selection from the file list to a name that matches exactly. Disable this feature to allow selection from the complete list of the folder's contents.
- ◆ Select a drive or folder to search from the Search pop-up menu. Click the Next Volume button to move to the next media drive.
- ◆ Check Reconnect All Files in Relative Path to automatically reconnect any other clips in the sequence that are associated with files in the same folder.

6. Click Choose to select the source media file(s) to be reconnected with the clip.

The Reconnect dialog box closes, returning you to the Reconnect Files window.

7. Back in the Reconnect Files window, repeat Steps 4-6 until you have located all the files. If FCP's Search cannot locate a source media file, the Reconnect dialog box does not appear. You should click the Locate button to try to find the file manually, or click the Skip File button to move on to the next file in your list.

8. Click Connect to reconnect all the clips listed in the Files Located list with the source media you specified (**Figure 20.34**).

Figure 20.33 Final Cut Pro searches your media drives for the first file in your selection, then opens the Reconnect window with that source file displayed in the file window. Files that don't match are dimmed. You may have to scroll down through the list to see your file.

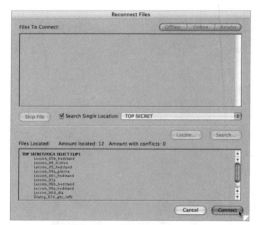

Figure 20.34 Click Connect, and all the clips listed in the Files Located list will be reconnected with the source media you specified.

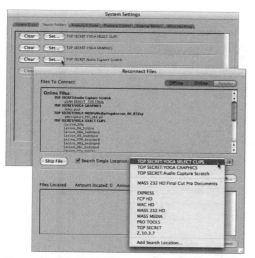

Figure 20.35 The folders you specify on the Search Folders tab of the System Settings window appear at the top of the Reconnect Files window's Search Single Location pop-up menu. Check the Search Single Location box, and you can restrict your search operation to the folder or drive you select from the pop-up menu. Your project's designated search folders appear right at the top of the pop-up menu list.

✔ Tips

- On the Search Folders tab of the System Settings window, you can pre-select which folders will appear in the Reconnect window's Search Single Location pop-up menu (**Figure 20.35**). Your project's designated search folders appear right at the top of the pop-up menu list, so it's easy to do speedy, efficient searches by restricting the search to a single folder.

- You can conclude a reconnection operation in the Reconnect dialog box at any point by clicking the Connect button. All files remaining in the Files to Connect list will be skipped, and the files listed in the Files Located list will be reconnected.

Reconnecting Online Files

The Reconnect Media feature offers an option to reconnect online as well as offline files. Reconnecting missing or offline clips is the most common use of the Reconnect Media command, but you could have occasion to reconnect online files, too—for example, when you want to replace the media in a clip you've used in a sequence with a revised version of the same media element or with another element entirely.

If you've been using low-resolution versions of your source media files to produce an edited version of your program, Reconnect Media is not the best way to redirect your sequence clips to high-resolution versions of the same media files. To avoid a settings mismatch between sequence settings and clip settings, you should use the Media Manager route described in "Offline RT and Media Management," earlier in this chapter.

If you do want to relink a clip in your sequence with an entirely different source media file, the new source file must be at least long enough to cover the current marked duration of the clip you're relinking it to. If your new source file is too short, you'll see an error message.

Using the Offline Files dialog box to reconnect

Final Cut Pro displays the Offline Files dialog box to alert you that media files have gone missing since the last time you saved a project. Any time you open a project or switch back to FCP from the Finder or another application, Final Cut Pro rechecks the status of your media files. If FCP detects missing files, the Offline Files dialog box appears to alert you and offer you options for restoring order to your project.

To reconnect using the Offline Files dialog box:

1. Final Cut Pro displays the Offline Files dialog box (**Figure 20.36**), which alerts you that media files are missing from the current project. This list could include:

   ◆ Missing source media files

   ◆ Render files lost because they reference a missing media file

   ◆ QuickTime reference movies made invalid by a missing media file

2. *Do any of the following:*

   ◆ In the Forget Files section, check the box next to a file type (**Figure 20.37**) if you want to change the status of the files from "missing" to "offline" (by clearing the file path listed in their Source property) and remove them from the list of missing files. If you don't use the Forget Files option, Final Cut Pro will continue to post alerts about missing media each time you launch the project, until you reconnect the media and clips or make the clips offline.

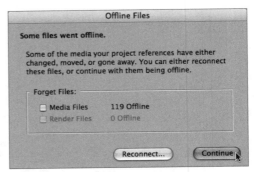

Figure 20.36 The Offline Files dialog box appears to alert you that media files have gone missing since the last time you saved your project.

Figure 20.37 Check the box next to a file type in the Forget Files section to change the status of missing files from "missing" to "offline."

Figure 20.38 Click the Reconnect button to access the Reconnect Media feature and try to locate and reconnect the missing files.

◆ Check Media Files if you want to change the status of all missing source media files "missing" to "offline." All clips referencing these files will be marked as offline clips in your project, but you can still relink the files later.

◆ Check Render Files if you want to mark all missing render files as offline. If you choose to forget (remove) render files, you won't have the opportunity to reconnect them later.

3. To finish the process, *choose one of the following options:*

◆ Click the Reconnect button (**Figure 20.38**) to open the Reconnect Files window feature, and then try to locate and reconnect the missing files. The Reconnect Files operation is described earlier in this chapter.

◆ Click Continue to exit the Offline Files dialog box. If you left the Forget Files options unchecked, FCP will continue to classify the files as missing or invalid. The next time you launch this project, FCP will display the Offline Files dialog box again, and you can choose to reconnect or to take files offline at that time.

✔ Tip

■ The Offline Files dialog box doesn't identify which clips FCP considers missing, so before you use the Forget option (which erases the Source property, the clip's link with its source media), try the Reconnect button. You can get a look at a list of the missing clips in the Reconnect Files window and decide if you really want to Forget them.

FCP Protocol: Offline vs. Missing Clips

Missing clips and offline clips look the same in the Browser, Viewer, Timeline, and Canvas.

What's the difference?

Offline clips have no file path listed in their Source property. They are listed as offline in your project's item tracking data, so Final Cut Pro doesn't look for them the next time you open that project.

Missing clips are listed as online in your project's item tracking data, but FCP can't find the clips' underlying media files at the location listed in the clips' Source property. FCP will search for missing files each time you open a project until you reconnect the files or make them official offline files by clicking Forget in the Offline Files dialog box.

FCP Protocol: Deleting Media

How do you delete media files from Final Cut Pro the right way?

Before you toss that folder full of source media files in the Trash, take a moment to review the way Final Cut Pro tracks files. Remember that the Browser clips you use to construct sequences in your project are not actually media files; they are pointers to the actual media files on disk, and Final Cut Pro's links to those underlying source media files are location dependent. If you open the Item Properties window for any clip in Final Cut Pro, you'll see the directory path to the underlying source media (the clip's directory path also appears in the Browser's Source column). If you've created subclips, repeated the same clip in a sequence, divided a clip with the Razor Blade tool, or created multiple versions of a sequence, you can have quite a few different clips all pointing to the same media file on disk.

If you delete a clip from the Browser bin or a Timeline sequence, you haven't thrown out the underlying media source file on disk. You can re-import the file to reconnect it to your project, or, if you've already used that clip in a sequence, you can drag a copy of the sequence version of the clip back into the Browser. Dragging a clip from an open sequence in the Timeline back into the Browser places a new master clip copy of the sequence version into your project.

Your source media files stay on disk until you use the Make Files Offline feature to move them to the Trash or delete them from your hard drive.

Using Make Files Offline is the recommended way to delete files from inside FCP. Should you need to delete source media files outside FCP by dragging them to the Trash, it's best not to delete media files linked to an open project while Final Cut Pro is running. You should save and close the project before you delete media files in the Finder. Determine your own comfort level here, but quitting Final Cut Pro before you trash any media files would be the safest course.

Once you've deleted a source media file, all clips referring to that file will be marked as offline. Final Cut Pro will warn you that the clips are offline each time you open the project until you delete the clip references, including any versions of the clips that appear in sequences, or tell FCP to "forget" the offline clips. See "Using the Offline Files window to reconnect," earlier in this chapter.

Use the Render Manager to delete render files. For more information, see Chapter 18, "Real Time and Rendering."

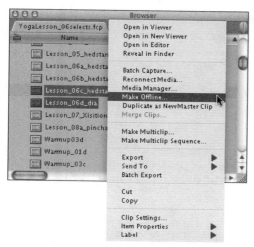

Figure 20.39 Control-click a selected item; then choose Make Offline from the shortcut menu.

Deleting Media

The Make Files Offline feature is the right tool to use when you want to remove clips and their associated source media from your project. It's acceptable to delete media files outside Final Cut Pro by dragging them directly from your media drives to the Trash, but using the Make Files Offline feature accomplishes the same thing and keeps the file tracking in your FCP project up-to-date.

Make Files Offline offers three options. Each of the options starts by making your selected clip or sequence offline. Making a clip offline breaks the link between that clip and its media file.

Once the clip has been decoupled from its media file, you can choose to move the media file to the Trash or delete it from your disk.

To make files offline:

1. In the Browser or Timeline, select the clips or sequences you want to make offline.

2. *Do one of the following:*
   - Choose Modify > Make Offline.
   - Control-click a selected item; then choose Make Offline from the shortcut menu (**Figure 20.39**).

continues on next page

DELETING MEDIA

3. In the Make Offline dialog box, choose one of the following three options; then click OK.

- ◆ Click Leave Them on the Disk to make the files offline and leave the original media files on your disk.

- ◆ Click Move Them to the Trash to make the files offline and move the source media files to the Trash (**Figure 20.40**). To finally delete the files, you'll need to empty the Trash manually. If you change your mind later, before you empty the Trash, and want to retrieve the files, drag them out of the Trash and reconnect them to your project by using the Reconnect Media command. If you empty the Trash, your files are finally deleted.

- ◆ Click Delete Them from the Disk to make the files offline, and then immediately delete the media files from your disk. This action cannot be undone. You'll have to recapture the media to restore your project.

4. If you choose to move or delete the files, a warning message tells you that the action cannot be undone. To continue, click OK.

The selected clips and all affiliated clips are made offline (**Figure 20.41**).

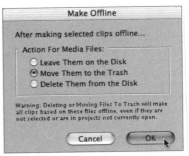

Figure 20.40 Click Move Them to the Trash to make the files offline and move the source media files to the Trash.

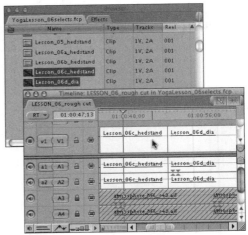

Figure 20.41 When you take clips offline, remember that any clips in your project that are affiliated with your selected clips will also be taken offline. In this example, taking the Browser master clips offline has caused the affiliated sequence clips to be taken offline as well.

Figure 20.42 Choose File > Save All to save the current version of the project.

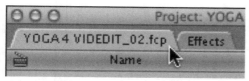

Figure 20.43 The new version of your project replaces the old one on the front tab of the Browser window.

Project Maintenance Tips

Even if you are not forced to reorganize your project's media elements because you have run out of disk space, it's a good idea to streamline a project as you go, especially if you're working on a long, complex project. As your project accumulates clips, sequences, edits, render files, multiple tracks of audio, and effects, more and more of your available RAM is needed just to open the project. At some point, you could experience a drop in Final Cut Pro's speed or video playback performance.

To streamline a project in progress:

1. With the project open in the Browser, choose File > Save All (**Figure 20.42**). The current version of the project is saved.

2. Choose File > Save Project As. The Save dialog box appears.

3. Navigate to the folder where you want to store your project file, enter a name for the new project version in the Save As field, and then click Save.

   The new version of your project replaces the older one on the front tab of the Browser window (**Figure 20.43**).

continues on next page

PROJECT MAINTENANCE TIPS

4. Remove all but the most current versions of your sequences, and delete any excess clips (**Figure 20.44**). If you are short of disk space, you could choose to delete the clips' source media files as well, but you don't need to delete the source media files to get the benefits of a streamlined project.

5. Choose Tools > Render Manager, and delete any obsolete render files. Remember that the Render Manager gives you access to render files for all your projects (**Figure 20.45**), so be careful as you select the files you want to delete.

6. With the new, streamlined project open in the Browser, choose File > Save.

7. If you streamlined your project to improve Final Cut Pro's performance, you'll need to close and then reopen the project to recapture the available RAM and start enjoying improved performance.

Figure 20.44 Remove all but the most current versions of your sequences and delete any excess clips. If you need old versions later, you still have them in the project version you saved in step 1.

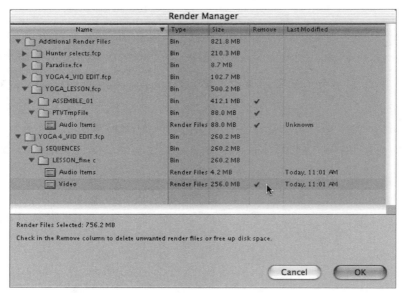

Figure 20.45 The Render Manager gives you access to render files for all your projects, so be careful which files you delete.

Editing in stages

If you are trying to assemble a long project in Final Cut Pro on a modest system, you may find that you have much more media than hard drive space to store it on.

The simplest approach to a staged editing process is to edit one sequence at a time, print it to video, clear off the media, and then edit the next sequence.

Here's a checklist for taking a completed sequence offline and preparing your drives for the next sequence:

◆ After you have completed a sequence and printed it to tape, make sure you save the project file that contains the final version of your sequence.

◆ You should also save a backup copy of the project file on a Zip disk, CD, or some other form of removable media.

◆ Back up any media elements in your sequence, such as graphics files or digital audio from a CD, that won't be restored in a batch recapturing process.

◆ In the Browser, select all the clips and sequences that reference media files you no longer need. Use the Make Offline command, described earlier in this chapter, to delete all the media source files you no longer need.

◆ The clips and sequences referring to the deleted media files will be marked offline, but the clip data will remain in your completed project file. This clip and sequence data takes up very little room, so you don't need to delete it; you can store it in a single Browser bin.

◆ Capture the next batch of media files and start work on your next sequence.

The Last Mile: Tips for Final Assembly of BIG Projects

You can tell when the size of your project is taxing the limits of FCP's performance. Everything takes longer—opening and saving the project, screen refresh, even moving around the Timeline. If you have no choice but to press FCP's capacity to handle large amounts of media and multiple long sequences, try this:

◆ Split your show into a series of separate sequences, and complete all rendering inside the individual sequences.

◆ Create a new project and drag just the finished individual sequences from your old projects into the new project; then close the old projects.

◆ Create the master sequence assembly of all your finished segment sequences in the brand-new project, including just the master sequence, and keep all other projects closed as much as possible.

◆ Back up your project file frequently.

Restoring a sequence

If you find that you need to go back and modify a sequence after you have deleted its underlying media files, you can use the sequence data you saved in the project file to batch recapture your footage and re-create the sequence.

All filters, motion paths, keyframes, transitions, nested items, and audio mixing are reconstituted when you batch recapture the media files for a sequence. Your render files will be gone, however, and you'll need to re-render any sequence material that requires them.

To restore a sequence:

1. Select the sequence in the Browser, and choose File > Batch Capture. If you want to recapture any Browser clips, select those as well (**Figure 20.46**).

2. Follow the steps in "To batch capture clips" in Chapter 5, and batch recapture your footage from tape.

3. Restore to your hard disk any media elements in your sequence, such as graphics files or digital audio from CD, that won't be restored in the batch recapturing process.

4. Select the sequence in the Browser and choose File > Reconnect Media.

5. Follow the steps described in "To reconnect offline files," earlier in this chapter, and reconnect the media elements you restored that were not part of the batch recapture operation.

6. To restore the render files, re-render any sequence material that requires rendering (**Figure 20.47**).

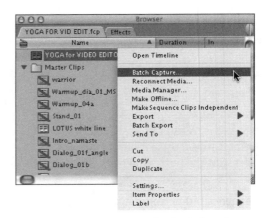

Figure 20.46 In the Browser, select the sequence plus any clips that you want to restore.

Figure 20.47 To restore the render files, you must re-render any sequence material that requires rendering.

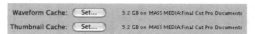

Figure 20.48 Looking for the Thumbnail and Waveform Cache folders? You'll find the directory path to their disk location listed on the Scratch Disks tab in the System Settings window.

Modifying an offline clip before recapture

Here's a technique that can streamline your project and save you some drive space. Let's say you have refined your edited sequence and discover that you are using just the audio track (or just the video) from a large number of audio+video clips. You can recapture your audio+video clips as audio only or video only without relogging by adjusting the clips' formatting in the Tracks column of the Browser. You need to take the clips offline first.

To learn how to modify the audio or video format (or other types of settings) for logged offline clips, see "Modifying logged clip data" in Chapter 5.

Tracking used and unused clips

If you just want to do a little housecleaning in your project's media file folder, it's handy to have an inventory of every clip that's currently being used in a sequence in your project and another list of every element in your project that remains unused. How can you create complete lists of used and unused elements in your project? It's simple. You can use the Find feature to assemble these lists—you can even inventory multiple projects in a single Find operation. Powerful stuff.

Removing a project from your drives

Final Cut Pro doesn't generate separate preview or temporary files when you use the Print to Video or Edit to Tape function. The only files you need to clean up after a project are the project file, media files, render files, and thumbnail and waveform cache files (**Figure 20.48**).

To get a complete list of elements used in a group of sequences:

1. Open all the projects you want to search.

2. On each project's tab in the Browser, Command-click to select the sequences you want to include in your search (**Figure 20.49**).

3. Choose Edit > Find; or press Command-F.

4. In the Find dialog box, configure the options as follows:

   ◆ Choose All Open Projects from the Search pop-up menu.

   ◆ Choose Used Media from the For pop-up menu and check the box next to In Selected Sequences.

   ◆ Choose Replace Find Results from the Results pop-up menu.

5. Click Find All (**Figure 20.50**).

   A list of all the clips used in the sequences you selected is displayed in the Find Results window.

✔ Tips

■ You can export your used clip list directly from the Find Results window and convert it to a text file. With the Find Results window active, choose File > Export > Batch List (**Figure 20.51**).

■ If your clip's name is different from the name of the underlying media file, you can find the underlying media file (and its location) in the clip's Item Properties window or the Browser's Source column.

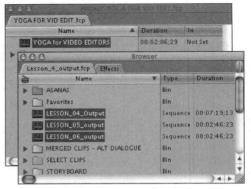

Figure 20.49 On each project's tab in the Browser, Command-click to select the sequences you want to include in your search.

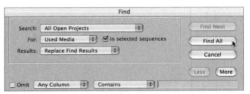

Figure 20.50 The Find dialog box, configured to find unused clips in selected sequences. Click Find All to perform the search.

Figure 20.51 Export a text file of your used clip list directly from the Find Results window.

PROJECT MAINTENANCE TIPS

KEYBOARD SHORTCUTS

General controls

FUNCTION	KEY COMMAND	FUNCTION	KEY COMMAND
Open file	Cmd O	Save all	Cmd Option S
Open selected item	Return	Undo	Cmd Z
Open Item in separate window	Shift Return	Redo	Shift Cmd Z
Open Item in Editor	Option Return	Audio scrub on or off	Shift S
Close window	Cmd W	Snapping on or off	N
Quit	Cmd Q	Toggle Loop Playback	Ctrl L
Save	Cmd S	Close Tab	Ctrl W
		Open text generator	Ctrl X

Opening application windows

FUNCTION	KEY COMMAND
Viewer	Cmd 1
Canvas	Cmd 2
Timeline	Cmd 3
Browser	Cmd 4
Audio Meters	Option 4
Effects	Cmd 5
Favorites bin	Cmd 6
Trim Edit	Cmd 7
Log and Capture	Cmd 8
Item Properties	Cmd 9
Sequence Settings	Cmd 0 (zero)
User Preferences	Option Q

Selecting, cutting, copying, and pasting

FUNCTION	KEY COMMAND
Copy	Cmd C
Cut	Cmd X
Duplicate	Option D
Select In to Out	Option A
Paste	Cmd V
Paste attributes	Option V
Paste Insert	Shift V
Select all	Cmd A
Deselect all	Shift Cmd A

Navigation

FUNCTION	KEY COMMAND
Forward one frame	→
Back one frame	←
Forward one second	Shift →
Back one second	Shift ←
Match frame in Master clip	F
Match frame in Source file	Cmd Option F
Next edit	Shift E or ' or Ctrl 8
Previous edit	Option E or ; or Ctrl 7
To next edit or In/Out	↓
To previous edit or In/Out	↑
Go to In point	Shift I
Go to Out point	Shift O

FUNCTION	KEY COMMAND
Next gap	Shift G
Previous gap	Option G
To beginning of media	Home
To end of media	End or Shift Home
To next marker	Shift ↓ or Shift M
To previous marker	Shift ↑ or Option M
Shuttle backward fast	J (tap repeatedly to increase speed)
Shuttle backward slow	J + K
Pause	K
Shuttle forward fast	L (tap repeatedly to increase speed)
Shuttle forward slow	L + K

Finding items

FUNCTION	KEY COMMAND
Find	Cmd F
Find Next (in Find results)	Cmd G or F3
Find previous (in Find results)	Shift F3

Scrolling

FUNCTION	KEY COMMAND
Horizontal scroll left	Shift Page Up
Horizontal scroll right	Shift Page Down
Vertical scroll up	Page Up
Vertical scroll down	Page Down

Screen layout and display

FUNCTION	KEY COMMAND
Custom Layout 1	Shift U
Custom Layout 2	Option U
Standard layout	Ctrl U

Projects and sequences

FUNCTION	KEY COMMAND
New project	Shift Cmd N
New sequence	Cmd N
New Sequence with Presets prompt	Cmd Option N
Import file	Cmd I

Browser

FUNCTION	KEY COMMAND
New bin	Cmd B
Open bin (List view)	→
Close bin (List view)	←
Make Favorite Effect	Option F
Logging Column Layout	Option B
Standard Column Layout	Shift B
Toggle Browser View	Shift H
Make Favorite Motion	Ctrl F

Timeline

FUNCTION	KEY COMMAND	FUNCTION	KEY COMMAND
Create or break link	Cmd L	Lock all video tracks	Shift F4
Create or break stereo pair	Option L	Lock audio track + track no.	F5 + track no.
Toggle track sizes	Shift T	Lock all audio tracks	Shift F5
Clip Keyframes on or off	Option T	Toggle Audio Waveforms	Cmd Option W
Clip overlays on or off	Option W	Linked Selection on or off	Shift L
Delete and leave gap	Delete	Modify Duration	Ctrl D
Ripple Delete (no gap)	Shift Delete	Zoom Timeline In	Option + (plus sign) or Option =
Ripple Cut to Keyboard	Shift X		
Fit sequence in window	Shift Z	Zoom Timeline Out	Option − (minus sign)
Lock video track + track no.	F4 + track no.		

Logging and Capturing

FUNCTION	KEY COMMAND
Log clip	F2
Batch capture	Ctrl C
Capture Now	Shift C

Playing video

FUNCTION	KEY COMMAND
Play	L or Spacebar
Pause/Stop	K or Spacebar
Play around current	\ (backslash)
Play every frame	Option P or Option \ (backslash)
Play here to Out	Shift P
Play in reverse	Shift Spacebar or J
Play In to Out	Shift \ (backslash)

In and Out points

FUNCTION	KEY COMMAND
Set In point	I or / (slash) on keypad
Set Out point	O or * (asterisk) on keypad
Clear In	Option I
Clear Out	Option O
Clear In and Out	Option X
Make selection an In or Out	Shift A
Mark clip	X
Mark to Markers	Ctrl A
Go to In point	Shift I
Go to Out point	Shift O
Set video In only	Ctrl I
Set video Out only	Ctrl O
Set audio In only	Cmd Option I
Set audio Out only	Cmd Option O

Markers

FUNCTION	KEY COMMAND
Add marker	M or ` (accent grave)
Add and name marker	M + M
Delete marker	Cmd ` (accent grave)
Extend marker	Option ` (accent grave)
Reposition marker	Shift ` (accent grave)

FUNCTION	KEY COMMAND
Next marker	Shift M or Shift ↓
Previous marker	Option M or Shift ↑
Clear All Markers	Ctrl ` (accent grave)
Mark to Markers	Ctrl A

Tool selection

Function	Key command	Function	Key command
Tool Selection	A	Tool Slide	S + S
Tool Edit Select	G	Tool Razor Blade	B
Tool Group Select	G+G	Tool Razor Blade All	B + B
Tool Range Select	G+G+G	Tool Hand	H
Tool Track Forward Select	T	Tool Zoom In	Z
Tool Track Backward Select	T+T	Tool Zoom Out	Z + Z
Tool Track Select	T+T+T	Tool Crop	C
Tool All Tracks Forward Select	T+T+T+T	Tool Distort	D or C + C
Tool All Tracks Backward Select	T+T+T+T+T	Tool Pen	P
Tool Roll Edit	R	Tool Pen Delete	P + P
Tool Ripple Edit	R + R	Tool Pen Smooth	P + P + P
Tool Slip	S		

Editing

Function	Key command	Function	Key command
Select Closest Edit	V	Split edit	[Option] Click In or Out point
Add Edit	[Ctrl] V	Set target video + track no.	[F6] + track no.
Toggle Ripple/Roll Tool Type	U or [Shift] R	Set target video to None	[Shift] [F6]
Add Default Video Transition	[Cmd] T	Set target Audio 1 + track no.	[F7] + track no.
Add Default Audio Transition	[Cmd] [Option] T	Set target Audio 1 to None	[Shift] [F7]
Extend edit	E	Set target Audio 2 + track no.	[F8] + track no.
Insert edit*	[F9]	Set target Audio 2 to None	[Shift] [F8]
Insert with transition	[Shift] [F9]	Trim backward one frame	[(left bracket) or , (comma)
Overwrite*	[F10]	Trim backward *x* frames	[Shift] [(left bracket) or [Shift] , (comma)
Overwrite with transition	[Shift] [F10]		
Replace*	[F11]	Trim forward one frame	] (rt. bracket) or . (period)
Fit to fill	[Shift] [F11]		
Superimpose	[F12]	Trim forward *x* frames	[Shift]] (rt. bracket) or [Shift] . (period)
Make subclip	[Cmd] U		
Slip edit	[Shift] Click In or Out point		

Same as key command for OS 10.3 Expose feature. Reassign keys for FCP or Expose to avoid conflict.

Output

Function	Key command
Show Current Frame on External Video	[Shift] [F12]
Print to video	[Ctrl] M
Toggle External Video	[Cmd] [F12]

Compositing and special effects

Function	Key command
Nest Items	[Option] C
Add Motion Keyframe	[Ctrl] K
Add Audio Keyframe	[Cmd] [Option] K
Next Keyframe	[Shift] K
Previous Keyframe	[Option] K
Make still frame	[Shift] N
Run FXBuilder script ()	[Cmd] K
Render selection	[Cmd] R
Render sequence	[Option] R
Disable Rendering	[Caps Lock]
Speed	[Cmd] J
Toggle Image/Wireframe view	W
Toggle RGB/RGB+A/Alpha	[Shift] W
Fit in window	[Shift] Z

Function	Key command
Nudge position down	[Option] [↓]
Nudge position left	[Option] [←]
Nudge position right	[Option] [→]
Nudge position up	[Option] [↑]
Sub pixel down	[Cmd] [↓]
Sub pixel left	[Cmd] [←]
Sub pixel right	[Cmd] [→]
Sub pixel up	[Cmd] [↑]
Zoom in	[Cmd] = (equal sign)
Zoom out	[Cmd] – (minus sign)
Add Motion Keyframe	[Ctrl] K
Add Audio Level Keyframe	[Cmd] [Option] K
Mixdown Audio	[Cmd] [Option] R

Quick Navigation Keys and Modifiers

This group of keyboard shortcuts for marking and navigation are arranged in what is known as a "Set-Clear-Go" scheme.

◆ The simple key command sets the edit, marker, or point.

◆ [Shift] plus the key command advances to the next edit, marker, or point.

◆ [Option] plus the key command advances to the previous edit, marker, or point.

KEY	NO MODIFIER	[Shift] + KEY	[Option] + KEY
I	Set In	Go to In	Clear In
O	Set Out	Go to Out	Clear Out
M	Set Marker	Next Marker	Previous Marker
E	Extend Edit	Next Edit	Previous Edit
G		Next Gap	Previous Gap
K		Next Keyframe	Previous Keyframe
[Ctrl] K	Add Motion Keyframe		

INDEX

INDEX

N

INDEX

INDEX